The ILLUSTRATED ENCYCLOPEDIA OF FIREARMS

The ILLUSTRATED ENCYCLOPEDIA OF FIREARMS

Ian V. Hogg

NEW BURLINGTON BOOKS

A QUARTO BOOK

Published by New Burlington Books
13 New Burlington Street, London W1

ISBN 0 906286 41 7

© Copyright 1978 Quarto Limited

First published 1978
Reprinted 1987

This book was designed and produced by
Quarto Publishing Limited
32 Kingly Court, London W1
Art Editor: Roger Daniels
Design Assistant: Marian Sanders
Text Editor: Donald Clarke

Phototypeset in England by
Vantage Photosetting Company Limited, Southampton
Printed in Hong Kong
by Leefung-Asco Printers Limited

Jacket front illustration by Jim Bamber

Endpapers
An international shooting competition
between America and Ireland, 1875

Frontispiece
An elaborate example of a cased pair of
pistols with matching accessories. They
are breech-loading centre-fire target
pistols with ebony stocks fitted with
mounts of chiselled iron in the Gothic
style. Austrian (Vienna), about 1860.

CONTENTS

FOREWORD

ALTHOUGH THE FIREARM has a long history, as the introductory section of this book outlines, the amount of technical progress during the first five hundred years was relatively small. Apart from the flintlock mechanism, there was little in a musket of 1800 which would have puzzled an arquebusier of 1400 had he lived to see one. But the opening years of the 19th century saw two significant advances: the adoption of the percussion principle and of rifling, and these began a revolution in weapons design. Ignition of the propellant became certain and instantaneous, and the flight of the bullet became accurate. Within a comparatively few years the revolver had taken shape, the bolt-action breech-loading rifle had been devised, and the metallic self-contained cartridge appeared. There has been more technical advance in the last 150 years than had taken place in the previous five hundred or so.

In order to keep this book to a manageable size, some decisions had to be taken about the scope of its contents, and the primary decision was of a date at which to begin our survey. After much discussion, we have selected 1830. Forsyth's percussion principle had been patented and was entering common use; percussion caps had appeared; Dreyse was working on his bolt-action Needle Gun and Lefaucheaux was developing the pinfire cartridge. From 1830 onward, the inventions and designs, stimulated by the inventive awareness of the 19th century and aided by the rapid improvements in machinery and manufacturing technique due to the Industrial Revolution, became an ever-widening stream.

Into this stream we have cast a very selective line; the sheer number of firearms designs patented since 1830 would fill several volumes, and we have, therefore, chosen those which

we think deserve mention for their innovation, their effect on firearms history and design, their wide use in war and recreation, and their outright fame. It might be thought that there is a bias toward military weapons rather than sporting ones, but the fact, unpalatable as it may be, remains that the far greater part of firearms development has its roots in military requirements, and it is after the military application has been seen to work that the idea then passes to the sporting side. In other hands, the mixture and balance might well have been different; but we believe that the following pages offer the reader the significant elements of the history of firearms in a convenient and concise form.

IAN V. HOGG

THE HAND GONNE

c.1350

THE EARLY HISTORY of firearms is, of course, allied with that of gunpowder, and it is a matter for regret among students and researchers that no-one in the Middle Ages appears to have been sufficiently impressed by either one to have made some reliable record of their first appearance. As a result, speculation has run rife, and it is only in the present century that most of the legend and conjecture has been exposed to detailed scrutiny and swept away, to be replaced by more reasoned conclusions.

In the past, the invention of gunpowder has been ascribed to such very varied sources as the Chinese, the Greeks, the Arabs and the Hindus, but none of these claims will withstand critical testing. One remarkable thing is that while each of these races has records and artifacts reaching back well before the period of interest to us, none can produce valid evidence of a knowledge of gunpowder or firearms any earlier than can be proved in Western Europe. Certainly the Greeks had 'Greek Fire' and the Chinese employed various pyrotechnic substances, but neither of these were gunpowder nor did they possess explosive properties: to argue otherwise is like asserting that automobiles must have existed in 1880 because there are records of bicycles at that date.

The first undisputed records of the existence of gunpowder occur in the writings of Roger Bacon, a Franciscan Friar of Ilchester; in about 1260 he buried the formula in an anagram,

Illustration from a manuscript c.1400, showing a hand gonne being ignited by a hot iron.

while in essays written in 1267–8 he referred to it openly as 'the powder, known in divers places, composed of saltpetre, sulphur and charcoal.' From that time on, records became more numerous and gunpowder (or black powder), though an expensive commodity, became more common.

But the question now arises: to what purpose was it put? Bacon refers to it being wrapped in parchment and ignited to give a 'blinding flash and stunning noise', and it seems probable that the earliest days saw it used principally as a novelty. How, and when, and by whom the ability to use it to propel a missile was discovered is not known with any certainty. For years the legend of 'Black Berthold', the mysterious monk of Freiburg, held sway; that one day he was preparing gunpowder in an apothecary's mortar when the mixture ignited and blew the pestle from the mortar.

From this, the story ran, he deduced the use of gunpowder in a closed vessel and invented the gun, and the use of the word 'mortar' for a particular piece of ordnance commemorates this occasion. Unfortunately, no two authorities seem to have agreed on when Berthold performed this vital experiment, and the earliest date ascribed to it is a good deal later than that of definite and proveable records of cannon. Moreover, the term 'mortar' was not to appear for many years, and recent researchers have suggested that Berthold never existed at all but was pure legend from start to finish.

The earliest incontestable record of a firearm is the famous 'Millimete Cannon', so-called from being depicted in a manuscript by Walter de Millimete of England and dated 1326. In the same year there is reference in the records of Florence to the provision of guns and shot for defending the town. It would thus seem that by 1326 the cannon was known across Europe and, by inference, must have been known for some time to allow such distribution to take place. The principal difficulty in identifying the early use of firearms is the haphazard use of the word 'artillery' interchangeably between mechanical engines — catapults, ballistae and mangonels — and firearms: since the one usurped the function of the other, it adopted the same generic term, and in the early

Hand gonnes accompanying full-sized cannon and archers in a 15th century siege. Explosive ordnance development was under way.

records of battles and sieges it is often almost impossible to say which of the two distinct types of 'artillery' were in use.

In the 1350s, though, we begin to see references to 'gunnis cum telar'—guns with handles—marking the emergence of the personal firearm. In the normal course of events we might reasonably expect that a new device would begin small and become larger as experience was gained, but with the firearm this natural order of things is reversed. The first firearms were cannon, albeit small cannon, and from this beginning design moved in two directions, upwards to make bigger and more powerful cannon, and downwards to make 'hand gonnes'.

Few weapons of this early period have survived; one of the best-known is that excavated from a well in Tannenburg Castle, and this weapon can be dated fairly accurately since it is known that the castle was razed in 1399. A similar weapon is the small bronze piece found at Loshult, Sweden, in 1861 and estimated to date

Above Two Swiss hand guns of the 14th century, one fitted with a recoil hook to become a 'hakenbuchse'.

Left A 14th century bronze hand gun from Loshult, Sweden.

GUNPOWDER

Gunpowder is an intimate mixture of saltpetre, charcoal and sulphur: the earliest formula, that of Roger Bacon, gives the proportions as 7:5:5, or 41% saltpetre, 29½% charcoal and 29½% sulphur. This gradually changed, the percentage of saltpetre increasing, until by the end of the 18th century it had reached its final form: 75% saltpetre, 15% charcoal and 10% sulphur.

The earliest powder was called 'serpentine' and was a finely ground powder. This had certain defects: packed tightly in a gun chamber it was difficult to ignite and slow to burn, and in storage and transport had a distinct tendency to separate out into its constituent parts. During the 15th

century the French invented 'corned' powder, in which the three substances were mixed together in the wet state (which was a much safer method than dry mixing) and the resulting paste dried. This was then crumbled and passed through sieves to produce granular powder. Such powder was more efficient in the gun, since the interstices between the grains allowed faster ignition and combustion, and since each grain was a solid compound the individual substances could not separate out. Early woodcuts show various stages in the making of powder: chopping the charcoal, wet-mixing the powder, breaking up the 'press-cake' and sieving the grains.

from the early years of the 14th century. Other examples have been excavated in Germany and Central Europe, and as a result these early hand gonnes can be seen to have several points of similarity. In general, they appear to have consisted of a wooden stave some three feet long to which a cast bronze or iron barrel was fixed by iron bands. The barrel varied in length from one to three feet, and the smooth bore was from a half to one-and-a-half inches in calibre. In some instances the barrel appears to have been cast as an open-ended tube, a plug being driven into the rear end in order to seal it. A vent, or touch-hole, was drilled through the metal at the rear end of the bore.

To fire, the hand gonne was charged with a quantity of powder and a ball or a handful of stones or small shot. Powder was then sprinkled in the vent, and the weapon grasped by its stave, tuck-

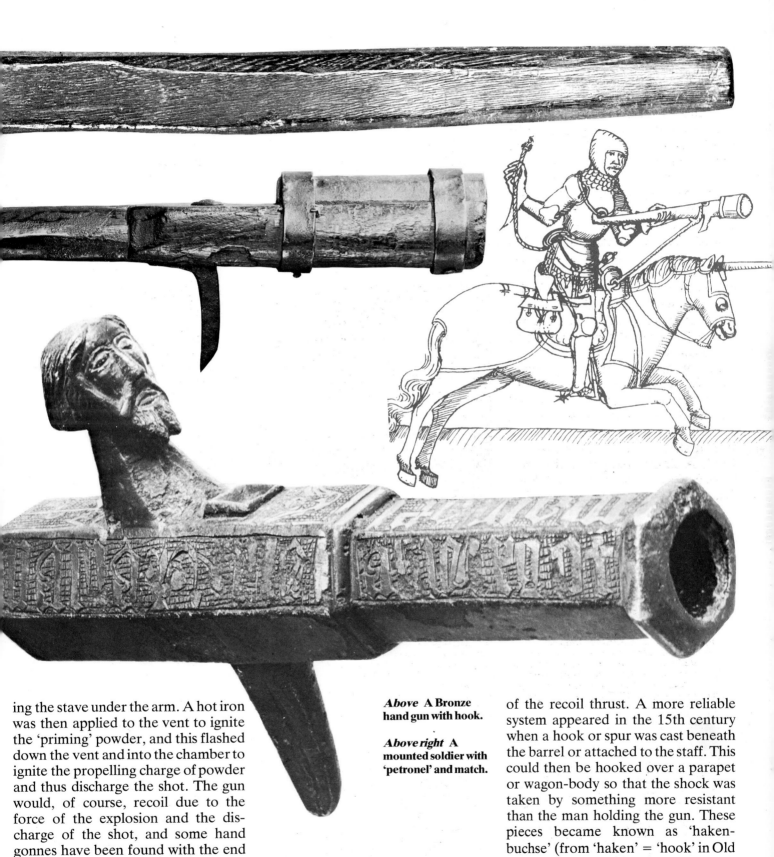

ing the stave under the arm. A hot iron was then applied to the vent to ignite the 'priming' powder, and this flashed down the vent and into the chamber to ignite the propelling charge of powder and thus discharge the shot. The gun would, of course, recoil due to the force of the explosion and the discharge of the shot, and some hand gonnes have been found with the end of the staff formed into a knob or ball, which, it is suggested, might have been rested on the ground to absorb some

Above **A Bronze hand gun with hook.**

Above right **A mounted soldier with 'petronel' and match.**

of the recoil thrust. A more reliable system appeared in the 15th century when a hook or spur was cast beneath the barrel or attached to the staff. This could then be hooked over a parapet or wagon-body so that the shock was taken by something more resistant than the man holding the gun. These pieces became known as 'haken-buchse' (from 'haken' = 'hook' in Old German) and this, in turn, was gradually corrupted to 'harquebus' or 'arquebus'.

9

THE MATCHLOCK
15th CENTURY

THE MOST INCONVENIENT thing about the early hand gonnes was the awkward system of ignition by hot iron; obviously a hand-gunner could not stray far from the brazier in which he heated his iron. For defensive purposes this was no great drawback, since braziers were placed on the ramparts of a castle or defensive work, but for field use the method was impractical. Some time towards the end of the 14th century the matter was resolved by the invention of 'slow match'. This consisted of loosely woven hemp cord boiled in a solution of saltpetre and then allowed to dry. Due to the impregnation, when ignited the cord would smoulder slowly and reliably,

always presenting a brightly burning end which could be used to ignite gunpowder. A hank of slow match could be carried more easily than a hot iron and, once ignited, could be carried for several hours, looped loosely in the fingers, so that the foot soldier now had a convenient form of ignition with which he could roam far and wide about the battlefield. He had to take care of it, though; Cyprian Lucar, an English gunner writing in 1588, observed that 'A Gunner . . . ought not, for any prayers or reward, lend any piece of his gunmatch to any other person, because it may be hurtful to him in time of service to lack the same. . .'

Even so, a hank of smouldering string was an inconvenient thing to be burdened with in the heat of battle; as with the hot iron, it still demanded the use of one hand and arm, which could not, therefore, be used to support the gun. Another point was that the gunner had to keep his eye on the gun so as to bring the match to the vent; if he kept his eyes on the target he might well miss the vent and plant the burning match on his wrist or fingers. Early in the 15th century these difficulties were ended by the invention of the matchlock. The earliest illustrated record is dated 1411 and shows a hand gonne with wooden staff, on which is mounted a long Z-shaped arm. At the

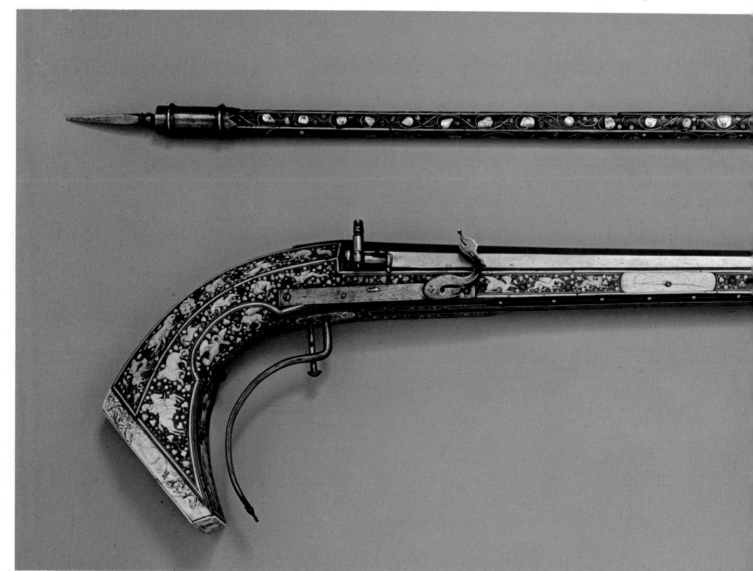

forward end of this arm is a piece of burning slowmatch, and this is being forced down into contact with the vent by the gunner pulling up on the other end, the Z being pivoted to the staff in its centre.

This was cumbersome, but it soon inspired improvement. As it happened, the contemporary crossbow used a similar Z-shaped catch to retain the bowstring and release it, and this was adapted to become the 'match lock'. The operation was the same but the device was more compact. In the first models the stock of the gun was slotted to allow the 'serpentine' (the Z-shaped piece) to pass through, and a pivot pin held it in place. The section

above the stock held the match, while the section below acted as the trigger, being pulled back to bring the match to the vent. In a very short time the gunsmiths simplified construction by placing the vent in the side of the gun and surrounding its outer end with a 'pan', a saucer-like depression into which the priming powder was placed. This allowed the serpentine to be attached to the side of the stock, doing away with the need to cut slots in the woodwork. Then the whole affair, serpentine and pan, became a self-contained unit 'lock', attached to the 'lock plate' which was in turn attached to the side of the weapon.

Further detail improvement fol-

lowed. A cover was placed on the pan; this could be slid forward to permit the priming to be loaded, then back to protect the powder from rain or spillage. When the time came to fire, the cover was opened again in order to allow contact of the burning match; when the cover was in place it was also a safeguard against sparks from the match inadvertently firing the gun before the firer was ready. More rapid action was achieved by the development of the 'snapping matchlock' in

An English musket rest of about 1630, the wooden shaft inlaid with mother-of-pearl and engraved staghorn. Below it a French matchlock of about 1575, the walnut stock inlaid with engraved and stained staghorn.

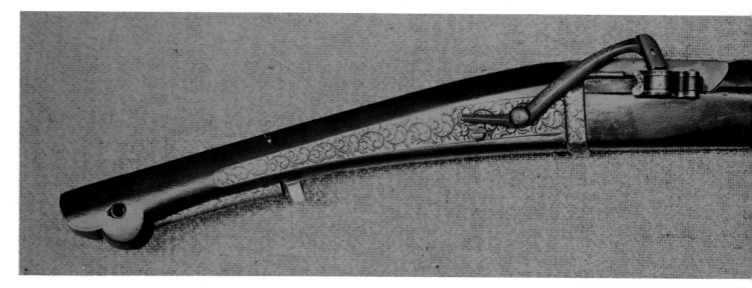

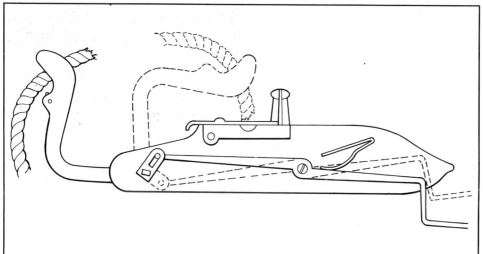

Top A Japanese 18th century matchlock musket with inset silver decoration.

Above right An Arquebusier takes aim; notice the 'cartouches' slung around his waist, each containing one charge of bullet and powder.

Above The basic matchlock mechanism.

Far right A breech-loading matchlock shield-pistol belonging to Henry VIII.

Right Figure with matchlock, from a manuscript dated 1411.

Above A German bronze matchlock, c.1500.

Below An early matchlock, from an imaginatively illustrated manuscript of 1468.

Loading a matchlock; a 16th century woodcut showing the way in which the hand-gonne's shaft had become shaped into a shoulder stock.

which the simple serpentine arm was replaced by a curved match-holder driven by a spring; the holder was drawn back and held by a trigger which, when pulled, released the holder to fly forward under pressure of the spring and carry the match into the pan. This type of matchlock, though soon superseded in Europe, was to remain in wide use in Japan until the 19th century. It had been taken there by Portuguese traders in the 16th century shortly before Japan cut herself off from the world, and since subsequent developments in firearms did not reach Japan, the snapping matchlock remained their normal ignition system far beyond its obsolescence in Europe.

The matchlock conferred benefits in other directions; now that the firer had no need to watch the match and vent to secure ignition, he could make some attempt at pointing the gun in the direction of the enemy more accurately. The stock of the weapon therefore changed from the round staff to a more flattened form which could be placed against the shoulder, one hand gripping the butt and operating the trigger while the other hand supported the barrel. Illustrations from the last quarter of the 15th century show this type of 'freehand' operation of matchlocks, but as a general rule the forked rest was still in wide use, principally because of the weight of the weapons. Arquebusses could weigh up to 20 lbs or more, and holding such a mass at the shoulder was not easy. 'Muskets' were somewhat lighter — about 15 lbs —and were easier to hold.

THE WHEEL-LOCK

16th CENTURY

WHILE THE MATCHLOCK was a moderately effective method of ignition, it still left a lot to be desired. One drawback was that if it chanced to rain, inevitably the match was extinguished and the army's firepower immediately fell to zero. Another tactical defect was that when a sentry was walking up and down at night, his movements were announced to the enemy by the glowing match, so that evading him became a very easy matter. But when it came to equipping armies, the matchlock had the supreme virtue of cheapness and simplicity; there was little involved in it, and even less in keeping it working in the field. And because of these advantages it stayed the standard infantry weapon for some two hundred years.

But there was an understandable desire on the part of gunsmiths to produce something more elegant, and in the opening years of the 16th century the wheel-lock was developed, probably in Germany. The origin of this mechanism is as indefinite as the origin of the gun itself: some authorities offer Leonardo da Vinci as the inventor on the strength of certain drawings which, though undated, have been reliably assessed as being from about 1508. These undoubtedly show a type of wheel-lock mechanism, but the concensus is that the device in question was a tinder igniter; an attempt to manufacture a gun lock to da Vinci's specification did not result in a working device. Another school of thought ascribes the invention to one Johann Kuhfuss or Kiefuss, a clockmaker of Nuremberg, and it certainly seems more likely that it originated with a clockmaker than with a gunsmith. But whoever was responsible, there are sufficient records to show that it was in use by 1510.

The wheel-lock mechanism is perpetuated in the cigarette lighter of today (or, rather, yesterday, since the arrival of the piezo-electric crystal)—a serrated wheel which is revolved rapidly in contact with a pyrophoric stone so that burning particles are thrown off. In the cigarette lighter the sparks strike a wick or a stream of gas; in the gun they were directed into the pan where they ignited the priming. The necessary impetus to the wheel was provided by a spring connected to the wheel's axle by a short length of chain. The axle had a square end on to which a 'spanner' could be placed and the wheel wound back so as to put the spring under tension. A locking pin then held the wheel against the spring's pull. When ready to fire the 'cock' was thrown forward; this was a hinged arm carrying a piece of iron pyrites in a jaw, so that the pyrites was held firmly against the wheel surface alongside the powder-charged pan. Pulling the trigger now released the wheel, striking off sparks from the pyrites and igniting the gunpowder.

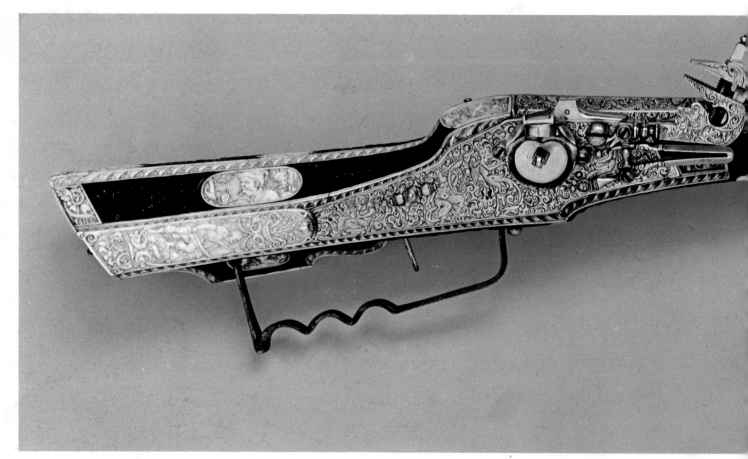

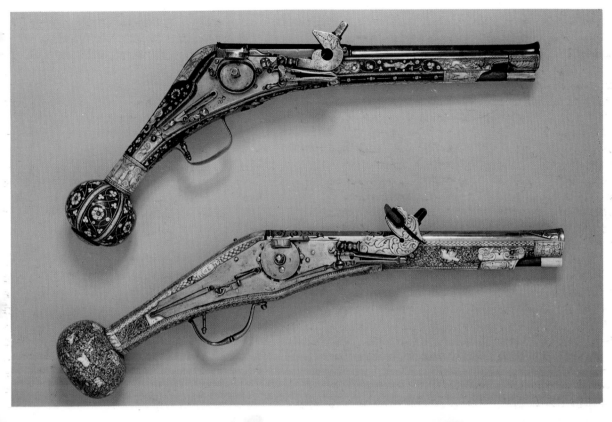

Left Two ball-butted pistols of characteristic German pattern, the stocks of both inlaid with engraved staghorn. The first example has a lock of French type with a separate mainspring; South German (Nuremberg), dated 1593. The second bears the initials of the stockmaker, B. H., and the barrel is engraved with maker's marks and dated 1579.

Below A wheel-lock rifle, the walnut stock applied with carved ebony and staghorn panels, probably by Peter Opel of Regensburg; South German, about 1600.

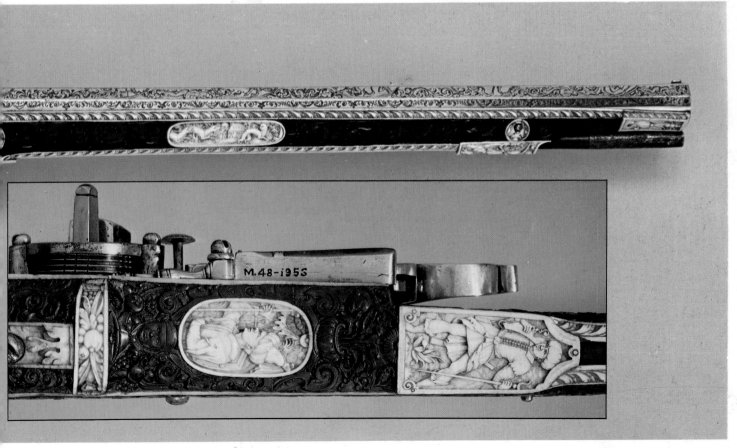

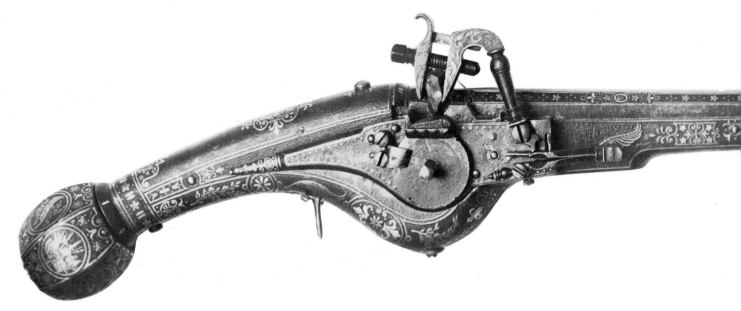

Needless to say, this basic design soon saw improvement. Pan covers which slid open as the cock was put into place were an early step; then came linking of cock and trigger so that as the trigger was pulled, the cock flew forward into contact, the pan cover opened and the wheel revolved. In order to relieve the firer of the need to wind up the wheel after each shot, the 'self-spanning' lock was invented, in which the cock was geared to the wheel in such a manner that pulling it back for a fresh shot would wind up the wheel again; this was an elegant mechanical idea but, due to the powerful leverage needed, was not very practical, and such locks were uncommon.

The wheel-lock was, as might be imagined, rather more expensive than the ordinary matchlock, and for this reason it was not widely adopted as a military arm. Instead, it became the preferred system for sporting and privately owned weapons, and the lock makers and gunsmiths were able to lavish their artistic talent upon wheel-locks. As a result some of the finest specimens of decorated weapons are from the wheel-lock period. Another, less laudable, consequence of the wheel-lock was that weapons could now be carried concealed. It had hardly been practical to try and conceal a matchlock complete with burning match beneath one's clothes, but a cocked and primed wheel-lock was a different matter. So much so that as

LEONARDO'S WHEEL-LOCK

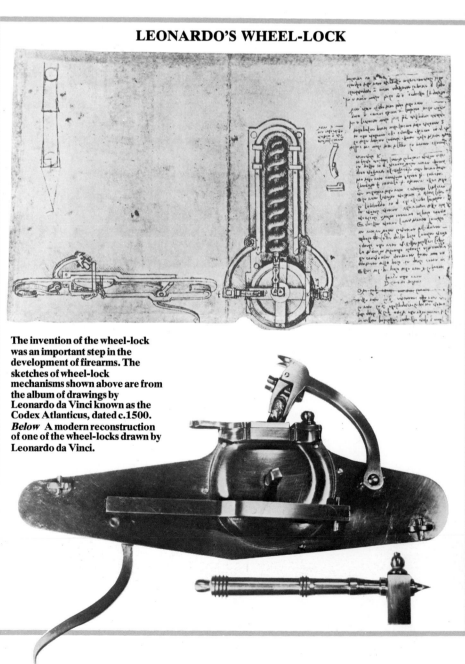

The invention of the wheel-lock was an important step in the development of firearms. The sketches of wheel-lock mechanisms shown above are from the album of drawings by Leonardo da Vinci known as the Codex Atlanticus, dated c.1500. *Below* A modern reconstruction of one of the wheel-locks drawn by Leonardo da Vinci.

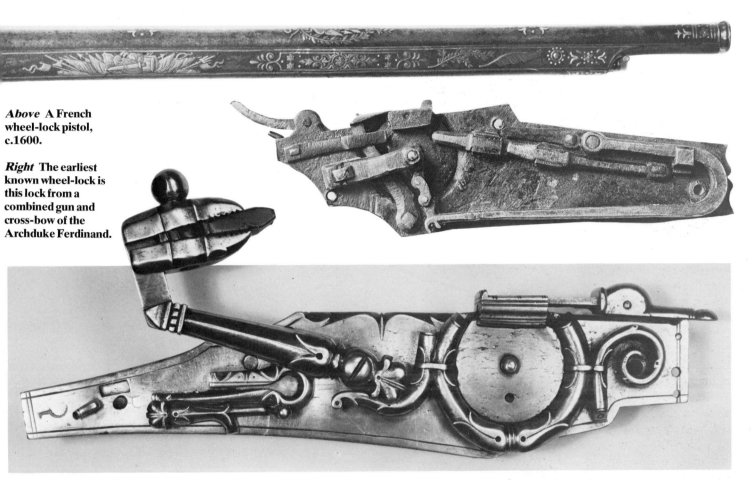

Above A French wheel-lock pistol, c.1600.

Right The earliest known wheel-lock is this lock from a combined gun and cross-bow of the Archduke Ferdinand.

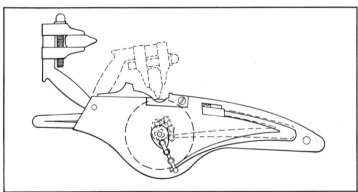

Above A self-spanning wheel-lock, c.1540.

Right The mechanism of a wheel-lock.

Below An interesting French 'pyrites lock' in which a curved arc replaces the serrated wheel.

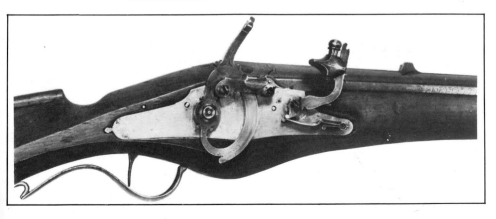

early as 1518 the Emperor Maximilian was being urged to pass laws to forbid the carrying of concealed weapons and 'guns which ignited themselves'.

Since it was inconvenient to attempt to conceal three or four feet of musket or arquebus beneath the coat, these laws suggest that by 1518 the pistol had appeared on the scene, a one-hand short gun capable of ready concealment. However, no dated pistol earlier than about 1560 is known, and it was not until the latter part of the 16th century that the pistol began to make an appearance as a cavalry weapon. Since the cavalry existed in smaller numbers than foot soldiers, and were less likely to damage their expensive weapons, the wheel-lock cavalry pistol soon gained acceptance and led to changes in cavalry tactics to allow the horsemen to discharge their pistols before getting down to business with their swords.

Decorated Stocks and Barrels

The 16th and 17th centuries saw the personal firearm develop from a crude piece of weaponry into a possession reflecting the wealth and prestige of its owner; barrels were often chiselled in relief and gilt, while stocks were fitted with mounts of gilt and inlaid bronze.

Right A wheel-lock rifle with ivory panels, c.1670.
Below Two Turkish flintlocks: 18th century (top) and 17th century (below).
Below right Detail of a German wheel-lock pistol, dated 1579.
Opposite top An Italian flintlock pistol, c.1690.
Opposite centre Designs for pistol ornamentation by Simonin of Paris, 1685.
Opposite right and bottom A flintlock pistol by an unknown French gunsmith, c.1690.

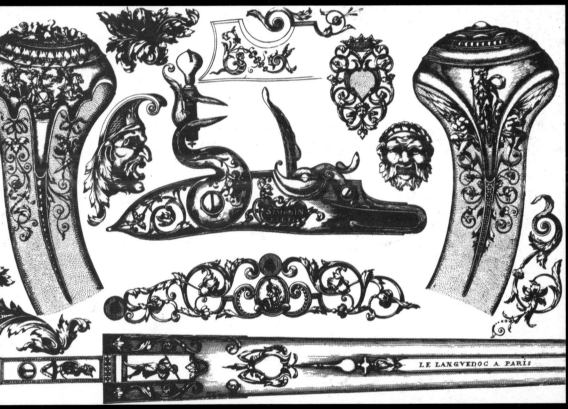

LE LANGVEDOC A PARIS

THE SNAPHAUNCE

LATE 16th CENTURY

IN THE 16th CENTURY, as ever since, the sure road to fame and fortune for any weapon designer or manufacturer was to obtain a contract for military supply, and therefore if the wheel-lock was not acceptable to the military, then something cheaper and simpler had to be found.

Once again, a precise time and place cannot be advanced for the snaphaunce, though every indication points to Germany as its birthplace. The basic mechanism was that of a spring-loaded arm, the 'cock', which carried a shaped piece of flint in jaws at its outer end. The pan was now covered by a steel 'frizzen', an arm which was hinged ahead of the pan and which had an upturned and concave face at its free end. The relative positions of cock and frizzen were so arranged that when the cock fell forward, under the impetus of its spring, the flint was driven hard across the curved face of the frizzen so as to strike sparks. At the same time, the curved face of the frizzen and its pivot point led to a complex interplay of forces in which the impact of the cock caused the frizzen arm to fly up so as to allow the struck sparks to pass into the pan and ignite the priming.

These locks were known as 'snaphaunce' locks; the origin of the term is in some doubt. Some writers claim that it comes from the Dutch 'snap Haens', meaning 'hen thief', ascribing this derivation to the early use of the lock by poachers. More likely is the derivation from German: 'Schnapphahn' or 'snapping hammer', which seems more feasible if the German origin of the lock is accepted.

Irrespective of its origin, the snaphaunce soon spread across Europe and certain local preferences and peculiarities emerged. The 'Swedish' or 'Baltic' version, for example, was characterised by an extremely long arm and jaw to the cock, which appears to have been derived from matchlock design. The Spanish lock, sometimes called the 'miquelet' lock, had the frizzen shaped to form a pan cover, so that the powder was not exposed until the actual moment of ignition. The Spanish lock also had a 'half-cock' position as a safety measure. With all snaphaunces the cock was drawn back with the thumb against spring pressure; the lower end of the cock was then rested on a cross-

bolt, or 'sear', actuated by the trigger, so that pulling the trigger withdrew the sear and allowed the cock to fall. In the Spanish lock there was a second sear which moved out beneath the toe of the cock as it was pulled back almost as soon as it began to move, and prevented fire being struck if the cock were accidentally slipped during the 'cocking' movement. Once this 'half-cock sear' was under the cock the weapon could be safely carried; the pan cover could be operated; and the trigger could not be pulled, since the trigger sear was not in play. The advantage here was that with the cock at 'half cock', the pan could be primed and the gun loaded and kept loaded in safety. Without the half-cock feature the pan could not be opened if the cock were left forward, but when the weapon was cocked and then loaded, it could only be carried in a most careful fashion for fear of accidental discharge. The Spanish lock's half-cock sear was withdrawn from its blocking position by cam action when the cock was drawn to 'full-cock' position.

The Dutch snaphaunce lock, which was probably derived from the Spanish, separated the frizzen and pan

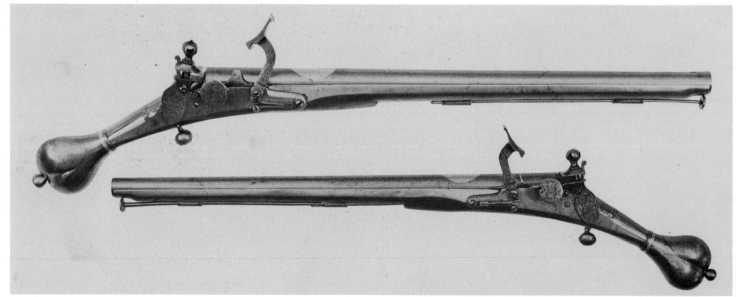

A typical Scottish-made pistol with ball trigger and heart-shaped butt, c.1671.

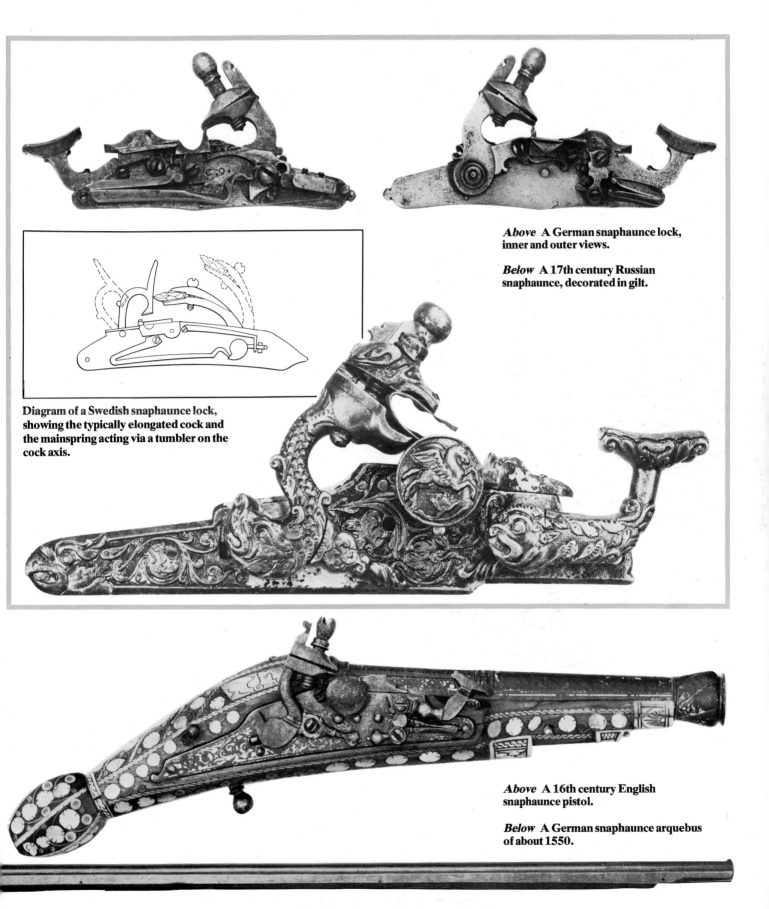

Above A German snaphaunce lock, inner and outer views.

Below A 17th century Russian snaphaunce, decorated in gilt.

Diagram of a Swedish snaphaunce lock, showing the typically elongated cock and the mainspring acting via a tumbler on the cock axis.

Above A 16th century English snaphaunce pistol.

Below A German snaphaunce arquebus of about 1550.

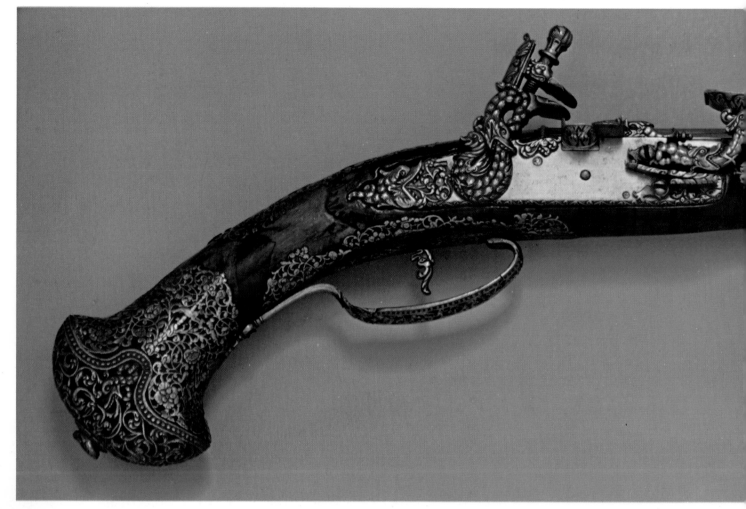

cover into two distinct components and linked the sliding pan cover to the cock by a simple lever. Thus as the cock fell, the pan cover was thrust open in time to receive the sparks. To carry the gun safely, the frizzen could be thrown up, out of the path of the cock, without exposing the priming.

The 'English Lock' used a combined frizzen and pan cover and took its nickname from the sear mechanism in which the cock was a notch in its lower edge into which a 'dog-catch' snapped by spring power as the cock was pulled back. This dog was withdrawn by the action of the trigger.

Some finely decorated snaphaunces are known. Although the snaphaunce lock became the standard method of ignition, it was also incorporated into highly ornamental weapons, carefully made for wealthy patrons.

Above A snaphaunce holster-pistol, the walnut stock inlaid with mounts of pierced iron, the barrels signed 'Lazarino Cominazzo'; Brescia, about 1650.
Below An English snaphaunce musket dated 1588.
Right A pair of snaphaunce pistols with mounts of chiselled iron by Giuseppe Guardiani of Anghiari. Italian, late 18th century.

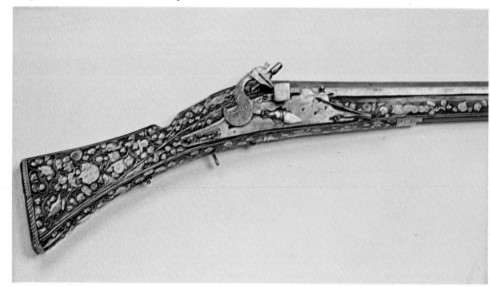

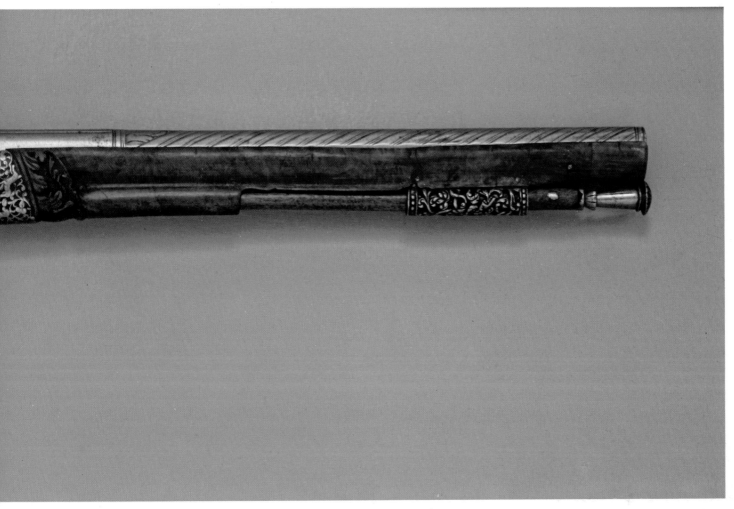

The 20th century concept of conspicuous consumption was present in earlier times in the form of ostentatiousness among the wealthy or the aristocracy. The ownership of beautiful objects has always been desirable in itself, but in earlier times the man who had wealth and power was required to demonstrate it in order to keep it. The lavishly decorated firearm has been common: what better way to flaunt both wealth and power?

Illustrated on these two pages are some of the finer examples of arms using the snaphaunce lock. The musket, inlaid with gold and silver, is English and dates from 1588; the holster pistol, with a stock of walnut inlaid with fretted iron, is from Brescia, Italy, and dates from about 1650; and the two pocket pistols are also Italian, dating from the late 18th century.

THE FLINTLOCK

1620–1635

THE SIMPLICITY and efficiency of the snaphaunce lock rapidly brought it into prominence throughout Europe and it fell to the French to bring together the best features of the various local designs and perfect the 'flintlock' early in the 17th century. The earliest references for perfected flintlocks occur in the 1620–1635 period.

Basically the 'true' flintlock, as perfected, exhibits the following points: the frizzen and pan cover are in one piece, retained in position by a strong spring; the sear moves vertically and engages in a 'tumbler' with two notches to give full and half cock; and the mechanism is entirely concealed on the inner side of the lockplate. The 'tumbler' was a steel cam attached to the axis shaft of the cock, so that movement of the cock was reproduced inside the lock by the tumbler, and the sear could perform its controlling functions by acting upon the tumbler instead of directly on the cock.

The flintlock rapidly assumed the premier position although some gunsmiths remained faithful to the earlier snaphaunce designs and continued to make them for many years. The principal area in which the flintlock prospered was in military firearms; here was a lock which was relatively simple, strong, not expensive, and as reliable as could be expected, and which put an end to the dangers of carrying burning slowmatch.

With the form of lock more of less settled, improvements and perfections appeared. Flint 'knapping' or forming became a major industry in those parts of the world where particularly sound flint occurred: Brandon in England, Cher in France, the Southern Tyrol and Transylvania were noted for the quality of their flints and exported them by the barrel. A good flint was generally considered to last for about fifty shots, after which it was generally discarded, since attempts to put a new edge on it were seldom successful. The actual fixing of the flint into the cock was quite a delicate matter, as this extract from the English

Exercises of the Firelock shows: 'In fixing flints, no uniform mode should be attempted; the flat side must be placed either upwards or downwards according to the size and shape of the flint and also according to the proportion which the cock bears in height to the frizzen, which varies in different muskets. This is observed by letting the cock gently down and observing where the flint strikes the frizzen, which ought to be at a distance of about one third from the top. Most diligent observation ought at the same time to be made whether every part of the edge of the flint comes into contact with the frizzen, so as to strike out fire from the whole surface. Each particular flint, therefore, requires its own particular mode of fixing so as to accommodate it to the particular proportions and conformations of each lock. Whenever a piece has been fired,

the first opportunity should be taken to examining whether the flint remains good, and fixed as it ought to be, and no time should be lost in correcting whatever may be found amiss. . .'

An important innovation which accompanied the flintlock was the prepared cartridge. Since the earliest days the soldier had been provided with a flask of powder and a pouch of bullets, and he loaded these items individually. An early attempt at standardisation had been the 'cartouche', a small container which held one bullet and sufficient powder for one loading. But now the complete bullet and powder combination was wrapped in a tube of paper. The use of the cartridge can be seen in this extract from the *Exercise of the Firelock*:
'Upon the command "Prime and Load", make a quarter face to the right . . . at the same time bringing the

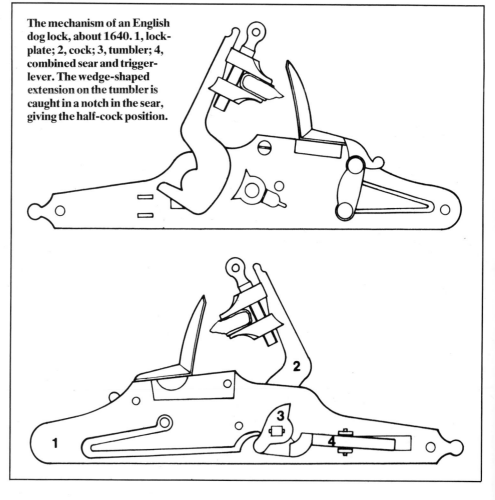

The mechanism of an English dog lock, about 1640. 1, lockplate; 2, cock; 3, tumbler; 4, combined sear and trigger-lever. The wedge-shaped extension on the tumbler is caught in a notch in the sear, giving the half-cock position.

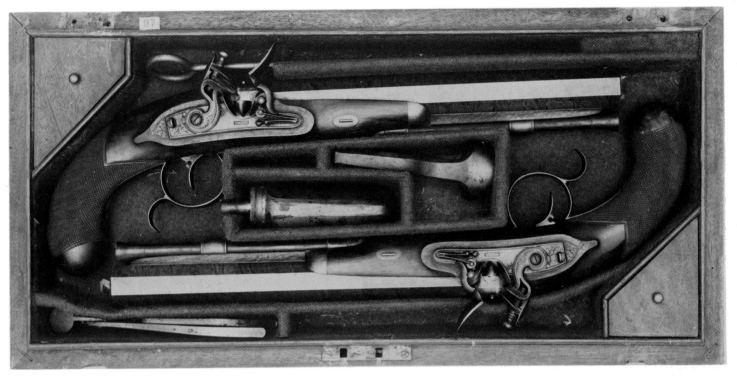

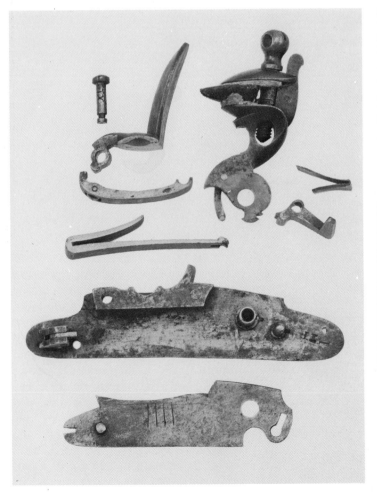

Above A pair of flintlock duelling pistols, cased, by Nock, c.1800
Left A gunmaker's label of 1809.
Far left Components of Nock's Screwless Lock from an English cavalry pistol c.1800.
Below Detail of the lock from a gun of Louis XIII made by le Bourgeoys c.1620.

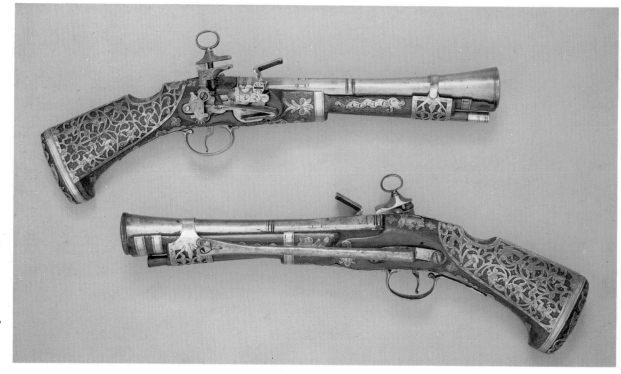

Right Two Spanish miquelet-lock blunderbusses, c.1690.

Below right A French gun of about 1770, with mounts of silver and gilded iron, the barrel inlaid with brass.

Below An early German cartridge box of embossed iron, with loops for attaching to the belt, c.1550.

Right A German powder flask of staghorn mounted in silver gilt.

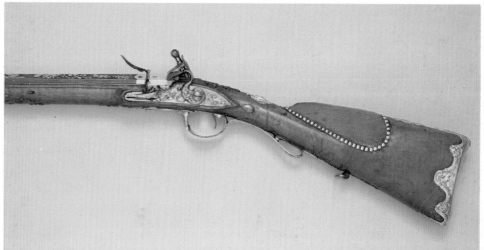

firelock down to the priming position ... Open the pan...'

'Upon the command "Handle Cartridge", 1st draw the cartridge from the pouch, 2nd bring it to the mouth, holding between the forefinger and thumb, and bite off the top of the cartridge.'

'Upon the command "Prime", 1st, shake out some powder into the pan and place the last three fingers on the hammer. 2nd shut the pan...'

'Upon the command "About", turn the piece nimbly round to the loading position ... Place the butt upon the ground without noise, raise the elbow square with the shoulder, and shake the powder into the barrel...'

'Upon the command "Draw Ramrods" force the ramrod half out and seize it back-handed exactly in the middle. 2nd, draw it entirely out, turning it at the same time to the front, put one inch into the barrel.'

On the command "Ram Down the Cartridge" ... push the ramrod well down to the bottom and strike it two very quick strokes with the ramrod.'

NICHOLAS BOUTET

A foremost French gunmaker Nicholas Boutet (below) who specialised in decorated firearms. Examples of his work are (top) a pair of pistols, c.1820, and (below) a garniture of arms presented to Napoleon in 1797.

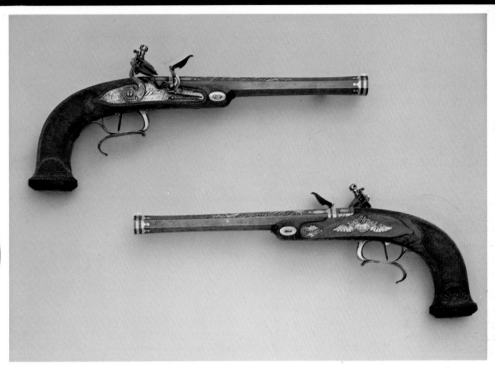

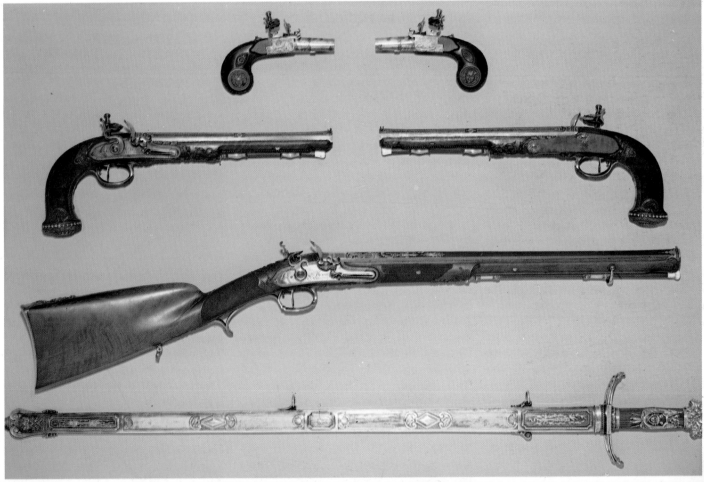

THE PERCUSSION PRINCIPLE

EARLY 19th CENTURY

THE FLINTLOCK, for all its virtues, had one inherent fault; its action was not instantaneous, but could be distinguished as three separate events: first the fall of the cock and striking of sparks; second the ignition of the priming; and third the explosion of the cartridge and ejection of the bullet. In the military application this led to long and intensive training of the recruit, since his normal reaction was to flinch as the priming fired, thus disturbing his aim before the cartridge exploded. In the sporting application the snap of the flint and the flash of the priming often alerted the game, which moved with lightning reaction and was no longer there when the bullet or shot arrived. Hunters became adept at forecasting how far and in which direction the game would spring or fly and aimed-off accordingly, but it turned hunting into a game of chance instead of a reliable method of filling the pot.

Among the hunters who suffered thus was the Reverend Alexander Forsyth of Belhelvie, Aberdeenshire. As well as ministering to his flock, Forsyth devoted his time to chemistry, mechanics and shooting, and he began to apply his mind to the problem of making a weapon capable of instantaneous discharge. In 1800 Edward Howard of the Royal Society had discovered fulminate of mercury, a sensitive substance which, when struck, detonated violently: doubtless Forsyth had heard of this, and he began making his own experiments. In 1807 he patented a system of ignition which relied upon a 'detonating powder' composed largely of potassium chlorate.

In Forsyth's lock, the frizzen and pan were replaced by a small revolving magazine resembling a flask—it became known as the 'scent bottle lock' from its shape—which contained a supply of detonating powder. This magazine pivoted around an axis which was bored through the side of the gun barrel to provide a vent into the chamber. The flint-carrying cock

The Reverend Alexander James Forsyth of Belhelvie, inventor of the percussion firearm.

was now replaced by a simple hammer. The gun was loaded with powder and shot in the usual way, and then the magazine was revolved a half-turn about its axis. This brought the powder receptacle above the vent and a small measure of detonating powder dropped down and charged the vent. The magazine was then turned back half a turn, which took the magazine section down to the 'blind' side of the vent and positioned a loosely-held pin above the powder in the vent. On pulling the trigger the hammer fell, striking the pin; this was driven down into the vent, crushing the powder and exploding it. The resulting flame ran down the vent and fired the gunpowder charge. There were some very surprised birds around Belhelvie in 1807.

Forsyth attempted to interest the government in his lock for military use, and he attracted the attention of the Master General of the Ordnance. For two years he had the use of a workshop in the Tower of London, but on a change of Master Generals his contract was terminated. He then set up a company, with James Purdey, a prominent gunsmith, and put the percussion lock on the market with

considerable commercial success.

It is questionable whether any other single innovation in the history of firearms is as significant as Forsyth's percussion principle, for without it much of the subsequent developments—metallic cartridges, automatic weapons, breech loading—could never have taken place. It marks the watershed between the long and slow development of the muzzle-loading arm—1326 to 1807—and the rapid and manifold developments of breech-loading and rapid-firing arms of all descriptions, much of which development was fundamentally completed by 1900.

Once Forsyth had shown the way, practical gunsmiths were quick to make improvements. Forsyth and Purdey changed the 'scent bottle' lock to a similar sliding pattern, linked to the hammer; as the hammer was cocked, so the magazine slid forward, bringing a firing pin into position to be struck by the hammer. Similar locks were produced by gunsmiths on the continent, but the use of loose detonating powder had its drawbacks and alternative systems of priming were soon to appear.

One early idea was to make up small pills of powder, coating them with varnish or gum. These were placed in the vent and struck by the hammer. Such a system came, of course, from contemporary apothecary's practice, as did an alternative system of sealing pinches of powder between two discs of paper, which has survived to this day in the caps or 'amorces' used by children in toy guns.

Stemming from the paper disc system came the 'tape' system invented by Maynard, an American dentist, in which small patches of powder were stuck to a paper or linen tape which could be pulled from a magazine and laid across the vent as required.

Another ingenious system was the placing of the powder at the closed end of a small copper tube. The open end was thrust into the vent, and the hammer fell so as to crush the closed

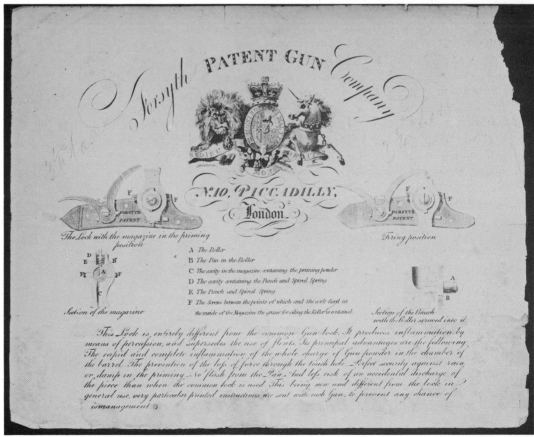

Above A Forsyth sporting gun in its case.

Right The label from the sporting gun case, showing details of the 'scent bottle' lock and instructions for its use.

Overleaf A pair of percussion pistols in a mahogany case with plated turn-off barrels and walnut stocks inlaid with silver. Signed 'Egg London', about 1830.

THE FORSYTH LOCK
1 is the magazine, which revolves around 2, the vent. The hammer 3 strikes the firing pin 4 to ignite the powder deposited in the vent.

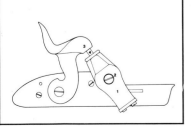

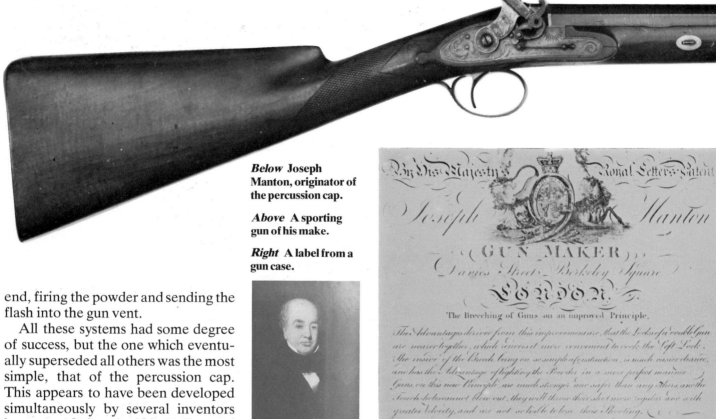

Below Joseph Manton, originator of the percussion cap.

Above A sporting gun of his make.

Right A label from a gun case.

end, firing the powder and sending the flash into the gun vent.

All these systems had some degree of success, but the one which eventually superseded all others was the most simple, that of the percussion cap. This appears to have been developed simultaneously by several inventors between 1818 and 1823. In England Joseph Manton and Joseph Egg perfected a system; in America Captain Joshua Shaw took out patents in 1822. The French gunsmith Prelat laid claim to the idea, as did Colonel Peter Hawker, a noted English sportsman. Whoever may have been first, the fact remains that in England Forsyth's patent of 1807 effectively prevented much progress prior to 1821.

After some false starts, the percussion cap settled down to a very simple pattern, that of a top hat of copper with a small coating of detonating powder inside the crown, secured there by a coat of varnish which also served to waterproof it. The gun vent now ended in an upturned 'nipple' with a central hole, upon which the cap was placed, open end down. The hammer fell, crushing the cap against the edges of the nipple and thus firing the detonating powder so as to send a powerful flash down the vent. A slight defect of the early caps was that, due to weak copper and strong powder, the caps frequently split, fragments

flying off and endangering the firer. This was countered by making the hammer face hollow, so that at the moment of ignition the cap was entirely surrounded by steel. Another system adopted to guard against the disintegrating cap was to place the nipple below the breech and arrange the hammer to strike upwards, so that the body of the gun was between the cap and the firer's face. These 'underhammer' guns enjoyed some popularity and actually appeared as military weapons in Scandinavia.

As usual with a new idea, there was no rush by the military to adopt it overnight. By the early 1800s most nations had a sizeable amount of money invested in arms, and to scrap the lot and replace with something entirely new was an unpleasant prospect. Fortunately, the percussion system lent itself to conversion; it was relatively simple to remove the flintlock from a gun and replace it with a percussion lock.

Above An early breech-loading percussion pistol.

Left A percussion lock, c.1830.

Below A pair of decorated percussion duelling pistols.

Below left A pair of pocket pistols in mahogany case, fitted with Forsyth's patent sliding primers.

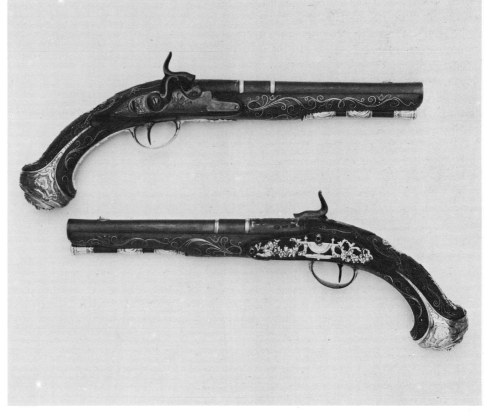

BREECH-LOADING FIREARMS

EARLY 19th CENTURY

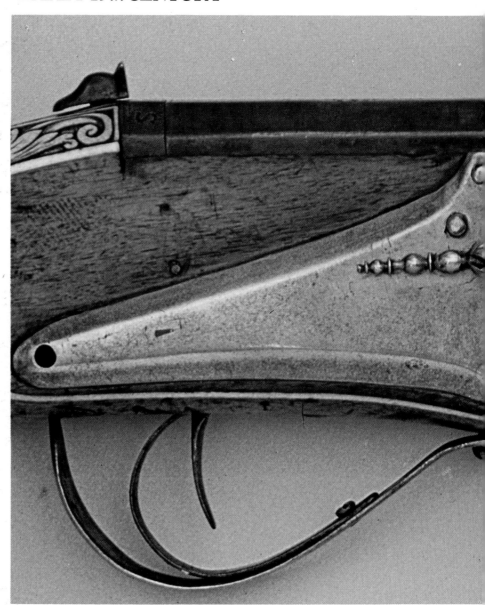

THE INDUSTRIAL REVOLUTION brought about many changes, but one of the least-appreciated (or so it seems) was that it now became respectable to be an engineer, and the 19th century saw the engineer reach a status he never enjoyed before nor has done since. Consequently many intelligent and ingenious minds, which otherwise might not have contemplated mechanical problems, suddenly discovered innumerable technical problems waiting to be solved, with the added stimulus of a sizeable fortune for the best solution. And many of these minds began studying firearms and how to improve them.

One way to improve them, most people agreed, would be to load them from the breech end and do away with the prolonged performance with powder, ball and ramrod. There was nothing new in this idea, since breech loading firearms had been attempted right from the earliest days, particularly with cannon. But in those early days there was little real understanding of what went on inside the gun when it fired or of the type and magnitude of the pressures and temperatures involved. Moreover the ability to machine metal to fine limits on a production basis simply did not exist; it was one thing to spend months carefully hand-fitting a pistol for sale at a high price to a noble patron, but a totally different matter to attempt to duplicate it on a scale suitable to equipping an army.

Some of the earliest known breech-loading small arms are two carbines and two shield pistols made for Henry VIII. The carbines used a trap-door at the rear of the barrel which could be lifted and an iron tube, charged with powder and ball, inserted. Ignition was by wheel-lock through a vent incorporated in the tube. The shield pistols used a similar loading system but were matchlocks—and that itself is remarkable, for only one other specimen of a matchlock pistol is known. But in spite of excellent workmanship for their time, the sealing of the

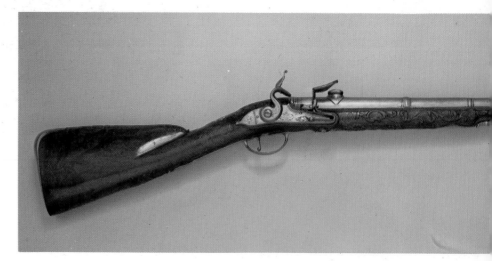

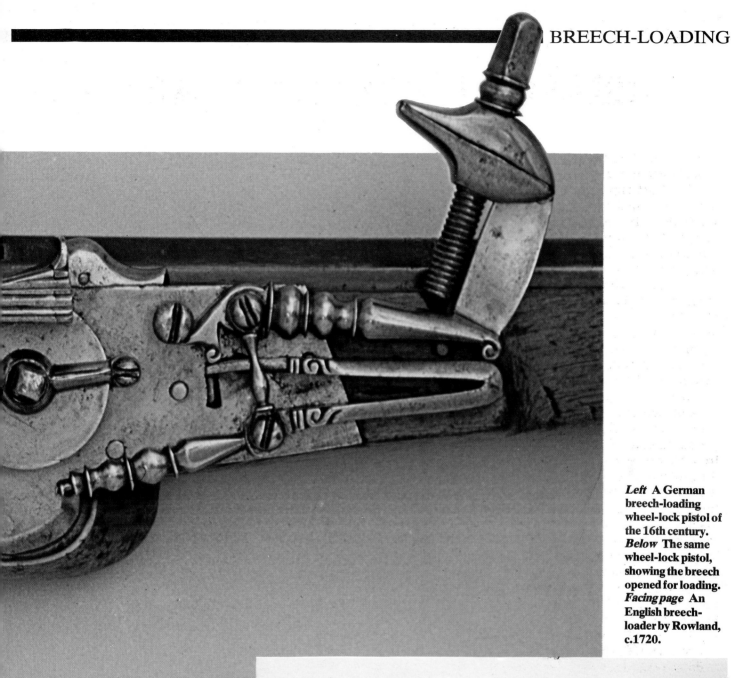

Left A German breech-loading wheel-lock pistol of the 16th century. *Below* The same wheel-lock pistol, showing the breech opened for loading. *Facing page* An English breech-loader by Rowland, c.1720.

breeches of these weapons left a lot to be desired.

The next attempt at breech-loading to amount to anything was an invention by de la Chaumette, a Frenchman; in 1704 he drilled a large vertical hole through the rear end of a musket barrel, cut a thread on it, and then closed the hole by a screwed plug inserted from below. The trigger guard formed a handle for the plug, and a few turns were sufficient to lower the top of the plug so that powder and ball could be inserted into the breech. The plug was then screwed up, and the gun was fired by the usual flintlock mechanism. Chaumette seems to have had relatively little success with the design, though some sporting guns were made on the principle, and it lay more or less neglected until revived and improved by Patrick Ferguson, a Scottish soldier, in the 1770s. Ferguson made the breech plug with a quick thread so that half-a-turn was enough to open the breech for loading; he also made the breech section of the plug with a smooth surface so that fouling could not jam the action, and he placed a greater thickness of metal below the breech to take the screw thread so that the plug could be lowered below the chamber level to facilitate cleaning the bore.

In 1776 Ferguson demonstrated his rifle in front of the Master General of the Ordnance. On a wet and windy day at Woolwich Marshes he fired his new gun at a steady rate of four or five shots a minute, and then capped this by walking towards the target, loading and firing as he went. As a result, one hundred 'Ferguson Rifles' were ordered to be made; a special 'Light Company' of 100 men was raised and,

commanded by Ferguson and armed with the rifles, was sent to America. But the first major engagement of the Ferguson rifle was destined to be its last, though from no fault of the rifle. Ferguson and his light company were part of a diversionary attack at Brandywine Creek on 11 September 1777; they acquitted themselves with distinction until Ferguson was wounded by an American bullet. With the moving spirit removed, the light company was dispersed and the hundred rifles disappeared. Ferguson recovered from his wound, but before he could make a start in reforming the light company, he was killed at the Battle of King's Mountain, and the Ferguson rifle was never revived. The greatest mystery of all is what happened to his rifles? Only one or two of that original hundred are known to exist today, though others, made by gunsmiths for the Honourable East India Company and for private owners, have survived.

The first nation to adopt a breech-loader as standard was the United States when, in 1819, it began issuing the Hall Carbine. This had the rear

Above Breech of a carbine made for Henry VIII, dated 1537.
Below A 'turn-off' pistol, breech-loaded by unscrewing the barrel.

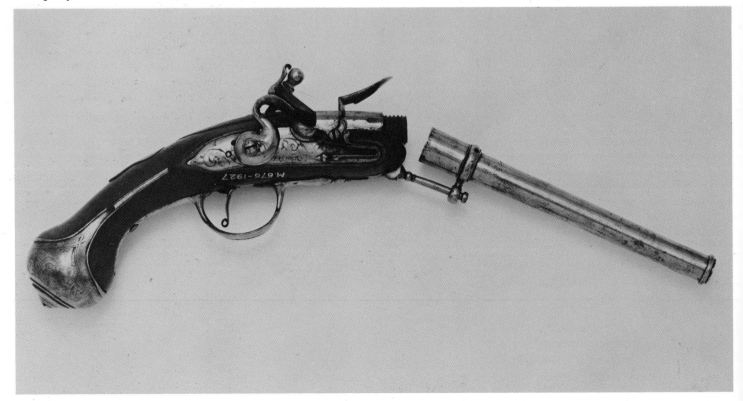

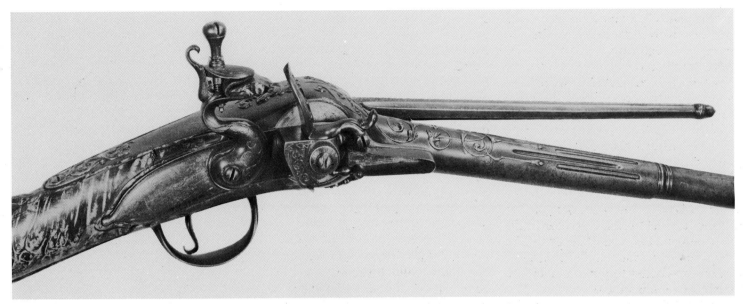

Above A breech-
loading magazine
gun, c.1680.

Right The Hall
breech-loading
carbine, with
removable breech
and lock unit.

Above A breech-
loading magazine
gun, c.1680.

Right The Hall
breech-loading
carbine, with
removable breech
and lock unit.

A flintlock pistol with
turn-off barrel and
breech-loading, self-
priming repeating action
on the Lorenzoni
system. The ball and
powder are taken from
the magazines in the butt
(1) and transferred by
gravity to the breech (2
and 3).

section of the barrel—the chamber
—separated from the rest and hinged
at the rear so that it could be tipped up
and loaded. Ignition was by percussion, and the chamber section also
carried the hammer and nipple, so that
the loaded chamber could be withdrawn from the rifle and carried in the
pocket to serve as an emergency pistol. Another innovative feature of the
Hall carbine was that it was manufactured by machinery on an assembly-
line principle, and the parts were interchangeable. It was far from perfect,
for the joint between chamber and
barrel soon began to leak due to the
erosive effect of the hot gases, but it
was to remain in service for almost
fifty years.

It was the self-contained cartridge
—i.e. a cartridge which held powder,
bullet and means of ignition—which
provided the complete answer to the
breech-loading puzzle, and it was not
until this apparently obvious point was
appreciated that progress began to be
made. The man who saw the cartridge
as the key was a Swiss, Johannes
Pauly.

Although Pauly's guns were greeted
with acclaim by such figures as
Napoleon and the Czar of Russia, they
failed to achieve commercial success,
and in 1814 he moved to London,
where he died three years later.

THE REVOLVER

THROUGHOUT THE HISTORY of firearms there were periodic attempts to devise weapons which could be loaded with several charges and bullets and then discharged repeatedly without having to reload between shots.

One obvious system was to provide the gun with several barrels, firing them separately or collectively as the situation demanded. The 'Ducksfoot' pistol, with five or six splayed-out barrels was one solution and one which, it is said, was particularly popular with sailors on boarding a ship or confronting mutineers. Another famous weapon was Nock's Volley Gun, a seven-barrelled short musket pro-duced for the Royal Navy in the 1780s. This consisted of a central barrel surrounded by a cluster of six more, all fired by a single flintlock mechanism. The lock fired the central chamber, from which ports communicating with the outer barrels fired the other six chambers simultaneously, which must have been something of a handful to control.

More practical was a gun firing one barrel at a time, and as early as the late 16th century there were examples of three-barrelled guns in which the group of barrels could be moved so as to bring each barrel into alignment with the matchlock in turn. In the 17th century came the idea of having one fixed barrel but placing a cylinder, containing a number of loaded chambers, behind it, discharging them one at a time through the barrel. The drawback here was the difficulty of arranging ignition; either a single pan and lock served each chamber in turn, having to be reprimed for each shot, or each chamber had its own loaded pan and frizzen; neither system was entirely satisfactory. Towards the end of the 18th century the 'Pepperbox' pistol became popular; this used a revolving cluster of barrels, fired by a flintlock, each barrel being hand-turned into alignment with the lock.

In 1818 Captain Artemus Wheeler of Concord, Massachusetts, obtained

a patent for a 'gun to discharge seven or more times', and this might be said to mark the birth of the revolver as we know it today. Wheeler's design was actually for a carbine or short musket, with a hand-revolved cylinder and flint ignition. It was examined by the U.S. Navy in 1821 but turned down. In the meanwhile, Wheeler's assistant, Elisha Collier, came to England and secured a patent for a 'firearm combining a single barrel with several chambers to obtain a succession of discharges from one loading.' Collier never denied that his inspiration came from Wheeler, but he incorporated some important features which lifted the design far beyond those which had

preceded it. The most innovative feature was the provision of a spring to revolve the cylinder when the hammer was cocked. Another important feature was that the cylinder moved forward, under spring pressure, so that the rear end of the barrel entered into the mouth of the cylinder to form a close joint and so prevent the escape of flame and gas on firing. Other mechanical linkages were provided so as to lock the cylinder in place against the recoil force.

Altogether, the Collier pistol was a considerable advance, and although he failed to get it adopted as a military weapon (it was refused as being 'far too complicated and expensive to be

applicable to the Public Service') the idea had some commercial success. Several English gunsmiths obtained licences from Collier to manufacture revolving pistols, shotguns and rifles to his patent. He then went into business as a gunsmith for a short time, but in 1827 he left the firearms field and turned to civil engineering for the remainder of his life.

It will be seen that the period of the Collier revolver spanned the time during which the percussion cap came into use, and his designs were accordingly changed in order to use this system of ignition, a far less involved matter than his original flintlock system. The percussion cap also revitalised the pepperbox revolver, and the 'bar-hammer' pepperbox, so called from the long hammer which stretched across the top of the pistol in order to reach the nipples on each barrel, became popular in England and America. The English designs were particularly important since they introduced trigger mechanisms which automatically rotated the barrel clus-

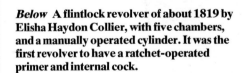

Below A flintlock revolver of about 1819 by Elisha Haydon Collier, with five chambers, and a manually operated cylinder. It was the first revolver to have a ratchet-operated primer and internal cock.

Left Collier's second model of about 1820 with improvements, including an external cock and fluted cylinder.

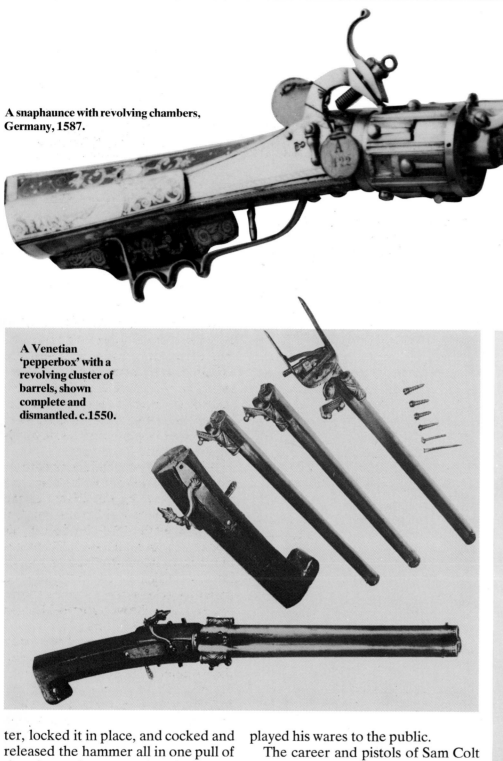

A snaphaunce with revolving chambers, Germany, 1587.

A Venetian 'pepperbox' with a revolving cluster of barrels, shown complete and dismantled. c.1550.

ter, locked it in place, and cocked and released the hammer all in one pull of the trigger, the so-called 'self-cocking' mechanism.

In spite of the efficiency of these arms, there was no great market for them. The London Proof House returns for the 1830–1850 period show that the average number of revolving arms submitted for proof (as they had to be before sale) was no more than about 300 a year. The revolver did not make a great appeal to the public until 1851, when the Great Exhibition was held in London and Samuel Colt dis-

played his wares to the public.

The career and pistols of Sam Colt are dealt with in greater detail in the body of the book, and will not, therefore, be repeated here. Suffice it to say that he had developed a percussion revolver and patented it in England in 1835 and in America in 1836. His patent was shrewdly drawn and effectively blocked any competitive development of a revolver with a mechanically-rotated cylinder in America until it expired in 1857. The English patent was never actively worked in England, and it is doubtful

Below The 'Defence' revolver invented by James Puckle (left) showing the square chambered cylinder for 'use against infidels'. *Inset* A printed patent for the 'Defence' revolver.

Left An English five-shot pepperbox pistol by Budding of Stroud.

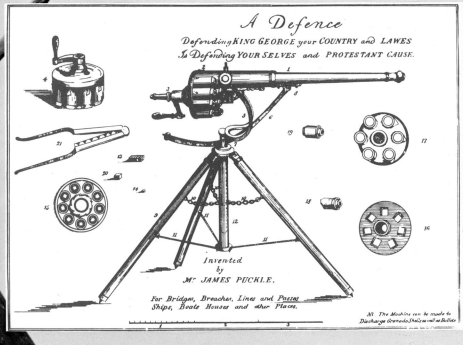

A Defence
Defending KING GEORGE your COUNTRY and LAWES
Is Defending YOUR SELVES and PROTESTANT CAUSE.

Invented by Mr JAMES PUCKLE.

For Bridges, Breaches, Lines and Passes
Ships, Boats Houses and other Places.

whether his claims would have withstood too close an examination; the existence of mechanically-rotated cylinders on pepperbox revolvers prior to 1836 would probably have invalidated much of his claim. But in any event, as we have already said, there was little public interest in revolvers in England.

After going into liquidation with his first revolver venture, Colt was given a second chance by the advent of the Mexican War of 1847, and from then on, aided by the 1849 Gold Rush, his company prospered. In 1851 his exhibits in London attracted enormous interest, which he carefully fostered by a variety of astute publicity stunts, and suddenly the western world began to clamour for revolvers.

Colt's revolvers were of the 'open frame' pattern; the butt frame carried the hammer and cylinder, and the barrel was affixed to the front of this frame by a removable key. Thus, there was no connection between the barrel and the upper portion of the frame and the top surface of the cylinder was exposed. By knocking out the key, the barrel could be removed, followed by the cylinder, for cleaning, after which the cylinder could be loaded with powder and ball or with prepared paper cartridges, caps placed on the nipples, and the gun re-assembled. To simplify re-loading, Colt later developed a lever-rammer which lay beneath the barrel and could be unclipped to allow the chambers to be reloaded without having to dismantle the weapon completely.

At the 1851 Exhibition, Colt's only serious competitor was Robert Adams of London. Adams had developed the 'solid frame' revolver in which the butt frame and barrel were forged as a single piece of metal, a rectangle being left in the frame into which the cylinder was fitted. This resulted in a much stronger form of construction. Adams also used a different firing mechanism to that of Colt. The Colt was a 'single action' pistol in which the hammer had to be manually cocked for each shot, being released by pressure on the trigger. The Adams was a 'self-cocking' pistol in which pulling the trigger lifted and dropped the hammer. Both systems have their advantages; the single action was better for accuracy, since the relatively light pull needed to release the cocked hammer was unlikely to upset the aim. The self-cocking lock, however, demanded a much greater effort to pull through on the trigger, and this invariably caused the pistol to waver off its aim. On the other hand, for rapid fire in action, the self-cocking lock was preferred since the firer merely kept on pulling the trigger.

Both Colt and Adams competed for military contracts, and Colt was, due to the better accuracy stemming from the single-action lock, fortunate in securing a contract to provide revolvers to the British Army and Navy. But the Crimean War showed the advantages of the Adams design in close combat, and when Lieut. Beaumont made an improvement to Adams' lock which allowed the user to select either single action or self-cocking action —the 'double-action' lock—the Adams supplanted the Colt in British service.

With the advent of metallic cartridges the revolver designers now had to devise methods of loading and unloading at the rear of the cylinder, and this led to a plethora of patented contraptions. Eventually three systems outlived the rest: gate-loading, in which the cartridges were inserted one at a time into the chambers, through a

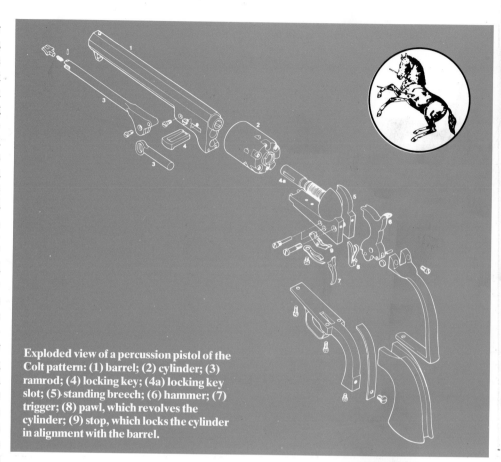

Exploded view of a percussion pistol of the Colt pattern: (1) barrel; (2) cylinder; (3) ramrod; (4) locking key; (4a) locking key slot; (5) standing breech; (6) hammer; (7) trigger; (8) pawl, which revolves the cylinder; (9) stop, which locks the cylinder in alignment with the barrel.

Above A typical Adams solid-frame ·45 revolver of 1872.

Right The English gunsmith Robert Adams loading the revolver of HRH the Prince Consort.

ADAMS' REVOLVING PISTOL.

Above The Smith &
Wesson 'New Century'
revolver in ·455 calibre.

Left Horace Smith and
Daniel B. Wesson.

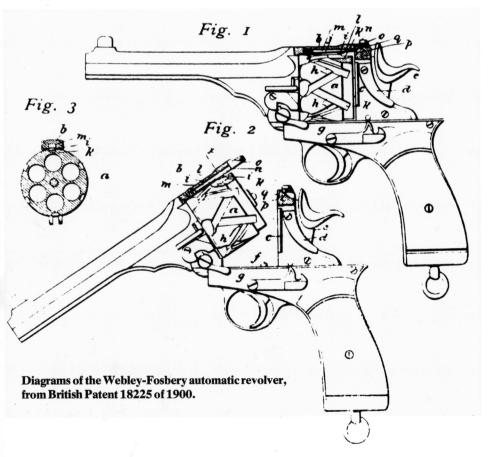

**Diagrams of the Webley-Fosbery automatic revolver,
from British Patent 18225 of 1900.**

gate or trap at the side of the breech; the hinged frame, in which the barrel and cylinder swung away from the frame to expose the rear face of the cylinder; and the side-opening solid frame revolver in which the cylinder was carried on a 'crane arm' and could be swung out to lie alongside the frame for loading. Extraction of the empty cases was achieved in the first case by a rod beneath the barrel which, thrust backwards, pushed the spent cases through the gate one by one, and in the other two cases by arranging a plate in the centre of the cylinder to move outward, catching beneath the cartridge case rims and thus ejecting them.

Except for aberrant forms such as the Webley-Fosbery automatic revolver, the Landstadt and the Dardick revolvers, the basic pattern for revolvers was settled by the early 1890s and development since then has largely been in matters of detail or improved systems of manufacture.

THE RIFLE

THE FACT THAT A spinning bullet could be made to fly more accurately than one fired from a smoothbored barrel seems to have been discovered some time late in the 15th century, but where and by whom is another unsolved mystery. The earliest known rifled arm is a matchlock hunting rifle owned by the Emperor Maximilian in 1500. Many hypotheses have been advanced to account for the development of rifling, but we can only continue to speculate. The most likely theory is that archers were accustomed to cant the feathers on their arrows in order to achieve some degree of spin (more probably, roll stabilisation), finding (probably by accident) that this improved the accuracy of flight, and thus the development of rifling in firearms was a logical follow-on. This is probably true; what is quite certain is that it was two or three hundred years before there was any sort of understanding of why rifled arms shot more accurately.

But even if the theory was absent, practical results spoke loud enough, and from the 16th century onwards, rifled arms were made. Not in great numbers, since rifling was a long and difficult—and hence costly—process, so that rifles were originally the property of wealthy hunters and sportsmen. Moreover the owners had to take some pains with their ammunition, casting their own bullets very precisely to ensure that they would fit the rifling grooves correctly, for the bullet which was too loose a fit was of little or no use. This, of course, led to problems after a few shots had been fired; the fouling set up by the residue from the burned gunpowder charge made it harder and harder to force the

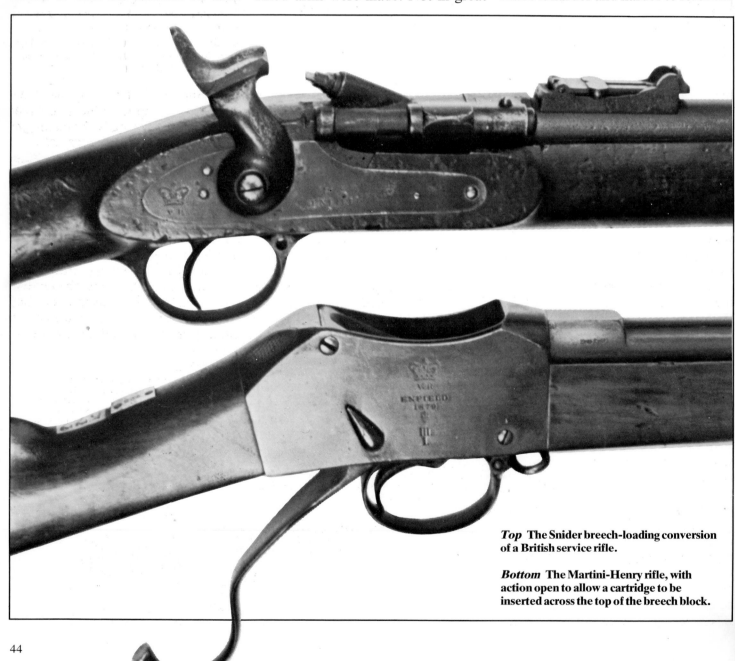

Top The Snider breech-loading conversion of a British service rifle.

Bottom The Martini-Henry rifle, with action open to allow a cartridge to be inserted across the top of the breech block.

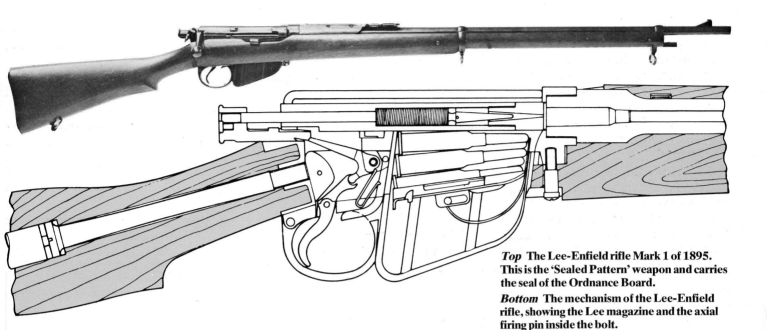

Top The Lee-Enfield rifle Mark 1 of 1895. This is the 'Sealed Pattern' weapon and carries the seal of the Ordnance Board.

Bottom The mechanism of the Lee-Enfield rifle, showing the Lee magazine and the axial firing pin inside the bolt.

ball down the barrel, and the bullet generally had to be 'started' in the muzzle by a wooden mallet. Eventually, the shooter had no alternative but to stop firing and thoroughly clean the barrel before he could continue.

Very soon it was found that a simpler way was to 'patch' the bullet; to enclose it in a cloth or thin leather wad which had been greased. The ball used with this system was of smaller calibre than the barrel and thus ball and patch could be easily rammed down. On firing, the patch would 'set up' and fill the rifling grooves behind the bullet, grip the ball and impart the desired spin, and then fall clear as it left the muzzle. This also helped to reduce the fouling, since the grease left in the bore softened the powder residue and the wad swept the grooves clean with each shot.

In spite of the extra expense involved in rifling a weapon, it was soon appreciated that in the hands of trained men a few rifles could be most effective in battle, and rifles began to appear in military service in the 17th century. King Christian IV of Denmark is generally credited with being the first to put the rifle into military service but he was soon followed by others. In some armies the would-be rifleman was required to provide his

own rifle, on the assumption that he would probably produce a better weapon than the military could afford and also that he would already be familiar with it and thus require little or no further training.

We have already discussed the Ferguson rifle when dealing with breech-loading, since it was the breech arrangement which made the Ferguson unique in its period. In America, had it survived, it would have been pitted against the legendary 'Kentucky Rifle'. The rifle had gone to America in the early years of the 18th century, as Swiss, German and Bohemian

gunsmiths emigrated to the New World and set up in business, and that business became largely the making of hunting rifles. These were, at first, heavy weapons with 7-grooved rifling in large calibre barrels—calibres of ·5 to ·7 of an inch were usual. Such weapons had answered well in European hunting, but conditions in America were somewhat different; a hunting trip was not an afternoon's walk in the woods but a protracted and strenuous expedition, and the hunters wanted lighter rifles. Moreover, they argued, a smaller calibre would kill game just as well and economise on

THE TARGET RIFLE

Competitive rifle shooting doubtless began with a simple contest between two men as to who could shoot straightest, but over the years it has become an extremely involved and compartmented occupation. There are contests for military rifles, single shot rifles, automatic rifles, contests in which the rifle must be held to the shoulder, in which it may be partially supported, and in which it is entirely rested on a bench; with open sights and with telescopes; in the condition it left the makers' hands and with every modification which

the owner can contrive. The present-day match rifle, as illustrated here, has become a high-precision machine for punching holes in targets and wholly impractical for anything else. The stock is carefully tailored to the individual so that he always holds it in precisely the same fashion; the trigger is adjustable for strength of pull; the sights compensate for drift, wind and, jump while the rifling and the barrel are prepared with surgical precision. The result is as accurate and consistent a firearm as it is possible to make.

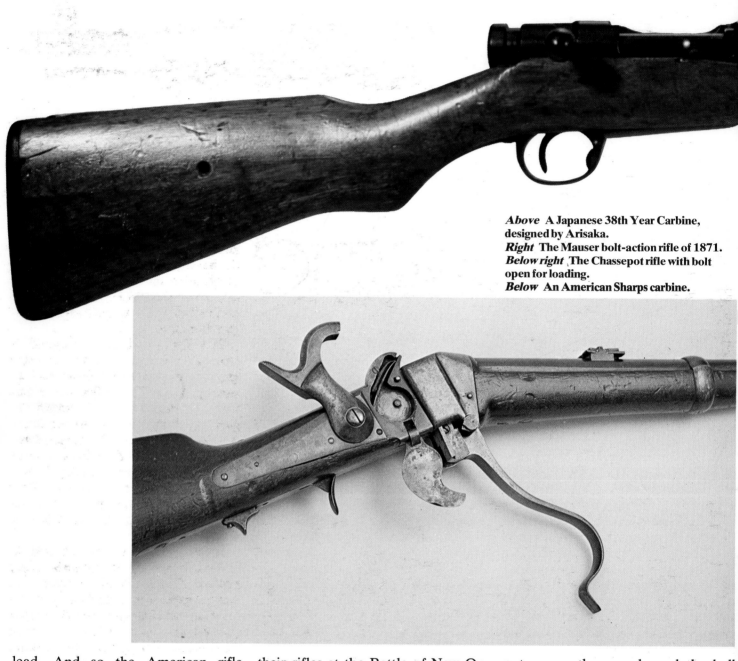

Above A Japanese 38th Year Carbine, designed by Arisaka.
Right The Mauser bolt-action rifle of 1871.
Below right The Chassepot rifle with bolt open for loading.
Below An American Sharps carbine.

lead. And so the American rifle evolved; a thinner and longer barrel of about ·45 inch calibre with a maplewood stock and with a unique 'patch box' incorporated in the butt for spare flints and bullet patches.

The majority of the gunsmiths specialising in these weapons settled in Pennsylvania, and the rifle is more properly known as the 'Pennsylvania Rifle'. Today they are more often, and incorrectly, called 'Kentucky' rifles due to a popular ballad from the War of 1812 which sang of Andrew Jackson's 'Kentucky Mountain Men' and

their rifles at the Battle of New Orleans. The accuracy of these rifles was legendary; one contemporary report speaks of putting eight consecutive shots into a 5 inch by 7 inch target at sixty yards' range, while a British officer who frequently found himself on the wrong end of these rifles gave his opinion that the average American marksman could hit an enemy in the head at 200 yards.

The principal drawback with the rifle as a military weapon was the slowness of loading, even with prepared cartridges. The patch had to be

put across the muzzle and the ball started truly down the bore and rammed. As a result, military riflemen were often accompanied by other soldiers armed with muskets so as to be able to produce some improved firepower in the event of a counterattack against the rifleman. The only answer to this would be to produce a bullet which would be of such small diameter that it would pass easily down the bore during loading but which would, by some means, expand to fit tightly into the rifling grooves.

In the 1840s a Frenchman, Thouve-

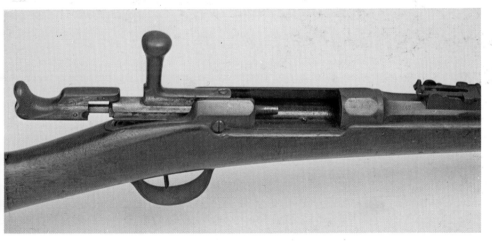

ios minor improvements, became the standard rifle bullet for the remainder of the muzzle-loading era.

Although the usual form of rifling is the 'polygroove' system in which a number of spiral grooves are cut into the barrel, there have been other ways of spinning the bullet and it is worth considering some of them, even if only to illustrate the boundless ingenuity of gun designers.

The Brunswick rifle, adopted in British service in 1835, had only two grooves, opposite each other and unusually deep. The bullet was a ball with a central raised belt which engaged with the grooves as the bullet was loaded and which imparted the spin as it was ejected. In theory it was a sound enough system, but the effect of the raised belt on the bullet's flight was such that it was impossible to hit anything at ranges greater than 400 yards.

Another idea, developed first in Denmark and later enthusiastically promoted in England by Lancaster, was to make the gun's bore oval instead of circular, and then develop it into a twist. An oval bullet was used and this, following the twisted bore, developed the necessary spin.

A similar idea was the Whitworth Hexagonal Bore in which the rifle barrel was a twisted hexagon in section, with the bullets shaped to suit.

With the arrival of breech loading most of the aberrant forms of rifling disappeared; most of them had been concerned with reducing the problems raised by powder fouling, and once it became practical to clean a rifle by passing a brush completely through the barrel, such problems diminished. Simple polygroove rifling became the standard pattern and has remained so.

nin, developed a pointed cylindrical bullet which was used in a special gun which carried a pillar in the centre of the chamber. The powder was loaded first and occupied the space around the pillar; the bullet was then dropped down the barrel so that its base rested on the tip of the pillar, whereupon a few sharp blows with the ramrod deformed the base of the bullet so that it spread out by impact on the pillar and expanded into the rifling.

This worked, but the deformation of the bullet was rather hit-and-miss and the pounding of the rammer upset

the head shape resulting in irregular flight. A better solution was to hollow out the base of the bullet and allow the explosion of the charge to expand the 'skirt' of the bullet into the rifling. This system was first proposed by William Greener, an English gunsmith, in 1835, but in spite of demonstrations the idea did not catch on. In 1846 Captain Minie, a French officer, developed a pointed bullet with a hollow base, and with a small iron cup in the base, which under pressure forced out the lower edge of the bullet into the rifling. The 'Minie bullet', with var-

THE MACHINE GUN

THERE HAS ALWAYS been a desire to increase the firepower of an army without increasing the number of soldiers to be clothed and fed, and this tendency can be discerned from the earliest times. In the 15th century the 'ribauldequin' was developed, a light two-wheeled cart carrying several small-calibre cannon barrels which could be touched off in a ragged volley to deliver a blast of shot. In 1718 James Puckle produced his 'defence' gun, a tripod-mounted revolver which allowed a rapid fire to be put down. Two cylinders were provided, one to fire round bullets against Christians, and one chambered for square bullets to be fired against infidels. A handful were made, two of which now remain, but Puckle's company went bankrupt and the idea fell by the wayside.

In 1851 a Belgian, Captain Fafschamps, invented a multiple-barrelled gun in which a cluster of barrels were enclosed in a cylindrical casing so that it resembled a cannon. A plate carrying a number of cartridges could be placed behind these barrels and clamped in position and the cartridges fired in succession through the barrels. He passed the idea to a manufacturer named Montigny who perfected it, and it was then adopted, in great secrecy, by the French Army as the 'Mitrailleuse' or 'grape-shot shooter'. Mechanically the idea was sound enough, but during the Franco-Prussian War it was tactically mishandled, which set the mitrailleuse idea back several years in military eyes.

It was the American Civil War which had given the machine gun its start. The first attempts were a reversion to the 'ribauldequin' or 'organ gun' idea, a collection of 25 rifle barrels on a wheeled carriage. Each barrel had to be muzzle-loaded, after which a priming of gunpowder was run across the 25 vents and ignited by a percussion cap and hammer. The result was a formidable volley, but this was followed by a long pause for re-loading, so the 'Billinghurst-Requa

A contemporary engraving of the Montigny Mitrailleuse, or 'grape-shot shooter'.

Battery Gun' found very few supporters among the military.

Somewhat more practical was the 'Ager Coffee Mill', which used a single breech-loaded barrel. Steel tubes were pre-loaded with powder and ball and had a percussion cap affixed to a nipple at the rear end, after which they were dropped into a hopper on top of the gun. Turning a hand crank fed the tubes one at a time into the breech, dropped a hammer on to the cap, and then extracted the fired tube; the gunner and his mate then had the job of picking up the empty tubes, cleaning them and re-loading them before the next engagement.

The most famous of the mechanical guns which appeared at this period was, of course, the Gatling Gun. Gatling appears to have appreciated the problem which had been pointed out by military critics of the Ager Gun; that firing a hundred shots a minute—or, as one commentator put it, '7500 grains of powder and seven pounds of lead every minute'—would raise the barrel to a very high temperature. To get round this, and also to simplify the mechanical problems of feeding and extracting at a high rate of fire, Gatling built his gun with six barrels which revolved. As any one barrel was at the topmost position, a cartridge was dropped behind the chamber, and as it travelled downwards this cartridge was gradually

chambered and the breech closed, until at the bottom-most point on its travel that barrel was fired. As it now moved up so the breech was opened and the fired case extracted, so that as it reached the top it was ready for another cartridge. In this way if the gun fired at, say, 600 rounds a minute, any one barrel fired at only 100 rounds a minute and spent the rest of its time travelling around to cool down.

In spite of inventing the gun during the Civil War, Gatling sold very few, largely because his political sympathies were suspected and because his factory was in Cincinnati, Ohio; it was thought that if he were given a contract to make guns for the Union Army, the Confederates might very easily promote a raid across the Ohio river and seize the shipment just as it was completed. After the war, though, the US Army and Navy both adopted the gun, and it was widely sold to Britain, France, Russia and many other countries.

Other mechanical machine guns which appeared in the 1870s were the Lowell, Gardner and Nordenfelt, all of which will be found in the Encyclopedia pages. Although the mechanical principle was superseded by the 1880s, the mechanical guns lingered into the early years of the 20th century before being scrapped. But the basic attraction of the Gatling—the division of work among a cluster of barrels—remained, and in the 1940s the idea was revived in order to produce a high-speed gun for aircraft use. When two fighter aircraft are dogfighting or a single machine is attempting to fire at a ground target, the period of time during which gun and target are aligned gets shorter and shorter as the aircraft gets faster and faster. With the speeds that jet aircraft were reaching the engagement time had dropped to about one second, and the contemporary machine guns, which in one second could fire only six or seven shots, were no longer effective. The Gatling, driven by an electric motor instead of a hand crank, could deliver up to 6000 shots a minute, 100 shots a second, and could thus produce a worthwhile volume of fire in a brief period of time. This line of thought led to the 20mm Vulcan cannon, and eventually to guns in rifle calibres.

But in the 1870s the only power available was manpower, or so it seemed. Then came Hiram Maxim, who brought an enquiring and inventive mind of the first order to bear on the problem and who rapidly realised that the recoil of the gun, which was usually cursed as a useless and unfortunate byproduct, was a source of untapped energy. By treating the recoil force as a source of power and using it to drive the gun mechanism, it would thus be possible to make an 'automa-

Two sailors operating a Gardner machine gun.

tic' machine gun, one which would continue to fire of its own volition so long as somebody held down the trigger and supplied it with ammunition.

Broadly speaking, there are two ways of driving an automatic weapon, be it machine gun, rifle or pistol: by means of the recoil force or the pressure of gas inside the barrel which is generated by the explosion of the cartridge. Within these two broad categories there are an infinite number of sub-divisions, though only a few of them will produce a practical weapon. The principal sub-division is whether or not the breech block is securely locked to the barrel when the gun is fired. With a low-powered cartridge in a short barrel there is no need to lock the breech; the inertia of the breech block is sufficient to resist the

Left An artist's impression of a Gatling-equipped 'camel corps'. The latter was intended to publicise a compact, short-barreled version known as the Camel Gun and there is little evidence to suggest that such a corps ever existed.
Above The manufacturer's nameplate on the breech of the Rotunda Gatling.
Below Richard Jordan Gatling (1818–1903), inventor of the first successful 'mechanical' machine gun.

opening force due to pressure on the back of the cartridge case, at least long enough to allow the bullet to leave the barrel and the chamber pressure to drop. Where more powerful cartridges are used, as, for example, in most military machine guns, it is necessary to lock the breech block since the longer barrel and heavier bullet mean that the pressure is retained longer and an unsupported breech would begin to open while the pressure was dangerously high. When this occurs, the cartridge case is ejected violently and, due to the pressure inside, usually bursts as it leaves the chamber. In other cases the interior pressure expands the mouth of the case so tightly that it refuses to move when the base of the case begins to leave the chamber and the case therefore splits in the middle. Either way, the result is not conducive to safety or to reliable operation.

Study of patents files shows that several inventors have realised the potentialities of gas and recoil but they were beaten before they began until the self-contained metallic cartridge was perfected. So long as a cartridge consisted of a handful of powder, a lead ball and a piece of flint or a percussion cap, it was futile to attempt any form of automatic feed and firing.

By the time Maxim had begun his studies the metallic cartridge had arrived, although it was a long way from perfection. By making a cloth belt with loops to hold the individual cartridges, Maxim was able to develop a weapon which would continue to fire, propelled by the force of its own recoil, feeding itself with cartridges, for as long as required. In his first model, it is interesting to note, he used air to cool the barrel. He soon changed this, developing the familiar water-jacket which surrounded the barrel and through which water could be circulated to absorb barrel heat. It is worth bearing in mind that of the energy produced by an exploding cartridge, only about 25% is expended in driving the bullet out of the muzzle; of the remainder, over half is muzzle blast and just under half is heat. A machine

Above French troops firing a Hotchkiss 8mm machine gun.

Right French officers being instructed in the details of a captured German Maxim '08 machine gun. The instructor has opened the receiver of the gun and holds the firing lock in his right hand.

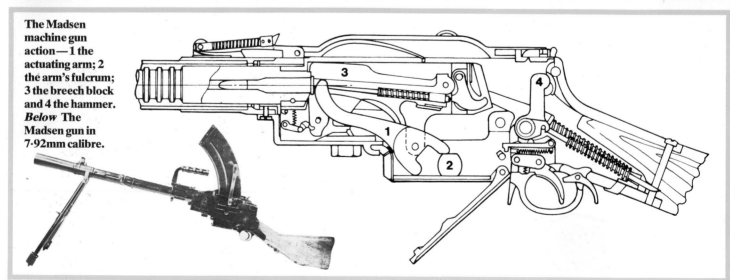

The Madsen machine gun action—1 the actuating arm; 2 the arm's fulcrum; 3 the breech block and 4 the hammer. *Below* The Madsen gun in 7·92mm calibre.

gun firing at 1000 rounds a minute generates about 200 horsepower. The Maxim gun would begin to boil the water in the jacket after about two minutes sustained firing.

Other water-cooled guns followed the Maxim, reflecting the current tactical views; the machine gun was a 'weapon of position' useful for beating off attacks from a prepared defensive post, and in this role it came to dominate the battlefield during the First World War. But that war also brought out the requirement for a light machine gun which could be carried by one man, and this class of weapon came into prominence in the post-war years as the Bren, Chatellerault and Vickers-Berthier (among many others) entered service. Portability argued against carrying gallons of water about, so air-cooling became the accepted method, with the additional feature of rapidly removable barrels, so that after sustained firing had heated the barrel, it could be quickly changed for a cool one and allowed to cool down.

During the Second World War the German Army introduced the concept of the 'general purpose machine gun', an air-cooled weapon which was all things to all men. It could be put on a tripod and used (with several spare barrels) for sustained fire, being belt fed.

The light Vickers-Berthier machine gun on a tripod.

AUTOMATIC PISTOLS

WHEN MAXIM DEMONSTRATED the ability to use the weapon's own recoil to actuate automatic action, it was an invitation for someone to try and condense the idea into a pistol. The difficulties were enormous, due to the small scale of the weapon and the consequently small size and strength of the component parts and also due to the difficulty (at that time) of producing reliable and consistent ammunition in pistol calibres. A difference in pressure or velocity from shot to shot in a revolver was of little concern to the action of the weapon, but inconsistent ammunition in an automatic pistol gave rise to erratic functioning.

The first automatic pistols designs involved tapping gas from the barrel to drive a piston back and thus cock a revolver hammer. Since the hammer controlled cylinder revolution, it can be seen that such a mechanism would re-cock the revolver and advance the cylinder after each shot. Weapons in this style were developed by Paulson in England (1885) and Orbea in Spain (1863) but were never put on the market. One important feature which both these inventors incorporated in their designs was a 'disconnector', a linkage which automatically disconnects the trigger from the rest of the firing mechanism after each shot and only re-connects them after the firer has consciously released the trigger and taken a fresh grip. Without a disconnector, the guns would have been truly automatic; they would have discharged all their chambers at high speed before the astonished firer had time to realise what was happening and release his grip on the trigger. And since this has applied to pistols ever since, it should be stressed that over 95% of the pistols we call 'automatic' should more properly be called 'self-loading'. The remaining 5% can be switched from the usual self-loading mode of operation so as to disconnect the disconnector and turn the pistol into a genuine automatic which will empty itself in seconds when the trigger is pressed, function-

ing as a sort of submachine gun. But fortunately these are extremely uncommon because for the most part they are grossly inefficient.

The revolver did not lend itself easily to being converted to an automatic pistol (though it was eventually done with some success in the Webley-Fosbery) and in the 1880s a number of inventors occupied their time in developing a new type of weapon, the 'mechanical repeater'. In almost every case, these used a bolt action, similar to that which had recently become popular in military rifles, and this bolt was propelled back and forth by a lever operated by the forefinger. The firer placed his finger in a ring at the end of this lever, which appeared where the trigger normally lived, and pushed forward; this opened the bolt. He then pulled back, which drove the bolt forward, chambered a cartridge from a magazine, locked the bolt and, at the last moment, released a firing pin to fire the cartridge. When they were new and clean and oiled, these weapons worked reasonably well, but when they were dirty or dry, they took a great deal of muscle-power in the

Right **The Czechoslovakian vz/38 automatic pistol, adopted by the Czech Army in 1939.**

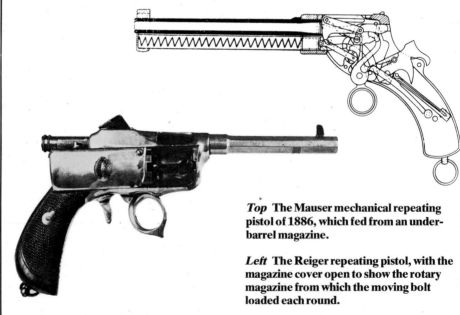

Top **The Mauser mechanical repeating pistol of 1886, which fed from an under-barrel magazine.**

Left **The Reiger repeating pistol, with the magazine cover open to show the rotary magazine from which the moving bolt loaded each round.**

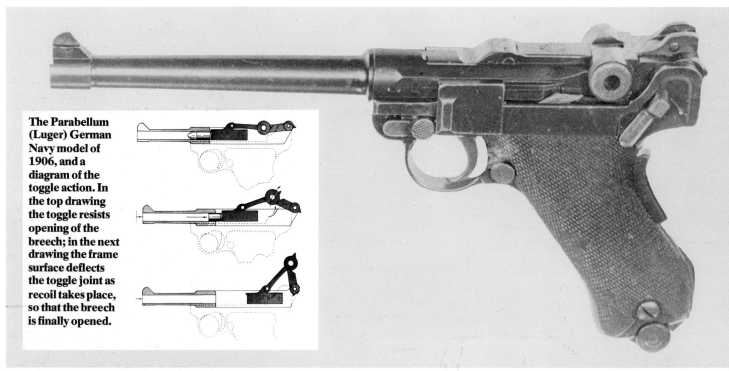

The Parabellum (Luger) German Navy model of 1906, and a diagram of the toggle action. In the top drawing the toggle resists opening of the breech; in the next drawing the frame surface deflects the toggle joint as recoil takes place, so that the breech is finally opened.

forefinger to operate them properly. As a result they did not prosper.

But it was one of these mechanical pistols, modified, which became the first automatic pistol. The Schonberger of 1893 had begun life as the Laumann repeating pistol; it was then altered so that the pressure in the cartridge case forced back the primer cap, so unlocking the breech, after which the remaining pressure in the case blew it back and opened the bolt. This was a remarkable system of operation which has never since been used in a production weapon, principally because it demands the use of special ammunition. And history tells us that guns which demand special ammunition, which cannot be bought over the counter at the local gunsmith, do not prosper. So the Schonberger didn't do very well in the marketplace, and the first pistol to become a commercial success was the Borchardt. This was recoil operated, with the breech locked by a most ingenious toggle system which was probably derived from study of the Maxim machine gun breech lock. After this, the designs came hard on each other's heels; the famous Mauser of 1896, several Berg-

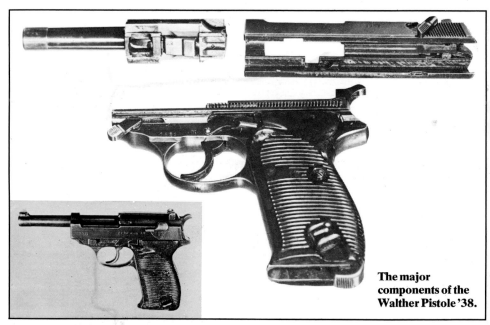

The major components of the Walther Pistole '38.

mann designs, and then the Luger, a refined Borchardt, in 1900.

The United States was strangely deficient of automatic pistol designs at this period—indeed, few good automatic designs have ever come from there—and it was not until John Moses Browning began to study the subject that any progress was made. His first pistols found little interest in

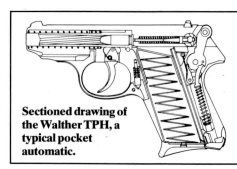

Sectioned drawing of the Walther TPH, a typical pocket automatic.

America, since they were developed as low-powered pocket weapons and no American manufacturer could see a market for then in competition with the multitude of cheap revolvers which were available there. He therefore disposed of his patents in Belgium, where they were transmuted into pistols with enormous success. What America wanted was a powerful automatic in keeping with their preference for large-calibre handguns, and Browning now sat down to develop a locked breech design of classic simplicity and ample strength, which eventually appeared as the Colt ·45 M1911 military pistol, service pistol of the US forces from that day to this and the oldest serving military weapon of any major nation.

This military decision in favour of an automatic pistol finally aroused American interest and a handful of local designs appeared as a result, but, as the manufacturers had feared, competition from inexpensive revolvers was a serious problem, and it was aggravated in the 1920s by an influx of cheap pocket automatics from Germany and Spain, which resulted in the gradual extinction of the American designs other than those of Colt.

Spain had become one of the foremost producers of automatic pistols, having pirated the Browning pocket designs shortly before the First World War. During the war the French and Italian governments, desperate for pistols, placed vast contracts for 7·65mm automatics with Spanish makers, and dozens of small companies sprang up to fill the demand. After the war these companies continued to turn out these 'Eibar' automatics (named from the centre of the Spanish gunmaking trade) and ex-ported them throughout the world at give-away prices. Some of them were good, but far more of them were poorly made of inferior metal, and they gave the Spanish gun trade a bad name which has taken them years to live down. Much of this 'cottage industry' disappeared in the Spanish Civil War.

The next major technical step came in 1929 when the Walther company of Germany popularised the double-action lock on automatic pistols. An advantage claimed for the double-action revolver over the automatic was that once loaded, it could be carried safely in an uncocked condition, then drawn and fired by simply pulling through on the trigger. An automatic, on the other hand, had either to be carried cocked, with the safety catch applied, or carried with an empty chamber and hurriedly charged and cocked when the need arose. With the Walther pistol it became possible to load the chamber, lower the hammer in safety, and then, when needed, pull through on the trigger to fire the first shot. The idea had been tried before, but Walther's design was better engineered than its predecessors and became a commercial success. It then went on to gain military acceptance; it was used in the Walther P-38, adopted by the German Army in 1937.

The late 1930s saw a number of new automatic pistols appear, either for the commercial market or for military adoption, and among them were some designs which have survived to the present day. The Walther P-38, above, is still in use by the West German Army. The French designer Charles Petter made some interesting modifications to Browning's locked breech design in a pistol for the French Army. His patents were later bought by a Swiss company and improved to produce the SIG pistols, currently enjoying a high reputation. Browning himself, before his death, made changes in his 1911 design, which later appeared as the 'Browning High Power', and is now probably the world's most widely-sold pistol.

Major parts of the Steyr M1912 pistol, in which breech locking is done by the rotation of the barrel, controlled by the curved rib on the barrel acting against slots in the pistol frame.

AUTOMATIC RIFLES AND SUBMACHINE GUNS

THE SUBMACHINE GUN bids fair to be the shortest-lived class of military weapon; it was born in the First World War, reached maturity in the Second, and there are indications that within another ten years it will have been discarded from the inventories of every major power.

The submachine gun is properly defined as a short-barrelled automatic weapon which is magazine fed and fires a cartridge normally associated with pistols. It was first developed in this form during 1917–18 for the German Army who wanted a weapon with which to arm their newly-formed 'Storm Troops'. The deadlock on the Western Front had led the Germans to devise a new tactical manoeuvre in which small groups of highly-trained soldiers would filter through the front line under cover of smoke screens and gas bombardments, and for this a weapon of short range but with a high rate of fire and a compact and handy form was wanted. The result was the 'Bergmann Musquete' or 'Kugelspritz' ('bullet-squirter') but the war was over before it had seen sufficient use to justify any tactical lessons being drawn from it.

The victorious Allies were in no doubt; it was not a military weapon, and they forbade it to the German Army, though the German Police forces were permitted to own them, probably due to the civil disturbances which were frequent in the immediate postwar years. It seems that the Army were not particularly distressed, since the military commanders of every nation in those days could see no military niche that the submachine gun could fill; it had been born of unusual tactical conditions which would not occur again, so that was that.

However, the prospect of a compact handful of fire power continued to fascinate some designers, among them the famous General John T. Thompson, who had been working on a small machine gun he called his 'Trench Broom' when the war ended. In an inspired moment he invented the term

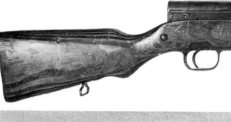

Far left US Infantryman carrying an Armalite AR15 in Vietnam; the belts are for a different gun.
Top left The Simonov SKS 46.
Left American troops using the AR15 in 1968.
Top right The Australian Owen Gun.
Right The Czech Skorpion submachine gun.

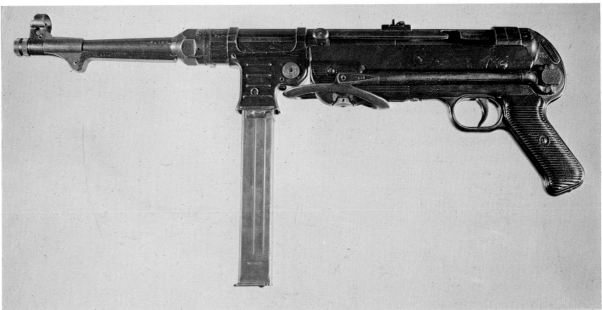

Top The Bergmann MP18, earliest submachine gun.
Above The Soviet PPSh-41 submachine gun of WWII.
Right The German MP40.

'sub machine gun': but his invention, in the hands of the Capone Mob, Machine Gun Kelly, Alvin Karpis and a few of their contemporaries earned it the sobriquet of the 'Tommy Gun', and that is the unfortunate General's memorial.

These American activities gave the submachine gun an unfortunate image, and for too long it was despised as a 'gangster gun' instead of being studied and assessed for a possible role. But the Spanish Civil War saw hundreds of submachine guns put into the field, and it was realised in some quarters that these weapons, simple to teach and use and relatively cheap to make, were the ideal weapon for arming hastily-trained mass armies. Interest in the submachine gun revived once more and in Germany and Russia designs were approved for mass production.

When the Second World War broke out the British Army, who had, in fact, studied the available designs of submachine guns in the 1930s but had been denied finance to equip with them, were forced to buy Thompson guns from the USA. These were expensive, and after the fall of France in 1940 efforts were made to develop a British design. This resulted in the famous Sten Gun, the epitome of cheap and expendable construction in firearms, a simple tube with a bolt working inside it, a short barrel on one end, a steel-tube butt at the other, and a magazine feeding into the side. At the height of wartime production these were being turned out for about £2.50 each, and as well as equipping British troops they were distributed wholesale to resistance groups throughout Occupied Europe.

Russia undoubtedly held the record for volume production, turning out submachine guns by the million and arming whole regiments with nothing else. Moreover, the submachine gun suited the Russian tactical doctrines; it was a weapon of attack, not of defence. The Americans also developed their own cheap expendable gun,

Above John Garand in his workshop.

Below The Garand rifle action. The bolt (1) is driven by a gas piston. The follower (2) forces rounds from the clip (3) into the bolt's path. When the trigger is pressed the hammer (4) strikes the firing pin (5).

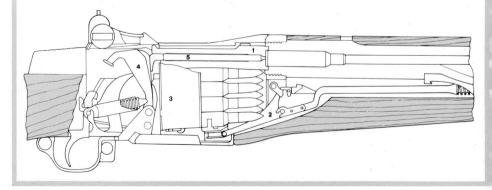

Above The Sten Gun in its 'Mark 2' version.
Below French Maquisard firing his Sten gun, air-dropped by the thousand to resistance groups all over Europe.

known as the 'grease gun' from its simple cylindrical shape. Strangely, the Japanese, who would have benefited immeasurably in their jungle and Pacific campaigns by having a good submachine gun, ignored the weapon and produced only a small number for use by their airborne troops.

After the war the general quality of guns improved, once the pressure was off, and the move was towards compactness, aided by the development of the 'overhung' or 'telescoping' bolt. In this design the front face of the bolt is hollowed out so that when the bolt is closed much of the mass lies ahead of the chamber mouth and actually surrounds the barrel. This allows the overall length of the gun to be reduced and also makes for a better-balanced weapon and one which can easily be used single-handed.

In the 1960s the small-calibre assault rifle became popular; due to its shorter cartridge this type of weapon was more handy than the 'traditional' rifle firing a full-size round, and many of the designs were capable of automatic fire. The Soviets adopted one of the first assault rifles in the late 1940s and they very quickly realised that it could do almost everything that a sub-machine gun could. Since it makes logical sense to reduce the number of different weapons in an army, the submachine gun was retired and the Kalashnikov rifle became the standard infantry weapon. As other armies gained experience with assault rifles they agreed with this view. In the United States Army the submachine gun has been relegated to the reserve, and if the British 4·85mm Individual Weapon, currently under evaluation, is adopted, it will replace the Sterling submachine gun as well as the FAL rifle. The submachine gun will have reverted to its 1920s gangster status.

THE FIREARMS OF THE FUTURE

INVITATIONS TO PROPHESY are generally invitations to disaster, but the firearms field is perhaps less liable than most to take flight in unexpected directions. Things have a habit of moving in cycles in the ordnance world; ideas seem to appear before they have the necessary technological backing, fade away, and then re-appear with amazing regularity, and it is largely a matter of seeing what went wrong last time in order to be able to guess what will be appearing shortly.

A case in point is the selective-fire automatic pistol. During the early parts of the First World War some experimenters tried taking the disconnector out of an automatic pistol and fitting it with an over-long magazine, the object being a one-hand rapid-fire weapon for early aviators. The result was not very practical, because the light weight of the recoiling parts set up a high rate of fire, and the reciprocating slide or bolt above the firer's wrist caused the muzzle to climb very rapidly into the air so that most of the shots were wasted. In the early 1930s the idea was revived in Spain, this time with the addition of a clip-on wooden butt which, it was hoped, would make the gun more controllable. It didn't.

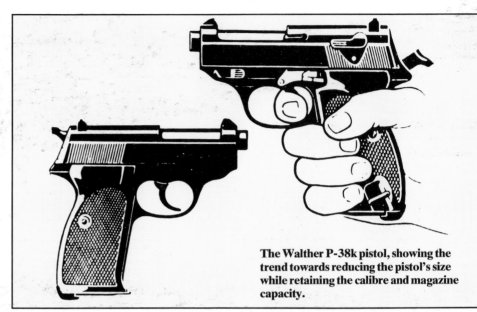

The Walther P-38k pistol, showing the trend towards reducing the pistol's size while retaining the calibre and magazine capacity.

The 9mm 'Mamba', a double-action automatic pistol in stainless steel.

The Heckler & Koch 'PSP'. The 'grip safety' in the front of the butt cocks the pistol immediately before firing.

Below The Heckler & Koch HK 36 assault rifle, an experimental weapon in 4·5mm calibre.

Left The Heckler & Koch VP-70 pistol with butt attachment. This pistol has a 'burst-fire' facility which allows it to function as a submachine gun.

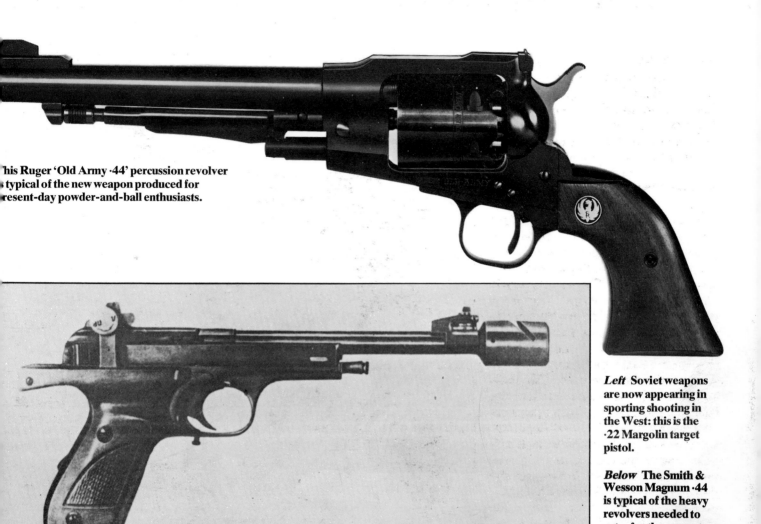

This Ruger 'Old Army ·44' percussion revolver is typical of the new weapon produced for present-day powder-and-ball enthusiasts.

Left Soviet weapons are now appearing in sporting shooting in the West: this is the ·22 Margolin target pistol.

Below The Smith & Wesson Magnum ·44 is typical of the heavy revolvers needed to cater for the current fashion in powerful pistol cartridges.

A 7·62mm caseless cartridge (right) compared to a standard 7·62 NATO round. The caseless design saves brass and weight, but at the expense of complication in the design of the weapon.

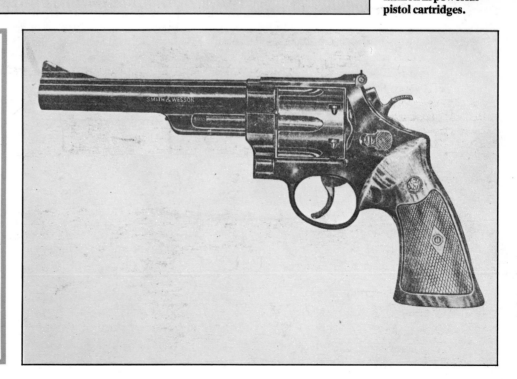

The 'machine pistol' appeared again in the 1950s when the Russian Army embraced the 'Stetchkin', but that soon faded away. Now the Heckler & Koch company of Germany have revived the idea but with a technical refinement: a controller which restricts a burst of fire to only three rounds every time the trigger is pressed. This prevents excessive rise of the muzzle and allows the firer to get back on target quickly for another burst; it also conserves ammunition. Reception of the idea seems to be mixed at the moment, and only time will tell whether the machine pistol is in for a new lease of life or is merely making one of its many temporary comebacks.

Military rifles can be expected to shrink both in calibre and in overall size as cartridges become smaller. This gradual move to 'miniature' ammunition has been gathering speed since the Germans introduced their 7·92mm 'Kurz' cartridge in 1943. Briefly, the arguments are that a large cartridge is superfluous since the soldier rarely shoots at anything more than 350–400 yards away; a short cartridge and small bullet will give satisfactory results at that range and will allow a smaller and lighter rifle to be used. The stumbling block was the demand that the bullet still had to do some worthwhile damage, and this appeared to demand the retention of a substantial calibre. The introduction of the 5·56mm (·223) cartridge in the 1950s, though, showed that small calibres could incapacitate just as effectively as large ones, provided the bullet was carefully matched to the weapon. With the 5·56mm bullet it was found that the twist of rifling and the amount of spin imparted to the bullet was critical; the bullet was spun so as to be just stable in flight, but it lost stability instantly when it encountered anything substantial. As a result, it toppled, gave up its energy rapidly, and dealt out severe wounds. From this starting point ballisticians began working downward, and at present

calibres as small as 4mm (0·157 inch) are being evaluated.

Similar studies have been applied to hunting ammunition, since much the same criteria appear to apply to shooting game as to shooting men, and if small calibres work for military rifles they should also work for hunting rifles. However, there is rather more to this than simple wound ballistics and calculations based on 'stopping power' might indicate. The man who designs the ammunition can never be sure what the man who buys it intends to shoot, and animals are vastly different from specie to specie; the bullet which will stop a deer may not necessarily stop a bison, and a great deal of the effectiveness of hunting cartridges is bound up with the degree of expertise of the hunter. Nevertheless, working on the assumption that a man willing to try out new ammunition must have some idea of what he is up to, new calibre and bullet weights are being introduced for those willing to try them. There was a rash of ·17 inch cartridges some fifteen to twenty years ago, most of which failed to survive; some of the new offerings are in this calibre area and it remains to be seen whether they will do any better. In our view these new calibres may well fill the bill for some particular applications and with some particular hunters, but as a general rule it is unlikely that they will make much impression on the popularity of the long-established hunting cartridges.

One of the more recent firearms phenomena is the revival of 'black powder shooting' using replicas of muzzle loading flintlock and percussion weapons. The reasons for this are extremely diverse, ranging from the simple enjoyment of an uncomplicated artifact, by means of the pleasure gained from shooting a home-made (or at least home-finished) gun, to the somewhat studied postures of the ecological brigade who feel that hunting with more primitive weapons gives the animal a better chance of survival. Whatever the reason, its

popularity is attested to by the increasing number of guns on the market and clubs being formed to shoot them, and since this form of shooting appears cheaper than some others, it should continue to prosper.

Pistol design scarcely moves these days, when just about every feasible way of making a pistol has been explored. The tendency is toward heavier calibres with more powerful loading—the Magnum cartridge—in order to produce either long range accuracy or short-range destructive power. Another present-day field of endeavour is the gradual reduction in size of the pistol without reducing the calibre. The Colt ·45 M1911 automatic is 8½ inches long and weighs 40 ounces, and it was always considered to be a difficult gun to master due to the powerful cartridge and heavy recoil. Yet a recently announced ·45 auto pistol, the Thomas, is 6½ inches long and weighs 32 ounces while the Spanish 'Star PD ·45' is 7 inches long and weighs an incredible 24 ounces. This tendency probably accounts for the current fashion for holding pistols with two hands, even though the makers are still putting only one handle on them.

Firearms have come a long way in the past 650 years: it would be tempting to think that they have reached the limit of their development, since it seems difficult to visualise any major innovation. But they probably thought the same thing when the flintlock was perfected. Leaving aside the emotive and psychological questions which firearms frequently invoke, it has to be admitted that the firearm is a considerable engineering feat—just think for a moment of what goes on inside a machine gun a thousand times a minute—and there is never likely to be a shortage of individuals who are convinced that they have discovered a better way of solving the basic mechanical problems. I am prepared to make a small wager that within the next ten years, something will have come along to surprise us all.

A-Z

OF THE
WORLD'S FIREARMS

AAT-52/*France*

Arme Automatique Transformable, Modèle 1952, a French Army general-purpose machine gun. Designed shortly after the Second World War, it operates on a delayed blowback system. The bolt is in two parts, a light bolt head and a heavier body; the head carries a lever, the short end of which is lodged in a recess in the gun body and the longer end in the rear bolt body. On firing, the pressure in the cartridge case forces the bolt head backwards, but because of the lever, the bolt body has to be moved at a considerable mechanical disadvantage, which effectively holds up the opening of the breech for a very short time. The inevitable tendency to difficult extraction, found in all delayed blowback weapons firing bottle-necked cartridges, is ameliorated by longitudinal grooving of the chamber, which allows the case to 'float' on a layer of gas as it is extracted. The remainder of the design is conventional, the belt feed being controlled by a system based on that of the German MG42.

ABADIE *(fl. late 19th C.)*

Belgian gunsmith, reputed to have been the originator of the common Belgian rod-ejection system for revolvers, in which the ejecting rod is housed in the hollow cylinder arbor and supported on a hinged arm, so that it can be pulled forward, hinged sideways, and then thrust back to eject spent cases singly through the loading gate. With more certainty his name is attached to a hinged loading gate and safety device used on various European revolvers from about 1880 to 1900. In this device the loading gate is linked with the pistol hammer so that opening the gate, to load or unload the pistol, draws the hammer back to a half-cock position and locks it there so as to prevent it accidentally falling forward and firing a cartridge during the loading process. Two revolvers with this device used Abadie's name; these were the Portuguese 9·1mm Service models of 1878 and 1886.

The Accles machine gun, an English-made Gatling with rotary feed drum patented by Accles.

ACCLES, James George *(b.1850)*

Firearms engineer, born in Australia of American parents. Apprenticed to Colt, he then worked in England on ammunition production. He established Gatling machine gun and ammunition factories in various countries, working for Gatling until 1888. Then Accles returned to England to work for the Gatling Arms & Ammunition Co. of Birmingham, a company independent of Gatling in America and holding the European franchise for the Gatling gun. This venture failed and Accles founded Grenfell & Accles marketing a variant of the Gatling gun which used a rotating feed mechanism patented by Accles. He later founded Accles & Pollock, a tube-making company which still operates, though Accles severed his connections in about 1903. He then worked as an independent firearms consultant until 1913 when he founded Accles & Shelvoke to make humane cattle killers and a pistols.

ADAMS, Robert (fl. 1850–1865)

English pistol maker and founder of the Adams Patent Small Arms Company in 1864. In 1855 the British Army adopted the Beaumont-Adams percussion revolver under the name of the Deane and Adams Revolver Pistol. This was basically an Adams design of cap-and-ball revolver with a double-action firing lock designed by Beaumont. Adams then developed a conversion system for this pistol, using a new cylinder, rammer and loading gate, so as to convert the weapon to breach-loading, and this was adopted for British service use in 1868. A solid-frame metallic cartridge revolver was produced by Adams and this was widely adopted by police and military forces.

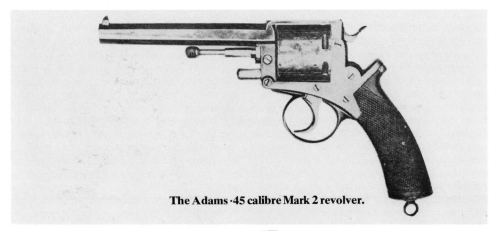

The Adams ·45 calibre Mark 2 revolver.

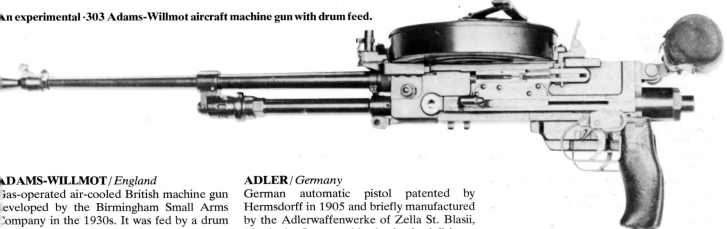

An experimental ·303 Adams-Willmot aircraft machine gun with drum feed.

ADAMS-WILLMOT / England

Gas-operated air-cooled British machine gun developed by the Birmingham Small Arms Company in the 1930s. It was fed by a drum magazine and was intended for use as an aircraft observer's flexible gun. It was tested in this role by the Royal Air Force in 1934 but rejected as being insufficiently reliable at that stage of its development. Small numbers were sold abroad for evaluation but no country adopted the weapon for service use.

ADEN / England

British aircraft cannon of 30mm calibre. The name derived from 'Armament Department, Enfield'. It was based on a German design of revolver cannon developed by Mauserwerke during the Second World War, and it entered British service in the early 1950s. The gun has a single barrel and a five-chambered revolver unit behind the barrel into which the cartridge is rammed during two steps of revolution, fired when aligned with the barrel, and extracted and ejected during the remaining two stages of revolution. Feed is by belt, and the gun is actuated by a combination of barrel recoil and gas piston operation which drives the ramming and ejecting mechanisms. The rate of fire is between 1200 and 1400 rounds per minute and the muzzle velocity is 2600 feet per second. Ammunition consists of high explosive shells with impact fuses and the cartridge cases are of alloy, with electrically-fired caps.

ADLER / Germany

German automatic pistol patented by Hermsdorff in 1905 and briefly manufactured by the Adlerwaffenwerke of Zella St. Blasii, Thuringia. It was a blowback pistol firing a unique 7mm bottle-necked cartridge and using a reciprocating bolt in the receiver. The patented feature was the method of construction of the receiver whereby the top and sides could be swung up and back to expose the breech and bolt for cleaning. A cocking lever protruded through a slot in the top of the receiver. The Adler was not an outstanding design in any way, and it did not achieve commercial success, manufacture coming to an end as early as 1907.

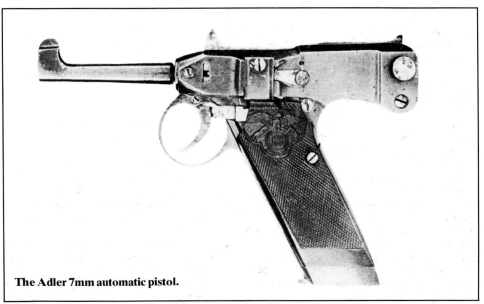

The Adler 7mm automatic pistol.

AGER COFFEE MILL / *USA*

American mechanical machine gun designed in the early 1860s by Wilson Ager and more correctly titled the 'Union Battery Gun'. It was a single-barrelled gun with a hopper above the breech and a crank on the side, and it was these two components, with their resemblance to the domestic coffee mill of the day, which gave rise to the gun's nickname. Ammunition for the gun had to be prepared before firing; it consisted of short steel tubes into which powder and a ·58 lead ball were loaded, a percussion cap being placed on a nipple at the rear end. These tubes were then dropped into the hopper above the chamber, and revolving the hand crank operated a bolt mechanism which loaded the steel tube into the gun chamber, fired it by means of a hammer against the percussion cap, and then extracted and ejected the tube prior to loading a fresh one. After firing, the tubes were cleaned and re-loaded. A rate of fire of 100 rounds per minute could be achieved, and the Ager gun was, for its day, a reliable and practical weapon. It was patented during the American Civil War and Ager offered it to the Union Army; they, however, could not make up their minds as to its utility and only fifty were purchased throughout the war.

AGNELLI, Giovanni *(fl. 1905–1914)*

Italian gun designer responsible for the design of the SIA machine gun; the initials are derived from the manufacturer, Societa Anonima Italiana G Ansaldo, Armstrong & Company. This was a retarded blowback gun in which the bolt was locked by the forward movement of the firing pin, which rotated the bolt as it struck the cartridge cap. Like all retarded blowback guns the SIA suffered from difficult extraction; Agnelli solved this problem by cutting longitudinal grooves or flutes in the gun chamber so that a small amount of gas leaked past the case mouth and 'floated' the case to prevent it sticking. He patented this idea, which has been widely used in subsequent weapon designs.

Agnelli's designs and patents were taken over by the Ansaldo company shortly before the First World War, but the gun was not developed into a practical weapon until the 1920s, by which time there were several other and better designs available. A small number were bought by the Italian Army for training.

AKM / *USSR*

Automatic Kalashnikov, Modified. This improved version of the AK47 rifle was developed in the early 1960s and is gradually replacing the earlier AK47 model. The principle of operation remains the same, as does the general appearance, the changes being largely concerned with simplifying and cheapening the manufacturing process. Where the earlier weapon was expensively and traditionally made with a carefully-machined body and components, the AKM uses a stamped steel body and has several internal components with a 'parkerised' dull finish instead of a bright polished steel finish. Several small changes in details have been made, all in the interests of speeding up manufacture. The wooden furniture — butt and fore-end — of the AKM are of laminated wood, resin-bonded, instead of solid birch or beech as in the AK47. The reliability and serviceability of the weapon are unchanged.

ALBINI-BRAENDLIN / *Italy*

·60 calibre rimfire rifle developed by August Albini (1830–1909), an Admiral in the Italian Navy. He designed the rifle in 1865, using a hinged breech section which could be lifted up to permit loading of the cartridge, after which it was dropped back into the action so as to align

AK47 / *USSR*

Automatic Kalishnikov, Model of 1947. This Soviet automatic rifle was developed by Mikhail Kalashnikov shortly after the Second World War. It was designed around a 7·62mm 'short' cartridge developed at the end of the war and based on the similar German 7·92mm short assault rifle round. Using a short cartridge allows the rifle to be smaller and more compact, due to the lower recoil energy and the shorter reloading stroke required. The AK47 uses gas operation, a piston above the barrel being driven back by a small amount of gas tapped from the barrel. This piston strikes a bolt carrier which starts to the rear, a cam surface inside it rotating the bolt so as to unlock it from the breech. Carrier and bolt then go to the rear, extracting the empty cartridge case and ejecting it. A return spring then forces carrier and bolt forward, chambering a fresh cartridge from the 30-shot magazine. As the carrier is forced home, it revolves the bolt and locks it. Pressure on the trigger now releases a hammer to strike the firing pin in the bolt, firing the weapon. A selector lever permits firing single shots or full-automatic fire at a rate of about 600 rounds per minute.

The AK became the standard Soviet service rifle, after which it was widely supplied to 'satellite' nations; it has been estimated that some 35 million have been made. It is certainly one of the best assault rifles ever made, being robust, simple and completely reliable in use.

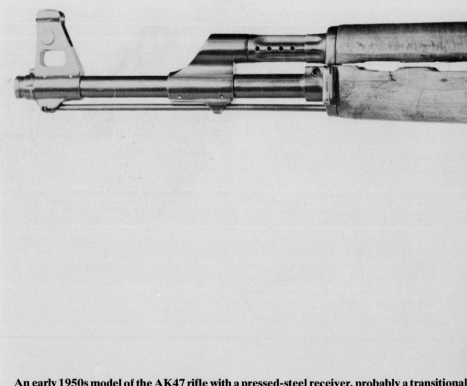

An early 1950s model of the AK47 rifle with a pressed-steel receiver, probably a transitional stage between the AK47 and AKM models.

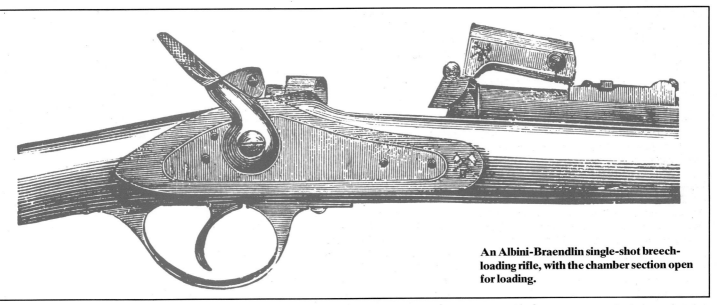

An Albini-Braendlin single-shot breech-loading rifle, with the chamber section open for loading.

with the bore and an external hammer struck a firing pin to fire the cartridge. The system could either be made as a new weapon or could be applied to existing muzzle-loading rifles to convert them to breech loading. Albini had the rifle manufactured by the Braendlin Armoury Company of Birmingham, England and it was adopted by the Italian Navy in 1866, followed in 1867 by the Belgian Army and the armies of Bavaria and Würtemberg. In addition, the Belgian Army converted numbers of muzzle-loaders to the Albini system. It was tested by the British Army in 1865, but as often happens to a perfectly good idea, it was turned down in favour of the Snider, a very similar design.

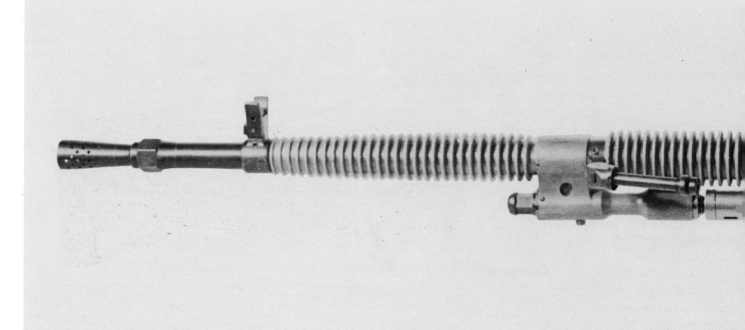

Alfa machine gun, removed from its tripod.

ALFA / *Spain*

Machine gun manufactured by the Fabrica de Armas Oviedo, Spain. The first to appear was the Model 1944, chambered for the 7·92mm Mauser cartridge, then standard in the Spanish Army, and the weapon was adopted by that Army. The Alfa was a conventional gas-operated belt-fed weapon, feeding from a cartridge box on the left side. Tripod mounted and air-cooled, it appears to be based on pre-war Breda practice and is generally employed as a medium machine gun for sustained fire support. Quantities of these machine guns were bought by the Egyptian Army in the early 1950s.

The ALFA model 55, currently in use by the Spanish Army, is the same weapon except that it is chambered for the 7·62mm NATO cartridge. It weighs about 87 lbs complete with tripod and has a rate of fire of about 750 rounds per minute.

ALLEN, Ethan *(d.1871)*

American gunsmith. He began by making walking-stick guns, then progressed to single-shot muzzle-loading pistols. In 1845 he patented a pepperbox pistol with top hammer which became extremely popular, particularly in the 1849 gold rush to California. With his brothers-in-law Charles Thurber and Thomas Wheelock he began manufacturing both pep-perboxes and the Allen & Thurber repeating pistol. In later years he turned to making percussion revolvers with conventional single barrels, marketing them as the Allen & Wheelock, and in the 1860s he produced a ·22 cartridge revolver with a 7-shot cylinder, though with this design he attracted litigation due to infringement of the Rollin White patent for bored-through cylinders. It is of interest that his two daughters married Sullivan Forehand and Henry Wadsworth and, on Allen's death, these two men took over his factory and operated it as Forehand & Wadsworth, manufacturing pistols for several years. After the death of the surviving partner in 1898 the company passed into the hands of the Hopkins & Allen company which continued to make revolvers until it, in turn, was taken over in 1915 by the Marlin Rockwell Company in order to use the plant for making machine guns.

ANCION-MARX, Leopold *(fl. late 19th C.)*

Belgian gunsmith of Liège, who built up a considerable business in the latter part of the 19th century, supplying weapons of all types. Of his own manufacture, his catalogue encompassed single and double-barrelled shotguns, single shot rifles, rifle-shotgun combinations, double rifles, and a wide variety of revolvers from pinfire models retailing at 5 francs to solid frame swing-out cylinder models for 35 francs.

In addition, he acted as agent for principal manufacturers and claimed to be able to supply any type or make of firearms. Much of his output was sold through the trade and reappeared with the names of retailers engraved upon them and no indication of their actual origin, and many weapons passed off as products of local gunmakers could be more accurately ascribed to Ancion-Marx. Like many gunsmiths, Ancion-Marx was primarily a businessman, and there is no evidence that he actually innovated any design features. The business did not survive the First World War.

ANDREWS / *England*

Submachine gun designed by Andrews, an Australian, and made in prototype form by the Birmingham Small Arms Company in 1943 for trial by the British Army. The gun body was rectangular, and the bolt was guided by two rods which passed completely through the bolt above and below the barrel and were anchored at the front of the body above and below the muzzle. These rods also carried the bolt return springs. The magazine was inserted from the right-hand side, a simple tubular pistol grip was fitted, and the butt was formed by a socket at the rear of the gun body which accepted a spare loaded magazine which then functioned as the butt. Chambered for the standard 9mm Parabellum cartridge, the Andrews did reasonably well in the trials, but at that time the Army were using the Sten gun quite happily and there was no production facility available for a new submachine gun; as a result, no fresh design was likely to be adopted, and since two other designs had performed better than the Andrews, no further action was taken.

ANSCHUTZ / *Germany*

An old-established company, the J. G. Anschutz Germania-Waffenwerk of Zella-Mehlis built up a considerable reputation before 1939 with its production of high-class target rifles and pistols, particularly adapted to Olympic and International competition shooting. These were single shot weapons, generally using Martini actions, and were available with almost any shape of grip, type of sight, degree of hair-trigger or other refinement that the purchaser wanted. After 1945 the company relocated at Ulm/Donau in the German Federal Republic and resumed production of precision weapons.

APACHE / *originally Belgium*

Type of pocket revolver invented by the Liège gunsmith Louis Dolne in the 1870s. It was a pepperbox revolver, the cylinder being much longer than the 7mm pinfire cartridge so that each chamber served as its own barrel. The design of the rest of the weapon was, however, unique: the butt was a steel or brass casting which was pierced with finger-holes and could be folded beneath the cylinder and frame. In this position the owner could grasp the cylinder in the palm of his hand and slip his fingers through the holes in the butt, the result being a very serviceable knuckle-duster. In addition, a dagger blade was hinged to the frame in front of the cylinder and could be folded into the frame or extended in front of the pistol, whereupon the weapon could function as a dagger.

There was said to be a variation of the Apache pattern manufactured by Delahaxe (believed to be a Parisian maker) in which the dagger folds but the knuckle-duster section is fixed at right angles to the cylinder axis so that both pistol and knuckle-duster are operable at the same time.

Note that the name 'Apache' is also applied to a 6·35mm automatic pistol manufactured in 1922 by Ojanguren & Vidosa of Eibar, Spain; and later to a ·38 revolver of Colt 'Police Positive' type made by the Fabrica de Armas Garantizada, also of Eibar.

ARISAKA / *Japan*

Japanese service rifle, 1897–1945, designed by a Colonel Arisaka who headed a commission of review charged with developing a replacement for the Murata rifle of 1887. The Arisaka rifle is largely a Mauser copy, though there are some differences in the design of the bolt; this is a two-part unit showing Mannlicher influence, and it differs principally in that the cocking action takes place during the closing of the bolt and not, as in Mauser actions, on the opening stroke. Numerous variants were produced over the years, and these were first known by the symbol and year of the current monarch's reign, as follows:

Meiji 30th Year (1897). 6·5mm infantry rifle.
Meiji 30th Year Carbine (1897). As above, but shorter.
Meiji 38th Year (1905). 6·5mm rifle designed after experience in the Russo-Japanese War.

Typical of the Arisaka design is this Meiji 38th Year carbine.

It improved the safety catch and bolt design, but was still a 'long' rifle.

Meiji 38th Year Carbine. Similar changes were made in the cavalry weapon in 1905.

Meiji 44th Year Carbine (1911). Similar to the 38th Year but with a folding bayonet beneath the fore-end.

Sometime in the late 1920s the system of nomenclature changed to conform to the Japanese calendar. In the 1930s experience in Manchuria led to the development of a heavier-calibre cartridge and various weapons to suit. This led to the following designs, which were still basically Arisaka rifles:

Type 99 (1939). Almost identical to the Meiji 38th Year rifle, this was chambered for a new 7·7mm cartridge and was made slightly shorter, conforming to the 'short rifle' designs which had been adopted by most other nations.

Type 99 Parachutist's Rifle (1940). This was a Type 39 rifle converted by placing an interrupted-screw joint in the barrel immediately in front of the chamber, so that the weapon could be dismantled into two short pieces for carriage by airborne troops. It was not entirely successful, and was superseded by the Type 2 (1942) which altered the method of joining up the barrel and action from a screw to a sliding wedge. This was rather more serviceable, but few were made.

In addition to service with the Japanese Army, a large number of Arisaka rifles were bought by the British Army in 1915 for use as training weapons; they were known as the 'Rifle, Magazine, 0·256in Pattern 1900' (for the Meiji 30th Year) or 'Pattern 1907' (for the Meiji 38th Year type). They were also bought by Mexico and Russia at various times.

ARMALITE / USA

This company was founded in 1952 by Charles Sullivan and George Dorchester, with the intention of making high quality sporting weapons. In 1954 it became the Armalite Division of Fairchild Engine & Airplane Corporation and Eugene Stoner was retained as designer. Prototypes of various sporting arms were made, but the company's first success came with the design of the AR-5 Survival Rifle for the US Air Force. This was a simple lightweight bolt action rifle chambered for the ·22 Hornet cartridge, which could be rapidly dismantled into its component parts, which could then be packed into the hollow butt. When so packed, the rifle would actually float if dropped in water. In 1958 a civil version, the AR-7, was produced; this was a blowback auto-loader chambered for the ·22 Long Rifle round, and like the AR-5 could be stripped and packed inside the plastic butt.

The company had already made prototypes of automatic rifles, and in 1955 began development of an assault rifle chambered for the 7·62mm NATO cartridge. This rifle used an unusual gas system in that the gas tapped from the barrel was piped back and vented directly into the bolt carrier, to drive the carrier back and, by cam action, rotate and unlock the bolt. The whole weapon was laid out in a 'straight line' configuration, which generates less of an upward couple when fired and thus allows the weapon to be kept more accurately on target when on automatic fire. In 1957 the Artillerie Inrichtingen Arsenal of Hembrug, Netherlands, agreed to manufacture this rifle, but since the Dutch Army were not interested in adopting it, tooling up proceeded slowly. Eventually some 5000 weapons were made being sold to Portugal, Nicaragua and the Sudan, but the weapon's full potential was never realised. One reason for this was that it appeared at a time when interest was turning to the smaller-calibre weapons.

In 1958 the AR-15 rifle was produced; designed by Stoner, this was chambered for a new cartridge, the 5·56mm (·223) round which was actually developed by Armalite for this rifle. Broadly speaking, the AR-15 was derived from the AR-10, using the same sort of gas operation and being laid out in much the same way. Tested by the US Army, it was taken up by the US Air Force as a suitable lightweight weapon for use by airfield guards. This led to its appearance in Vietnam, where the Vietnamese Army decided that such a small and light weapon would be ideal for their troops who were small of stature. Large numbers were purchased, which in turn led to more being bought by the US forces. The Colt Company obtained a license to make the AR-15 in 1959 and produced several hundred thousand in subsequent years.

In military service the AR-15 was desig-

The Armalite Explorer shown dismantled and ready for use.

ARMAGUERRA / *Italy*

Submachine gun designed by Giovanni Oliani and manufactured in prototype form only by the Fabricca Armas de Guerra of Cremona, Italy, during the Second World War. The first model was the OG42, and it is credited with being the first submachine gun to utilise the 'overhung' bolt configuration, in which the bolt is shaped so that the majority of the mass lies above and in front of the actual bolt face and thus overhangs the barrel when the breech is closed. This configuration permits the gun body behind the breech face to be shorter than normal, though it demands a casing above the barrel to accommodate the mass of the bolt. Oliani made various improvements to the design and produced the OG44 version in two models, one with a fixed wooden butt and one with a folding butt. One specimen of each is known to exist today. The Armaguerra was a well-designed weapon, but it appeared at a time when most nations were adequately served with submachine guns and speculative manufacture was not possible.

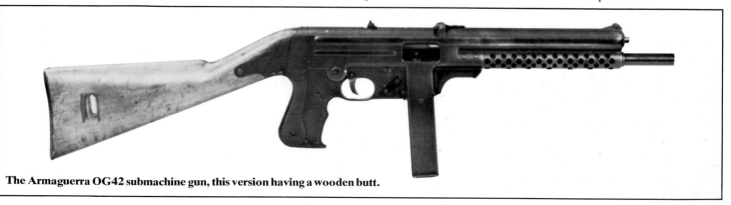

The Armaguerra OG42 submachine gun, this version having a wooden butt.

nated the M16, and it was found that it gave considerable trouble in service. The trouble was eventually traced to a change in the cartridge propellant which introduced excessive fouling, coupled with a publicity campaign which unfortunately had stressed that the rifle never needed cleaning. These two facts were mutually incompatible, but once this had been cleared up, the M16 proved quite reliable in service use.

In 1959 Stoner left the Armalite company to work for Colt, and a new designer, Arthur Miller, took his place. At that time the AR-15 rifle was a success, but the company decided to develop a new design which became the AR-18 rifle. The system of gas operation changed, in that a conventional piston and rod mounted above the barrel were used, the piston rod thrusting back against the bolt carrier. The gun body is of pressed steel, suitably welded, while many of the major components are steel stampings rather than expensive forgings. The whole design has been worked out with the aim of permitting the gun to be manufactured by light engineering shops with no special gun-making knowledge or facilities. Chambered for the 5·56mm cartridge, the AR-18 was tested by the US Army and found satisfactory, but with the heavy commitment to the AR-15 there was no point in adopting a different weapon.

A Japanese company, the Howa Machinery Co. of Nagoya, obtained a licence to make the AR-18 in 1967 but found sales difficult due to political considerations and Japanese law. It has been made by the Armalite company in Costa Mesa, California, and it has recently been licensed to the Sterling Armaments Company of Dagenham, England.

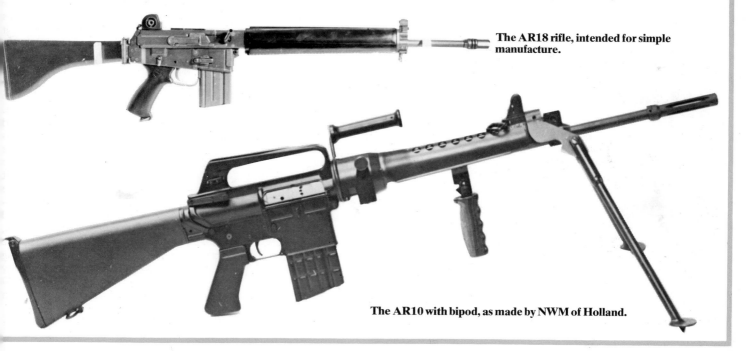

The AR18 rifle, intended for simple manufacture.

The AR10 with bipod, as made by NWM of Holland.

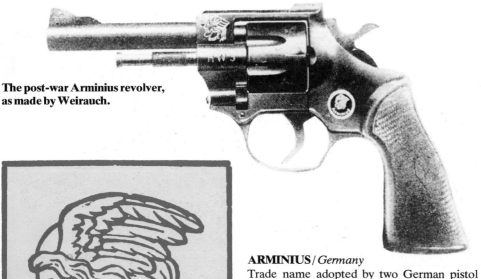

The post-war Arminius revolver, as made by Weirauch.

ARMINIUS/ *Germany*

Trade name adopted by two German pistol makers. It was first used by Friedrich Pickert of Zella-Mehlis and applied to a wide variety of pocket revolvers made prior to 1939. These were all at the cheaper end of the market and were available in most of the common small calibres, from ·22 to ·38, in hammer or hammerless designs. After the Second World War the name was taken over by the firm of Hermann Weirauch of Mellrichstadt, Bavaria and applied to a range of revolvers. These are solid frame, swing-out cylinder designs of average quality, chambered in popular calibres from ·22 to ·38 and available with various finishes.

ASTRA/ *Spain*

Trade name adopted by the Spanish compan of Unceta of Guernica and principally applie to pistols. The name was first used in 1911 for 7·65mm copy of the Browning 1903 automati pistol, but it became prominent in 1921 wit the Spanish Army's adoption of the Astr Model 400 as their service Model 1921 pisto. This model was derived from the Campo-Gir design, and was a blowback automatic cham bered for the 9mm Bergmann-Bayard car tridge, known in Spain as the 9mm Largo. Th pistol's shape was unique, a long tubular barre and jacket resembling a water pistol more tha a firearm, and this outline was perpetuated i subsequent models. Notable among these wa the Model 600 in 9mm Parabellum, manufac tured in 1942 for the German Army.

The name was also used for a series of pistol based on the Mauser C/96 Military pattern an introduced in 1928. Externally resembling th Mauser, the internal mechanism was simplifie and three variants were produced; one used 20-shot integral magazine, one with a 10- o 20-shot removeable magazine, and one cham bered for the 9mm Largo.

In the 1950s the company began productio of revolvers under the name Astra Cadix These are solid frame models with swing-ou cylinders, based generally on Smith & Wesso practice.

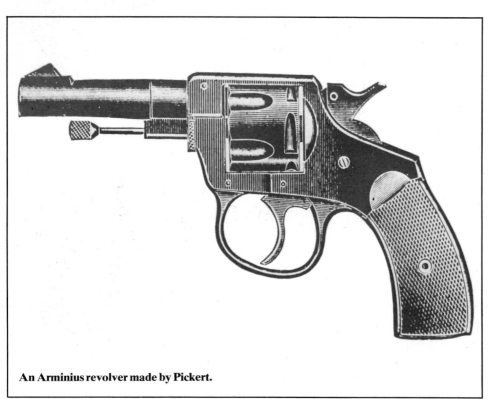

An Arminius revolver made by Pickert.

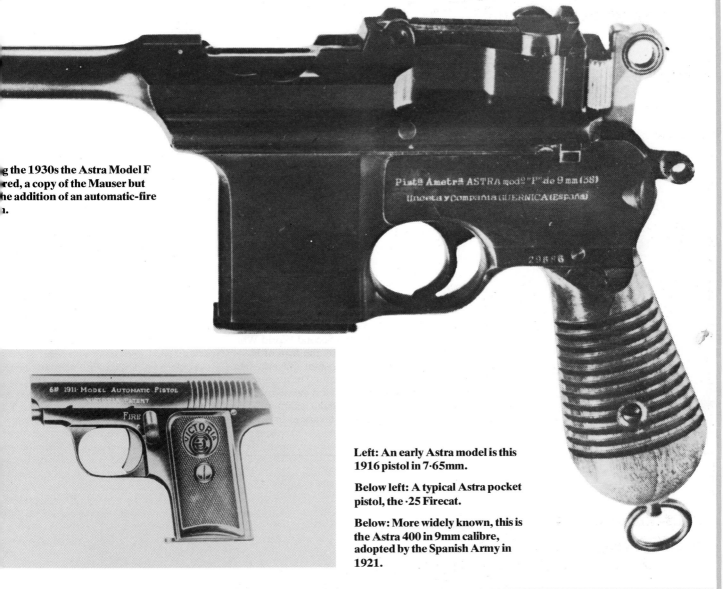

g the 1930s the Astra Model F
red, a copy of the Mauser but
he addition of an automatic-fire
.

Left: An early Astra model is this
1916 pistol in 7·65mm.

Below left: A typical Astra pocket
pistol, the ·25 Firecat.

Below: More widely known, this is
the Astra 400 in 9mm calibre,
adopted by the Spanish Army in
1921.

The Star SI35 submachine gun, offered to the US and British governments as the 'Atlantic'

ATCHISSON, Maxwell G. (fl. 1955–)

American gun designer, responsible for the development of a replacement bolt assembly for the US Rifle M16 which permits the firing of ·22 cartridges as a training expedient. He worked for the Military Armaments Corporation of Powder Springs, Georgia, and later developed a submachine gun which used ·22 cartridges, also for use as a training device. In 1957 he designed a 9mm submachine gun of extreme simplicity and light weight in which the box magazine actually functions as the pistol grip. This design has, however, never been placed in production.

Atchisson next turned to the problem of improving infantry firepower and devised an improved version of the US Rifle M16A1, modifying it to use a heavy barrel, fire from an open bolt, and mount three box magazines side-by-side with a quick-change device, so as to convert the rifle into a passable squad light machine gun. Another design is of an automatic 12-bore shotgun styled in the manner of an assault rifle; he devised this weapon because, as shown by action in Vietnam, the point man in an infantry section needs a weapon which can deliver heavy short-range firepower in the event of an ambush. Both weapons have been evaluated by the US Army but no decision as to their adoption has been announced.

ATLANTIC / Spain

Submachine gun, actually the Star Model TN-35 manufactured by Star-Bonifacio Echeverria of Eibar, Spain, prior to 1939. It was offered to the British and US governments in 1942 for possible supply. Chambered for the ·38 Auto Colt cartridge, it was unusual in having a two-position switch which allowed two rates of automatic fire, 300 or 700 rounds per minute. Military tests in both countries showed that it was below acceptable standards of reliability and robustness, and it was not accepted for service.

ATMED / USA

Submachine gun designed by George Hyde and built by the Atmed Manufacturing Company of New York. It was submitted for trial to the US Army in September 1942. In general form it resembled the Thompson submachine gun, having a wooden stock, rectangular body, finned barrel, wooden fore-end and box magazine feeding from below. Chambered for the ·45 Auto Colt cartridge, the gun worked on the normal blowback principle, using advanced primer ignition. It survived some of the military tests with good marks, but was found generally unreliable and was not considered to be worth further development.

AUSTEN / Australia

Australian submachine gun designed by Ua[ ] Riddell in 1941 and manufactured by Dieca[ ]ers Pty Ltd and W. J. Carmichael in M[ ]bourne, 1942–1945. Total production [ ] about 20,000 guns. The name is derived fr[ ] 'Australian Sten'.

The design is basically that of the Sten g[ ] with the folding butt and telescoping bolt a[ ]embly of the German MP40 incorporated. [ ] forward pistol grip was added to the desi[ ] and the resulting weapon became the Aus[ ] Mark 1. Riddell then made radical alteratio[ ] for the Mark 2 model. The tubular gun b[ ] was enclosed in an aluminium frame, a meth[ ] of assembly which simplified manufacture a[ ] made the weapon resistant to damage with[ ] adding greatly to the weight. Though [ ] model went into production in 1944, relativ[ ] few were made.

Although the Austen was sound enough[ ] was never well-liked by the Australian troo[ ] who preferred the Owen Gun; this may ha[ ] been due to the fact that the Austen used t[ ] Sten magazine, the one component which w[ ] the weak link in the Sten design since it w[ ] prone to jamming.

The Owen was considered more reliab[ ] and in the Pacific campaign reliability wa[ ] greater asset than light weight.

The Mark 2 version of the Austen, which used a light alloy casing around the receiver.

AUTO-MAG / *USA*

American automatic pistol manufactured by the TDE Corporation of El Monte, California. This pistol was designed around a 'wildcat' cartridge, the ·44 Auto Magnum, produced by marrying a ·44 revolver bullet to a cut-down 7·62mm NATO rifle cartridge case. This round was developed as a technical exercise in the mid-1950s, at which time no gun existed to fire it. In the early 1960s Max Gera began work on an automatic pistol designed to fire this cartridge, and this was eventually announced as the Auto-Mag early in 1970. It is a recoil-operated pistol with a rotating bolt head controlled by cam tracks in the pistol frame. Firing a ·44in 240 grain bullet, it develops a muzzle velocity of 1640 ft/sec and a muzzle energy of 1455 lbs.

The Auto-Mag Company of Pasadena was set up to make the gun in late 1970, though at that time commercial ammunition was not available and purchasers of the gun would have had to make their own rounds. This company got into financial difficulties, and since that time the patents and rights for the pistol have passed through several hands. The latest information is that the TDE Corporation (a division of the Thomas Oil Company) are making the pistol, while the High-Standard company are assuming responsibility for distribution. It is currently available in ·44 Auto Magnum calibre and also in ·357 Auto Magnum, a similar combination of ·357 revolver bullet and cut-down 7·62mm case. It is an extremely powerful pistol and has gained acceptance as a hunting weapon, used with a telescopic sight.

The ·44 Magnum Auto-Mag pistol, the most powerful automatic pistol currently made.

AUTOMATIC ARMS COMPANY / *USA*

Company set up in Buffalo, New York, in the early years of the century in order to promote and manufacture machine guns. They obtained a number of patents, most of which appear to have been worthless, but managed to acquire those of Samuel MacLean and O. M. Lissak relating to the MacLean-Lissak Light Rifle. This was a machine gun design which MacLean and Lissak had developed but which did not arouse any military interest. The design was for a gas operated rifle, the actuating mechanism of which was assisted by a muzzle gas trap. It was not particularly successful, and the Automatic Arms Company retained Captain Isaac N. Lewis, lately retired from the US Army, to work on the design and improve it. This Lewis did, eventually producing the design which came to be known as the Lewis Gun. Although Lewis owned stock in the company, in exchange for his technical assistance, he eventually took the gun to Belgium and set up a company there, while the Automatic Arms Company disappeared.

AUTO-ORDNANCE CORPORATION / *USA*

Company formed in 1919 to develop and market the Thompson Submachine gun. Principal shareholders were Thompson, his son, and Thomas F. Ryan, who provided most of the money. The company's function was assembly and sales of the gun, manufacture being done by the Colt company under contract. In 1930 Ryan bought out the Thompsons, and in 1938 he sold out to Russell Maguire. In 1940, with large European orders for the Thompson gun,

Maguire placed fresh manufacturing contracts with the Savage Arms Company, since Colt declined to make any more; this being insufficient, Maguire then built his own manufacturing plant. After the war the name, stock and goodwill were sold to the Kilgore Company who hoped to sell the Thompson in foreign countries, but the surplus cheap submachine guns of war origin ruined this market and they sold out in 1961 to the Numrich Arms Company. The Auto-Ordnance Company is still trading, supplying spare parts for original Thompson guns and also manufacturing a semi-automatic long-barrel version of the Thompson for commercial sale.

AVTOMAT / USSR

Light automatic rifle designed by Vladimir Fyodora, a prominent arms designer in Tsarist Russia who later became well-known in Soviet arms circles. Prior to the First World War he experimented with various automatic rifle designs but was hampered by the standard Russian rifle cartridge of the day, the 7·62mm Mosin-Nagant round, a rimmed and bottle-necked cartridge of awkward shape. After the Russo-Japanese War, the Russians acquired a number of Japanese 6·5mm Arisaka rifles and a large quantity of ammunition, and since these 6·5mm cartridges were more slender and less powerful than the Mosin-Nagant round, Fyodora designed a selective-fire rifle around them. The rifle used short recoil of the barrel to actuate the loading cycle, and was fitted with a forward pistol grip and box magazine. It was, in fact, the fore-runner of the modern 'assault rifle' in almost every respect.

The Avtomat was put into production in 1917, but this was cut short by the October Revolution and, as a result, the rifle was never seen in action against the German Army. It was revived after the revolution, under Soviet control, and appears to have remained in production until 1924, while Fyodora and his design team continued to make improvements until about 1928. Reports on its use in the Civil War are unknown, and specimens outside Russia are extremely rare.

AYDT, Carl Wilhelm (fl. 1870–)

Gunsmith of Suhl, Germany, who in 1884 patented a rifle breech mechanism which used a solid breechblock pivoted underneath the chamber and swinging backwards in a downward arc on operation of a side under-lever. On closing, the curved rear face of the block slides in guides in the gun body which serve to firmly lock the block against the breech face. It is not well adapted to high pressures, but is has been widely used in Europe for small-calibre target rifles produced by specialist makers.

BABY BROWNING / Belgium

Sales name for two 6·35mm automatic pistols manufactured by the Fabrique National d'Armes de Guerre of Herstal, Liège, Belgium, to the patents of John M. Browning. The first was introduced in 1906 and was called the 'Browning Baby' model in early sales literature, though the name was later dropped and this pistol is more generally known simply as the Model 1906. It was a simple blowback pistol weighing 13 ounces with a 6-shot magazine, and it was provided with grip and magazine safety devices. A manual safety catch was later added, the model then being advertised as the Triple Sûreté model.

The second model, known from its inception as the Baby Browning, is similar in general design but smaller in all dimensions, having been introduced in the early 1920s in order to meet the demand for very small pocket pistols and also to counter the competition from other small models such as the Menz Liliput. It

The 6·35mm 'Baby Browning' pistol.

weighed 10 ounces, retained the six-shot magazine, but did without the grip safety. The outline was generally more 'square' and compact than that of the 1906 model. It is still in production, and both models have, over the years, attracted innumerable copies, notably from small Spanish firms.

BABY NAMBU / *Japan*

Colloquial name for a Japanese service pistol. Essentially, it was a smaller version of the service Nambu 4th Year model, chambered for a special 7mm cartridge. Being lighter and smaller than the service pistol, these models were favoured by Japanese Staff officers and aviators, and it has also been referred to as the 'Officers Model'. Introduced early in the 1920s, it has been estimated that no more than about 3–4000 were made, though the study of serial numbers and other markings tends to throw some doubt on this. They are uncommon, and, of course, ammunition for them is no longer manufactured.

BACON, Thomas K. *(fl. 1850–1880)*

American gunsmith; set up the Bacon Arms Company in Norwich, Connecticut, in about 1862. His early production consisted of ·32 single shot pistols and ·36 percussion revolvers, both of which were used in small numbers during the American Civil War. He later negotiated a licence agreement with Smith & Wesson to make cheap rimfire cartridge revolvers; the licence was necessary since the Rollin White patent, owned by Smith & Wesson, would otherwise have prevented Bacon from making cylinders with bored-through chambers. On subsequent years he continued to produce these revolvers, all solid-frame non-

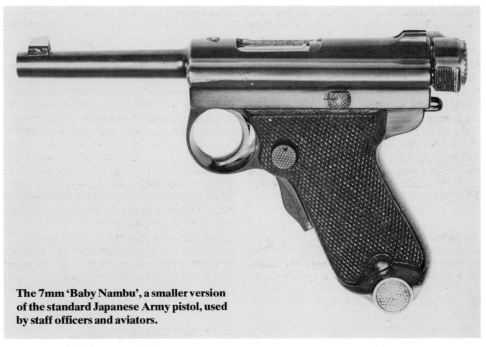

The 7mm 'Baby Nambu', a smaller version of the standard Japanese Army pistol, used by staff officers and aviators.

ejecting models with sheathed triggers, under such names as the 'Gem', 'Bonanza', 'Conqueror', 'Governor', 'Guardian' and 'Little Giant'. The market for this class of weapon eventually dwindled, and Bacon went out of business in 1891.

BALLE D / *France*

French military rifle bullet, developed for the 8mm Lebel rifle and introduced in 1898. It was the first pointed and boat-tailed bullet to be adopted as a military standard and was unusual for being an homogeneous bullet of copper-zinc alloy and not, as was usual at the time, a compound bullet using a lead core and copper alloy jacket. The shape was intended to reduce air drag both at the nose, by being pointed, and at the base, by the boat-tailing, this improving the bullet's performance and accuracy through the entire range of velocities. The solid construction was claimed to have been introduced in order to avoid the tendency of compound bullets to 'set up' or deform under the pressure of the gas generated by the cartridge, thus becoming cylindrical and defeating the designer's object. Balle D remained the service standard throughout the life of the 8mm rifle, until the end of the Second World War.

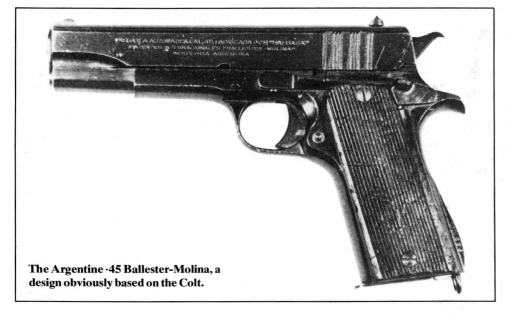

The Argentine ·45 Ballester-Molina, a design obviously based on the Colt.

BALLESTER-MOLINA / *Argentina*

·45 calibre automatic pistol manufactured by the Hispano-Argentine Fabricas de Automobiles SA (HAFDASA) of Buenos Aires. It was produced in 1935–1940 for the Argentine government and was a close copy of the US Army's ·45 Colt M1911 model, the only significant mechanical difference being the omission of the Colt's grip safety. The name was derived from Carlos Ballester, designer for the HAFDASA company.

As well as being the official Argentine Army pistol during the 1940s, numbers were bought by a British Purchasing Mission in 1941 and were supplied to SoE and other clandestine organisations in Europe.

This pistol was also made chambered for the ·22 Long Rifle cartridge, to the same dimensions as the ·45 model, and used as a military training weapon. These ·22 Long Rifle variants were also sold commercially as the 'La Criolla' ('the Creole').

BALLESTER-RIGAUD / *Argentina*

Semi-automatic carbine manufactured c.1944–1946 by the HAFDASA (see above) company of Buenos Aires and employed in limited numbers by the Argentine Army and national police force. In 9mm Parabellum calibre, it was a simple blowback weapon, wooden-stocked and with a 54-round magazine. It is understood that the original design was of a machine carbine or submachine gun which incorporated automatic fire, and it is believed that some of the early army issues were to this pattern. The change to a self-loading carbine, without automatic fire capability, came with the adoption of the weapon by police and internal security forces.

BANG, Soren H. *(fl. 1900–1925)*

Danish designer of an automatic rifle. Bang took out a series of patents from 1901 up to the early 1920s which covered a rifle operated by muzzle blast. A sliding cone over the rifle muzzle was driven forward by the rush of gas following the bullet ejection, and this movement was communicated via an operating rod to a breech bolt carrier unit. By a lever arrangement the carrier was driven to the rear, and cam surfaces within the carrier rotated the breech bolt, unlocking it from the barrel and then opening the breech. A return spring then forced the carrier back to load a fresh cartridge from the box magazine and then rotate and lock the bolt. The muzzle cone was repositioned at the same time, ready for the next shot.

The Bang rifle was tested by the US Ordnance Department in 1911 and was favourably reported on, though it displayed a tendency to overheat the barrel and was considered to be too expensive a manufacturing proposition for service adoption. It reappeared in a lighter and improved form in the 1920s and was again tested in the USA and also in Britain. Lightening the weapon had, however, impaired the robustness, and in both countries it suffered component breakages during the trials and was turned down for military adoption. Bang made no further attempts to improve the weapon thereafter. The muzzle cone system of operation was later used by the Walther company in their experimental Gewehr 41(W) for the German Army in 1941. It was no more successful than it had been in the hands of Bang.

BÄR / *Germany*

German multi-shot pistol manufactured by J. P. Sauer & Sons of Suhl and invented by Burkhardt Behr, a Russian resident in Switzerland,

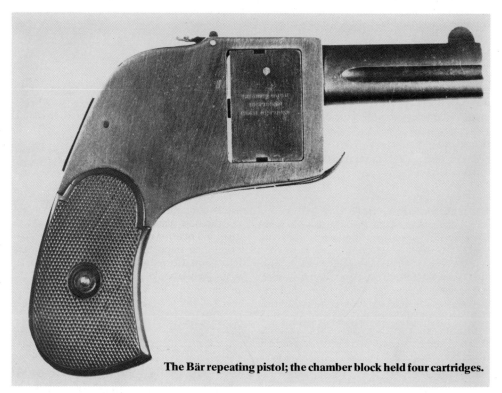

The Bär repeating pistol; the chamber block held four cartridges.

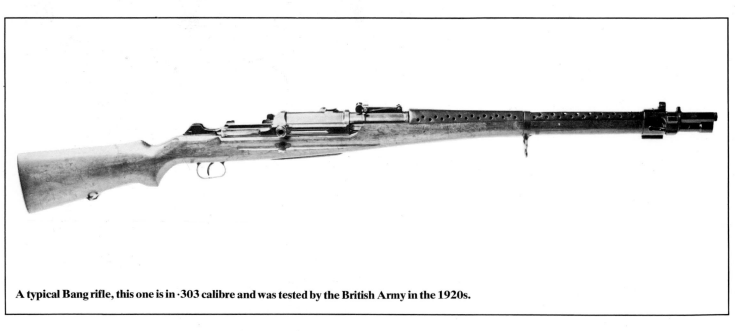

A typical Bang rifle, this one is in ·303 calibre and was tested by the British Army in the 1920s.

in 1898. Behr was a prolific inventor in many fields; in firearms he patented several breech mechanisms, recoil buffers and cattle killers in the early years of the 20th century.

The Bär pistol was a self-cocking weapon with two superposed barrels of two inches length. Behind the barrels, in the solid frame, was a rectangular block bored with four superposed chambers, the top pair of which were aligned with the pistol's two barrels. This block was centrally pivoted on its longitudinal axis and could be swung through 90° sideways so as to expose the chambers for loading. The block was then swung back and aligned with the frame, after which the first pull on the trigger would cock the internal hammer and fire the top cartridge through the top barrel. The second pull automatically re-aligned the internal firing pin to fire the cartridge in the second, lower, chamber, discharging the bullet through the lower barrel. The block was then rotated through 180° to bring the two bottom chambers to the top and into alignment with the barrels. These were then fired in the same manner.

Due to the flat chamber block, the Bär was a very slender weapon and much easier to pocket than most contemporary revolvers, and for this reason it achieved great popularity as a self-defence pocket pistol. It sold well from 1899 to about 1907, after which the pocket automatic pistols began to oust it from the market. Originally chambered for a special 7mm rimmed cartridge, some of the last production were chambered to take the 6·35mm automatic pistol cartridge.

BAUER / USA

Trade name on pistols sold by the Bauer Firearms Company of Fraser, Michigan, USA. These pistols are actually the 6·35mm Baby Browning model, and are marketed by Bauer in two grades: the Model SS in satin-finish stainless steel, and the Model SB in blued stainless steel. Production began in 1972.

BAVARIAN LIGHTNING / Bavaria

Popular name applied to a cavalry pistol adopted by the Bavarian Army in 1870 and derived from their service rifle of 1869. The invention of Johann Werder, both weapons were single-shot models derived from the Peabody hinged breech block action, in which the block, hinged at its rear end, is swung down at its front so as to expose the chamber for loading. In the Peabody design (and in the Martini, which is derived from it) the movement of the block was performed by an under-lever, but Werder appreciated that under-levers were difficult to operate when the firer was lying on the ground, as in military use, and he modified the action so that the block was moved by pushing forward on a finger-lever inside the trigger guard of the rifle. After the rifle was adopted, it was seen that this system lent itself to one-handed operation, and it was therefore adapted to a cavalry pistol. Both weapons fired an 11·3mm central fire cartridge, and both were soon to become obsolete.

BAYONNE / France

The Manufacture d'Armes Automatique de Bayonne, of Bayonne, France, began production of automatic pistols in 1921 and has continued to the present day. The original designs were based on the well-known Browning blowback patterns and were in 6·35mm, 7·65mm and 9mm Short calibres. The Model A was a 6·35mm copy of the Browning 1906, with triple safety. Model B, also in 6·35mm, differed in appearance, having an open-topped slide which exposed the upper surface of the barrel. Model C in 7·65mm and 9mm Short resembled the Browning Model 1910, having the recoil spring round the barrel retained by a muzzle locking ring. Model D was a C with lengthened slide and barrel.

All these models were in production in 1940 when the German occupation took place, and the factory was then placed under German supervision, much of the production going to German service use. At the end of the war the owners repossessed the factory and production was re-started for the commercial market. New models introduced since 1945 are the 6·35mm Model E, resembling the Model D; the Model R, again resembling the Model D but having an external hammer and chambered for 7·65mm ACP or 7·65mm French Longue cartridges; the Model D Para, chambered for the 9mm Parabellum cartridge and internally modified so as to incorporate breech locking controlled by a rotating barrel; and the Model F, a ·22 pistol generally using the Model D frame but with a variety of barrel lengths for target shooting. This company also produced the Echasa Model GZ for the Spanish company of Echave & Arizmendi; this was a slighlty modified Model D. The Model F when provided with an external hammer is sold as the 'Le Chasseur'.

These pistols are generally called 'MAB' pistols after the maker's monogram moulded into the butt plates. In the United States they are found bearing the monogram 'WAC', indicating their importation and sale by the Winfield Arms Corporation of Los Angeles. The various models take new names for the American market: The Model C became the 'Le Cavalier', the Model D the 'Le Gendarme' and the Model R the 'Le Militaire'.

All these pistols were commercial, but in the 1970s the Model R Para has been slightly modified so as to accept a special 15-shot magazine and is issued to the French Army as the Model PA-15. There is also a Model PAPF-1 with an extended barrel and slide and provided with precision sights.

The MAB Modele C pistol in 7·65mm calibre.

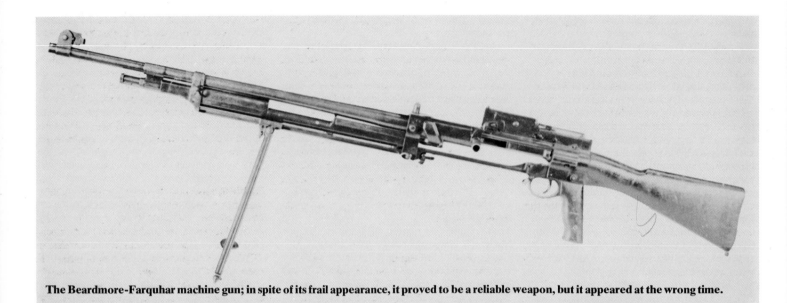

The Beardmore-Farquhar machine gun; in spite of its frail appearance, it proved to be a reliable weapon, but it appeared at the wrong time.

BEARDMORE-FARQUHAR/ Scotland

Machine gun, invented by Colonel M. G. Farquhar and manufactured by the William Beardmore company of Glasgow. Farquhar was also associated with the Farquhar-Hill automatic rifle, and it is difficult to determine which of the many patents taken out by these two men (and others in association with them from time to time) apply to the machine gun and which to the rifle; there is undoubtedly some overlap. Farquhar's earliest patent appears to be in 1906 and this was for a rifle, but it contains the essential elements of the machine gun mechanism.

The gun was gas operated, but instead of the gas piston acting directly on the breech closure, it worked through the medium of a spring. This spring was compressed by the gas piston, and was then held in this state until the gas pressure in the breech had dropped to a safe level, whereupon the energy stored in the spring was used to rotate and unlock the bolt and send it to the rear. During this recoil stroke, a return spring was loaded, and it then returned the bolt, chambering a fresh cartridge and locking the bolt.

It will be appreciated that the balance of power of the two springs was critical to the design, but the gun worked successfully and was of exceptionally light construction, this being made possible by the recoil-absorbing properties of the springs. It was drum fed, weighed 16¼ lbs and fired at about 500 rounds a minute. Air cooled, it was submitted as a possible observer's gun for use in aircraft, and it was tested in this role by the Royal Air Force in 1919. Though favourably received, this was the wrong time to try to sell guns; retrenchment and economy were the slogans of the times, and the Beardmore-Farquhar gun was turned down on these grounds. It was submit-

ted again in 1940, but by that time its performance and general approach were both obsolete, and it was once more refused for service.

BEAUMONT, De/ Holland

De Beaumont was a Dutch manufacturer with a factory at Maastricht which produced a number of service revolvers for the Netherlands Army from 1873 until some time in the early 1900s. They were all solid frame, gate-loaded, double-action models of no particular novelty or virtue other than their robustness. The calibre was always 9·4mm centre-fire, and while all were basically the Model 1873 there were some minor variations; the Old Model had no attached ejector, a cleaning and ejecting rod being carried in the holster; the New Model added a rod-ejector beneath the barrel; and the Klein Model had a shorter barrel. In 1891 the KNIL Model was introduced for the use of the Colonial Army in the Netherlands East Indies; this was also in 9·4mm calibre, had a 114mm barrel, rod ejection, much improved lockwork and a simpler method of assembly.

BEAUMONT, LT. F. B. E. (1838–1899)

Lieutenant Frederick B. E. Beaumont, RE, patented a double-action revolver lock, an improvement based on Adam's self-cocking lock, in 1855. This appears to have been developed in conjunction with Adams, and was rapidly adapted to Adam's design of solid-frame percussion revolver, which then became known as the 'Beaumont-Adams' pattern. The advantage of the Beaumont lock was that the revolver could now be fired in either of two ways: by pulling the trigger, which raised the hammer to the full cock position and then dropped it to fire the cartridge, or by pulling back the hammer to full cock with the thumb, to be released by a light pressure on the trigger.

The former method was advantageous for rapid action, the latter for more deliberate and accurate fire. The original Adams lock had been a self-cocking lock in which the trigger was pulled to cock and fire in one action, and while this feature appealed to soldiers for its advantages in a *mêlée*, it was not accepted by the authorities because it did not permit accurate aim to be taken. The Beaumont lock now gave both options, which satisfied everybody, and within a month of Beaumont's applying for a patent, the Board of Ordnance ordered 100 pistols with the lock for extensive trials. Subsequently it became the British service revolver.

Pistols with the Beaumont lock were also made by Adams for the commercial market, and other manufacturers adopted the lock.

BECKER/ Germany

Aircraft cannon invented by two brothers named Conders, employees of the Stahlwerke Becker of Reinickendorf, Germany, in 1916. Of 19mm calibre, it was an automatic weapon firing a high-explosive projectile and working on simple blowback lines, relying upon differential locking to achieve safety. Feed was from a vertical 15-shot box magazine and it could be fired in the single-shot mode or at a rate of 300 rounds a minute. Development continued throughout the war, though weapons were produced for service use throughout the period of development. They are reported to have been installed in Gotha bombers, and 131 were issued to the German Army anti-aircraft battalions. The precise number made is not known; records of the Allied Disarmament Commission show that

392 guns were confiscated and scrapped after the war.

After 1918 the Stahlwerke Becker were forbidden to engage in weapon manufacture, and they therefore sold their patents to a Swiss company, the Maschinenbau AG of Seebach. This company made some small improvements, changed the calibre to 20mm, and placed it on the market as the Semag-Becker Cannon, a lightweight infantry support gun and anti-tank gun on a small two-wheeled carriage. It failed to sell and in 1924 the company went into liquidation. The patents, plus the existing weapons and machinery and many of the technical staff, were acquired by the Oerlikon Machine Tool Company, and the gun was then redesigned and marketed as the Oerlikon Gun, in which form it eventually achieved great success and founded the fortunes of the Oerlikon company.

BEHOLLA / Germany

7·65mm automatic pistol developed by Becker & Hollander of Suhl, Germany, in 1915. It was taken into use by the German Army as a substitute standard weapon, the entire production going to the Army and none ever being offered commercially. The design was later, by Army orders, contracted to other manufacturers and made as the Leonhardt, Menta and Stenda. The latter version, by Stendawerke, was continued into the post-1918 period as a commercial design.

The Beholla was a fixed-barrel blowback pistol of no particular merit, but it was unusual in its method of assembly. The barrel was retained in the pistol frame by a cross-pin which had to be driven out through holes specially made in the slide. As a result, it was not possible to dismantle the pistol without using a bench vice and a thin punch to drive out the pin, a defect which meant that field cleaning must have been cursory. Apart from this, the Beholla was a robust and serviceable weapon. Study of serial numbers suggests that upwards of 100,000 may have been made under the various names.

BEKHEART, Philip B. (fl. early 20th C.)

A San Francisco gun dealer who, in 1908, persuaded the Smith & Wesson company to manufacture a ·22 target revolver on the frame of the ·32 police revolver. At that time, ·22 revolvers were considered almost as toys, and were, in consequence, built on small frames which prevented a decent grip being obtained for target shooting. The company were not sure of Bekheart's reasoning, but he guaranteed to take and sell a thousand pistols, and the design was made. The guns were sold extremely rapidly by Bekheart, were instantly popular, and the company went into production of the Bekheart Model or ·22/·32 Hand Ejector in 1911. It was to remain in production until 1953, interrupted only by the war years. Basically it is the ·32 frame mounting a special ·22 barrel and cylinder chambered for the ·22 Long Rifle Cartridge. Over-sized grips were fitted, and target sights provided. It was replaced in 1953 by the ·22/·32 Target Model 35 which is simply the same design with some slight improvements in manufacturing methods.

BENET, Lawrence Vincent (fl. 1875–1895)

American designer, son of General Benet, Chief of Ordnance US Army. In 1887 he became chief engineer to the Hotchkiss company of France, after the death of Hotchkiss. In 1892 he was responsible for purchasing the patents of Odkolek, and from these basic designs he developed the Hotchkiss machine gun, one version of which, designed with the assistance of Mercie, a French machinist, became the Benet-Mercie machine gun as used briefly by the US Army. This was a gas-operated weapon which relied upon the use of a 'fermeture nut' to lock the breech. This was a sleeve surrounding the breech of the weapon and provided internally with interrupted threads. The bolt was fitted with suitable lugs. The gas piston rotated the nut so that the bolt could then be withdrawn, the lugs passing through

The German Beholla 7·65mm automatic pistol, issued as a military pistol during World War One.

the interruptions in the threads. On return, the bolt was locked by rotation of the nut through a small arc. The design was later used for the 'light' Hotchkiss machine gun which was extensively used by cavalry in the British and French armies in 1914–1918.

BERDAN, Hiram S. (d.1893)

Colonel, US Army Ordnance Department; retired in 1864 to design firearms and ammunition. Notable for the Berdan primer, a percussion cap for use in drawn brass cartridge cases and in which the cap anvil is formed as part of the case. The design was widely adopted in Europe. He also developed a single shot breech-loading rifle using a front-hinged lifting (trap-door) breech block and known as the Berdan I. Russia adopted this weapon in 1868, together with a Berdan-designed cartridge. It was later modified to a bolt action by Tula Arsenal and thence known as the Berdan II from about 1871 onward.

The Berdan Model I.

BERESIN / USSR

Soviet aircraft machine gun designed by Mikhail Evgenevich Beresin, a designer on the staff of Tula Arsenal. The design was largely based on that of the Finnish 20mm Lahti aircraft cannon and entered service in 1940. It was a gas-operated gun in 12·7mm calibre, belt fed, and firing at rates between 700 and 1000 rounds a minute; the rate of fire could be adjusted within these limits to cater for various rates of synchronisation required in different aircraft applications. The action was locked by a transversely moving bolt lock actuated by the gas piston. The gun first saw service as the 'BS' for 'Beresin Samolotni' (Beresin Aircraft) and it was intended, from the start, to be an expendable gun, being scrapped as soon as a malfunction occurred; this was considered to be cheaper and easier than having a more expensive design and repairing it. The design was later modified into the BT for flexible installation in turrets; the BK for fixed installation in wings; and the UBS for synchronised installation within the propellor arc.

The Beresin gun served throughout most of the Second World War, but in about 1942 it was obvious that a heavier-calibre weapon was needed. The Beresin was scaled-up to 23mm calibre by two designers Volkov and Yartsev, becoming the VYa cannon.

BERETTA / Italy

Firm of Pietro Beretta, founded in 1680 in Brescia, Italy; became one of the leading gunmakers during the following century. Its products were confined to sporting rifles and shotguns until the outbreak of the First World War, when the factory turned to military weapons. In 1919 it returned to the manufacture of sporting weapons, though retaining some capacity for military arms, and this capacity was, of course, expanded once more during the Second World War. Since 1945 the company has produced a diverse array; its sporting weapons are of the highest class and sold worldwide, while its military weapons are also of the first quality and as well as arming the Italian forces are widely exported to outfit other armies.

Pistols

The first Beretta pistol was the Model 1915, a wartime product which was, therefore, somewhat below the usual standard of Beretta products. It was a 7·65mm blowback which exhibited a characteristic which was to become standard on Beretta designs: the front of the slide was cut away so as to expose the upper surface of the fixed pistol barrel. Shortly after this pistol appeared, a 9mm version, chambered for the Glisenti cartridge, was made; this had a stronger recoil spring plus a buffer spring to soften the slide return action. This model is easily recognised by the large safety catch and the presence of an ejection port in the top of the slide.

The Model 1915/19 was an improved Model 1915 in which the front ends of the slide sides were swept over the barrel to carry the foresight, and this design feature has been retained ever since. It was produced only in 7·65mm calibre.

The Model 1919 was the first pistol to be offered commercially; it was simply a 6·35mm version of the 1915/19 with the addition of a grip safety in the butt backstrap.

The Model 1923 was a 1915/19 modified to use an external hammer. Chambered for the 9mm Glisenti round, it was only made in small numbers, originally for military use and later for commercial sale. It was followed by the

Model 1931 which reverted to the 1915 pattern but added an external hammer. Most of these were issued to the Italian Navy and are generally found with wooden grips with a small medallion carrying the naval emblem, RM divided by an anchor. Those sold commercially have black plastic grips with the monogram PB.

The Model 1934 is probably the most common Beretta, having been made in vast numbers for the Italian Army. It is little more than a 1931 chambered for the 9mm Short cartridge. Military weapons will be found marked RE (Army) RA (Air Force) or RM (Navy) while police weapons are marked PS. It was also sold commercially, but in small numbers since most production was taken by the services.

The Model 1935 was a 1934 in 7·65mm calibre, used by the Air Force and Navy. Commercially it was sold as the Model 935.

Since 1945, several commercial models have been sold under various names—the Jaguar, Minx, Puma etc. These are almost all variants of the basic 1934 design, chambered for ·22, 6·35mm or 7·65mm cartridges. The last important military design was the Model 951 or Brigadier, which was the first locked-breech pistol from Beretta. The general form is still that of the M1934, but it is larger in all dimensions and chambered for the 9mm Parabellum cartridge. Breech locking is done by a wedge beneath the barrel which holds barrel and slide together until unlocked by striking the frame after a short recoil—very similar to the system used on the Walther P-38 pistol. This model has also been made under license in Egypt as the Helwan pistol.

In 1977 several new designs were announced, including the Model 81 in 7·65mm, the Model 84 in 9mm Short and the Model 92 in 9mm Parabellum; these are all fitted with double-action lockwork, and have large capacity magazines, the model 92 taking 15 shots and the other 12 shots.

Rifles

Sporting rifles in all the usual commercial calibres were made by the company for several years, but the first military rifle design came

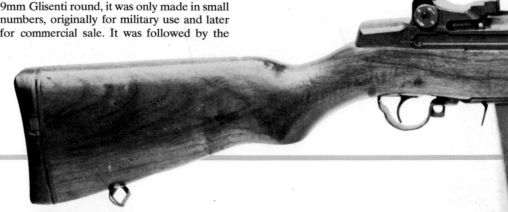

about after the company had been making the American M1 Garand rifle under an off-shore procurement contract in the 1950s. These were made for the Italian Army and were also sold to Indonesia. With the adoption of the 7·62mm NATO cartridge, it was decided to overhaul the basic Garand design and eliminate some of the less-liked features, notably the eight-round clip loading. The Beretta BM59, as the result is known, uses the basic Garand mechanism but with a new 7·62mm barrel, a 20-shot removable magazine which can be 'topped up' from chargers while in place on the rifle, a new trigger and firing mechanism, and a grenade-launcher on the muzzle. Three variant models were produced: the standard; the Alpini with a cut-down stock, pistol grip and folding butt; and the Parachutist's model, which is much like the Alpini but with a removable grenade-launcher and flash-hider.

When the 5·56mm cartridge became popular, Beretta built a completely new rifle. This, the AR70, is an Assault Rifle, gas-operated via an overhead piston and bolt carrier, and is very much in the modern idiom, being largely made of steel pressings welded together. It can fire single shots or automatic fire at a rate of 700 rpm.

Submachine Guns

The Beretta company's involvement with submachine guns began in 1917 when they were asked to make a more practical weapon out of the Vilar Perosa machine gun. The designer Tullio Marengoni did this by splitting the twin Vilar Perosa in two and mounting each half into a wooden stock resembling the standard army carbine. It used the overhead magazine of the V-P, and was fitted with two triggers, one providing single shots and the other automatic fire at 900 rpm. A folding bayonet was fitted, and a semi-automatic version with a single trigger was also produced for police use. In 1930 this design was modified by using a 25-round magazine feeding from beneath the gun to become the M1918/30.

In 1938 Maregoni produced the Model 1938A, which used a short wooden stock, a perforated barrel jacket, muzzle compensator, and bottom-feeding box magazine. This was an extremely good design and remained in production, in various modifications, until about 1950.

After Maregoni's retirement, a new designer, Domenic Salza, set to work to produce a model which would be easier and cheaper to make, and this resulted in the Model 12. This is quite different from its predecessors, a simple steel tubular body with two pistol grips and a folding butt-stock. It relies on an 'overhung' bolt, in which the bolt face is recessed so that much of the bolt mass surrounds the barrel when the bolt is closed, to reduce the length of the weapon and improve the balance.

Shotguns

It would be impossible to tabulate all the shotguns made by the Beretta company throughout its life, since they have been produced to every conceivable specification. At present they offer a single-barrel 'trap' gun; double-barrelled guns in side-by-side and over-and-under configuration in 12 and 20 gauge with barrels ranging from 26 inches to 30 inches; and a gas-operated automatic shotgun in 12 and 20 gauge in various weights and barrel lengths. All are of the finest possible quality.

The Beretta Model 34 pistol, standard arm of the Italian forces during World War Two.

The Beretta 38/42 submachine gun; one of the best, if less well-known, wartime designs.

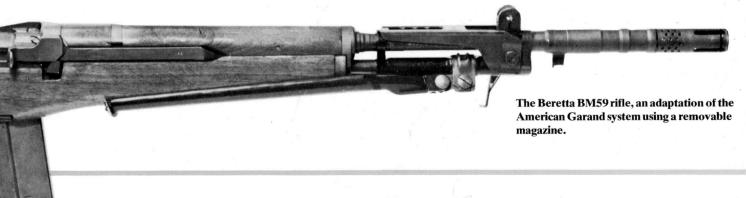

The Beretta BM59 rifle, an adaptation of the American Garand system using a removable magazine.

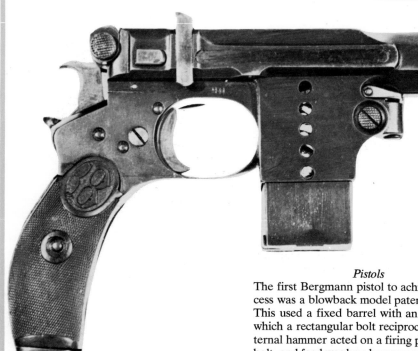

This Bergmann 11mm locked-breech pistol was submitted for British trials in 1902.

BERGMANN / Germany

The Theodor Bergmann Waffenfabrik of Suhl, Thuringia, lends its name to a variety of pistols and submachine guns which were designed by Louis Schmeisser, an employee of the company. Bergmann's first pistol patent was taken out in 1892 in conjunction with Otto Brauswetter, a watchmaker from Szegedin, Hungary. This covered the revolver-lock trigger, hammer mechanism and clip-loading magazine which later became standard features of Bergmann designs. It also used a locked breech controlled by a laterally-displaced bolt. It is probable that only this bolt is Brauswetter's, the remainder coming from Schmeisser; the point is academic since the design was never manufactured.

Pistols

The first Bergmann pistol to achieve any success was a blowback model patented in 1893. This used a fixed barrel with an extension in which a rectangular bolt reciprocated. An external hammer acted on a firing pin inside the bolt, and feed was by a box magazine ahead of the trigger guard which was loaded with a clip of five cartridges. An unusual feature was that the cartridges, in 5mm calibre, had no form of rim for extraction; ejection from the chamber was by residual gas pressure, and the case was bounced out of the feedway upon striking the next round in the magazine. This was not entirely reliable and was replaced in 1897 by a conventional rimless cartridge with a groove for the extractor. These models were eventually produced in 5mm, 6·5mm and 8mm calibres. Pistols could be had with various barrel lengths, sights, and grips, and it was even possible to have them chambered for other types of ammunition, as a result of which there is a bewildering variety of early models.

In 1901 a locked-breech pistol was developed which used a laterally-sliding locking piece to secure the bolt during firing. It was chambered for a new 9mm cartridge of Bergmann design, and was offered for sale as the Mars; it was accepted for service with the Spanish Army in 1905, but Bergmann was unable to manufacture the number needed and subcontracted the work to the V. Ch. Schilling company of Suhl. They were then taken over by the Heinrich Krieghoff concern who repudiated the contract, leaving Bergmann with a fat contract and no means of fulfilling it. He therefore sold the design to the Pieper company of Liège and retired from the pistol business, while Pieper produced the pistol as the Bergmann-Bayard Model 1908.

After Bergmann's death in 1915 the company was absorbed by the A. G. Lignose, who continued to use the Bergmann name, marketing various pocket pistols, notably those derived from the patents of Chylewski. In 1937 the Lignose organisation also purchased the moribund Menz company of Suhl and for some time thereafter marketed various Menz pistols under the Bergmann name, calling them the Bergmann-Erben (see below).

Machine Guns

The first Bergmann machine gun was patented in 1900 and was probably, like the pistols, the work of Schmeisser. Production on a limited scale followed as the Model 1902, and it was then improved to become the Model 1910. This gun was a water-cooled medium gun mounted on a tripod, operated by short recoil. Locking was done by a vertically-moving block, and the design incorporated a quick-

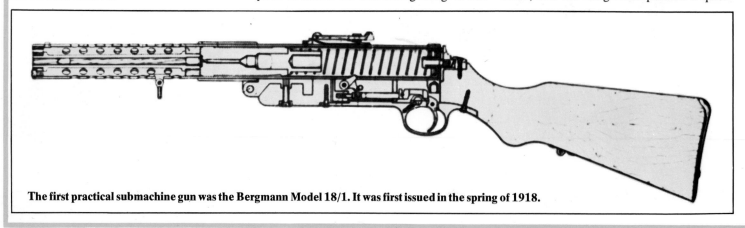

The first practical submachine gun was the Bergmann Model 18/1. It was first issued in the spring of 1918.

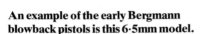

An example of the early Bergmann blowback pistols is this 6·5mm model.

change barrel, a remarkable innovation in a weapon of that class at that time. Belt fed, it fired the standard 7·92mm Mauser round at about 500 rpm. Although a very sound design, it never gained the acceptance it appears to have deserved, largely because the German Army were then thoroughly committed to the Maxim Gun. But in 1915, with a shortage of machine guns, they were happy to accept a modified version, the MG15nA (nA = neuer Art = new pattern). This removed the water jacket and replaced it with a perforated barrel jacket so that the gun was now air-cooled and considerably lighter. A pistol grip and light tripod were fitted, and the 200 round belt fed from a drum carried on the right side of the gun. This was issued to German and Austrian troops on the Italian front and appears to have been a well-liked and reliable weapon.

Submachine guns

The Bergmann submachine gun was designed by Schmeisser after Bergmann's death, and became the prototype for almost all the submachine guns which followed. A simple blowback weapon using differential locking, it comprised a tubular receiver with heavy bolt, perforated barrel jacket, and 9mm barrel which was actually the barrel of the Long 08 Luger pistol. The magazine was the 'snail' magazine which had been produced for the same pistol, and was entered into the left side of the gun at an angle. Some 30,000 of these were made.

After the war the submachine gun was proscribed for military forces, though it was permitted to be retained by police forces in Germany. The design was then changed by removing the snail magazine and its sloping housing and replacing it with a right-angled magazine housing and a straight-forward box magazine feeding into the left side as before.

The MP18/I, as the original design was known, could only be used on automatic fire, at a rate of about 400 rpm. The design was later taken over by the C. G. Haenel company, for whom Schmeisser had gone to work, and given a selector mechanism which allowed the firing of single shots. This became the Model 28/II and was offered for commercial sale by Haenel with great success. Numbers of them appeared in the Spanish Civil War where they drew the attention of the military to the potential of the submachine gun.

The Bergmann MP28/II was copied outright by the British in 1940 as the Lanchester submachine gun, used by the Royal Navy.

The Bergmann Model 15nA machine gun, with belt-feed box. Had it been available it could have been a useful light infantry weapon.

BERGMANN-BAYARD / *Belgium*

Locked-breech automatic pistol invented by Bergmann (see above) and manufactured by the Ancient Etablissments Pieper of Liège, Belgium, who purchased the rights from Bergmann. The suffix 'Bayard' represents the trade-name of the Pieper company, their trademark being a mounted knight, engraved on the pistols. The Bergmann-Bayard name was also attached to the special 9mm cartridge developed for this pistol, somewhat longer and more powerful than the 9mm Parabellum round; this cartridge was to become the standard Spanish Army pistol round, known there as the 9mm Largo. This Spanish adoption came from their adoption of the pistol in 1906; though they later adopted other makes of pistol, they adhered to the cartridge.

The Bergmann-Bayard was also adopted by the Danish Army as their Model 1910, supplies being provided by Pieper. When the First World War interrupted supply, the Danes made arrangements to manufacture their own pistols and commenced doing so in 1922. The Danish version differed slightly from the original Belgian pattern, having much larger grip plates of wood or black plastic.

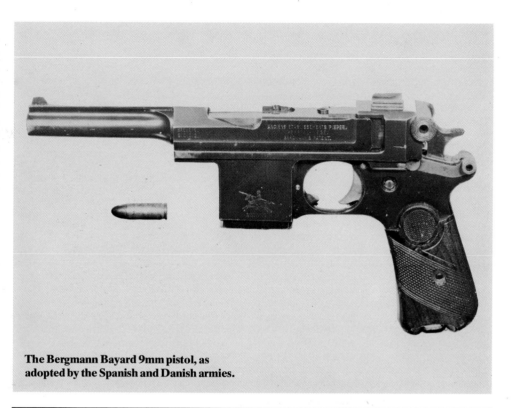

The Bergmann Bayard 9mm pistol, as adopted by the Spanish and Danish armies.

BERGMANN-ERBEN / *Germany*

Pistols marked 'Theodor Bergmann Erben' were marketed in 1937–1939 by the A. G. Lignose of Suhl. 'Erben' translates as 'successor' or 'heir' and this nomenclature appears to have been no more than an attempt to trade on the goodwill inherent in the Bergmann name. The first models so marked were actually the contemporary Menz PB Spezial, which had been in production when the Menz company was absorbed by the Lignose organisation. The 6·35mm Model II which followed was based on an earlier Menz design. It seems probable that both pistols were assembled from stocks of spare parts in existence at the time of the Menz take-over in 1937. The quantity produced was small and the Bergmann-Erben pistols are quite uncommon today.

The Bergmann Erben pistol, actually a Menz design trading on the Bergmann reputation.

BERN / *Switzerland*

The Eidgenossische Waffenfabrik Bern, of Bern, Switzerland, is the Swiss Government Arsenal and has been concerned with the manufacture of pistols, rifles, machine guns and submachine guns for many years, though most of the weapons are known by other names. For a description of the various weapons, see under Schmidt-Rubin (rifles); Schmidt (pistols); Parabellum (pistols); and Furrer (Machine guns and submachine guns). The arsenal has produced various prototype weapons, notably a series of automatic pistols during the Second World War, but only those which saw service received names.

BERNADELLI / *Italy*

The Bernadelli company of Gardone Valtrompia, Italy, entered the firearms business in 1865 when Vincenzo Bernardelli set up in business as a barrel maker. Later, aided by his son, he progressed to the manufacture of sporting arms and pistols. Primarily a manufacturer of high-grade shotguns, pistol making began as late as 1928 with the manufacture of the 10·4mm Italian service revolver, details of which will be found under Bodeo. After the Second World War production of automatic pistols and revolvers was begun.

As with all shotgun manufacturers, tabulation of their products is virtually impossible,

owing to the great diversity of types produced over the years. Their current production covers double guns in both side-by-side and over-and-under styles, in all the standard bores and with degrees of quality governed only by the prospective buyer's pocket. An interesting detail is their recent re-introduction of outside-hammer shotguns.

Bernadelli revolvers are generally based on Smith & Wesson practice, using solid frames with side-swinging cylinders locked by the ejector rod fitting into a lug beneath the barrel. The internal arrangements of the lockwork are also much the same as those on Smith & Wesson revolvers. The first models appeared in about 1950, in ·22 and ·32 chambering; later models appeared in 1958, but, although well made, they do not seem to have attracted much commercial success.

The automatic pistols began in 1945 with the 'Vest Pocket' model, a tiny 6·35mm weapon with strong similarities to the Walther Model 9. This was then scaled up, in 1947, to produce the Pocket Model in 7·65mm calibre. This was originally produced with an 85mm barrel having an enveloping slide, but it was followed by various models with the barrels extended beyond the front of the slide in lengths up to 250mm. These barrels were provided with foresights built on to a collar which slipped over the muzzle and was locked there by a screw; this was necessary in order that the sight could be removed to allow the slide to slip over the muzzle when dismantling the pistol.

In 1949 the first of a number of ·22 pistols appeared, known as the Baby model. This was, in effect, no more than the 1945 Vest Pocket model modified so as to take the rimfire cartridge. The Standard model, also introduced in 1949, was similarly the Pocket model modified for ·22 ammunition; like the Pocket model, it could be had with a variety of barrel lengths.

In 1950 the VB appeared, a further scale-up of the Pocket Model, chambered for 9mm Browning Long or 9mm Parabellum. Since this is a blowback weapon, the 9mm Parabellum loading is a little powerful for it and, because the recoil spring has to be exceptionally powerful to cope with the heavy loading, it is rather too strong for reliable functioning with the weaker cartridge.

Later models are all variations on the earlier designs, improved in small matters and with slightly more streamlined appearance. These include the Model 60, Model Arm and Model 62 in the usual blowback calibres.

BERTHIER, Gen. A.V.P.M (fl. 1885–1920)
A French Army officer who was responsible for two significant firearms designs, the Berth-

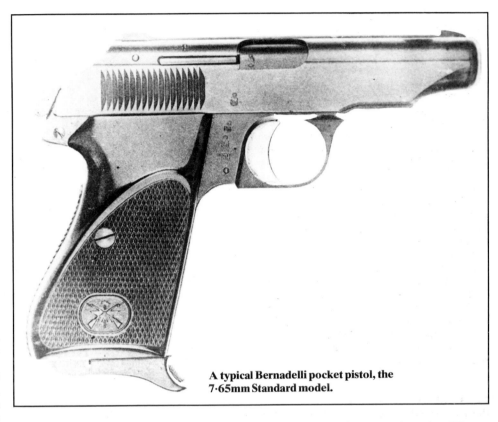

A typical Bernadelli pocket pistol, the 7·65mm Standard model.

ier rifle and the Vickers-Berthier machine gun. The former was a bolt-action rifle of conventional form which used a Mannlicher-type clip for loading to a box magazine below the action. The earlier Lebel rifle had used a tubular magazine below the barrel, which was slow to load, and the Berthier design was adopted in order to keep abreast of clip-loading weapons introduced in other countries. The first such weapon was the Cavalry Carbine M1890, and this was followed by minor variations such as the Carabine de Gendarmerie and the Mousqueton d'Artillerie. The first full-length rifle on the Berthier system was the Fusil des Tirailleurs Indo-Chinois Modele 1902, which was

again followed by small variants for different forces.

In 1915 the French Army expressed a preference for the Berthier design over the original Lebel, which was still the primary infantry weapon, and large numbers of the Colonial Model 1907 rifle were removed from their Colonial owners and issued to the French Army in France, being called the Fusil Mle 07/15. But the prime drawback with the Berthier design was that the clip only carried three rounds; by comparison, the German Mauser held five and the British Lee-Enfield ten. In 1916 therefore the design was modified and a new five-round clip issued, a change which

The French Army Mousqueton d'Artillerie Mle 1892, a typical Berthier bolt-action design.

necessitated placing a short sheet-metal extension on the bottom of the magazine. These rifles were to serve the French Army for several years, and numbers of them were again modified in 1934 to accept the new 7·5mm cartridge which replaced the 8mm Lebel round.

Berthier also became interested in automatic rifles, taking out patents in Britain and Belgium in 1905. But from this starting point he later modified his intentions and produced a machine gun, which was manufactured for him by Pieper of Liège in 1908. It was among the first weapons which could properly be called a light machine gun; it was shoulder-fired, from a bipod, and fed from an overhead box magazine. It was gas-operated and used a tipping bolt locking into the receiver; in fact,

more than one observer has noted the similarities between Berthier's design and the later design by Browning of his Automatic Rifle—both of which were developed within a few miles of each other in Liège. One of the most remarkable innovations of the Berthier design was the method of cooling; the barrel was surrounded by a thin jacket, and water was pumped back and forth through this jacket by two rubber bellows units operated by the gunner's assistant.

Berthier visited the USA in 1916 in an attempt to organise production of this machine gun. The US Army ordered several thousand shortly after the American entry into the war, and Berthier arranged for manufacture to be done by the Hopkins & Allen company of Norwich Connecticut. Unfortunately, the

company set up to organise production, the United States Machine Gun Company, who controlled the Hopkins & Allen factory, had run into severe financial trouble due to underestimating the cost of producing a batch of rifles for the Russian Government. While they were still attempting to sort this out, the factory was requisitioned by the Marlin-Rockwell corporation who wanted it in order to make Browning Automatic Rifle parts. With no factory, and no other source of production in sight, the Berthier machine gun failed to appear. The war ended and Berthier then went to Britain and sold the manufacturing rights to Vickers. It thereafter became the Vickers-Berthier gun (*qv*) and General Berthier left the firearms scene, no doubt in some disgust at the difficulty of doing business.

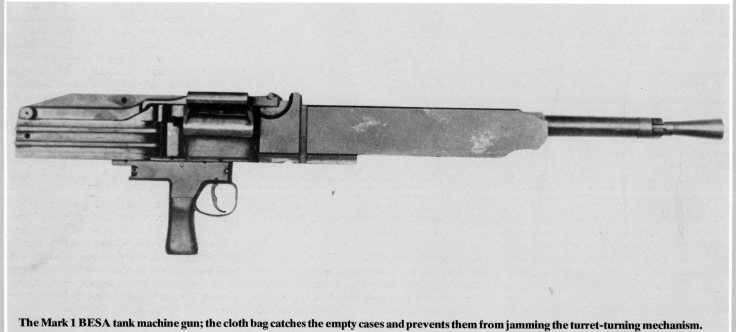

The Mark 1 BESA tank machine gun; the cloth bag catches the empty cases and prevents them from jamming the turret-turning mechanism.

BESA / *England*

British tank machine guns, the name being derived from their manufacture by the Birmingham Small Arms Company. The first gun to assume this name was the Czechoslovakian ZB53 model, designed by Vaclav Holek in 1937. It used a gas operation similar to that of the ZB-26 light machine gun and was chambered for the 7·92mm Mauser round. A heavy-barrelled gun, it was belt fed and could be set to produce two rates of automatic fire, 450 and 750 rpm. The British Army decided that this was the most suitable gun for use in tanks and the manufacturing rights were purchased. But since time was short, and since the conversion of the ZB-26 into the Bren gun had included its

conversion from 7·92mm rimless ammunition to ·303 rimmed ammunition and had been a difficult task, it was decided to retain the 7·92mm calibre and arrange for the manufacture of suitable ammunition in Britain. Since the gun was solely for use in tanks which would have their own channels of supply, this decision was logistically acceptable.

The BESA gun is unusual in that as well as being gas operated, the barrel also recoils, and the mechanism is so arranged that the round is fired while the barrel is still moving forwards, which reduced the recoil blow. The first models were exactly as the Czech original, but BSA later modified the design in order to simplify production and in the process did away with

the adjustable rate of fire, setting the rate at 800 rpm. A later version had the rate set at 500 rpm. The BESA was renowned for its accuracy and reliability and remained in service until replaced by the ·30 Browning gun in the 1950s.

The second BESA gun was based on the Czech ZB-60, a very heavy 15mm gun which was simply an enlargement of the 7·92mm model. It was solely for use as the primary armament in armoured cars. It fired at a rate of 450 rpm and was an extremely effective gun, but only 3200 were ever made; it does not seem to have been popular, largely due to its size (80 inches long) and weight (125 lbs). It was considered to be obsolete not long after the end of the war.

The Mark 1 Besal machine gun, a utility design which was held in reserve in case Bren production failed during the war.

BESAL / *Britain*

British design of light machine gun developed by the Birmingham Small Arms Company in 1940–1941. During the Second World War the entire British production of Bren light machine guns was concentrated at the Royal Small Arms Factory, Enfield, and it became apparent that one air raid on the factory would have serious repercussions on the supply of machine guns. As a result, the BSA company were asked to develop a design of 'utility' light machine gun which could be put into production rapidly in an emergency. Their chief designer Harry Faulkner developed this gun, originally called the Besal but later, to avoid confusion with the BESA gun, called the Faulkner gun. It was a gas-operated gun with a rectangular breech block which locked into the body on similar lines to the Browning automatic rifle. The piston was also square in section, so that all manufacturing could be done on milling machines without needing lathes. Two models were designed; the first had the normal sort of cocking handle on the right side, the second was cocked by pulling on the pistol grip, a modification of the system used on the BESA gun. Although somewhat unprepossessing, the Besal was a sound and reliable design which would have been very easy to manufacture. The designs were proved in prototype form, accepted, and then placed in reserve in case they were needed. No emergency arose, and the Besal was, therefore, never produced.

BETHEL-BURTON / *USA*

Bethel-Burton, of Brooklyn, New York, produced a number of military rifle designs in the 1880s. The first of these was a bolt-action repeater using a tubular magazine beneath the barrel which carried eight rounds. Except that the bolt locked into the receiver by means of interrupted lugs at its rear end (a theoretically poor arrangement) it was no different from several other tubular magazine designs of the period. Next, a side-mounted box magazine was produced which fed by gravity, dropping the cartridges into the same lifting arrangement as had been used with the tubular magazine. Finally, these ideas were combined and a box magazine added to the tubular magazine to give the gun a total magazine capacity of twenty rounds; a cut-off device on the box magazine prevented those rounds feeding until the tubular magazine had been emptied. Both designs were tried by the US Army in 1884 and by the British Army in 1885, but they were not considered to be sufficiently advantageous to be worth adopting.

BILLINGHURST-REQUA / *USA*

A 'battery gun' consisting of twenty-five rifle barrels mounted in a wheeled carriage. The rear end of the barrels was closed by a steel breech-piece which carried twenty-five chambers. These were loaded with powder and ball, and the breech piece then clamped in place with the chambers entering the rifle barrels. Each chamber had a vent, and a train of fine gunpowder was now trickled along the breech-pipe to connect the vents. At the centre was a percussion cap nipple and a hammer. To fire the battery, the hammer was dropped on to the cap; this ignited the gunpowder train and the individual chambers were then touched off in a volley. Due to its concentrated fire it was ideal for covering narrow approaches such as bridges and it was frequently referred to as a 'bridge gun'. It was of ·52 calibre and the complete equipment weighed 1382 lbs.

The gun was the invention of Dr. Joseph Requa, and was built by William Billingshurst of New York. It was demonstrated there in 1862 in an endeavour to attract sufficient capital to allow production to begin, but it had little success. A small number were built and used in the American Civil War. One gun was examined and reported on by the British Ordnance Select Committee in August 1863; they were of the opinion that such weapons 'could never be effectually substituted for field guns of any description' and that their 'utility would be very questionable'.

BIRKIGT, Marc *(fl. early 20th C.)*

Swiss designer, primarily remembered for his work in designing Hispano-Suiza cars, but who also collaborated with the Italian designer Scotti in developing a heavy machine gun intended for aircraft use. Work is said to have begun in 1919, and in the middle 1920s it was updated to become a 20mm cannon which was specifically designed to fit between the cylinder banks of the Hispano-Suiza aircraft engine in order to meet a French specification for fighter aircraft. The weapon eventually became the Hispano-Suiza cannon.

BITTNER, Gustav *(fl. 1850–1890)*

A gunsmith of Wiepert (Vejprty), Bohemia, who set up in business with his brother as the Gebruder Bittner in about 1850. He was principally concerned with the manufacture of sporting guns in small numbers, though in conjunction with other gunsmiths of the locality he formed a consortium in 1886 to produce Mannlicher rifles on contract. He is principally remembered for a design of mechanical repeating pistol patented in the early 1890s. Like most of this class of weapon of that period, it was a bolt action pistol, the bolt operated by means of finger pressure back and forth in a ring trigger at the end of an operating arm. Cam surfaces on the arm rotated the bolt to unlock, then withdraw it; on the return stroke, a round was collected from the box magazine

Italian Bodeo revolver, model of 1889.

The Borchardt 7·65mm automatic pistol, forerunner of the Parabellum.

ahead of the trigger, the bolt rotated to lock and the striker cocked. Further rearward pressure on the ring trigger then pressed on a firing trigger which released the striker. These pistols were chambered for a special 7·7mm cartridge designed by Bittner for the pistol and not used in any other weapon. Like all other pistols of this type, it was rendered obsolete with the arrival of the automatic pistol in the middle 1890s, and it did not achieve much commercial success; nevertheless, it was made in sufficient quantity for it to be probably the most common of mechanical repeating pistols to be found in collections today.

BIWARIP / *Britain*
Submachine gun submitted to the British Army for trial in August 1938; records no longer exist to show who invented it or who was responsible for its submission. It was in 9mm Parabellum calibre and resembled an elongated pistol with a perforated jacket around the barrel and short magazine feeding in from the left side. It had no butt. It worked, but it was too light to be controllable and was not capable of accurate fire.

BLISH, John *(fl. early 20th C.)*
Commander John Blish, USN (Retired), was the patentee of a breech locking system in 1915. The system is said to have occurred to him after observing that the breech screws of heavy guns had a tendency to unlock as the breech pressure dropped after firing (they were apparently badly designed). He postulated an imbalance of pressures such that high pressure would cause two inclined faces to adhere, but at a lower pressure the adhesion would fail and the two surfaces would be able to slide across one another. This became the 'Blish system of slipping inclined faces' and was adopted by General John T. Thompson for incorporation into an automatic rifle he was trying to design. Thompson and Blish, with a

financier named Ryan, formed the Auto-Ordnance Corporation (*qv*) to promote this rifle. The design failed and eventually became the Thompson submachine gun (*qv*).

In the Thompson gun the Blish lock was in the form of a loose 'H-Piece', so-called because it resembled the letter H. This rode in a slot in the bolt, inclined at an angle of about 25°. At each side of the H-Piece were lugs which engaged in slots in the gun receiver at an angle of about 40°. When the gun fired, the rearward movement of the bolt, under high breech pressure, jammed the H-Piece in the bolt and the lugs in the receiver slots. When the pressure dropped, the bolt movement caused the H-Piece to slide up and disengage the lugs from the receiver, thus allowing the bolt to recoil. There was always debate about the efficiency of the Blish lock, and late models of the Thompson dispensed with it entirely, without impairing their action in any way. At best, it can only be considered as a form of delayed blowback mechanism and not a positive lock.

BODEO / *Italy*
The Bodeo revolver was adopted as the Italian service side-arm in 1889 and remained in first line employment until its replacement in 1910 by the Glisenti automatic pistol (*qv*). It was of standard design for its period, being a solid frame pistol with double-action lock, gate loading and rod ejection. It was chambered for a 10·4mm cartridge. On opening the loading gate, the hammer was locked in a safe position, the mechanism being based on the patents of Abadie (*qv*); little else of the design was original. The only unusual feature is a hammer block which prevents the hammer falling far enough to strike the cartridge unless the trigger is pulled fully back; it is this item which causes the pistol to be called Bodeo, since Sgr. Bodeo was at the head of the commission which drew up the specification and he is believed to have been responsible for this device.

The pistol appeared in two forms: one had an octagonal barrel, a folding trigger and no trigger guard; the other had a cylindrical barrel and a normal trigger and guard. The former was for troops, the latter for NCOs and officers. Both patterns were in production at the same time; in the past the fixed-trigger model has been called the Model 1894 but there appears to be no warrant for this distinction.

Both designs were made in numerous factories and are marked accordingly.

BORCHARDT, Hugo *(c.1850–1921)*
Hugo Borchardt was born in Germany and emigrated with his parents to America in 1865. His next few years there are lost to us, but in 1872 he became Superintendent of Works for the Pioneer Breechloading Arms Company; in 1874 he was a foreman for the Singer Sewing Machine Company. He then moved to the Colt Patent Firearms Company, and in March 1875 became Works Superintendent of the Sharps Rifle Company. While occupying this post he invented the Sharps-Borchardt rifle, a single shot weapon with dropping breech block known as the Model 1878.

In 1876 Borchardt appears in the employment of the Winchester Repeating Arms Company, where he designed a number of six-shot solid frame revolvers, the later models of which incorporated an ingenious swing-out cylinder design which pre-dated the Colt application by over ten years. One model, a solid frame with rod ejection, was tested by the US Board of Fortification and Ordnance in 1876 but turned down, and the other designs were never commercially exploited; this may be due to the legendary deal between Colt and Winchester, in which Winchester revealed the Borchardt revolver designs, which were far in advance of anything Colt had at that time, and threatened to put them on the market if Colt persisted in its intention to produce rifles which would have competed with Winchester designs. Colt thereafter stuck to pistols and Winchester to rifles, and the Borchardt designs went into Winchester's museum, where they still are.

Doubtless upset by this turn of events, Borchardt, who had by this time taken American citizenship, returned to Europe in about 1882 and worked for a time with Rudolf Frommer in the Femaru Fegyvergyar factory in Budapest. It is probable that it was here that he became interested in automatic weapons. He returned briefly to the USA in 1890 but in 1892 appeared in Berlin, where he displayed the drawings of his automatic pistol to the Ludwig Löwe company. He entered Löwe's employment and patented his pistol in September 1893, there-

after superintending its manufacture in the Löwe factory. He remained in the company's employment, and with its successor the Deutsche Waffen und Munitionsfabrik until he retired in 1919. From about 1900 onward he took less and less interest in his pistol design, and spent most of his time pursuing various designs of automatic rifle, basing them on the toggle-joint principle used in his pistol. None were ever manufactured, except as prototypes.

Borchardt was undoubtedly a brilliant designer, but he tended to lose interest once the design had been made to work. He was less than pleased when others pointed out possible improvements and tried to urge them on him.

BORCHARDT PISTOL / Germany

Automatic pistol invented by Hugo Borchardt (see above) and patented in September 1893. Although not the first automatic pistol to be placed on the market—it was preceded by the

Schonberger—it was certainly the first one to be a commercial success, some 3000 being made between 1894 and 1899 when manufacture ceased.

The action of the Borchardt pistol relied upon the Maxim toggle lock in modified form. The toggle relies upon the fact that when laid flat, with the central joint below the line of

thrust and braced against the pistol frame, it forms a solid strut behind the exploding cartridge and thus securely locks the breech. In the Borchardt action, the toggle unit was 'broken' by the action of the barrel and locked toggle recoiling together across the frame of the pistol until the rear end of the toggle, carrying a roller, struck a curved surface and was deflected downwards. This caused the other end of that toggle arm to rise and thus break the joint. At this point the pressure on the base of the cartridge could force open the breech, causing the toggle to rise still further and place tension on a spring. The stored energy of the spring later closed the toggle, forcing a cartridge out of the magazine and into the chamber as the toggle was once more straightened out and locked.

The greatest difficulty lay in developing a suitable cartridge to work with this action, and Borchardt, doubtless assisted by engineers of the Deutsche Metallpatronenfabrik, a company which had affiliations with Löwe, developed a bottle-necked rimless case with a 7·65mm jacketed bullet. Some authorities seek to credit the cartridge design to Georg Luger, but evidence for this is tenuous.

The Borchardt was generally provided with a wooden butt-stock which could be clamped to the rear of the frame to convert the pistol into a species of self-loading carbine. With a barrel length of 190mm this was a feasible idea, but it was somewhat weakened by the absence of any form of adjustable rear sight.

The early production Borchardt pistols were marked 'Waffenfabrik Löwe Berlin/System Borchardt' on the frame side. About 800 were made, and then the Löwe company amalgamated with Deutsche Metallpatronenfabrik to become the Deutsche Waffen and Munitionsfabrik. The marking on the pistol then changed to 'System Borchardt/Deutsche Waffen und Munitionsfabrik/Berlin' in three lines on the right side of the frame. About 2200 are thought to have been made under DWM management.

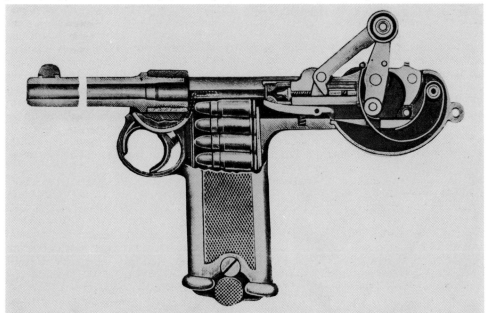

The action of the Borchardt, showing the toggle unit and the curved recoil spring.

BOREALIS / *Canada*

Submachine gun developed in Canada by the North American Arms Company of Toronto in 1950. It was based on the NAACO Brigadier pistol, a ·45 version of the Browning GP35 firing a specially developed high-power ·45 cartridge. This pistol was to be fitted into a stock frame and a special 20-round magazine inserted into the butt. A selective-fire trigger unit was fitted and the pistol then became the Borealis submachine gun. It is probable that a prototype was made, but since the pistol design never succeeded in interesting anybody, the submachine gun was stillborn.

BOXER, Edward M. *(1819–1898)*

Colonel Boxer was an officer of the Royal Artillery who became the Superintendent of the Royal Laboratory (that section of Woolwich Arsenal concerned with ammunition) in 1857. His primary concern was with artillery equipment and he made several notable improvements in ammunition, among them the Boxer Improved Diaphragm Shrapnel Shell, the Boxer Parachute Light Ball, a variety of time fuses of hitherto unknown reliability and accuracy, and some of the first projectiles for rifled artillery. In the small arms field his name is best known in connection with the Boxer Primer, or cap used with centre-fire cartridges, which he developed for the compound metal-and-cardboard case for the ·577 Snider rifle and which was approved for service on 20th August 1866. In the Boxer primer, which is widely used in American ammunition today though less so in European designs, the anvil, against which the weapon's firing pin crushes the sensitive composition, is contained within the primer and is not, as in the Berdan design, formed as part of the cartridge case. Though somewhat more difficult to manufacture, caps of this type are much easier to use when re-

loading fired cases, the complete cap unit being easily expelled from the case and replaced by a new unit; replacement of Berdan primers is more difficult due to the non-central multiple fire channels and the necessity to fit the cap carefully around the fixed anvil at a carefully regulated distance.

BOYS RIFLE / *Britain*

British anti-tank rifle named for Captain H. C. Boys, head of the design team which developed the rifle, and who died a few days before the rifle was approved for service in November 1937. It was a bolt-action rifle in ·55 calibre which used a belted cartridge case. The rifle was five feet long, weighed 36 lbs, propelled its bullet at 3250 ft/sec, and could penetrate 21mm of armour at 300 metres range. A five-round magazine was mounted above the action, and the barrel was permitted to recoil in the gun frame; a muzzle brake was fitted and the butt was heavily cushioned, all measures to

try to mitigate the recoil force. In spite of this, though, it was still a fearsome weapon to fire.

In 1940 a tungsten-cored bullet was developed, and in 1942 a shortened model, intended for use by parachute troops, was briefly tried. But the anti-tank rifle had, by 1941, outlived its usefulness. At the time of its design, the Boys was capable of piercing any contemporary tank, though it is questionable what damage it would have done once it had penetrated. By 1941, though, it had been left behind by improvements in armour and was quite ineffective; it was left in the infantry's hands simply because there was no other weapon which could be offered to take its place. Once the light-weight projectors for hollow charge bombs appeared, the Boys, like other anti-tank rifles, rapidly disappeared from service.

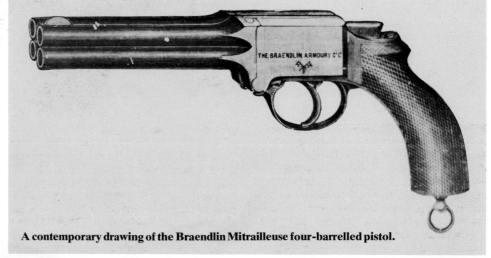

A contemporary drawing of the Braendlin Mitrailleuse four-barrelled pistol.

The ·55 Boys anti-tank rifle.

The Breda Model 38 machine gun, showing the loading strip.

BRAENDLIN ARMOURY LTD. / *Britain*

A Birmingham gunmaker trading in the 1860–1888 period as Braendlin, Sommerville & Co. and later as the Braendlin Armoury Ltd. This latter company was liquidated in 1888 and appears to mark the end of Braendlin's active career, though the company name was continued, under different ownership, until 1914.

Braendlin appears to have been a jobbing gunsmith largely concerned with contract manufacture of other people's designs. He made the Albini-Braendlin rifle (*qv*) and with Sommerville and Galand patented and manufactured the Galand and Sommerville Patent Self-extracting Revolver in 1868–1870. In 1880 he began making the Martin-Marres-Braendlin Mitrailleuse, a four-barreled pistol of similar type to the better-known Lancaster. Though noticed favourably by various contemporary reviewers, the design did not prosper.

BREDA / *Italy*

The Société Anonyme Ernesto Breda of Brescia, Italy, was a heavy engineering company specialising in railway rolling stock until it accepted a contract from the Italian Government to manufacture the FIAT-Revelli machine gun. This apparently convinced the company that there was a future in armaments manufacture, and after the war they set about attempting to design a machine gun.

In 1924 they produced a 6·5mm light machine gun, the Tipo 5C, which operated on a combination of recoil and blowback. The bolt was locked to the breech by a 'fermeture nut' of similar type to that used in the light Hotchkiss guns; this nut, or collar, encircled the rear end of the barrel and the front end of the bolt, and, by interrupted lugs, held the two together. On firing, the barrel recoiled a short distance during which a cam revolved the nut to release the bolt which was then free to be blown back by residual chamber pressure. A somewhat unusual feature was that the magazine was fixed to the side of the gun and was hinged forward in order to be loaded from rifle clips. Some 2000 of these guns were bought by the Italian Army as their Model 1924.

In 1930 the Breda company acquired the SAFAT concern, a subsidiary which had been set up by FIAT to produce weapons; the FIAT company, for their part, had decided to quit the firearms field. Henceforth the weapon production of Breda was properly called Breda-SAFAT though this correct name is not always applied. At the time of this amalgamation, the Breda Model 1930 machine gun was being introduced into Italian service. This was simply the Model 24 with some small improvements. It was made in 6·5mm calibre for the Italians and in 7·92mm calibre for export.

With the acquisition of the SAFAT concern, Breda now developed an aircraft machine gun in 7·7mm calibre which was quite successful and widely exported as well as becoming the standard Italian aircraft gun. This was followed, in 1931, by a 13·2mm heavy machine gun, gas operated, for use in tanks and on a tripod as a heavy infantry support gun.

In 1937 came the 8mm Model 37 which was adopted as the standard Italian Army machine gun. This was gas operated and fired from a 20-round strip; the mechanism is remarkable for the fact that it replaced the spent cases in the strip instead of ejecting case and strip separately. In spite of its complication, the gun enjoyed a reputation for reliability throughout the Second World War. Also in 1938 came an 8mm tank machine gun, which used the same basic mechanism but had a top-mounted box magazine and a heavy barrel to permit sustained fire without overheating.

While serviceable, the Breda guns all suffered from one basic defect; the designers did not ensure a slow unseating of the fired cartridge case prior to a rapid extraction and ejection. All the Breda guns attempted to extract violently, before the pressure had dropped, and it was necessary to either lubricate the cases or groove the inside of the gun chamber so as to float the cases on a layer of gas. Neither solution was completely satisfactory.

BREN / *Great Britain*

Light machine gun adopted for service in August 1938. The Lewis gun had remained the standard British light gun since the First World War, but it was not without its defects, and in 1930 action began on selecting a successor. The Vickers-Berthier, already in use with the Indian Army and in current production in Britain, was highly favoured; other possible candidates included the Madsen, the Browning Automatic Rifle, the Chatellerault and the Darne guns. The final choice appeared to lie between the Vickers-Berthier and the Madsen, but then the British Military Attaché in Prague drew the attention of the War Office to a Czech gun, the ZB26, which he had just seen demonstrated. He was so persuasive about the weapon's merits that the sum of £135 was laid out to buy a specimen gun and 10,000 rounds of 7·92mm ammunition.

This gun was tried, with good results, but one basic demand was that whatever gun was selected, it had to use the British standard ·303 rimmed cartridge, and in 1931 a ZB30 gun, a ZB26 modified to use the British ammunition, was obtained and tested. Some defects were found, most of which were due to the ammunition, and Holek, the designer, returned to Eng-

The Mark 3 Bren gun, a lightened and shortened wartime version.

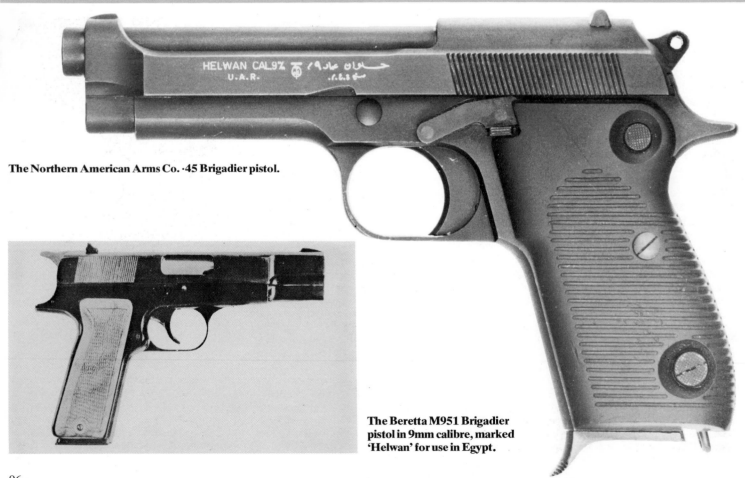

The Northern American Arms Co. ·45 Brigadier pistol.

The Beretta M951 Brigadier pistol in 9mm calibre, marked 'Helwan' for use in Egypt.

land in 1932 with a new weapon, the ZGB32, for trial. This gun had the gas port moved back down the barrel so as to reduce the fouling from the cordite cartridges and used a new curved magazine which was better-suited to the rimmed ·303 cartridge. More small modifications resulted in the ZGB33 and ZGB34 models, which were finally tested in competition with the Vickers-Berthier and Madsen guns in August 1934. These tests proved quite conclusively that the ZGB34 was the superior gun.

Arrangements were then made for manufacturing the gun at the Royal Small Arms Factory, Enfield, and it was this which led to the somewhat contrived name: BR from Brno and EN from Enfield, commemorating the birthplace and the place of manufacture. Drawings to British tolerances and measurements were prepared by January 1935, and the first gun left the new production line in Enfield in September 1937. Production had reached a level of 400 guns a week by the outbreak of war in 1939 and eventually reached its peak of 1000 guns a week in 1943. Guns were also made by the Inglis company of Canada (who also made them in the original 7·92mm configuration for supply to the Chinese Nationalist Army) and

by the Lithgow Small Arms factory in Australia. In the 1950s, when the 7·62mm NATO cartridge was adopted as the British standard, the Bren design was modified accordingly, and it is still in service with the British and other Commonwealth armies.

Four versions of the Bren have seen service. The Mark 1 was the Czech design re-dimensioned; it had a bipod with telescopic legs, a drum-set rear sight, and a hand grip beneath the butt with an over-the-shoulder steadying plate. The Mark 2 removed these refinements, substituting a fixed-length bipod, a much simpler leaf pattern rear sight and no fittings on the butt. The Mark 3 was a simplified and lightened Mark 1 with a shorter barrel, while the Mark 4 was a Mark 2 with shorter barrel. A somewhat luxurious tripod was provided, but rarely used, while a 100-round drum magazine conversion was made for anti-aircraft purposes.

The Bren gun became a legend in its own time and was probably the most liked and respected weapon the British Army had during the war. The reasons for this are its absolute reliability, simplicity and accuracy; given those three attributes, there is no need for anything more.

BRESCIA / Italy

An Italian government arsenal, the Fabricca Nazional d'Armas Brescia operated from the 1880s until the Second World War and was principally concerned in contract production of Italian military rifles of the Mannlicher-Carcano type. It also manufactured numbers of Bodeo service revolvers and, in the 1930s, was responsible for most of the prototypes of the automatic pistol of Guilio Sosso. The company's markings will also be found on some Glisenti automatic pistols made prior to 1918.

BRIGADIER / Canada/Italy

This name has been applied to two distinct pistol designs. The first, manufactured in 1950 by the North American Arms Company (NAACO) of Toronto, Canada, was a copy of the Browning GP35 automatic. It was generally larger than the Browning, had a light alloy frame, a removable trigger mechanism module, and a safety catch on the slide which physically blocked the movement of the firing pin. It was chambered for a ·45 cartridge of greater power than the usual ·45 ACP round, which developed a muzzle velocity of 1600 ft/sec. By suitable modification the pistol could be converted into a submachine gun known as the Borealis (qv). The development never got beyond the prototype stage, there being no military interest in the design. The second Brigadier pistol was the Beretta M951

military pistol in 9mm Parabellum calibre, details of which will be found under Beretta.

The 9mm Brixia pistol, a slight improvement on the 1910 Glisenti model.

BRIXIA / Italy

The Metallurgica Bresciana Tempini of Brescia, Italy, appears to have been responsible for the development of the Brixia automatic pistol in about 1911. This was a slightly improved version of the Glisenti M1910 service pistol which had defects that the Brixia set out to cure. The receiver design was changed in the hope of stiffening it and the grip safety was discarded. A small number of pistols was taken by the Italian Army as their Model 1912 but on a trial basis and not as a replacement for the Glisenti. A few were then sold commercially, but the outbreak of war in 1914 terminated production.

The exact relationship between this company and the Siderurgica Glisenti has never been successfully determined; one suggestion is that MBT was another name for Glisenti re-organised, which might account for their desire to improve the Glisenti pistol.

BRNO / *Czechoslovakia*

The Ceskoslovensko Zbrojovka (Czech Arms Company) was formed in 1919 in Brno, using the talents of various Czech designers and engineers who had previously worked in Austro-Hungarian arsenals. Formed as a state-owned firm, with a branch in Prague, it found difficulty in building up an export trade due to political restrictions, and in 1924 it was liquidated and then set up anew as a limited liability company. The first major production was of Mauser rifles, resulting in the Czech army's Model 1924 short rifle, one of the last and best of Mauser weapons of this type. The Mauser company sent one of their engineers, Josef Nickl, to Brno to assist in setting up production, and he persuaded CZ to produce a pistol he had designed. This was a modification of the Mauser 1910 model in which the barrel was completely concealed inside the slide and was rotated to lock and unlock the breech. Mauser licensed CZ to make this pistol, which then became the Czech Army M1922. In 1923, after some 10,000 had been made, the design and machines were passed across to Ceska Zbrojowka of Strakonitz and CZ gave up the manufacture of pistols to concentrate on rifles and machine guns.

In about 1921 Vaclav Holek, the chief designer, became interested in machine guns and eventually designed a gas-operated light gun, the Praga Model 1924, which was then improved to become the ZB26. This weapon had a long finned barrel with an ingenious quick-release latch which allowed a hot barrel to be removed and a fresh one fitted in a few seconds; a long gas cylinder through which a piston acted on the breech block, tilting the rear end up to lock into the receiver; and an overhead box magazine. Very small improvements, added as experience was gained, resulted in the ZB27 and ZB30 models, and all were extremely successful, being adopted by no less than 24 countries. Probably the most famous and most widely used of this series was the British Bren gun (*qv*).

Holek then designed a medium machine gun for tank use, in which the principle of differential locking was modified; the gun was gas operated but the barrel and working parts were allowed to recoil and the cartridge was fired during the counter-recoil movement. This meant that the explosion of the cartridge had to arrest the forward movement before it could begin the recoil stroke, and in this way the effective recoil blow on the gun mounting was reduced. The design was adopted into the Czech Army as the ZB37, a tripod-mounted and belt-fed infantry gun. It was also taken into use by the British Army as a tank gun where it was known as the BESA (*qv*). Holek's 15mm ZB60 was also called the BESA in Britain.

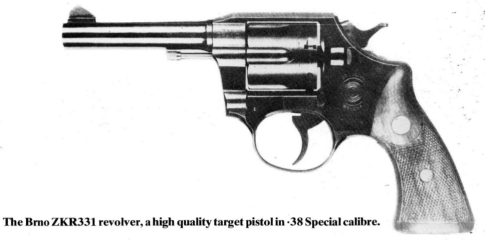

The Brno ZKR331 revolver, a high quality target pistol in ·38 Special calibre.

The company entered the submachine gun field in 1933 with the ZK383, designed by the brothers Josef and Frantisek Koucky. While externally resembling the Bergmann MP18, with wooden stock and perforated barrel jacket, the ZK383 incorporated an ingenious method of adjusting the rate of fire by adding or removing a weight in the bolt assembly. It also had a quick-change barrel and a bipod, so that it could be used in the light machine gun role. It was a successful design and was used by the Bulgarian army and by several South American countries. The Koucky brothers went on to design several more submachine guns, but none of them achieved the success of the ZK383 and most never got past the prototype stage.

The next successful submachine gun was developed by Holek at the end of the war and became the CZ23 and CZ25 models. These are important designs in the development history of the submachine gun since they were the first production weapons to incorporate the 'overhung' or 'wrap-around' bolt. The face of the bolt was deeply recessed, so that when the breech was closed some six inches of the bolt actually surrounded the barrel. This method of construction reduced the overall length of the gun and also kept the centre of balance within a relatively small compass at all times. Due to the short bolt stroke the pistol grip was brought forward to a position where it could also function as a magazine housing. The CZ23 had a wooden stock, the CZ25 a folding metal stock; both were chambered for the 9mm Parabellum cartridge. Some 100,000 were made and they were widely sold abroad.

In about 1952 the Czech Army standardised on Soviet calibres of ammunition, and had to adopt the 7·62mm pistol round in place of the 9mm Parabellum. The CZ24 and CZ26 guns were the result of this decision; they were

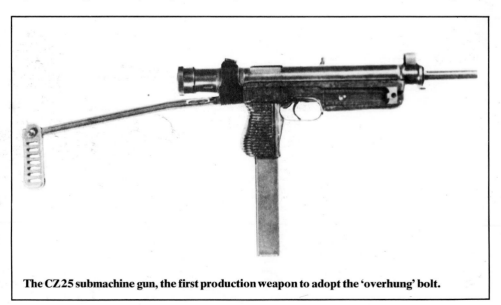

The CZ25 submachine gun, the first production weapon to adopt the 'overhung' bolt.

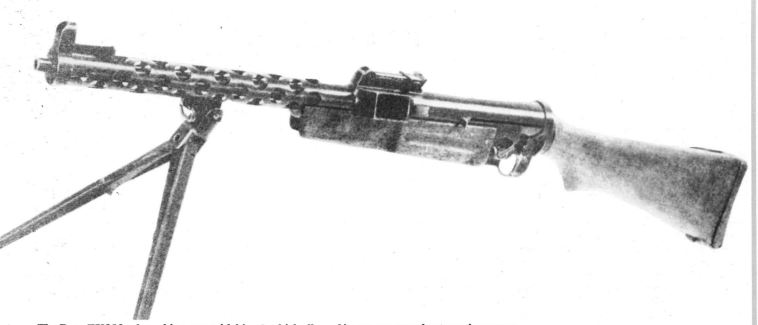

The Brno ZK383 submachine gun, with bipod, which allowed its use as a squad automatic weapon.

simply the CZ23 and CZ25 re-barrelled for the new cartridge.

The final model of the ZB26 machine gun appeared in 1952 as the VZ52 model, firing the 7·62mm short Czech cartridge; it was later modified to fire the 7·62mm short Soviet M1943 cartridge, becoming the VZ52/57 model. Broadly speaking, it was the ZB26 design with the addition of a feed mechanism which allowed the firing of ammunition in belts as an alternative to using the usual box magazine, and it also had a dual trigger system for single shots or automatic fire. It was

Holek's last design; he died in December 1954.

Automatic rifle design had been pioneered by Holek's brother, Emmanuel Holek, who developed the gas-operated ZH29 rifle in the middle 1920s. It was a sound and reliable weapon but it was never adopted in any numbers. The Koucky brothers then took up the challenge during the 1930s and produced their ZK420 rifle in 1942. This was also gas operated, using a bolt carrier to rotate the bolt, but although a good design, it achieved no success, largely because it appeared at the wrong time. The first CZ automatic rifle to meet with milit-

ary approval was the VZ52, an unremarkable gas-operated weapon which did not stay in service for long. It was replaced in Czech service by the VZ58, a much better design which externally resembles the Soviet AK47 but which uses different internal arrangements, having a tilting bolt rather than a rotating one.

In postwar years the company (now known as Zbrojovka Brno) has developed a range of sporting weapons, principally to the designs of Augustin Necas. These include single shot target pistols, target revolvers, target rifles, sporting rifles and shotguns.

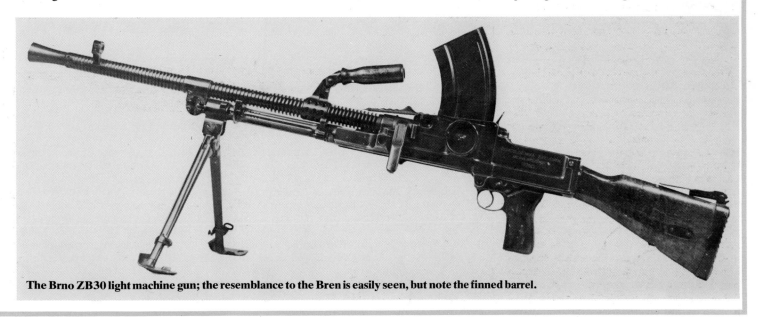

The Brno ZB30 light machine gun; the resemblance to the Bren is easily seen, but note the finned barrel.

BRONDBY / *Denmark*

Series of automatic rifles, machine guns and submachine guns designed in Denmark 1930–1939. All were gas-operated, with the gas cylinder above the barrel, and used a vertically-moving breech locking plate. An unusually large muzzle brake was generally fitted to these weapons, which may have helped operation but which generated uncomfortable amounts of back and side blast. Tested in Britain in 1938, the designs were considered to 'show promise', but they were never heard of again.

The Browning Nomad ·22 target pistol.

BROWNING, John Moses *(1855–1926)*

John M. Browning was America's and one of the world's foremost firearms inventors. He is reputed to have built his first rifle while still a boy, and his first patent, for a breech-loader, was obtained when he was 24 years old. His expertise covered all types of weapon, from pocket pistols to anti-aircraft artillery. Weapons to his design were manufactured by Remington, Winchester, Colt, and the Fabrique National d'Armes de Guerre of Herstal, Liège, Belgium, the products of this latter company being the only ones to carry the Browning name.

Browning Pistols

Browning was responsible for two basic pistol designs, a pocket blowback and a military locked-breech automatic. The former and a variant of the latter were produced by FN of Liège in the following models:

Browning 1900 or 'Old Model' A 7·62mm blowback automatic using a recoil spring mounted in the slide above the barrel and having the recoil spring acting also as the mainspring for the firing pin.

Browning 1903 Originally produced in 9mm Browning Long calibre, this pistol used a new method of construction in which the barrel was attached to the pistol frame by ribs beneath the chamber; this allowed the pistol to be dismantled very easily by pulling back the slide and rotating the barrel to free the ribs. The system was so simple that it attracted innumerable copyists, particularly in Spain.

Browning 1906 A smaller version of the 1903 model, in 6·35mm calibre, also widely copied.

Baby Browning See separate entry.

Browning 1910 A complete change of design, this 7·65mm pistol had the return spring arranged around the barrel and had the slide shaped in a roughly tubular form.

Browning 1922 The 1910 with slide and barrel lengthened.

Browning GP35 This was a locked breech military pistol, development of which began immediately after the First World War. It was patented in 1927, the year after Browning's death, the development having been completed by FN's engineers. It was introduced in 1935 and was adopted by the Belgian Army and also purchased in small numbers by other countries. During the war, manufacture continued in Liège under German supervision, and was carried out in Canada by the John Inglis company. In postwar years it has become the standard military pistol of most countries outside the Communist bloc, has been made under license in Argentina and in Indonesia as the Pindad pistol.

The GP35 (Grand Puissance, 1935) uses Browning's system of locking breech to slide by ribs on the top of the barrel which engage into cuts in the undersurface of the slide. Barrel and slide thus have to recoil locked together. A forged lug under the barrel has a shaped cutout which engages with a cross pin in the pistol frame, and the action of the shaped cutout on the pin is such that the rear of the barrel is pulled down after a short recoil, thus freeing the lugs from their grooves. This unlocks the breech, and the barrel is held while the slide is free to recoil and complete the unloading-loading cycle. This use of a forged lug beneath the barrel in place of Browning's original swinging link has been widely copied, notably in the designs of Petter, SIG and in the Polish VIS-35 pistol (*qv*).

The Browning pistols which do not carry his name are made by the Colt company (*qv*).

A Brondby gas-operated automatic rifle; his submachine gun design was on similar lines.

The Browning 1906 6·35mm calibre Baby Browning.

The Browning 1922 model had the recoil spring wrapped around the barrel.

The High-Power or GP-35 locked breech 9mm pistol.

The Browning 1900 or 'Old Model' pistol.

Browning machine guns

Browning's first practical machine gun design was manufactured by Colt as their M1895 and was a gas-operated weapon; see under Colt for further details.

He then abandoned gas operation for short-recoil operation and designed a completely new mechanism which he built into a water-cooled medium gun. This mechanism locked the breech by a vertically-moving key and incorporated an accelerator to provide greater impetus to the bolt during its recoil stroke so as to provide a reserve of power. The gun was belt-fed, in ·30 US Service calibre, but Browning was unable to interest the military until the entry of the USA into the First World War in 1917, after which the gun was adopted as the M1917. It was subsequently modified into an air-cooled version for use as an aircraft weapon, and this model was later taken into use as a ground machine gun. A version in ·50 calibre was developed during the 1920s.

The Browning machine gun, in one form or another, is probably the most widely-distributed machine gun in the world.

Browning automatic rifles

At the same time that he introduced his M1917 machine gun, Browning offered the army a gas-operated magazine-fed weapon which he called his Automatic Rifle, and this was adopted by the US Army in 1918. It could fire single shots or automatic, and the original conception was for the soldier to carry it at his hip, on a sling, firing it as he advanced across No Man's Land. This idea was abandoned and it came to be used as a light machine gun, being adopted in post-war years by Belgium, Sweden and other European countries. Nevertheless, it was not well suited for this role since it lacked an interchangeable barrel and the 20-shot bottom-mounted magazine was inconvenient when the weapon was being fired from the prone position. But in lieu of anything better, its owners persisted with it, the US Army retaining it as their squad automatic until after the Korean War.

In the sporting field, Browning developed a self-loading ·351 rifle which was made in the USA by Remington as their Model 8 in 1906. It was also made for European sale by FN of Liège. This was a blowback weapon, and it remained in production for many years. A ·22 version was later made, first by FN in 1914 and later by Remington as their Model 16.

Browning shotguns

Browning patented his first automatic shotgun in 1900 and it was placed on the market by FN. In 1903 it was introduced into the USA, and, with slight changes, has remained in production ever since. It was a long recoil weapon in which the barrel and breech recoiled together a distance greater than the length of a cartridge, at the end of which stroke the breech was unlocked and held while the barrel returned. Once the barrel was back in the forward position, the breech lock was released and loaded the next round from a five-shot tubular magazine.

Other shotguns bear the Browning name; an over-and-under double gun introduced in 1931, a short-recoil automatic of 1954, a single gun of 1970 and a gas-operated automatic

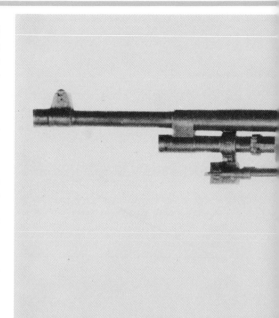

The Browning Automatic Rifle, widely adopted as a

Browning demonstrating his recoil-operated machine gun, which later became the US Army's Model 1917.

An air-cooled Browning machine gun, the M1919A6, used by the US Army in World War Two as a squad light machine gun.

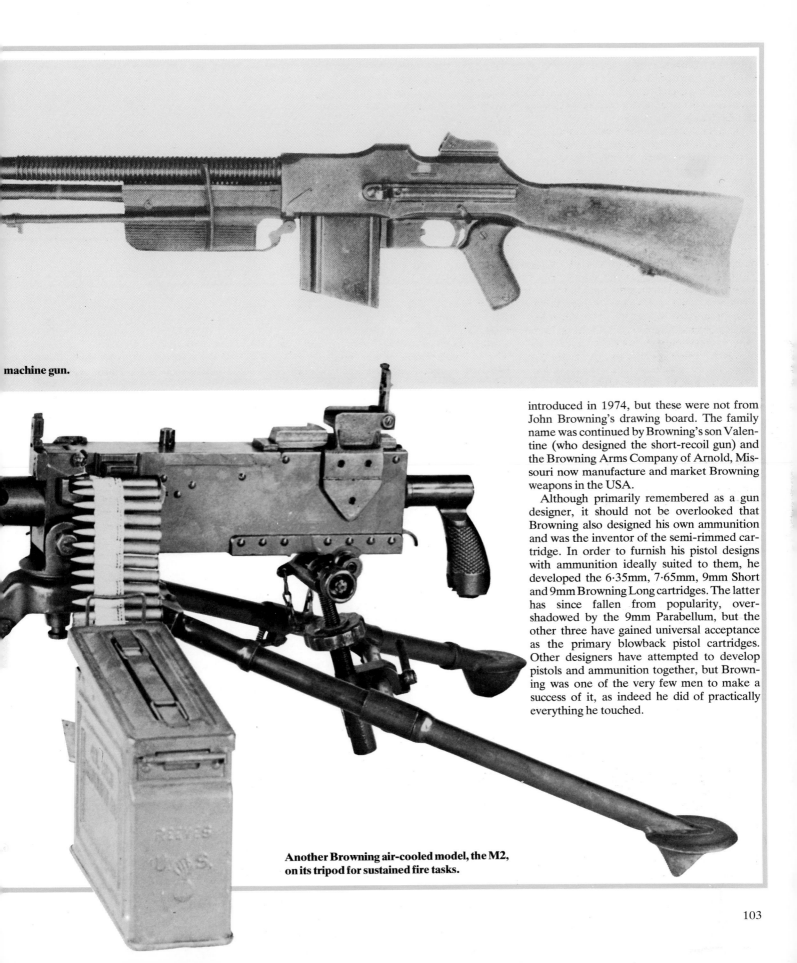

machine gun.

introduced in 1974, but these were not from John Browning's drawing board. The family name was continued by Browning's son Valentine (who designed the short-recoil gun) and the Browning Arms Company of Arnold, Missouri now manufacture and market Browning weapons in the USA.

Although primarily remembered as a gun designer, it should not be overlooked that Browning also designed his own ammunition and was the inventor of the semi-rimmed cartridge. In order to furnish his pistol designs with ammunition ideally suited to them, he developed the 6·35mm, 7·65mm, 9mm Short and 9mm Browning Long cartridges. The latter has since fallen from popularity, overshadowed by the 9mm Parabellum, but the other three have gained universal acceptance as the primary blowback pistol cartridges. Other designers have attempted to develop pistols and ammunition together, but Browning was one of the very few men to make a success of it, as indeed he did of practically everything he touched.

Another Browning air-cooled model, the M2, on its tripod for sustained fire tasks.

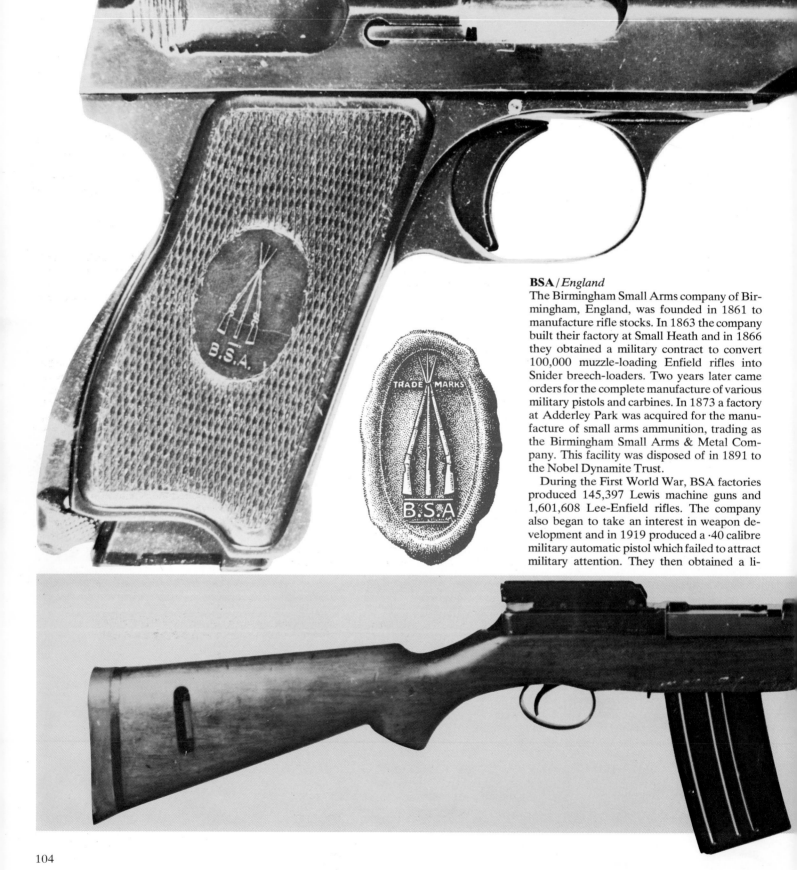

BSA/*England*

The Birmingham Small Arms company of Birmingham, England, was founded in 1861 to manufacture rifle stocks. In 1863 the company built their factory at Small Heath and in 1866 they obtained a military contract to convert 100,000 muzzle-loading Enfield rifles into Snider breech-loaders. Two years later came orders for the complete manufacture of various military pistols and carbines. In 1873 a factory at Adderley Park was acquired for the manufacture of small arms ammunition, trading as the Birmingham Small Arms & Metal Company. This facility was disposed of in 1891 to the Nobel Dynamite Trust.

During the First World War, BSA factories produced 145,397 Lewis machine guns and 1,601,608 Lee-Enfield rifles. The company also began to take an interest in weapon development and in 1919 produced a ·40 calibre military automatic pistol which failed to attract military attention. They then obtained a li-

This BSA ·40 automatic was developed just after World War One but never went into production.

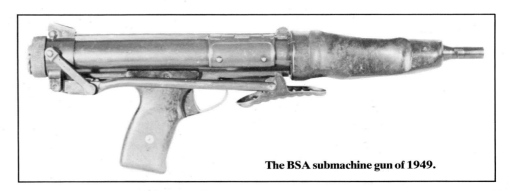

The BSA submachine gun of 1949.

cence to develop the Thompson submachine gun patents in Europe and produced a number of prototype automatic rifles based on the Thompson designs, again without much commercial success. Another venture was the Adams-Willmott machine gun. Before the outbreak of the Second World War the company had set up for production of the BESA tank machine gun and during the war developed the Besal or Faulkner machine gun. Anti-tank rifles, aircraft cannon and submachine guns, were also produced.

In postwar years the BSA submachine gun was developed, as was a 7mm automatic rifle, but neither gained military acceptance. Some of the 7·62mm FN rifles adopted after Britain standardised on the 7·62mm NATO cartridge were made by BSA.

After the First World War the company had entered the sporting gun field with an inexpensive shotgun, and they later followed it up with sporting and target rifles. Air rifles had formed part of the firm's output since the early 1900s, and they were the developers of an unusual air rifle modelled on the service Lee-Enfield rifle and intended for inexpensive training of cadets and militia units.

The BSA submachine gun, submitted for trials in 1946–1949, was a compact and ingenious design in which the cocking action was done by rotating the forward handguard, thrusting it forward and back, and rotating it again to lock into place. This system meant that the firer retained his grip of the weapon throughout the cocking action, which was advantageous in the event of a feed stoppage. Of 9mm calibre, the gun had a magazine which, with its housing, could be folded forward alongside the barrel giving compact dimensions for packing and, again, allowing rapid action in the event of a malfunction. But in competitive trials, it suffered from having had less development time than its competitors and was rejected for military service. The same fate befell the P-28 automatic rifle, a weapon of great promise. It was an exceptionally clean design, using a laterally-locking bolt, but the abandonment of the projected British ·280 cartridge in favour of the 7·62mm NATO round put an end to its chances.

BUCHEL/*Germany*
Ernst Buchel of Zella-Mehlis, Thuringia, was active prior to 1939 in the manufacture of single shot ·22 target pistols of various types and of ·22 bolt-action target rifles. His best-known products were the Tell and Luna free pistols, with 12 inch barrels and Martini dropping block actions, but his Ideal with rotary breech and WB with fixed breech and dropping barrel were also popular in competitions on the Continent.

BUHAG/*East Germany*
Trade name of the Buchsenmacher Handwerke Genossenschaft GmbH. The company manufactures a variety of guns for competitions, rarely seen outside Eastern Europe.

BURNSIDE, Ambrose E. *(1824–1881)*
US Army officer, retired in 1853 and set up the Burnside Arms Company in 1855. In 1856 he patented a breech-loading single-shot carbine, using a conical metal cartridge with a hole in its base to accept ignition from a percussion cap placed on an external nipple, and fired by a side hammer. 55,000 carbines and 21 million cartridges were purchased by the US Government for use by Union forces during the American Civil War. Burnside returned to the army during the war and became a General in the Union Army; he was Governor of Rhode Island 1866–1869 and Republican Congressman 1866–1881. In 1871 he organised, and became the first President of, the National Rifle Association of America.

The BSA P-28 automatic rifle, developed in the late 1940s for the British Army 7mm short cartridge.

CADIX / *Spain*

Sales name for revolvers manufactured by Unceta y Cia of Guernica, Spain (for details of which company see under Astra). The Astra Cadix series appeared in 1958 in three calibres: ·22, ·32 and ·38 Special. The ·22 revolvers had a nine-shot cylinder, the ·32 six-shot and the ·38 five-shot; barrel lengths of 2, 4 or 6 inches were available. Later the Model 357 was introduced which, as the name implies, was chambered for the ·357 Magnum cartridge. Like the earlier models this was a solid-frame revolver with swing-out cylinder, but was of heavier construction and with a six-shot cylinder. A Model 960 was then produced, this being essentially the Model 357 chambered for the ·38 Special cartridge, intended for those people who required a heavier revolver than the ·38 Cadix. All Cadix revolvers are currently in production, based generally on Smith & Wesson practice, and are of good quality and workmanship.

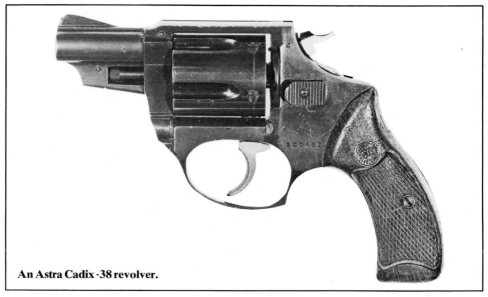

An Astra Cadix ·38 revolver.

CARL GUSTAV / *Sweden*

The Carl Gustav Stads Gevarsfaktori of Eskilstuna, Sweden, is the Swedish government arms manufacturing plant and it has produced a wide variety of weapons over the years. In the small arms field its principal output has been of Mauser rifles, Ljungman rifles (both dealt with under their respective headings) and the Carl Gustav submachine gun. Like many armament factories, it is operated with a sharp eye to expenses and when military contracts permit, commercial sporting rifles of high quality, using the basic Mauser action, are also made.

The first Carl Gustav submachine gun was simply a license-built copy of the Finnish Suomi M1931 (*qv*) with slight modification to suit the Swedish Army's requirements. During the Second World War, however, it became imperative to develop a native design more amenable to rapid manufacture, and the result was the Carl Gustav M45. Fabricated from heavy-gauge steel stampings, this was a simple blowback gun with a tubular body and short barrel and jacket, the mechanism being based on that of the Sten gun, and with a folding tubular steel butt. The first models were designed to take the Suomi magazine, since this was in wide service use in Sweden, but in 1948 the company developed a new 36-shot magazine, a highly efficient two-column design which has since been widely copied, and in order to be able to fit either the new or the old magazines to the gun, a removable magazine housing was produced. By 1951 there were sufficient of the new magazines available to allow the Suomi design to become obsolete, and thereafter the Carl Gustav was made with its own integral magazine housing.

In addition to its use by the Swedish Army the Carl Gustav was widely sold abroad. It was made under license in Egypt in the 1950s as the Port Said. A slightly modified version has been made in the United States by Smith & Wesson and was converted to fire their electrically-ignited caseless ammunition in the late 1950s, though this project met with no success.

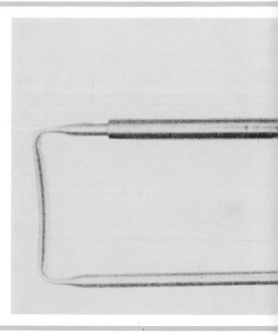

CAL / *Belgium*

Carabine Automatique Légère. A light assault rifle developed by the Fabrique National d'Armes de Guerre of Herstal, Belgium. While it generally resembles that company's well-known FAL rifle, its internal arrangements are somewhat different. The CAL is a 5·56mm calibre weapon and has a gas cylinder above the barrel; a piston in this cylinder is driven back on firing, and the piston rod strikes a bolt carrier and then returns to its original position in the cylinder. This brief impulse given to the bolt carrier is sufficient to drive the carrier backwards against the resistance of a return spring. As the carrier moves, a cam track cut in its top and side engages with a lug on the bolt and revolves the bolt to unlock it from the barrel; once the bolt is unlocked it is carried back by the bolt carrier and then returned by spring action. As it returns it picks up a fresh cartridge from the 20-shot bottom-mounted magazine and loads it into the chamber, after which the continued forward movement of the bolt carrier turns and locks the bolt once more. In addition to permitting single shots or automatic fire, the mechanism on early models contained a 'burst fire selector' which allowed three shots to be fired for a single pressure on the trigger.

The CAL was designed with an eye to mass production, making extensive use of steel stampings and plastics, and is a sound and reliable weapon. It appeared in the early 1970s but has not been adopted by any major nation.

CAMPO-GIRO / *Spain*

Spanish service pistol adopted in January 1914. It was invented and patented by Lt. Col. Venancio Lopez de Ceballos y Aguirre, Count of Campo Giro, between 1900 and 1904, and prototypes were made by the Fabrica de Armas de Oviedo in 7·65mm Parabellum and 9mm calibres, the latter being an experimental cartridge special to the pistol. An improved model was then developed, chambered for the standard Spanish service pistol round, the 9mm Largo or Bergmann-Bayard. This became the 1910 Model, of which 1000 were bought for extended trial by the Spanish Army. So far the Campo-Giro had been a locked-breech weapon with a laterally-sliding bolt lock beneath the chamber, but after the Army tests several modifications were made to the design, the most important being the removal of the breech locking system so as to turn the pistol into a simple blowback type. Operation was controlled by an exceptionally strong return spring, together with shock absorbers in the frame to buffer the powerful recoil arising from the heavy cartridge.

The new design, known as the Model 1913, was adopted by the Army in the following year, and manufacturer was undertaken by Esperanza y Unceta of Eibar, some 13,200 being made. A slightly modified version, the changes lying mainly in the functioning of the safety catch, was later introduced as the Model 13/16, and after the First World War the designation was changed to Model 1921. Shortly after this it was replaced by the Astra Model 400, which was itself an improved version of Campo-Giro's design. It is uncommon outside Spain.

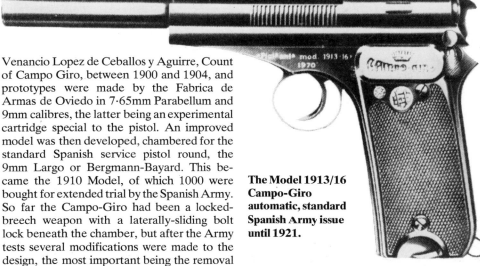

The Model 1913/16 Campo-Giro automatic, standard Spanish Army issue until 1921.

CARCANO / *Italy*

Salvatore Carcano was an inspection engineer at the Italian Arsenal at Turin who developed a military rifle for the Italian Army in 1867. This was a bolt-action single shot weapon derived largely from the German Needle Gun of Dreyse and using a cardboard cartridge and a hollow-based lead bullet of 11mm calibre. It was later superseded by the Vetterli-Vitali.

Carcano's name next appeared with the Mannlicher-Carcano rifles (*qv*) which he designed in about 1886–1890. His own contribution to the design appears to have been the safety catch, which is in the form of a sleeve surrounding the firing pin and terminating in a thumb-operated catch at the right side of the bolt. The rest of the rifle was an amalgam of Mannlicher and Mauser principles.

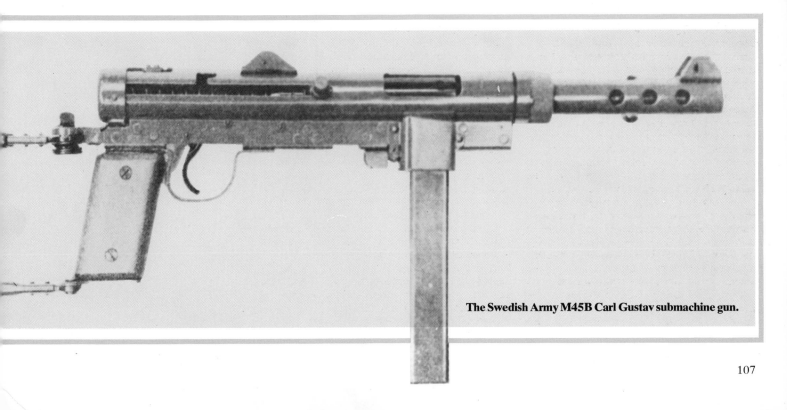

The Swedish Army M45B Carl Gustav submachine gun.

CEI-RIGOTTI/*Italy (fl. 1890–1905)*
Captain Amerigo Cei-Rigotti of the Italian Army invented a self-loading rifle in 1895 and, attracting official approval, was given facilities to develop it. He demonstrated it at Brescia in 1900, revealing it to be gas-operated by a piston beneath the barrel which acted, through a cam, to rotate and unlock the bolt. It was chambered for the Italian service 6·5mm cartridge and fed from a clip-loaded magazine beneath the action; various sizes of magazine, up to 50 rounds capacity, were provided. During the demonstration Cei-Rigotti fired the weapon as an automatic, discharging 15 shots in one second, and also showed that by operating a selector it could fire single shots.

His patents were taken up by the Glisenti-Bettoni company who announced their intention to manufacture the rifle in quantity. In 1901 Cei-Rigotti visited England and demonstrated his rifle to the Small Arms Committee, but the report of the Committee shows that the weapon jammed repeatedly and it was decided that more trials would be needed before an opinion could be given on its suitability for service. But difficulties arose over the provision of ammunition and the trial never took place; the actual rifle, one of the very few surviving specimens, is today in the Museum of the School of Infantry. No military interest

could be aroused in the design, and no production took place; although the weapon, as tested, had defects, it was basically a sound design and with some development could easily have become the first selective-fire automatic rifle in military service.

CETME/*Spain*
Centro dos Estudios Technicos de Materiales Especiales, Madrid. This is a Spanish government facility for weapons development and there, in the early 1950s, a rifle design was developed by a design team headed by Ludwig Vorgrimmler. Vorgrimmler had been an engineer with Mauserwerke during the war and had worked on the Sturmgewehr 45 assault rifle project. After the war, the French took an interest in this weapon and retained Vorgrimmler to work on it, but they later lost interest and Vorgrimmler took himself off to Spain to work for CETME. There he continued the development, finally producing the CETME Type A rifle in 7·92mm calibre, using a special cartridge with a short case and an exceptionally long spire-pointed bullet.

The rifle uses a delayed blowback system of operation, having a two-piece bolt; the light head is separated from the heavier bolt body by two rollers, and as the bolt closes these are

forced outwards by the heavy bolt body into recesses in the barrel extension. On firing, the pressure on the bolt head forces the head back; this movement is resisted by the rollers, but due to the shape of the recesses they are able to be forced out of engagement, eventually allowing both sections of the bolt to move to the rear. The delay so imparted is minimal, but sufficient to allow the bullet to clear the barrel and breech pressure to drop.

Foreign interest was aroused, and a Dutch company was granted a licence to manufacture. It aroused the interest of the German Army in the design, but since the Germans preferred to have subsequent development take place closer to home, the licence was transferred to the Heckler & Koch company (*qv*) and in their hands the design was modified until it emerged as the G3 rifle, adopted by the German Army in 1959 and subsequently by many other countries. These are several variants of the original G3 design, described under the entry for Heckler & Koch.

Meanwhile CETME had made improvements in their design, and in 1958 the Model C was adopted by the Spanish Army. As issued, the Model C uses a 7·62mm cartridge, the Spanish variant of the 7·62mm NATO round, which uses a lighter bullet and less powerful charge than the NATO standard.

The original CETME rifle of 1957, with bipod for use as a light machine gun.

A typical Chamleot-Delvigne design is this Italian service revolver of 1872 in 10·35mm calibre.

CHAFFEE-REECE / USA

A magazine repeating rifle submitted to the US Board of Ordnance in 1882 by General J. N. Reece, US Army. It was a bolt-action rifle with a tubular magazine inside the butt, loaded by a trapdoor in the butt-plate. Seven cartridges could be loaded, and a series of ratchet levers, actuated by the movement of the bolt, moved the cartridges up the tube, feeding one up in front of the bolt whenever it was drawn back. A magazine cut-off was fitted, which could be applied to disconnect the ratchet mechanism and thus prevent the contents of the magazine being fed forward, so that the magazine could be carried as a reserve while the rifle was operated as an ordinary single-shot weapon. Chaffee had originated this design as a lever action rifle and it appears probable that General Reece was responsible for the change to bolt action.

One thousand rifles were manufactured at Springfield Armoury and issued for service in 1884, the first magazine rifle to be adopted by the United States Army. Experience showed, however, that the magazine feeding mechanism was insufficiently robust to stand up to military service, and the Chaffee-Reece design was abandoned.

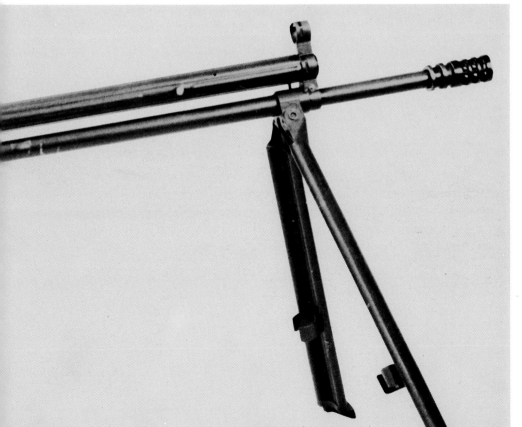

CHAMELOT-DELVIGNE / France

Descriptive title applied (frequently in error) to a variety of military revolvers produced on the Continent in the 1870s. The names of Chamelot and Delvigne, both obscure French gunsmiths, attach to a patented revolver lock mechanism which was widely copied and modified, and thus almost any revolver with this double-action lock has come to be called a Chamelot-Delvigne. Those appearing to adhere most closely to the original patent include the Belgian 11mm Model 1871, the Netherlands 9·4mm and French 11mm models of 1873 and 1874, and the Italian 10·4mm Model of 1879. These were all solid-frame, gate-loaded, rod-ejecting revolvers. In 1872 the Swiss adopted a derivation designed by Stabsmajor Schmidt in 10·4mm rimfire chambering, calling it the Chamelot, Delvigne and Schmidt model; it was modified to 10·4mm centre-fire in 1879.

CHAMPION / Czechoslovakia

A single-shot target pistol with a hinged drop-down barrel and exposed hammer, designed by the Koucky brothers and manufactured by the Zbrojovka Brno company at their factory Uhersky Brod, Czechoslovakia. Also known as the ZKP-493, it is popular with competition shooters in Central Europe.

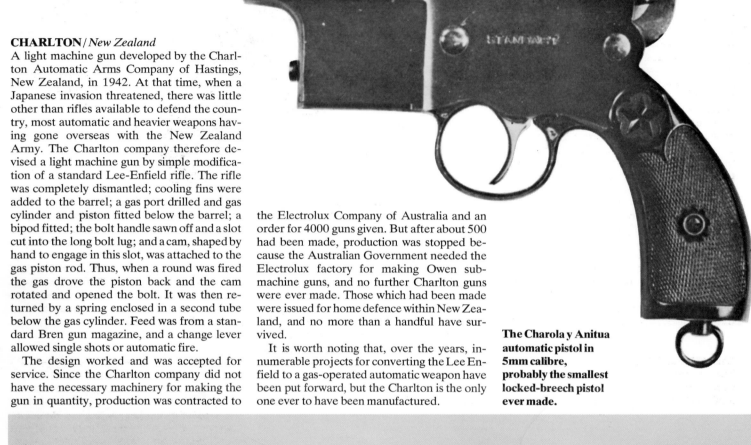

CHARLTON / *New Zealand*

A light machine gun developed by the Charlton Automatic Arms Company of Hastings, New Zealand, in 1942. At that time, when a Japanese invasion threatened, there was little other than rifles available to defend the country, most automatic and heavier weapons having gone overseas with the New Zealand Army. The Charlton company therefore devised a light machine gun by simple modification of a standard Lee-Enfield rifle. The rifle was completely dismantled; cooling fins were added to the barrel; a gas port drilled and gas cylinder and piston fitted below the barrel; a bipod fitted; the bolt handle sawn off and a slot cut into the long bolt lug; and a cam, shaped by hand to engage in this slot, was attached to the gas piston rod. Thus, when a round was fired the gas drove the piston back and the cam rotated and opened the bolt. It was then returned by a spring enclosed in a second tube below the gas cylinder. Feed was from a standard Bren gun magazine, and a change lever allowed single shots or automatic fire.

The design worked and was accepted for service. Since the Charlton company did not have the necessary machinery for making the gun in quantity, production was contracted to the Electrolux Company of Australia and an order for 4000 guns given. But after about 500 had been made, production was stopped because the Australian Government needed the Electrolux factory for making Owen sub-machine guns, and no further Charlton guns were ever made. Those which had been made were issued for home defence within New Zealand, and no more than a handful have survived.

It is worth noting that, over the years, innumerable projects for converting the Lee Enfield to a gas-operated automatic weapon have been put forward, but the Charlton is the only one ever to have been manufactured.

The Charola y Anitua automatic pistol in 5mm calibre, probably the smallest locked-breech pistol ever made.

The ·303 Charlton machine gun, a gas-driven conversion of the Lee-Enfield rifle.

CHAROLA Y ANITUA / *Spain*

One of the earliest automatic pistols, the Charola y Anitua appeared in 1897, manufactured by Garate, Anitua y Cia of Eibar, Spain. No patent relative to this pistol has been traced, but it seems likely that Charola invented the basic idea and the Anitua company turned this into a workable pistol. The butt and trigger are based on contemporary revolver practise, with an external hammer, but the rest of the design—a box magazine in front of the trigger, exposed barrel, and bolt moving inside the barrel extension—are reminiscent of Bergmann or Mauser designs and may have been inspired by them. The Charola had the distinction of being the smallest-calibre pistol ever to employ a positively-locked breech; it fires a tiny 5mm bottle-necked cartridge of low power and breech locking is quite superfluous, though at such an early stage of pistol design this might not have been appreciated. The breech lock was a swinging wedge pinned to the pistol frame and entering a recess in the bolt.

The Charola was made in Spain for a few years, after which it was made in Belgium by an unknown company. It is said to have enjoyed a good export market in Russia, even though the Belgian product was of poor quality. It is extremely uncommon today.

CHARTER ARMS / *USA*

The Charter Arms Corporation of Bridgeport, Connecticut, was set up in 1964 by Douglas McClenahan, an engineer with experience of

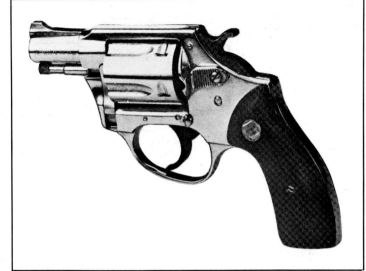

The Charter Arms 'Undercover' ·38 revolver.

firearms design and production acquired with the Colt, High-Standard and Ruger companies. McClenahan saw an opening in the market for a short-barrelled pocket revolver and, since his employers were disinclined to back his opinion, went into business for himself. The company's first product was the Undercover revolver which, as the name implies, was a short-barrelled weapon intended for concealed carrying by police officers. It was a five-shot model, chambered for the ·38 Special cartridge, and it was later followed by the Undercoverette, a policewoman's version chambered for the ·32 cartridge. The Pathfinder model moved away from law-enforcement to provide a hunting and general sport weapon in ·22 calibre. In response to requests from police officers for a pocket revolver combining maximum ballistics with minimum bulk, the 'Bulldog' appeared, a ·44 Special five-shot model with a 3 inch barrel. This is a formidable weapon, which received some unfortunate publicity when it was used by the 'Son of Sam' killer in New York in 1977.

CHASSEPOT, Antoine Alfonse (*1833–1908*)

Chassepot was an employee of the French Artillery Arsenal who designed the breech-loading rifle which bears his name and which was adopted by the French Army in 1866. The Chassepot Rifle, of 11mm calibre, was an improvement on the Dreyse Needle Gun, using the same sort of bolt action but considerably simplifying the mechanism. The self-contained paper cartridge carried a percussion cap on its base, instead of at the base of the bullet as in the Dreyse design, and the paper was supposed to be entirely consumed in the explosion of the cartridge; in practice, residue was almost always left in the chamber to make the loading of the next cartridge difficult. Sealing of the breech was done by a rubber ring around the head of the bolt; on firing, the steel face of the bolt was thrust back by the explosion pressure and squeezed the rubber ring outwards to make a gas-tight seal against the chamber walls. Effective enough when new, the rubber seal was liable to damage in use and was adversely affected by the heat of the explosion, leading to eventual leakage and the need for replacement at frequent intervals. Nevertheless, the Chassepot was a notable step in military rifle design and gave a good account of itself in the Franco-Prussian war. When the metallic cartridge appeared in the early 1870s, numbers of Chassepot were converted to this type of loading.

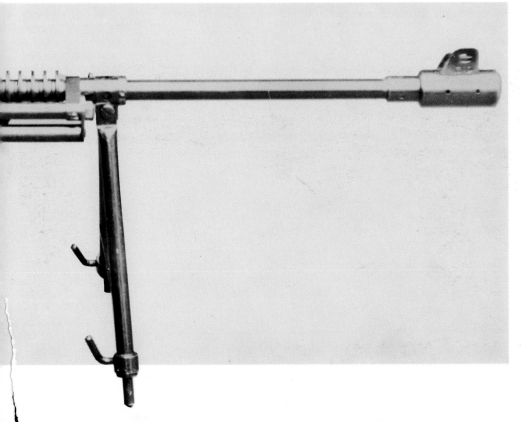

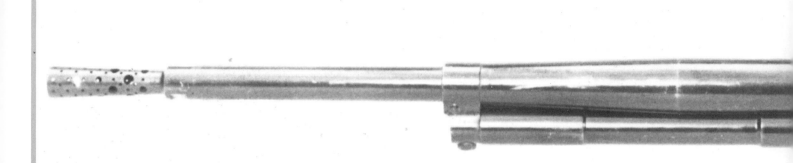

A variant of the Chatellerault machine gun was this Modele 1931 intended for use in fortifications and tanks, and using a side-feeding drum magazine.

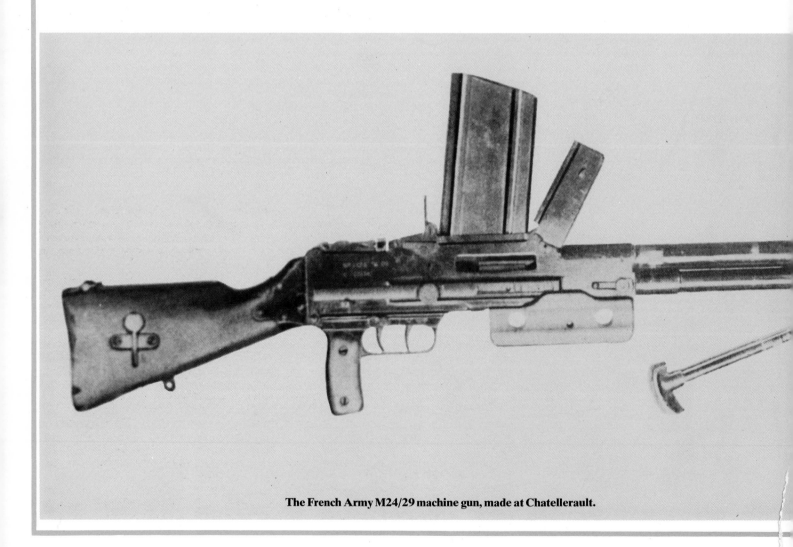

The French Army M24/29 machine gun, made at Chatellerault.

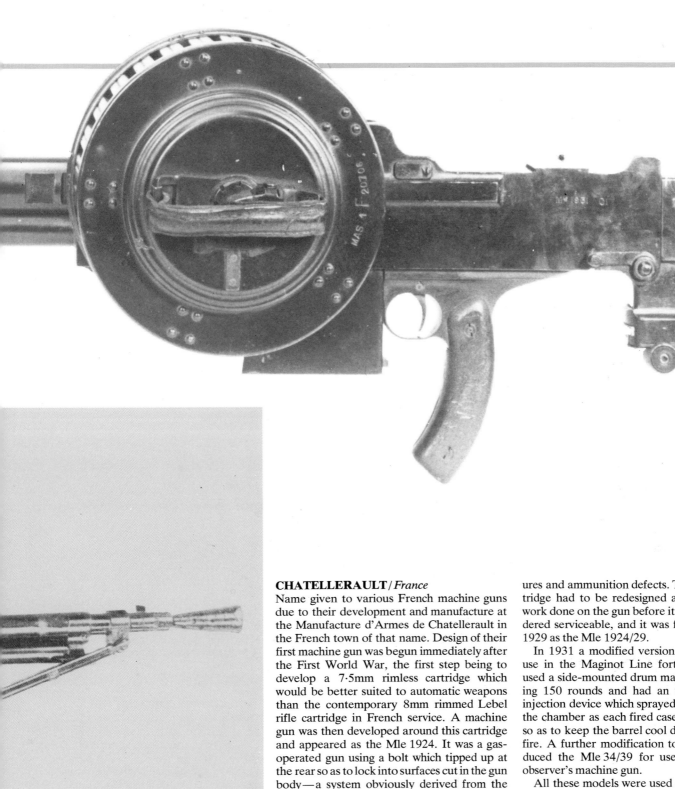

CHATELLERAULT / *France*

Name given to various French machine guns due to their development and manufacture at the Manufacture d'Armes de Chatellerault in the French town of that name. Design of their first machine gun was begun immediately after the First World War, the first step being to develop a 7·5mm rimless cartridge which would be better suited to automatic weapons than the contemporary 8mm rimmed Lebel rifle cartridge in French service. A machine gun was then developed around this cartridge and appeared as the Mle 1924. It was a gas-operated gun using a bolt which tipped up at the rear so as to lock into surfaces cut in the gun body — a system obviously derived from the Browning Automatic Rifle. Feed was from a top-mounted box magazine. Unfortunately, the French Government, anxious to amortize expenses, began touting the gun abroad before development work was complete; military commissions from Jugoslavia and Roumania came to France to see it, but the demonstrations were disastrous due to mechanical fail-ures and ammunition defects. The 7·5mm cartridge had to be redesigned and much more work done on the gun before it could be considered serviceable, and it was finally issued in 1929 as the Mle 1924/29.

In 1931 a modified version was issued for use in the Maginot Line fortifications. This used a side-mounted drum magazine containing 150 rounds and had an unusual water-injection device which sprayed cold water into the chamber as each fired case was extracted, so as to keep the barrel cool during sustained fire. A further modification to belt feed produced the Mle 34/39 for use as an aircraft observer's machine gun.

All these models were used during the Second World War, the Mle 1931 being adopted as a tank gun in addition to its role as a fortress weapon, and both it and the Mle 1924/29 were used by the German Army after the occupation of France. The Mle 1924/29 continued to be used by French Colonial Forces for several years after 1945, and it can still be found in the armies of former French colonies.

CHAUCHAT

The 8mm French Army Chauchat machine gun. The American version, in ·30 calibre, had a rectangular box magazine. The rimmed French cartridge necessitated a semi-circular type.

The Chinese Army Type 64 silenced submachine gun.

CHAUCHAT/France

A French light machine gun, taking its name from a Col. Chauchat, president of a design commission which developed the weapon in 1914. It was undoubtedly the worst machine gun ever issued to any army at any time in history. The basic design was sound enough, if unusual; it was a 'long recoil' (*qv*) weapon in which the barrel and bolt recoiled, locked together, for a distance greater than the length of a complete round of ammunition. At the end of this stroke, the bolt was unlocked and held, while the barrel was allowed to run back to the firing position. As the barrel came to rest, it released the bolt, which then ran forward, chambering a fresh round from the semi-circular magazine beneath the gun. But while the design was sound, its execution was cheap and slipshod, the gun being made from stamped and turned components with excessive tolerances, much hand-fitting of parts, and absolutely no interchangeability of spares. It

was unusual for a gun to achieve more than one or two short bursts before jamming, and when this happened it invariably had to be completely dismantled to rectify the stoppage.

In addition to being adopted by the French Army in 1915, it was also, in an unguarded moment, adopted by the United States Army in 1917, a time when they were enchanted with all things French. Almost 16,000 in 8mm calibre and a further 19,200 in ·30 calibre were purchased under an agreement which stipulated American acceptance after the guns were passed by French inspectors. Nine American divisions were armed with the weapon, and it has been estimated that fully fifty per cent of them were thrown away after their first stoppage. After the war the Belgian and Greek governments adopted the weapon under the name Gladiator, it having been manufactured by the Gladiator Arms Company. Their last recorded appearance was during the Spanish Civil War, in the hands of some unfortunate

International Brigade units; testimony of some of the Brigade members indicates that the passage of time had done nothing to improve the Chauchat.

CHICAGO PROTECTOR/USA

This was the Turbiaux (*qv*) palm-squeezer pistol as manufactured under licence by the Chicago Fire Arms Company in 1892–1895.

The American licensee for the Turbiaux was originally the Minneapolis Fire Arms Company, and they made and sold a ·32 seven-shot model in the late 1880s. A salesman of this company called Peter H. Finnegan considered that the design could be improved; further, he envisaged good sales prospects in the forthcoming Chicago World's Fair of 1894, and so in 1892, together with a partner named Corrigan, he set up the Chicago Fire Arms Company and purchased the license to the Turbiaux patent. He then negotiated with the Ames

Sword Company of Chicopee Falls, Massachusetts, to make 25,000 pistols to his improved design. The Ames company employed a man named Crouch to set up production, and Crouch, together with Finnegan, perfected some small improvements which Finnegan patented in 1893. These improvements were a matter of more robust general construction and a grip safety device.

Crouch now left the Ames employ to set himself up as a sub-contractor to make the Chicago Protector, as the pistols were now known, for Ames to supply to Finnegan. But he was unable to produce the quantity demanded in the time stipulated in the contract, delivering only 1500 pistols by late 1894. By this time the World's Fair had ended, and Finnegan's hopes of sales had ended with it. A most involved lawsuit followed, with claims and counterclaims thick on the ground. The result was a judgement in favour of Finnegan, and as part of the settlement the Ames Company had to

purchase the patents and licence. They attempted to salvage something from the wreckage by manufacturing the pistol until 1910, but without much success.

CHINESE WEAPONS
Due to the nondescript systems of nomenclature used by various Chinese regimes, it is convenient to consider a number of weapons under this heading.

No native design of weapon appeared from China prior to the 1950s. In the early years of modern firearms, the Chinese governments were content to purchase western designs; their first cartridge rifle was the Mauser Model 1888, originally bought from Germany, later locally made in Hanyang Arsenal. This was followed by other Mauser designs, some of which are probably still in use. In similar manner the Maxim and Brno machine guns were first bought and then copied, as were Madsen

and Hotchkiss machine guns, the Browning Automatic Rifle and the Thompson submachine gun.

In the private field, the Chinese were assiduous copyists of a variety of pistols, most notably the Mauser C/96 Military model and the Browning M1900 Old Model; these latter will often be found with a fine crop of spurious trademarks, particularly that of the Mauser company.

At the present time the Chinese Nationalist Army is outfitted entirely with American designs, some purchased and some locally made on Taiwan, while the People's Republic leans to Russian designs, many of which have been slightly modified and given fresh nomenclature; thus the Soviet Simonov SKS carbine becomes the Type 56 in Chinese service. In recent years, though, a number of native designs have appeared, as follows:
Type 64 Silenced Pistol An unusual weapon, which appears to have little purpose other than

115

as an assassination weapon, the Type 64 is a blowback 7·65mm pistol with an integral silencer of high efficiency. The 7·65mm cartridge is of rimless type and unique to this pistol; while apparently similar to the common 7·65mm ACP cartridge, it is of slightly different dimensions and not semi-rimmed. A refinement of the pistol's design is the ability to lock the slide to the barrel so that it cannot recoil in the usual blowback way and the pistol thus becomes, in effect, a single shot weapon; locking the pistol in this fashion ensures that there is no mechanical noise or ejected case to betray the firer. Where this is of less importance, the slide is unlocked and the pistol functions as a self-loader.

Type 64 Silenced Submachine gun This is a submachine gun of the usual blowback type, chambered for a special low-velocity 7·62mm pistol cartridge and with a long Maxim-pattern silencer permanently installed around the barrel. It uses a 30-round magazine and can be fired at either single shots or automatic fire. The silencer contains a large number of plastic discs to reduce the noise of discharge, and is quite effective.

Type 68 rifle This is a Chinese amalgam of two Russian designs; in outline it appears to be based on the Simonov SKS carbine, but the gas-operated mechanism uses a rotating bolt in a carrier, based on the Kalashnikov AK-47 rifle. It fires the Soviet 7·62mm × 39 short cartridge from a 15-round box magazine and can be used for single shots or automatic fire.

Type 67 Light machine gun A gas-operated belt fed gun on a bipod mounting, firing the 7·62mm × 54R Mosin-Nagant cartridge. The design incorporates a number of features identifiable with other machine guns, and it appears that the Chinese have successfully managed to extract the features they preferred and weld them together into a functioning weapon. The gas piston and bolt mechanism are based on the Bren or ZB guns; the trigger, fire selector and safety catch are from the Soviet Degtyarev DP; the quick-change barrel comes from the Soviet Goryunov SG machine gun; while the belt feed appears to have been adapted from the Czech vz/52 design of machine gun. In spite of this heterogeneous assembly, the Type 67 is a serviceable weapon and was extensively employed by the Communist forces in Vietnam.

CHUCHU / *Brazil*

An obscure Brazilian designer, Chuchu patented, in 1884, a four-barrelled pistol with fixed breech and drop-down barrels generally resembling the better-known Lancaster (*qv*) design. However, Chuchu's design allowed the barrels to be folded further than usual so that they could lie beneath the butt and thus make an extremely compact unit for carrying in the pocket. A special retaining plate ensured that

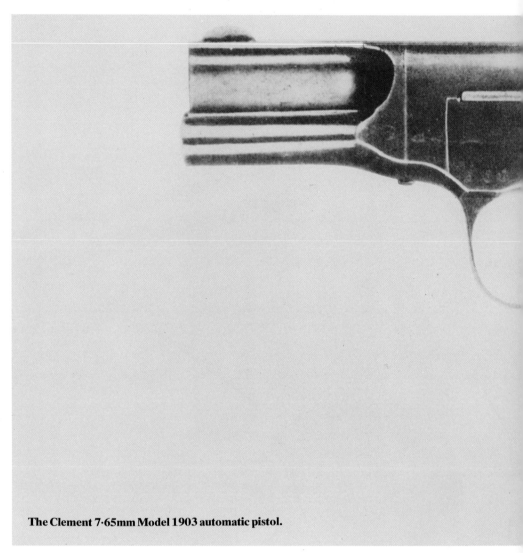

The Clement 7·65mm Model 1903 automatic pistol.

the four ·22 cartridges would not drop out of the chambers while the pistol was being carried in this manner. A self-cocking internal hammer struck the four firing pins in succession as the trigger was pulled.

CHYLEWSKI / *Austria*

Witold Chylewski designed an automatic pistol which could be operated entirely by one hand. Almost every automatic pistol demands two hands to place it in operating condition: one hand to hold the pistol while the other hand is employed to pull back the slide or breech block to charge a cartridge into the chamber and cock the firing mechanism. Chylewski's pistol had a slide retracting lever which formed the front edge of the trigger guard; by gripping the pistol in the normal way, the forefinger could be placed around this lever and squeezed, which drew back the slide to cock and load. After releasing the lever, the finger could be transferred to the trigger, and for subsequent shots

the slide retracting lever did not move.

About a thousand pistols are reputed to have been made for Chylewski by the Société Industrielle Suisse in Neuhausen, and using these as samples, as well as marketing them, Chylewski tried to interest a manufacturer in buying the rights and making the pistol in quantity. Unfortunately, he chose the aftermath of World War One to try this, and had no success. His patents expired in 1921; shortly afterwards the idea was adopted by Th. Bergmann, who produced the Lignose (*qv*) pistol to Chylewski's design; in this manifestation it was called the Einhand. What happened to Chylewski is not known.

CLAIR / *France*

The Clair brothers, Benoit, Jean Baptiste and Victor, of St. Etienne, France, are frequently advanced as being the inventors of the self-loading or automatic pistol, but the evidence is not in their favour. 1880 is put forward as the year which saw the start of their development,

but the absence of proof was ably dealt with by R. K. Wilson in his *Textbook of Automatic Pistols* as follows: 'It is said ... that the brothers were simple-minded mechanics who shunned publicity and who were apparently too ingenuous to patent their ideas. If this was so, they were indeed unusual inventors, and quite unlike any other of the breed ever seen in the gun trade.'

The first record of their activity is in a patent filed in Britain in February 1889 in which they claimed novelty on the entire principle of gas operation, but since this idea had been anticipated by several other inventors, no patent was granted to them. In 1893 came their first patent for actual weapons, a gas-operated shotgun and a gas-operated pistol.

Some weapons were certainly produced, though they were not precisely as depicted in these patents. The actual date of production is in doubt; some historians offer 1887, others give 1893 or 1895, while one contemporary writer gave 1900. The wording of the 1893 patent suggests that no more than rough experimental models had been made at that time, and if the pistol had been produced as early as 1887 it seems odd that they would have waited six years before trying to patent it. The pistols were in 8mm calibre, clumsy and unreliable, and they were unable to compete with other designs appearing at that time, such as the Bergmann, Borchardt and Mauser pistols. And since the Schonberger (1892) Paulson (1886), Schwarzlose (1892) and Borchardt (1893) designs had all been patented prior to the Clair design, there is small warrant for any claims of precedence for the Clair brothers.

CLEMENT / *Belgium*

Charles Clement, a Liège gunsmith, patented an automatic pistol in 1903, a blowback design using a fixed barrel and a bolt which moved back and forth inside the action body, appearing through the rear end of the body on recoil. It was chambered for an unusual 5mm bottle-necked cartridge which originated with the Charola y Anitua pistol (*qv*) and which, due to its association with the Clement pistol and the demise of the Charola, became known as the 5mm Clement cartridge.

In 1907 Clement revised his design. A major feature of his patent had been the assembly of the action body by means of an upstanding metal lug at the rear of the frame; in the 1903 design the lug was offset to one side and the bolt passed alongside it, but in the 1907 model the lug was placed centrally and the bolt slotted to pass around it. In this design Clement abandoned the 5mm cartridge and the pistol was chambered for either the 6·35mm or 7·65mm cartridges.

Minor changes were incorporated in later years until in 1912 he abandoned the patented design entirely and produced a fresh model which was no more than a copy of the Browning Model 1906 in 6·35mm calibre. Shortly after this, Clement died and the business was taken over by Neumann Frères of Liège, who continued to manufacture and sell under the Clement name until they closed down in 1914 under the German occupation. Under Neumann's ownership a revolver was marketed as the Clement, a ·38 calibre copy of the Colt Police Positive model; relatively few were made before the company ceased to trade.

COLONEY, Myron *(late 19th C.)*

Coloney, of whom little is known, was an inventor from New Haven, Connecticut who attracted the attention of Dr. James H. MacLean of St Louis, Missouri. MacLean was a Doctor of Medicine who appears to have amassed a small fortune from patent nostrums, while Coloney was a self-confessed mechanical genius with a special bent for firearms. Between them in the 1880s, they issued impressive prospectuses, obtained patents and sold stock, claiming to have perfected a wide variety of ever more improbable weapons, collectively known as MacLean's Peace Makers. These included such trivia as a 48-shot repeating pistol, a 128-shot rifle, three-barrelled pistols, machine guns and repeating artillery, none of which were ever actually manufactured.

It is of interest to see that MacLean's British patent 5613 of 1881, while claiming protection for a wide spectrum of unlikely weapons, managed to show a rimless grooved cartridge case, designed to facilitate extraction; this appeared long before the rimless cartridge achieved production, but MacLean failed to appreciate Coloney's brainwave and the idea lay fallow until independently developed elsewhere. It was the only workable idea the pair ever had, and they missed it. Both MacLean and Coloney vanished into obscurity, doubtless a few steps ahead of their creditors and investors, in the early 1890s.

COLT, Samuel (1814–1862)

Colt was undoubtedly the man who put the revolver on the map, though he played little part in its actual invention. He was primarily an organiser and salesman; he was an early advocate of mass production and standardisation of design to allow interchangeability of parts. Before Colt, the manufacture of firearms was done in traditional fashion, with skilled gunsmiths fashioning the individual parts and assembling them into complete weapons, hand-fitting each component to work properly with the others. After Colt, the task was a matter of making individual parts by semi-skilled labour with machine tools, each part carefully dimensioned and checked so that assemblers could put weapons together from boxes of components without the need for bench fitting, and customers throughout the world could order spare parts with the assurance that they would fit the gun. Given a sound mechanical design to begin with, the gunsmith was no longer required, machinists taking his place.

At the age of 16, Colt was cabin boy on the brig *Corvo*; according to legend he occupied his spare time in carving a revolver from scrap wood, his inspiration for the mechanism coming from the ship's wheel. This tale seems to have been a later invention by the infant public relations industry. After his seagoing stint was over, he went ashore and is next heard of as Doctor Coult, running a medicine show, travelling around America titillating the yokels with laughing gas and patent medicines. With the proceeds of this activity, he went to New England and engaged a mechanic named Anson Chase, gave him his ideas and instructed him to make up a revolver. Chase, a poor craftsman, turned out some crude specimens, at least one of which is said to have exploded upon being fired, and Colt took the work away from him. Eventually he found a better craftsman in John Pearson of Baltimore and in 1834 Pearson managed to produce what Colt had envisaged. As soon as he had a satisfactory weapon, Colt took ship for England and took out English patent No. 6909 on 22nd October 1835. He then returned to America to take out US Patent 9430X on 25th February 1836. He was just 21 years of age.

Colt's patents (the English one was never used and expired in 1849) covered his method of rotating the revolver cylinder by a hand linked to the hammer and engaging a ratchet on the rear face of the cylinder, and a method of locking the cylinder in alignment with the barrel for the period of discharge. The American patent succeeded in preventing any competitor from developing any sort of mechanically-revolved cylinder arm until the patent expired in 1857. In the long run this was to give Colt a commanding lead in revolver

The famous Frontier, or Peacemaker, in ·45 calibre.

manufacture, but his early days gave little hint of prosperity to come. America was, at that time, in a relatively settled and peaceful period, and there was little demand for revolvers. Colt set up his Patent Fire Arms Manufacturing Company in Paterson, New Jersey, in 1836 and began making pistols, rifles, shotguns and carbines, all on the revolving principle. But sales were slow, his financial backer went bankrupt, and in 1843 the company went to the wall.

In 1847, however, the Mexican War stimulated the demand for firearms, and General Zachary Taylor, impressed with the Colt revolvers owned by some of his officers, despatched a Captain Sam Walker to see Colt (who was then working on developing an electric telegraph system) and arrange for the production of a military revolver. Walker suggested certain improvements, Colt produced a design, and in January 1847 he was given an order for 1000 pistols. Having no factory, he subcontracted the order to Eli Whitney, a noted Massachusetts manufacturer of arms and inventor of the cotton gin; a second order for another 1000 pistols was given in November 1847, and from the proceeds of these orders Colt was able to open another factory of his own.

From then on, he occupied himself primarily with travelling and promoting his designs world-wide. In 1849, just as his new factory was ready, the California Gold Rush began and the drive to open up the West followed; and every prospector and adventurer outfitted himself with Colt's weapons. In 1851 he went to London to exhibit his arms at the Great Exhibition, arousing considerable interest and eventually persuading the British Army and Royal Navy to buy several thousand revolvers. In 1853 his London Armoury was opened, largely because the American factory was unable to produce weapons fast enough to meet domestic and foreign demands. But in 1855 he opened a new large factory at Hartford, Connecticut, a plant capable of volume production sufficient to meet any demand, and in the following year he closed down his London factory.

Subsequent to Colt's untimely death at the age of 47, the company was run by a succession of directors who were, in general, sufficiently astute to keep the company prosperous, though they exhibited, at times, a surprising reluctance to adopt new ideas or abandon old ones, which led to some dubious designs and outdated models. Nevertheless, the quality and reliability of Colt arms, particularly pistols, carried the firm across the odd rough patch.

It would be impossible, in the space available, to give details of all the different designs developed by Colt over the years; there are several specialised publications which perform this valuable historical function in admirable

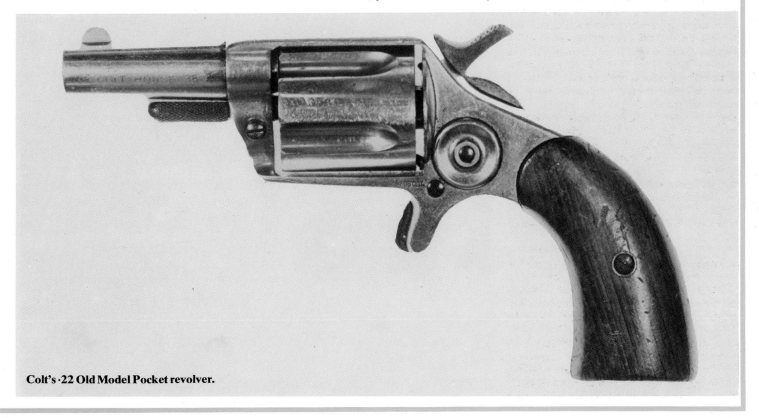

Colt's ·22 Old Model Pocket revolver.

detail. All that can be done here is to mention some of the more important designs and indicate the trend of development.

Colt's first product was the Paterson revolver, of ·34 calibre with a five-shot cylinder. It was, of course, a percussion weapon, with nipples recessed into the back of the cylinder, which was mounted on a central arbor. The 5½ inch octagonal barrel was forged with a lug which passed over the front end of the arbor and which was located firmly on the front end of the pistol frame. It was then locked in place by a cross pin which passed through slots in the barrel lug and the arbor. Since the top of the cylinder was thus exposed, this form of construction has given rise to the term 'open frame'. A thumb-cocked hammer was fitted, and a folding trigger without a guard, which automatically unfolded as the hammer was cocked. To load it was necessary to dismantle the pistol by removing the cross pin and the cylinder; as a result, the pistol was sold with a spare cylinder which could be carried ready-loaded and quickly subsituted for a fired cylinder. In 1839 Colt patented a lever-rammer which was fitted beneath the barrel, allowing the cylinder chambers to be loaded in the pistol.

The rifles and shoulder arms produced by Colt used the same basic mechanism: in effect, they were revolving pistols but with long barrels and a stock suited to firing from the shoulder. By and large, these were less popular than the pistols; it is said that, due to the larger charges used in the rifles and shotguns, there was a greater tendency for 'flash-over', the flame from the exploding charge leaking past the cylinder/barrel joint and igniting the charges in the other chambers, generally to the detriment of the firer's forward hand.

The order for pistols for the Mexican War led to the Walker (after the suggestions from Captain Walker) or Whitneyville (from the place of manufacture) model. This used the same general form of construction but with a conventional trigger and guard. Being intended for military use it was much larger and more powerful than the Paterson, being of ·44 calibre with a nine-inch barrel and six-shot cylinder and weighing over 4½ lbs. Subsequent percussion models—the Dragoon and Pocket models of 1848, the 1851 Navy, 1860 Army and 1862 Police, were little more than variations on the same open-frame design. The only notable change in design was due to Elisha Root, Colt's factory manager, who developed a solid frame revolver with side-mounted hammer, sold as the New Model Pocket Pistol from 1855.

Also in 1855, Rollin White (*qv*) obtained his patent for 'cylinders bored end to end' to allow breech loading, and this patent was acquired by the Smith & Wesson company. As soon as Colt's master patent expired in 1857, Smith & Wesson went into production with a breech loading cartridge revolver and they, in turn, now had a master patent which effectively stifled competition. Fortunately for Colt, ballistic development was in its early days, and those first metallic cartridges were relatively weak, allowing the percussion revolver, with its ability to handle powerful charges and heavy bullets, to survive for several more years. In an endeavour to emulate the rapid-loading facility of the breech-loading pistol (since they had been unable to come to terms with Smith & Wesson over a licence to the White patent) Colt developed a special cylinder which accepted a metallic cartridge inserted from the front of the chamber, the assembly being called

The Colt ·38 New Police Model of 1895, popularly known as the 'Cop and Thug'.

An early Colt automatic was the 1902/08 model in ·38 ACP calibre.

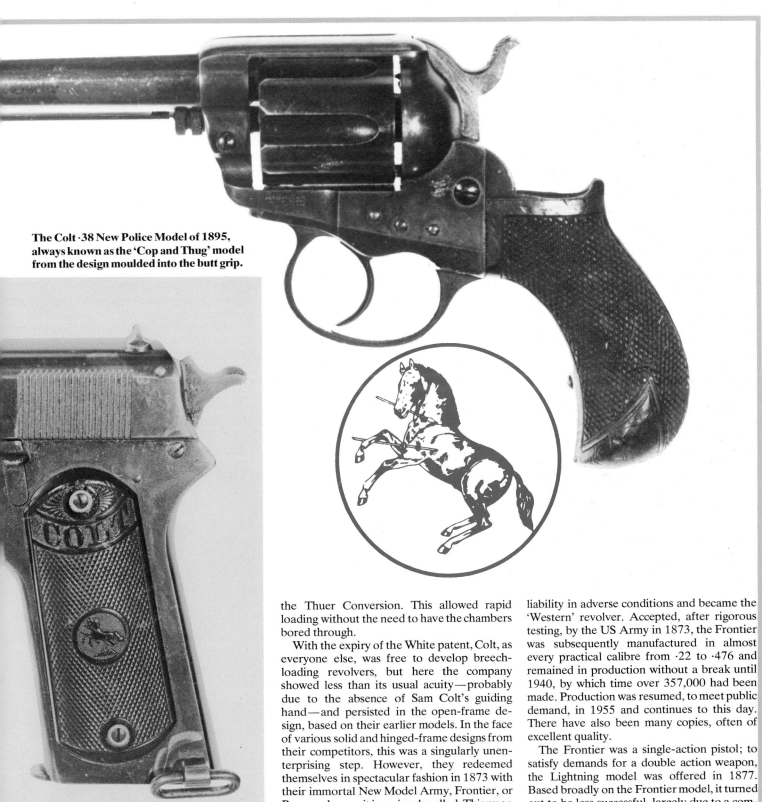

The Colt ·38 New Police Model of 1895, always known as the 'Cop and Thug' model from the design moulded into the butt grip.

the Thuer Conversion. This allowed rapid loading without the need to have the chambers bored through.

With the expiry of the White patent, Colt, as everyone else, was free to develop breech-loading revolvers, but here the company showed less than its usual acuity—probably due to the absence of Sam Colt's guiding hand—and persisted in the open-frame design, based on their earlier models. In the face of various solid and hinged-frame designs from their competitors, this was a singularly unenterprising step. However, they redeemed themselves in spectacular fashion in 1873 with their immortal New Model Army, Frontier, or Peacemaker, as it is variously called. This was a solid-frame, rod-ejecting, six-shot revolver in ·45 calibre which, in spite of minor flaws, rapidly gained an invincible reputation for re-

liability in adverse conditions and became the 'Western' revolver. Accepted, after rigorous testing, by the US Army in 1873, the Frontier was subsequently manufactured in almost every practical calibre from ·22 to ·476 and remained in production without a break until 1940, by which time over 357,000 had been made. Production was resumed, to meet public demand, in 1955 and continues to this day. There have also been many copies, often of excellent quality.

The Frontier was a single-action pistol; to satisfy demands for a double action weapon, the Lightning model was offered in 1877. Based broadly on the Frontier model, it turned out to be less successful, largely due to a complicated lock mechanism which soon broke and was virtually unrepairable. It was replaced, to some extent, by the Double Action Army of

1878, though even this improved and stronger weapon failed to attract much enthusiasm.

In addition to heavy military revolvers, Colt also produced a wide selection of pocket pistols; notable among these was the Cloverleaf series, which gained this popular name from the deeply indented four-shot cylinders of the first models, a configuration selected so as to allow the cylinder to be part-turned and present a thinner bulk for carrying in the pocket.

Colt's next major step was the introduction of a solid-framed revolver with the cylinder mounted on a crane arm, allowing it to be swung sideways from the frame for ejection and reloading. This first appeared on the Navy Model of 1889, gaining this name from the US Navy having bought 5000 of them. This became the pattern for subsequent designs, and, apart from the perpetual Frontier model, all Colt revolvers since that time have used this solid-frame configuration, minor improvements in the method of retaining the cylinder, locking it or revolving it being added from time to time. Their last important innovation was their introduction of the Positive Safety Lock, an addition to the trigger mechanism which positively blocked the falling hammer unless the trigger was correctly pulled back. This prevented accidental firing such as could occur if

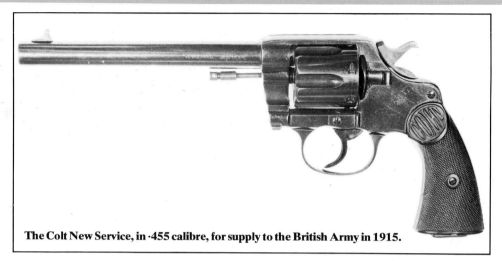

The Colt New Service, in ·455 calibre, for supply to the British Army in 1915.

the hammer were let slip during thumb cocking or if the pistol was dropped so as to land upon the hammer. This is similar to the Iver Johnson (qv) safety idea, and would ultimately be required by US legislation in 1971.

When the automatic pistol began to appear in Europe in the 1890s, Colt was one of the few American companies to take note, quickly realising that if a reliable pistol could be produced they could establish a lead in that field as commanding as the one they made in the revolver field. They achieved their aim, and have sustained that lead ever since. Lessons from the past indicated that the road to success lay in obtaining good patents, and they rapidly acquired several, notably those of John M. Browning, and these laid the foundation of their development work. As with revolvers, they set out from the start to produce a weapon acceptable to the military, submitting their first

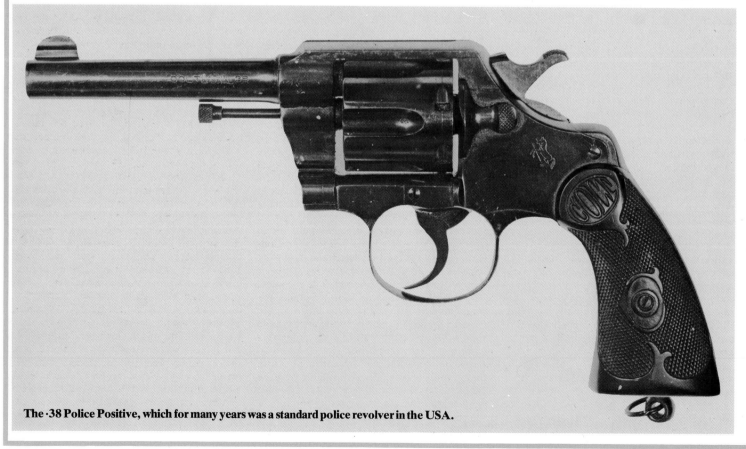

The ·38 Police Positive, which for many years was a standard police revolver in the USA.

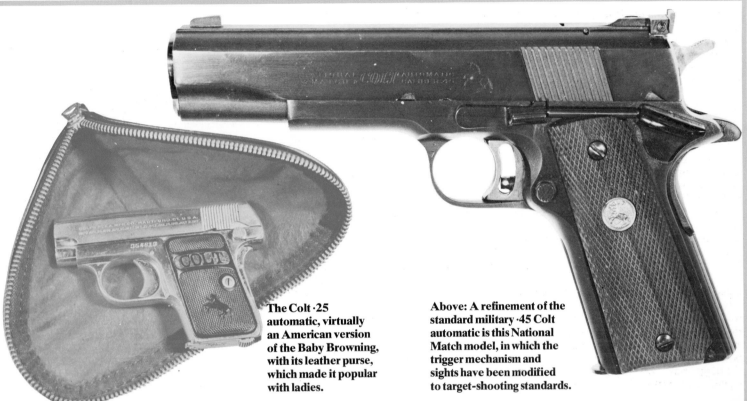

The Colt ·25 automatic, virtually an American version of the Baby Browning, with its leather purse, which made it popular with ladies.

Above: A refinement of the standard military ·45 Colt automatic is this National Match model, in which the trigger mechanism and sights have been modified to target-shooting standards.

design for test in 1898. This used the Browning-patented 'swinging link' system of breech locking, in which the barrel was attached to the pistol frame by two hinged links, one at the breech and one at the muzzle. The upper surface of the barrel carried two lugs which, when the pistol was at rest, engaged in two grooves in the interior of the slide. On firing, recoil made the barrel move back; due to the engagement of lugs and grooves, the slide—which formed the breech block—moved back in sympathy, so that the breech was held securely closed. Due to the links, continued movement of the barrel carried it downwards, still parallel with the frame, and disengaged the lugs so that the breech was free to open and the slide to recoil.

The first pistol to be marketed, the Model 1900, was chambered for a ·38 rimless cartridge of considerable power. The US Army and Navy bought some 250 for trial and others were sold commercially. Changes were then made as experience showed the need; in 1905 the US Army came firmly to the decision that nothing less than a ·45 calibre would be acceptable as a military sidearm, and Colt therefore developed a new ·45 rimless cartridge and a suitable design of pistol. In 1907 an exhaustive test by the Army found the Colt design worthy of further development, and eventually the Model 1911 was accepted by the Army as their service pistol; with minor changes in the 1920s

it remains so to this day, the longest-serving military weapon currently in use. Including commercial sales, over two and a half million have been made.

While the military aspect was of prime importance, Colt did not neglect the civilian market for the automatic pistol of lesser power, and produced a number of simple and reliable pocket blowback pistols, also based on Browning patents. Their Model 1903 was essentially the same as that made in Belgium as the Browning 1903, Colt and Fabrique National reaching agreement over sales so that their products did not compete. In a similar manner the Colt ·25 model 1908 was the Browning 1906. In more recent years, the rising costs of production led Colt to contract their ·25 design to a Spanish manufacturer, but the Gun Control Act of 1968 placed obstacles in the way of importation, and Colt resumed manufacture in the USA. Another well-known Colt automatic pistol series is the Woodsman ·22 hunting and target model.

In 1895 Colt entered the machine gun field with a gas-operated design by Browning; it is said that Browning allowed Colt to use their name on the gun simply because he had a better design in mind and wanted to use his own name on that one. It was unique in that the gas did not drive the usual type of parallel gas piston, but blew a hinged arm downward; linkage from this arm actuated the bolt and belt

feed mechanism. It was adopted by the US Navy and, to a lesser extent, by the US Army; while serviceable, it was an awkward weapon to use in the field, due to the need to ensure adequate clearance beneath the gun for the downward swing of the actuating arm. Failure to ensure such clearance led to its nickname—'the potato digger'.

Browning's better design was the recoil-operated gun discussed under his name, and Colt manufactured these, commencing with the water-cooled M1917 model. They also made the original batch of Thompson submachine guns for the Auto-Ordnance Corporation. After the Second World War they acquired the rights to the Armalite (qv) rifle designed by Eugene Stoner, and from this design, with Stoner as consultant, have developed their own CAR (Colt Automatic Rifle) series. More recent ventures include the CMG-2 machine gun, a belt-fed weapon currently being evaluated by military authorities, and the 'Imp' (Individual Multi-Purpose Weapon), a compact submachine gun in ·221 calibre. This began as a survival rifle for the US Air Force, and is unconventional in that it dispenses with the usual type of stock and relies on the firer's forearm to give the necessary support to the body of the weapon. An evaluation is currently in progress, the weapon having been taken into US service as the 'Rifle, Caliber ·221, GUU-A/P'.

COMMANDO / *USA (1)*

Submachine gun manufactured by Colt. The success of the Colt-manufactured M16A1 rifle, particularly in US Army hands in Vietnam, led to speculation as to the utility of a shorter and more handy model, and the Commando was the result. Basically, it is an M16 rifle with the barrel shortened from 20 inches to 10 inches and with a telescoping tubular butt, giving the weapon an overall length of 28 inches with the butt collapsed. The only drawback is that since the 5·56mm cartridge was designed for use in a full-length shoulder arm, it is not developing full power in a half-length barrel, and some of the propelling charge is unconsumed at the time of bullet ejection, leading to excessive flash and blast. This has been partly countered by an outsized flash suppressor on the muzzle. By the same token, the short barrel leads to rather irregular ballistics and thus to a greater dispersion of fire than with the rifle, but this is perhaps not a bad thing in the submachine gun role, and the Commando is at least as accurate as any other weapon in this class. It is currently in use by US troops as the 'Submachine gun XM177E2'.

COMMANDO / *USA (2)*

A self-loading carbine in ·45 calibre, currently made by the Commando Arms Incorporated of Knoxville, Tennessee. In general appearance it resembles the Thompson submachine gun, but uses a different mechanism which fires from a closed breech. The barrel is 16½ inches long, giving greater accuracy than the submachine gun, and there is a wide variety of optional magazines, grips and stocks available to suit the purchaser.

COMMISSION RIFLE / *Germany*

Popular name for the German service rifle Model 1888; also called the Mauser & Commission Rifle. This terminology arises because the rifle was designed by the Military Rifle Testing Commission at Spandau Arsenal.

The service rifle in use in the early 1880s was the Mauser M71/84, a repeating bolt-action weapon using a tubular magazine beneath the barrel and firing an 11mm black-powder cartridge. The tubular magazine had certain drawbacks, notably a shifting balance of the rifle as the magazine was emptied, the need to load it

one round at a time, and a potential hazard in that the point of one bullet lay in contact with the percussion cap of the next cartridge. With blunt-nosed lead bullets, this latter item was less of a problem, but in 1886 the French Army had introduced the Lebel rifle, using pointed small-calibre bullets and smokeless powder, and the Germans were anxious to adopt these features. The principal objection from the troops was the slowness of loading, and the Commission were particularly concerned with adopting a packet loading system.

The rifle which they designed had a fixed magazine below the bolt, into which a clip with five cartridges could be inserted. A 'follower arm' forced the cartridges upwards within the clip, presenting each one to the bolt in turn. Once the last cartridge had been loaded, the empty clip fell out of the magazine via a hole in the bottom. The action was basically the Mauser bolt, improved by the adoption of two locking lugs on the bolt head, while the clip-loading system was based on Mannlicher's design; it was an improvement insofar as the Mannlicher system used an asymmetrical clip which could only be loaded into the magazine one way, while the Commission's design used a symmetrical clip which could be dropped in either way up. The defects of any clip loading system are that once a clip is in the magazine, there is no way to 'top up' the magazine with loose rounds when it is half empty, and that it cannot be used as a single loader while retaining a full magazine.

The cartridge produced for this rifle was the 7·92mm×57 rimless, frequently called the '8mm Mauser', firing a 226 grain jacketed bullet by means of a smokeless powder charge. It was to remain, with slight modification, the standard German service rifle and machine gun cartridge until 1945, and it is still widely used as a military and sporting cartridge.

For the pistol developed by the Commission, see under Reichsrevolver.

COOK / USA

Submachine gun designed by Loren Cook, a US soldier, in 1951–1952. It was a simple design mainly constructed of tubular steel sections; barrel, tubular receiver and tubular butt-stock were all in prolongation of one another. The magazine housing acted as pistol grip, and a knurled tubular front grip was clamped to the

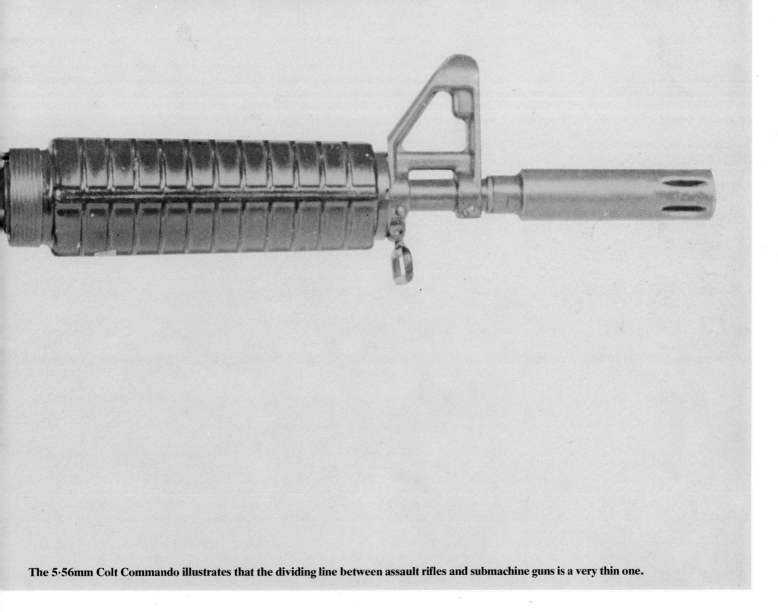

The 5·56mm Colt Commando illustrates that the dividing line between assault rifles and submachine guns is a very thin one.

The Cristobal ·30 Model 2 submachine gun; there are obvious affinities with the Hungarian M39, which was also designed by Kiraly.

barrel. Prototypes were made in 9mm Parabellum and ·45 calibres, and the magazine housing was designed to accept the standard British Sten or American M3 submachine gun magazines in accordance with the calibre. Cook was unable to sell in his design, and he abandoned it in about 1955.

CORUNA, LA / Spain
Name given to the Rexim-Favor (qv) submachine gun when marketed by the Spanish Fabrica de Armas de Coruna. This company had made the weapons for the Swiss firm SA Suisse Rexim, but Rexim went bankrupt leaving the Spaniards with the better part of 5000 submachine guns on their hands. They renamed it the La Coruna, and endeavoured to sell them to the Spanish government, but without success. After this they managed to dispose of them slowly through commercial channels. Most of them appear to have ended up in the hands of various African guerilla groups.

CRISPIN, Silas (fl. 19th C.)
Silas Crispin was a New York gunsmith of whom very little is known other than that he invented an unusual revolver and cartridge, which he patented in October 1865. Like many other would-be inventors of the time, Crispin was faced with the problem of circumventing the Rollin White patent, which gave Smith & Wesson the American monopoly of breech-loading revolvers. He solved this by splitting the revolver cylinder into two halves, the rear half with 'blind' chambers—i.e. not bored through the full length—and the front half with bored-through chambers.

The revolver was a hinged frame model in which the barrel hinged down and took the front half of the cylinder with it, leaving the rear half fixed to the frame. The cartridge was a self-contained metallic case and bullet with a raised annular rim around the case about three-quarters of its length back from the bullet tip. To load, the revolver was opened and the cartridges inserted nose first into the cham-

bers of the front half of the cylinder, so that the annular rim, which contained the percussion composition, was resting on the face of the cylinder half. The revolver was then closed, and the rear portions of the cartridge were positioned inside the blind chambers of the rear portion of the cylinder. The sensitive annular rim was thus at the cylinder joint, and at this point each chamber had a short slot in the side. As each cylinder reached alignment with the barrel, this slot lined up with a firing pin inside the top strap of the frame, which was struck as the hammer descended and transmitted the blow to the annular rim, firing the composition inside.

Only one specimen of Crispin's revolver is known to exist, and it is obvious that it never achieved commercial success, probably because it appeared just as the American Civil War ended; had he managed to get it into production a year or two earlier, he might have done very well out of it. As it was, by the time it could have been ready for production the Rollin White patent had expired and its raison d'etre vanished. But Crispin cartridges in ·31 calibre (for the revolver) and ·44 calibre are known to collectors, and a ·50 version was used in a modified model of the Smith Breech-Loading Carbine.

CRISTOBAL / Dominican Republic
After the Second World War the Hungarian designer Kiraly (qv) left Hungary, and in 1948, working for the Dominican Government, he set up an arms factory at San Cristobal. Here were produced two weapons, the Cristobal Model 2 carbine and the Model 62 rifle.

The Model 2 was a combination of Beretta and Kiraly design features; the general appearance, with wooden stock and tubular receiver, resembles the Beretta Model 38 submachine gun, but the forward-sloping magazine and the delayed blowback mechanism relying on a two-part bolt are unmistakably Kiraly, being almost identical to the Hungarian 39M submachine gun (for details of which see under Danuvia). The carbine fired at single shots or

automatic and was chambered for the US ·30 Carbine cartridge, a somewhat unusual choice. A later version used a folding metal butt and perforated barrel jacket.

The Model 62 rifle was a full-sized shoulder arm chambered for the 7·62mm NATO cartridge. It used a gas piston derived from the US Army's M1 rifle, allied to a tipping bolt mechanism similar to that employed on the FN FAL rifle. It was never put into quantity manufacture.

CUTTS COMPENSATOR / USA
A device invented by Col. Richard M. Cutts (USMC Retired) and his son Richard M. Cutts Jr. (USMC) and intended to stabilise an automatic weapon during sustained fire. It was a muzzle attachment with a number of slots cut in the top surface; as the bullet passed through the device, a portion of the gas following the bullet was deflected upwards through the slots. This caused reaction which forced the muzzle of the weapon down.

One of the common complaints with submachine guns is that when fired at automatic, the turning effect of the recoil, forcing the weapon against the firer's shoulder or grip, tends to make the muzzle rise so that only the first few shots are in the target area. The effect of the Cutts Compensator was, it was claimed, to counter this tendency and thus make the weapon more controllable and more accurate. It was adopted for the Thompson submachine gun in 1928 and never used on any other weapon, although several other submachine guns have used devices of similar intent in order to achieve the same ends.

Opinions vary as to the worth of the device; the British Small Arms Committee tested one on a Thompson in 1928 and reported that it had no appreciable effect, yet, as noted above, others have felt it necessary to add similar devices to their weapons. Perhaps the best that can be said is that it might do good and certainly does no harm; the principal British objection to it was that it added $20 to the already high price of the Thompson in 1939.

D

DANUVIA / *Hungary*

The Danuvia Company of Budapest was set up in the early 1930s to manufacture military weapons, and employed Paul Kiraly (*qv*) as their principal designer. Their activities appear to have been largely confined to contract manufacture of other people's inventions, but in 1938 they developed a submachine gun to Kiraly's design. This was a delayed blowback weapon using a two-piece bolt; the front section of the bolt carried a lever arm which, when the bolt was closed, was engaged in a recess in the gun body. On firing, the rearward thrust of the cartridge case forced the bolt head back but had to overcome the mechanical disadvantage of this lever as it was revolved against the mass of the heavier bolt body, and this gave sufficient delay to allow the bullet to leave the barrel. The gun was stocked like a rifle, fired the 9mm Mauser Export cartridge, and had a fixed magazine. It was also provided with a rate-of-fire controller of surpassing complexity, described by one critic as a 'watchmaker's dream'.

In May 1939 this weapon was offered to the British Army, the Birmingham Small Arms company having acquired a license to manufacture; they claimed that they could produce the gun for not more than £5 provided they left out the rate-reducing device, but although the

weapon performed well on trials, no action was taken by the authorities and the project got no further.

Kiraly modified his design in accordance with criticisms voiced in England, removing the rate reducer and also arranging the magazine so that it could be folded forward into a slot in the stock, and it was accepted for service by the Hungarian Army as their M39. Some 8000 were made, and in 1943 the design was changed to incorporate a folding metal butt, upon which change the designation became the M43. This is believed to have remained in production until 1945.

Danuvia were also responsible for the Gebauer machine gun, designed by the scientist of that name (*qv*) and Kiraly. It was extremely complicated, fired at an astronomical rate and was totally unreliable.

During the war the company were active on German Army contracts, but they vanished from sight in 1945.

DARDICK / *USA*

The basic idea of this pistol was conceived by David Dardick in 1949, and the 'Open Chamber' idea represents one of the few innovations in pistol design of modern times. Dardick spent several years perfecting the idea

before marketing it in 1954, but in spite of its theoretical advantages, it failed to prosper.

The weapon is in the form of a revolver but instead of the conventional cylinder there is a 'star wheel' with three triangular cut-outs in place of chambers. The magazine is in the pistol butt, and spring power forced the top round from the magazine into one of the star wheel cut-outs. Pressure on the trigger revolved the star wheel through 120° to align the cartridge with the pistol barrel and then dropped the hammer to fire it in the usual manner. The novelty of this design lay in the fact that the cartridge was not contained in a conventional chamber but in an 'open chamber', two sides of which were formed by the cut-out in the star wheel and the third side by the top strap of the revolver frame. The next pull on the trigger revolved the star wheel again, bringing up the next cartridge from the magazine and also carrying the spent case around and ejecting it through a port on the right side of the pistol.

Due to the triangular shape of the cut-out, and also due to the open chamber construction, the cartridge case had to be triangular and had to be capable of withstanding much more pressure than normal. These ends were achieved in the first models by forming the cases of extruded triangular aluminium section, but later cartridges were made of polycarbonate plastic.

The Hungarian M39 submachine gun, chambered for the 9mm Mauser cartridge, and one of the more successful designs to come from the Danuvia company.

Triangular adapters were made into which ordinary commercial cartridges could be placed so as to convert them into 'trounds' (Dardick's name for his triangular rounds) for use in the pistol.

Apart from novelty there was little advantage in the Dardick as far as the user was concerned, and in comparison with conventional pistols they were expensive. It is doubtful if more than 50 pistols were ever made, and the company went into liquidation in 1960. The principle of the open chamber gun has some advantages and the idea is currently being explored by a company who have licensed it from Dardick in the hope of applying it to machine guns and aircraft cannons.

DARNE / *France*

The brothers Regis and Pierre Darne, after some years of work as gunsmiths, perfected their unique shotgun in 1895. Instead of the usual drop-down form of double-barrelled gun, the barrels are rigidly attached to the frame and the breech unit is withdrawn to the

rear by operating a lever in the centre of the breech block. This opens the breech and extracts the empty case. The Darne shotgun was, and still is, of the highest possible quality and refinement and has always been rated as one of Europe's premier sporting guns.

Under the pressures of war the Darne company accepted a contract to make Lewis machine guns for the French Army in 1915. This appears to have stimulated their interest in military arms, and the Darne brothers developed a machine gun of their own design in 1917. After the war they continued to develop it, eventually producing an aircraft observer's

The Model 1100 Dardick pistol, an attempt to introduce new concepts into revolvers, but which failed to gain popularity.

gun, fixed aircraft guns, infantry guns and a heavy anti-tank machine gun. Only the aircraft guns were successful, being used by the French, Brazilian, Spanish and Italian Air Forces in the 1920s and 1930s. In marked comparison with the quality of their shotguns, the Darne machine guns were cheap and of extremely poor quality materials and workmanship. This was decried at the time, but hindsight indicates that the Darne company may have been among the first to realise that the traditional standards of engineering and gunsmithing were out of place on an expendable weapon.

DAUGS, Willi *(fl. mid-20th C.)*

Willi Daugs was the production manager of Tikkakoski Arsenal in Finland during the Second World War, and was responsible for the design and manufacture of the Finnish M-44 sub-machine gun, which itself was a copy of the Soviet PPS-42. At the end of the war Daugs fled to Sweden, taking the drawings of the M-44 with him, and then turned up in Holland, where he tried to interest various manufactur-

ers in the weapon, without success. He then moved to Spain and met Ludwig Vorgrimmler, a German designer, at the Fabrica de Armas de Oviedo. Together they redeveloped the M-44 design, calling it the Dux (*qv*) submachine gun. The German Army expressing interest in the design, Daugs then went to Germany to work there as a consultant to J. G. Anschutz, who were attempting to improve the weapon. But difficulties arose over licensing agreements and Daugs left Germany. He is believed to have gone to South America, but has not been active in the small arms design field since the early 1960s.

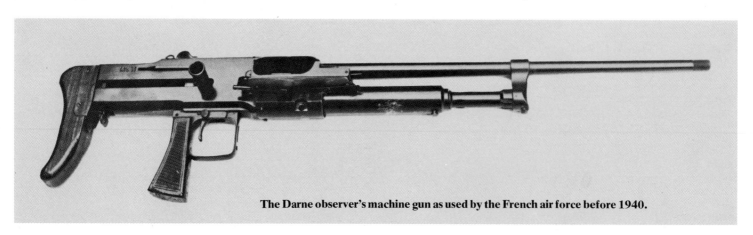

The Darne observer's machine gun as used by the French air force before 1940.

DAW, George Henry (fl. 19th C.)

G. H. Daw's early history is unknown; he presumably served the usual apprenticeship, but his first recorded appearance is as a partner in the firm of Witton, Daw & Co., of London, in 1851. This partnership survived until 1861, when Daw left to set up on his own. After his death in 1889 the business continued as the Daw Gun Company until 1892.

Daw's principal claim to fame was his introduction into Britain of the centre-fire shotgun cartridge, having acquired rights to the patents of Schneider of France. There was, however, a vast amount of litigation over these patents and Daw was forced to give up his exclusive rights to the design as a result of a lawsuit by Eley, the cartridge manufacturers; the decision (according to W. W. Greener) was due to Schneider's failure to maintain patent protection in France. Daw subsequently published a pamphlet entitled *The Central Fire Cartridge before the Law Courts, the Government and the Public* (1867) in which he took pains to explain his point of view. He had previously published *Daw's Gun Patents* (1864), a general resumé of firearms patents and a compendium of advertising matter for himself. One is led to the conclusion that Daw liked litigation better than he liked gun-making, and liked advertising himself better than either.

Daw made muzzle-loading rifles and duelling pistols, which he exhibited at the Great Exhibition of 1851, and towards the end of the 1850s manufactured the Lang (*qv*) gas-seal revolver. On setting up in business on his own, he acquired an interest in patents taken out by two Birmingham gunsmiths, Charles Pryse and Paul Cashmore, which related to a double-action revolver lock, and in the 1860s he made percussion revolvers incorporating this lock, selling them as the Daw Revolver. He also made revolving rifles, using the same lock action, though these are less common today.

With his espousal of the centre-fire shotgun cartridge, in the early 1860s, he seems to have gradually moved away from revolvers and concentrated upon shotguns and sporting guns generally, exhibiting samples at the International Exhibition in 1862. His shotgun design is distinguished by an underlever beneath the trigger guard which, when pressed down, withdraws a locking bolt and permits the barrels to be swung down for loading. Both external hammer and hammerless designs were produced, the latter being a true hammerless in that it used axial strikers which were cocked by the action of the underlever as the gun was opened.

This hammerless version was, by contemporary account, a clumsy and complicated gun and did not achieve much commercial success; the hammer gun was better and appears to have been the company's mainstay until its closure in 1892.

DEANE AND ADAMS / Britain

Name under which the percussion revolvers of Robert Adams (*qv*) were sold. It arose from Adams' partnership with John Deane and his son John Deane Jr. as 'Deane, Adams and Deane', which company was set up to exploit Adams' various patents covering rifles and revolvers. The firm displayed revolvers at the Great Exhibition of 1851, and the subsequent interest in these and in the exhibits of Colonel Colt led them to concentrate on pistol production. Its acceptance by the British Army as the Deane and Adams Pistol set the seal of approval on it, and it was widely sold for several years.

DECKER, Wilhelm (fl. early 20th C.)

Wilhelm Decker of Zella St Blasii, Germany, patented an unusual pocket revolver in 1912. It was a solid frame six shot model in 6·35mm calibre, and hammerless, using an axial firing pin which was cocked and released by a single pull on the plunger-type trigger. The trigger was beneath the barrel, on the end of an operating rod which ran beneath the cylinder; when the trigger was pulled, movement of this rod rotated the cylinder by means of a pawl and then locked it while the stroker fired the cartridge. Loading was done by a gate on the right side, ejection of spent cases being performed by pushing them out of the cylinder, through the gate, by a pin carried inside the cylinder arbor.

Relatively few appear to have been made when production ceased in 1914. In the spring of that year it was advertised in England as the Mueller Patent Revolver but no specimen so marked has ever been found. Decker reappeared after the war as a patentee of various automatic pistol mechanisms between 1919 and 1922, but none of these were ever manufactured and he dropped from sight.

DEER GUN / USA

Where this weapon got its name is not clear; certainly it has nothing whatever to do with deer hunting. The Deer Gun was a 9mm calibre single shot pistol which is believed to have been fathered by the American CIA with the intention of flooding South East Asia with pistols during the Vietnam war. It was based on the same concept as the Liberator (*qv*) pistol of the Second World War, a simple weapon capable of being used by the uninstructed and capable of killing at short range. To load the Deer, the barrel is unscrewed from the diecast frame, and a 9mm Parabellum cartridge placed into the chamber. The barrel is then screwed back into the frame. On pressing the trigger a striker is cocked and released to fire the cartridge. The barrel is then unscrewed once more and the spent case ejected by poking it out with any convenient twig before loading. A supply of cartridges could be carried in the hollow butt. A 'comic-strip' set of instructions, comprehensible by the completely illiterate, was packed together with a supply of ammunition and a pistol into a polystyrene package ready for air-dropping. Several thousand were apparently made in 1964, but a change of political policy supervened and, with the exception of a few kept as museum pieces, the lot were scrapped.

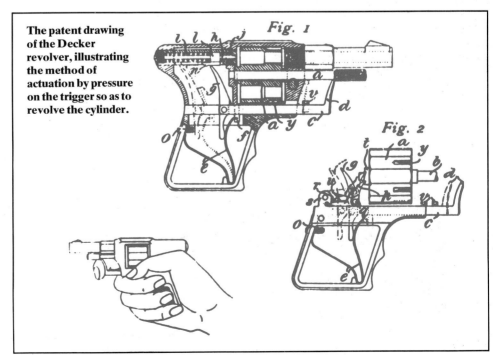

The patent drawing of the Decker revolver, illustrating the method of actuation by pressure on the trigger so as to revolve the cylinder.

DEGTYAREV, Vasily Alexeyevitch (1879–1949)

Degtyarev came from a family of gunsmiths and served his apprenticeship in the Imperial Arms Factory at Tula. In 1906 he became assistant to Federov (*qv*) at the Sestorets Small Arms Factory, where he was introduced to automatic weapons. In 1921 he began designing a light machine gun which became the standard Soviet infantry weapon. He later designed submachine guns, medium and heavy machine guns, and collaborated with Shpagin in the design of a heavy machine gun. Degtyarev eventually became a Major-General in the Artillery Engineering Service, Doctor of Technical Sciences, won four State Prizes, and became a Deputy of the Supreme Soviet, no mean achievement for a boy who left school at the age of eleven.

The Degtyarev DP (Degtyaryova pakhotnyi — Degtyarev Infantry) machine gun was adopted in 1926 after two years of inten-

sive tests. It was a gas-operated gun using the Friberg-Kjellman (*qv*) bolt-locking system in which two flaps are forced out by the passage of the firing pin, securing the bolt to the gun body at the instant of firing. It was a simple and robust design, highly resistant to dirt and poor maintenance and simple to manufacture. Feed was from a distinctive 47-shot flat drum magazine and the gun could only fire automatic, no single shot ability being provided. Its only mechanical defect was the positioning of the return spring, around the gas piston and immediately beneath the barrel, where it was liable to soften due to overheating in sustained fire. This fault became more apparent during the Second World War and the design was changed, placing the spring in a tubular extension behind the gun body. This meant that the gunner could no longer grip the small of the butt to press the trigger, so a pistol grip was provided. The bipod was also improved, and the gun became the DPM (DP Modified).

After adoption of the DP, the DT (T=Tank) for use on armoured vehicles was introduced. This was the same mechanism but used a pistol grip and telescoping butt for more convenient handling inside the tank, and had a deeper 60-round magazine, Then came the DA (A=Aviation) for use as an aircraft observer's gun; this was much the same as the DT and was made in single and twin versions. The aircraft guns remained unchanged throughout the war years, but the DT was modified by moving the return spring and became the DTM.

In 1934 came the DK (K=krupnokalibyerni=heavy calibre) a 12·7mm gun, belt fed, intended principally as an air defence weapon for the infantry. This was made only in prototype and acted as the basis for the improved model, the DShK (Sh indicating the collaboration of G. Shpagin in the design). Shpagin developed a rotary feed system which stripped cartridges from the belt and presented them to the bolt for loading. This, also a

The Soviet DT tank machine gun, a shorter version of the infantry squad weapon.

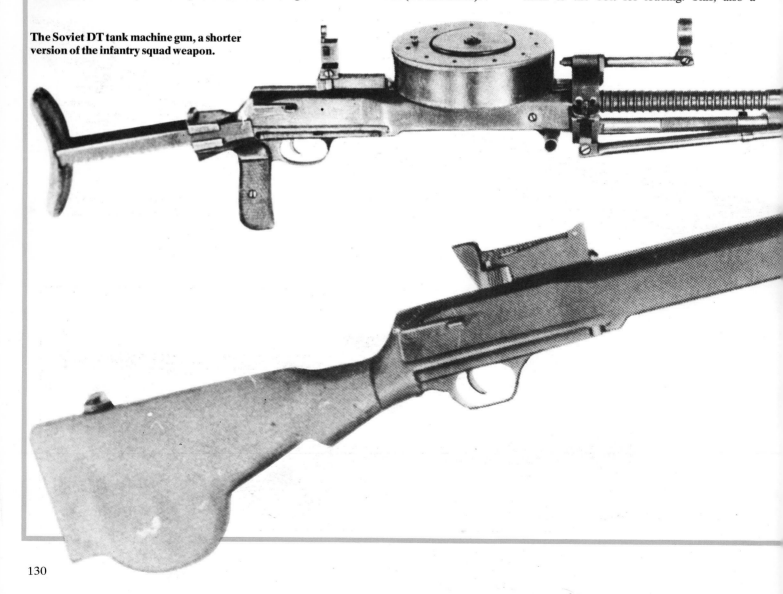

12·7mm gun, was introduced in 1938 and served throughout the war as an anti-aircraft and ground heavy gun. In 1946 it was modified to become the DShKM by changing the feed system to a more simple pawl system. Both DShK and DShKM guns are still widely used by satellite armies.

Having dealt with the light and heavy requirements, Degtyarev turned to the medium machine gun field, but here he lost his touch. The 1939 DS was more or less an enlarged DT but using belt feed. It had a heavy finned barrel suited to sustained fire, and used the standard 7·62 Soviet rifle cartridge. It proved, though, to be a difficult manufacturing proposition and was never made in quantity.

In postwar years the DP design was slightly improved to produce the RP46 in 1946. This modified the feed mechanism so that either the 47-round DP drum or a 250-round belt could be used. By this time, though, the 7·62mm M1943 short cartridge had come into Soviet

service, and it was desirable to have a machine gun which fired this round; as a result, the final Degtyarev machine gun design was the RPD, introduced in the early 1950s. Again, it was the DT brought up to date, using belt feed from a drum carried beneath the gun.

In the submachine gun field Degtyarev produced his first design in 1934, an amalgam of features of the Bergmann MP 28 and the Suomi M1931, using a 71-round drum magazine. The gun was originally designed for a 25-round box magazine and the magazine housing, therefore, could not take the standard Suomi drum; a special drum, with an elongated extension on its top so that it would fit the box magazine housing, was developed. Numerous minor variants of this design appeared as small improvements suggested themselves but it seems that production was relatively slight until 1938, when the reports from observers in the Spanish Civil War drew Soviet attention to the virtues of the submachine gun. Production

was then increased, but the PPD34, as the design was known, was expensive and time-consuming to manufacture, and in 1940 Degtyarev produced the PPD-40 design. This simplified manufacture and also abandoned the box magazine, using the Suomi drum.

Degtyarev's anti-tank rifle, the PTRD of 1941 was a 14·5mm weapon using a simple bolt action. The barrel and action, however, could recoil in the stock, and this movement forced the bolt handle over a cam which rotated and unlocked the bolt. As the barrel and action returned to the forward position, the bolt was held and was thus pulled open and the spent case ejected. All the firer had to do was place a fresh cartridge in the feedway and close the bolt. It was a simple and robust design and was used throughout the war by Soviet troops, long after comparable designs had been abandoned elsewhere. The bullet had a tungsten core, travelled at 3300 feet a second, and could pierce 25mm of armour at 500 metres range.

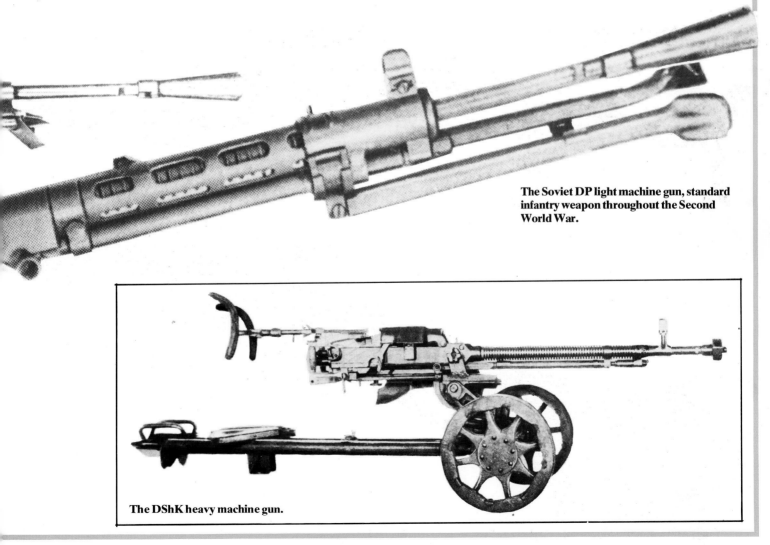

The Soviet DP light machine gun, standard infantry weapon throughout the Second World War.

The DShK heavy machine gun.

DE KNIGHT / USA

Machine gun invented by Victor De Knight of Washington DC in 1898. It was a water-cooled, tripod-mounted gun of conventional appearance, though the water jacket concealed not only the barrel but also a gas cylinder and piston. This actuated a swinging breech block, broadly similar to the Peabody or Martini rifle breech. Feed was from a belt, and the gun was chambered for the US service ·30-40 Krag cartridge. Prototypes were made by the Pratt & Whitney Engineering Company, but De Knight was unable to raise any interest in the gun and the design was eventually abandoned.

DE LISLE / Britain

The De Lisle Silent Carbine was manufactured at the Royal Small Arms Factory, Enfield Lock, during the Second World War. It was intended solely for use by Commando and clandestine forces, as a method of dealing with sentries who might otherwise sound an alarm at an inconvenient moment. Broadly speaking, it was the bolt action of the Lee-Enfield rifle, attached to the barrel of the Thompson sub-machine gun, and with a permanently attached Maxim-pattern silencer of great size and effi-

ciency. The Lee-Enfield magazine was replaced by the magazine from the Colt M1911A1 automatic pistol and the weapon fired the standard ·45 ACP cartridge. It was, without any doubt, the most silent weapon ever used during the war; the only sound was the snap of the firing pin striking the cap. It was accurate to about 300 yards range. Two versions were made; the first with a wooden stock based on that of the Lee-Enfield rifle, and the second with a pistol grip and folding metal stock for easier carriage by parachutists.

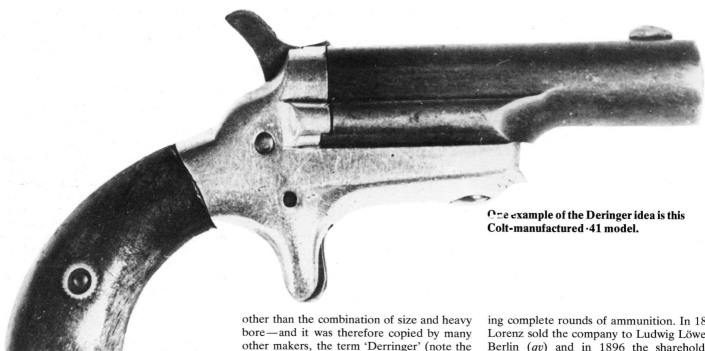

One example of the Deringer idea is this Colt-manufactured ·41 model.

DERINGER, Henry (1789–1868)

Deringer was the son of a German gunsmith who had emigrated to America. In 1806 he set up his own shop in Philadelphia and made a variety of muzzle-loading rifles and pistols. In 1825 he produced a short, heavy calibre, single shot pistol which could be easily concealed, and this attained great popularity, not to mention notoriety after John Wilkes Booth used one to assassinate President Lincoln. He failed to patent his design—indeed, it is doubtful whether he could have claimed any novelty in it

other than the combination of size and heavy bore—and it was therefore copied by many other makers, the term 'Derringer' (note the different spelling) being loosely applied to any short-barrelled single shot pistol.

After his death, the name was continued in the Deringer Revolver and Pistol Co. until 1879, producing cheap ·22, ·32 and ·38 rimfire revolvers on tip-up frames, loosely copied from the contemporary Smith & Wesson designs. The Colt company then acquired rights to the name and manufactured cartridge breech-loaders for several years under the Deringer name. Numerous 'Derringer' pistols in various calibres are still made today by several companies in Europe and the USA.

DEUTSCHE WAFFEN UND MUNITIONSFABRIK / Germany

This company, known more compactly as DWM, began in 1872 as Henri Ehrmann & Cie, manufacturing metallic cartridge cases. It went through various organisational changes, becoming the Deutsche Metallpatronenfabrik Lorenz in 1878, and by 1883 was manufactur-

ing complete rounds of ammunition. In 1889 Lorenz sold the company to Ludwig Löwe of Berlin (qv) and in 1896 the shareholders bought out Löwe and rechristened the firm DWM. By this time it had acquired factories for smokeless powder, primers and detonators and other facilities, and it had various working agreements with such companies as Alfred Nobel and Fabrique National of Belgium. With the acquisition of Löwe's engineering factories, DWM was no longer solely concerned with ammunition, but entered into weapons manufacture as well. Their telegraphic address was 'Parabellum Berlin' and they used this name on machine guns and pistols; though the latter were familiarly known as the Luger (qv).

After the First World War the arms business went into a decline for some years, and DWM were taken over by a holding company and known as the Berlin-Karlsruher Industrewerke (BKIW) until 1936 when it resumed the DWM title. In 1949 it changed once more to become Industriewerke Karlsruhe (IWK) and is currently in business manufacturing ammunition.

The DWM pistol went into production in

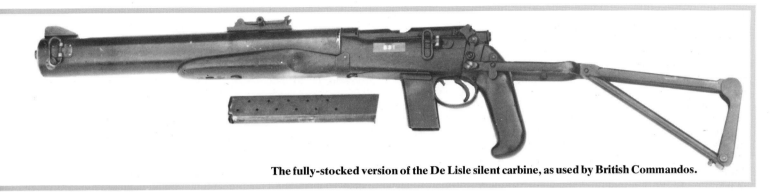

The fully-stocked version of the De Lisle silent carbine, as used by British Commandos.

1921; the provisions of the Versailles Treaty placed difficulties in the way of producing the Parabellum (Luger) pistol, and a product more aligned with the civil market was indicated. The design was simply the Browning Model 1910 in 7·65mm calibre, and it was produced by DWM with only slight changes in the contour of the grip and operation of the magazine catch. Production continued until 1929; it has been suggested that production stopped because of patent difficulties with Fabrique National, but they had long-standing business links, and it seems improbable that production would have continued for seven years in the face of outright infringement. It is more likely that production ceased because of the general trade depression of the times.

DIMANCEA, Haralamb (1855–1890)

Major, Romanian Artillery; Sub-Director of Military Pyrotechnics 1887–1890. Patentee (Br. Pat 9973/1885) of a revolver which was made in small numbers by the Gatling Arms & Ammunition Co. of Birmingham. The novelty of his design lay in the extracting and firing arrangements. On releasing a latch, the barrel and cylinder could be swung sideways and then drawn forward, a fixed extractor plate then pulling the empty cartridge cases from the chambers. The firing mechanism, entirely concealed within the frame, was a sliding firing pin which was cocked and released by a six-armed 'paddle wheel' rotated by successive pulls of the trigger. Manufacture is believed to have taken place between 1886 and 1890, and specimens in ·38 and ·45 calibre are known.

DODGE, William C. (fl. 19th C.)

Dodge was a patents examiner at the US Patent Office who gave up this occupation to devote himself to firearms design. His most important contribution was his patent covering the application of simultaneous ejection of spent cases from revolvers. This was done by a plate or star-shaped ejector which, on swivelling or hinging the revolver barrel and cylinder away from the frame, could be forced out by a lever to simultaneously eject all the cases in the cylinder by catching on their rims. His first extractor patent was taken out in 1865 and it was rapidly followed by one covering the general principle of hinged-frame revolvers. The Smith & Wesson company were quick to see the value of these, and acquired the sole rights to them in 1868. Other patents by Charles A. King allowed the ejection movement to be made automatic on the breaking open of the pistol, and the whole system was first used on the Smith & Wesson No. 3 Army revolver.

Dodge later patented a smoothbore revolver intended for the firing of buckshot or multiple-ball loads; a specimen was made and tested unsuccessfully by the US Army in 1879.

DRAGUNOV / USSR

A Soviet Army sniping rifle, first issued in the late 1960s. It is in 7·62mm calibre, firing the old rimmed rifle cartridge from the Mosin-Nagant rifle, doubtless in the interests of greater accuracy at long range than is possible with the M1943 short cartridge. The mechanism is semi-automatic, based on the Kalashnikov AK rifle (qv). It is made to an extremely high standard and is always issued with a telescope sight. The trigger mechanism has been carefully refined to give a smooth pull-off and the Dragunov is capable of the highest accuracy. A commercial version, the Medved, is on open sale, usually chambered for the 9mm×54R sporting cartridge.

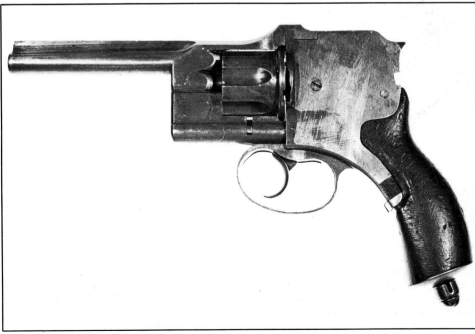

The Dimancea revolver, made by the Gatling Arms & Ammunition Company of Birmingham.

The Dreyse 9mm pistol used a very strong recoil spring which could be disconnected for easier cocking and loading.

DREYSE / *Germany*

Niklaus von Dreyse (1787–1867) was the inventor of the Needle Gun (*qv*), the bolt action breech-loading rifle which introduced breech loading as a viable military system and which paved the way for every bolt action rifle. He founded the Waffenfabrik von Dreyse in 1841 to manufacture needle guns, revolvers on the needle gun principle, and percussion revolvers. But after von Dreyse's death, and when the needle-gun was replaced in military service after the Franco-Prussian War, the company's fortunes declined until in 1889 it was taken over by a majority shareholder and re-organised as a joint stock company. Two years after this it failed completely, and the remains were bought up by the Rheinische Metallwaren und Maschinenfabrik of Dusseldorf. This was a heavy engineering company and it diversified into many fields, staying out of the firearms business for many years. At about the turn of the century, though, it re-entered the firearms field and, in memory of the illustrious forebear, used the name Dreyse as a trade name on their products. Although the company continued in the firearms business, eventually adopting the name Rheinmetall (*qv*) and

later Rheinmetall-Borsig (which it remains today), it has not used the Dreyse style on any weapons made since 1918.

The Dreyse weapons were actually designed by Louis Schmeisser, at that time in the company's employ, and the first pistol appeared in 1907. It was an unusual design; the slide was cranked, the major portion lying on top of the fixed barrel and the shorter section forming the breech block and lying behind the barrel, enclosed in a slab-sided casing at the rear of the frame. The recoil spring was around the barrel, linked to the slide, and pulling back the upper portion of the slide caused the breech block section to appear through a hole at the rear of the frame. Produced only in 7·65mm calibre, it continued to be made throughout the First World War, numbers being taken by the German Army as substitute standard weapons.

A 6·35mm pistol appeared next; this was of fairly conventional form, resembling the Browning 1906 in appearance but somewhat different in construction. The third model was a 9mm pistol, an enlarged version of the 7·65mm type but chambered for the 9mm Parabellum cartridge. Since the pistol was a blowback, this demanded a very strong return

spring, and to cock the pistol in the normal way by pulling back the slide was extremely difficult. Schmeisser overcame this by fitting a rib on top of the slide, linking the slide to the return spring: this rib could be lifted, uncoupling the slide from the spring and allowing the slide to be pulled back to cock and charge the pistol. With the slide returned to its forward position, the rib was pressed down to re-engage slide and return spring ready for firing. This pistol was developed in 1911 for commercial sale but met with little success; offered to

The German Army MG13, a conversion of the 1910 Model Dreyse to provide a light machine gun in the 1930s.

The Schmeisser-designed Dreyse 7·65mm pocket pistol.

the German Army in 1914 it was turned down, and less than 2000 were made before production ended in 1917.

The Dreyse machine gun was patented in 1907. This was a short recoil gun, the breech being locked and unlocked by being moved up and down by cam tracks inside the gun body. An accelerator was fitted, to speed up the rate of fire, and the weapon, as was common in those days, was water-cooled and belt fed. It was produced as the MG10 but the German Army were firmly committed to their Maxim '08 model and bought only a few of the Dreyse weapons. During the First World War, though, the shortage of machine guns led to numbers of Dreyse models being taken by the Army, and a number were modified by fitting a bipod and shoulder stock to turn them into rudimentary light machine guns for use in the Middle East, and in this form they were known as the MG15.

After the war the remaining Dreyse MG10 and MG15 guns were dismantled and rebuilt into air-cooled, magazine-fed weapons and issued to the Reichswehr as their squad light machine gun, the MG13. These were later replaced by more modern designs and were sold to the Portuguese Army in 1938.

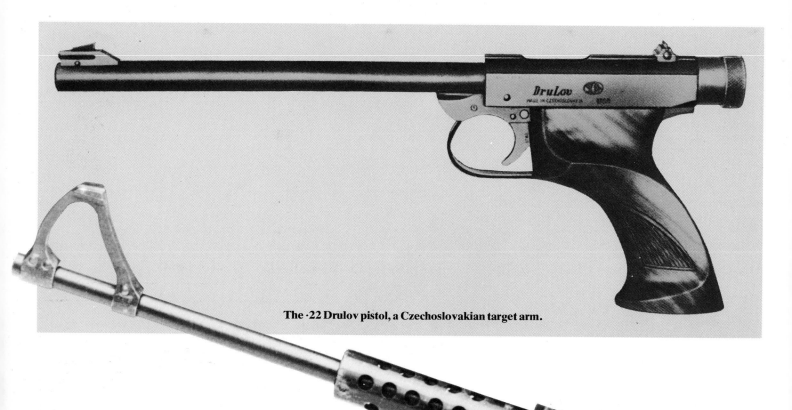

The ·22 Drulov pistol, a Czechoslovakian target arm.

DROR/*Israel*
A recoil-operated light machine gun developed in Israel in the late 1940s, and apparently based on the Johnson M1944 (*qv*) design. It was not successful, the principal defects being the side-mounted magazine, which tended to upset the balance of the weapon, and the recoiling action of the barrel in its slide which, in a desert environment, led to excessive wear and reduced accuracy. Chambered for the 7·92mm Mauser cartridge, it was later superseded by the Fabrique National MAG machine gun.

DRULOV/*Czechoslovakia*
A single-shot ·22 pistol for competition shooting; originally made by Druzstvo Lovena of Prague, it is now made by the Dilo National-Cooperative of Svratovch and distributed by the Omnipol export agency. Breech closure is done by a rotating bolt operated by a knurled grip at its rear end; inside the bolt is the usual axial striker and spring. The barrel is 25cm long and the front and rear sights are fully adjustable. In spite of its export status, it is rarely seen outside Central Europe.

The DROR machine gun, an adaptation of the Johnson design, briefly used by the Israeli Army.

DUX / *Spain*

A submachine gun manufactured by the Fabrica de Armas de Oviedo, Spain. The basic design was that of the Finnish M-44, which in turn was derived from the Soviet PPS-42, and the weapon was designed by Willi Daugs (*qv*). Daugs had manufactured the Finn weapon and left Finland at the end of the war, taking the drawings with him. He eventually arrived in Spain, and in conjunction with Vorgrimmler, an ex-Mauser engineer, designed the improved M-44 which he called the Dux. One thousand DUX-53 guns were bought by the West German Border Police in 1954, and the German Army then took an interest in the design. They bought 25 guns and passed some of them to various German manufacturers to have them modified in various ways for trial. After tests of these modified guns, J. G. Anschutz were given a contract to develop an improved model, and Daugs went to Germany to act as a consultant. Anschutz eventually produced an improved version, the DUX-59; this had various small changes to the magazine housing, buttstock, safety catch and barrel jacket, but it was still recognisably a descendant of the PPS-42. But at about the time that Anschutz perfected this design, Daugs left Germany and withdrew the licensing rights from Anschutz. The German Army, having already waited five years and now apparently doomed to wait an indeterminate time until Daugs and Anschutz settled their differences, gave up the Dux project completely and opted for a different weapon. Anschutz washed their hands of the whole affair, Daugs vanished, and the Dux submachine gun expired.

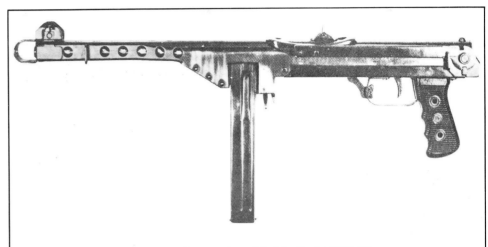

The Dux-53 submachine gun, an improved model of the Soviet PPS-43.

Though dressed up with a new stamped body and a new barrel jacket, the Dux-59 is really not much different from the original PPS model.

ECHASA / *Spain*

Trade name of Echave y Arizmendi SA of Eibar, Spain, manufacturers of pistols. The company was established about 1911 and concentrated entirely upon automatic pistols; their early products were of moderate quality, but in the 1930s this improved and they were one of the few pistol makers allowed to restart after the Civil War. Much of their trade was exported, but this was severely curtailed by the American Gun Control Act of 1968 and the company went out of business in 1970.

The early pistols were copies of the Browning Model 1906, cheap and simple blowback pocket automatics in 6·35mm and 7·65mm calibres, sold under the names Bronco, EA, Lightning, Pathfinder, Protector and Selecta. The Selecta was the last of this line and was of somewhat better quality than the others. After the Second World War they produced a completely new model, first known as the Fast, a 7·65mm blowback with double-action lock, resembling the German Walther Model PP

pistol. In the early 1950s the Echasa trademark was adopted, and the Fast pistol was then marketed as the Echasa; from the markings seen on different pistols, it seems that the Echasa was for European sale and the Fast for export to the USA. Finally, in the late 1950s, the company produced the Lur Panzer, a ·22 blowback pistol resembling the Luger; it had a much simpler toggle mechanism, however, which appears to have been based on the German patents of the Erma company.

ECHEVERRIA / *Spain*

Star-Bonifacio Echeverria SA, of Eibar, Spain, a company manufacturing a variety of firearms under the trade name Star. The firm began in about 1908, making an automatic pistol; it later developed a wide range of pistols and then added sporting guns and submachine guns, but the company's records were destroyed during the Spanish Civil War and precise details of their products are no longer known. After that war, the company were one of the few permitted to continue with the manufacture of firearms.

The original automatic pistol, produced in 1908, was a blowback weapon based broadly on the design of the Mannlicher Model 1901 pistol, but with a detachable magazine in the butt. Improvements in detail took place, and the type remained in production until 1929, but in the early 1920s a model based on the lines of the Colt M1911 US Army pistol, using the Browning method of breech locking, was

A pocket pistol by Echeverria, the Star 'Starlet' model in 6·35mm calibre.

introduced as the Star Model A, and this pattern gradually superseded the earlier one. The subsequent pistols of this type were in a lettered series—A, B, C, etc.—and can be found in every commercially viable calibre. Among the more notable have been the Model D in 9mm Short calibre, used by the Spanish police forces; the Model F, a sporting and competition ·22 pistol; the Model MD, which had a selector to allow full automatic fire; and the Model PD, a recently-introduced ·45 pistol of remarkably small dimensions. The Super B model in 9mm Parabellum calibre is currently the standard pistol of the Spanish army.

During the 1930s the company began developments of submachine guns, the designers being V. Suinaga and Isidor Irusta. Their first effort was the SI-34, a self-loading carbine which fired the 9mm Largo pistol cartridge. This was then modified to allow automatic fire and was designated the SI-35; it was unusual for having a control mechanism which allowed the rate of fire to be changed at will from 300 to 700 rounds a minute. This mechanism was unduly complex, and the design was then simplified to produce the RU-35 model and finally the rate-of-fire regulator was removed entirely for the TN-35 model. All these weapons were of the delayed blowback type, using a wedge-block to slow the opening of the bolt; they were chambered for the 9mm Largo cartridge and used 30-round box magazines. Small numbers of the SI-35 and RU-35 were used in the Spanish Civil War, but production never reached a level sufficient to arm major units.

In 1942 the company acquired mechanical drawings of the German MP-40 submachine gun and, using these as a basis, developed their Model Z-45. It resembled the German weapon but incorporated a perforated barrel jacket and a muzzle compensator. Production began in mid-1944 and it was adopted by the Spanish armed forces and sold overseas. The Z-45 has since been replaced by the Z-62, a lighter weapon, easier to manufacture, and which incorporates an automatic safety device which prevents accidental firing.

EGG / Britain

English gunmaking family, active from c.1750 to c.1880. The most famous member was Durs Egg, who worked in London at the latter part of the 18th century and was responsible for numbers of fine duelling pistols, ingenious double-barrelled pistols, and a breech-loading military carbine issued to four Dragoon regiments in 1784–1785, although it was not further adopted. He was also associated with the French gunsmith Pauly (*qv*) when the latter came to England in 1812, and Egg is believed to have made a compression-ignition pistol to Pauly's design.

Joseph Egg, another member of the family, claimed to have been one of the originators of the percussion cap, and doubtless had a hand in the perfection of the idea. Charles, Henry and a second Durs were in business as gunsmiths in London at various dates until 1880.

The Star 9mm Model B, a locked-breech pistol currently used by the Spanish armed forces.

EM/*Britain*

Initials standing for Enfield Model and applied to a number of experimental weapons during the period 1940–1950. The most important were as follows:

EM1 In 1945 the British Army decided to adopt a self-loading rifle. As a first step, an 'Ideal Calibre Committee' sat and recommended ·276 inch (7mm) as the new calibre, together with a short-case cartridge. This (frequently known as the ·280 cartridge) was developed, and work began on a suitable rifle, the EM1. This was gas-operated and used a roller locking system similar to that later seen on the CETME (*qv*) rifle. The design was quite unusual, the 'bull-pup' configuration being adopted. In this layout, the bolt and breech are as far back on the rifle as possible, close to the end of the butt, so that they are actually behind the firer's face when he takes aim. This allows the maximum barrel length to be acommodated within a given length of rifle and, in effect, allows the overall length of a rifle to be reduced without affecting the working length of the barrel. Other features which follow from

this are the location of the magazine behind the pistol-grip, and the need to raise the sight line well above the weapon to compensate for the 'straight-line' layout. To avoid an easily-damaged post foresight, the EM1 used a unity-power optical sight contained in a permanently-attached carrying handle above the barrel. Steel pressings and plastic material were incorporated in the design in order to simplify production and reduce expense. However, difficulties arose in manufacturing specimens for trial, and due to the mechanical complexities of the design, it was abandoned.

EM2 This was developed at the same time as the EM1 but by a different design team. It, too, was of the 'bull-pup' type, and gas operated, but it used a less complicated breech locking system which resembled that of the Russian Degtyarev machine guns, two locking plates being forced sideways out of the bolt by the passage of the firing pin. During 1949 the EM2 was extensively tested in Britain, and in 1950 in the USA, giving excellent results in all its trials. The US Ordnance Department, however, were apparently unable to comprehend

the reasoning behind the small calibre/short cartridge concept, and insisted that the cartridge was insufficiently powerful for military use. In 1951 it was announced that the EM2 would enter British service as the Rifle No. 9, but later in that year, after meetings of Defence Ministers of the UK, USA, Canada and France, this decision was revoked and a fresh agreement reached to develop a new cartridge to become the NATO standard round. In 1957 the 7·62mm cartridge was adopted; attempts were made to adapt the EM2 design to this round, but they were not successful and the project was brought to an end.

MCEM1 Machine Carbine EM1 was no relation to the rifle EM1; this was designed by Turpin, co-inventor of the Sten gun, in about 1944. It was a compact weapon with removeable stock, perforated barrel jacket, and an ingenious double-column magazine. It was abandoned in favour of the EM3 model.

MCEM2 Submachine gun design by Lieut. Podzenkowski of the Polish Army, a member of the Polish design team working at Enfield during and after the war. It was very short, and

The first British assault rifle design, the Enfield EM1.

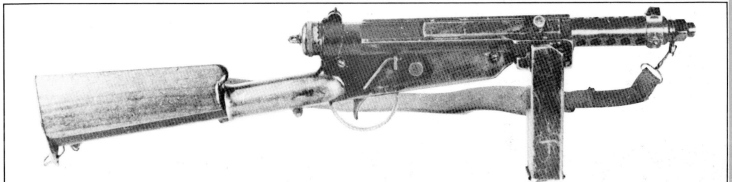

Top: The MCEM6 submachine gun designed by Podzenowski.
Centre: The MCEM1 submachine gun designed by Turpin.
Bottom: The EM2 automatic rifle.

the stock could be removed and the rest of the gun placed inside it for carriage. The most notable feature of this design was the bolt, which was hollowed out at the front end so as to enclose the breech when closed. In the firing position, some seven inches of the barrel were inside the bolt, and this 'overhung' bolt is among the first of its kind. However, the weapon had other defects, notably a very small magazine and far too high a rate of fire, and it was not further developed.

MCEM3 Turpin's improved MCEM1, using a single-column magazine and a faster rate of fire.

MCEM4 Silenced submachine gun of which little record survives; it was probably de-veloped by Lieut. Kulikowski, another of the Polish design team, in 1945.

MCEM5 Another submachine gun design of which no record now exists.

MCEM6 Podzenkowski's improved MCEM2 design. It was slightly longer and used a heavier bolt to bring the rate of fire down to a practical figure. Comparative tests of the MCEM2, 3 and 6 took place in 1946, after which it was decided to concentrate on improving the MCEM3. Work continued for another year, but in the end it was seen that the EM3 had an insoluble overheating problem, becoming too hot to hold when fired for any length of time, and the whole Enfield submachine gun de-velopment programme was brought to a close.

ENFIELD/*Britain*

Name applied to various British military arms, derived from their inception or production at the Royal Small Arms Factory, Enfield Lock, Middlesex, which was founded in 1856.

The first weapon to bear the name was actually designed before the factory was built to produce it; this was the Enfield Rifle Musket, Pattern 1852, a ·577 muzzle-loading single shot percussion rifle firing a Pritchett expanding bullet. The first rifle to be generally issued to British troops, and the last muzzle-loader, it was a highly successful weapon which gave good service in the latter part of the Crimean War and in India. It was replaced by the Snider (*qv*) conversion and then by the Martini-Henry (*qv*) breechloaders, and the Enfield name next appeared on an Enfield-Martini ·402 rifle of 1886, which used Metford (*qv*) rifling; but due to impending improvements, though 70,000 of these were made they were never issued.

In 1879, due to difficulty in obtaining a supply of revolvers from trade sources, the factory received instructions to develop a service revolver, and in only 16 days produced drawings and had them approved. The prototypes were sent for trial in January 1880, and the design was approved in August as the 'Pistol, Revolver, Breech-loading, Enfield, Mark 1'. It was a six-shot, hinged-frame revolver in ·476 calibre, with an unusual extraction system; hinging the barrel down pulled the cylinder forward but left the extractor plate in place, in effect drawing the cylinder off the empty cases. As might be expected, the defect

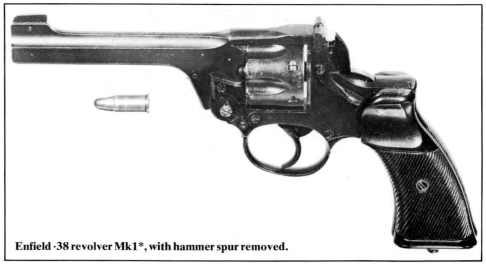

Enfield ·38 revolver Mk1*, with hammer spur removed.

in this system was that the bottom case frequently failed to drop out of the frame. Small improvements were seen to be needed and a Mark 2 pistol was issued in March 1882; the principal changes were the tapered-boring of the chambers to improve accuracy, and the installation of a hammer lock to prevent the pistol being accidentally fired while loading.

The Lee-Enfield rifle was the next weapon to bear the Enfield name; details will be found under that heading. But the Lee-Enfield ran into severe criticism during the early 1900s (most of which was quite unjustified) and Enfield were instructed to develop a new rifle. This took the form of a ·276 weapon using a

Mauser-type bolt and magazine and an extremely powerful cartridge. It was not a success on its first trials, but development was hurriedly shelved on the outbreak of war in 1914. The grave shortage of rifles, however, led to this Pattern 1913 design being re-modelled to take the standard ·303 service cartridge, and contracts for the manufacture of several million rifles were given to three American companies. This course was adopted because the new rifle (now called the Pattern 1914) was easier to mass-produce than was the Lee-Enfield.

When the United States entered the war in 1917, it too was faced with a rifle shortage and, since the machinery for producing the Pattern

The newly-developed 4·85mm Individual Weapon.

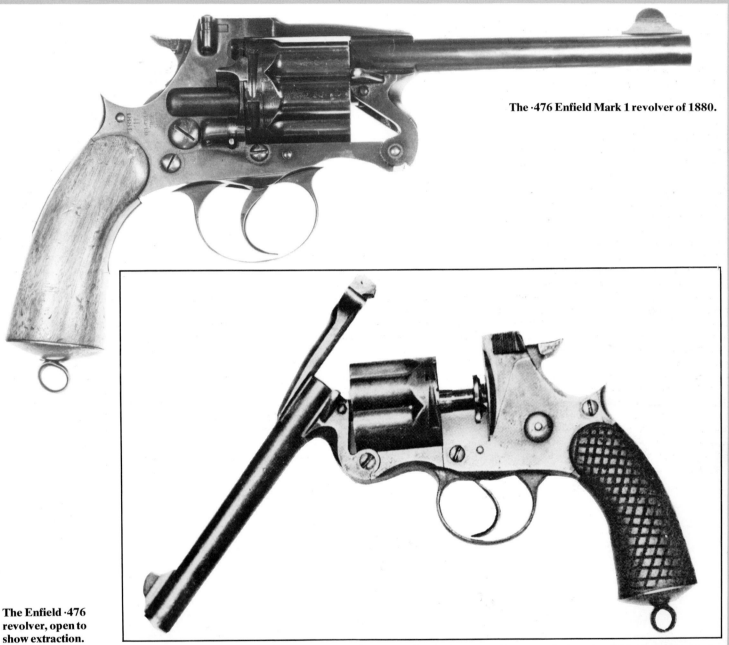

The ·476 Enfield Mark 1 revolver of 1880.

The Enfield ·476 revolver, open to show extraction.

1914 was in existence in America, the US authorities modified the design once more, this time to accept the American Army's ·30 cartridge. In this form it was put into production as the Enfield Rifle M1917 or, in British nomenclature, the Pattern 17. By this time production of Lee-Enfield rifles in Britain was keeping pace with demand, and the British Government were happy to terminate their contracts and free the US manufacturing plant for production of the American model.

In the post-First World War years the British Army elected to abandon the ·455 calibre for revolvers and adopt a ·38 instead. A design by Webley (who had provided all the service revolvers since the demise of the original Enfield in the late 1880s) was turned down and an Enfield design adopted. In broad terms it was a copy of the Webley but with some small modifications to the lockwork. This remained the service sidearm until the adoption of an automatic pistol in the 1950s.

Enfield was the principal manufacturing plant for the British Army, and produced such weapons as the Bren light machine gun (qv) and the Boys anti-tank rifle (qv). At the same time it initiated design studies on automatic rifles and submachine guns, which will be found detailed under EM, the abbreviation adopted for 'Enfield Model' experimental weapons.

The latest designs to emerge from Enfield are the 4·85mm Individual Weapon (rifle) and Light Support Weapon (light machine gun) which were announced in 1976. Both bear some resemblance to earlier EM designs but have a much different mechanism and both use a number of common components. They are currently (with their 4·85mm cartridge) undergoing evaluation in a comparative NATO trial to determine the standard small-arm calibre for the 1980s.

ERMA/*Germany*

Acronym derived from the full title: Erfurter Maschinenwerke B. Giepel GmbH, a German company which originated in Erfurt after the First World War and which is now located in Dachau, West Germany.

The company is probably best-known for the series of submachine guns developed from about 1925 onward, designed by Heinrich Vollmer and Berthold Giepel. The principal design feature was the collection of the bolt, firing pin and return spring into a self-contained unit enclosed within a telescoping tubular casing; this patented feature made assembly of the weapon very easy and also proofed the most vital parts against dust and dirt. The first submachine gun incorporating this unit was produced in 1930 and achieved limited overseas sales. It featured a wooden stock, a short vertical wooden handgrip, a side-mounted magazine and a comparatively long, tapering barrel. In about 1934 an improved model, using a perforated barrel jacket, was introduced as the EMP (Erma Machine Pistol). First production went to the Yugoslavian Army and was fitted with a bayonet; it was later adopted by the German Army in some quantity, and numbers appeared in the Spanish Civil War.

In 1938, in response to a military demand, Erma produced a totally new model, the MP-38, which was immediately adopted by the

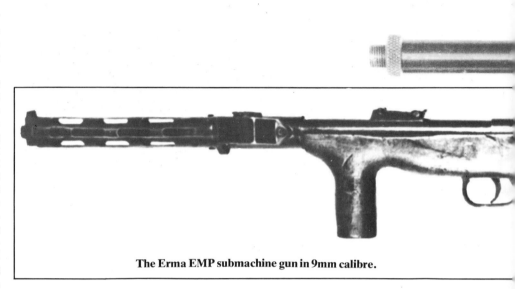

The Erma EMP submachine gun in 9mm calibre.

German Army, and became the virtual trademark of the Wehrmacht soldier. It broke new ground by being the first military weapon to eschew the use of wood; it was entirely made of steel or plastic. It was also the first weapon to have a folding metal butt-stock. Although produced in quantity, it was still an expensive production task, and after the outbreak of war it was slightly simplified and redesigned so as to

make manufacture quicker and cheaper, and in this form it became the MP-40. The external differences were small; the easiest recognition feature is the magazine housing which is smooth-sided and pierced with a large hole in the MP-38, but corrugated and without a hole in the MP-40.

The Erma MP-38/40 was one of the most familiar weapons of the Second World War.

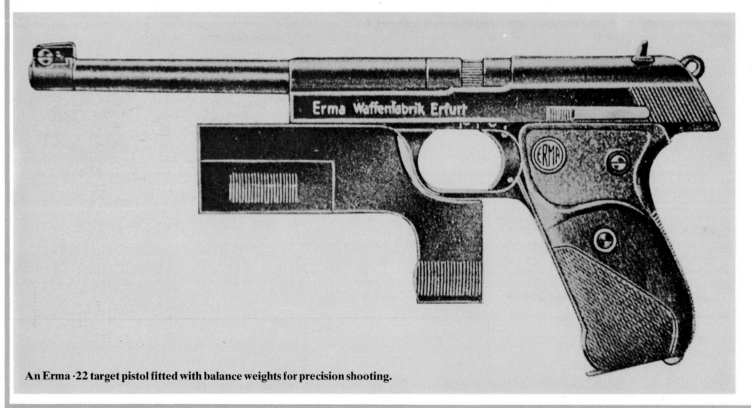

An Erma ·22 target pistol fitted with balance weights for precision shooting.

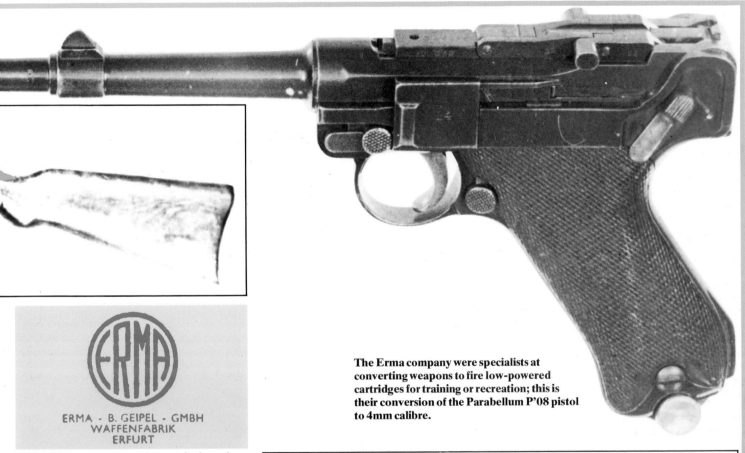

ERMA - B. GEIPEL - GMBH
WAFFENFABRIK
ERFURT

The Erma company also made ingenious conversion units comprising a special barrel and breech mechanism, which could be fitted into the standard army rifle and the Luger 08 pistol to permit their use with special 4mm calibre training ammunition. They then went on to manufacture a ·22 automatic pistol for target-shooting and then ·22 rifles for sporting and competitive shooting, until 1939.

In postwar years the company returned to the submachine gun field in the late 1950s, producing a number of limited-production models for evaluation by the Bundeswehr. None were found suitable and no more submachine gun designs have been produced since the early 1960s. Instead, Erma reverted to the pistol field and patented an ingenious variation of the Luger toggle lock, based on the mechanism used in the pre-war training devices, and then incorporated this into a design of pistol based on the Luger. In fact the breech is now no longer locked but operates in the blowback mode, the lines of force on the toggle acting so as to open it by spent case pressure alone. Since the introduction of the ·22 calibre EP-22 in 1964, other models in 7·65mm and 9mm Short calibre have been placed on sale. Production of all types is understood to have reached some 70,000 within ten years.

The Erma company were specialists at converting weapons to fire low-powered cartridges for training or recreation; this is their conversion of the Parabellum P'08 pistol to 4mm calibre.

The Erma KGP-22 pistol, based on the lines of the Parabellum but with a simpler action.

EVANS, Warren (*fl. 1860–1885*)
American inventor who patented a repeating rifle in 1868. Chambered for a ·44 rimfire cartridge, it featured a somewhat oversized butt-stock which concealed an Archimedean screw ammunition carrier which contained 26 cartridges. An under-lever operated the breech mechanism and rotated the carrier, the

pitch of the screw being sufficient to deliver one cartridge for each stroke of the lever. The Evans Magazine Rifle Company was set up in Mechanic's Falls, Maine, in 1871 and the rifle was favourably received. It was tested by various military authorities, and in 1878 the Russian Rifle Test Commission recommended the adoption of the Evans Carbine for the Russian

Navy. It is unlikely that many were so adopted, since the company went out of business in 1880. The principal defect of the Evans, so far as military service was concerned, was the slow and cumbersome process of loading up the ammunition carrier; only if it was fully loaded and rotated by 26 strokes of the operating lever was the first round delivered to the breech.

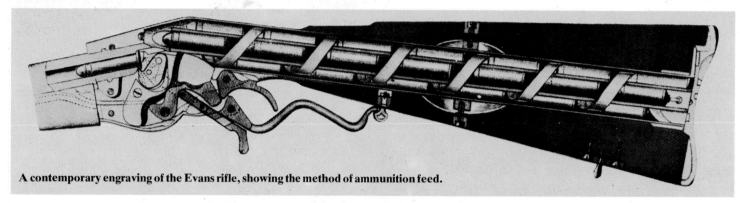

A contemporary engraving of the Evans rifle, showing the method of ammunition feed.

FABRIQUE NATIONAL/*Belgium*
Fabrique National d'Armes de Guerre of Herstal, Belgium (usually referred to in abbreviated form as 'FN') was founded in 1889 for the purpose of manufacturing Mauser rifles under license, to equip the Belgian Army. In 1900 John M. Browning (*qv*) joined the company, whereupon it began production of automatic pistols under the Browning name, then

automatic shotguns and sporting rifles, and later produced the military Browning Automatic Rifle for sale in Europe. Until the late 1930s contract manufacture of these and other military designs built under license occupied the factory, but shortly before the Second World War a design team began working on a fresh generation of weapons. This work was interrupted by the war and the subsequent German

occupation, but was resumed in 1945.
    The SAFN (Semi-Automatic, FN) rifle was the first result of this work. It was designed by Dieudonne Saive with the intention of providing the Belgian Army with a new semi-automatic rifle in 1940; in the event, it appeared in 1949, was accepted by the Belgian Army, and was then widely sold overseas in a variety of calibres. It was gas operated, a cylin-

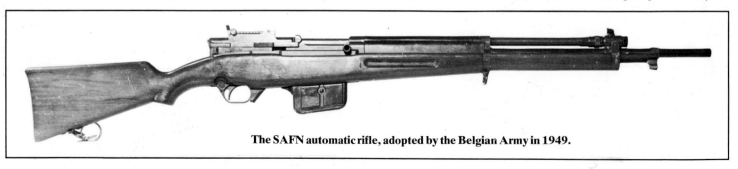

The SAFN automatic rifle, adopted by the Belgian Army in 1949.

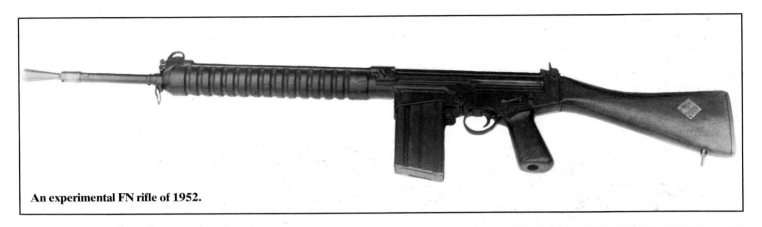

An experimental FN rifle of 1952.

The MAG general-purpose machine gun on tripod mounting.

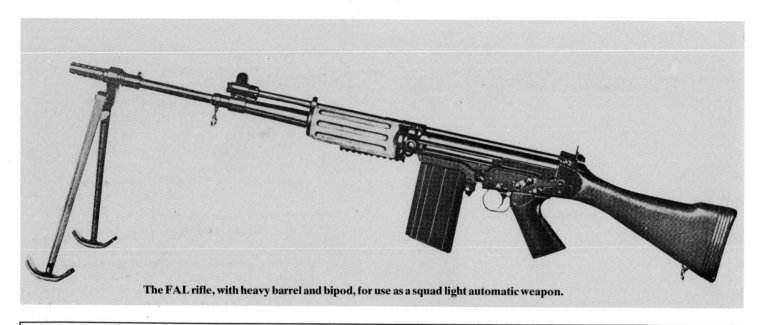

The FAL rifle, with heavy barrel and bipod, for use as a squad light automatic weapon.

The 5·56mm CAL rifle.

der above the barrel carrying a short-stroke piston which moved back only sufficiently to strike the bolt carrier and impart movement. Thereafter the impetus drove the carrier back and cam tracks inside it lifted the bolt out of engagement with locking surfaces in the gun body.

Although the SAFN achieved considerable success, it did not entirely satisfy Saive who, assisted by Ernest Vervier, eventually produced a fresh design, chambered for the new 7·62mm NATO cartridge. This became the FAL—Fusil Automatique Légère—which was subsequently adopted by armies throughout the world, including those of Britain, Canada, the Netherlands and India. The FAL is gas operated, using a bolt carrier with tipping bolt much as the SAFN. Various models with heavier barrels, bipods, and facility for automatic fire are used in the light machine gun role by several countries.

With the growing popularity of assault rifles in the 5·56mm calibre, a new design based on the general outline of the FAL and known as the CAL (qv)—Carabine Automatique Légère—has recently been developed.

The FN company have, of course, manufactured all the various types of Browning machine guns at one time or another, and produced the Browning Automatic Rifle in a number of variant styles to suit the requirements of different countries. In the early 1950s Ernest Vervier developed the completely new MAG—Mitrailleuse à Gaz—a gas operated, belt-fed weapon designed as a general purpose machine gun, i.e. one which can be carried by the soldier as the squad automatic weapon or used as a tripod-mounted heavy support weapon, as the situation dictates. Normally found in 7·62mm NATO calibre, it has been produced in other chamberings to suit particular countries. Widely adopted as an infantry machine gun, it has recently been taken into service in the US Army as a tank machine gun.

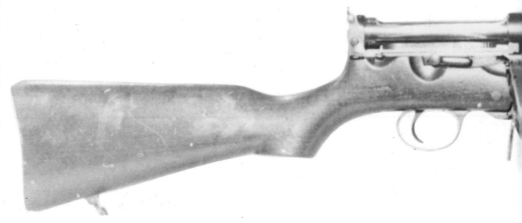

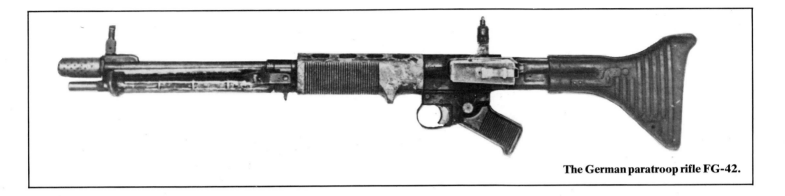

The German paratroop rifle FG-42.

FAFSCHAMPS, Captain *(fl. c.1850)*

A Belgian Army officer of whom little is recorded except that he was the original inventor of the Mitrailleuse (*qv*) machine gun. In 1851 he submitted drawings and a working prototype to the Belgian engineer Joseph Montigny. Montigny saw that the design had promise, but he also saw that it needed considerable improvement, and he bought Fafschamp's design outright. He then renamed the improved weapon the Montigny Mitrailleuse, and Fafschamp's part in it was soon forgotten.

FAGNUS / *Belgium*

The company of A. Fagnus et Cie of Liège was established in the early 19th century and manufactured a range of inexpensive solid-frame pinfire revolvers, many of which were exported and which appeared on the market bearing local gunsmith's names. In the 1870s they produced a hinged-frame centre fire revolver in which the barrel unit was pinned to the frame behind the standing breech and opened upwards. Frame and barrel unit were locked together for firing by a long actuating lever which formed the major part of the trigger-guard and was pivoted in front of the cylinder. Forcing this lever down released the barrel unit, which could then be swung up to expose the rear of the cylinder; further pressure on the lever would then thrust the extractor unit out from the cylinder and eject the empty cases. Like many patent extracting systems, it was too unwieldy to compete with the more conventional downward-hinged frame or side-opening cylinder types, and the Fagnus company ceased production in the late 1880s.

FALLSCHIRMGEWEHR 42 / *Germany*

The FG42 was a selective-fire automatic rifle designed specifically for use by German airborne troops. A requirement was stated in 1940, and two companies Rheinmetall and Krieghoff, produced prototypes. The Rheinmetall design was accepted, but since that company could not find space for production, manufacture was done by Krieghoff.

The weapon was designed to be an automatic rifle which could also function as a light machine gun. It was gas operated and fired the standard 7·92mm Mauser cartridge. The bolt was rotated to lock into the breech, and the firing mechanism was so arranged that for single shots the bolt was closed before the firing pin was struck, but in automatic fire the bolt was held open between bursts of fire so that the barrel and breech could cool down. This gave better accuracy for single-shot fire while reducing the chance of a 'cook-off' after a burst of automatic fire. The gun was fed from a box magazine at the left side.

By the time the FG42 was perfected, though, the German airborne troops were of less importance, and only about 7000 rifles were ever made. Nevertheless, it was an important step in the development of selective-fire rifles, and it achieved the near-impossible feat of being a serviceable automatic rifle of light weight yet firing an old-fashioned full-power cartridge.

FARQUHAR-HILL / *Britain*

Designed by Col. M. G. Farquhar of Aboyne (Scotland) and A. H. Hill of Birmingham, this rifle was first patented in 1906, though many subsequent patents overlapped with this and modified it, and several of them were equally applicable to the Beardmore-Farquhar (*qv*) machine gun. The first design was recoil-operated, but in 1909 this was changed in favour of gas operation. Like the machine gun design, the gas piston placed a load on to a spring which then exerted force on the breech block, a system which absorbed recoil and made the weapon very smooth in its action. Models with various arrangements of stock and magazine were produced and submitted for military test between 1912 and the early 1920s, but they were not found suitable for service.

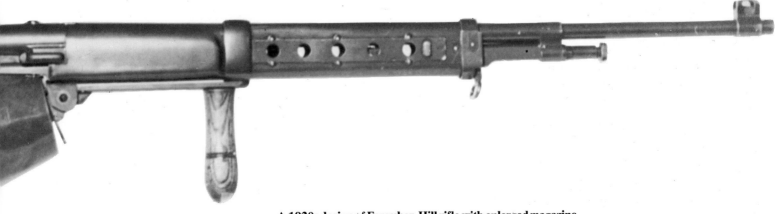

A 1920s design of Farquhar-Hill rifle with enlarged magazine.

FAULKNER GUN/*Britain*
Name applied to the Besal machine gun design so as not to invite confusion with the existing BESA gun. For further details see under BESAL.

FBP/*Portugal*
Fabrica do Braca do Prato, Lisbon; manufacturing arsenal of the Portuguese Government, which lends its name to the FBP submachine gun produced there in the 1950s. It was designed by Major Cardoso of the Portuguese Army in 1948 after analysis of successful designs and is an amalgam of features taken from other weapons. The bolt and operating spring are enclosed in a telescoping casing, as in the Vollmer-designed German MP38, and the attachment of the barrel and the cocking lever are also copied from the same gun. The pressed-metal frame and telescoping wire butt are from the American M3, while the stepped barrel and bayonet attachment are of Cardoso's design. The result was reliable and robust, though users have spoken of poor accuracy. Manufacture ceased some years ago.

FEDEROV, Vladimir G. *(1874–1942)*
Vladimir Federov (sometimes spelled Fyodorov) entered the Russian Artillery Academy in 1897, graduating in 1900, and was assigned to the Arms Test Commission for duty. In 1905 he produced his first design, a gas-actuated conversion of the Mosin-Nagant bolt action rifle, and then produced a completely new design for a recoil-actuated self-loading rifle. This latter was approved in principle, and Federov, together with Degtyarev (*qv*) constructed a prototype. He soon realised that the existing 7·62mm service cartridge was ill-suited to an automatic rifle design and he began afresh, using the Japanese 6·5mm cartridge as the basis of a new design. In 1916 he produced the Avtomat (*qv*) rifle. Production was barely begun before it was interrupted by the Revolution, but after some delay work was resumed under Soviet control, and numbers of

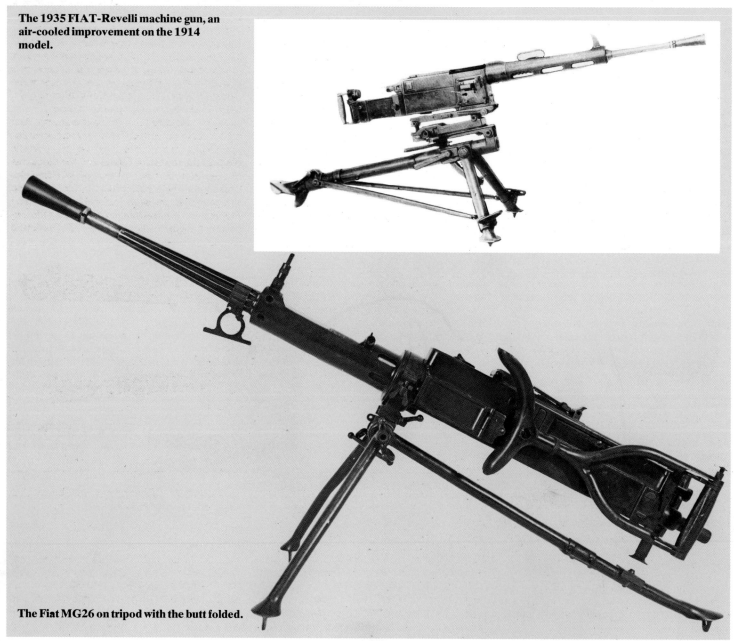

The 1935 FIAT-Revelli machine gun, an air-cooled improvement on the 1914 model.

The Fiat MG26 on tripod with the butt folded.

the Avtomat were made for the Red Army.

After the Revolution, Federov was given an arms factory to manage, and under his control and encouragement such designers as Degtyarev, Shpagin and Simonov were to develop the weapons which armed the Soviet forces during the Second World War. In 1943 he was promoted Lieutenant-General of the Artillery Technical Service, and he was to receive many awards and decorations, including the Order of Lenin. In addition to his eminence as a designer and administrator, he wrote several notable historical and technical works on firearms and their development, though, unfortunately, none have ever been translated into English.

FIAT / *Italy*

Originally the Fabricca Italia de Automobiles Torino, or F.I.A.T., this form was changed to FIAT in 1906. The company is, of course, more widely-known for its cars, but during the First World War it became involved in arms production, manufacturing the Revelli (*qv*) M1914 machine gun. A separate company, known as SAFAT (Société Anonyme Fiat Armamente, Torino) was set up to develop and produce military weapons, but during the 1920s Fiat changed their minds and decided there was little future in this field, and sold SAFAT to the Ernesto Breda company. But in 1934 the Fiat company were asked to put the Revelli machine gun into production once

more, but modified to accept the new 8mm cartridge just adopted by the Italian Army. The necessary modification was done, and, in addition, the design was totally changed from a magazine-fed water-cooled weapon to a belt-fed air-cooled one. A fluted chamber was incorporated to overcome the M1914's extraction problems, but without much success, and, in general, the Fiat Model 35 machine gun was worse than the 1914 gun it had set out to improve upon.

FIDJELAND / *Norway*

Terje Fidjeland was a gunmaker of Iveland, Kristiassand, Norway, who was an assiduous inventor and patentee in the 1900s. Together with Johan Schwarz, he formed the Schwarz-Fidjelands Gevaersyndikat to promote various of these patents; among them were such items as a rotary rifle magazine, ammunition storage in a butt compartment, and a retractable permanently-fitted bayonet. None of these ideas appear to have prospered. He was also active in developing (again with Schwarz) an automatic rifle; this was demonstrated successfully in London in July 1905 but does not appear to have been taken further. Two of Fidjeland's patented features in this gas-operated weapon are worthy of recognition, since they were widely adopted in later years and hailed as new, their origin being forgotten. His British Patent 5439 of 1901 covers the application of a perforated jacket around a rifle barrel in order to allow the escape of heat; such jackets have appeared on innumerable weapons since, and are often ascribed to Schmeisser, who used one on the first Bergmann submachine gun. Fidjeland's British Patent 28066 of 1903 relates to tapping gas from the muzzle of the rifle and directing it back through a tube to act directly on the breech block. This has come into general use in recent years, and has usually been credited to the Swedish designer Ljungmann. The Kalashnikov (*qv*), for example, the most widely distributed rifle in history, is gas-operated.

FINNEGAN, Peter H. *(fl. 1885–1895)*

Sales agent for the American Minneapolis Fire Arms Co. c.1890, dealing in the Turbiaux repeating pistol. In 1892 Finnegan formed the Chicago Firearms Co. and purchased the Turbiaux patent, tools and stock from the Minneapolis company. He then negotiated with the Ames Sword Company for them to make him 25,000 pistols. The Ames Company employed one E. M. Crouch to design the necessary machinery, and Crouch made some improve-

ments to the pistol which Finnegan patented, notably a grip safety device. Crouch then set up independently as a sub-contractor to make the pistols for Ames but failed to produce the quantity demanded in the time specified. An involved lawsuit ensued, which Finnegan won, the Ames company buying the patents, etc. from Finnegan by way of reparation. Ames then attempted to market the pistol until about 1910, though without much success.

FLOBERT, Louis *(fl. mid-19th C.)*

Louis Flobert was a Parisian gunsmith who, in 1845, placed a small bullet in the mouth of a percussion cap and thereby invented the rimfire cartridge. His object was to produce a low-powered round for indoor target shooting, and the 'Flobert cap' and his associated single-shot pistols and rifles became immensely popular. He also developed a simple rolling-block breech mechanism in which the breech was closed by a block hinged below the axis of the barrel. After cocking an external hammer, the block could be swung open by a thumb-lever, exposing the chamber for loading, and then pushed back to close. The falling hammer automatically provided a strut support for the block at the instant of firing, and the block was pierced to permit the passage of the firing pin. This system was only suited to low-powered cartridges, but it was simple and foolproof. The Flobert cap has continued, with minor dimensional changes, to become the BB (Bulletted Breech) cap of today, and it can still be found in ·22 and 9mm rimfire calibres.

FNAB / *Italy*

Fabricca Nazionale d'Armas Brescia. Although this establishment produced other weapons under the name Brescia (*qv*), the initials FNAB were used on a submachine gun developed in 1943 and of which about 7000 were made in 1943–1944. It was a compact

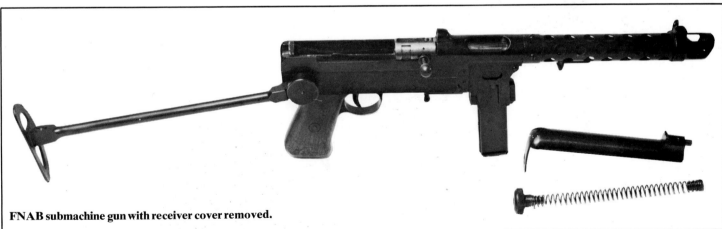

FNAB submachine gun with receiver cover removed.

weapon in which both the butt and the magazine could be folded to lie alongside the barrel and thus make a convenient handful for carrying or stowage. The gun was exceedingly well made, machined from solid steel, and with a perforated barrel jacket and muzzle compensator. The mechanism was unusual, being a delayed blowback fired from a closed bolt.

The FNAB-43 was issued to German and Italian units in Northern Italy in 1944 and remained in use until the end of the war. The design was not further developed.

FOOTE, John P. *(fl. 20th C.)*

John P. Foote, an American gun designer, was for some time with the Military Armaments Corporation of Georgia, and developed two submachine guns in the 1960s. The MP61 was a very basic blowback gun in ·45 calibre, using the magazine of the US M3 gun. The receiver was of seamless steel tubing, with front and rear pistol grips and a folding butt. The design failed to attract attention, and was followed by the MP-970, in 9mm Parabellum calibre. This used an overhung bolt to reduce overall length, and was principally fabricated from rectangular sheet-metal pressings welded together. Although a sound and compact design, it seems to have had as little success as its predecessor.

FOREHAND & WADSWORTH/*USA*

American company operated by Sullivan Forehand and Charles Wadsworth. They married the daughters of Ethan Allen (*qv*), a noted New England gunsmith, and on his death in 1871 took over his existing workshop and changed the name. Their first products were a continuation of the ·22 single-shot pistol which Allen had been making since 1865, but they then turned to the manufacture of cheap solid-frame rimfire revolvers. After 1888 they began production of hinged-frame revolvers in ·32 and ·38 centre-fire calibres; these used a ribbed barrel and a spring catch above the standing breech to lock barrel and frame together, and in this respect they were very similar to several contemporary designs from other makers. One solid-frame revolver in ·44 calibre was named the Russian, an obvious attempt to ride on the coat-tails of the successful Smith & Wesson ·44 Russian; although the Forehand & Wadsworth model had a superficial resemblance, it was a much cheaper weapon.

Wadsworth took less and less interest in the company and appears to have sold his interest to Forehand some time in the late 1880s, and the firm was re-organised as the Forehand Arms Company in 1890. Wadsworth died in Brazil in 1892, and Forehand died in Worcester, Massachusetts, in 1898. On his death the

business was bought up by Hopkins & Allen (*qv*) who used the name until 1902.

FORSYTH, Alexander *(1768–1843)*

A minister of the Church of Scotland who, interested in natural science and shooting, devised the first percussion lock mechanism, using a fulminate or chlorate mixture. In 1805 he submitted the invention to the Master-General of the Ordnance and was given facilities in London to continue development. In 1807, on a change of Master-Generals, Forsyth was evicted and returned to his home in Belhelvie, Aberdeenshire, to continue his work, patenting his lock in 1808. In collaboration with the gunsmith James Purdey he set up a company to manufacture guns and locks, upwards of 20,000 being made. In 1842 he was, after much wrangling, awarded £200 by the Board of Ordnance in recognition of his invention, and after his death a further award of £1000 was distributed among his heirs.

FOSBERY, George Vincent *(1834–1907)*

A British officer commissioned into the Bengal Army, Fosbery won the Victoria Cross on 30 October 1863 during the Umbeyla Expedition to the North-West Frontier of India. He

The ·32 Safety Hammer DA revolver, from Forehand & Wadsworth's 1896 catalogue.

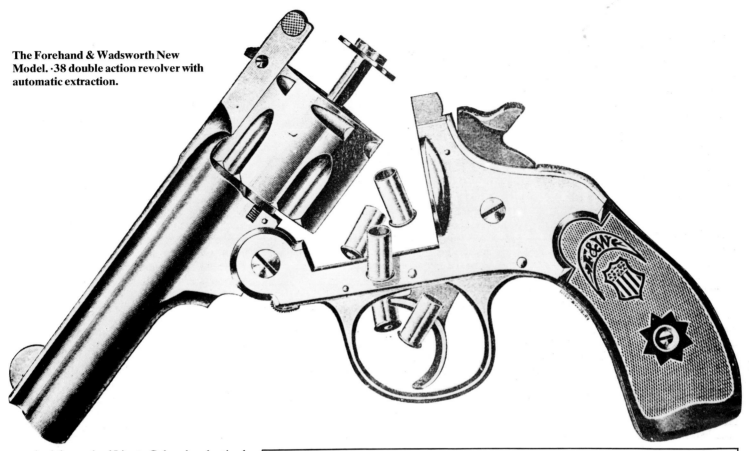

The Forehand & Wadsworth New Model. ·38 double action revolver with automatic extraction.

reached the rank of Lieut.-Colonel and retired in 1877. He had been interested in firearms throughout his life, patenting breech-loading rifles and cartridges in 1866, but his name attaches particularly to the Webley-Fosbery automatic revolver. He first took out patents for this in 1895, basing his design on a Colt Frontier single-action pistol, rebuilt so as to allow the barrel and cylinder to recoil across the frame. A cam attached to the hammer cross-shaft struck a lug on the frame during recoil, cocking the hammer and revolving the cylinder for the next shot. In 1896 he took out fresh patents, changing the method of rotation of the cylinder to operation by a fixed pin on the frame engaging in zig-zag grooving on the outside surface of the cylinder. He later assigned the patent to the Webley & Scott Revolver and Arms Company who refined the design and applied it to their standard military pattern hinged-frame revolver.

FRANCHI/ Italy

Luigi Franchi SpA of Brescia was founded in 1868 and has since become one of the foremost European firearms makers, specialising in sporting guns. At the present time their output is devoted to over-and-under double guns and recoil- or gas-actuated automatic shotguns. These are provided in all popular bores and in varying degrees of refinement and expense.

In about 1950 the company decided to venture into the military arms field and developed

The Franchi LF57 submachine gun.

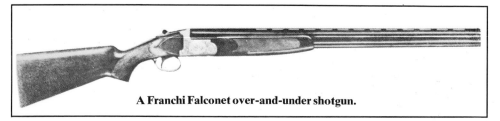

A Franchi Falconet over-and-under shotgun.

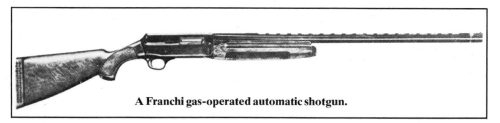

A Franchi gas-operated automatic shotgun.

a submachine gun, the LF-57. This was well designed, fabricated almost entirely of metal pressings, and used an overhung bolt. In spite of this its only sales success was its adoption in limited numbers by the Italian Navy in the early 1960s. Production then ended and the Franchi company, their curiosity satisfied, returned to the shotgun business.

FRANCOTTE / *Belgium*

Auguste Francotte of Liège was one of the foremost revolver makers of Europe during the latter half of the 19th century; in the 1890s his catalogue advertised over 150 different models, ranging from open-frame pinfires to heavy military models, and a detailed tabulation of all the variations in calibre and finish would be impossible here. He appears to have begun in the 1860s by making licensed copies of successful designs; he produced numerous Adams and Tranter revolvers, almost indistinguishable from the British-made models, and turned out respectable copies of early Smith & Wesson designs. One of his more lucrative lines was a pinfire revolver based on the Lefaucheux (*qv*) pattern; he then made improvements of his own to produce the Lefaucheux-Francotte model of open-frame revolver in pinfire and centre-fire calibres. Among these were the 11mm Swedish M1871 Trooper's Model; the 10mm Danish M1882 Trooper's Model; and the 9mm Danish M1886 Officers' Model.

With the arrival of the hinged-frame revolver, Francotte adopted the Pryse (*qv*) locking system in which two transverse pins, operated by spring arms, lock the barrel and frame together. By the 1880s most of Francotte's considerable output was to the wholesale market, selling pistols to small gunsmiths who then stamped their own names on them; the only identification with Francotte is the initials AF stamped in some inconspicuous place in the frame.

In the 1890s he designed a mechanical repeating pistol of the usual reciprocating bolt pattern, operated by a ring trigger and feeding from a magazine in the butt. The drawings indicate that it was a rather better design than most of this class, but it is doubtful if many were made; equally rare is a four-barrelled repeating pistol patented in 1885, though this design was probably licensed out and later appeared under the name of Braendlin (*qv*).

In 1912 he produced a 6·35mm blowback automatic pistol of somewhat unusual design; instead of the usual Browning copy with enveloping slide, this pistol used a reciprocating bolt moving in an upper extension of the frame. Few of these were made before war broke out in 1914, when Francotte went out of business under the German occupation.

FRENCH ORDNANCE REVOLVERS/*France*

The first revolver to be adopted by the French services was a Lefaucheux (*qv*) pinfire model, approved for issue in 1856 to the French Navy. It was an open-frame model with gate loading, an unusual combination, in 12mm calibre and was a reliable weapon. Although only issued to the Navy, many Army officers acquired them, and, with experience, this led to a demand for an Army revolver. In 1873 an 11mm centre-fire revolver of the Chamelot-Delvigne type was issued for cavalry troopers, followed in 1874 by a similar model, but with shorter barrel for general issue to officers. These were acquired from 'trade' sources, and in 1886 the St. Etienne arsenal began work on a design to replace the 1873 model so as to concentrate armament supply in government hands. The eventual result was the Model 1892, frequently, though wrongly, called the 'Lebel' revolver and more correctly known as the 'Model d'Ordonnance' (*qv*). As illustrated here, the Mle 92 was a solid-frame weapon with swingout cylinder in 8mm calibre, robust and accurate. An unusual and practical feature was the construction of the frame so that one side could be opened out to allow access to the mechanism for repair or cleaning.

FRIBERG-KJELLMAN / *Sweden*

Lieut. D. H. Friberg was an officer in the Swedish Army who, in 1872, patented a system of breech locking for automatic arms in which two lugs in the bolt were forced outwards by cams so as to wedge into recesses in the gun

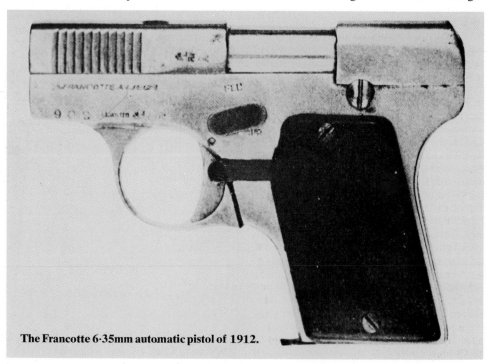

The Francotte 6·35mm automatic pistol of 1912.

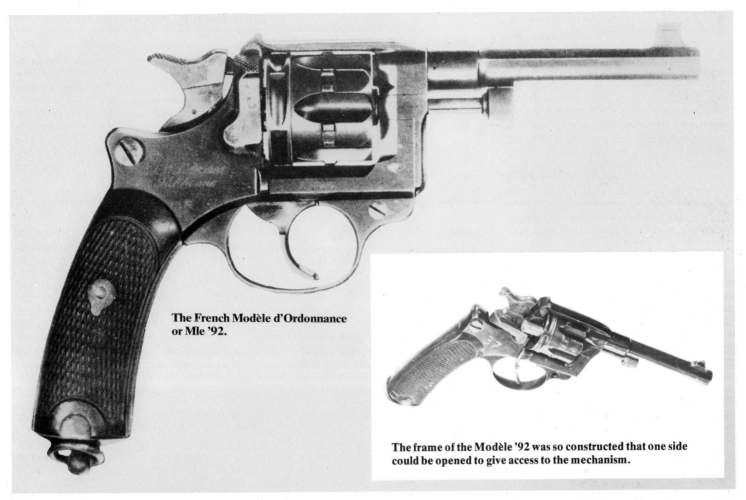

The French Modèle d'Ordonnance or Mle '92.

The frame of the Modèle '92 was so constructed that one side could be opened to give access to the mechanism.

body. Like so many patented ideas of the time, it was in advance of current firearms technology and it lay fallow for over thirty years. In the late 1890s Friberg began working on an automatic rifle, and he demonstrated a prototype in 1900 with some success. It was a gas-operated weapon using his lug locking system. Friberg had enlisted the aid of Rudolf Kjellman, Superintendent of the Stockholm Small Arms Factory, and when Friberg died in 1905, Kjellman continued development of the rifle. In 1906 he patented a short-recoil rifle in which he modified Friberg's lock so that it was actuated by the forward movement of the firing pin; this ensured that the bolt had to be closed and securely locked before the pin could reach the cartridge, and this modified locking system became known by both names.

Kjellman next incorporated the lock into a machine gun which he submitted for trial by the Swedish Army in 1910, but it was not adopted for service, and Kjellman appears not to have pursued the design any further. The Friberg-Kjellman lock, however, has survived; it was used in the Soviet Degtyarev machine guns; in the Rolls-Royce machine gun; and in the German Gewehr 43 automatic rifle.

French officer's model 1874 revolver in 11mm calibre.

FROMMER, Rudolf *(1868–1936)*
After qualifying as an engineer, Frommer joined the staff of the Hungarian Fegyver es Gepgyar Reszvenytarsasag (Arms and Machinery Company Ltd) in 1896. In 1906 he became manager, and he retained this position until his retirement in 1935. He was a first-class engineer with an original mind and was responsible for many firearms ideas and patents. He was, perhaps more than any other designer, attracted by the long recoil system of operation and he managed to make a success of it, something few others have achieved. Although he designed various military and sporting automatic rifles and some machine guns (the egregious Chauchat is said to have been derived from a Frommer design—probably one he threw away), Frommer is principally remembered for his automatic pistols. They were all far too complicated for what they did, and they are often criticised as being too delicate and prone to malfunction, but this accusation is not borne out by the record. They would not have survived so long in military service had they not been reliable.

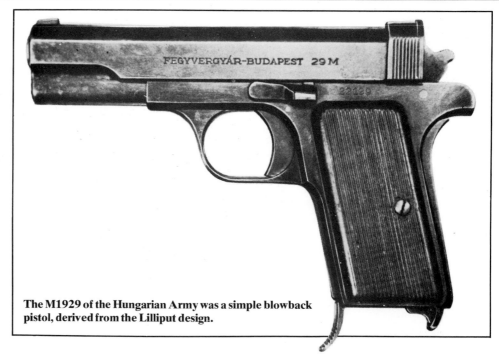

The M1929 of the Hungarian Army was a simple blowback pistol, derived from the Lilliput design.

The much simpler Frommer M1937 pistol adopted by the Hungarian Army; this version is in 7·65mm and was made for the German Luftwaffe.

The Frommer Lilliput automatic pistol.

Frommer's first pistol appeared in 1901, a long-recoil model using a rotating bolt. It was entered for various military trials and placed on sale, but it was a cumbersome article and was not a success. A modified version appeared in 1906, more compact, using the same mechanism, and chambered for a peculiar 7·65mm cartridge designed by Roth *(qv)* instead of an even more peculiar 8mm from the same stable. In 1910 the design was changed to accept the standard 7·65mm ACP cartridge, but even so it sold in only small numbers, and none of these early models are common today. In 1912, though, he produced the Stop model; this still used the long-recoil and rotating bolt system but was a much more compact and reliable weapon chambered for the 7·65mm ACP cartridge. It was first adopted by the Austro-Hungarian Army in 1912 and later by the Hungarian Army when that became a separate entity in 1919, and it remained in service and police use until the end of the Second World War. It was also sold widely on the commercial market, a 9mm Short version being added in 1919.

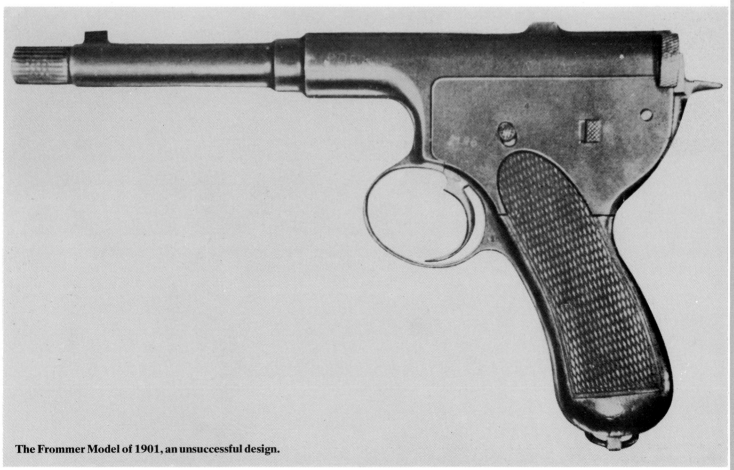

The Frommer Model of 1901, an unsuccessful design.

The Frommer 'Baby', which in spite of its small size still used the long recoil locking system.

At the same time as the Stop was introduced, a smaller model called the Baby appeared, still in 7·65mm calibre and using the same method of actuation. The object here was the provision of a more pocketable weapon, the Stop being seen as primarily a holster pistol.

In about 1921 he introduced the Lilliput model, his first move away from the long recoil system and the use of locked breeches which, when all was said and done, were superfluous in the calibres he was using. The Lilliput was a 6·35mm simple blowback weapon, featuring an external hammer and grip safety but using a fixed barrel and conventional type of slide. In 1929 an enlarged version, in 7·65mm calibre, was introduced simply as the Frommer M1929 and was immediately adopted by the Hungarian Army. It was robust and simple, and as a combat weapon was undoubtedly better than the Stop.

Finally, a year after Frommer's death, came the M1937, which was little more than a simplified and cleaned-up M1929 but in 9mm Short calibre. This, too, was adopted by the Hungarian Army, and during the Second World War several thousand were made in 7·65mm calibre for the German Air Force.

The Stop pistol of 1912 became a prominent military pistol in spite of its complicated action.

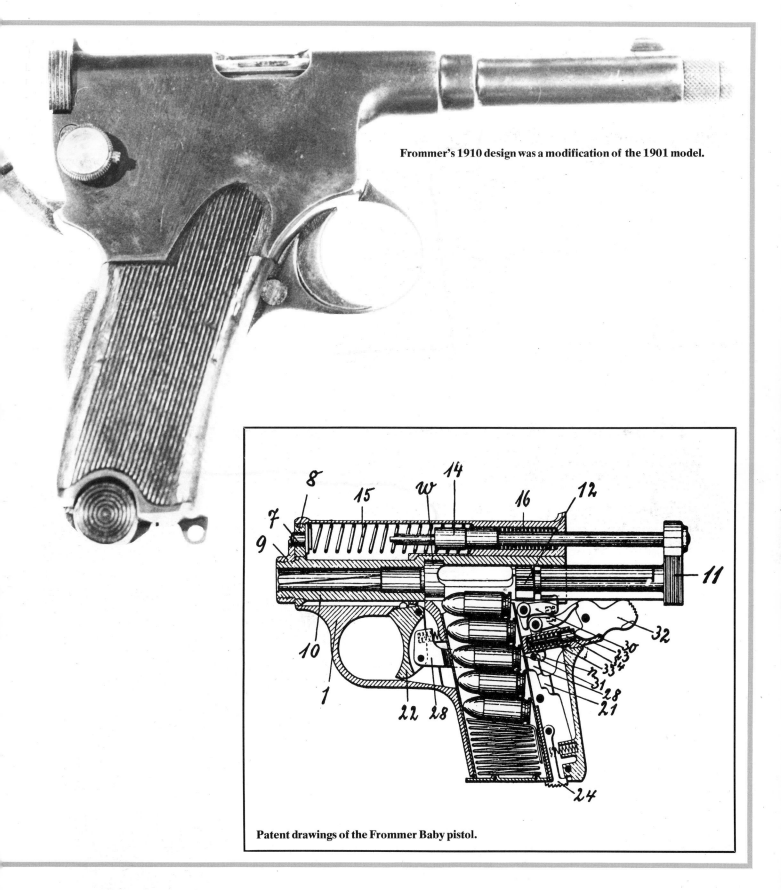

Frommer's 1910 design was a modification of the 1901 model.

Patent drawings of the Frommer Baby pistol.

Furrer MP41 submachine gun, original version.

FURRER, Adolf *(fl. 1920–1940)*
Colonel Adolf Furrer of the Swiss Army was Director of the Eidgenossische Waffenfabrik Bern, the Swiss Government arsenal, from 1921 to 1940. In addition to superintending production of various service weapons, he was in charge of design, and he produced two of the most complicated and expensive weapons in military history, a brace of designs which would never have survived the test of combat had they been put to it.

During the early 1920s the Bern factory was making Luger pistols for the Swiss Army, having gone into production on their own account in 1918 when pistols could not be obtained from Germany. It seems probable that, having the necessary machinery available to make the Luger toggle joint breech action, Furrer decided to put it to greater use. He designed a light machine gun which used a toggle joint rather like that of the Luger but arranged on its side so that the joint broke to the right side of the gun rather than upwards. This entered Swiss service in 1925 and, in spite of the diffi-culty of manufacture, stayed until 1951.

In the late 1930s the Swiss Army demanded a submachine gun and, in spite of being offered a better design, the testing board chose a weapon designed by Furrer, the MP41. This used an extremely involved variation of the toggle lock allied to a recoiling barrel, the toggle breaking to the left of the gun and the magazine being entered from the right-hand side. The first hundred of these were ordered in December 1940 and were not completed and delivered until the spring of 1942, evidence of

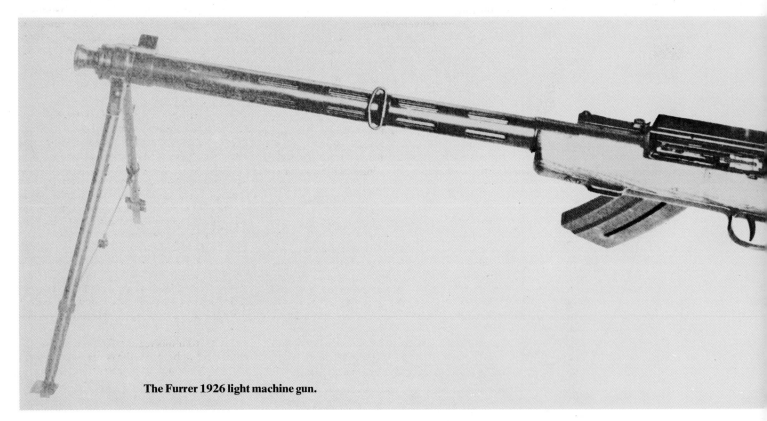

The Furrer 1926 light machine gun.

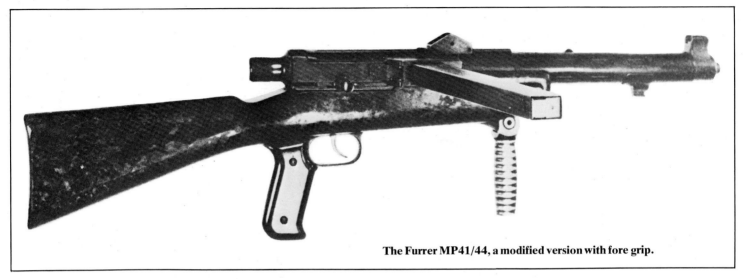

The Furrer MP41/44, a modified version with fore grip.

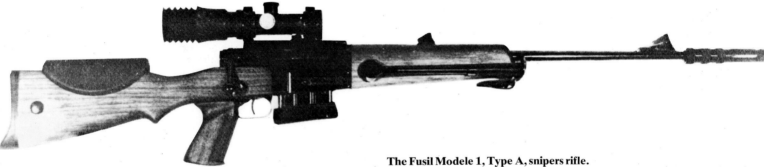

The Fusil Modele 1, Type A, snipers rifle.

the difficulty of manufacture. Eventually some 4800 were delivered during 1943. By comparison, in that same year the Erma company produced 234,000 MP40 submachine guns for the German Army, and the British were turning out 20,000 Sten guns a month from one factory alone. The Furrer MP41 was the most expensive and difficult design of submachine gun ever seen, and its adoption in the face of better designs without even the formality of a competitive trial was irresponsible, to say the least. It would be interesting to know whether this was carelessness or influence on the part of the arsenal's director.

FUSIL F1 / *France*

The Fusil F1 is a modern bolt-action magazine rifle currently used by the French Army as their sniper weapon. Produced by the Manufacture National d'Armes de St. Etienne, it is offered in three versions; Modèle A, the service weapon; Modèle B for competition shooting; and Modèle C for hunting. Modèles B and C are, of course, commercially available. The difference is primarily one of the attachments and accessories; Modèle A has a pistol grip, bipod, flash-hider and image-intensifying sight, as befits a specialised military weapon. Modèle B has a more conventional stock and

micro-adjustable target sights; while Modèle C has more ordinary 'iron' sights plus a telescope sight and can be had in chamberings other than the 7·62mm NATO or 7·5mm French service calibres.

FYRBERG / *USA*

The American gunsmith Andrew Fyrberg was primarily an inventor rather than an actual manufacturer of firearms and he remained one for much of his active career in the industry. Over a thirty year period from 1880 he patented many mechanisms relating to firearms which he then licensed to other manufacturers. Among these were an ejector mechanism used by Harrington & Richardson and, probably the most important, the safety hammer for Iver Johnson.

In 1903, though, Fyrberg began producing revolvers under his own name, from an address in Hopkinton, Massachusetts. These were ·32 and ·38 hinged-frame pocket revolvers, their particular novelty being a frame latch patented by Fyrberg in 1903.

Apart from this feature they are practically indistinguishable from the contemporary products of Iver Johnson, and it is likely that Fyrberg had the pistols made for him rather than making them himself.

GABILONDO / *Spain*

This company was founded in 1904 as Gabilondos y Urresti, in Guernica, manufacturing cheap revolvers. In about 1911 they added an automatic pistol, the Radium, to their line. This was a simple blowback, based on the Browning 1903 design, but with an unusual magazine arrangement in which the butt grip was slid down, taking the magazine follower and spring with it, and rounds then tipped loosely into the magazine cavity. Sliding the plate back up placed the rounds under compression from the spring. In 1914 they introduced a larger model, using a conventional magazine, called the Ruby. Early in 1915 they received an open-ended contract from the French Army to provide 10,000 Ruby pistols in 7·65mm calibre every month, a figure which was soon increased to 30,000. This was far beyond the capacity of their factory, so much of the work was sub-contracted, which gave several small gunsmiths a useful start in life and laid the foundations for the flood of cheap automatic pistols which appeared in the 1920s.

After 1918 the company moved to Elgoibar and became Gabilondo y Cia, producing a new design of rather better quality, based on the Browning 1910 model and marketed as the Buffalo or Danton pistols. In 1931 they intro-

duced a completely fresh range under the trade name of Llama, all these being external-hammer types copied from the Colt M1911 outline, though some of the smaller calibres dispensed with the locked breech feature. These were of far better quality than their fore-runners and have continued to be manufactured up to the present day. They have also been sold under the names Mugica and Tauler, both being the names of sales agents in Spain.

In more recent (post-1950) years, the Ruby name has been revived and a number of revolvers named Ruby Extra have been introduced. These are generally of Smith & Wesson pattern: solid frame, double-action weapons with side-opening cylinders and in ·38 or ·38 Special chambering. Revolvers have also been made under the Llama name, these being of rather better finish (and higher price) than the Ruby line.

GALAND / *Belgium*

Charles Francois Galand was a Belgian gunsmith, established in Liège, who invented and patented numerous improvements to revolvers. In 1872 he patented a double-action lock generally known since as the Schmidt-Galand lock and which was widely adopted; he developed a unique extractor mechanism which was used by many other gunmakers under licence; and he invented the Velo-Dog, one of the most-copied designs in history. Although principally active in Liège, he moved to Paris after the 1870 War, and the Velo-Dog revolvers, produced in the 1890s, bore the inscription 'Galand Arms Factory Paris'. The company did not survive the First World War.

Galand's basic revolver (which, according to its licensees, can also be found as the 'Galand & Sommerville' or 'Galand & Perrin' or in similar combinations) was an open-

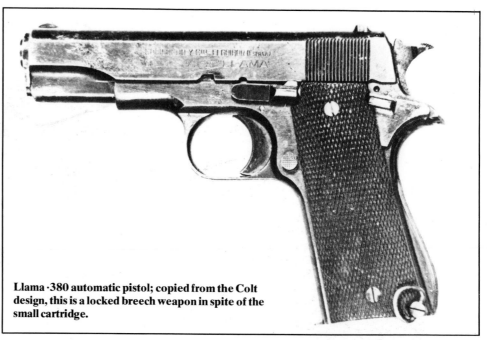

Llama ·380 automatic pistol; copied from the Colt design, this is a locked breech weapon in spite of the small cartridge.

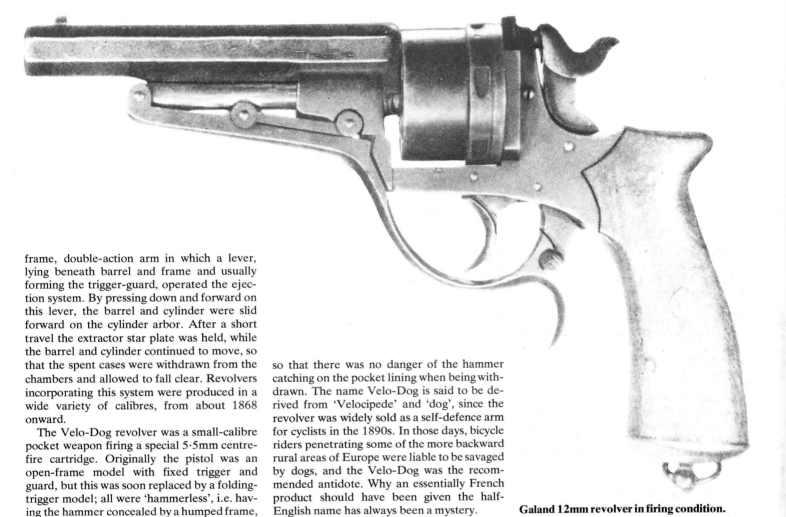

Galand 12mm revolver in firing condition.

frame, double-action arm in which a lever, lying beneath barrel and frame and usually forming the trigger-guard, operated the ejection system. By pressing down and forward on this lever, the barrel and cylinder were slid forward on the cylinder arbor. After a short travel the extractor star plate was held, while the barrel and cylinder continued to move, so that the spent cases were withdrawn from the chambers and allowed to fall clear. Revolvers incorporating this system were produced in a wide variety of calibres, from about 1868 onward.

The Velo-Dog revolver was a small-calibre pocket weapon firing a special 5·5mm centre-fire cartridge. Originally the pistol was an open-frame model with fixed trigger and guard, but this was soon replaced by a folding-trigger model; all were 'hammerless', i.e. having the hammer concealed by a humped frame, so that there was no danger of the hammer catching on the pocket lining when being withdrawn. The name Velo-Dog is said to be derived from 'Velocipede' and 'dog', since the revolver was widely sold as a self-defence arm for cyclists in the 1890s. In those days, bicycle riders penetrating some of the more backward rural areas of Europe were liable to be savaged by dogs, and the Velo-Dog was the recommended antidote. Why an essentially French product should have been given the half-English name has always been a mystery.

The Galand Le Novo folding revolver; the trigger holds back, and the butt is a hollow steel pressing which folds forward to envelop the bottom of the frame.

GALESI / *Italy*

The Industria Armi Galesi, of Collebeato, Italy (more recently known as 'Rigarmi') commenced the manufacture of pistols in 1914. Until the 1950s it was largely confined to the Italian market, but since that time it has exported widely, notably to North and South America.

Their early pistols were simple pocket blowback models based on the Browning 1906 design, in 6·35mm and 7·65mm calibres. In 1930 a new model, based on the Browning 1910 pattern, appeared in 6·35mm and 7·65mm, and in 1936 a 9mm Short version was produced which was adopted by the Italian Army as a substitute Standard pistol. In 1950 some small mechanical changes were made in the design, to facilitate dismantling and cleaning, and a ·22 rimfire version was added to the line. Known as the Model 9, this series has been available since then in a wide range of finishes. In the late 1960s, under the Rigarmi name, a fresh model appeared, a design based on the Walther PP and with a similar double-action lock.

GALIL / *Israel*

Service rifle of the Israeli Army, adopted in 1973. Designed by Israel Galili and Yakov Lior of Israeli Military Industries, it was first field-tested in 1969 and was introduced as the basic infantry weapon, intended to replace the existing semi-automatic rifle, the submachine gun and the light machine gun in the squad automatic role. The Galil is basically an assault rifle, but when fitted with a bipod it can fill the light machine gun position; with a front pistol grip and short barrel it can be used as a submachine gun; and when fitted with a special launcher it can be used to fire anti-tank and anti-personnel grenades. It fires the 5·56mm cartridge from 35 or 50 round magazines, and the standard version is provided with a folding metal butt, folding bipod, and carrying handle. There is also an SAR (Short Assault Rifle) version which has a short barrel and an optional front pistol grip. The Galil is gas-operated, with a rotating bolt, and fires single shots or at a rate of 650 rounds/minute. It has been exported and is being evaluated by NATO.

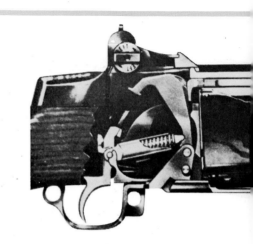

GARAND, John C. *(1888–1974)*

Garand was a mechanical engineer who, during the First World War, became interested in military firearms and designed a light machine gun in which the mechanism was actuated by the set-back of the cartridge primer due to chamber pressure. This small movement was amplified and used to unlock the breech, after which blowback action completed the firing cycle. Although the design was embryonic, it was favourably received by the authorities, and in 1919 Garand became a designer at Springfield Armory. There he developed an automatic rifle, using the same primer setback system, but he had to abandon this line of thought when the Army's standard cartridge propellant powder was changed to one with different pressure characteristics. He then began developing a gas-operated rifle using a rotating bolt, chambered for the ·276 cartridge developed by Pedersen (*qv*). In 1929, after a severe competitive trial, Garand's rifle was selected for further development as the potential US Army service rifle. By 1932 the design had been perfected, but General MacArthur,

The US Army's Garand M1 rifle in ·30 calibre.

The Galesi ·22 automatic marketed as the 'Hijo Militar'. Inset: The Galesi Model 6 automatic pistol.

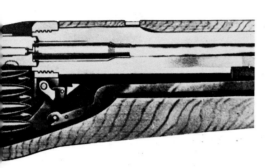

The action of the Garand rifle; cartridges are forced from the clip by a follower arm, and the recoiling bolt re-cocks the hammer.

then Chief of Staff, opposed the adoption of the ·276 cartridge on the grounds that the Army had a vast investment in ammunition and machinery for its production which could not be wasted. Garand therefore redesigned his rifle to operate with the regulation ·30 cartridge, and on 9th January 1936 his design was formally approved as the US Rifle M1, thus becoming the first automatic rifle to be the standard infantry arm of a major army.

The Garand rifle uses a gas piston beneath the barrel to drive an operating rod which, by a cam arrangement, rotates and opens the bolt. It fires from a 8-round clip which is automatically ejected after the last shot of the clip has been fired, the bolt then being held back so that the rifle is ready for reloading. It proved to be extremely reliable throughout the Second World War and, undoubtedly, this reliablility was instrumental in accelerating the universal adoption of automatic rifles by every army in post-war years. The current US service rifle, the M14, is little more than a Garand with removable 20-shot magazine and chambered for the 7·62mm NATO cartridge.

John C. Garand.

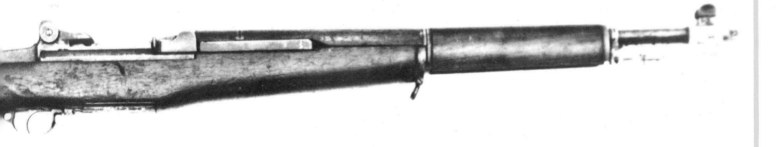

GARDNER, William *(fl. 1860–1885)*

Gardner was a soldier in the Union Army during the American Civil War and eventually rose to the rank of captain. During the war he had come into contact with various battery guns and the Gatling Gun, and he decided to invent something better. He patented a design but, having no finance or facilities for production, sold the patents to the Pratt & Whitney engineering company. Pratt had worked for Colt and had some knowledge of firearms design and manufacture, and he took Gardner's idea and turned it into a working gun.

The basic Gardner gun consisted of two barrels side-by-side, with the two bolts at the rear ends driven by opposed cranks driven by an exterior handle. As this handle was turned the cranks rotated and, by means of connecting rods attached to the bolts, opened and closed the breeches. One bolt would run forward, chambering a cartridge from the overhead magazine, close the breech, fire the cartridge, and then extract the empty case on the rearward throw of the crank. Since the two cranks were opposed by 180°, as one breech was being fired, the other was ejecting the spent case and the two barrels thus fired alternately. By altering the angular separation of the crank throws it was possible to build guns with up to five barrels.

In spite of impressive demonstrations of reliability, the US government showed no interest; they had adopted the Gatling and were in no mind to change. In 1880 Gardner went to England where the Royal Navy rapidly adopted a five-barrel and then a two-barrel model. The Army also adopted the gun in two-barrel form, but in spite of this accolade, Gardner had little success in selling the gun elsewhere.

GASSER, Leopold *(1836–1871)*

Gasser came from a family of gunsmiths and set up in business in Vienna in 1862, making Beaumont-Adams revolvers under license. He then designed an open-frame revolver which was adopted by the Austro-Hungarian Army, and he eventually operated two factories, turning out more than 100,000 revolvers a year for military and commercial markets. After his death in 1871 the business was carried on by his son Johann, who made a number of improvements on his father's designs.

The Montenegrin Gasser revolver is probably Gasser's most renowned product. This was an enormous 11mm weapon, originally an open-frame gate-loader, later a hinged-frame auto-ejecting model. They derived their name from their wide distribution in the Balkans and to the story that every able-bodied male in Montenegro was obliged by law to own one.

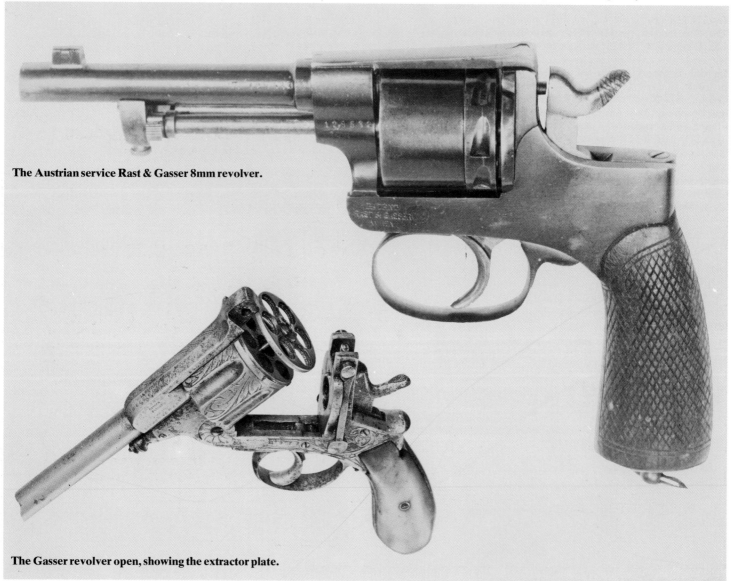

The Austrian service Rast & Gasser 8mm revolver.

The Gasser revolver open, showing the extractor plate.

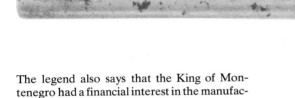

The legend also says that the King of Montenegro had a financial interest in the manufacture, but this has never been authenticated.

In later years the Rast & Gasser solid-frame revolver became the standard Army and Police pistol in the Austro-Hungarian Empire and was also sold commercially in large numbers. The adoption of automatic pistols for the Army in 1908 and 1912 ended the demand for service revolvers and the Gasser concern did not survive the First World War.

GAST / Germany

The Gast machine gun was the invention of Carl Gast, a German engineer, and was manufactured by the Vorwerke company of Barmen-Eberfeld. Development began early in 1917 as a result of a demand from the German Air Force for a fast-firing observer's machine gun. Gast's design consisted of two inter-dependent guns mounted in a common casing. Operation was by recoil, and the guns were cross-connected so that the recoil of one gun provided the power to feed and fire the other gun. Each half was fed by its own 192-round drum, and the gun had an effective rate of fire of 1300 rounds/minute. Issues for active service evaluation began in the summer of 1918, and after some minor modifications the design was accepted for service, but the war ended before it could be put into quantity production. 1314 guns were found and destroyed by the Allied Disarmament Commission, and specimens of the Gast gun are comparatively rare. The design was ingenious, but the principal drawbacks were the fact that parts were not interchangeable; that if a stoppage occurred in either gun, both would stop firing; and the magazines were 'handed' to suit only one side of the gun and could not be interchanged. According to reports, a design in 13mm calibre had been prepared, but all the service guns were in 7·92mm calibre.

The Gasser Montenegrin revolver in 11mm calibre.

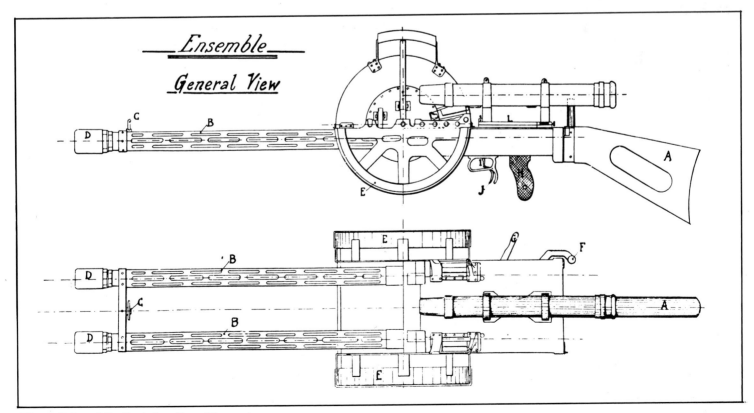

Plan and view of the Gast aircraft machine gun.

GATLING, Richard Jordan *(1818–1903)*
Gatling qualified as a Doctor of Medicine in 1848 but never practised that profession; it has been said that he qualified solely that he might better protect his family during a smallpox epidemic. His true forte was mechanical engineering, and he filed his first patents, for a rice-sowing implement, in 1844 and thereafter developed a variety of agricultural devices. In 1861 he began work on a machine gun, using a feed system similar to that of the Ager (*qv*) gun, with metal tubes pre-loaded with powder and ball and fitted with percussion caps. The weapon had six barrels which revolved round a central arbor as a crank was turned, and the various actions of feeding, firing and extracting took place in each barrel at a specific part in the travel. He demonstrated this gun in 1862 and raised sufficient interest for him to prepare six specimen guns for despatch to the Secretary of War in Washington, but all six guns, together with all the drawings, were destroyed by fire at the factory. After this setback he redesigned the gun to use a rimfire cartridge and obtained

Early engraving of a Gatling gun on field carriage.

A US Navy ·50 Gatling on field carriage, 1875.

A ·42 Gatling at Woolwich Arsenal, with 368-round drum magazine.

some small sales, but was unable to interest the Union Army, largely because his political affiliations were (quite wrongly) suspected.

In 1864 he built a much-improved model which at last gained acceptance. The US Army adopted it in 1866 and the Colt company began manufacture under an agreement with Gatling. The British Army adopted a 10-barrel version in ·45 calibre in 1874 and the Royal Navy later adopted one in ·65 calibre.

In 1893 Gatling made a gun chambered for the US ·30 service cartridge and drove the barrels by an electric motor, attaining a rate of fire of 3000 rounds a minute. This feat was to be recalled over fifty years later and inspired the development of the Vulcan (*qv*) gun.

His last design, in 1895, rotated the gun barrels by gas pressure tapped from the gun muzzle, thus converting one of the best mechanical machine guns into an automatic model. As a technical exercise it was a success, but it was far too cumbersome when compared with the Maxim or any of the other automatic designs, and it was therefore never adopted.

Contemporary engraving of a Gatling gun.

A ·65 calibre Gatling gun on naval carriage.

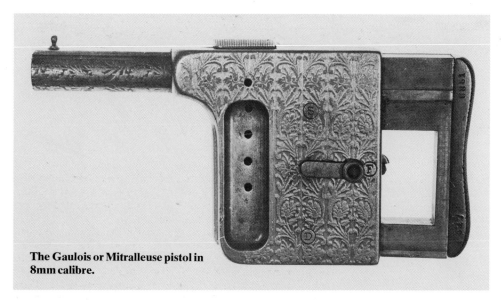

The Gaulois or Mitralleuse pistol in 8mm calibre.

The Gebauer machine gun with the cover lifted to show some of the complicated mechanism.

GAULOIS / *France*

French 'palm-squeezer' repeating pistol patented in 1893 by Mimard and Blachin and manufactured by the Manufacture d'Armes et Cycles de St. Etienne. In 8mm calibre, and firing a special short cartridge, it consisted of a flat action body and short barrel with a 'squeeze' grip at the rear end. Five bullets were placed in the box magazine inside the body and the weapon was then gripped in the hand so as to squeeze in the rear grip. This chambered and fired a cartridge, and as the hand's squeeze was relaxed, so a spring drove the grip out so as to eject the spent case and position the next cartridge for loading. As a short-range home defence weapon it was effective enough and proved quite popular, remaining on sale until 1914. It was originally marketed as the Mitrailleuse, the name being changed in 1903.

GEBAUER, Jan *(1889–1945)*

Gebauer is primarily remembered in Central Europe as a ballistics expert and scientist. After military service in 1914–1918 as an anti-aircraft artillery officer, he worked in the Czech War Department and afterwards became Professor of Mathematics and Ballistics at the Technical High School in Prague. He later returned to the War Department to become responsible for all ballistic research, the compilation of range tables, and the direction of technical ordnance development.

In addition to all that, he collaborated (in the early 1930s) with Kiraly (*qv*) in the design of the Gebauer machine gun for fixed synchronised installation which used a combination of short recoil and gas operation. The mechanism was extremely complicated and the rate of fire was 2000 rounds a minute. It promised much, but whenever it was tested it displayed a lack of reliability which always led to its being turned down for service use. The Gebauer demonstrated once more that the best gun designer is not necessarily the man with the most impressive scientific background.

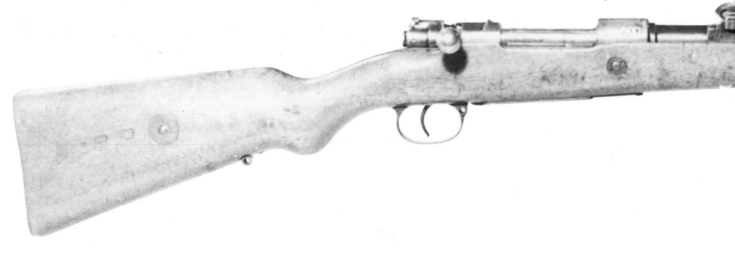

The short rifle version of the Gewehr 98, known as the Karabiner 98k.

GEWEHR 41 AND 43/Germany

In 1941, faced with the fact that the American and, to a lesser extent, the Soviet armies were issuing semi-automatic rifles as the primary infantry weapon, the German Army at last issued a set of specifications for something similar, and two experimental models resulted. The Gewehr 41 (M) was designed by Mauser and used a muzzle cone to trap gas and thus force a piston rod backwards. Movement of the rod was imparted to the rear portion of a two-piece bolt which, on moving backward, rotated the bolt head so as to unlock and then withdraw it. Both sections of the bolt were then thrust back by the piston so as to extract the spent case and, in returning, chamber a fresh round. It was not a good design; some critics have said that it was virtually an amalgam of every bad automatic rifle design which Mauser had thought up in the previous fifty years. Whatever the cause, it was turned down by the Army after a very short trial.

The Gewehr 41 (W) was made by Walther. This also used a muzzle trap which deflected gas backwards to drive an annular piston surrounding the barrel. This, in turn, drove back an actuating rod to operate the bolt. Breech locking was done by lugs forced sideways from the bolt by the passage of the firing pin, an adaptation of the Friberg-Kjellman system. Although this was, in truth, very little better than the Mauser design, if performed sufficiently well on test for it to be provisionally adopted for service, but it was later discovered

that the muzzle trap and annular piston system was prone to jamming due to corrosion from powder fouling and from differential expansion of the barrel and piston, and its acceptance for service was cancelled.

Since the bolt-locking mechanism appeared to be the only sound part of the weapon, the rest of it was completely redesigned, changing the gas actuation system to a more conventional piston system, tapped above the barrel. This was adopted as the Gewehr 43 and proved to be completely successful, remaining in production until the end of the war, though the quantity produced was never enough to allow the weapon to become a general issue, and most were fitted with telescope sights and used as sniping rifles.

GEWEHR 98/Germany

The Mauser Gewehr 98 and its variant models were the standard infantry rifles of the German Army from 1898 until 1945, and might well be considered the definitive Mauser military design, since every rifle which came afterward was merely a minor modification of this basic type. It was a bolt-action rifle with an integral five-round magazine; the bolt was locked by one rear and two forward lugs, and the striker was cocked by the opening movement of the bolt.

As a full-length infantry rifle, it originally fired the same 7·92mm cartridge that had been introduced with its predecessor, the M1888

Commission (qv) rifle. The Gewehr 98 was accompanied into service by a short version, the Karabiner 98, for use by mounted troops, artillery and pioneers.

In the early 1900s the British and American armies introduced 'short rifles'—weapons which fell between the traditional long infantry rifle and the cavalry carbine, and which could be used as a universal army weapon. The German Army saw the sense of this and a short version of the Gewehr 98 was adopted in 1904. The barrel was shortened from 30 to 24 inches and the bolt handle was turned down instead of protruding at right-angles from the action. This was formally adopted in 1908 as the Karabiner 98a, issues being first made to artillery and pioneer troops.

In 1903–1904 a new pointed bullet of slightly larger diameter was developed for the 7·92mm cartridge; most early Gewehr 98s were modified by fitting new barrels, while the Kar. 98a models were designed for this new bullet from the outset.

After the First World War the Gewehr 98 was modified by adopting the turned-down bolt handle and making some small alterations in the sights, after which it was confusingly renamed the Karabiner 98b, though it was still a full-length rifle. In 1934 a final design was drawn up, little more than the Kar 98a with slight changes to suit the manufacturer's convenience; this was adopted as the Karabiner 98k (k for kurz—short) and became the standard rifle of the Wehrmacht.

The standard Mauser Gewehr 98, service rifle of the German Army.

The 9mm Glisenti with its cartridge.
Inset: The Italian Glisenti automatic pistol, showing the bolt in the fully recoiled position.

GLISENTI / *Italy*

Standard automatic pistol of the Italian Army, adopted in 1910; although largely superseded by the Beretta in 1934, numbers remained in use until 1945. It was a locked-breech pistol in 9mm calibre, the lock being a pivoting wedge in the frame. The 9mm cartridge was of the same dimensions as the 9mm Parabellum, but less powerfully loaded, a modification probably due to the construction of the pistol. The frame is open on the left side, merely covered with a plate, and thus the pistol lacks stiffness, a defect which more powerful ammunition would rapidly search out. The firing mechanism was unusual in that the pistol was re-loaded by

the recoil stroke of the bolt but not re-cocked; the striker was a self-cocking unit, tensioned and released by pulling the trigger. This has some appeal as a safety measure, since the pistol can hardly be fired accidentally, but it makes for a long and 'creepy' trigger pull and a lack of accuracy in shooting.

GODSAL / *Britain*

The Godsal rifle was an experimental model put forward for possible military adoption by Major P. T. Godsal, a retired infantry officer and target-shooting enthusiast who had frequently represented England at international

shooting matches in the 1900s. He began developing his rifle in the later 1880s and persisted into the early 1900s without much success. Like many other target shooters of the period, he was convinced that the Lee-Enfield was a bad rifle, largely because breech locking was done by lugs at the back end of the bolt; in theory this permits some compression of the bolt during firing and can lead to slight ballistic irregularity. To a target shooter like Godsal, this was a vital point, but in combat applications it had no significance, being far outweighed by the advantages of the Lee action.

Godsal called his breech locking system a 'travelling block', but to the uninitiated it still looked like a bolt; it was, in fact, a two-piece bolt in which the small head carried the locking lugs and the handle and rotated independently of the rest of the bolt which carried the firing pin. This positioning of the lugs gave the necessary support to the cartridge immediately behind it, avoiding the compression fault. Godsal also set the bolt as far back on the stock as he could so as to obtain a greater length of barrel within the rifle's overall length, another move to gain accuracy, and this configuration brought the rifle's magazine behind the trigger, which was somewhat inconvenient. As a target rifle it doubtless met all Godsal's desires, but as a combat weapon it was too complex, too frail and awkward to handle, and although specimens were tested by the Small Arms Committee from 1895 to 1903, no further action was taken.

Godsal appeared again in 1916 with a heavy anti-tank rifle, using the same bolt action. This fired a ·500 bullet from a necked-down ·600 Express rifle cartridge case, developing a high muzzle velocity, and the rifle was fitted with a muzzle brake intended to reduce the recoil thrust on the firer's shoulder. A few were made for trials, and one survives today, but they were never adopted for service; nevertheless, Godsal deserves recognition for being the first man to design an anti-tank weapon, since the Mauser Tank-Gewehr, usually quoted as being the first of this class, did not appear until 1918.

GORLOFF/Russia

Gorloff was a Russian General who was sent to the United States in 1871 to head a purchasing commission and to superintend the manufacture of 400 ·42 Gatling Guns for the Russian Army. Very astutely, he had new brass nameplates cast, bearing his own name, and had these affixed to the guns in place of the Gatling plates before they were shipped. As a result, the Gatling gun has since been known as the 'Gorloff' in Russian service, and credited as being a Russian invention plagiarised by Gatling. These guns were last used at the Siege of Port Arthur during the Russo-Japanese War, probably the last time that Gatlings were ever used.

The Goryunov SG43 machine gun on its Sokolov wheeled mounting.
Inset: The Tank version of the SG43 machine gun.

GORYUNOV, Piotr Maximovitch
(1902–1943)

Goryunov began as a locksmith and later served with the Red Army during the Revolution and the subsequent Civil War. After the war he went into the arms industry and worked as a gunsmith under Federov, Degtyarev and other designers. In 1940 he began designing a heavy machine gun to replace the existing Maxim 1910 model. The result was the SG43 machine gun which entered service in 1943 and of which numbers are still in use today among various satellite nations. Goryunov unfortunately died a few months after his design was

adopted, and subsequent development and improvement was done by his brother, M. M. Goryunov.

The SG43 was gas-operated, using an unusual form of breech locking. A shaped post on the end of the gas piston engages with a cam slot in the breech block, and as the gas piston runs forward to close the bolt, the movement of the post through the cam slot forces the rear end of the bolt sideways so that it is locked in front of a shoulder in the gun body. Rearward movement of the piston, on firing, reverses the action and pulls the bolt clear of the shoulder before opening it. Feed was from a belt, and

the barrel could be quickly changed when it became overheated. The design was later improved into the SGM version by the addition of dust covers, longitudinal ribs on the barrel to assist the dissipation of heat, and a new type of barrel lock. SGMT and SGMB versions, for tank and vehicle mounting respectively, were later developed.

Although some of Goryunov's design features were frowned on by theorists—e.g. the sideways locking of the bolt gives rise to unbalanced stresses in the gun body—the SG series were renowned for their reliability in action, a design feature typical of Soviet weapons.

GRAS / France

The Gras rifle, Model of 1874, was the first French service rifle to use a metallic cartridge. In essence, it was a conversion of the Chassepot bolt action rifle, but with the sealing of the breech performed by a brass case instead of by the rubber ring of the original Chassepot design. The bolt was redesigned to incorporate an extractor to suit the rimmed case, while the sights were changed to match the ballistics of the new cartridge. A single-shot weapon in 11mm calibre, the Gras remained in service until replaced by the Lebel magazine rifle in 1886. After that, the Gras was sold to various Balkan countries and to Japan, where it was the inspiration for the Murata design of 1881.

attract the attention of any manufacturer or military service, and after all the partners had lost considerable sums of money the Syndicate was wound up. Although unsuccessful, the Griffiths & Woodgate rifle appears to have been the first practical design for an automatic rifle to have originated in Britain.

GRISWOLD & GUNNISON / USA

Samuel Griswold and Alfred W. Gunnison formed this company in Griswoldville, Georgia, during the American Civil War and subsequently became the most prolific producers of revolvers for the Confederate States Army. Between July 1862 and November 1864 the

extensive contract manufacturers of military small arms prior to and during the Second World War, and they were also responsible for two original designs. From 1938 to 1940 they worked on the development of a 7·65mm automatic pistol in the hope of obtaining a contract to supply German police forces. In spite of presenting a specimen to Adolf Hitler in 1940, no contract came their way and the pistol was abandoned.

In 1944, in response to a military demand for a cheap semi-automatic rifle, the Volksgewehr was designed. This was an unusual design in which a sleeve surrounded the barrel and was connected to the breech-block. Holes in the barrel allowed gas, from behind the bullet, to

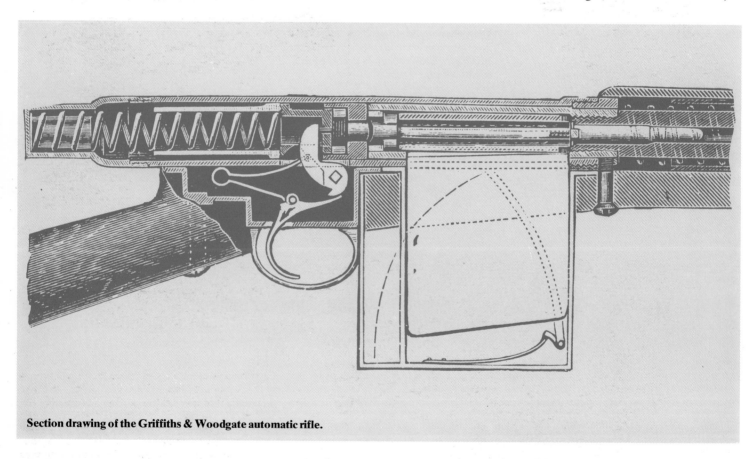

Section drawing of the Griffiths & Woodgate automatic rifle.

GRIFFITHS & WOODGATE / Britain

Major H. F. Woodgate and Mr. Griffiths patented an automatic rifle in 1891 and, together with a Mr. Ristori, founded the Automatic Rifle Syndicate Ltd. Woodgate continued to improve the original design and also to patent fresh ideas, until rifles with rotating bolts, toggle locks, and long and short recoil actions had been designed, the final patent (in 1905) using a storage-spring system resembling that later seen on the Beardmore-Farquhar machine gun. In spite of the designs being quite sound, the Syndicate was unable to

company made over 3600 open-frame revolvers in ·36 calibre, basically copies of the Colt Navy model. As a result they are probably the most common of Confederate revolvers to be found today; though it should be noted that reproductions of the design have been made in recent years. Original models do not carry the Griswold & Gunnison name, while reproductions do.

GUSTLOFF / Germany

The Waffenfabrik Gustloffwerke of Suhl were

enter the sleeve and thus create a forward pressure, tending to hold the sleeve and resist the rearward movement due to the breech-block being forced back in the usual blowback manner. This delayed the opening of the breech until the bullet was clear of the barrel, and when the block and sleeve finally were able to recoil, the trapped gas was exhausted to the open air. The rifle fired the 7·92mm Short cartridge and used the magazine of the StuG 44 assault rifle; it was cheaply made of metal pressings and was intended to arm the Volkssturm (Home Guard).

The 7·65mm Gustloff prototype automatic pistol.

The 13mm Gyrojet 'pistol'.

GYROJET / USA

The Gyrojet 'pistol' was a hand-held rocket launcher which resembled a pistol and fired a spin-stabilised rocket. It was developed by two Americans, Mainhardt and Biehl, operating as M.B. Associates of San Ramon, California, in the early 1960s. The rockets were of 13mm calibre and about 30mm long, and they contained a solid-fuel propellant in the rear section, together with a percussion igniter. The base of the rocket was sealed by a plate in which were four angled venturis so that the rocket efflux drove the rocket forward and also spun it to give flight stability. The 'pistol' carried a supply of rockets in a magazine in the butt; pressing the trigger caused a spring-impelled hammer to fly up and strike the top-most rocket on its nose. This drove it back to impinge on a fixed firing pin, thus firing the percussion igniter and igniting the propellant to launch the rocket. As the rocket moved off, so it over-ran the hammer and cocked it ready for the next shot. Pistols and carbines were built around this basic mechanism and were offered for military evaluation and placed on sale. Although some pistols were sold as curiosities, the design failed to gain acceptance. The principal objections were the low initial velocity and striking power, rapid fall-off in velocity at ranges over about 300 yards, and poor accuracy.

H

HAENEL / *Germany*

C. G. Haenel Waffen- und Fahr-radfabrik, Suhl, established as a light engineering company in 1840. It then progressed to the manufacture of sporting arms and continued with this until 1945 when it lost its identity, being nationalised and merged with other gunmaking concerns to become the VEB Ernst Thälmann-werke. Haenel were particularly noted for high-grade double shotguns and for target rifles, using the Aydt rolling block breech; their sporting rifles were generally built around Mauser or Mannlicher bolt actions.

In the 1880s they were allied with other Suhl gunmakers in producing the Reichsrevolver service pistol. In 1921 Hugo Schmeisser, designer for Bergmann, moved to Haenel as designer and chief engineer and the company began manufacture of a 6·35mm automatic pistol patented by Schmeisser. Apart from the patented method of assembly it was an unremarkable though well-made weapon. By the early 1930s the company had become more and more involved in contract production of military weapons, and pistol manufacture ceased, though the production of sporting weapons continued until 1939.

In the military field the company had made an early start in the submachine gun line by producing the Schmeisser-designed Bergmann MP-28. It later made numbers of the Erma-designed MP-38 and MP-40, and also designed and made a variant model, the MP-41. This was basically an MP-40 action mounted on the wooden stock of the MP-28. In 1941 Schmeisser began development of an automatic assault rifle, the Maschinen Karabiner (MKb) 42, which was later improved to become the MP-43 and StuG-44; this was one of the most outstanding weapon designs of the war and was the starting point for the whole family of assault rifles.

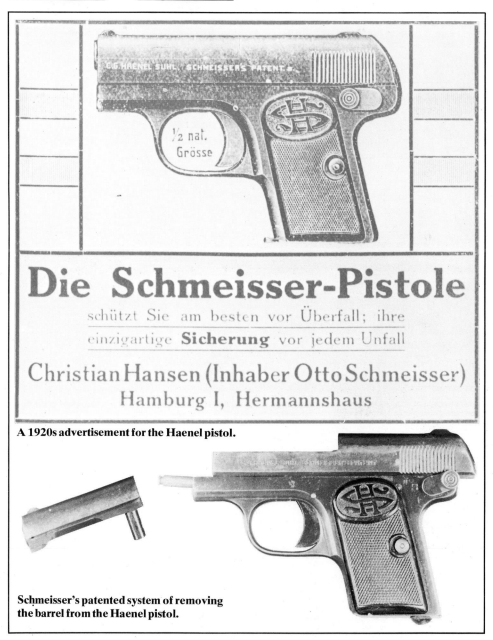

A 1920s advertisement for the Haenel pistol.

Schmeisser's patented system of removing the barrel from the Haenel pistol.

HAKIM / *Egypt*

Egyptian service semi-automatic rifle which was actually the Swedish Madsen-Ljungmann AG42 made in Egypt in the early 1950s. The principal changes in design from the Madsen original were its alteration to 7·92mm calibre instead of 6·5mm, the addition of an adjustment for the gas piston pressure so as to compensate for varying qualities of ammunition or, in emergency, to shut off the gas system completely and convert the rifle to a hand-operated weapon; and some alterations in the styling and contour of the rifle and the muzzle brake. A smaller weapon, chambered for the Soviet 7·62mm short cartridge was developed as the Rashid rifle, but few of these were made, since it made better economic sense to buy AK47 rifles from Russia.

HALCON / *Argentina*

Halcon is the trade name of Metalurgico Centro SCpA (Armas Halcon) of Banfield, Beunos Aires, and it was applied to a series of submachine guns developed between 1943 and 1960. The first model was heavy and ungainly, with a heavily finned barrel, over-sized muzzle compensator, and an odd-shaped pistol grip-cum-buttstock. It was employed in limited numbers by the Argentine Army and Police forces. An improved version, somewhat lighter and with a folding steel stock, appeared in 1946 and was again adopted in small numbers. A completely new design was put forward in 1957, a simple cylindrical receiver and pistol grip with a hinged metal buttstock, though the essential simplicity was compromised by using a hammer-fired firing pin separate from the bolt. Finally a 1960 model introduced dual triggers instead of a fire selector switch, the front trigger giving single shots and the rear trigger giving automatic fire. These later models were not adopted by the military service, and the company turned its attention to other fields of endeavour.

HAMMERLI / *Switzerland*

Hammerli SA, of Lensberg, Switzerland, have long enjoyed the highest reputation for their production of target rifles and pistols. These range from off-the-shelf models suited to particular types of contest—e.g., the Olympic 300-metre rifle match—to custom-built rifles and pistols specifically tailored to the requirements of individual marksmen. The appearance of many of these weapons is a trifle un-

settling to anyone unfamiliar with the highest reaches of the target shooting world, since they lack the graceful lines and easy symmetry of the conventional rifle or pistol and, without pretence to appearance, are target-punching machines pure and simple. Adjustable shoulder stocks, thumb-hole stocks, 'set' triggers,

Another Hammerli target pistol, the Model 210, showing a muzzle compensator in place.

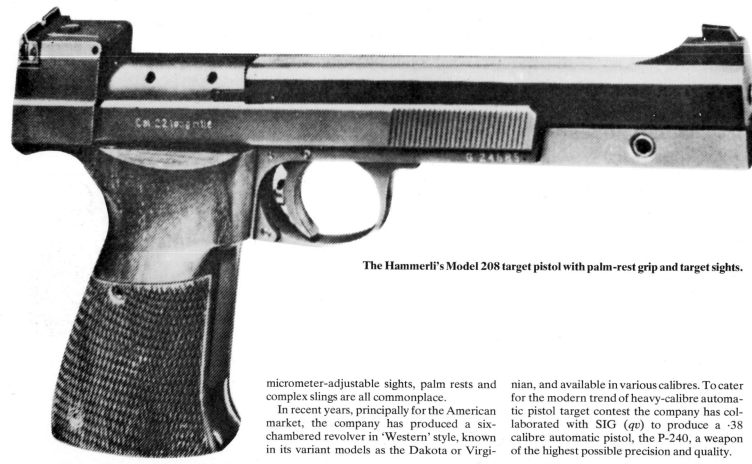

The Hammerli's Model 208 target pistol with palm-rest grip and target sights.

micrometer-adjustable sights, palm rests and complex slings are all commonplace.

In recent years, principally for the American market, the company has produced a six-chambered revolver in 'Western' style, known in its variant models as the Dakota or Virginian, and available in various calibres. To cater for the modern trend of heavy-calibre automatic pistol target contest the company has collaborated with SIG (*qv*) to produce a ·38 calibre automatic pistol, the P-240, a weapon of the highest possible precision and quality.

The Hammerli Model 230 target automatic in ·22 Short calibre.

HARRINGTON & RICHARDSON / *USA*

Gilbert H. Harrington and William A. Richardson began manufacturing revolvers in 1874, and within a few years had added shotguns to their products. Both died in 1897, but after a re-organisation in 1905 the company has continued to the present day, establishing a reputation as a major manufacturer of quality arms, produced at reasonable prices.

The company's first products were the usual cheap single-action solid-frame revolvers in ·22, ·32 and ·38 rimfire calibres, but in 1887 they obtained patents for a double-action lock and commenced the manufacture of a solid-frame revolver known as The American Double Action. Later models incorporated a patented Safety Hammer, in which the hammer had no projecting spur but used a serrated rear surface which could be gripped by the thumb after the hammer had been 'started' by slight trigger pressure, after which the hammer could be thumb-cocked. The 'safety' term referred to the freedom from the danger of catching the hammer spur in the lining of a pocket when drawing the pistol in a hurry.

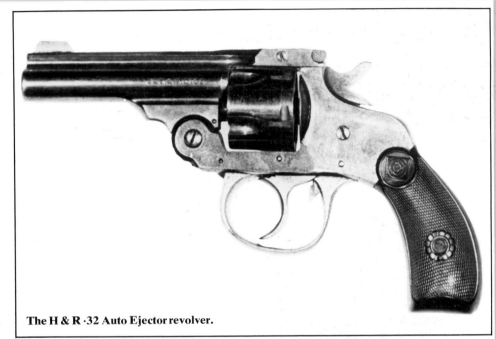

The H & R ·32 Auto Ejector revolver.

The H & R Defender ·38 revolver.

H & R ·32 Hammerless automatic pistol.

In about 1897 a line of hinged-frame revolvers was introduced as the Automatic Ejecting series, having the usual type of cam-actuated star plate in the cylinder which ejected the empty cases as the revolver was opened. An odd variant of this was the Knife Model, a four-inch barreled ·32 or ·38 pistol with a 2½ inch knife blade attached to the muzzle and folded beneath the barrel when not required.

During the period 1910–1914 the H & R Self-Loading Pistol was marketed; this was actually the contemporary ·25 Webley & Scott (*qv*) Hammerless model, made under licence from the Birmingham company, though there were one or two detail differences from the original British model. A ·32 pistol was also made which, though based on the Webley & Scott design, was not a counterpart of any Webley model. This appeared in 1913 and was made until the early 1920s, but neither of these pistols attained much popularity in the USA and the company have never essayed an automatic pistol since then.

In the years after the First World War new revolver designs appeared, and in 1929 came a single-shot target pistol, the USRA Model which achieved great popularity and success in competition shooting. Since 1945 the company has produced a wide range of solid and hinged-frame revolvers as well as maintaining its production of inexpensive shotguns.

The H & R Sentinel.

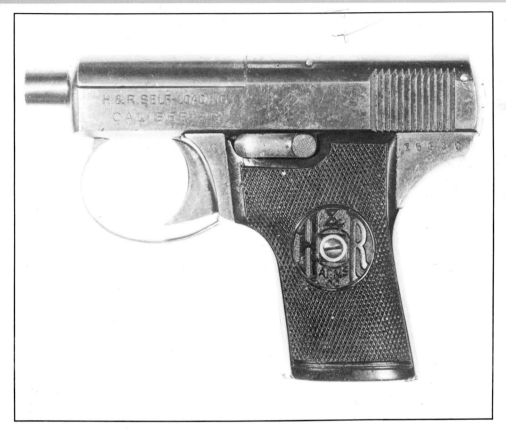

This ·25 H & R automatic was based on the Webley & Scott model of 1909.

A typical H & R shotgun.

The H & R Premier ·22, an inexpensive target pistol.

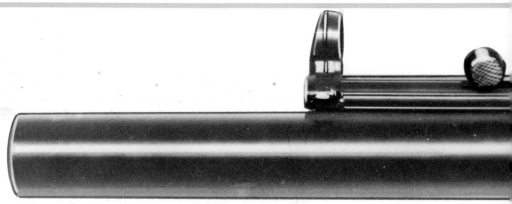

HECKLER & KOCH / *Germany*

After the Second World War the Mauser factory at Oberndorf was dismantled by the French, the contents being removed as war reparations. The buildings then stood idle until the early 1950s when, with the revival of arms manufacture in Germany, they were taken over by a newly-formed company, Heckler & Koch GmbH.

At that time the German Army had expressed interest in the CETME (*qv*) rifle, which had been offered to them by a Dutch company, Nederlands Waapen & Munition. Some further development was desirable and since the Bundeswehr preferred to have the work under their hands the CETME license was re-negotiated, and Heckler & Koch took over responsibility. They eventually produced an acceptable design, which entered German service as the Gewehr 3 (G3) in 1959 and which has since been widely adopted in other countries.

The G3 uses a delayed blowback system of operation in which the opening of the breech is resisted by two rollers in the bolt assembly which engage in recesses in the barrel extension. Gas pressure on the bolt face, via the fired cartridge, tends to force the bolt head and rollers back, but movement of the rollers is resisted by a shaped face in the bolt body, and thus the rollers must force the heavy bolt body to the rear before they can allow the bolt head to open the breech. As is common with this type of action, the bolt opening is abrupt and the chamber is longitudinally fluted so as to 'float' the empty case on a layer of gas and thus prevent it sticking in the chamber and failing to extract cleanly.

There are a number of variant models of the G3; the basic rifle is fitted with plastic butt and fore-end, is in 7·62mm NATO calibre, and has a 20-round magazine. The G3A3ZF model is fitted with a sighting telescope, while the G3A4 has a retractable butt-stock of tubular steel and the G3SG carries a variable-power rangefinding telescope and a lightweight bipod for use by snipers. The basic mechanism has also been incorporated into a machine gun design, available as the HK21 in belt-fed form or the HK11 in lightweight drum-fed form.

With the growing importance of the 5·56×45mm (·223) cartridge, Heckler & Koch modified their rifle and machine gun designs to suit: the rifle became the HK33, the machine guns the HK21 and HK13 in this calibre. Finally the growing number of countries which had adopted the Soviet 7·62×39mm short cartridge led the company to produce the HK32 rifle and HK12 machine gun, both chambered for this calibre.

The gradual merging of the functions of the assault rifle and the submachine gun is to be

The H&K Model P9S automatic pistol.

The sniper version of the German Army's standard rifle is the G3ZF model shown here.

The silenced version of the H&K MP5 submachine gun.

The MP5 with silencer removed to show the perforations in the barrel which reduce the muzzle velocity.

seen in the Heckler and Koch development; their first step appears to have been to develop a shortened version of the G3, but in 9mm calibre, calling it the MP5. They then shortened the HK33 rifle, gave it a collapsible butt and a 40-round magazine, and called it the HK33K (K for *kurz*—short) rifle, and then followed this with an even shorter version which became the HK53 submachine gun. The difference between the submachine gun and the short rifle lies merely in the length of the barrel; the HK33 barrel is 390mm long, the HK33K 322mm long and the HK53 211mm long.

Most recently the company have gone into production with a sporting rifle, based on traditional lines but incorporating the G3 roller-locked action. Three variants have been advertised, the difference lying in the operating stroke of the action: Model HK630 is for cartridges of 63mm length, HK770 for 77mm cartridges and HK940 for 94mm cartridges. Broadly speaking these cater for the 5/6, 7/8 and 9/10mm ranges of calibres and the rifle can be chambered in any of the standard commercial calibres.

The company has also developed a number of automatic pistols, ranging from the HK4, a blowback pocket model largely based on the pre-war Mauser HSc model, to the P9, P9S and VP70 pistols which are intended principally for police and military users. The P9 uses delayed blowback locking, the system using rollers and being obviously derived from the G3 rifle de-

sign. Chambered for the 7·65mm or 9mm Parabellum cartridges, the P9 pistol has an internal hammer and the normal single-action lock. The P9S, on the other hand, uses a double-action lock with a thumb-operated cocking/de-cocking lever on the left grip, and this model has recently been produced in ·45 calibre as well as in the two Parabellum calibres. The VP70 is a blowback pistol in 9mm Parabellum with some notable features; the magazine holds 18 rounds; the pistol striker is cocked and released by trigger pressure and no safety catch is fitted; and by clamping a plastic butt-stock on to the rear of the frame and grip, a 'burst-fire' counter is brought into play which fires three shots for each pressure of the trigger and turns the pistol into a controllable form of quasi-submachine gun.

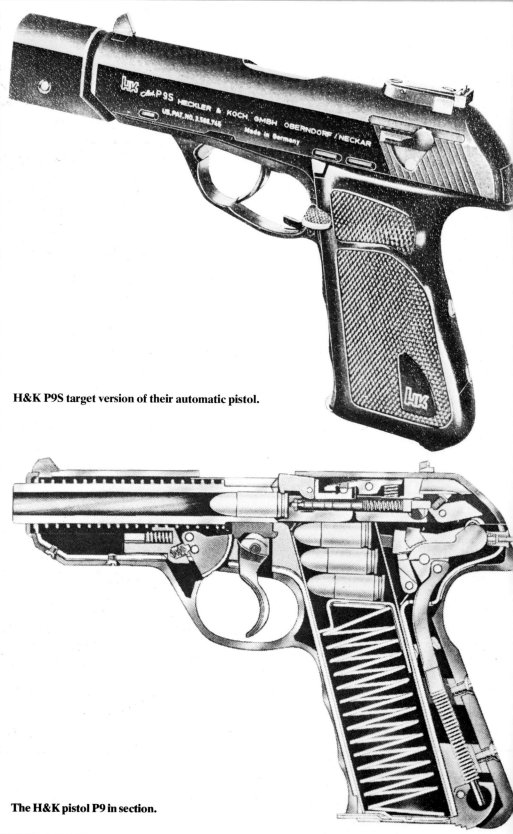

H&K P9S target version of their automatic pistol.

The H&K pistol P9 in section.

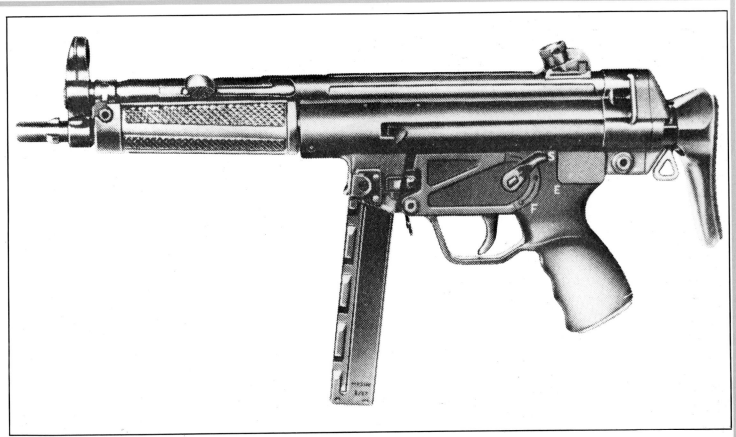

The H&K MP5 submachine gun.

The H&K13 5·56mm light machine gun.

HENRY, Alexander (d. 1900)

Alexander Henry was a Scottish gunsmith who became famous for his target rifles. These were muzzle-loaders and incorporated a rifling system which was basically a twisted polygonal section. In the 1870s he moved to London, following the adoption of his rifling system in the service Martini-Henry rifle in 1871, and he operated there as a gunsmith as well as running the Henry Rifled Barrel Company, providing barrels for other gunsmiths' actions.

HENRY, Benjamin Tyler (1821–1898)

Henry was apprenticed as a gunsmith and spent his life working at the trade, revealing at an early age an affinity for repeating arms, several of which he improved. In 1855 Oliver Winchester, a prosperous haberdasher, decided to invest in the arms business and bought shares in the Volcanic Rifle Company; when this went bankrupt in 1857 he bought the remains and established the New Haven Arms Company. The company's sole asset was the Volcanic (qv) rifle, which was not entirely successful, and Winchester instructed Henry to improve it and turn it into a saleable product. In October 1860 Henry patented a new design of lever-action rifle to fire a ·44 rimfire cartridge which he had also designed. The mechanism involved a toggle lock beneath the breech bolt which, activated by the lever, withdrew the bolt and then raised a cartridge from a tubular magazine beneath the barrel. The return movement of the lever rammed the cartridge, closed the breech, and firmly locked the toggle. An external hammer fired the rifle,

having been automatically cocked by the backstroke of the breech block. This 15-shot repeater was sold as the Henry rifle in ·44 calibre and it was highly successful; it was later improved into the Winchester design (qv). In commemoration of this pioneering design, which founded the company's fortunes, every rimfire cartridge made by the Winchester company since that time has the letter H impressed on its base.

HIGH STANDARD / USA

This company was founded in 1926 to manufacture gun barrel drills and rifling equipment, but in 1932 they purchased the stock and tools of the bankrupt Hartford Arms Company. Hartford had been making a ·22 automatic pistol intended for target and recreation shooting, and High Standard continued to make this weapon, merely changing the name. They later made sundry improvements to the design and

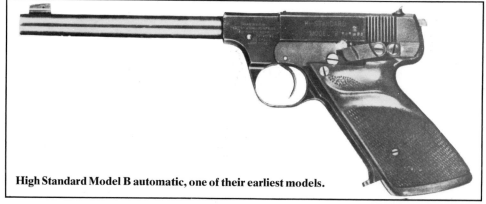

High Standard Model B automatic, one of their earliest models.

by the early 1940s had acquired a good reputation for inexpensive but accurate pistols. During the war the pistol was produced as a training and recreation weapon for the US Army and a silenced version was provided for the Office of Strategic Services and for use by various clandestine organisations. In postwar years the line was expanded to produce a variety of pistols to suit particular applications; thus, the Olympic ISU model is in ·22 Short calibre and tailored to the needs of the Olympic competition shooter, while the Dura-Matic model is a cheaper weapon intended for casual 'plinking' and for carrying on hunting trips.

In the 1950s the company began producing revolvers, beginning with a ·22 Kit Gun, a nine-shot model on a solid frame intended for field use. This was later replaced by the Sentinel series, which extended the range of available calibres to ·357 Magnum.

The second line of revolvers are based on

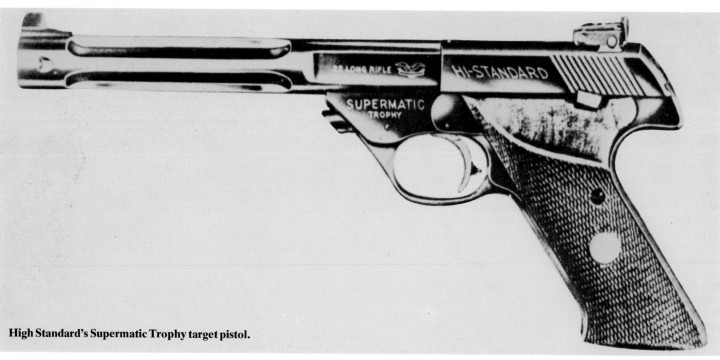

High Standard's Supermatic Trophy target pistol.

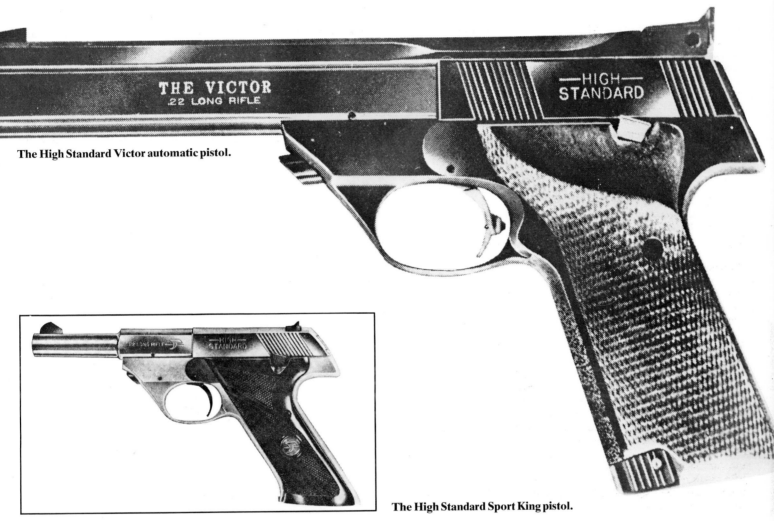

The High Standard Victor automatic pistol.

The High Standard Sport King pistol.

the lines of the Colt Frontier. The Double Nine uses a nine-shot cylinder in ·22 Long chambering, and is supplied with a spare cylinder for the ·22 Winchester Magnum Rimfire cartridge. Variations on this model, differing in barrel length, sights, etc., include the Durango, Longhorn and High Sierra models.

HILL, W. J. (fl. 1870–1885)

W. J. Hill was a small Birmingham gunmaker who developed a collective ejection system for revolvers in which the frame was top-hinged in front of the hammer. The revolver was 'broken' upwards, so as to expose the rear of the cylinder which rose with the barrel, and further upward movement of the barrel caused it to pivot about a second hinge, just above the chamber. This second movement allowed two 'horns' to drive an extractor plate from the centre of the cylinder so as to eject the spent cases. Revolvers marked 'Hill's Patent' can be found, made by various gunmakers of the period, but the only patent recorded in Hill's name (1878) relates to a revolver lock mechanism and not to this sytem of extraction.

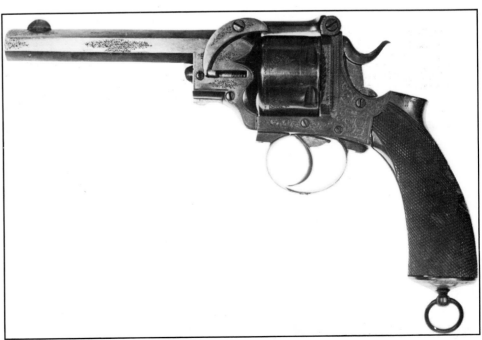

Typical revolver showing Hill's patented system of extraction.

HINO-KOMURA / *Japan*

The Hino-Komura pistol was patented in 1907 by Tomisiro Komura and K. Hino, having been developed in the aftermath of the Russo-Japanese War, when the Japanese Army had expressed a requirement for a self-loading pistol. The design was most unusual, being best described as a blow-forward mechanism. The barrel was a moving component in front of a solid breech unit; on firing, the pressure on the base of the cartridge case, plus the drag imparted by the passage of the bullet up the rifling, caused the barrel to be impelled forward. The empty case was held by the extractor on the fixed breech and was thus stripped from the chamber as the barrel moved away. A spring then returned the barrel, which collected and chambered a fresh cartridge from the butt-mounted magazine before coming to rest against the breech face. A firing pin was cocked during the barrel's movement, and the pistol was thus ready to fire the next shot. The appearance of the pistol was equally odd, with a long, thin barrel, an exposed trigger without any form of guard, and a grip safety unit in the grip. About 1200 pistols in 7·65mm calibre are believed to have been made in the years 1907–1912, but they were not accepted for military service and are extremely uncommon.

HOPKINS & ALLEN / *USA*

In 1868 two Hopkins brothers and C. H. Allen set up a company to make revolvers; after being out-voted by shareholders they lost control of the firm and in 1898 it became the Hopkins & Allen Arms Co. After a disastrous fire in 1900 they merged with the Forehand Arms Company in 1901, though the Hopkins and Allen name was retained after the

merger. In 1917, while engaged in manufacturing rifles on contract to the Belgian Government they ran into financial difficulties and were taken over by the Marlin Rockwell Corporation, and the company name vanished.

The principal product throughout the company's life was a series of revolvers of varying quality; some were cheap solid-frame 'suicide specials' produced under such names as Captain Jack, Mountain Eagle, Defender and Universal. Others, sold under the Hopkins & Allen name, were better quality hinged-frame auto-extracting revolvers in ·32 and ·38 centre-fire calibres. Their last model, the Triple Action Safety, used an ingenious system of pivoting the hammer on an eccentric pin so that the face of the hammer normally rested on the pistol frame and prevented the firing pin touching the cartridge; only when the trigger was correctly pulled was the eccentric revolved so as to bring the hammer lower and thus align it with the cartridge.

Hopkins & Allen also produced revolvers for the Merwin, Hulbert Company, a New York sporting goods firm. These were the normal H & A revolvers but marked with the Merwin, Hulbert name, and also a design of heavy open-frame revolver in ·44 calibre intended as a military or police weapon.

The Hopkins & Allen Ranger No. 2 in ·32 rimfire calibre.

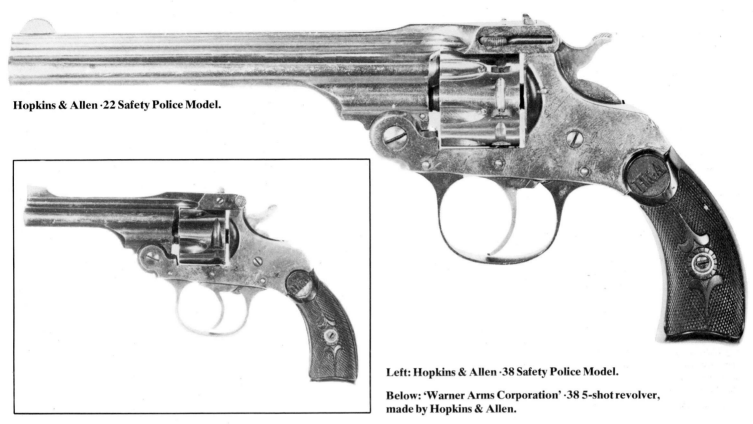

Hopkins & Allen ·22 Safety Police Model.

Left: Hopkins & Allen ·38 Safety Police Model.

Below: 'Warner Arms Corporation' ·38 5-shot revolver, made by Hopkins & Allen.

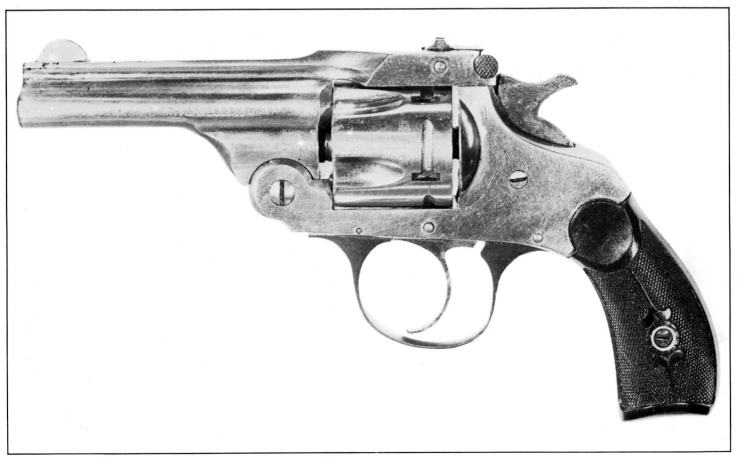

HOTCHKISS / *France*

The company of this name was founded by Benjamin Berkely Hotchkiss (1826–1885), an American ordnance engineer. His early years were spent with the Colt company, and in 1856 he designed a rifled field gun for the Mexican Army. During the American Civil War he was in charge of New York City Arsenal, and in 1867 he went to France to promote a metallic cartridge of his own design. After the war of 1870 he perfected a 'revolver cannon' and in 1875 set up the company in order to manufacture this weapon in various calibres, largely for sale to navies. It was a five-barrelled gun which resembled the Gatling and was similarly hand-cranked, though the internal arrangements were considerably different. The revolver cannon was produced in calibres from 37mm to 57mm and qualified as artillery rather than small-arms; the company then went on to develop some of the earliest quick-firing artillery guns, using sliding block breeches and metallic cartridge cases.

In the 1870s, Hotchkiss developed a bolt-action magazine rifle which had a tubular magazine in the butt; in 1876 the Winchester company took up this design in the USA and in 1878 the Winchester-Hotchkiss rifle was adopted by the US Army and US Navy.

The Hotchkiss machine gun, one of their most famous products, was not, however, invented by Hotchkiss; after his death in 1875, technical development came into the hands of Laurence V. Benet, another American, and in 1893 Benet was approached by Baron von Odkolek of the Austro-Hungarian Army. Odkolek had invented a machine gun which managed to avoid conflict with the Maxim patents by using a gas cylinder and piston beneath the barrel, and Benet realised that this was a great commercial opportunity. He also realised that Odkolek's basic idea needed much refinement and, driving a hard bargain, he bought the patents outright, refusing any sort of royalty arrangement.

The basic Hotchkiss machine gun was gas-operated, with a reciprocating bolt locking into the body by a lug which was forced up from the bolt by the action of the gas piston. Feed was done by a pressed-metal strip carrying the cartridges, entered into the right side of the gun. The first models overheated badly, but Benet made the chamber area more massive and added a series of heavy brass cooling fins to the barrel, which alleviated the trouble. In 1897 the gun was adopted by the French Army and soon afterward by the Japanese, who used it to good effect in the Russo-Japanese War. In 1908 Benet, assisted by Henri Mercie, a French engineer, designed a new version which employed a new system of locking the breech, the fermeture nut. This was a rotatable collar around the gun breech which carried interrupted threads; the head of the bolt was provided with lugs which passed through the interruptions in the thread as the bolt closed. The collar—or 'nut'—was revolved by the action of the gas piston so as to lock and unlock the bolt at each stroke. This model, which Hotchkiss called their Portative model, was first adopted by the American Army as the Benet-Mercie Light Machine Rifle, and it later became the first light machine gun to be adopted by the British and French Armies during the First World War.

Hotchkiss machine guns were still widely used up to and during the Second World War. Since then, however, no Hotchkiss gun has seen military service. The company developed a submachine gun in the 1950s which did not achieve much success.

French service 8mm Hotchkiss M1914 machine gun.

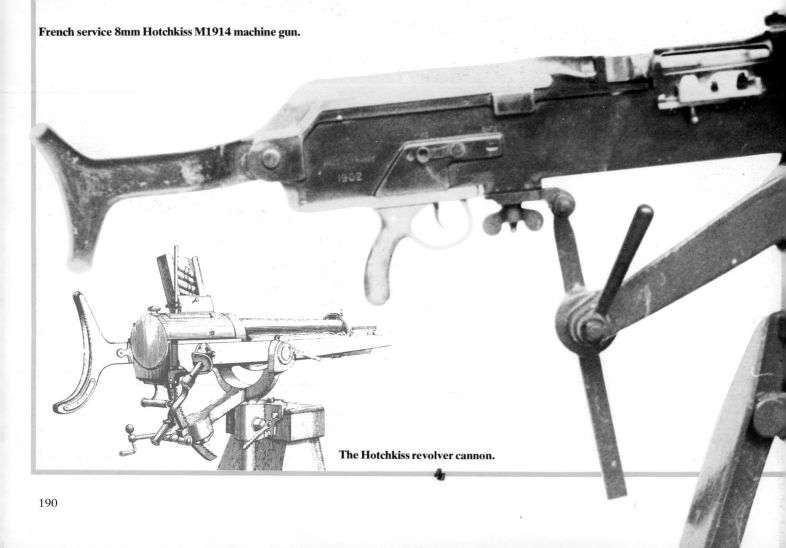

The Hotchkiss revolver cannon.

British service Hotchkiss Mark 1 ·303 machine gun.

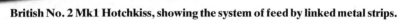

British No. 2 Mk1 Hotchkiss, showing the system of feed by linked metal strips.

HUGHES / USA

The Hughes Helicopter Division of the Summa Corporation are currently developing a new type of heavy machine gun. It is a mechanically-operated gun, driven by an electric motor, and the rate of fire is variable between one and 1000 rounds a minute simply by varying the speed of the motor. A reciprocating bolt is driven back and forth by an endless chain passing round four toothed sprocket wheels, one of which is driven by the motor. A shoe on the chain engages in a transverse slot in the bolt carrier so that the forward part of the shoe's travel closes the bolt and the rearward part opens it. The lateral movement of the shoe as it crosses from the forward to the rearward motion causes it to traverse the slot and thus hold the bolt closed during the firing interval. Bolt locking is done by lugs on the bolt head which are revolved by a cam unit within the bolt carrier. Feed is by either a disintegrating link belt or loose rounds fed through a chute; these are marshalled and fed to the bolt by rotary mechanisms which are gear-driven from the chain drive so as to keep the feed synchronised with the rate of fire. The Hughes Chain Gun, as it is called, was first developed in 30mm calibre as a potential helicopter weapon; it has since been built in 7·62mm calibre for trial as a tank machine gun.

HYDE, George J (d. 1964)

George Hyde was born in Germany and was employed on gun design during the First World War. In 1926 he emigrated to the USA and obtained employment as a gunsmith. Early in the 1930s he began to develop a submachine gun, and his first model appears to have been in ·22 calibre and built up from commercial rifle components. His first serviceable gun was the

Model 35 (of 1935) which, like most American submachine gun designs, appears to have been influenced by the Thompson, as can be seen by the finned barrel, twin pistol grips and wooden butt. Though it performed quite well on test, the US Army disliked some of its mechanical features, particularly the rear-mounted cocking handle which reciprocated with the bolt and came back to within half an inch of the firer's eye with each shot. Internally it was a simple blowback gun, chambered for the ·45 cartridge and using a box magazine.

Hyde next developed the Atmed gun, for the corporation of that name; this was a slightly modified Model 35 with a rectangular receiver which resembled the Thompson even more than the 35 had done. It also performed well on test, but it offered so little advantage over the existing Thompson design that the Army did not consider it worth developing.

Hyde now collaborated with the Inland Division of General Motors to produce the Hyde-Inland gun, which reverted to the tubular receiver of the Model 35, used a side-mounted cocking lever, and a wooden stock and fore-end. Some small modifications were made and it was accepted for service as the US Army's M2 submachine gun in 1942. Arrangements were made for 164,450 guns to be manufactured by the Marlin Firearms Corporation, but they ran into difficulty finding sub-contractors to produce some of the parts, which were designed to be pressed from sintered metal. It became necessary to re-design these components to be made by machining from bar steel, but results with the re-designed weapon were poor and since, by that time, the M3 submachine gun had been approved, the M2 project was cancelled in June 1943.

The M3 gun came about because the US Ordnance Department despaired of finding a

commercially-designed submachine gun which could meet their demands for accuracy, reliability and cheapness. Colonel Studler of the Ordnance Department called on George Hyde to design a gun and also called on Frederick W. Sampson, chief engineer of General Motors Inland Division to advise on those aspects of design which affected mass-production. Their final design was as utilitarian as the British Sten gun; indeed, a close study was made of the Sten gun in order to reap the benefits of British experience. The resulting weapon looked like its nickname—the 'Grease Gun'—a cylindrical receiver and stubby barrel, telescoping wire stock, all put together by welding of stamped components. Over 750,000 M3 and M3A1 guns were eventually produced. Hyde produced no more major designs after this.

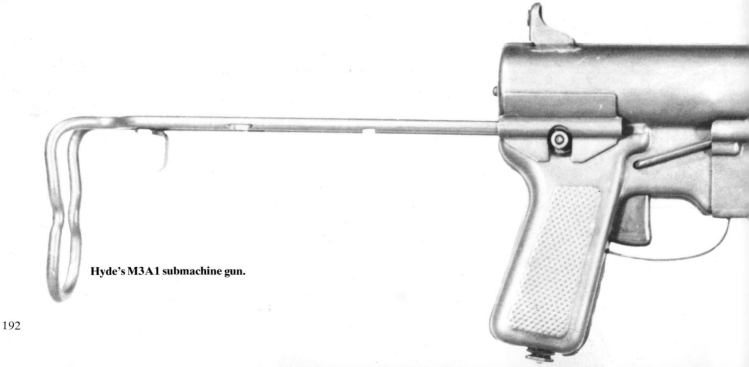

Hyde's M3A1 submachine gun.

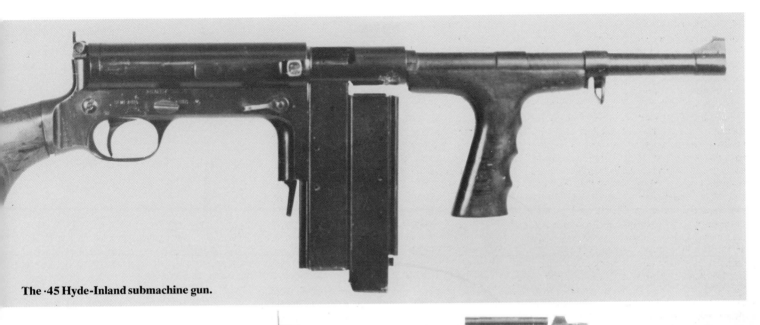

The ·45 Hyde-Inland submachine gun.

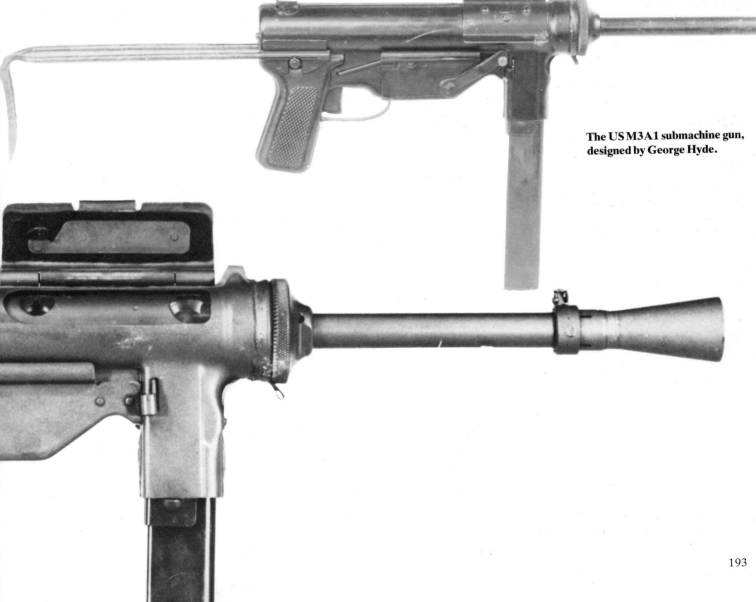

The US M3A1 submachine gun,
designed by George Hyde.

INA / *Brazil*

Industria Nacional de Armas SA of Sao Paulo, Brazil. This company has existed since the 1930s, primarily as a maker of sporting arms for local sale. A six-shot ·38 revolver based on the well-known Smith & Wesson Military & Police design was made in the 1950s and extensively adopted by Brazilian police forces, and in 1950 the company produced the MB50 submachine gun. This was actually a slightly-modified Madsen M1946 submachine gun in ·45 calibre, and was adopted by the Brazilian Army and by the National Police. In 1953 an improved model, the INA953, appeared; this was somewhat heavier and stronger and had the cocking handle moved from the top to the right side of the receiver.

INGRAM / *USA*

Gordon Ingram served in the US Army during the Second World War and returned to civilian life convinced that he could make a better submachine gun. In order to avoid confusion with the existing US M1, M2 and M3 submachine guns, and to allow for a possible M4, he called his first design the Model 5. This appeared in 1946 but found no takers. With some friends he then formed the Police Ordnance Company in Los Angeles, improved his design, and in 1949 offered the Model 6. This was a sound and simple weapon, the receiver made from seamless tubing, and was available in three variants: the Guard model with smooth barrel and wooden fore-end; the Police model with finned barrel and a forward pistol grip; and the Military model which was fully stocked and supplied with a bayonet. In ·45 calibre, the Model 6 sold quite well to various American police authorities and also to Cuba and Peru.

A Model 7 came next; this was the Model 6 with modifications to the bolt to allow it to be fired from a closed bolt condition, but the idea never got beyond a prototype. The Model 8 came after the Police Ordnance Company had been disbanded in 1952; the Government of Thailand expressed interest and Ingram made some small changes in the Model 6 and went to Thailand in 1954 to supervise the setting up of production. A Model 8 with telescoping stock became the Model 9, but only a prototype was made.

In 1969 Ingram joined Sionics Incorporated, a company involved in the manufacture of 'sound suppressors' for firearms. In the following year Sionics became the Military Armaments Corporation and Ingram designed a new, compact, submachine gun using stamped metal components, an overhung bolt of sheet steel weighted with lead, and with the barrel threaded to take a Sionics-pattern silencer. The Model 10 was made in 9mm Parabellum and ·45 calibres, while the Model 11 was the same design but smaller in all dimensions and chambered for the 9mm Short cartridge, a somewhat unusual choice. These weapons are extremely compact and well suited to use by Airborne or Commando-type troops. They have been sold to Chile and Yugoslavia and are being evaluated by other nations.

Ingram Model 10 submachine gun.

·45 and 9mm short versions of the Ingram Model 10, with 'Sound Suppressors'.

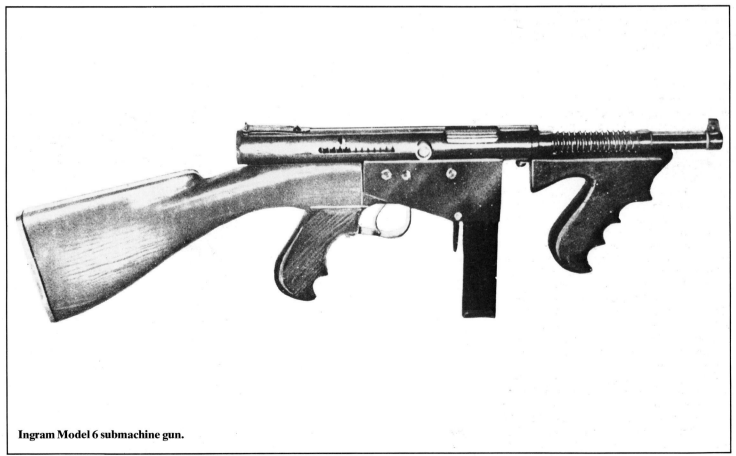

Ingram Model 6 submachine gun.

IVER JOHNSON

IVER JOHNSON/USA

This company began in 1871 as Johnson & Bye, making cheap solid-frame revolvers. Bye sold his interest to Johnson in 1883, after which the company became the Iver Johnson Arms & Cycle Works. In ensuing years it produced firearms, bicycles, roller skates, airguns, handcuffs and signal cannon.

The firearms products have been inexpensive but sound shotguns and revolvers, the sort of weapons to be found in rural communities, and the company's reputation in this field has always been high. Their principal contribution to firearms design was the adoption of a Patent Safety Hammer which had been invented by Andrew Fyrberg in 1896. In this mechanism an additional limb was fitted to the trigger, and the firing pin was no longer integral with the hammer but was mounted in the standing breech. When the hammer was at rest, a protrusion above the face abutted against the frame of the pistol and thus prevented contact between the hammer face and the firing pin. When the trigger was drawn back so as to trip and release the hammer, the additional limb was raised so as to interpose itself between the hammer and the firing pin. When the hammer fell, it struck the top part of this limb, and the blow was thus transferred to the firing pin so as to fire the cartridge. Dropping the pistol, or letting the hammer accidentally slip during thumb-cocking, would not cause a discharge since the 'transfer bar' would not be in place behind the firing pin unless the trigger were properly pressed.

The Iver Johnson company adopted the slogan 'Hammer the Hammer', together with an appropriate drawing, to publicise this device and it became a highly successful selling point.

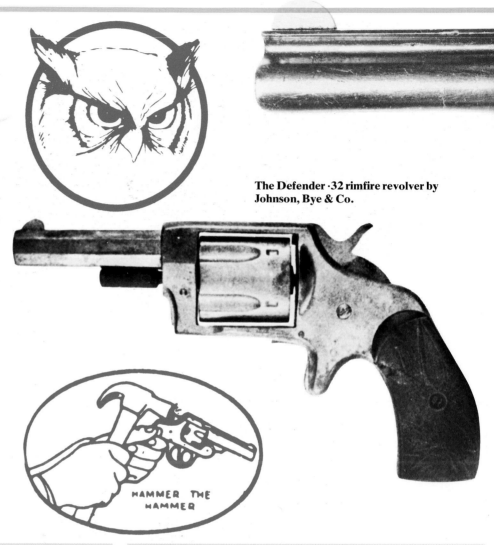

The Defender ·32 rimfire revolver by Johnson, Bye & Co.

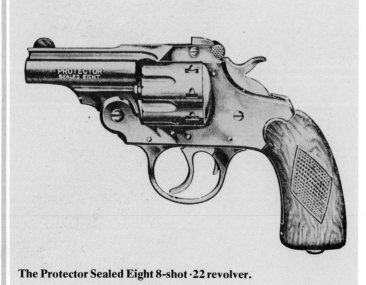

The Protector Sealed Eight 8-shot ·22 revolver.

The Iver Johnson Bulldog revolver, produced in ·22 and ·38 calibres.

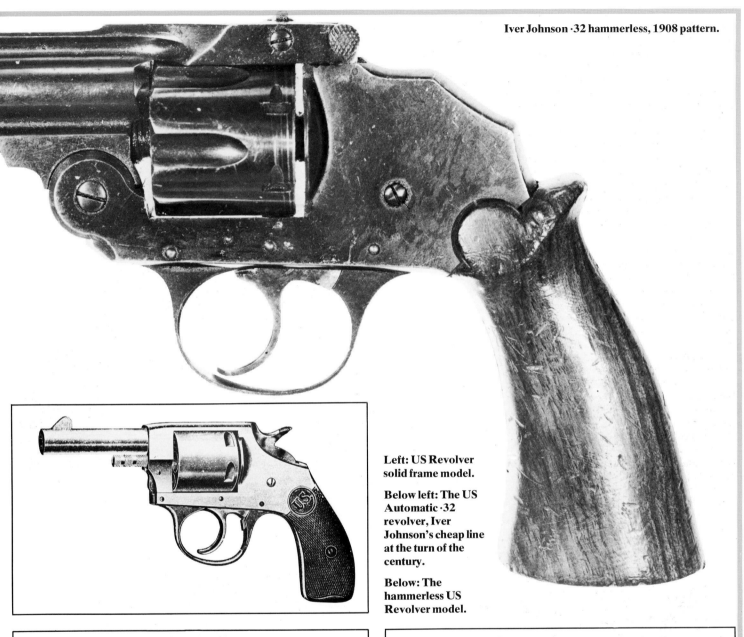

Iver Johnson ·32 hammerless, 1908 pattern.

Left: US Revolver solid frame model.

Below left: The US Automatic ·32 revolver, Iver Johnson's cheap line at the turn of the century.

Below: The hammerless US Revolver model.

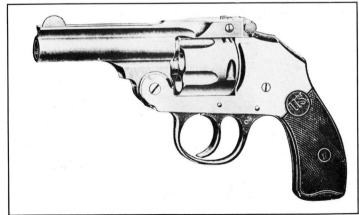

J

JÄGER / *Germany*

The Jäger pistol was made during the First World War by Franz Jäger of Suhl. It was an unusual pistol, well in advance of its time since it was largely put together from stamped metal components, a technique which did not meet with general approval until the 1940s. The pistol was built up from two steel sideplates which made up the butt and frame sides. Inside these plates locating pins held the parts of the firing mechanism, while two holes accepted a crossbar on the barrel breech and positively located the barrel. The sideplates were held at the correct spacing by front and back straps held in place by pins and screws. The slide was a pressed-steel unit with the solid breech-block held inside by screws. The calibre was 7·65mm and a butt-mounted magazine carried 7 cartridges. It is believed that fewer than 6000 were made, and little is known about their distribution. It is probable that the design was intended to be offered to the Army, but it failed to meet with official approval and was sold commercially to officers and soldiers.

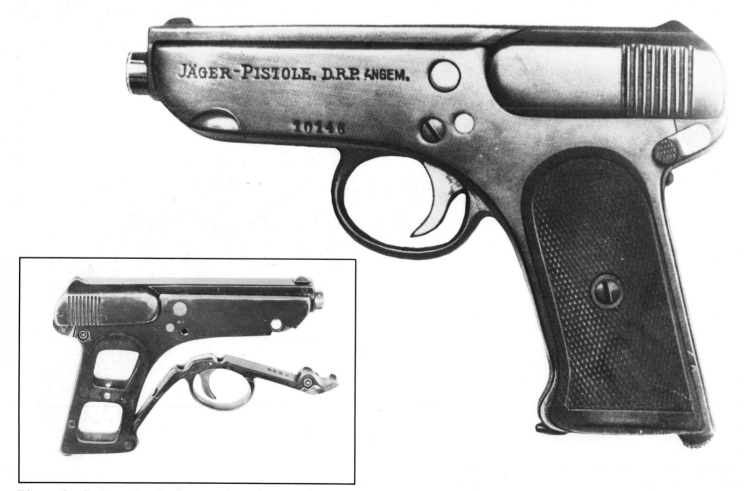

JÄGER-PISTOLE. D.R.P. ANGEM.

10146

Dismantling the Jäger, showing the pressed-metal construction.

The Jäger 7·65mm automatic pistol.

JAPANESE ARMS

Those Japanese weapons which had individual names attached—Arisaka, Hino-Komura, Nambu, Murata—will be found under those headings. This section serves to mention those military weapons which were merely described by Type or Model numbers. The number attached to a Japanese weapon's nomenclature always indicates the year of its adoption, but the method of notation changed in 1927. The original system was to use the number of the year within a particular Emperor's reign; thus, the 38th Year rifle was introduced in 1905, the 38th year of the Meiji Era. In 1927 this system was changed to one which used the last two digits of the year in the Japanese calendar; fortunately the last digit corresponds with the last digit of the year in the Gregorian calendar, so that mental translation of 'Type' numbers is easier than of 'Year' numbers. Thus, the Type 96 machine gun was introduced in 1936 and the Type 1 in 1941.

The 26th Year (1893) revolver is an example of the nationalist strain which runs through Japanese weapon design. At that time there were several excellent revolvers available, but the Japanese preferred to develop

The 14th Year Nambu pistol.

their own, a mixture of various foreign features. The hinged frame and frame lock were copied from Smith & Wesson designs, the double-action lock is a Galand type, and the

hinged plate covering the lockwork is taken from the French Mle 1892 revolver. It was chambered for a peculiar 9mm rimmed cartridge never seen outside Japan, and in general

Japanese service Type 26 revolver.

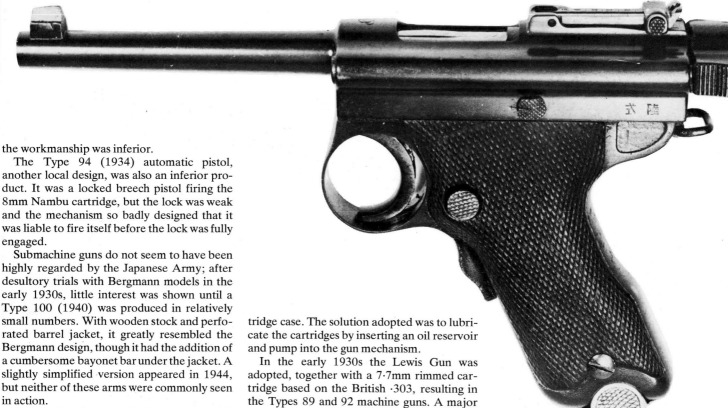

the workmanship was inferior.

The Type 94 (1934) automatic pistol, another local design, was also an inferior product. It was a locked breech pistol firing the 8mm Nambu cartridge, but the lock was weak and the mechanism so badly designed that it was liable to fire itself before the lock was fully engaged.

Submachine guns do not seem to have been highly regarded by the Japanese Army; after desultory trials with Bergmann models in the early 1930s, little interest was shown until a Type 100 (1940) was produced in relatively small numbers. With wooden stock and perforated barrel jacket, it greatly resembled the Bergmann design, though it had the addition of a cumbersome bayonet bar under the jacket. A slightly simplified version appeared in 1944, but neither of these arms were commonly seen in action.

The machine guns used by Japan were originally licensed copies of Hotchkiss designs, even to the cooling fins on the barrel. But these guns, in Japanese service, were all prone to difficult extraction, a fault due to a combination of excessive headspace (due to poor dimensioning during design and lack of quality control during manufacture), abrupt breech opening, and the shape of their 6·5mm car-

tridge case. The solution adopted was to lubricate the cartridges by inserting an oil reservoir and pump into the gun mechanism.

In the early 1930s the Lewis Gun was adopted, together with a 7·7mm rimmed cartridge based on the British ·303, resulting in the Types 89 and 92 machine guns. A major improvement came with the Army's adoption of the Type 97 machine gun, which was copied from the Czech ZB26 gun, numbers of which had been captured in China. This was very similar to the British Bren Gun and proved to be one of the most reliable weapons in the Japanese armoury and one which managed to do away with the need to lubricate the ammunition.

The Fourth Year Nambu automatic pistol.

The Type 100/1944 Japanese submachine gun.

Typical of later Japanese machine guns, the Type 96, based on a Czech design.

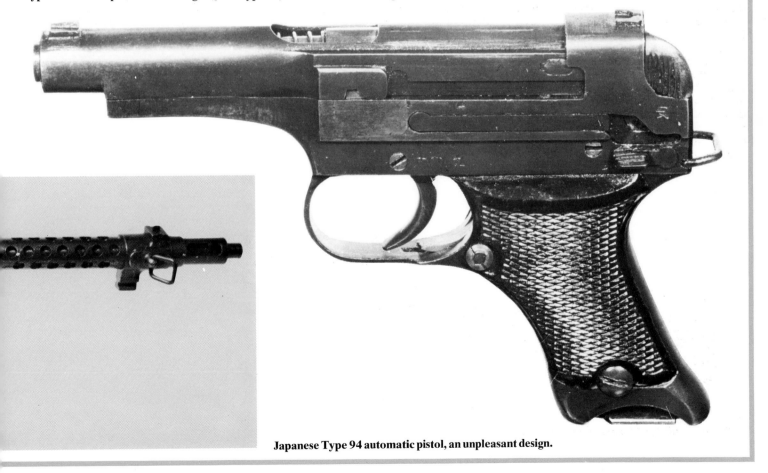

Japanese Type 94 automatic pistol, an unpleasant design.

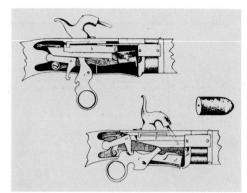

Contemporary drawings of Jennings rifle.

JENNINGS, Lewis *(fl. 1845–1860)*

Lewis Jennings was a little-known New England gunsmith who perfected a lever-action repeating rifle with a tubular magazine, which was ingenious in itself and important as being the forerunner of the Henry and Winchester designs. Jennings took a rifle which had been designed by Walter Hunt of New York in 1849, an impractical weapon, and simplified the design so as to turn it into a commercially viable product.

Operation of the breech was by a ring lever beneath the stock, which unlocked and withdrew the breech bolt. A tubular magazine beneath the barrel contained up to 20 bullets, each of which had a recessed base containing the charge of powder. The muzzle of the gun was raised during the operation of the lever so that gravity caused a bullet to slide from the magazine on to a lifter controlled by the lever. On pulling the lever back the breech bolt was driven forward to chamber the cartridge. The hammer was now manually cocked and a percussion cap placed on the nipple. When the hammer fell, the flash passed through the vent, through a passage in the bolt, and ignited the powder in the bullet's base.

The principal drawback was, of course, the lack of efficient sealing at the breech, but apart from that it was a mechanically sound weapon. It should be noted that the breech bolt was securely locked by a prop-up lever which was thrust up behind the bolt by the action of the ring lever. Claims that Jennings invented the toggle lock have no basis in fact.

JIEFFECO/*Belgium*

Automatic pistol designed and patented by H. Rosier in 1908. The patent was then assigned to Jannsen Fils & Cie, who in turn licensed the Manufacture Liegoise d'Armes a Feu Robar & Cie of Liège to actually make the pistols; the name of the pistol stems from the Jannsen involvement.

The Jieffeco was a 7·65mm blowback automatic on similar lines to the Browning 1901 model, with the return spring above the barrel. It was marketed in 1911, and in 1912 a 6·35mm version was introduced. Production ceased in 1914. The same design was also sold under the name Melior in this period, markets being arranged so that the two brands did not compete. In 1921 the Jieffeco name was revived on a fresh design, which had the recoil spring around the barrel, and this was sold in the USA by the Davis-Warner Corporation until about 1925.

The Jieffeco automatic pistol.

JOHNSON, Melvin M. *(1909–1970)*

Melvin Johnson was a law graduate who found firearms more interesting, and in the middle 1930s he developed an automatic rifle, followed by a light machine gun, both of which were recoil operated. The barrel recoiled a very short distance, during which the bolt was rotated to unlock, after which blowback force completed the bolt movement. The rifle was provided with a rotary magazine which could be loaded from the standard 5-round charger or with single rounds at any time, whether the bolt was closed or open. The rifle was undoubtedly quite a good design, but the US Army had, in 1936, committed themselves to the Garand, and since the Johnson design offered no advantages, it was turned down. It was, however, purchased by the Dutch government in 1941 for use by the Netherlands East Indies army and some 50,000 were made; the loss of the Indies to the Japanese prevented completion of delivery, and the US Marines took the remaining rifles since they were having difficulty in obtaining their share of Garand production at that time.

The Johnson machine gun operated in the same way as the rifle except that it had a box magazine on the left side of the action; it, too, could be 'topped up' at any time. Once again the gun was turned down by the US authorities, largely since it showed no improvement over the existing Browning automatic rifle and could not be adapted to belt feed, which the Army insisted had to be a feature of any new machine gun design. Again, the Dutch ordered a quantity for the East Indies and, as with the rifle, the Japanese prevented delivery of the latter part of the contract. As with the rifle the remaining guns went to the US Marines and a number to the US Army.

Johnson was a prolific writer and publicist of his ideas and designs, and the newspapers of the time tended to stress the controversial aspects of the struggle to have the Johnson rifle and machine gun adopted, but there was nothing nefarious in the Army's refusal; it was simply that the guns offered no advantage over designs already in production, and 1941 was no time for changing horses in mid-stream.

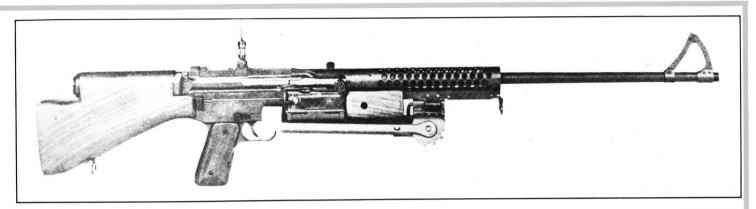

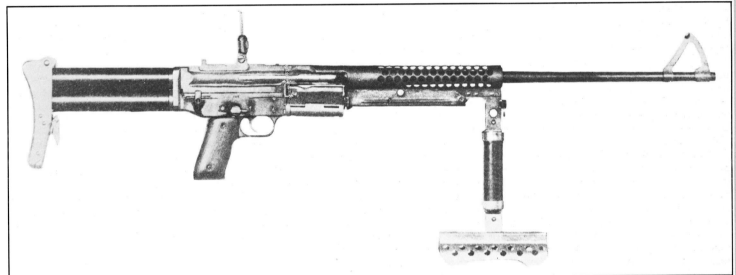

From top to bottom:

The Johnson 1941 light machine gun, with wooden butt and folded bipod.

The Johnson 1944 machine gun with monopod and tubular steel butt.

The Johnson automatic rifle of 1938.

Johnson's improved M1941 design of rifle with rotary magazine.

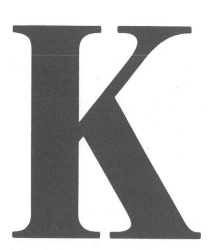

KALASHNIKOV, Mihail *(b.1920)*

Kalashnikov was born in a remote Siberian village and at the age of 17 obtained employment as a railway clerk. He was conscripted in 1939 and entered a tank regiment. In 1941, on the invasion of Russia by Germany, he was a Senior Sergeant and Tank Commander and was soon awarded the Order of the Red Star for gallantry in action. In July 1941 he was severely wounded at Bryansk, hospitalised, and eventually invalided out of the service. During his convalescence he began to study arms design and put forward designs for a submachine gun and a carbine, neither of which were accepted. Undeterred, Kalashnikov continued to design and in 1947 put forward an automatic rifle which was introduced into Soviet service in 1953 as the AK-47 *(qv)*. He later improved the design into the AKM, which was introduced in 1960.

The Kalashnikov rifle has undoubted claim to be one of the finest assault rifle designs ever seen and one of the great firearms designs of history. Precise figures are impossible to obtain, but Western intelligence sources have estimated that upwards of 35,000,000 AK and AKM rifles have been made in the 25 years since its introduction. Kalashnikov deservedly received the title Hero of Soviet Labour, has been awarded various Lenin and State Prizes, and is a Deputy of the Supreme Soviet.

KIMBALL / *USA*

This pistol was designed by John W. Kimball of Detroit, Michigan, in 1955 and was intended to fire the ·30 US Carbine cartridge. It operated on the delayed blowback principle, the delay being obtained by allowing the barrel and breech slide to recoil locked together for a short distance, after which the slide was unlocked and was able to continue recoiling while the barrel was held. The chamber was also grooved to resist extraction of the case and assist in the delay.

The design was introduced in the hope of attracting military interest, but the US Army turned it down. It was then marketed commercially in ·30 Carbine and ·22 Hornet chambering, but it suffered from two defects; firstly, the ·30 cartridge had been designed for use in a rifle and was ballistically inconsistent in a short pistol barrel; and secondly the frame was insufficiently strong, leading to metal fractures and the slide being blown from the frame. Less than 300 pistols were made before the company ceased operation in 1958.

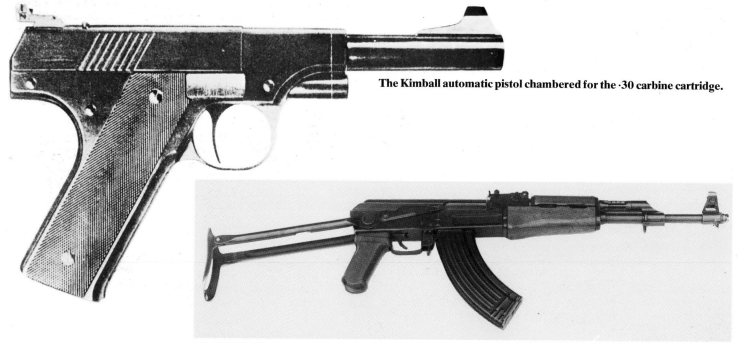

The Kimball automatic pistol chambered for the ·30 carbine cartridge.

The Kalashnikov assault rifle designed for the short 7·62mm cartridge.

KIRALY, Paul de *(1888–1964)*

Kiraly is a somewhat enigmatic figure who appeared at intervals to make some contribution to firearms development and then vanished again. His first recorded appearance was in 1912 when, in conjunction with J. Lovasz, a fellow-Hungarian, he patented a two-part breech block for an automatic weapon, a design which was to be his ace-in-the-hole for the rest of his career. The block carried a lever arm, the pivot of which was positioned so that one section of the lever was shorter than the other; the short section protruded below the bolt and engaged in a recess in the gun body. The lever pivot was on the lightweight bolt head; the heavier bolt body was behind this, and the two parts of the bolt were separated by the long section of the lever. When the gun was fired the pressure on the cartridge case forced the bolt head back; this caused the lever to be turned about its fulcrum, which was the recess in the gun body, so that the long end had to push back the heavy bolt body at considerable mechanical disadvantage. This effectively slowed down the opening movement of the

Top: The Kiraly-Ende KE7 light machine gun.

Close-up of the Kiraly automatic rifle breech.

bolt and produced a delayed blowback system.

Having patented this, Kiraly vanished from sight and was next found working for SIG in Switzerland, where he collaborated with a designer named Ende to produce the SIG KE-7 (Kiraly-Ende) machine gun in the early 1930s. This was a light recoil-operated gun with few working parts which was offered commercially and sold in small numbers. He then worked on the design of the SIG MKMO submachine gun, in which his two-part bolt appeared, though using a different system of delay. In about 1935 he appeared in Hungary, working for the Danuvia company (*qv*) in Budapest, where he was associated with Gebauer (*qv*) in the design of the latter's aircraft machine gun.

In 1939 he offered, through a firm of importers, a submachine gun to the British Army. This used his 1912 two-part bolt design and the BSA company obtained a license to manufacture it. But it was turned down by Britain, and after modification it was made by Danuvia as the Hungarian Army's Model 39M.

Upon the Soviet occupation of Hungary, Kiraly fled to South America and in 1948 contracted with the Government of the Dominican Republic to supervise the setting up of an arms factory in San Cristobal. There, with the assistance of technicians from P. Beretta of Italy, the Cristobal (*qv*) carbines and rifles were made, using the now-familiar two-part bolt mechanism.

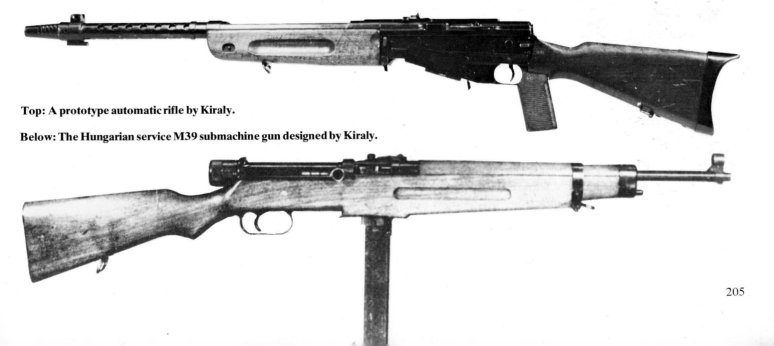

Top: A prototype automatic rifle by Kiraly.

Below: The Hungarian service M39 submachine gun designed by Kiraly.

The German Knorr-Bremse 7·92mm machine gun.

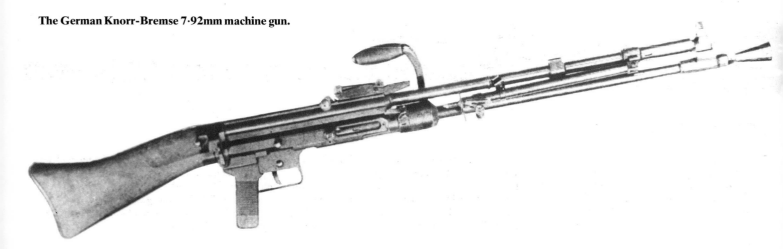

KNORR-BREMSE / Germany

As the name implies, the Knorr-Bremse AG of Berlin was concerned with the manufacture of automobile brakes, but in the 1930s it occurred to the directors that there was a possibility of profit in supplying weapons to the renascent German Army. Accordingly, they acquired the rights to a Swedish-designed light machine gun, the LH33, which the inventor had been unable to sell to the Swedes, made some small changes, and began manufacture in 1935. The German Army bought a small number as the MG35, using them as training weapons until they could obtain better designs. The gun had some drawbacks; the safety catch, if wrongly applied, would fire the gun unexpectedly, and the butt was liable to fall off during firing. A number of guns finally found their way to Sweden in 1940, when the Swedes were rather desperate, but Knorr-Bremse never achieved the success they sought and returned, sadder but wiser, to the brake business.

KOLIBRI / Austria

The Kolibri automatic pistol was made by Georg Grabner of Rehberg, and goes down in history as the smallest-calibre pistol and cartridge ever made. The design was based on a pistol called the Erika, which was already small; Grabner decided to make a miniaturised version and promote it as a self-defence gun for ladies, capable of being carried in any handbag or purse. What the lady was to defend herself against is open to some question; the 3-grain bullet produced about two foot-pounds of muzzle energy, which would probably have proved decisive against an enraged cockroach.

The Kolibri was produced in 2·7mm or 3mm calibres, the barrel being smooth-bored due to the expense and difficulty of rifling such a tiny calibre. A five-shot magazine went into the butt and the pistol was 65mm long and weighed 220 grammes fully loaded.

The tiny Kolibri 3mm automatic, so small as to be almost useless in any context.

KOMMER / Germany

The Theodor Kommer Waffenfabrik of Zella Mehlis began manufacture of a 6·35mm automatic pistol in 1920. It was little more than a copy of the Browning 1906 design but was of good quality. This became the Kommer I and was followed in the middle 1920s by the II and III models; these were virtually the same design, but they had the butt enlarged to hold seven and eight cartridges respectively.

In 1936 the company introduced a Model 4 which again leaned heavily on Browning for inspiration, in this case the 1910 model with the recoil spring around the barrel and retained by a screwed muzzle cap. This was in 7·65mm calibre and was a well finished and reliable pistol. Production of all pistols ceased in 1940 and the company no longer exists.

The Soviet KPV heavy machine gun.

KPV/*USSR*
A Soviet heavy anti-aircraft machine gun designed by Vladimirov and adopted in the early 1950s. It was specifically designed to use the heavy 14·5mm cartridge which had been developed during the Second World War for use in anti-tank rifles. Operation of the KPV is by short recoil assisted by a muzzle gas booster. During recoil the bolt head is rotated by a cam, unlocking it from the barrel, and allowing it to continue to the rear to complete the loading cycle. Feed is from a metallic belt and the rate of fire is about 600 rounds per minute. The weapon is generally found in multiple mountings; the ZPU-2 carried two guns on a trailer mount, the ZPU-4 four guns on a trailer. Self-propelled mountings have also been reported by Western observers.

KRAG-JORGENSEN/*Norway*
Ole H. J. Krag (1837–1912) joined the Norwegian Artillery in 1857 and served principally in the Kongsberg Arsenal, becoming Director in 1880. He became Master-General of the Ordnance in 1895 and retired in 1902. He was a first-class designer and he took out numerous patents for rifle and pistol mechanisms; one of his last was for an automatic pistol which could be cocked and charged by one-hand action, a design very similar to that later perfected by Chylewski *(qv)*.

Krag's name, however, is always united with that of Erik Jorgensen, Works Superintendent of Kongsberg Arsenal and co-patentee of the Krag-Jorgensen rifle. This was a bolt-action magazine rifle with a unique form of magazine which passed horizontally under the bolt and then came up on the left side of the bolt-way. A trap-door on the right side of the action could be opened and the cartridges dropped into the magazine cavity. On closing the trap-door a spring-loaded follower attached to it then placed pressure on the loose cartridges and fed them through the magazine and up to the bolt-way where they were stripped off, one at a time, as the bolt was manipulated. An advantage of this system was that the trap could be opened and the magazine topped up at any time, irrespective of whether the bolt was open or not.

The Danish Army adopted the Krag-Jorgensen rifle in 1889 and used it until 1945. The American Army were the next to adopt it, in 1892, though they soon replaced it with the Springfield. The Norwegians adopted it in 1894 and, like the Danes, retained it in use until the end of the Second World War.

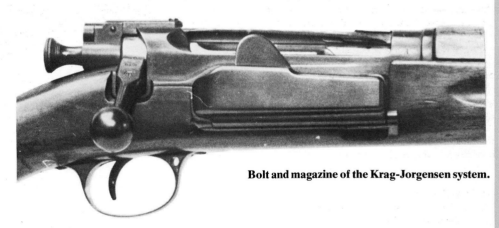

Bolt and magazine of the Krag-Jorgensen system.

6·5mm Norwegian service Carbine M1895.

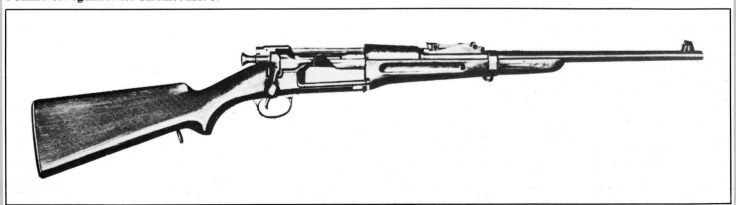

KRNKA, Karel (1858–1926)

Karel Krnka was from a gunmaking family, and served in the Austro-Hungarian Infantry, achieving the rank of Captain. While so serving, he devised a 'quick loader' for single-shot military rifles which attained great popularity throughout Europe. This was a sheet-metal compartmented box which clamped to the right side of the rifle and contained ten cartridges, which were presented to the firer's hand by spring power. It was thus easier for the soldier to re-load when firing from the prone position than it would have been if he had to use the usual waist-belt pouch of the day.

In 1887, in conjunction with his father Sylvester Krnka, he developed a bolt-action rifle with a detachable box magazine which, though considered a better design, was turned down by the Austro-Hungarian Army in favour of a Mannlicher model. He retired from the Army after this and went to England to become the chief engineer of the Gatling Arms & Ammunition Company of Birmingham, where he was instrumental in organising production of the Dimancea (qv) revolver. When that company went into liquidation in 1890 he returned to Bohemia and set up in business as a Patent Agent until 1898 when he became manager of the Georg Roth ammunition works. In collaboration with Roth he developed several automatic pistol and rifle designs. After Roth's death in 1909, Krnka went to the Hirtenberg

possible methods of making automatic weapons work. The most successful of his designs were those he did in conjunction with Roth, all of which were marketed under the Roth name and are discussed under that heading; these included the Roth-Sauer and the Roth-Steyr.

KROPATSCHEK, Alfred (1838–1911)

Kropatschek joined the Austro-Hungarian artillery as a cadet in 1854, and from the late 1860s was largely concerned with weapons design and production. In 1874 he developed a repeating rifle mechanism which used the Gras (qv) turnbolt action allied to a tubular magazine beneath the barrel. Withdrawing the bolt caused a lifter to raise a cartridge from the magazine to the chamber, and the action of closing the bolt first rammed the cartridge and then lowered the lifter to receive the next cartridge from the magazine. His design was accepted by the French, who adopted it in 1878 as the Gras-Kropatschek, issuing the rifles principally to the French Navy. It was also taken into use by the Hungarian Army and by some of the smaller Balkan states.

Kropatschek then left the small arms field to concentrate on artillery equipment, which he did quite successfully. He was knighted and received numerous decorations for his work in improving his country's armaments.

KRUMMLAUF / Germany

Krummlauf (lit. 'curved path') was the name given to a series of barrel attachments developed in Germany in 1943–1945 and intended to deflect the path of a bullet as it left the gun muzzle and thus enable the gun to literally shoot round corners. The original requirement was for a weapon which would permit infantry to fire out of trenches or around obstacles without exposing themselves to return fire; this was then expanded to include a requirement for a weapon to be carried in tanks which would allow fire to be directed downwards so as to cover the immediate vicinity of the tank. In the normal course of events, a tank's machine gun could not depress far enough to protect the area immediately around the tank from close-in infantry attack.

Experiments were first done with the standard Gew 98 rifle, but since the 7·92mm short cartridge of the StuG 44 assault rifle had a shorter bullet which could be turned more easily, the device was finally perfected for the assault rifle. Three designs were projected; the J (Jager or infantry) model which deflected the bullet through 30°; the P (Panzer) which turned it through 90°; and the V (versuchs—experimental) which turned it through 40°. Only the J model was made in quantity; some 10,000 are said to have been

Cartridge Company and remained there until 1922, after which he returned to Czechoslovakia and became a designer with Ceska Zbrojovka until his death in 1926.

In 1888 he had developed a mechanical repeating pistol of the usual reciprocating bolt type, fed by a rotary magazine, but realised that there was little future in that class of weapon and turned to the design of automatic arms. In 1895 he patented a design which included two features which eventually were to become almost his trademark: the pistol operated by long recoil, and the magazine was integral with the pistol butt and had to be loaded by a charger through the open bolt. A handful of these were made but it was never offered commercially. In 1902 he published an important book—*Die Prinzipiellen Eigenschaften der Automatische Feuerwaffen* under the pseudonym 'Kaisertreu'—in which he carefully analysed and classified the various

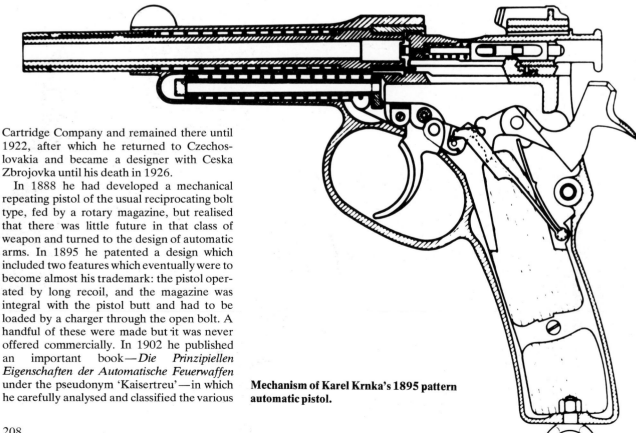

Mechanism of Karel Krnka's 1895 pattern automatic pistol.

A Krummlauf curved barrel attachment, together with its cumbersome prismatic sight, attached to the muzzle of a Sturmgewehr 44 assault rifle.

ordered, though considerably less than this were made. The P type demanded special fittings in the tank, and since tank production was at a standstill by the time the device was perfected, none were ever made. The V type was still under development when the war ended.

The mechanism was surprisingly simple; merely a section of rifled barrel, bent to the desired angle, and attached to the muzzle of the weapon. This was sufficient to deflect the bullet with acceptable accuracy for short range firing. Holes were drilled in the outer surface of this extension, not to relieve pressure behind the bullet but to give an escape of gas which pushed on the muzzle to counteract the movement due to centrifugal force on the bullet as it took the curve. A prismatic sight deflected the line of aim through the same angle as the bullet. The device was used in some numbers during street-fighting in Europe, but the idea has not been developed further.

KYNOCH / Britain

The Kynoch Gun Factory was located in Aston, Birmingham, and was founded by George Kynoch in 1888 after severing his connection with the ammunition company of the same name. He made a number of sporting rifles but then concentrated on manufacture of a revolver patented by Schlund, a Birmingham engineer with whom Kynoch was connected in other business ventures. This revolver was a

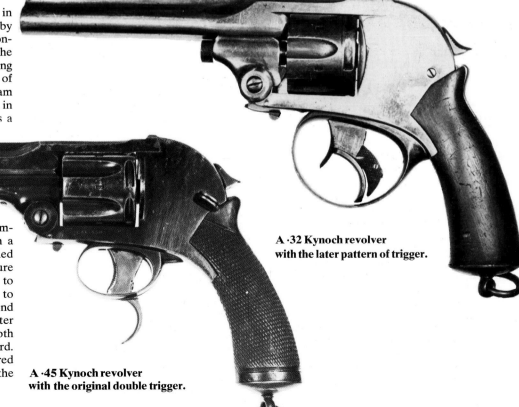

A ·32 Kynoch revolver with the later pattern of trigger.

hinged-frame six-shot weapon, with the hammer concealed inside the frame and with a double trigger. The lower trigger was pulled back to cock the hammer, after which pressure on the upper trigger released the hammer to fire the pistol. Kynoch revolvers built to Schlund's original 1885 patent had the second trigger pendant below the trigger guard; later models, to a patent taken out in 1886, had both triggers inside an enlarged trigger guard. About 600 of these pistols were manufactured before Kynoch's death in 1890, after which the Kynoch Gun Factory ceased to operate.

A ·45 Kynoch revolver with the original double trigger.

LAHTI, Aimo Johannes *(fl. 1910–1940)*

Aimo Lahti was the Director of the Finnish Arsenal (Valtion Kivaarathedas) for many years between the two World Wars and was responsible for a handful of important military small arms designs as well as many artillery developments. Perhaps the most outstanding characteristic of his designs was their absolute reliability under the most adverse conditions.

Development of the Lahti pistol began in 1929 and it was adopted by the Finnish Army in 1935. Although the appearance of the butt and tapering barrel invite comparison with the Luger, the mechanism of the Lahti is totally different, using a rectangular bolt moving inside the receiver and locked by a vertically disposed yoke. An unusual feature of this pistol is the provision of an accelerator which, driven by the recoiling barrel, turns with considerable mechanical advantage to impart a high rearward speed to the bolt as it is unlock-

ed. This gives the bolt a positive impetus and ensures reliable working in Arctic temperatures. The pistol is chambered for the 9mm Parabellum cartridge and is a very high quality weapon, relying on high-grade material and careful manufacture. In 1940 the Swedish Army decided to adopt it, but since the Finns were unable to produce the numbers required, manufacture was licensed to the Swedish Husqvarna company. Some small changes were made in the design in order to suit the Swedish methods of manufacture and to accommodate the slightly different material available in Sweden, and although over 80,000 were made, these pistols were never as good as the original Finnish-made models.

Lahti's most famous design was the Suomi submachine gun, a weapon which was, for many years, the standard by which all the others were judged and which was used all over the world. After one or two experimental de-

signs he produced a Model 1926 which was adopted by the Finnish Army in that year, making them among the first to take the submachine gun as a standard weapon. This model fired the 7·65mm Parabellum cartridge, had a quick-change barrel and an unusual air buffer which could be adjusted so as to vary the rate of fire. This was followed by the Model 1931, the one which achieved fame and wide distribution. The bolt mechanism was slightly changed and the variable rate of fire abandoned; the gun was chambered for the 9mm Parabellum cartridge, and it could use either a double-column box magazine holding 50 rounds or a 71-round drum magazine.

The Lahti-Saloranta machine gun was developed in 1926 with the hope of selling it abroad, but although it was a good design, there was little market interest at that period and only the Finns adopted it. A recoil-operated light gun in 7·62mm calibre, it could fire from either a 20-round box or a 75-round drum magazine, and had a quick-change barrel. It was one of the first post-war generation of light machine guns, and, for its day, was an excellent weapon. It remained in use by the Finnish Army until after World War Two.

LAMPO / *Italy*

A 'palm-squeezer' mechanical repeating pistol developed by Sgr. Catello Tribuzio of Turin in 1890. It was manufactured and sold in small numbers in 1891–1895. Chambered for the 8mm Gaulois cartridge, it could be concealed in the palm of the hand, the third finger engaging in a ring trigger and the barrel protruding between the fingers and thumb. Pushing the trigger outwards withdrew the bolt, and pulling it inwards closed the bolt, chambered a cartridge and then fired the pistol.

LANCASTER, Charles / *Britain*

Charles Lancaster was a barrel-maker who set up in business as a gunsmith in London in 1826. He died in 1847 leaving two sons,

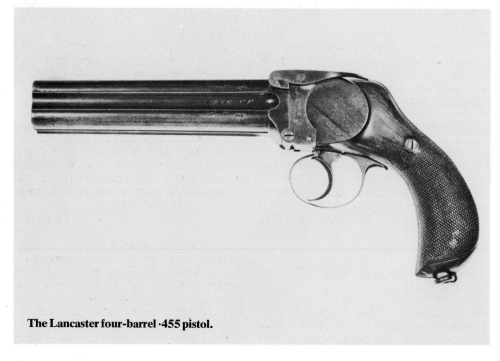

The Lancaster four-barrel ·455 pistol.

The 7·65mm Langenhan Army Model pistol.

Charles William and Alfred, who continued the family business until 1860, when they split up. Alfred went into business on his own, which he continued until his death in 1892. Charles William ran his side of it until he died in 1878. Charles William had, in 1870, taken one Henry A. A. Thorn as his apprentice and, at the time of his death, was arranging to take Thorn into partnership. Thorn bought the business from the executors and, in remembrance of his benefactor, adopted the trading name of 'Charles Lancaster'. On the death of Alfred Lancaster, his business reverted to Charles's, and the company continued under the Lancaster name until Thorn's death in 1914. This somewhat involved explanation is necessary because a reference to 'Charles Lancaster' can mean different people at different times.

Charles William had developed a cartridge-loading shotgun in 1852 which enjoyed considerable success. It was a drop-down gun, the barrels being locked and unlocked by an under-lever, and it fired an ingenious cartridge of Lancaster's design. This had a cardboard body and a copper base perforated with four holes. The base was covered by a plain copper disc, and between the two discs was a thin coat of detonating compound. The shotgun's hammer drove a broad firing pin forward to strike

the base of the cartridge, crushing the composition between the two copper surfaces and causing the flash to pass through the four holes to ignite the powder inside the case.

Henry Thorn developed a useful single trigger mechanism which allowed the two barrels of a shotgun to be fired in succession from one trigger; he was not the only one to develop this idea, but his was certainly one of the better and more reliable designs. He also showed a liking for multi-barrelled guns; his four-barrelled shotgun—virtually two double guns superimposed—found little favour since it was a cumbersome and heavy weapon to manipulate quickly against flying birds, but his four-barrelled pistol was extremely popular with Army officers. Patented in 1881, it had four ·455 or ·476 barrels in a drop-down unit, with a self-cocking firing mechanism which fired the barrels in succession for repeated pulls of the single trigger.

LANDSTADT, Halvard Folkestad
(fl. c.1900)
Landstadt was a Norwegian engineer and patentee of an automatic revolver made in small numbers in 1899–1900. A solid-frame weapon, it used a flat-sided, two-chambered

'cylinder' and a removable box magazine in the butt. Pulling back and releasing a spring-loaded breechblock caused the top cartridge in this magazine to be loaded into the bottom chamber by means of a projection on the underside of the block.

On pulling the trigger, the 'cylinder' rotated 180° to position the loaded cartridge behind the barrel, after which the firing pin in the breechblock was released. The explosion of the cartridge drove the breechblock back, extracting and ejecting the fired case, and on the return stroke the lower chamber was reloaded and the firing pin cocked. The principal feature claimed by Landstadt was that there could never be a cartridge in front of the firing pin except when the trigger was pulled in the conscious act of firing. Specimens of his revolver are extremely rare today.

LANGENHAN/Germany
Friedrich Langenhan set up a gunsmith's business in Mehlis, Thuringia, in 1842, making percussion pistols and, later, revolvers and sporting guns. The business was continued by his son Hermann and moved to Zella St. Blasili (later Zella Mehlis). Military revolvers were manufactured for the various German states

211

prior to 1870 and the manufacture of single-shot pistols for target shooting continued until the 1920s.

In 1915, doubtless under the pressure of war, Langenhan began making an automatic pistol, a 7·65mm blowback, which was taken by the German Army as a substitute standard weapon. It was a peculiar design and one which was inherently unsafe; the breechblock was a separate component, retained in the rear of the slide by a locking stirrup and screw. When new, this design was probably sound, but once wear had set in there was a danger that the vibrations of firing the pistol would loosen the screw and stirrup and allow the block to be blown from the rear end of the pistol into the firer's face.

After the war a scaled-down version in 6·35mm calibre was produced; this had a more secure method of retaining the breechblock, using a positive cross-bolt. It was followed by

an even smaller model, attempting to gain some of the market in vest-pocket pistols which were popular at that time. Both these were made in small numbers until about 1929, after which the company returned to the manufacture of sporting guns and bicycles.

LEBEL, Nicolas (1838–1891)
Lebel joined the French Army in his youth and had attained the command of an infantry Battalion by 1876. He was then detailed to command a small arms training school, and, finding an interest in his new post, began studying firearms and drawing up designs. He was then promoted to Lt. Col. and appointed member of a commission charged with designing a new infantry rifle. Lebel applied himself particularly to the design of the cartridge, realising that this was the essential part of the whole design.

Fortunately, the chemist Vielle had just perfected the first smokeless powder, and Lebel allied this to a drawn-brass cartridge case and a small-calibre jacketed bullet to produce the 8mm Lebel cartridge, which was to remain the French standard until the late 1920s. The rifle adopted by the commission to fire this cartridge was little more than a strengthened Kropatschek (qv) design, using a tubular magazine under the barrel.

The new rifle and cartridge were adopted in 1886. Lebel was promoted to Colonel and given command of the 120th Regiment d'Infanterie, which he retained until his death five years later. The 1886 rifle was to remain in service in diminishing numbers until the Second World War, though its place in the first line had largely been taken over by the Berthier (qv) designs from the early years of the century.

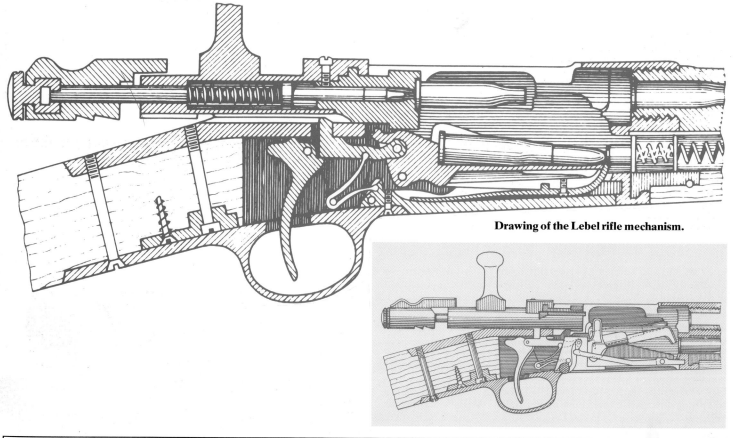

Drawing of the Lebel rifle mechanism.

A Model 1907/15 Lebel-Berthier made by the Remington company.

LEE, James Paris *(1831–1904)*

James P. Lee was born in Scotland, emigrated with his parents to Canada, and then went to the United States to work as an engineer. He set up the Lee Firearms Company in the 1860s and in 1879 patented a rifle with a removable box magazine beneath a bolt action, the first of its kind.

His first rifle was a ·45 weapon for the US Navy, and since Lee's original backers had lost heart and handed the contract over to Remington, Lee went to work for that company and developed a number of designs of military and sporting rifles using his magazine and bolt action. In 1888 the British Army adopted the Lee system, producing the Lee-Metford (*qv*) and Lee-Enfield (*qv*) rifles from it.

Lee then developed a straight-pull bolt action in which the bolt was locked by a cam operated by a handle which resembled the conventional bolt knob. It was a safe and efficient system but somewhat awkward to operate. The US Navy adopted it in 6mm calibre in 1895, and the Remington company produced a number of commercial rifles, but there is a psychological resistance to straight-pull bolts, which never seem safe to people trained on turnbolts, and the design failed to prosper.

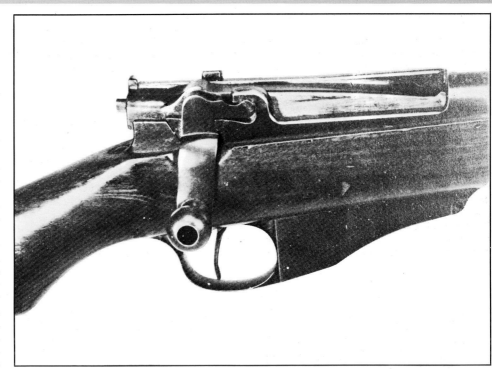

The Lee straight pull bolt action.

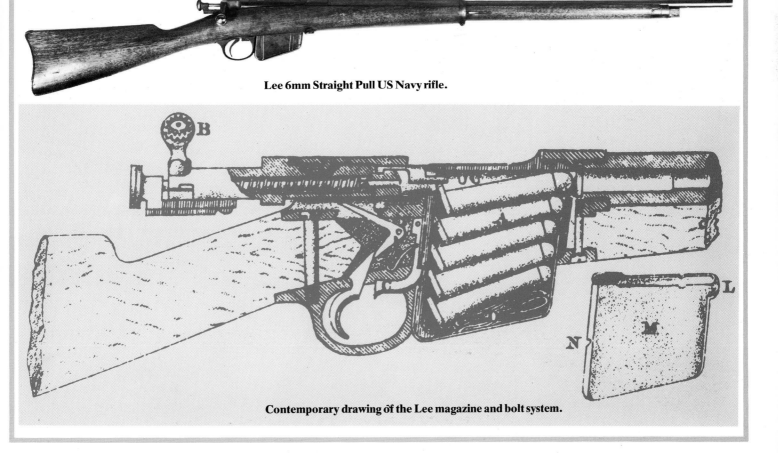

Lee 6mm Straight Pull US Navy rifle.

Contemporary drawing of the Lee magazine and bolt system.

LEE-ENFIELD / *Britain*

The Lee-Enfield rifle was introduced into British service in 1895 as the successor to the Lee-Metford (*qv*). It was essentially the same weapon except that the rifling had been changed. The adoption of cordite propellant was found to be wearing out Lee-Metford barrels after as little as 4500 rounds had been fired through them, and the solution was to adopt a deeper form of rifling.

In all there were 24 rifles and two carbines in the Lee-Enfield series, introduced between 1895 and 1949, but undoubtedly the most famous of these was the SMLE, or 'Rifle, Short, Magazine, Lee-Enfield' introduced in 1903. This was developed as a 'short rifle' to replace, as a general issue, the 'long' rifle used by infantry and the carbine used by cavalry and artillery. In addition it had a deeper magazine to accommodate ten cartridges instead of five, and was arranged for faster loading by means of a charger of five cartridges. Although subjected to severe criticism by many self-styled 'experts' of the day, it proved, during the First World War, that it was probably the best all-round combat bolt action rifle ever made. The rear locking lugs of the bolt, while theoretically unsound and, if badly adjusted, conducive to inaccuracy, nevertheless allowed the bolt to be manipulated much faster and more easily than any other system, contributing to an aimed rate of fire in excess of 40 rounds a minute. Its only real defect was that it was a slow and intricate manufacturing proposition, and after 1918 various experimental models were made in order to settle on a design which retained the reliability and handiness of the SMLE but which was better suited to mass production. The result was the Rifle No. 4 (the system of nomenclature had been changed in the 1920s), which appeared shortly after the outbreak of war in 1939 and became the standard British rifle. The visible changes included the adoption of an aperture sight at the rear of the action instead of a U-sight in front of the chamber,

and the exposure of about three inches of barrel in front of the wooden stock. The traditional sword-bayonet also vanished, in favour of a nine-inch spike.

The Australian Army which, like all Commonwealth armies, used the Lee-Enfield, had been experimenting with a short version for more convenient use in jungle warfare, and this development was taken up at Enfield, resulting in the Rifle No. 5, or Jungle Carbine. This had a very dashing appearance, being a No. 4 rifle shortened by about five inches and with a shortened stock resembling that of a sporting rifle. Shortening the barrel gave rise to excessive muzzle flash and blast and a bell-shaped flash suppressor had to be fitted. The lightness of the weapon led to a fierce recoil which was countered to some degree by fitting a rubber pad to the butt. While reasonably satisfactory in jungle conditions, the No. 5 was found to suffer from a rare malady known as 'wandering zero', which meant that it was liable to suddenly lose its accuracy without warning. After much investigation the disease was pronounced incurable, and the Jungle Carbine was removed from service.

The Lee-Enfield was officially replaced as the standard rifle in 1957, but it is still in service, re-barrelled to 7·62mm NATO calibre, as a sniping rifle.

LEE-METFORD / Britain

In 1883 the British Army's Small Arms Committee was instructed to report 'as to the desirability, or otherwise, of introducing a magazine rifle' and 'as to the best pattern of such an arm'. They began by canvassing service opinion, which was divided on the subject, and then moved to testing a collection of magazine weapons, and their final decision was to the effect that they thought a magazine weapon was needed and that the Lee bolt action and magazine offered the best solution. At about the same time as this decision was reached, the French introduced their 8mm Lebel rifle, and in 1888 in Germany the German Commission (qv) magazine rifle appeared chambered in 7·92mm calibre. These two major powers had adopted small-calibre weapons using smokeless powder and, faced with this, in 1888 a new British rifle was approved for trials. It used the Lee bolt and box magazine allied to a barrel rifled according to a design by William Metford, an engineer and notable rifle enthusiast and designer. Metford's rifling was shallow-grooved, the groove edges being rounded in order to avoid sharp angles which encouraged the collection of powder fouling. For in spite of the appearance of smokeless powder on the Continent, the Royal Laboratory were not yet satisfied that a reliable and consistent powder had been produced, so that the ·303 cartridge for the new rifle used a charge of compressed gunpowder.

The official name of the new weapon was the Magazine Rifle Mark I, but the British soldier has always preferred a familiar name to an impersonal nomenclature, and it became the Lee-Metford Rifle. In all, there were four models of rifle, differing in minor features, and a carbine for cavalry use.

Gunpowder has liabilities as a gun propellant. It is liable to damp, gives off a dense cloud of white smoke, and generates a quantity of fouling which can soon jam a weapon. In 1891 the Royal Laboratory finally perfected a smokeless powder, a combination of nitro-glycerin and nitro-cellulose called cordite, and a ·303 cartridge loaded with cordite was issued. This was virtually smokeless, free from fouling, and more powerful than gunpowder, all of which were good points· but the temperature of the explosion was much higher than that of gunpowder, leading to erosion of the first part of the rifling. This made the weapons inaccurate, since it soon washed away the gentle contours of the Metford rifling and the bullet was no longer spun correctly. A new pattern of rifling, developed at the Royal Small Arms Factory, Enfield, was developed and adopted for the service rifle, which, by virtue of this change, became the Lee-Enfield (qv). The Lee-Metford was officially superseded in 1895, though it continued to be used for re-·serves and training until the 1920s.

Top: The Rifle, Short, Magazine, Lee-Enfield, or SMLE of 1907.

Centre: The Number 4 rifle, designed for mass-production.

Bottom: Rifle, Magazine, Lee-Enfield, Mark 1 of 1895.

LEFAUCHEAUX, Casimir (fl. 1820–1860)

Casimir Lefaucheaux was a Parisian gunsmith who, in 1836, developed a hinged-frame breech-loading shotgun which is the ancestor of all double guns. The two barrels were joined side by side and to a 'lump' or block of metal beneath the breech end; this block had a semi-circular cut-out at its front edge and a rect-angular one at its rear.

The semi-circular cut fitted around a cross-pin in the gun's fore-end and acted as a pivot and to locate the barrels, while the rectangular slot received a cross-bolt operated by an under-lever to lock the barrels in place in front of the standing breech. The gun was cham-bered for a pinfire cartridge, the pins of which protruded through slots in the top edge of the chamber face and into the air above the breeches when the gun was closed, so that they could be struck by the falling hammers. It was necessary to cock the hammers and pull them clear before opening the gun, and the empty cartridge cases were removed by using the pins. By modern standards the gun was crude and unsafe, but it was a notable advance for its period and cheap shotguns of this pattern were widely sold throughout Europe for the remain-der of the 19th century.

In 1854 he patented a breech-loading pinfire revolver which became the French Navy's standard issue weapon and was later widely adopted throughout Europe.

LE FRANCAIS/France

The Le Francais automatic pistol is made by the Manufacture Française d'Armes et Cycles de St. Etienne, now known as Manufrance. The company has, in fact, made a wide variety of sporting arms over the years, but the Le Francais is perhaps the most interesting of their products.

All the Le Francais models are to the same basic design: a blowback automatic in which the barrel is hinged to the frame so as to drop down in shotgun fashion when released by a side lever. This movement is also linked to the magazine, so that as soon as the magazine is withdrawn the barrel flies open, a certain method of ensuring safety while reloading. The breech block is conventional in appearance, but the return spring lies vertically in the front edge of the butt grip and is linked to the breech by a bell-crank, one arm of which engages in the block and the other hooks to the spring. Firing is done by a self-cocking striker which is forced back against a driving spring by the first movement of the trigger and then released to fire the cartridge. Upon firing the breech block is forced back and the empty case is ejected from the chamber by residual pressure, there being no form of positive extraction.

The first Le Francais was a 6·35mm model which appeared in 1914 as the Modele de

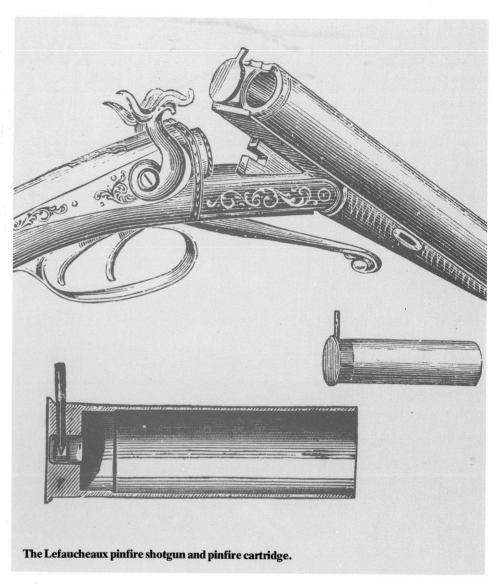

The Lefaucheaux pinfire shotgun and pinfire cartridge.

Poche, followed by a 6·35mm Policeman model with a longer barrel. In 1928 a Military model, chambered for the 9mm Long Brown-ing cartridge, appeared, in the hope of a milit-ary contract, but although the French Army purchased some for trials, it was not adopted. Currently, models in 6·35mm and 7·65mm are manufactured.

LE MAT, François Alexandre (1824–1883)

Dr. F. A. Le Mat was a French-born American whose title of 'Doctor' seems as obscure as his later-adopted 'Colonel'. His first appearance on the firearms scene came with his obtaining a patent in 1856 in which the arbor pin of a revolver, the axis about which the cylinder revolved, was in the form of a large-calibre gun barrel from which a charge of shot could be fired. A number of these revolvers appear to have been made in New Orleans in 1860, but

on the outbreak of the American Civil War Le Mat went to France where, in conjunction with a partner named Girard, he organised produc-tion of Le Mat revolvers for shipping to the Confederate Army. The first batch were made in Paris but they were found to be so faulty that subsequent production took place in Birming-ham, England.

In addition to these revolvers, Le Mat pro-duced some rifles on the same principle, though these are rarely seen, and as the percus-sion era closed he obtained patents covering the application of his idea to breech-loading metallic cartridge pistols. He continued to make improvements in the design until his death, though the revolver seems to have gone out of fashion in the late 1870s.

Percussion Le Mat revolvers are usually nine-chambered and of ·40 calibre, with an 18-bore shot barrel; pinfire and central-fire types are in a variety of commercial calibres.

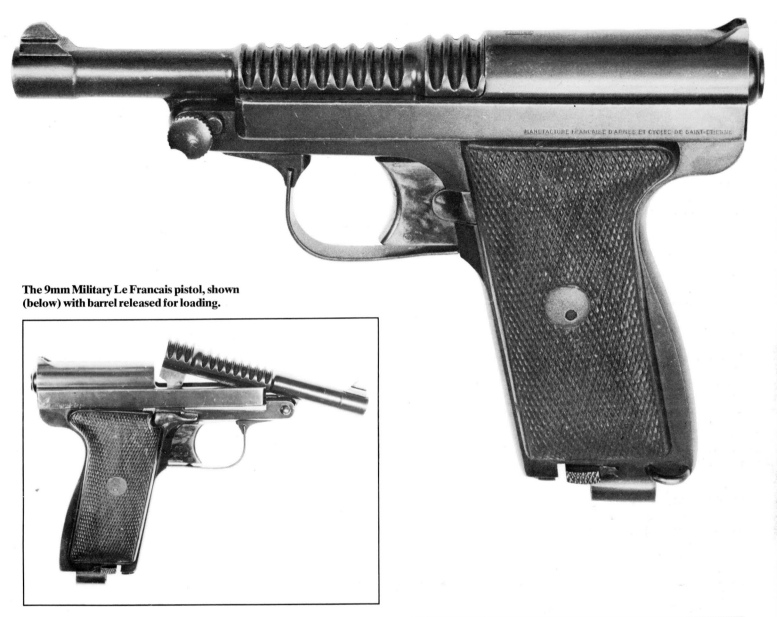

The 9mm Military Le Francais pistol, shown (below) with barrel released for loading.

The combination revolver designed by François Le Mat (1824 – c.1883) was produced in a variety of different guises, from a baby revolver to a carbine. Shown here is a late model revolver.

LEWIS, Isaac Newton (1858–1931)

Colonel I. N. Lewis graduated from West Point in 1884 and entered the Coast Artillery Corps, from which he retired in 1909. In 1910 the Automatic Arms Company of Buffalo, New York, asked him to develop a machine gun for them. This company had purchased patents from Samuel MacLean (qv) which needed further work to turn them into a workable gun. Lewis took up the challenge and by 1911 had five working guns available for demonstrations which took place at Fort Myer in front of various military authorities. Four guns were handed to the Board of Ordnance & Fortification for test, but the Board seemed curiously reluctant to come to any decision, and eventually Lewis took them back and went off to Belgium where he set up a company, the Armes Automatique Lewis in Liège in 1913. In 1914 most of the staff fled to Britain where they were given facilities to continue production at the BSA factory in Birmingham, and when the British Army, shortly afterwards, adopted the Lewis Gun, the entire BSA factory was given over to its manufacture.

The Lewis gun was used by the British, Belgian and Italian armies in great numbers and it later became one of the most important aircraft machine guns of the war. It remained in use until replaced by more modern designs in the 1930s, but even so there was still a place for it in the Second World War, when it was used by the British Royal Navy and Merchant Navy and also by the Home Guard.

In spite of all this, the American Army was peculiarly opposed to the Lewis; this may have been because the first ·30 Lewis Guns turned out to be defective due to their hasty modification from the British ·303 design. This was easily corrected, but no more than 2500 Lewis guns were taken into use by the Army, and even these were kept solely as training guns.

The US Marines adopted the Lewis, but on their arrival in France their Lewis guns were taken from them and replaced by the egregious Chauchat. The root of the matter appears to have been a personality clash between Lewis and Major General Crozier, Chief of Ordnance, US Army. After Crozier's retirement in 1918 things changed, and the Lewis gun became the standard Army Air Corps weapon.

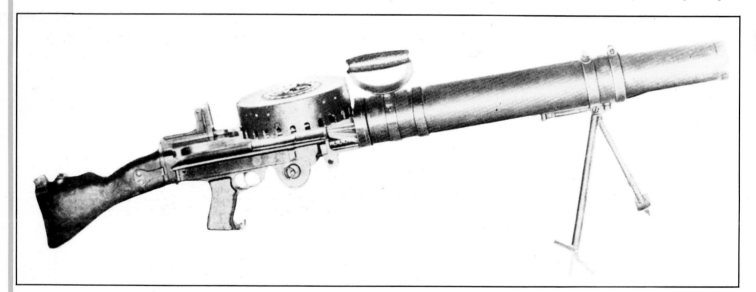

When this Lewis machine gun was used in training, a rattle was fitted to simulate firing.

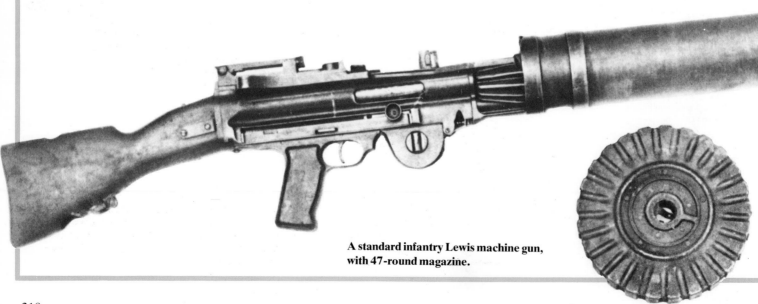

A standard infantry Lewis machine gun, with 47-round magazine.

Amends were finally made when a Second World War 16 inch gun Coast Artillery Battery in the Harbor Defenses of New York was named after Lewis, a traditional way of honouring illustrious Coast gunners.

The Lewis Gun was gas operated, using a piston under the barrel. The rear end of the piston rod carried an upright 'piston post' which engaged in a helical slot in the bolt so that as the piston moved back the bolt was first revolved to unlock and then drawn back. The firing pin was attached to the post, and struck the cartridge as the piston reached its forward position. Feed was from a flat drum on top of the gun; the original drum held 47 rounds, but

a deeper 97-round drum was developed for air use.

Ground guns were cooled by a peculiar system; the barrel was surrounded by longitudinal fins enclosed in a tubular shroud and open at the ends. The blast of gas at the muzzle as the gun fired drew air in at the rear of the casing, passed it over the fins, and expelled it at the muzzle. Aircraft guns dispensed with the fins and shroud, since the passage of the aircraft through the air gave the necessary cooling flow. During the Second World War many ex-aircraft guns were pressed into ground service, whereupon it was found that they showed no tendency to overheat, and Lewis's complicated cooling system was discovered to have been quite unnecessary.

The Soley Lewis, a modification designed in Britain in 1941, using the Bren gun magazine.

The aircraft and tank Lewis gun, with spade grip and a 97-round magazine.

The Lewis machine gun, manufactured by the Savage Arms Co during the First World War as an aircraft gun, and converted in the Second World War into a ground gun for the Home Guard.

The ·45 inch Flare Projector or Liberator pistol.

LIBERATOR/*USA*

In 1942 the American Office of Strategic Services hit upon the idea of producing a cheap and expendable single-shot pistol which could be distributed to disaffected elements in enemy countries and enable them to irritate their oppressors. Called, for security's sake, the ·45 Flare Projector, the design adopted was of a stamped metal frame mounting a smoothbore ·45 barrel, a hand-operated breech and a hand-cocked striker. The butt was hollow and could be used to carry spare cartridges. In use, the breech was opened and a ·45 cartridge inserted; it was then closed, and the striker cocked. Pulling the trigger discharged the shot, after which the breech was opened and the empty case ejected by poking down the barrel with a pencil or convenient twig. At short range it was quite effective; it needed to be, since if the first shot missed, there would be little chance to go through the emptying and reloading performance before retaliation descended.

Production was done by the Guide Lamp Division of General Motors, who knew little about pistols but a lot about stamping things out of sheet metal, and they produced a million in three months. They were provided with a 'comic strip' set of graphic instructions and ten cartridges, all in a waterproof bag for $2·10 apiece, and they were liberally distributed throughout Europe and the Far East. The name Liberator was given retrospectively when the gun was no longer confidential.

LIGNOSE/*Germany*

The Lignose Pulverfabrik was a German company manufacturing explosives and, in particular, smokeless powder for small arms ammunition. In 1920 the company expanded, buying up smaller firms and forming a consortium, Lignose AG. Among the companies so absorbed was the Theodor Bergmann Waffenfabrik of Suhl. Bergmann had died in 1915; Louis Schmeisser, the talent behind the firm, had left for other employment, and the company was in poor shape. Its output was henceforth known under the name of Lignose and the pistols and sporting guns were so marked. The best known of the Lignose products was the Einhand automatic pistol.

These pistols were derived from the patents of Chylewski (*qv*); he had toured Europe trying to sell his design with little success, and in mid-1921 the patents expired. The Bergmann company immediately began manufacture, but before many had been made under the Bergmann name the Lignose move took effect.

The special feature of the Einhand was the ability to cock and charge the pistol with one hand. The front edge of the trigger guard could be drawn back, cocking the slide and, when released, allowed the slide to run forward to chamber a cartridge. Thus the pistol could be

The Lignose Einhand one-handed automatic pistol.

carried unloaded and safe, and charged and cocked as it was drawn from the pocket. It was only successful in 6·35mm calibre; prototypes in 7·65mm and 9mm Short were made, but the additional strength of return spring needed for these more powerful cartridges needed a much more powerful grip to cock the pistol, and this made them impractical.

LITTLE TOM / *Austria*

The Little Tom automatic pistol was designed and manufactured by Alois Tomiska (1861–1946), a Bohemian gunmaker who had set up in business in Vienna in the 1890s. He patented it in 1908 and placed it on the market in the same year, producing models in 6·35mm and 7·65mm calibres. It was a simple blowback automatic, well made, and was noteworthy for being the first successful automatic pistol to use a double-action lock in which the first shot could be fired by pulling through on the trigger to cock and release the hammer. He continued to make and sell this design until the latter part of the First World War, but after the war he sold his patents to the Weiner Waffenfabrik of Vienna and went to Czechoslovakia to become designer and engineer with the Ceska Zbrojovka company until his retirement.

The Wiener Waffenfabrik, an obscure company, made some minor alterations in the appearance of the Little Tom and continued to manufacture it until about 1925. It has been estimated that about 15,000 were made by Tomiska and another 10,000 by Wiener Waffenfabrik.

LÖWE, Ludwig *(1837–1886)*

Löwe was an engineer who, by the 1860s, was running a small machine-tool company in Berlin. In 1870, after visiting the USA, he began the mass production of sewing machines, but during the course of the Franco-Prussian war accepted contracts for the manufacture of weapons and their components. Löwe realised that, given the political condition of Europe, there was probably more money to be made from arms than from sewing machines, and from then on he moved more and more towards munitions production. In the late 1870s the company received a substantial contract to make replicas of the Smith and Wesson ·44 'Russian' revolver for the Russian Army, and these were made under license from the American firm and reputedly with tools acquired from them. By the 1890s the factory was turning out Mauser military rifles by the thousand, both for the German Army and for overseas sale, having formed a business link with the Mauser company. Löwe had close connections with many contemporary armament companies and is said to have been instrumental in arranging the merger between

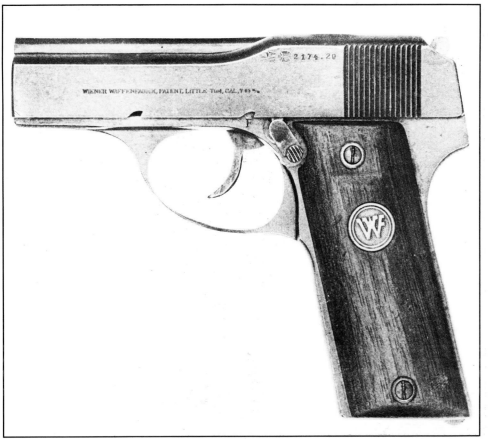

The later Little Tom as made by the Wiener Waffenfabrik.

The first Little Tom model, made by Tomiska.

The Lowell machine gun, showing the barrel cluster raised, ready to be turned to line up a cool barrel.

Vickers and Maxim. His most considerable contribution to firearms history came in 1892 when he employed Hugo Borchardt *(qv)* and produced the Borchardt pistol, a considerable act of faith which paved the way for the subsequent development of the Parabellum *(qv)*, or Luger pistol. In 1896 Löwe retired, and his company merged with others to become the Deutsche Waffen und Munitionsfabrik (DWM). Borchardt stayed on with DWM until he retired in 1919.

LOWELL/USA

The Lowell Manufacturing Company of Lowell, Massachusetts, was set up in 1875 by a Mr. De Witt C. Farrington in order to manufacture a mechanical machine gun of his design, sold as the Lowell gun. Superficially, it resembled the Gatling gun but the mechanism was entirely different: the Lowell had four exposed barrels but only one was used at a time and the barrel cluster did not rotate. When the barrel in use became too hot, the framework carrying the barrels could be moved round 90° and a cold barrel lined up for firing. The gun was operated by a hand crank at the rear which, by worm

gearing, drove the bolt back and forth. Feed was from an overhead magazine, a simple slotted upright in which the cartridge rims were engaged.

The gun was tested by the US Navy in 1876. Farrington was so sure of the soundness of his design that he asked for the services of two unskilled labourers, gave them a brief course of instruction, and then allowed them to fire the demonstration. They fired 2100 shots in $8\frac{1}{2}$ minutes, including changing the hot barrel round. This and subsequent demonstrations showed that the Lowell had claim to being one of the best mechanical guns ever designed; but like so many other excellent inventions, it appeared at the wrong time. The American forces had just outfitted with the Gatling gun and had no finance or inclination for anything else. The British had the Gardner and Nordenfelt, the French the Hotchkiss, and none of them wished to change simply for change's sake. Apart from 20 to Russia and small numbers to various American police and prison forces the Lowell failed to sell and the company closed down. The only Lowell gun known to exist is in the Royal Artillery Museum, a sample gun bought for trial in 1876.

LUGER, Georg *(1849–1923)*

Luger was born in the Tyrol and in 1865 became a Cadet in the Austro-Hungarian Army. He retired in 1872 in order to marry, and then took up employment as a railway engineer. His military service had, however, given him an interest in firearms and in 1875 he collaborated with F. von Mannlicher *(qv)* in designing a rifle magazine. He continued to design rifles and in 1891 joined the firm of Ludwig Löwe *(qv)* in Berlin, becoming a consultant designer. There he met Hugo Borchardt and, in due course, began to develop improvements to Borchardt's pistol design, the result being the Parabellum *(qv)* or Luger pistol, one of the world's most famous firearms.

In the past it has been accepted that Luger was the sole source of the improvements to the Borchardt, but more recent research indicates a degree of cooperation between the two men, though without doubt it was Luger's more practical viewpoint and more single-minded application that took the pistol to its final peak of design. Borchardt was apparently reluctant to refine a design once it worked; at any rate, the two produced a pistol which is still in production 60 years later.

MADSEN / *Denmark*

The Madsen gun was devised in the 1880s by Captain W. O. Madsen of the Danish Artillery, assisted by a Mr. Rasmussen, engineer at the Royal Arsenal at Copenhagen. In 1896 it was adopted as an automatic rifle by the Danish Navy, thus giving them the distinction of being the first force to adopt such a weapon, but it does not appear to have been a success. In the same year the Dansk Rekylriffel Syndikat was set up to promote the Madsen abroad, and a light machine gun version was introduced in 1902. Almost immediately it was bought by the Russian Army, who used it in the Russo-Japanese War, and this publicity attracted more orders. The Danish Army adopted it in 1904, and thereafter it was produced in every military calibre and adopted by armies throughout the world, remaining essentially unchanged until production ended in the 1950s.

The Masden was a remarkable weapon, quite unlike any other; indeed, one respected authority on the machine gun, the late Major F. W. Hobart, once said that the remarkable thing about the Madsen was not that it worked well, but that it worked at all. The mechanism relies on a rear-pivoted dropping breech block derived from the Martini *(qv)* action. Operation of this block is controlled by a stud on its side which travels in a groove cut in a switch plate which forms the right side of the gun body.

On firing, the barrel, barrel extension and breech block recoil. The stud on the block reaches a fork in the switch plate groove and is deflected upwards, lifting the front of the block away from the breech. An extractor claw beneath the chamber now strikes a cam surface and is drawn up and back so as to extract the empty case and eject it from the chamber; the case is deflected by the curved under-surface of the breech-block and is expelled through the bottom of the gun. By this time the stud has reached the end of the switch plate; the recoiling unit has cocked the gun's hammer and compressed a return spring which now begins to force everything back to the original position. During the recoil stroke a feed arm, pivoting at the bottom of the gun body, has been swung to the rear and now snaps in place behind a fresh cartridge which has entered the gun body from the overhead magazine. The forward movement of the recoiling parts now causes the stud to move down in the switch plate groove, dropping the face of the breech block below the mouth of the chamber. As the parts go forward, the feed arm drives the new cartridge into the breech; the stud then rides up in the switch plate, so raising the face of the block and closing the breech behind the cartridge. The final part of the forward movement carries the stud into a straight section of groove, locking the block firmly in place ready for the hammer to fall and fire the cartridge.

After the Second World War the Dansk Industrie Syndikat, as the company was now called, began to manufacture submachine guns. The first (1945) model was a mechanical oddity which used an all-enveloping recoiling slide rather in the manner of an over-sized automatic pistol. It was not a success, and in 1950 a completely new design appeared. This was of conventional form, using a bolt moving inside a rectangular receiver and a box magazine below the gun, but it maintained Madsen's record for originality by having the gun body pressed from sheet steel in two halves which were hinged together at the rear end.

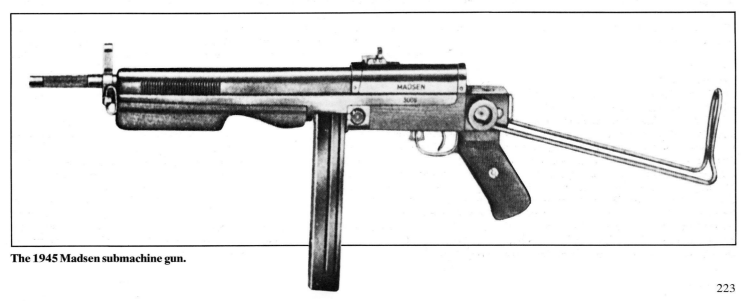

The 1945 Madsen submachine gun.

The barrel dropped into a prepared groove and the two halves were kept together by the barrel retaining nut. Removing this allowed the entire gun to be opened up like a book, giving unrivalled access for cleaning and maintenance. This, and the subsequent 1953 model which exhibited slight differences, sold in vast numbers throughout the world.

In 1956 the company produced two more designs, a light automatic rifle and the Madsen-Saetter machine gun. Both were gas-operated and both were very sound weapons, but the timing of their arrival was such that most countries had just completed re-armament with new infantry weapons and there was little market for the Madsen designs. After vainly trying to promote these new models for some time, the company gave up and retired from the firearms business in 1970.

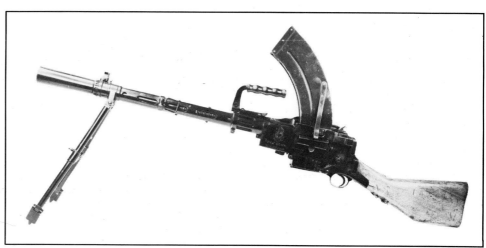

A typical Madsen light machine gun.

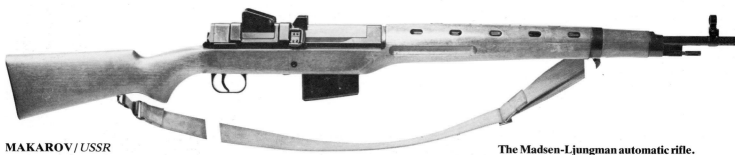

The Madsen-Ljungman automatic rifle.

MAKAROV / *USSR*

The Soviet Makarov pistol appeared in the late 1950s and is, by and large, an enlarged version of the Walther Model PP, with the same fixed barrel and double-action lock. There are, though, some minor internal differences in the mechanism; the safety catch moves in the opposite way, the trigger linkage is different, and the mainspring is a leaf rather than a coil. But the principal interest lies in the calibre: it is chambered for a special 9mm×18 cartridge known in the west as the 9mm Makarov or the 9mm Soviet Auto Pistol round. In both size and power it falls midway between the 9mm Short and 9mm Parabellum cartridges, and it would appear to have been designed to be as powerful as possible without demanding a locked-breech pistol. It is also used in the Stetchkin *(qv)* Soviet pistol, and a cartridge of similar dimensions and performance has recently been produced in West Germany, known there as the 9mm Police.

The Makarov pistol has been adopted by several other countries in the Communist bloc; it is known in East Germany as the Pistole M and in China as the Type 59.

MANN / *Germany*

The Fritz Mann Werkzeugfabrik of Suhl operated before and during the First World War as a supplier of gun components to gunmakers. In 1918 Mann decided to go into the pistol business, and did so with an unusual 6·35mm blow-

The Soviet Makarov automatic pistol.

back automatic pistol. At that time the vest pocket pistol was all the rage, and the Mann pistol weighed no more than nine ounces and at 4·02 inches overall was one of the smallest ever made. It was a solid-frame design with removeable barrel and separate bolt, and it was extremely difficult to dismantle or clean. It appears not to have sold well, and in 1924 he replaced it with a more conventional design based largely on the 1910 Browning pattern, with the recoil spring around the barrel. It was of far better quality than its predecessor and was made in 7·65mm and 9mm Short calibres until about 1929, when the Mann company closed down.

MANNLICHER, Ferdinand, Ritter von
(1848–1904)

Mannlicher was trained as an engineer and, obtaining employment with the Austrian Northern Railways, became their Chief Engineer. In 1876 he attended the World Exposition in Philadelphia and suddenly discovered an interest in firearms. He became associated with Austrian Arms Factory at Steyr and eventually retired from the railway to become a full-time weapons designer. He was knighted for his development of the Austrian Army service rifle.

Between 1875 and 1904 Mannlicher developed over 150 different weapons; many of these were never taken beyond the prototype stage, but the remarkable thing is that every one was actually made and fired. Numerous inventors have put scores of designs on paper, but Mannlicher stands unrivalled for the quantity of weapons he actually produced in metal.

Mannlicher's particular study was the repeating rifle and his first design, in 1880, was for a bolt-action rifle with three tubular magazines concealed within the butt. He abandoned this and developed a box magazine below the bolt, then a tubular magazine below the barrel, and then a gravity-fed overhead magazine, all of these within two years. In 1884 he broke new ground by producing a bolt action in which the bolt handle was pulled straight back, without having to turn it, to open the bolt. In the following year he improved this design and added a box magazine loaded with a clip of cartridges. The clip remained in the magazine, the cartridges being fed out one by one, until the last round had been fired, whereupon the clip was ejected upwards, past the open bolt.

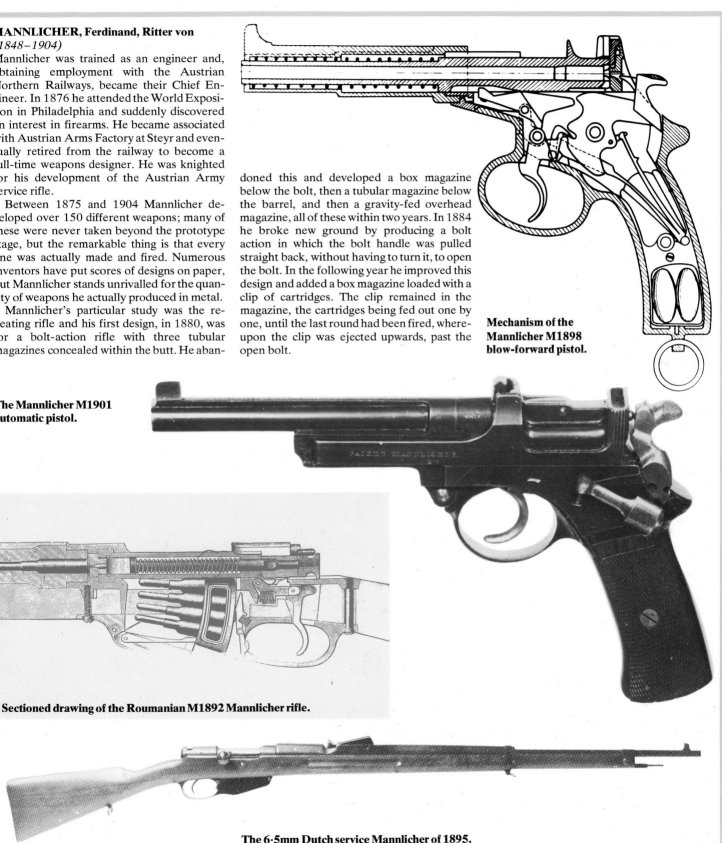

Mechanism of the Mannlicher M1898 blow-forward pistol.

The Mannlicher M1901 automatic pistol.

Sectioned drawing of the Roumanian M1892 Mannlicher rifle.

The 6·5mm Dutch service Mannlicher of 1895.

The Austro-Hungarian M1895 Mannlicher rifle.

His first success was the Austrian M1886 service rifle in 11mm calibre, a straight-pull bolt action, clip-loaded, the clip dropping through a slot in the bottom of the magazine after the last cartridge had been chambered. In 1887 he devised a turnbolt rifle with a revolving box magazine devised by Spitalsky, and then improved it by adopting a rotary magazine invented by Otto Schoenauer of the Steyr factory. These Mannlicher-Schoenauer actions were extensively used on sporting rifles as well as in military weapons, and a list of the individual nations who adopted Mannlicher rifles would take up far too much space. It is probably fair to say that with the exception of the British Lee-Enfield and the Danish Krag-Jorgensen systems, any country which didn't adopt a Mauser rifle adopted a Mannlicher, and the recently adopted Austrian Army sniping rifle is merely an up-dated version of Mannlicher-Schoenauer.

As early as 1885 he had an automatic rifle, recoil-operated, working successfully, and he later developed a number of delayed-blowback rifles, but such was the military conservatism of the time that none of them ever met with approval. His automatic pistol designs included a blow-forward model which achieved little success; a delayed blowback (the M1901) which is surely the most elegant and best-balanced automatic pistol ever made; and a locked breech model (the M1903) with a box magazine resembling that of the Mauser. But with his pistols he was less successful, largely because they were all chambered for unique cartridges of Mannlicher's own design instead of for more easily-found commercial types, and because they tended to be less robust than their competitors.

The 6·5mm Roumanian 1893 carbine.

The 7·92mm Hungarian Army Mannlicher M98/40.

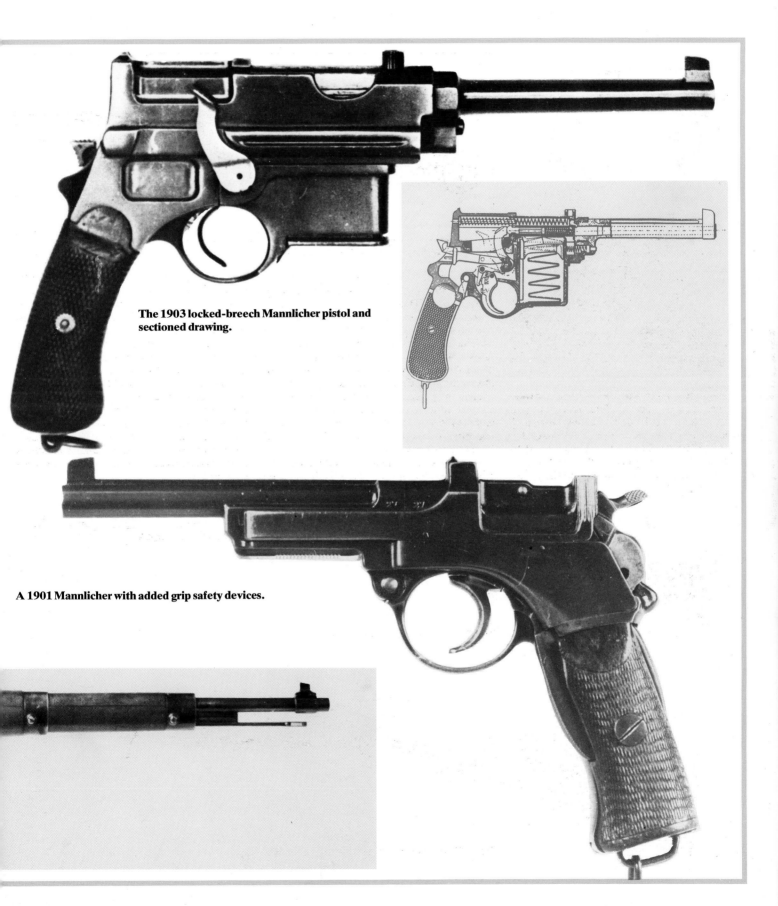

The 1903 locked-breech Mannlicher pistol and sectioned drawing.

A 1901 Mannlicher with added grip safety devices.

MANURHIN/*France*

The Manufacture de Machines du Haut Rhin of Mulhouse has principally been concerned with machine tools, though there has always been a close connection with the firearms world, since the company manufactures some of the world's best machinery for the production of small arms ammunition.

In the years after the Second World War the company obtained a licence from Walther to manufacture the Walther PP and PPK automatic pistols. These were made to standards equally as high as those of Walther and except for the markings were indistinguishable from the originals. When the licence agreement ended and Walther went back into the arms business, Manurhin continued to make the pistols on contract for several years; these were shipped to Walther and there given the usual Walther markings.

More recently the company has introduced the MR73 revolver, the first new revolver design to appear in France for many years. It is a solid-frame, double-action model with side-swinging cylinder, in ·357 Magnum calibre. Two versions are made; the Combat, with short barrel lengths and fixed sights, and the Target, with barrels of up to eight inches length and micrometer-adjustable rear sight. The Target model is also made in ·22 calibre.

The Walther pistol produced by Manurhin under license.

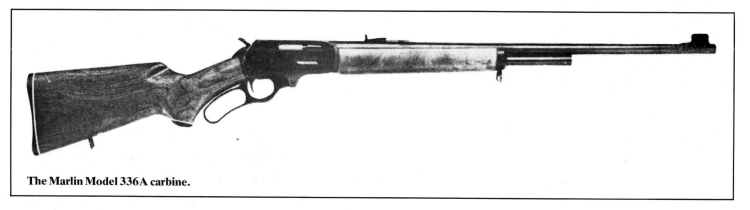

The Marlin Model 336A carbine.

MARGOLIN, Mikhail *(b. 1904)*

Margolin is a designer of target and sporting pistols which have achieved international recognition, and this is the more remarkable since he was blinded in 1923 while on military service. It is reported that his design technique is to make models of components in wax or modelling clay and gradually build up a complete model mechanism, after which drawings are prepared and the parts made in metal. Margolin then 'studies' them with his finger-tips, suggests modifications, and thus the design is perfected.

In general, the Margolin models are fixed-barrel ·22 automatic pistols with external hammers; they are, of course, carefully made to fine tolerances, and are fitted with micrometer

sights, balance weights, adjustable triggers, anatomical grips and all the other refinements that high-quality competitive shooting demands.

In 1956 the Soviet competitors in the Olympic rapid-fire matches at Melbourne used a remarkable Margolin design in which the mechanism was inverted, so that the axis of the barrel was below the trigger and the recoil force was aligned with the centre of the firer's hand and arm, so eliminating much of the tendency of the pistol to jump when fired. Subsequently, the Olympic Committee changed the rules to ensure that only conventional pistols could be used in the rapid-fire event; unconventional weapons are catered for in the 'free pistol' classes.

MARLIN, John Mahlon *(d. 1901)*

John Marlin was an out-worker in the gun trade in the 1860s; that is to say he would contract with a gunsmith to manufacture certain components and make them in his own workshop. In the early 1870s he began making cheap solid-frame rimfire revolvers and single-shot pistols, and then moved on to include single-shot falling-block rifles. His activities prospered, and in 1881 the Marlin Firearms Company was formed and a lever-action rifle was introduced. This rifle had a tube magazine below the barrel and superficially resembled the contemporary Winchester, but the breech action is much different. Instead of using a toggle mechanism, the lever moves the breech block by direct linkage and the block is locked

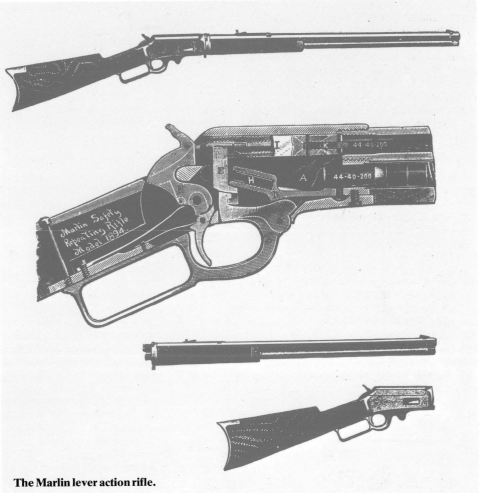

in place by a vertical locking strut which, actuated by the lever, moves up and enters a recess in the lower side of the block. The lever also operates the usual sort of cartridge lifter. This rifle, in a variety of calibres, has remained the mainstay of the company ever since, though in 1898 shotguns were added to the firm's range.

In about 1887 a double-action hinged-frame revolver went into production, but contemporary reports give an unfavourable opinion of this weapon and the company discontinued it in the late 1890s, concentrating on shoulder arms thereafter. In recent years they have added self-loading sporting rifles to their products.

During both World Wars the company manufactured military weapons on contract, both for the US Army and for various Allies. The Marlin machine gun, used by the US Army between the wars as an aircraft and tank gun, was Marlin's redesign of the Colt M1895 machine gun, substituting a conventional gas piston for the swinging arm actuator.

The Marlin lever action rifle.

MARS / Britain

The name 'Mars' has attracted a number of pistol makers; Th. Bergmann used it for commercial sales of the design known as the Bergmann-Bayard; Kohout & Co. of Czechoslovakia produced copies of the Browning 1906 and 1910 models under this name; and the Manufacture d'Armes de Pyrenees of Hendaye used it as a sales name for the Unique series of automatic pistols. But these all fade into the background when compared with the English Mars, one of the most powerful, complicated and rare pistols in history.

The Mars was designed by Hugh Gabbett-Fairfax of Leamington Spa. He was a prolific inventor of automatic firearms, taking out numerous patents between 1895 and 1923, though few of his designs ever got off the paper. In 1895 he patented a long-recoil pistol with rotary magazine, of which one specimen is known to exist, but he then changed his design to one with a conventional butt magazine. In 1897 he offered the design to Webley & Scott, but they did not adopt it, though they were willing to manufacture it for Gabbett-Fairfax

to sell. Accordingly, he organised the Mars Automatic Fire-Arms Syndicate in 1901, but shortly after this Webley changed their minds and gave him back the designs. Manufacture was then arranged with an unknown Birmingham gunsmith, pistols were made, and they were placed on sale and also submitted for military trial. After exhaustive tests they were turned down; since the Syndicate had gambled on military acceptance, this refusal brought about their liquidation and Gabbett-Fairfax's bankruptcy in 1903. A fresh Mars Automatic Pistol Syndicate was formed and a few more pistols made, but this venture failed in 1907 and the Mars vanished. It has been reliably estimated that no more than about eighty pistols were ever made, and from the specimens

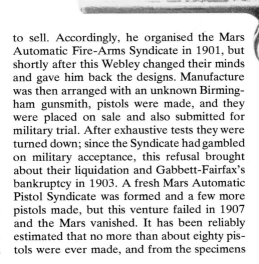

The Mars automatic pistol in ·45 calibre.

which remain it is likely that few of them were alike, since modifications were made from time to time as ideas suggested themselves.

The novelty of the Mars—and its downfall—lay in its mechanism and in the ammunition which Gabbett-Fairfax designed for it. It was a long-recoil pistol of considerable ingenuity. On firing, the barrel and bolt, securely locked, recoiled about two inches along the top of the frame, cocking the external hammer as they came to rest. The bolt was then revolved to unlock it from the breech, and the barrel ran back to the forward position. As it did so, the empty cartridge case was extracted and a mechanical ejector knocked it clear of the feedway. During the recoil stroke a cartridge carrier had withdrawn a cartridge from the magazine, backwards, and now lifted it up to align with the chamber. All this happened in a split second, and now the firer relaxed his grip on the trigger preparatory to taking the pressure for the next shot; this released the bolt, which ran forward, chambering the cartridge and then revolving to lock into the breech. At the same time, the cartridge carrier dropped down and grasped the next cartridge in the magazine.

The Mars was produced in 8·5mm, 9mm, ·36 and ·45 calibres, and all of them fired special bottle-necked cartridges of exceptional power; the 9mm, for example, fired a 156 grain bullet at 1650 feet a second to give a muzzle energy of 943 foot-pounds. Bearing in mind that the US Colt ·45 automatic delivers only 370 foot-pounds, it is obvious that the Mars was a handful in every respect. Its epitaph appears in the records of the trial: 'No one who fired once with this pistol wished to shoot with it again.'

MARTINI, Friederich von *(fl. 1860–1880)*
Martini was a skilled engineer rather than a gunsmith. In 1867 the Swiss government bought 15,000 Peabody rifles from the USA, but, having got them, the Swiss Army felt that they might be improved, and they asked von

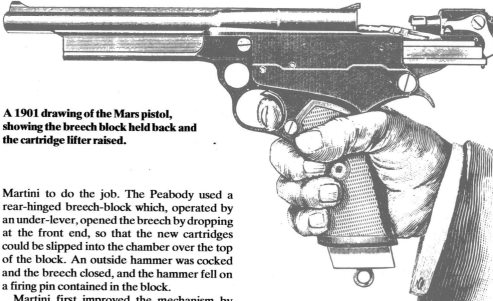

A 1901 drawing of the Mars pistol, showing the breech block held back and the cartridge lifter raised.

Martini to do the job. The Peabody used a rear-hinged breech-block which, operated by an under-lever, opened the breech by dropping at the front end, so that the new cartridges could be slipped into the chamber over the top of the block. An outside hammer was cocked and the breech closed, and the hammer fell on a firing pin contained in the block.

Martini first improved the mechanism by arranging for the hammer to cock automatically as the breech was opened. He then went one better and threw away the hammer, putting a firing pin inside the breech block and cocking it automatically as the breech was opened. Not only was this neater, but it reduced the 'lock time'—the time between pulling the trigger and having the cartridge explode; the shorter the lock time, the less chance there is of the rifleman's aim wandering, and thus the better the accuracy of the rifle system. For that reason the Martini action is still used today in target small-bore guns. Since it also has attributes of strength and simplicity, it has been used in single-barrel shotguns. The greatest military application of this system came with its adoption in Britain for use in the Martini-Henry rifle.

MARTINI-HENRY / *Britain*
In 1867 the British Army began examining competing breech-loading systems in order to settle on a replacement for the Snider conver-

sion. After examining several weapons, they chose the Martini breech action described above and allied it with a barrel rifled to a design proposed by Alexander Henry (*qv*). The Martini-Henry rifle in ·45 calibre was adopted in April 1871. Several variant models of rifle and carbine followed, and after the adoption of the ·303 cartridge and the Lee-Metford rifle, many Martinis were taken into workshops and re-barrelled in ·303 calibre for use by Territorial and Militia units until sufficient magazine rifles were available. When so modified they became known as Martini-Enfield or Martini-Metford, according to the type of barrel fitted, and they remained in use until the First World War. Original Martini-Henry rifles in ·45 calibre were still in use by local defence forces in the Suez Canal area as late as 1950.

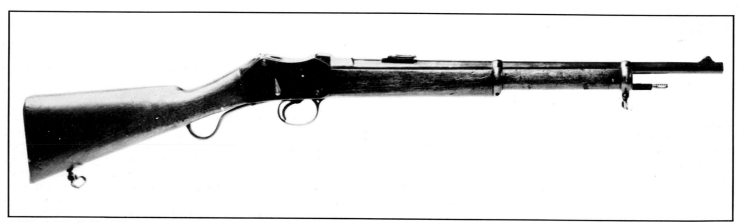

A Martini-Enfield carbine, derived from the Martini-Henry by having a ·303 Enfield barrel in place of the original ·45.

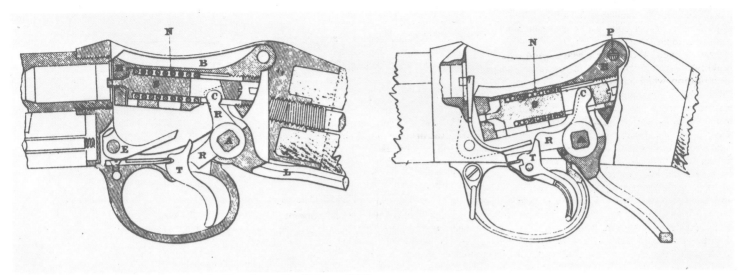

The action of the Martini-Henry, from the *Treatise on Small Arms*, 1888.

MAS/*France*
Gunmaking began in St. Etienne, on the Loire, in 1535, and the Manufacture National d'Armes de St. Etienne (known as MAS) was founded in 1669. Since that time it has been concerned in the manufacture of every sort of military weapon and the design department has been responsible for several important weapons. Not all its efforts have been successful; the St. Etienne machine gun of 1907, for example, set out to replace the Hotchkiss by indulging in some questionable mechanical

larly over-complicated and fragile weapon, though it managed to survive until the middle 1930s before it was retired.

Better designs have, however, made up for the occasional mistake. In the early 1930s the St. Etienne factory assumed major responsibility for the automatic pistol designed by Petter (*qv*) and produced it as the MAS 1935. This was a first-class pistol, using a similar system of locking to the Browning GP35 model, and its only disadvantage was that it was chambered for a somewhat ineffectual cartridge, the

cartridge and intended to replace the miscellany of 8mm Lebel and Berthier rifles and carbines then in service. This was the last bolt-action design to be adopted by a major power, and opinions on it differ. From the purely mechanical standpoint it is strong and simple, though simplicity was carried rather far by the omission of a safety catch. But it was an ugly weapon and, due to the positioning of the bolt and trigger, it was necessary to bend the bolt lever acutely forward, which many people find awkward to operate.

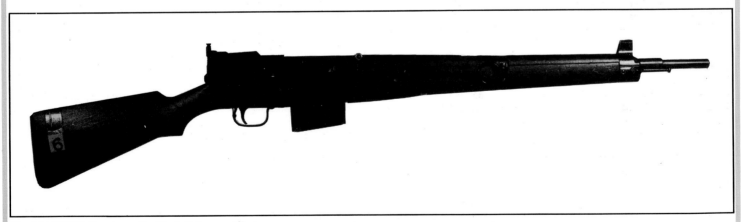

The MAS M1949 automatic rifle in 7·5mm calibre.

aberrations. The gas piston was blown forward and hence had to operate a rack and pinion device in order to reverse the direction of motion and thus propel the breech-block backwards. It was adopted for service but was rapidly replaced by the standard Hotchkiss in 1914 when war showed up its deficiencies. The Model 1917 automatic rifle, of which over 80,000 were made in St. Etienne, was a simi-

7·65mm French Long. This was eventually amended in 1950 when the MAS1950 pistol appeared, more or less the 1935 model suitably modified to accept the 9mm Parabellum cartridge.

The 1930s saw a great deal of activity in France as the Army, rather belatedly, began to demand new weapons. In 1936 the MAS36 rifle appeared, chambered for the new 7·5mm

After this the St. Etienne arsenal turned to the design of a submachine gun, the MAS38. This also has an odd look about it, because the axis of the barrel and of the body and stock are divergent by several degrees, giving the weapon a peculiarly 'bent' look. The reason for this was that for the sake of compactness of the body, the bolt had to recoil inside a tube let into the buttstock; and since the butt had to 'drop'

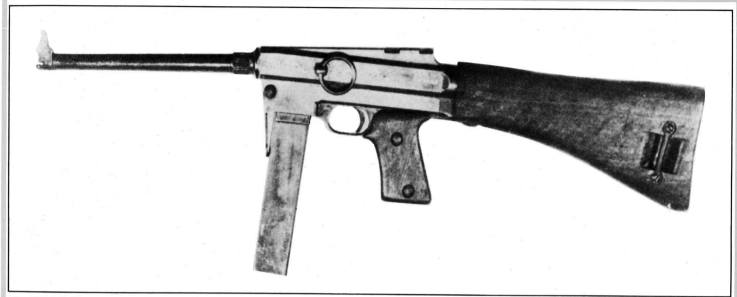

The MAS 7·65mm submachine gun of 1938.

to give a natural aiming stance, the receiver had to be realigned. As a result, the face of the bolt is cut obliquely so that although it approaches the breech at an angle it closes evenly on the cartridge. This weapon, too, was chambered for the 7·65mm Long cartridge. Both the rifle and the submachine gun were quite sound designs, but the war came along so soon after their introduction that sufficient were never produced for general issue.

During the war and the German occupation, the design staff quietly worked away on a new automatic rifle and by 1944 were able to make prototypes. After tests and changes this appeared in 1949 as the MAS49 and was adopted throughout the French Army, giving them a lead over every other European nation. This was a 7·5mm gas-operated rifle in which the bolt was tilted down at the rear to lock into the gun body. No gas piston was used, the gas being piped back to impinge directly upon the bolt carrier. With a ten-round magazine and an integral grenade launcher at the muzzle, it was a robust, if somewhat heavy, rifle. It was modified in 1956 by shortening the wooden stock and adding a muzzle brake.

The latest MAS product to be put forward is the MAS 5·56; this is an automatic assault rifle in 5·56mm calibre, gas operated and capable of automatic fire. It is extremely modern in layout, designed as a straight-line 'bull-pup' with the bolt actually behind the firer's eye. This allows the maximum length of barrel to be got into the minimum length of rifle. The weapon is under evaluation; there seems to be little doubt that it will replace the MAS49.

MAT/*France*

Manufacture National d'Armes de Tulle, a French government arsenal established in the 17th century. While manufacturing all manner of armaments and accessories to government specification, the factory attached its name to an extremely good submachine gun, the MAT–49. Production began in 1949 and continued for several years, and the MAT–49 is currently in wide use by French military and police forces.

It is a solid and strong weapon, largely made of sheet steel stampings, a conventional gun firing the 9mm Parabellum cartridge. The butt is in wire form, telescoping alongside the receiver, and the magazine housing and magazine can be folded forward to lie under the barrel jacket, forming a compact unit for carrying. The bolt design is unusual in that the front face has a reduced diameter section which enters a recess in the breech face, so that the cartridge is completely surrounded by steel at the instant of firing. A grip safety locks the bolt and trigger, so that the gun cannot be accidentally fired should it be dropped.

The MAT 9mm submachine gun of 1949.

MAUSER / *Germany*

Peter Paul Mauser (1838–1914) and his brother Wilhelm (1834–1882) were two of the thirteen children of Franz Andreas Mauser, a gunsmith of Oberndorf-am-Necker. They were both apprenticed in the Royal Wurttemberg Arms Factory at Oberndorf, and in 1865 began to develop improvements to the Needle Gun. While attempting to interest various government departments in their invention, they fell in with an American entrepreneur, Samuel Norris, who persuaded them to set up a workshop in Belgium and there continue the development of their new rifle, patents for which were taken out jointly in the names of Norris and the two Mauser brothers. Norris was intent upon selling the Mauser design to the French, in the hope of replacing their ageing Chassepot rifle, but the French were not interested, and Norris withdrew his financial support in 1869 and allowed the patent to lapse.

The Mausers returned to Oberndorf, submitted their latest design to the Prussian Rifle Test Commission at Spandau, and in 1871 it was accepted for service. The resulting orders for the new rifle led to the formation of the Gebruder Mauser & Cie. Peter Paul attended

Paul Mauser

Wilhelm Mauser

to manufacture, while Wilhelm was the administrator and salesman until his unfortunate early death. After this, Peter Paul took on the entire burden of design and administration,

and remained in harness to the end of his life. His death in 1914 was due to complications which set in after he caught a chill while range-testing his latest automatic rifle.

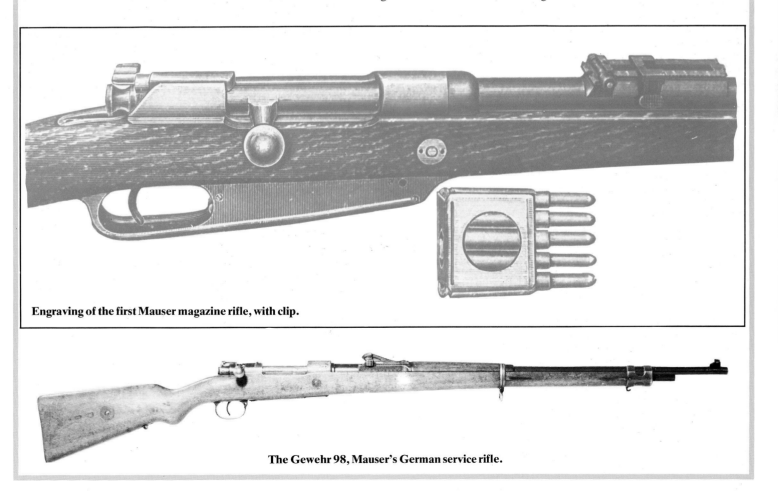

Engraving of the first Mauser magazine rifle, with clip.

The Gewehr 98, Mauser's German service rifle.

In spite of the astronomical number of Mauser rifles adopted throughout the world, the actual basic design changes were comparatively few. The Model 1871 service rifle was a single shot turnbolt weapon in 11mm calibre. Locking of the bolt was done by the bolt handle being turned down in front of a shoulder in the action body; the firing pin was withdrawn as the bolt opened and fully cocked on the closing stroke, and a manual safety catch was fitted to the rear end of the striker.

With the arrival of repeating rifles, Mauser developed a conversion of the 1871 design which used the same bolt and added a tubular magazine below the barrel and the usual type of bolt-actuated cartridge lifter. This was adopted in 1884, but the German Army wanted a 'packet-loading' system and in 1888 the Commission Rifle (qv) went into service, using the Mannlicher system of clip loading. The bolt action was much as before, but with a vitally important alteration in the method of locking; this was now done by two opposed lugs on the bolt head which engaged in recesses in the breech face as the bolt was rotated. (Mauser had developed this system of locking on a 9·5mm rifle supplied to Turkey in 1875.)

Mauser was far from pleased at seeing his rifle displaced by what he felt to be an inferior design, and he set about developing his own packet-loading rifle. Instead of the currently popular retained clip, he chose to use a five-round 'charger' which was lodged in the bolt-way and the five cartridges swept out and into the magazine by thumb pressure. (A distinction must be made here: properly speaking, a 'clip' becomes part of the magazine, and the gun cannot be operated without it, whereas the 'charger' is only a cartridge-holder, though often called a clip nowadays.) A box magazine below the bolt took the cartridges and they were forced up by a spring-loaded arm. This system, together with a one-piece bolt with forward locking lugs, was used first in the M1889 Belgian service rifle. The next major improvement came with the M1893 Spanish

Army rifle in which the magazine became a more compact unit concealed within the rifle stock instead of being a metal box in front of the trigger guard.

In 1898 the German Army discarded the Commission Rifle in favour of a Mauser design, the Gewehr 98 (qv). The principal change here was the incorporation of a third, rear, locking lug on the bolt. There were no further major changes in Mauser rifle design after this; subsequent Mauser bolt-action rifles developed by the Mauser company or by other countries—eg, the Belgian and Czech 1924

models—were merely changes in detail.

Having perfected the bolt action, Mauser turned to the development of automatic rifles. Various systems were explored; short recoil, long recoil, turning bolts, locking by flaps and cams, but few designs ever went beyond the prototype stage. The German Army tested the various designs without accepting them, but in 1915 took a number of Mauser's last design into use as the Flieger Selbstlader Karabiner 1915 and issued them as aircraft observer's guns. They were soon superseded by machine guns, however.

The Mauser Zig Zag revolver, opened to show the method of extracting and loading.

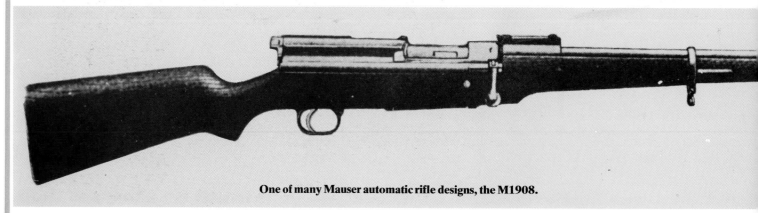

One of many Mauser automatic rifle designs, the M1908.

Mauser's development of pistols began badly, with a single-shot weapon in 1877 which achieved limited production. In the following year he produced the Zig Zag revolver, which gained this nick-name from the grooving on the outer surface of the cylinder. As the pistol was cocked, a pin in the frame moved back and forth and, riding in the zig-zag groove, rotated the cylinder. Mauser had hopes of a military contract, since the Army was anxious to adopt a revolver, but his design was turned down as being too expensive and complicated and the Army settled for the more primitive Reichsrevolver (*qv*).

In 1886 he produced designs for a mechanical repeating pistol, with a tubular magazine below the barrel and a finger-actuated mechanism of watch-like complexity; it is doubtful if many were made. It was not until 1896, with the Mauser Military Pistol, that he

Mauser military pistol, 1895 pattern.

achieved anything like success in the handgun field, and it must be said that this pistol was not his idea, but had been developed by the Superintendent of his factory, one Herr Federle. Although it was to sell by the million in later years, the Military (and its variant successors) was never adopted as the official service arm by any major power.

The Mauser Model 1908 pistol, produced in small numbers.

235

The Military relied on a reciprocating bolt inside a square-section receiver; it was locked to the breech by two heavy lugs which entered the bottom of the bolt, since the pistol fired a powerful 7·63mm cartridge. Ten rounds were charger-loaded into a box magazine ahead of the trigger, and a wooden holster-case could be clipped to the butt to form a shoulder-stock, after which the pistol could perform as a sort of carbine. It was invariably beautifully made and finished, and in spite of an unprepossessing appearance it is, in fact, a comfortable and accurate pistol to shoot. The variant models were principally changes in barrel length, sights and safety catch, but during the First World War the German Army placed a con-tract for 150,000 pistols chambered for the 9mm Parabellum cartridge, the only time the pistol was ever made in other than the 7·63mm calibre. The only other major change came in the early 1930s when, in response to competition from Spanish gunmakers who were marketing imitation Mauser pistols, Mauser produced a full-automatic version which, when fitted with its butt-stock, became a species of submachine gun.

In 1910 came the first Mauser pocket pistol, a blowback automatic in 6·35mm calibre, followed in 1914 by a 7·65mm version. These were rather larger than might be expected for pocket weapons of such calibres, but they were robust and well-made weapons which were adopted in numbers by various continental police forces. In 1934 the design was brought up to date by adopting a better-shaped grip and making some manufacturing changes, but this model was eclipsed by the Model HSc of 1938. This was a 7·65mm pistol of modern appearance, with double-action lock, obviously produced in answer to the competing Model PP by Walther.

The vest pocket market was also catered for by two *Westentaschenpistole* in 6·35mm, one appearing in 1918 and the other in 1938.

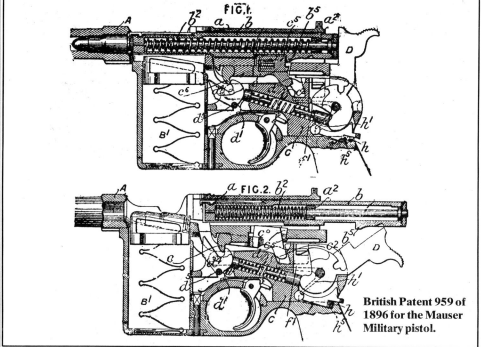

British Patent 959 of 1896 for the Mauser Military pistol.

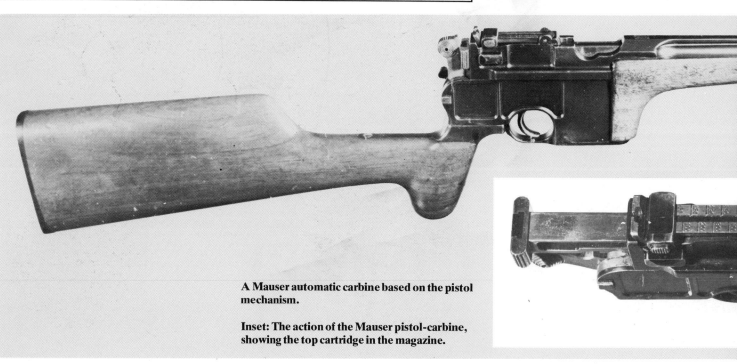

A Mauser automatic carbine based on the pistol mechanism.

Inset: The action of the Mauser pistol-carbine, showing the top cartridge in the magazine.

Mauser Model HSc double-action automatic pistol.

The Mauser Westentaschenpistole 2 6·35mm pistol.

The Mauser Model 912 selective-fire pistol.

During the Second World War Mauser were, of course, concerned in the production of all types of arms, from pistols to artillery. Their principal contribution to the military field was the MG34 machine gun, derived from a Swiss-made gun offered to the German Army in 1932. This was given to Mauser to improve, though their subsequent improvement amounted to a total re-design. It became one of the best machine guns of the war and introduced two radical concepts: that of the general purpose machine gun which could be used either as the squad light automatic or as a heavy sustained-fire weapon; and the idea of using a belt-fed gun as the squad automatic. Unfortunately it was an expensive gun to make, and Mauser later developed the MG42, no less effective but easier to mass-produce.

After the war the Mauser factory was under French control for some time, after which work more or less came to a halt. But the company survived and currently manufactures sporting arms. In addition, the Parabellum pistol has been put back into production.

The Mauser was chosen by some officers as an alternative to the Parabellum. This 1934 example has a German Navy badge.

An engraved Mauser HSc with its clip, in presentation box.

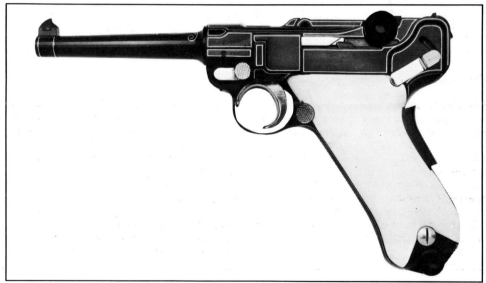

The famous Parabellum is still available from Mauser. This is the De Luxe model, with ivory grips.

The Mauser Sturmgewehr 45, prototype model, which acted as inspiration for many postwar designs, among them the CETME and G3 rifles.

The original Maxim machine gun.

MAXIM, Sir Hiram Stevens (*1840–1916*)

Hiram Maxim was apprenticed to a coach-builder, and went on to work in an engineering shop and a ship-yard. He then displayed a talent for electrical engineering and patented innumerable inventions in that field. In 1872 he designed a helicopter, and in 1894 he successfully demonstrated the aerodynamic principle of lift, using a steam-powered aircraft on rails. He became a naturalised British subject and was knighted in 1901.

Whatever else Maxim may have done, he is most famous for his machine gun. He experimented at various times with automatic rifles and pistols, but did not pursue them; however the machine gun, in his hands, changed from a hand-cranked curiosity to a self-powered weapon which changed the nature of warfare.

In 1881 Maxim attended an Electrical Exhibition in Paris; according to legend, he was there told by a friend that the quickest road to fame and fortune would be to abandon the electrical business and 'make something that will enable these fool Europeans to kill each other quicker'. Whatever the truth of the matter, Maxim came to London and set up a workshop in Covent Garden; he then carefully studied firearms, took out patents on every operating principle that looked feasible, and in 1884 demonstrated his first automatic gun. While this weapon worked, startlingly well to most observers, Maxim was still not satisfied; he was also given some good advice, by British Army officers, on such things as reliability, simplicity and ease of maintenance, features which inventors, then as now, often overlooked.

In 1885 he produced a new model which became the basic Maxim design and underwent no significant changes thereafter. It was a recoil-operated gun, belt fed and water-cooled, in which the breech block was locked by a toggle joint. It was first used in action by a British detachment in Gambia in November 1887, and by that time Maxim was travelling Europe, demonstrating and selling. By the turn of the century it had been adopted by the Russian, German, Belgian and Swiss armies, as well as the British, and more armies would follow suit. Maxim guns were used in every quarter of the globe and they were to remain in first-line service with some nations until the end of the Second World War.

In 1884 Maxim had approached Vickers, a British ship-building firm, and with Albert Vickers as Chairman had set up the Maxim Gun Company. In 1888 it joined with the Nordenfelt company to form the Maxim Nordenfelt Gun Company, and in 1892 Vickers took over and formed Vickers, Sons & Maxim.

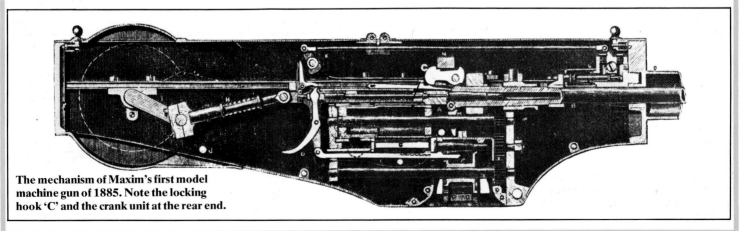

The mechanism of Maxim's first model machine gun of 1885. Note the locking hook 'C' and the crank unit at the rear end.

Maxim continued to invent, developing 37mm and 40mm automatic guns which were enlargements of the machine gun; the former was to become famous as the 'Maxim Pom-Pom' in the Boer War. His son Hudson Maxim began development of a weapon silencer in the early 1900s which Sir Hiram carried to a successful conclusion, and most weapon silencers since then have been based on his design. No better example of his versatility can be given than this extract from the trade magazine *Arms & Explosives* for March 1902: 'Sir Hiram Maxim is not only a prolific inventor but versatile withal. One of his latest patents does not deal with electric lighting, flying machines, ordnance or explosives, but with a new system of roasting coffee whereby the natural aroma of the berry is retained. . . .'

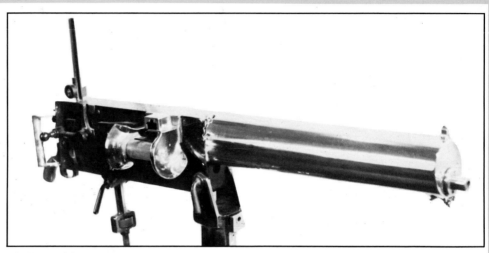

An early British Maxim gun in ·45 calibre.

Maxim's automatic pistol, an ingenious design which was never put into production.

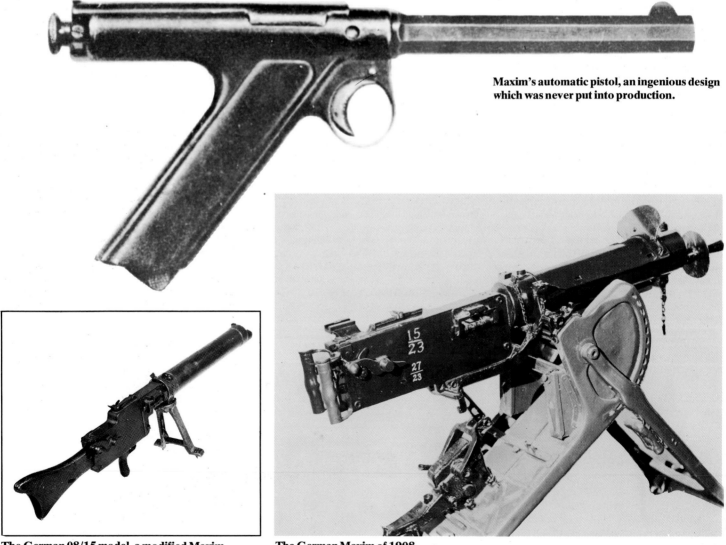

The German 08/15 model, a modified Maxim.

The German Maxim of 1908.

MAYNARD, Dr. Edward

Dr. Maynard was a Washington DC dentist with an interest in firearms. In 1845 he patented a 'percussion tape' in which pellets of detonating composition were spaced along a paper or linen tape. These tapes were coiled in a small magazine alongside the weapon lock, with a feed mechanism linked to the hammer, so that as the hammer was cocked, so sufficient tape was fed out to position a pellet of composition on top of the breech nipple. The system was quite successful and was extensively used on carbines and rifles from about 1850 onward. It was, of course, the inspiration for the familiar roll of explosive 'caps' now sold for children's toy pistols.

With the advent of breech-loading Maynard patented a metallic cartridge with a hole in the base instead of any form of cap. It was to be used with the usual percussion ignition system, more specifically with his 'percussion tape primer', and the flame from the nipple passed into the hole in the cartridge to fire the charge. Several thousand carbines using this system were made during the American Civil War. Maynard also developed a breech-loading rifle with drop-down barrel to suit his cartridge, which was sold as a sporting rifle for many years.

McLEAN, Samuel N. *(fl. 1900–1915)*

There are two McLeans who appear as patentees and inventors in firearms history; this is the sane one. The other, Doctor James H., was a lunatic dentist who, in collaboration with Myron Coloney (*qv*) invented ever more improbable firearms to amaze successive generations of students. Samuel, however, was a much more practical man, though as with many firearms inventors, success always seemed to elude him. In conjunction with Colonel O. M. Lissak, a respected ordnance engineer, he developed a useful 37mm cannon in 1903 which was somewhat before its time and never gained acceptance. They then went on to devise a machine gun mechanism which, failing to interest the US Army, was sold to the Automatic Arms Company who later transformed it into the highly successful Lewis (*qv*) machine gun.

In the pistol field, McLean espoused the mechanical repeater, and in 1892 patented a design covering a pistol with a cluster of tubular magazines beneath the barrel. The trigger caused a lifter to raise a cartridge to the breech, where a reciprocating breech block chambered and fired it. When one tubular magazine was empty, another was moved into place. It is understood that prototypes were made but none are now known to exist.

After his disappointment over the Lewis gun design, McLean abandoned the firearms field and turned to other forms of mechanical engineering.

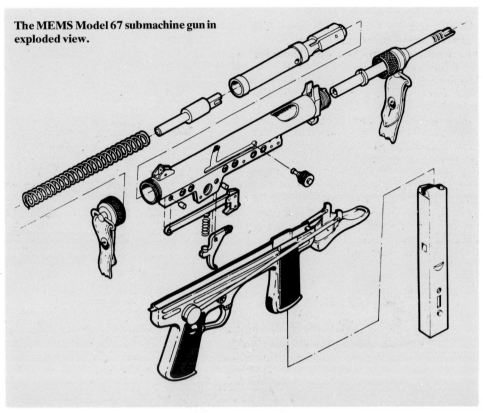

The MEMS Model 67 submachine gun in exploded view.

MEMS / *Argentine*

The MEMS submachine gun was designed by Prof. Miguel E. Manzo Sal (from whence the name is derived) and is manufactured by Arms & Equipos SRL of Cordoba. In current form it is the perfection of several earlier models dating from 1952. The mechanism is a conventional blowback gun using a box magazine, the design of receiver and barrel being broadly based on the Erma MP40. The magazine housing is larger than usual and shaped to form a front grip. The standard infantry model (M75/I) uses a wooden stock, while the Parachutist model (M75/II) has a folding metal stock. The MEMS has been extensively tested by the Argentine Army and police forces.

MENDOZA / *Mexico*

Rafael Mendoza was a designer employed by the Mexican National Arms Factory who, in the 1930s, developed a light machine gun which was adopted by the Mexican Army as their M1934 model. It was a gas-operated gun with a rotating bolt, the mechanism being generally similar to that of the Lewis gun. One novel feature was a double-ended firing pin; in the event of a broken pin, one of the most common faults, the bolt can be withdrawn and the pin reversed to allow firing to continue. This is perhaps no quicker than putting in a new pin, the usual remedy, but more practical, since there is less likelihood of finding that you forgot to bring the spare pin. Mendoza improved his design from time to time in small details, but none of the improved models were adopted.

In the late 1950s he developed a submachine gun which, like the early Madsen (*qv*), used an all-enveloping slide instead of the conventional receiver and bolt. In many ways it was little more than an overgrown automatic pistol with a buttstock fitted. It was used in limited numbers by the Mexican Army for a short time.

The Mexican Army's Mendoza RM2 machine gun.

MERWIN, HULBERT & Co./*USA*

Merwin, Hulbert & Co. were a substantial New York company selling sporting goods of every sort in the 1870s, and they were a principal agency for the sale of Hopkins & Allen revolvers. The company had acquired various revolver patents and had revolvers incorporating the patented features made for them by Hopkins & Allen. The novelty of these designs lay in the method of extraction of the fired cases; the barrel was pivoted to the front of the cylinder arbor and was unlocked by a rotary movement which swung the top strap sideways, away from the standing breech. The barrel was then pulled forward, carrying the cylinder with it, while the extractor plate stayed still. A number of more conventional open-frame revolvers were also made. The company got into serious financial difficulties in 1880; it was re-organised as Hulbert Brothers & Co., but failed completely in 1896.

MINIÉ/*France*

Minié was an otherwise unremarked Captain in the French Army who, in 1847, developed a bullet for use in muzzle-loading rifles. It was a lead cylindro-conoidal bullet with a recess in the base; into this recess fitted an iron cup. On loading, the bullet had sufficient clearance to pass down the rifle barrel; when fired, the cup was forced into the base so as to press the sides of the bullet outwards and thus grip the rifling to seal and spin the bullet. It was widely adopted; the British Government, for example, paid £20,000 for the use of the invention in British service ammunition. It has, though, been suggested that Minié was not quite as inventive as was thought, a viewpoint reinforced by the British award of £1000 to W. W. Greener, the gunsmith, in respect of an expanding bullet which he had designed and demonstrated to the Army as far back as 1836.

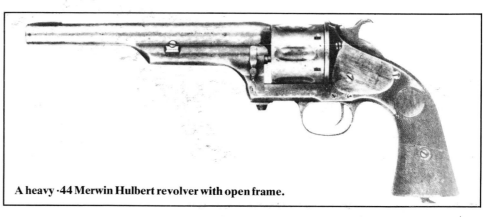

A heavy ·44 Merwin Hulbert revolver with open frame.

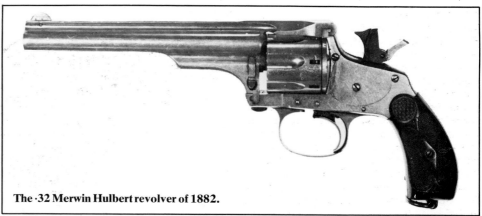

The ·32 Merwin Hulbert revolver of 1882.

MINI-GUN/*USA*

The Mini-Gun is a 7·62mm version of the Vulcan (*qv*) cannon, developed by the General Electric Company of America. It is a power-driven multi-barrel gun which uses the same basic mechanical principle as the Gatling (*qv*), having six barrels, each with its own bolt. The barrel and bolt unit revolves inside a casing in which a cam track engages the bolts and actuates the feed and fire cycle on each barrel.

Feed is from a 4000-round belt, and a rate of fire of up to 6000 rounds a minute can be reached. Due to the bulk of the ammunition and power supplies, and the fact that the electric motor driving the gun demands 28 volts at 130 amperes, the Mini-Gun is only a practical proposition when mounted in a vehicle or aircraft. As a helicopter armament system with the US Army, it helps to make the helicopter gunship an awesome weapon.

The General Electric Mini-Gun, a high-speed 7·62mm version of the Gatling gun.

The Fabrique National's new Minimi 5·56mm machine gun.

MINIMI / *Belgium*

This is a 5·56mm machine gun developed by Fabrique National of Liège and currently undergoing evaluation by several countries. It is gas-operated, firing from an open bolt, and has a quick-change barrel. In basic form it is belt-fed, the belt being contained in a pre-packed plastic box which clips beneath the gun to become an integral part of the weapon. The box material is transparent so that the gunner can always see just how much ammunition is left inside. A recent modification allows the US Army's standard M16 rifle magazine to be inserted obliquely into the gun body to act as a feed system when no belted ammunition is available. Other advantages claimed for the Minimi are ease of handling, since it is shorter than many rifles and weighs only 6½ kg; simplicity of maintenance; and a low price.

MIROKU / *Japan*

The Miroku Firearms Company of Kochi, Japan, began operations in the middle 1960s, manufacturing shotguns and revolvers. The shotguns are either side-by-side or over-and-under double guns and are available in a selection of grades and finishes to suit every depth of pocket; they have been exported to Britain and the USA in considerable numbers in the 1970s. The two revolvers are likewise of sound quality; solid-frame double-action, swing cylinder models and in ·38 Special calibre. In the USA they are sold under the names Liberty Chief and Liberty Special Police.

MITRAILLEUSE / *France*

French 'battery gun', an early type of machine gun, invented by a Belgian named Fafschamps (*qv*) and perfected by Joseph Montigny, a Belgian engineer. He demonstrated it to Napoleon III, who adopted it for the French Army. It was manufactured in great secrecy and kept under wraps until the Franco-Prussian War.

The Mitrailleuse was a collection of 25 rifle barrels in a cylindrical casing, mounted on a wheeled carriage so that it resembled a cannon.

The Miroku Liberty Chief ·38 revolver.

A Specimen of the Montigny Mitrailleuse in the Rotunda Artillery Museum, Woolwich.

At the rear end a breech block could be drawn back by a lever and a plate, pierced with holes matching the pattern of the barrels and carrying 25 Chassepot cartridges, was dropped into the gap. The breech block was then thrust forward so that the cartridges entered the barrels. Rotating a crank on the breech block now released 25 firing pins to discharge the cartridges; the speed at which they were fired depended upon how fast the gunner turned the crank. When all the cartridges had been fired, the block was withdrawn and the plate removed; it was then banged down onto 25 pins on the trail and the cases thus ejected, after which it could be re-loaded. With a supply of ready-loaded plates to hand, a well-drilled team could keep up a fire of about 350 shots a minute. The whole equipment weighed about two tons.

In the war of 1870 the Mitrailleuse failed to live up to its promise, largely because of uncertainty as to its proper tactical role and how to handle it. It was usually deployed as a form of field gun, and since the Prussian field artillery could comfortably out-range it, the Mitrailleuse batteries were generally shot to pieces before they could make their presence felt. Occasionally, they were intelligently handled; as for example at Gravelotte, where they were held concealed until the advance of the Prussian infantry; 72 officers and 2542 men of the 38th Prussian Infantry Brigade fell casualties in a matter of minutes. But in general the inept handling of the Mitrailleuse was to set the machine gun idea back in European military thought for several years.

MODELE D'ORDONNANCE / France

The Modèle d'Ordonnance revolver, or Modèle 1892, was the official French service revolver from 1892 until shortly before the Second World War, and even after its official replacement by an automatic pistol in 1935, several thousand remained in use by police and military, and it is believed that limited numbers were manufactured as late as 1945.

In 1886 the French Army adopted the Lebel rifle, using an 8mm smokeless powder cartridge. It seemed logical to follow this with an equally modern revolver, and in order to economise in barrel-making machinery the same 8mm calibre was chosen. The first design was no more than a re-work of the existing 11mm Chamelot & Delvigne M1873 pattern revolver and was merely a stopgap, since the

A contemporary print of the Montigny Mitrailleuse on its field carriage and showing the plate, loaded with cartridges, being inserted into the breech.

St. Etienne arsenal, responsible for design, had their hands full with getting the Lebel rifle into production. Once that was done the new revolver was designed and introduced in June 1892.

The Mle '92 was a solid-frame, double action revolver with the cylinder swinging out to the right-hand side for loading and ejection, probably the only revolver ever made in quantity which opened in this direction. The most novel feature lay in the construction of the side frame which was hinged at the front end and could be opened out to reveal the lockwork for cleaning or repair. While the weapon was robust and serviceable, the choice of 8mm calibre was a poor one, making the bullet too small to be an effective man-stopper, which, after all, is the primary purpose of a military revolver.

MONDRAGON / Mexico

General Manuel Mondragon of the Mexican Army patented a gas-operated automatic rifle in 1903, while he was serving as Military At-

taché in Paris. Since there were no facilities in Mexico, the rifle was manufactured in Switzerland by the SIG company, and it was adopted by the Mexican Army as the Fusil Porfiro Diaz, Systema Mondragon, M1908. It was in 7mm calibre and fitted with an 8-round box magazine. Operation was by a gas piston which drove a rotating bolt, and a particular feature of the design was that the gas could be shut off and the weapon operated as a hand-loader.

In addition to filling the Mexican contract, SIG appear to have been granted rights to sell it elsewhere, and they produced a model with a 20-round magazine and bipod, but there were few purchasers. At the outbreak of war in 1914 the German Army purchased their entire stock and issued them to infantry, but the conditions in Flanders soon clogged the action and they were withdrawn. They were then issued to aviation units for use by observers until sufficient machine guns were available, after which they were withdrawn and scrapped. Their length of service in the Mexican Army is not known, but it is not believed to have extended beyond the early 1920s.

Swiss-made Mondragon automatic rifle, with large magazine as used by German aviators in 1915.

MORRIS, Richard *(fl. 1875–1890)*

Inventor of the 'Morris Tube', a small-calibre training device widely used by the British Army. His patent was taken out in 1881 and covered a removable barrel of small calibre which could be inserted into the barrel of a larger weapon—eg, a service rifle—and retained there by a muzzle screw. The subcalibre barrel carried its own extractor but the cartridge was secured and fired by the bolt and firing pin of the parent weapon. Similar conversions for revolvers, using a barrel insert and chamber liners, were also proposed. The original designs were for a special bottle-necked centre fire cartridge in ·230 calibre, but in later years the ·22 rimfire cartridge was adopted. The Morris Tube was used until about 1908, when the British Army began to adopt permanently-fitted ·22 barrels inserted into service rifles. It remained in use by civilian rifle clubs until the middle 1920s.

MOSIN-NAGANT / *Russia*

S. I. Mosin (1849–1902) was a Russian artillery officer who became Director of the Imperial Arsenal at Tula. Emile Nagant was a Belgian gunsmith. In 1883 the Russian Rifle Test Commission announced a competitive trial to select a new service rifle, and after some considerable time had elapsed in testing they were left with two designs, one by Mosin and one by Nagant. After more deliberation it was decided to construct a rifle using the bolt action designed by Mosin allied to the magazine from the Nagant design. The final result was the Model 1891 rifle.

Basically it is a straight-forward turnbolt action with box magazine, but there are some interesting details. The bolt, which locks by two lugs in breech recesses and one lug at the rear end, is of an odd three-piece construction, unnecessarily complicated and probably designed that way in order to avoid infringing current patents. The magazine has an unusual control latch which secures the second and lower cartridges in the magazine and thus relieves the top round of spring pressure during the loading action of the bolt. Once the bolt has closed, the latch moves out and allows the next cartridge to rise to the undersurface of the bolt, and as the bolt is opened the latch moves in once again. The object of this was to keep the second cartridge down and thus reduce the likelihood of the rims jamming during loading.

Several variant models of the Mosin-Nagant appeared over the years, the last being a carbine issued in 1944, but during its life there was no significant change in the mechanism.

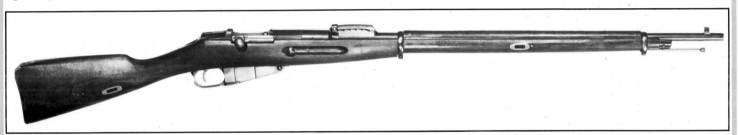

The Mosin-Nagant rifle M1891, by Remington Arms Co.

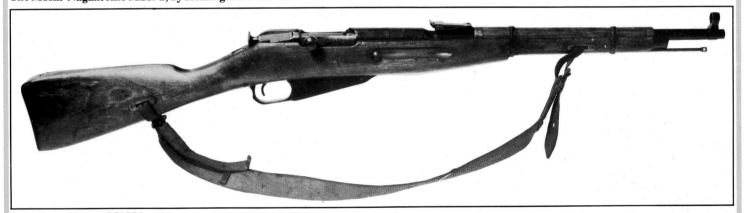

The Mosin-Nagant M1938 carbine.

MOSSBERG / *USA*

O. F. Mossberg & Sons Inc. of New Haven, Connecticut have, since the 1880s, made a speciality of providing inexpensive but reliable sporting guns and rifles. Their output of ·22 rifles must run into astronomical figures, and generations of shooters were introduced to the sport by way of a Mossberg rifle. They also make sporting rifles in heavier calibres and their current list of shotguns covers bolt or slide action patterns in all the standard gauges.

Oscar Mossberg was associated with Iver Johnson and other revolver makers in the latter part of the 19th century, and took out several patents which he licensed to them. His only venture into the pistol field was an odd four-barrelled repeating pistol which he patented in 1906. It had four barrels in a drop-down block and was fired by squeezing the butt grip. Mossberg assigned this patent to the C. S. Shattuck Company who sold it as the Shattuck Unique until they went out of business during the First World War. The patent reverted to Mossberg and lay dormant until the 1930s when, fitted with a conventional butt and trigger so as to resemble an automatic pistol, it was sold as the Mossberg Brownie until the next war stopped manufacture.

NAGANT/*Belgium*

The brothers Emile and Leon Nagant were gunsmiths of Liège. Emile appears first, manufacturing the usual sporting guns, saloon rifles and single-shot pistols in the 1870s, after which he took out patents for various improvements in revolver design and began to produce military revolvers. These attained considerable popularity throughout the world; his first success was the 9mm Belgian service revolver of 1878, and this was followed by contracts for the Argentine, Brazilian, Norwegian and Swedish Armies. He then turned to the development of magazine rifles, but none of his designs was adopted as it stood, though his controlled box magazine was used on the Russian Mosin-Nagant (*qv*) rifle of 1891.

Leon Nagant followed his brother into the business and his claim to fame comes from the gas-seal revolver which he patented in 1892, one of the few such designs ever to achieve success. The long-standing objection to revolvers was that, in order to permit the cylinder to turn, it was necessary to have a finite gap between the face of the chamber and the rear of the barrel, and through this gap some of the propelling gas was bound to leak, reducing the theoretical efficiency of the pistol. In a 'gas-seal' revolver, arrangements are made to seal this gap and thus produce 100% efficiency.

Nagant's system actually owes a great deal to the patents of Pieper (*qv*) and there seems little doubt that had Pieper not allowed his patents to lapse, Nagant would never have succeeded. In the Nagant revolver, the cylinder was allowed to move back and forth in the frame, its movement governed by a linkage from the hammer. The face of the chamber was bell-mouthed, and the rear of the barrel tapered. In addition, the cartridge was specially designed for the revolver; the bullet was concealed within an elongated cartridge case, the mouth of which was slightly bottle-necked. The operation was as follows: when the hammer was cocked—either by the thumb or by pulling the trigger—the cylinder was thrust forward so that the end of the barrel entered into the mouth of the chamber. As this occurred, the

Loading the Russian M1895 revolver through the side gate.

The Russian M1895 Nagant revolver.

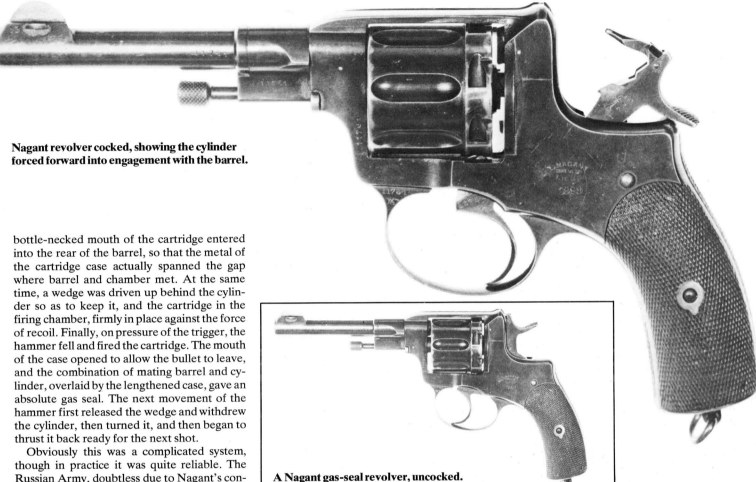

Nagant revolver cocked, showing the cylinder forced forward into engagement with the barrel.

A Nagant gas-seal revolver, uncocked.

bottle-necked mouth of the cartridge entered into the rear of the barrel, so that the metal of the cartridge case actually spanned the gap where barrel and chamber met. At the same time, a wedge was driven up behind the cylinder so as to keep it, and the cartridge in the firing chamber, firmly in place against the force of recoil. Finally, on pressure of the trigger, the hammer fell and fired the cartridge. The mouth of the case opened to allow the bullet to leave, and the combination of mating barrel and cylinder, overlaid by the lengthened case, gave an absolute gas seal. The next movement of the hammer first released the wedge and withdrew the cylinder, then turned it, and then began to thrust it back ready for the next shot.

Obviously this was a complicated system, though in practice it was quite reliable. The Russian Army, doubtless due to Nagant's connection with the service rifle design, adopted it as their 1895 model, and it remained in use with them until the end of the Second World War. Whether the final result was worth all the mechanical effort is another matter. It has not proved possible to make a perfect comparison between a gas-seal and non-sealing revolver of exactly similar specifications, but various tests tend to indicate that the benefit achieved might be as much as an additional 50 feet per second on to the muzzle velocity. In terms of the Russian 1895 revolver, which fired a 108 grain bullet at 1000 feet a second, this means a reduction in muzzle energy of about 23 foot-pounds, which is neither here nor there. Other people probably did similar sums, for the gas-seal revolver was never adopted by any other army of importance.

Nagant continued to make and sell gas-seal revolvers on the civil market in the 1890s, but in 1900 the Russian government purchased the entire rights to the patent and put the pistol into production at their Tula Arsenal. The Nagants therefore turned to the manufacture of conventional solid-frame revolvers, meanwhile working on a new design of gas-seal model which used a swing-out cylinder and thus avoided the question of conflict with the Russian license. This was finally achieved and marketed in 1901, but by that time the novelty had worn off and sales were minimal. In the following year the brothers went into the automobile business, forming the 'Fabrique d'Armes et Automobiles Nagant Freres', but they appear to have had little success in that field. After the First World War they returned to the manufacture of sporting guns and continued in business until 1941.

NAMBU / *Japan*

Major (later General) Kirijo Nambu of the Japanese Army first demonstrated his automatic pistol in 1909. The Japanese Army, while approving of it in principle, was not prepared to authorise its general issue until it had been proven, but officers were permitted to equip themselves with it if they wished. The first few hundred pistols were made by the Kayaba Industrial Company, but in 1915 the pistol was adopted officially and manufacture was taken over by official arsenals. It is formally known as the Nambu Type A, but is more usually referred to as the Fourth Year Model, referring to its adoption in the Fourth Year of the Taisho Era, ie 1915.

The Nambu was a locked breech pistol in 8mm calibre, the lock being done by a pivoted block beneath the bolt. Although superficially resembling the Parabellum, the mechanism bears closer affinities to the Italian Glisenti (*qv*) and was probably copied from it. The breech-block return spring was set to one side, in a tunnel in the frame, which gave the pistol a lop-sided appearance, and the only safety device was a grip safety set in the front of the butt.

In 1925 a modified version was adopted as the standard service pistol, under the name of 14th Year. This simplified various details in order to ease manufacturing problems, adopting two return springs, one at each side of the receiver, instead of one, and a manually-operated safety catch in place of the grip safety. This latter feature was badly conceived, since the safety could only be applied by using two hands, the catch being too far forward to be operated by the firing hand. Some 320,000 14th Year pistols were made by the three major Japanese arsenals before the end of the Second World War.

NEW NAMBU/*Japan*

This is a trade name adopted by the Shin Chuo Kogyo company of Tokyo, possibly as a mark of respect to the esteemed position held by the Nambu pistol in Japanese history. The weapons produced under this name have absolutely no connection, hereditary or mechanical, with the original Nambu designs.

The New Nambu Model 57A is a 9mm Parabellum locked-breech pistol which is little more than a copy of the Colt ·45 M1911A1 automatic. This was put into production in 1957 in order to supply the Japan Self-defence Force and police. It was followed by the Model 57B automatic, in 7·65mm calibre, which is largely based on the Browning 1910 design but with the addition of an external hammer. In 1958 came the Model 58, a five-shot solid-frame revolver with swing-out cylinder and two-inch barrel, based on Smith & Wesson practice. They are rarely seen outside Japan.

NORDENFELT, Torsten Wilhelm
(1842–1920)

After university training, Nordenfelt set up a hardware company which rapidly expanded, and he later went into banking. In about 1879 an inventor named Heldge Palmkranz approached Nordenfelt with a design for a

The 7·65mm New Nambu automatic pistol.

Nordenfelt machine gun at the Rotunda, Woolwich.

mechanical machine gun, seeking financial backing for its manufacture. On the understanding that the gun would now be named Nordenfelt, Palmkranz got his backing and thereafter faded from the scene. Nordenfelt applied his flair for business and advertising and promoted the design vigorously, founding the Nordenfelt Gun and Ammunition Company, with factories in Sweden, Britain and Spain. A five-barrelled version was adopted by the Royal Navy in 1884 and a three-barrelled model by the Army in 1887. It was adopted by many other European nations, particularly as a naval weapon intended for sweeping the decks of enemy ships. Finding naval armaments profitable, Nordenfelt went on to develop light artillery, ammunition and submarines before merging with Maxim in 1888 to form the Maxim-Nordenfelt Gun & Ammunition Company.

The Nordenfelt gun appeared in various configurations, from two barrels to 12, but all worked in the same manner. Ammunition was fed via a hopper and fell into a carrier block having the same number of partitions as there were barrels. As the gunner pushed forward on a lever, the carrier block moved across to line up with the barrels; a breech block moved forward and chambered the cartridges; and finally an 'action block' moved in behind the breech block and, containing the necessary number of firing pins, discharged the barrels in sequence. Reversing the movement of the handle withdrew the action block, then withdrew the breech block and extracted the empty cases, and finally moved the carrier block to receive a fresh charge of cartridges. The speed of operation obviously depended upon the speed at which the handle was pushed, but an average figure appears to have been 100 rounds per minute per barrel.

Nordenfelt also offered a single-barrel lightweight gun worked by two men. It weighed only 13 lbs, a remarkable figure for the period, but was considered to be a novelty rather than a serious weapon and was never accepted.

NORWICH PISTOL CO./ *USA*

This company was set up 1875, in Norwich, Connecticut, by the Maltby, Curtiss & Co. sporting goods firm of New York. The company was to manufacture cheap revolvers, roller skates, tools and general hardware which would then be sold through the Maltby and Curtiss stores and associated dealers throughout the United States. It was an entirely independent concern, apart from the initial financing, so much so that it went bankrupt in 1881. The remains were then bought outright by Maltby and Curtiss, who re-christened it the Norwich Falls Pistol Co., put in new management, and continued. The company finally folded in 1881, with the failing fortunes of the parent company. In that year the latter company became Maltby, Henley & Co., and thereafter there is an absence of records to indicate the final disposition of the Norwich concern.

In its twelve years of existence, the Norwich company turned out a vast number of pistols under a wide variety of trade names—America, Chieftain, Defiance, True Blue and so forth. All have two things in common; their low quality, and the presence of the patent date 23 April 1878 stamped on them. They were all solid-frame, sheathed-trigger rimfires in all calibres from ·22 to ·44.

Left: 4-barrel Nordenfelt gun on naval mounting, Military Museum of Lisbon.

Below: Breech and elevating mechanisms of Nordenfelt gun at Rotunda Museum.

OBREGON / *Mexico*

The Obregon automatic pistol, made by the Fabrica de Armas Mexico of Mexico City, was a ·45 pistol made during and shortly after the Second World War. It outwardly resembles the Colt M1911A1 model, with the same general outline and external hammer, but the front section of the slide is rather more tubular than is usual with Browning designs, copies of which are quite common.

The difference lies in the method of breech locking; the Obregon uses barrel rotation to hold the barrel and breech-block together. A helical lug on the bottom of the barrel engages in a slot in the pistol frame, while a square lug on top of the barrel engages in a recess in the slide. On firing, the top lug locks slide and barrel together; as the two recoil, the helical lug is drawn through the frame slot, causing the barrel to rotate until the top lug is disengaged from its recess in the slide. When this occurs, the movement of the barrel is halted and the slide is free to recoil, completing the firing cycle in the usual way.

The Obregon is said to be robust and accurate; it was used by the Mexican Army, and small numbers were sold commercially, but it is rarely seen in Europe.

ORBEA HERMANOS / *Spain*

The Orbea brothers were among the earliest Spanish pistol makers and they are notable for the gas-operated automatic revolver attributed to them and exhibited in the Eibar Museu de Armas. This pistol, made in 1863, used a gas piston beneath the barrel which cocked the hammer, rotated the cylinder to bring a fresh round into the firing position, and ejected the empty case. It was never put into production but it reflects the ingenuity of its maker and gives the Spanish gunmaking industry a sound claim on the invention of the automatic pistol.

Possibly daunted by the lack of enthusiasm generated by this design, the brothers thereafter settled for safer products. In 1894 they were making the Spanish Army's service revolver, which was virtually a copy of the Smith & Wesson ·44 Russian, and from then on their range of products were all thinly-disguised copies of current Colt and Smith & Wesson pistols. They also produced a cheap blowback automatic pistol, the La Industrial, during the 1920s, though it is possible that this was made elsewhere and merely sold by Orbea. The company failed to survive the Civil War.

ORTGIES / *Germany*

Heinrich Ortgies was a German, resident in Liège; whether he was actively connected with the firearms industry there is not certain, but during the First World War he designed and patented an automatic pistol. After the war he returned to Germany, and set up a factory in Erfurt, manufacturing the Ortgies pistol in 7·65mm calibre. He made upwards of 10,000 pistols, which were a success on the market, and in 1921 he received an attractive offer from the Deutsche Werke company of Erfurt. Ortgies accepted, the Deutsche Werke took over the tools, plant and goodwill, and they continued to manufacture the pistol until late in the 1920s.

The Ortgies was an extremely well-made striker-fired blowback model, and after Deutsche Werke took over it was made in 6·35mm, 7·65mm and 9mm Short calibres. The method of construction was unusual, in that the barrel was attached to the frame by a bayonet-joint under the breech, and the wooden grips were attached by concealed spring catches. The only safety device was a grip safety which, once pushed in by the hand, was retained in the firing position until released by a push-button. These latter features were abandoned when the 9mm Short model was introduced in 1922; the grips were retained by the usual screws, and a manual safety catch was added.

OVP / *Italy*

Officine Vilar Perosa; this company was set up during the First World War to manufacture the Vilar Perosa (*qv*) submachine gun, designed by Revelli. Due to various shortcomings of the

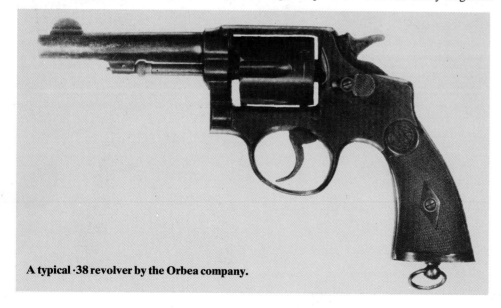

A typical ·38 revolver by the Orbea company.

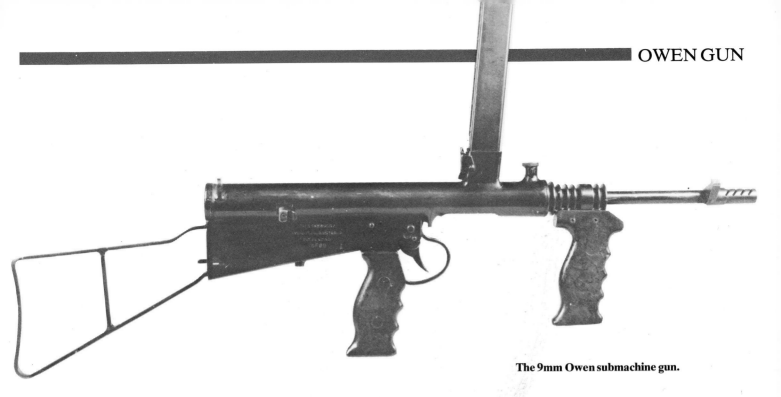

The 9mm Owen submachine gun.

Vilar Perosa gun, the Italian Army asked the company to redesign it into a handier weapon, much on the lines of the Beretta M1918 submachine gun. OVP complied, removing one barrel of the V-P gun and mounting it into a wooden stock. The barrel was lengthened, and an unusual cocking sleeve installed around the receiver; to cock the gun it was necessary to grasp this knurled sleeve and pull it back. This drew back the bolt and cocked it, after which the sleeve was released to go forward and remain there during firing. Two triggers were fitted; the forward trigger gave single shots and the rear automatic fire. The conversions were completed in 1919–1920 and numbers of these guns survived to be used in the early part of the Second World War.

OWEN GUN / *Australia*

The Owen gun was a submachine gun designed by a Lieutenant Evelyn Owen of the Australian Army in 1940. Prototypes were made in 9mm Parabellum, ·38 Super, ·45 and 7·65mm calibres and given to troops for practical trial. The 9mm Parabellum version was the most popular, and it was officially adopted in November 1941. Production continued until September 1944, by which time some 45,000 had been made. Three slightly different models were produced; the Mk 1/42 had cooling fins on the barrel; the Mk 1/43 had lightening holes cut in the frame, behind the pistol grip; and the Mk 2/43 was fitted with a bayonet. Only about 200 of the latter were made, as bayonets are not often useful on an automatic weapon.

The most noticeable feature of the Owen gun is that the magazine enters from the top, the feed being by spring with the assistance of gravity. It looks odd but is most effective and was well-liked by troops since it did make magazine changing that much easier; in fact, the Owen is among the most highly-respected soldier's guns in history, by which we mean that whatever theoretical criticism might be levelled—the overhead magazine, heavy weight, offset sights—these never bothered the men who used it and they preferred the Owen. The ultimate proof of a weapon is the soldier's opinion of it; the Owen was used by Australian troops throughout the war and for many years afterwards, in Malaysia and Vietnam.

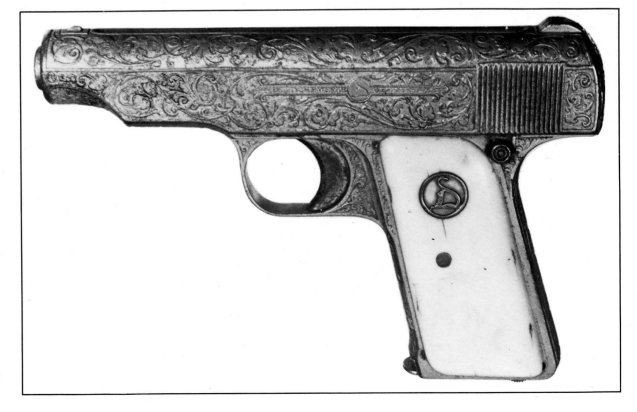

An engraved specimen of 7·65mm Ortgies pistol.

P

PARABELLUM / *Germany*

'Parabellum' was the telegraphic address of Deutsche Waffen & Munitionsfabrik of Berlin (*qv*) and they also applied it as a trade-name to various weapons. Of these, the most famous and important is undoubtedly the pistol developed by Georg Luger (*qv*) and marketed as the Parabellum, though universally called the Luger.

As explained under BORCHARDT, the DWM company had taken over the manufacture of the pistol along with the Löwe company factory, and Georg Luger then collaborated with Borchardt to improve its design. His principal concern was to turn it into a more practical weapon, making it more handy and reliable, in the hope of securing a military contract. The principal change came with the modification of the toggle breech mechanism so that the toggle was broken by the interaction of two finger-grips striking a ramp in the fixed pistol frame after a short recoil. This threw up the centre of the toggle, and broke the resistance to the recoil force of the cartridge; thereafter the breech block was driven back as the toggle rose, so as to extract the fired case and, propelled by a leaf spring concealed within the pistol butt, then returned to strip a cartridge from the magazine and chamber it. A striker within the block was cocked during this latter movement.

After several trials, the first Luger pistol was adopted by the Swiss Army in May 1900, the pistols being chambered for a bottle-necked 7·65mm cartridge known thereafter as the 7·65mm Parabellum. The pistol was actually given the name Parabellum by DWM in the spring of 1901. After the Swiss adoption, the pistol was tested in several countries; the US Ordnance Department purchased 1000 for trials, the British Army bought a handful but lost interest when they were told that the maximum calibre which could be managed was only 9mm; the Belgian and Dutch armies tested it. The most common objection was to the 7·65mm bullet, since military opinion at that

A Swiss trial model Parabellum pistol of 1900, 7·65mm.

time inclined to calibres in the order of 11mm or ·45 inch in order to achieve the greatest shock power with a single shot. Luger therefore opened out the neck of the 7·65mm case to turn it into a straight case and inserted a 9mm bullet, and in 1902 offered this calibre as an alternative. After more trials the German Navy adopted this calibre in 1904.

In 1905 came a major change in design with the adoption of a coil spring in the butt to return the toggle, instead of the original leaf spring. In 1906 a few, perhaps as many as 15, were made in ·45 calibre for trials in the USA which took place in the spring of 1907, trials which, in the end, led to the American adoption of the Colt pistol. In fact the Parabellum performed so well that the US Army wished to purchase a further 200 specimens in ·45 for troop trials, but the DWM company refused to make them; at that time they were tooling up for the German Army's requirements, and the amount of special work needed to make 200 odd-calibre pistols was not commensurate with

its chances of adoption by the US Army.

The adoption, in 1908, of the Pistole '08 by the German Army set the final seal on the Parabellum's acceptance. In 9mm calibre with a 4 inch barrel, the quantity demanded was far in excess of DWM's capacity and the additional pistols were made by the Government arsenal at Erfurt. It has been reliably estimated that by 1918 over one and a half million pistols had been made. During these years an additional model, the Long '08, was adopted; this had a 200mm barrel, long-range sights and a large 'snail' magazine carrying 32 rounds which extended below the butt.

In addition a wooden butt-stock could be fitted to the weapon, turning it into a type of carbine. It was issued to artillery units, machine gunners, and to crews of coastal motor-boats in some numbers. The wooden butt-stock was a feature of many of the Parabellum designs, most pistols being fitted with a shoe at the rear of the butt-grip into which this stock fitted.

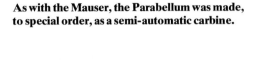

As with the Mauser, the Parabellum was made, to special order, as a semi-automatic carbine.

When the First World War ended, the manufacture of Parabellum pistols came to a halt; under the provisions of the Versailles Treaty, DWM were forbidden to manufacture them and in any case 9mm calibre was proscribed in Germany except for a small number of pistols permitted as replacements for the Army. Simson of Suhl (*qv*) were designated as official contractors for these replacements and DWM supplied stocks of parts to them; Krieghoff (*qv*) also became official suppliers, and in this case complete weapons, assembled by DWM from wartime parts, were provided to them for re-marking.

In 1923 manufacture began once more; DWM began making guns partly from new components and partly from old stock until the latter was exhausted, whereupon the guns became all-new. Vickers of Britain supplied between 6000 and 10,000 to the Dutch Government for their Far Eastern army, but how Vickers obtained them has never been publicly explained. Much of the new production was exported to the USA and the principal importer, A. F. Stoeger & Co., very astutely registered the name Luger as a trade-mark, so that strictly speaking, only weapons made for and sold by him can be called Luger pistols. (The company has retained the name and currently market a ·22 blowback pistol, resembling the Parabellum in outline, as the Stoeger Luger.)

In 1930 the production of the Parabellum was reorganised; at that time DWM was in the hands of a holding company, Berliner-Karlsruhe Industriewerke (BKIW), who were also controlling Mauser. A policy of rationalisation led to all small arms production being concentrated in the Mauser factory at Oberndorf, leaving the DWM plant for other things, and in consequence the Parabellum machinery and production line was moved to Oberndorf early in 1930. Although Mauser were now solely responsible for production, the pistols still carried the DWM monogram on the toggles, either because it was not considered wise to advertise the change or because Mauser wished to avail themselves of the DWM goodwill.

The Swiss government continued to use the Parabellum as their standard pistol, but due to difficulties in obtaining supplies during the War, in 1918 they had set up their own production facilities in the Arsenal at Bern, continuing to produce the last (1906) pattern which had been purchased from DWM. By 1928 they had come to the conclusion that at a unit cost of SF220 the Parabellum was too expensive; but they liked the design, and set the Arsenal technicians the task of modifying it so as to reduce the manufacturing cost. This was done by eliminating many 'cosmetic' machining steps; knurling on the finger grips was omitted, the frame contours were made more simple, the front strap of the butt made straight, and so forth. This brought the price down by 30% and the new design went into production in 1929 as the Pistole 06/29. About 30,000 were made before production finally ended in 1947.

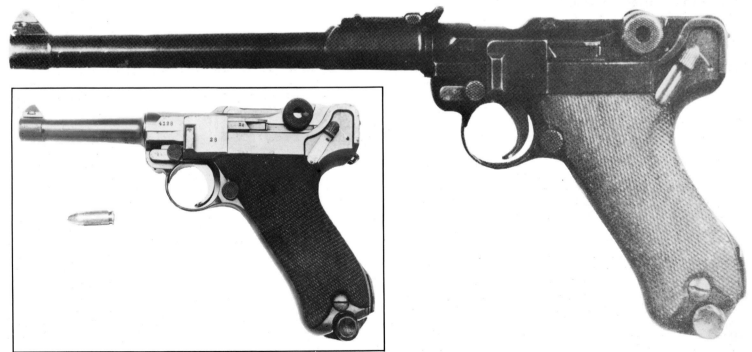

German Army Pistole 08 in 9mm calibre.

The Long 08 or Artillery model.

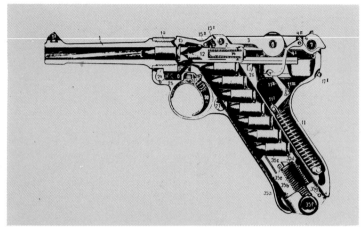

Sectioned drawing of the Parabellum action closed.

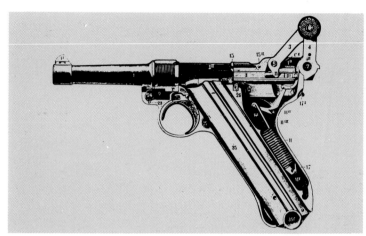

Sectioned drawing of the Parabellum action in recoil.

In Germany, similar thoughts had led to the development of the Walther (qv) Pistole 38 as the replacement for the Parabellum, but such was the demand for pistols that Mauser continued to manufacture the Parabellum until June 1942. Even then there were sufficient parts on hand to permit assembly to continue on a major scale until December 1942 and it is reported that small numbers continued to be assembled until late 1944. In 1945 the French Army seized the factory and under French control it continued to make Parabellum pistols, assembling them from available parts, most of which went to the French Army.

That seemed to be the end of the Parabellum; many of the machines at Mauserwerke had been adapted to other tasks, others had been destroyed and it seemed impossible for production of new pistols to be re-started. But in the years after the war the demand for Parabellum pistols seems not to have abated. In the 1960s negotiations opened between the American Interarmco company and Mauser, with the result that new machinery was assembled and in 1970 a new Parabellum pistol appeared. This was based on the Swiss 06/29, the simplified design. It was then followed, in 1973, by a model based on the Pistole '08, with the swelled-out front edge to the grip. The quality and finish is of the highest class, but the problems of manufacturing a complicated design in relatively small quantities is reflected in the price—over $400 at the time of writing.

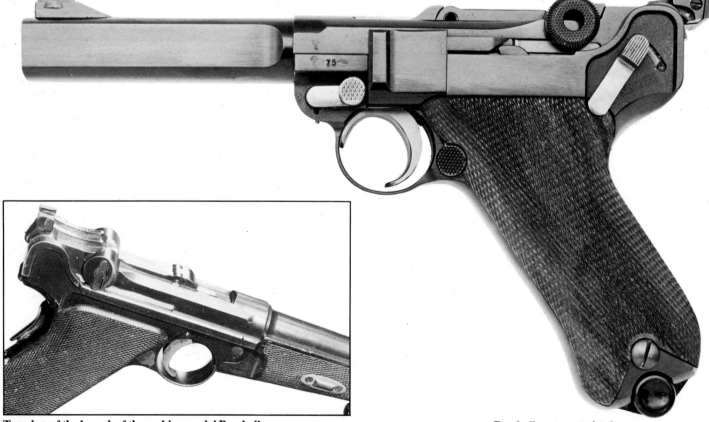

Parabellum target pistol.

Top view of the breech of the carbine model Parabellum.

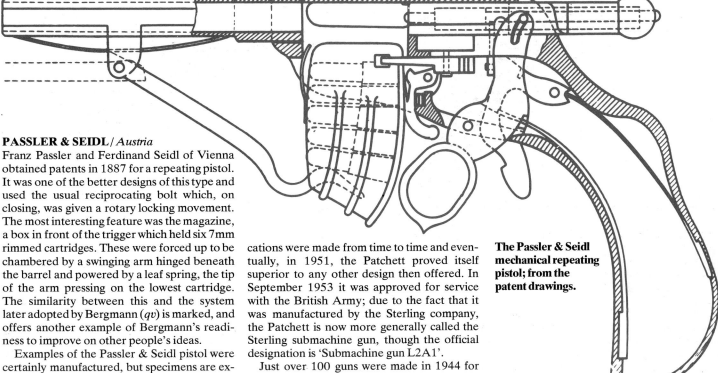

PASSLER & SEIDL / *Austria*

Franz Passler and Ferdinand Seidl of Vienna obtained patents in 1887 for a repeating pistol. It was one of the better designs of this type and used the usual reciprocating bolt which, on closing, was given a rotary locking movement. The most interesting feature was the magazine, a box in front of the trigger which held six 7mm rimmed cartridges. These were forced up to be chambered by a swinging arm hinged beneath the barrel and powered by a leaf spring, the tip of the arm pressing on the lowest cartridge. The similarity between this and the system later adopted by Bergmann (*qv*) is marked, and offers another example of Bergmann's readiness to improve on other people's ideas.

Examples of the Passler & Seidl pistol were certainly manufactured, but specimens are extremely uncommon.

PATCHETT / *Britain*

George William Patchett patented a submachine gun in 1942, had a prototype built by the Sterling Engineering Company, and demonstrated it to military officials in September of that year. It was described as 'essentially a Lanchester without butt or sights' but had a trigger mechanism designed by Patchett. The gun functioned well but Patchett was advised to take it away and fit a butt and sights, and then re-submit it.

In February 1943 it was again tested, together with other designs which had been put forward; it was inaccurate and failed to survive the 'mud-test' in which the weapon was thrown into mud, roughly cleaned and then fired. Patchett then re-designed the weapon, adding helical grooves to the outer surface of the bolt so that they cut away any mud or dirt which entered the gun body and drove it out through a special slot in the body. Various other modifi-

cations were made from time to time and eventually, in 1951, the Patchett proved itself superior to any other design then offered. In September 1953 it was approved for service with the British Army; due to the fact that it was manufactured by the Sterling company, the Patchett is now more generally called the Sterling submachine gun, though the official designation is 'Submachine gun L2A1'.

Just over 100 guns were made in 1944 for extended troop trials and a number of these were used in combat at Arnhem by airborne troops. Since official adoption it has passed through a number of modification stages and the current service model is the L2A3. A silenced version, the L34, is also on limited issue. Similar guns, slightly modified to suit preferences, are used in various Commonwealth armies, and the gun has been sold to over 70 countries. The Sterling company also produce a single-shot police model.

PAULSON, Richard *(fl. 1880s)*

Richard Paulson described himself as an engineer in his patent applications, but beyond that we know nothing of him. He deserves recognition for being one of the pioneers of automatic action in pistols, developing a gas-operated revolver in 1884–1886. He took out patents which related to gas- and recoil-operated weapons of various types, but his 1886 patent is significant since it detailed the action of a revolver in which a gas piston

The Passler & Seidl mechanical repeating pistol; from the patent drawings.

beneath the barrel was forced back, upon firing, to abut against the revolver hammer. The rod passed through the cylinder axis and, since the pawl was connected to the hammer, cocking the pistol also revolved the cylinder ready for the next shot. A spring then forced the piston rod back, but Paulson realised that unless some mechanical device was interposed, the return of the rod while the firer was still pressing the trigger would release the hammer and fire another shot, and so on until the revolver was empty. He therefore arranged for a 'disconnector' which prevented the rod from returning until the trigger had been released so as to hold the hammer cocked.

In spite of the idea's simplicity and practicality it failed to interest any manufacturer, and Paulson allowed his patent to lapse at the end of the statutory five-year renewal period. Though a specimen pistol must have been made, none is known to survive.

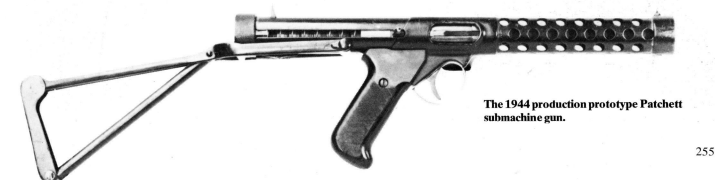

The 1944 production prototype Patchett submachine gun.

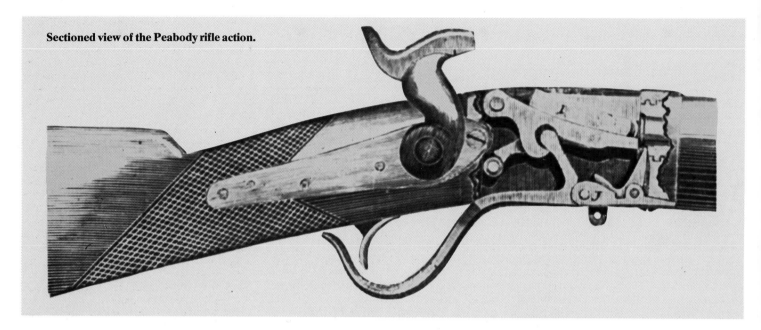

Sectioned view of the Peabody rifle action.

PEABODY / *USA*

Henry O. Peabody of Boston was the originator of a system of breech closure in which a block, lying in prolongation of the barrel axis, was hinged at its rear end so that by suitable levers it could be lowered at the front end to expose the chamber for loading. The cartridge could then be introduced across the top of the block, and the block closed; once closed, the axis pin at the rear end resisted any opening force. Peabody patented this idea in 1862, and produced a rifle in ·44 rimfire calibre. The breech block carried a firing pin which was struck by the conventional outside-mounted hammer of the day. The action of the block was controlled by a lever which formed the trigger guard. An upward extension of this lever acted as a prop to the block in the closed position and, when forced down, ran back to engage in a hooked portion of the block's undersurface so as to pull the block down.

In spite of Peabody's superior design, it was not accepted by the US forces; it was 1865 before it was properly tested in competition with other systems, and by that time the Civil War was over and no expenditure on arms was contemplated. However the Canadian government bought 3000 rifles in 1865 and, heartened by this, Peabody began to promote the rifle overseas and achieved considerable success; it was purchased by several countries, among them France who bought 39,000 rifles for use in the Franco-Prussian War.

It was also purchased by the Swiss who, not entirely satisfied with it, gave Martini (*qv*) the task of improving it, and his subsequent improvement was such that it eclipsed Peabody's original design. Ever since, the hinged falling block has been called the Martini action.

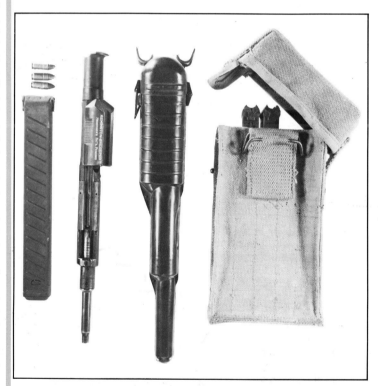

The Pedersen Device, which, fitted into a Springfield rifle in place of the bolt, turned it into an assault rifle.

PEDERSEN / *USA*

J. D. Pedersen worked as a designer with Remington in the early part of the century, making notable contributions to the Remington line of repeating shotguns and developing their Model 51 automatic pistol. During the First World War he was responsible for designing the Pedersen Device, or Automatic Pistol, Caliber ·30, M1918. This was a self-contained bolt and return-spring unit which could be installed into the action of a standard Springfield rifle after removing the bolt. The unit consisted of a tubular·receiver, bolt, return spring, chamber and barrel; the barrel was externally the same size as the standard ·30 rifle cartridge, so that it fitted inside the

PERINO / *Italy*

Captain Giuseppe Perino was an inspector at the National Artillery Arsenal in Rome who invented a machine gun in 1901. It was operated by recoil, assisted by the muzzle blast which impinged on a fixed plate so as to give the barrel an additional boost to the rear; the bolt was actuated by a bell-crank mechanism, and a most unusual feature was that the barrel acted as an hydraulic pump as it recoiled and pumped cooling water around inside the jacket and also as an air pump to force cold air past the breech. Feed was originally by a metallic chain, but this was soon abandoned for a method using metal strips of 12 cartridges, laid in five layers in a box on the left side. The bottom strip fed into the gun, the cartridges were removed, fired, and the cases replaced, and the strip was ejected from the right side. The gunner could keep the magazine topped up by dropping a fresh strip on top of the others at any time.

The Perino gun was offered to the Italian Army and also offered commercially; one was tested by the British in 1911 but they turned it down as being over-weight, though in all other respects it seems to have been a satisfactory weapon. The Italians wasted time in a long series of repetitive trials against other weapons, so that when the First World War came along they were forced to buy what machine guns they could find, instead of having the Perino already in production. Even so, it would probably have paid them, in the long run, to build the Perino in preference to some of the other designs they adopted, but in fact the Perino design was hastily abandoned in 1914.

PETTER, Charles *(fl. 1930s)*

Very little is known about Charles Petter; it is said that he served with the French Foreign Legion in the 1920s and was invalided out after being wounded in North Africa. In any event, he became an engineer with the Societé Al-sacienne de Constructions Mechanique at Cholet in Alsace some time in the early 1930s; it has been suggested that he was a director of the company, but this has never been satisfactorily resolved. In 1934 he took out patents covering a design of automatic pistol; basically, this was of the same type as the Colt M1911 or Browning GP35, a locked-breech weapon in which slide and barrel were locked together by lugs and unlocked by the action of a cam beneath the breech which, engaging in a cross-bolt in the pistol frame, pulled the barrel free of the slide after a short recoil stroke. Petter's patents covered the lockwork, which he improved by building into a removable module, and the return spring, which was fully supported throughout its length. The design was submitted for trial to the French Army and was adopted by them as the MAS-35 pistol, being made by the state arsenal at St. Etienne as well as by the state arsenals at Chatellerault and Tulle and by SACM themselves.

The pistol was a sound design, though ham-

The Pedersen ·276 automatic rifle.

chamber of the rifle, while the remaining parts sat in the boltway. An obliquely-fitted overhead magazine slotted into the device, and the rifle was thus transformed into a species of submachine gun. The ammunition fired was a special ·30 short cartridge, slightly longer than a normal 7·65mm ACP pistol cartridge. The object behind this was to permit front-line troops to convert their rifles into fast-firing weapons which could then be fired from the hip during the advance across No Man's Land. 65,000 devices were made in great secrecy for issue to US troops in France in 1919, but the war ended before they could be used. They were also made for use in the Enfield Rifle and in the Russian Mosin-Nagant, though only prototypes of these two were made. In 1923 they were withdrawn and scrapped, no more than about two dozen now remaining.

In that same year, Pedersen went to work for Springfield Arsenal and developed a delayed-blowback rifle using a toggle-joint breech mechanism. The angles of the toggle unit were carefully calculated so that instead of positively

The toggle action of the Pedersen rifle.

locking the breech, as in the Maxim and Borchardt toggles, this one merely slowed down the blowback action. The rifle was in ·276 calibre, but, like most blowback weapons using bottle-necked cartridges, gave trouble with extraction, and Pedersen developed a dry-wax method of lubricating the cartridges which cured the extraction trouble. Unfortunately, lubricated cartridges are not a solution to which military authorities take kindly, and although the Pedersen rifle was an excellent design, it was turned down for service in favour of the Garand (*qv*). The patents were licensed to Vickers and Britain and the rifle was produced by them as the Vickers Auto rifle for military trials, but was not accepted.

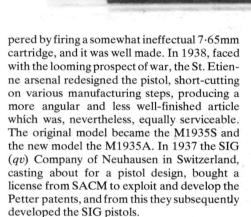

pered by firing a somewhat ineffectual 7·65mm cartridge, and it was well made. In 1938, faced with the looming prospect of war, the St. Etienne arsenal redesigned the pistol, short-cutting on various manufacturing steps, producing a more angular and less well-finished article which was, nevertheless, equally serviceable. The original model became the M1935S and the new model the M1935A. In 1937 the SIG (*qv*) Company of Neuhausen in Switzerland, casting about for a pistol design, bought a license from SACM to exploit and develop the Petter patents, and from this they subsequently developed the SIG pistols.

PICKERT / *Germany*

The Friedrich Pickert 'Arminius' Waffenwerke of Zella Mehlis was principally known for its production of cheap revolvers and pistols under the trade name Arminius (*qv*). These revolvers were also sold under the name Illinois Arms Company, and probably others. The company also made small-calibre sporting and saloon rifles, but this side of the business was secondary to pistol production. It is believed that the company was dismantled and re-formed with others into a co-operative after the Communist take-over in East Germany.

PIEPER, Henry *(1840–1898)*

Pieper was born in Westphalia and served an apprenticeship with a heavy engineering firm. He then went to Belgium to gain experience and worked in a machine shop. In 1866 Pieper saw that the gunmakers of Liège could not produce rifles fast enough to meet their orders, and he set up a small factory to specialise in making rifled barrels. This expanded to take in bolt mechanisms and other components, and eventually the business reached a considerable size. He then went on to manufacture sporting guns and took out patents for various specialised machines and for designs of repeating rifles.

In 1886 he patented a 'gas-seal' system for revolving arms, applicable to pistols or revolvers; the cylinder and barrel were mated together by moving either one, and a specially-lengthened cartridge case bridged the gap to provide sealing. Small numbers of rifles were

The M1935 pistol, designed by Charles Petter, is a modification of the Browning design.

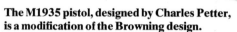

made on this system, but Pieper unaccountably allowed the patent to lapse, leaving room for Nagant (*qv*) to develop a similar design.

After Henry's death, the business was continued by his son Nicolas, the company being now known as the Societé Anonyme Etablissments Pieper. In 1905 the company was again reorganised, this time as the Ancien Etablissments Pieper and Nicolas took out patents for an automatic pistol. In 1908 the company obtained the license for the Bergmann (*qv*) Military pistol and, since Bergmann could not cope, took over the contract to supply the Spanish

A Pickert Model 10 revolver, typical of this company's pre 1939 products.

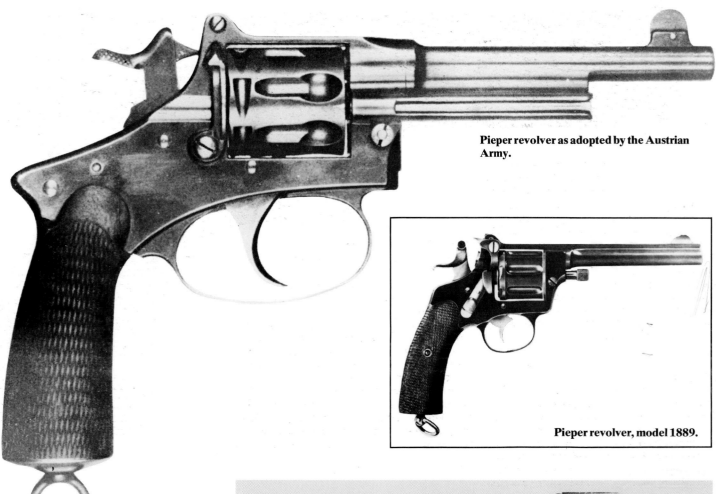

Pieper revolver as adopted by the Austrian Army.

Pieper revolver, model 1889.

The Pieper 6·35mm automatic of 1907.

Army, re-naming the pistol the Bergmann-Bayard, since 'Bayard' was the long-standing trade-mark of the firm. At about the same time a pocket automatic pistol called the Bayard was produced, this being to patents taken out by Bernard Clarus in 1907.

The Pieper automatic pistol was a unique design with a tip-down barrel unit; the recoil spring was contained in a tunnel above the barrel and connected to the breech block by a hook which engaged automatically as the barrel was tipped up into the firing position. The details of construction varied between models as improvements were incorporated, but the basic design remained the same. This form of construction led to an unusually slender pistol and it was a commercial success until the late 1920s. The demise of the design is understood to have been due to the high cost of manufacture in the face of cheaper competition. The patent was licensed to the Steyr (qv) factory in Austria and produced there until shortly before the Second World War.

The PPSh Soviet submachine gun designed by Shpagin.

PISTOLET PULYEMET / *USSR*

The term 'Pistolet Pulyemet' means 'machine pistol' and the abbreviation 'PP' is applied to all submachine guns produced in Soviet Russia.

The first submachine gun to appear in Russia was a design by Tokarev, submitted for test in 1926. It was a simple blowback weapon using two triggers to give single shot or automatic fire and it was chambered for the 7·62mm Nagant revolver cartridge. This cartridge was ill-suited to automatic weapon functioning and the design was dropped. In 1930 S. Korovine, a designer who had worked for many years in Belgium, developed a semi-automatic weapon in 7·63mm Mauser calibre; it is said to have been a complicated weapon, and since Korovine had taken out some patents in Belgium for involved lock mechanisms for pistols, this is quite likely. The weapon was, however, never developed since the Red Army showed no interest in it.

The first successful model was designed by Degtyarev and was adopted as the PPD-34 in 1934, being manufactured until 1940. In general, the design was taken from the Bergmann MP-28, with some minor changes. The most noticeable change was the adoption of a drum

magazine; Degtyarev's first design used a 25-round box magazine, with a magazine housing under the gun, and in order to suit a drum magazine to this housing it was necessary to make the drum with a short extension which fitted the box magazine housing. The drum held 71 rounds and its mechanical arrangement appears to have been copied from the Finnish Suomi submachine gun magazine.

This magazine arrangement was cumbersome and prone to damage, and in 1940 an improved weapon, the PPD-40, appeared. The wooden stock was cut away so that the magazine could be slid sideways into engagement, so that there was no longer any need for the extension to the magazine. The use of box magazines was abandoned, and the modified drum now became the standard. Otherwise, the PPD-40 was much the same as the PPD-34, and many of the parts were interchangeable.

The Degtyarev designs were sound enough weapons but they were built on traditional lines, machined from solid steel and slow to manufacture. In 1941 Georgii Shpagin produced the PPSh-41 which, while using much the same sort of basic blowback mechanism as the PPD models, utilised stamped and welded components so as to speed up manufacture at

the cost of finish. A perforated barrel jacket was made as an extension to the gun body and was also shaped to form a simple muzzle compensature. The old 71 round drum was retained, and the PPSh became the standard Soviet submachine gun throughout the war years, over five million being made.

The last model to appear was the PPS-42, designed by A. I. Sudayev of Leningrad in 1942. The city was under siege and short of weapons, and Sudayev designed this gun to be made as simply and quickly as possible out of what materials were available. Again, it relied heavily on stamped and welded components; it had a folding steel butt, and instead of the 71-round drum used a curved 35-round box magazine, since machinery for making drum magazines was not available. This weapon was slightly improved into the PPS-43 in the following year, but it was never made in such quantities as the PPSh, and most of the stocks were disposed of to satellite countries in postwar years; it was commonly found in the hands of Chinese and North Korean troops in the Korean War.

No Soviet submachine gun has been developed since 1943; in postwar years the assault rifle has taken its place.

The PPS-42 Soviet submachine gun.

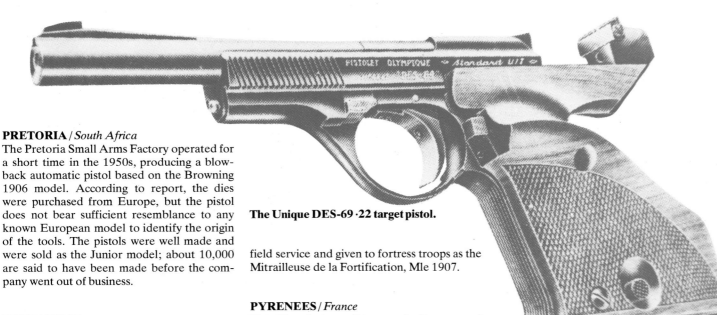

The Unique DES-69 ·22 target pistol.

PRETORIA / *South Africa*

The Pretoria Small Arms Factory operated for a short time in the 1950s, producing a blowback automatic pistol based on the Browning 1906 model. According to report, the dies were purchased from Europe, but the pistol does not bear sufficient resemblance to any known European model to identify the origin of the tools. The pistols were well made and were sold as the Junior model; about 10,000 are said to have been made before the company went out of business.

PUTEAUX / *France*

The Atelier de Construction de Puteaux was a French military arsenal, more usually concerned with artillery weapons. In the early 1900s, however, the French Army were anxious to produce a machine gun of their own, rather than have to depend on a commercial house (Hotchkiss) for their supplies, and the Puteaux arsenal was given the job. The weapon they produced was little more than a revamped Hotchkiss, using the same form of strip feed, but with a peculiar rate-of-fire controller which was theoretically capable of varying the rate between eight and 650 rounds a minute. It rarely worked with any precision. Another enhancement was the adoption of brass cooling fins along the length of the barrel. In service it was found to overheat faster than the standard Hotchkiss and the mechanism constantly gave trouble. After two years it was withdrawn from field service and given to fortress troops as the Mitrailleuse de la Fortification, Mle 1907.

PYRENEES / *France*

The Manufacture d'Armes de Pyrenees of Hendaye began in 1923 and has continued until the present day. The principal product has been a range of blowback automatic pistols in 6·35mm and 7·65mm calibres, the basic model being called the Unique. However, these weapons were widely sold throughout Europe in the years 1924–1939 under a variety of names peculiar to various dealers.

Broadly speaking, the Unique pistols divide into two groups; those made before 1940, which were principally copies of Browning designs, and those made since 1945 which are more original. The period between 1940 and 1944, when the German Occupation controlled the factory, saw the standard Unique Model 17 made for German orders, and these can be easily identified by the marking '9 Schuss' impressed into the black plastic butt-plates.

Since 1945 the company has placed less emphasis on the 6·35mm/7·65mm range and has turned to the manufacture of ·22 target pistols in a variety of styles and degrees of refinement. Their Des-69 model, with long barrel, wide trigger, balance weights, special grips, extended sight base, micrometer rear sight and other features is particularly popular with target shooters throughout Europe, and models with somewhat less sophistication are widely used in the less serious competitive fields.

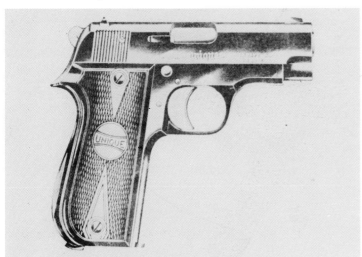

The post-war Pyrenees Model Rr-51 7·65mm pistol.

The Unique Model 17 pistol.

RADOM / *Poland*

The Fabryka Broni w Radomu, of Radom, was the principal Polish arms factory, founded shortly after the First World War. Manufacture there was principally of rifles to Mauser design, but the name is generally associated with the automatic pistol, made there from 1936 onward. In the early 1930s the Polish Army decided to adopt a standard design of pistol, since at that time there was a wide variety of weapons in use, largely left over from the War. A competition was held and a design by two Polish engineers, Wilniewczyc and Skrzypinski, was selected, being put into production as the VIS-35 model, though it is more generally known as the Radom.

The pistol was of modified Browning design,

using a fixed cam surface beneath the breech to disconnect slide and barrel on recoil, as in the contemporary Browning GP-35 pattern. A grip safety was fitted, but no manual safety catch; instead, there was a hammer release catch on the slide which allowed the hammer to be dropped safely on to a loaded chamber. The pistol could then be carried fully loaded, and merely had to be thumb-cocked to bring it into firing condition. It was quite large and heavy for its calibre, which was 9mm Parabellum, and was a robust and accurate weapon.

Original Polish production was marked on the slide with the Polish eagle; but in 1939, after German occupation, production was continued for the German Army, and these were marked Pistole P35(p) without the eagle. The

quality, under German supervision, gradually dropped below the pre-war standard. Manufacture continued until late 1944 when the Russian Army approached; the machinery was then evacuated to the Steyr factory in Austria, but little more than 5000 pistols were made there before production ceased with the end of the war.

REICHSREVOLVER / *Germany*

The Reichsrevolver of 1879 was designed to specifications laid down by a Committee formed by the Prussian Army and charged with producing a modern weapon to replace the single-shot pistols of the time. Two models were eventually produced, the M1879, some-

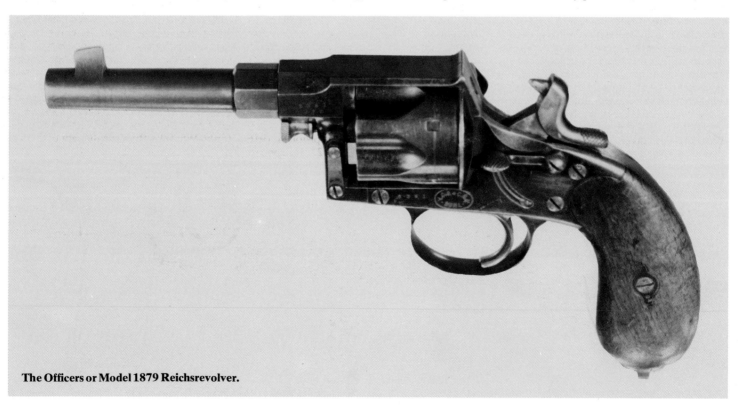

The Officers or Model 1879 Reichsrevolver.

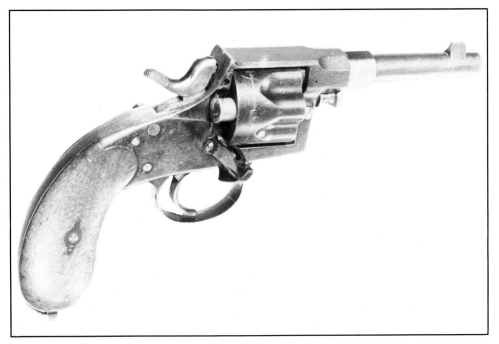

The 1883 'Infantry' or 'Officer's' Reichsrevolver shown here had a narrower barrel than the 1879.

times called the Cavalry or Troopers model, and the M1883, or Infantry or Officers model. The basic difference is that the M1879 had a 183mm barrel, while the M1883 had a 126mm barrel. Both were single-action, gate-loaded, solid frame revolvers; the cylinder was removed by taking out the arbor pin and using the pin to punch out the empty cases. A safety catch was fitted on the left side of the frame, a superfluity on a single-action revolver.

The adoption of such an antiquated design as late as 1879 has always been considered to have been a triumph for conservatism over technical advance. The American Smith & Wesson Russian model, a top-break revolver with automatic extraction, had been introduced in 1870 and there were any number of commercial revolvers which pointed the way to more modern designs. In spite of all this, the

Reichsrevolver became the standard issue and it remained so until the adoption of the Parabellum pistol in 1908. They were then placed into reserve stocks and were brought out in 1914, and some of them even reappeared in 1944–1945 in the hands of German Volkssturm units.

Manufacture was carried out by various commercial companies, whose names or initials always appear in an oval on the left of the frame. The butt backstrap is frequently marked with codes indicating military units who owned the pistols.

REISING, Eugene C. *(fl. 1915–1942)*
Eugene Reising, of New Hartford, Connecticut, patented an automatic pistol in 1916 and, with improvements, in 1921. He appears

to have begun production of the pistol in about 1919, since early models are marked only with the 1916 patent date. It was a ·22 calibre blowback automatic with tip-down barrel, intended for competition and sporting use, and seems to have sold reasonably well at first. So much so that in 1922 the Reising Arms Co. moved to New York and became the Reising Corporation. Thereafter, however, the novelty wore off and sales died away, and probably not more than 5000 pistols were sold in all. The company stopped production about 1924.

Reising next appeared in about 1938, with a design of submachine gun which he eventually patented in 1940. He was, by this time, connected with the Harrington & Richardson company, and they manufactured the Reising Model 50, as the gun was known, commencing in December 1941. The gun was tested and accepted for service use by the US Marine Corps, who bought most of the 100,000 which were produced. The balance were taken by the British purchasing commission and were shipped to Russia. A Model 55 was also made; this differed from the Model 50 only in having a folding wire stock.

The Reising was an odd design which fired from a closed bolt by means of a rotating hammer which struck a firing pin in the bolt. The bolt was delayed in opening by having to tilt so as to disengage from a locking surface in the body. Feed was from a 20-round box magazine beneath the body, and the gun was cocked by inserting a finger into a slot beneath the fore-end to pull back a lever. Though the gun performed reasonably well in range tests, it failed miserably in action, due to dirt entering the body and preventing the bolt from locking into the body recess. Most of the guns taken to Guadalcanal by the US Marines were dumped in a convenient river, and it was withdrawn from service shortly afterwards. Numbers were given to police and security agencies within the USA, and in this role they functioned satisfactorily. What the Russians thought of them has never been disclosed.

The Reising Model 60, a semi-automatic carbine version of the Reising submachine gun.

REMINGTON / *USA*

The Remington concern was founded in 1816 in Ilion, New York, by Eliphalet Remington, a barrel-maker, and his sons. Their first products were flintlock rifles which soon gained a high reputation and by the time of the Civil War they had progressed sufficiently to be able to manufacture rifles by the thousand for the Union Army. In the 1850s they began making pistols, becoming the second largest percussion pistol makers in America after Colt. But in 1886 the company, which had remained in the Remington family, got into financial difficulties and was taken over by a New York finance house, and in 1888 re-appeared as the Remington Arms Company. After this it specialised in shoulder arms, though in the 1920s it was to produce an automatic pistol which many authorities consider to be the best such pistol to emanate from America. This, unaccountably, failed to prosper, and the company went back to making rifles and shotguns, which it has continued to do until the present day with considerable success. In 1902 the company was merged with the Union Metallic Cartridge Company to become Remington-UMC Co., and finally it was given its present name, the Remington Arms Co. Inc. Due to the amalgamation, the company is a major producer of ammunition as well as weapons, and has made several innovations in the ammunition field.

With a history as long and involved as this, and with the vast output of arms, it would be impossible to detail every model produced, and therefore we can only afford space to mention some of the more important Remington designs. Undoubtedly the first of these was the 'rolling block' rifle; this originated with a patent by one Leonard Geiger, in 1863, and was subsequently modified by Joseph Rider, a designer working for Remington; in consequence of which it is often called the Remington-Rider rifle. It was a breech-loader, for metallic cartridges, and used a pivoted breech block which swung up into place behind the chamber. The rear surface of the block was curved in such a way as to mate with a curve on the front face of the hammer, which was pivoted directly behind the block. The cartridge was inserted into the chamber and the block hinged up, a spring holding it snugly against the base of the cartridge. When the trigger was pressed, the hammer fell, and during its fall the curved face on the hammer breast passed beneath the curved rear of the block so as to support it when the recoil force tried to push it back as the cartridge fired. It was a very positive and safe lock, capable of withstanding heavy loads, and proved to be extremely popular. It sold first to the US Navy who bought 12,000 in 1866, and was then adopted by Denmark, Sweden, Norway, Spain, Argentina, Egypt and China, as

Remington Model 51 automatic pistol.

Remington XP-100 bolt action single shot pistol.

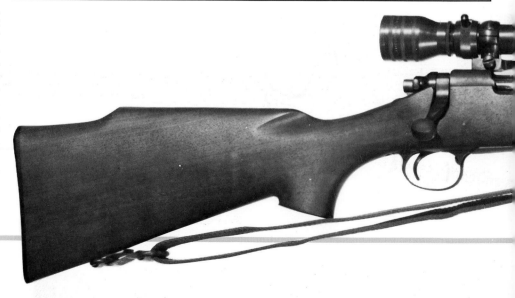

well as being widely used by many other armies. In all, over a million of the rolling block rifles and carbines were sold throughout the world, and it continued to be used on inexpensive rifles until past the end of the century.

Their next major step was the adoption of the Lee (*qv*) bolt action and magazine in 1880 and the company developed several military and sporting rifles around the Lee system, though the American Army turned its face against the Lee system on the ground that the detachable box magazine was 'too fragile' for military service.

John M. Browning (*qv*) became associated with Remington at about the turn of the century and for them he produced a semi-automatic rifle mechanism which was first offered in ·22 and then in more powerful calibres, and followed it with a slide-action repeating shotgun, and these proved to be profitable designs which, with periodical refinement, have survived to the present day.

In the pistol field their earliest memorable design was the ·44 New Model Army revolver of 1874. This was a single-action six-shot, gate-loaded weapon which was obviously intended to compete with the Colt Frontier of 1873, and it can always be recognised by the peculiar triangular web beneath the barrel. It was a first-class arm, but somehow never managed to achieve the popular esteem of the Colt. Production continued until 1894, but after the collapse of the original Remington company in 1888 pistol manufacture tapered off, probably due to economic reasons. They were not able to compete with the flood of cheap revolvers on the market, nor were they organised so as to make a major assault on the position of Colt or Smith & Wesson, so the wisest course was to abjure the pistol field and concentrate on shoulder arms, which they did outstandingly well. The exception to this was a single-shot target pistol which they produced from 1891 to 1909 and which was popular with competition shooters of the day.

Remington ·36 percussion revolver of the 1860s.

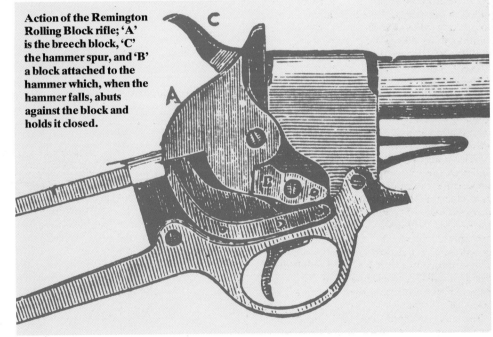

Action of the Remington Rolling Block rifle; 'A' is the breech block, 'C' the hammer spur, and 'B' a block attached to the hammer which, when the hammer falls, abuts against the block and holds it closed.

Remington Model 700 rifle in 7·62mm NATO calibre, as used by the US Army as a sniping rifle.

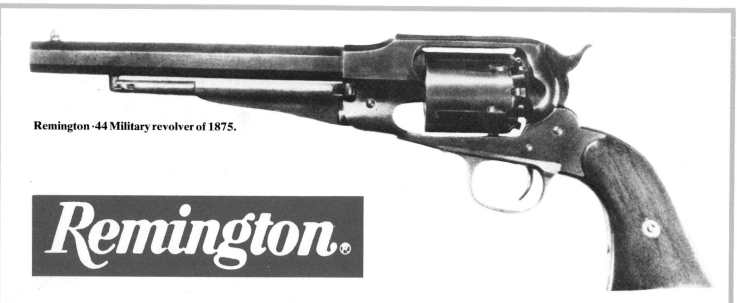

Remington ·44 Military revolver of 1875.

During the war, they employed J. D. Pedersen (*qv*) and he produced a design of automatic pistol which, in ·45 calibre, was submitted for military approval. It was a delayed blowback model with external hammer, and after tests the US Navy expressed their willingness to accept it as their standard pistol, leaving the Colt M1911 to the Army; but the government, understandably, saw no benefit in having two types of standard pistol and turned the idea down. Remington then set Pedersen to work to turn his design into a pocket pistol for the post-war commercial market, and late in 1919 it was introduced as the Model 51. It was a fixed-barrel automatic with a slide enveloping a separate breech block. On firing, the block recoiled for a short distance, pushing the slide back, until it was stopped by an abutment on the frame. The slide was free to continue to the rear, and after a further short movement a shaped surface inside the slide lifted the breech block away from the abutment so that it could recoil with the slide; the barrel remained stationary throughout. On the return stroke the block was closed up against the breech and then, by the shaped surfaces in the slide, forced down so as to be aligned ready to strike the abutment on the next shot. In 9mm Short calibre, and later produced in 7·65mm, the Remington Model 51 was a high-quality weapon and notable for being well-shaped for instinctive shooting. But it was an over-complicated design for the calibre it used, and this was reflected in the price. Manufacture was discontinued in 1934.

One other design deserving of mention is the XP-100 pistol. In 1963 the idea of using powerful pistols for hunting was beginning to gain ground in the USA and Remington were quick off the mark to produce a weapon specifically designed for this. The XP-100 was simply a shortened version of their current bolt-action rifle mechanism allied to a 10½ inch barrel and all installed on a nylon-based plastic stock. The fore-end of the stock was hollowed out so that weights could be installed to balance the weapon for the individual owner, and the sights were fully adjustable. It was chambered for the ·221 Remington Fireball cartridge, giving 2600 feet a second with a 50-grain bullet and being capable of producing one-inch groups at one hundred yards range. It was several years before a similar pistol appeared, and Remington's has been quite successful.

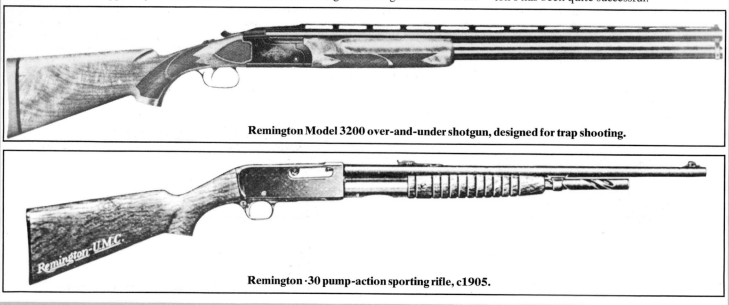

Remington Model 3200 over-and-under shotgun, designed for trap shooting.

Remington ·30 pump-action sporting rifle, c1905.

The Model 1914 Fiat-Revelli machine gun, showing the unusual magazine system.

REVELLI, Abiel Bethel *(1864–1930)*

Revelli was an officer in the Italian Army who became interested in automatic weapons. In 1909 he developed a self-loading rifle known as the Revelli-Terni, which was not adopted though tested by the Italian and Swiss Armies. He then turned to machine gun design and produced a mechanism which used a combination of short recoil and blowback; the breech was locked to the barrel by a simple lever which, after very short recoil, was thrown clear to allow the breech block to move back. In fact, the period of locking was so brief that the weapon is classed as a delayed blowback rather than as a locked breech. The Army adopted the weapon and passed it to FIAT (*qv*) to manufacture as the M1914, and it is therefore often referred to as the FIAT-Revelli gun.

Revelli then concluded that a lighter weapon was required for use in aircraft, and he designed a pistol-calibre machine gun, patented in 1915, which, from its place of manufacture, has always been known as the Vilar Perosa (*qv*) gun. As an aircraft gun it was a failure; it was then put forward as a light machine gun for use by Alpini troops, in which it was little more successful, and it finally found its right level as one of the first submachine guns.

After the war Revelli continued to work on automatic rifle designs and produced a model for test shortly before his death. It was not accepted for service, but in the 1930s his son, who was connected with the Armaguerra company, improved it and offered it again in 1939. It was again refused, and this marked the last Revelli design.

REXIM / *Switzerland*

The firm of Rexim SA of Geneva placed a submachine gun design on the market in 1953, a model known as the Rexim-Favor, a name reputedly derived from its designer, a Colonel Favier. According to an unconfirmed tale, the basic design was stolen from a French arsenal by a mysterious (and doubtless beautiful) lady spy in the late 1940s. The Rexim company were in no position to manufacture, and they had the guns made for them in the Spanish arsenal at La Coruna, 5000 being made in the first batch. These were then hawked round Europe in 1954–1955 without success, and in 1957 Rexim went bankrupt, leaving the Spaniards with the better part of the 5000 guns on their hands. They offered them for sale as the La Coruna and most of them appear to have gone to various African nationalist forces active at that period.

The failure of the Rexim design was due to its complication. The gun fired from a closed bolt; when cocked, the bolt ran forward to chamber a round, propelled by the usual sort of return spring. When the trigger was pressed, a second spring sent a cylindrical hammer unit forward to strike the firing pin and fire the round; the recoil force of the spent case thus had to overcome both springs to perform the loading cycle. Due to the closed bolt feature it tended to suffer from 'cook-off' when left loaded after a prolonged burst of fire. It was also expensive. Obviously not a good day's work by the lady spy.

The Rexim Favor submachine gun.

RHEINMETALL / *Germany*

This company was founded as the Rheinische Metallwaaren und Maschinenfabrik of Sommerda in 1889 and was a general engineering company. In 1901 it purchased the remains of the bankrupt Waffenfabrik von Dreyse (*qv*) but at that time the company felt no desire to enter the firearms field and the Dreyse factory was used for other products. In 1905, however, Louis Schmeisser, the chief designer, patented an automatic pistol and in 1907 this was marketed as the Dreyse (*qv*) to commemorate the famous name. A light machine gun also produced under this name.

Production of the Dreyse pistol stopped during the First World War and in the postwar years the compnay produced a pistol under the name Rheinmetall, an acronym which they had adopted. This retreated from the novelties of the Schmeisser design and was no more than a slightly modified copy of the Browning M1910. This survived until about 1927, by which time the company were becoming more and more involved with heavier weapons.

In the late 1920s the company began to form links with foreign firms, beginning with an association with Steyr of Austria and then selling surplus military weapons through a company called Hollandische Artillerie-Industrie und Hemboltsmaatschappisch, or HAIHA, though this latter firm went bankrupt in the early 1930s. For some years around this time, Rheinmetall operated a design agency in Moscow called BUTAST, part of the clandestine agreement with the Soviets which the German government had in order to conceal weapons development. In 1929 Rheinmetall bought a moribund Swiss engineering company in Solothurn and established the Waffenfabrik Solothurn AG, and then helped to set up another company, Steyr-Solothurn AG, to act as a Swiss sales office. The net result of all this was that the Rheinmetall factory in Germany now acted as a design agency, the Solothurn plant was the development engineering facility, production in quantity could be done at Steyr, and the Steyr-Solothurn AG acted as the world sales agents from an innocuous Swiss address. All this was, of course, well concealed at the time, and led to some entertaining conclusions being drawn by Allied intelligence agencies during the war when various German weapons were described as being based on Swiss designs while they had in fact originated in the Rheinmetall drawing office. In January 1936 Rheinmetall merged with Borsig AG, a well-known German company in the heavy engineering field to become Rheinmetall-Borsig AG. By the end of the Second World War the company had twelve major production plants and its own proving ground and range facility at Unterluss on the Luneberg Heath. After the war it practically ceased to exist for several years, but in the 1950s it was reconstituted.

After abandoning their pistol in 1927 the company turned more and more to military weapons. In 1929 it developed an automatic rifle with toggle lock designed by Heinemann, but this was not successful. It then, via the Solothurn link, developed a machine gun designed by Louis Stange of their Dusseldorf office. This novel design was an early indication of the trend to making weapons which were easy to mass-produce. Most of the gun could be produced on lathes or screw-cutting machines without the need for special machine tools. It was laid out in a straight line, the butt bayoneting to the end of the receiver, and by removing the butt and bolt the barrel could be removed through the receiver for changing. The German Army did not accept it, but the Austrian and Hungarian armies adopted it in 1930 and 1931 respectively. The Germans were impressed enough with it to hand it to the Mauser company for improvement; under Mauser's hand several details were changed and it re-emerged as the MG34 to become the Army's standard machine gun.

Rheinmetall thereafter concentrated on developing machine guns for aircraft. The Stange design, slightly altered, became the MG15 and was then modified so as to be more easily synchronised and became the MG17. During the war, when a shortage of infantry machine guns threatened, numbers of MG15 were fitted with bipods for use as ground weapons. It was

Rheinmetall-Selbstlade-Pistolen

1406–800

Sämtliche Munition für Jagd- und Sportzwecke Verkauf nur an Wiederverkäufer

Rheinmetall DÜSSELDORF

A 1920s advertisement for Rheinmetall.

also adopted by the Japanese Air Force as their Type 98 aircraft gun. The company then moved to heavier weapons, developing the MG131 in 13mm calibre for the Luftwaffe, and this design went into many variant models. The only other major company development in the small arms field was the Fallschirmgewehr 42 (*qv*), the German parachutist assault rifle. Apart from that, their wartime production was concerned principally with heavier weapons for the Luftwaffe and with artillery. At the present time they are not involved in small arms production.

ROBINSON, Russel S. *(fl. 1940s)*

Robinson was a designer with the Shepherd Robinson Arms Development Company of Sydney, Australia, who developed a most unusual submachine gun, the SR Model 11 in 1943. Robinson had an idea that it would be possible to smooth out the succession of firing impulses from an automatic weapon into a sustained thrust against the hand which would be easier to resist and which would allow more accurate fire to be maintained. The gun looked like a large automatic pistol with an extended barrel in front of the slide; this barrel had helical grooves on the outside which, as the slide was blown back, caused the barrel to rotate and thus counter the torque effect of the bullet going up the barrel. This also helped to smooth out the firing impulses, and the SR11 could, indeed, be fired automatic from one hand. A telescoping metal stock fitted at the rear and the whole thing was extremely light and handy; the 16-shot magazine in the butt was automatically ejected when it became empty.

The SR11 was tested in Britain in 1944 and found to be very accurate when fired automatic but very erratic when fired single shot, as a pistol. Robinson changed the design to improve the pistol performance but there was no requirement for the weapon and it was not further developed. Mr. Robinson then joined the staff at Enfield and produced an ingenious heavy machine gun which used a sliding breech block and a rammer to load the cartridges from a belt. The design was not accepted in England and he later went to the USA where it became the basis of the M73 tank machine gun.

ROLLS-ROYCE / *Britain*

The Rolls-Royce company were primarily concerned with the production of aircraft engines during the Second World War, but through this they were privy to various facets of the aircraft production programme. In 1941 there were problems with the provision of ·50 Browning machine guns for use in bomber turrets, and so Rolls-Royce decided to develop a machine gun of their own. In order to reduce weight and

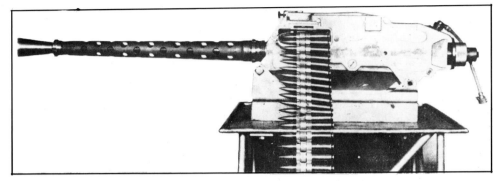

The Experimental ·50 calibre Rolls-Royce machine gun.

size, so as to make turret installation easier, it was to be five inches shorter in the barrel and have the body made of Hiduminium alloy. As finally developed it was recoil-operated, using a locking flap system similar to that of the Russian Degtyarev machine gun, with, of course, some Rolls-Royce-engineered refinements. The gun was tested in March 1941 but required the addition of a large flash-hider, was prone to stoppages and finally broke its extractor. A month later Rolls-Royce had the idea of redesigning the gun around the ·55 Boys anti-tank rifle cartridge, which would have produced a formidable weapon. The Air Ministry concurred and 2000 rounds were furnished for trial, but thereafter the supply of Browning guns improved, Rolls-Royce found they had enough to do producing engines, and the project was finally abandoned in March 1942.

ROSS, Sir Charles Henry Augustus Frederick Lockhart (1872–1942)

Sir Charles Ross was a Scottish landowner and reputedly one of the richest men in Britain in the 1890s, but he was not inclined to merely live on the income of his vast estates, and was an engineer, businessman, agriculturalist and inventor. His particular interest was in firearms, and he took out numerous patents for rifles and automatic pistols in the period 1895–1914. His automatic pistol used a toggle lock which, unlike the Maxim and Borchardt locks, was folded up when the breech was closed and opened out during the recoil stroke; it was ingenious, but never got past the pro-

totype stage. His automatic rifle, patented in 1896 and constantly improved over the years, was equally ingenious and unsuccessful. His bolt-action rifles, however, were a different story.

He took out his first bolt-action patent in 1893 when he was an engineering student at Cambridge; this was a straight-pull bolt action of complex design which never got any further. But in 1896 he patented a more practical model which was made for him by the London gunmaker Charles Lancaster, who also sold it for him. The straight-pull bolt action appeared to fascinate Ross, and from then on he kept perfecting his design. His 1897 model used a sleeve around the bolt, the sleeve being provided with a handle. This sleeve rode in straight grooves in the receiver. Internally, the sleeve had helical grooves which mated with lugs on the bolt, so that as the sleeve moved straight back it imparted a rotary motion to the bolt and unlocked the lugs on the bolt head from recesses in the barrel.

In 1897 Ross went to Canada and there developed an improved model, which he then made in the USA as the Model 1900 Sporter; the principal difference was that the 1897 design had used a hammer to strike a loose firing pin in the bolt while the 1900 used a spring-loaded striker. He also submitted the rifle for test by the Canadian Army, but his development was now temporarily halted by his serving in the South African War. On his return from South Africa he set about designing a military rifle, and for this, with the cooperation of Eley Brothers, the ammunition makers, he began developing a ·280 high velocity car-

tridge. The rifle, of course, used the Ross straight-pull bolt, and since the British Army was known to be contemplating a new rifle, Ross pushed it very hard. The Harris controlled magazine (qv) was used, and the weapon was extremely accurate, but the British preferred the Lee-Enfield and Ross's hopes were dashed. Nevertheless he continued to produce sporting rifles from the Ross Rifle Company which he had founded in Quebec, and he also managed to interest the Canadian Army in his military rifle design. In 1902 the Minister of Militia had ordered 12,000 rifles, to be followed by 10,000 per year for five years. Shortly after this the rifle was tested in Britain with unfavourable results, but Ross was able to convince the Militia that this was due to the different characteristics of the British ammunition, and production of the Ross military rifle, in ·303 calibre, got under way. There were a number of changes in detail as production went on; one Canadian expert has recognised no less than 85 distinct models. But the basic problem was that they were far too complicated and delicate for the rough and tumble of active service, and when the Canadian Army went to France in 1914 this began to be obvious. The rifles jammed in the mud, were frequently thrown away, and troops were found to be arming themselves with Lee-Enfields picked up on the battlefields rather than rely on the Ross. Another fatal defect was that it was possible to assemble the bolt incorrectly and still fire the rifle, resulting in the bolt being blown out into the firer's face. After much waste of time in face-saving manoeuvres, the Ross was finally withdrawn on the orders of Sir Douglas Haig in 1916. Production of rifles ceased, the factory was wound up, with compensation to Sir Charles, and the Ross rifles were relegated to training roles.

During the Second World War quantities of these training rifles were shipped to Britain for use by the Home Guard; they were not particularly popular, since many of the Home Guard men remembered its reputation from 1915.

As a target rifle and big-game rifle, the Ross was supreme; the Canadian teams made a great impact at Bisley in the years prior to the First World War, taking as much as 91% of the prize money in 1913. But as a military rifle it failed the test of practicality.

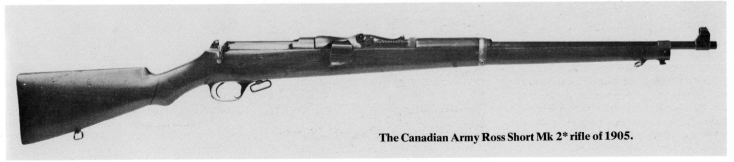

The Canadian Army Ross Short Mk 2* rifle of 1905.

ROTH, George (d.1909)

George Roth was primarily an ammunition maker, with a factory in Vienna which began production in the 1870s. In 1898 Karel Krnka (*qv*) went to work for him and in addition to superintending the ammunition factory managed to interest Roth in his automatic pistol designs. Whether Roth became actively interested and joined with Krnka in developing designs is something not likely to be resolved at this late date, but certainly Roth took out patents for automatic rifles in his own name as well as in association with Krnka. None of these were particularly successful, however, and he is today remembered for various pistol designs, though there is little doubt that they emanated from Krnka's drawing board.

Having no facilities for production, Roth allied himself with established gunmaking companies, and as a result the pistols usually have someone else's name attached. The first to appear was the Roth-Sauer, patented in 1900 by Roth and Krnka and manufactured by J. P. Sauer & Son of Suhl. Like most of Krnka's designs it was over-complicated, a long-recoil pistol with locked breech but firing a weak 7·65mm cartridge which had been designed by Roth.

In 1904 the two men produced another pistol, this time using a rotating barrel as a means of locking the breech. After various prototypes, this was adopted by the Austro-Hungarian cavalry in 1907, the first adoption of an automatic pistol by one of the then major armies of the world. This pistol was made by the Steyr factory and hence became known as the Roth-Steyr; again, it used a unique cartridge designed by Roth, an 8mm round of moderate efficiency. Both these pistols exhibited a feature which seems to be unique to Austrian designs; the magazine was in the butt, in the now-accepted manner, but instead of the customary removeable box, it was integral in the structure of the pistol and could only be loaded by pulling back the action of the pistol, inserting a charger into guides and then forcing the cartridges home into the magazine with the thumb.

The obvious drawback to this is the task of emptying the magazine without firing; the action has to be worked back and forth for however many cartridges remain, a procedure which reeks of potential accident. To avoid this, the pistols were provided with a spring retaining lip at the top of the magazine which, in normal use, controlled the feed of rounds to the bolt. But when depressed by an external catch, the lip moved away and permitted the force of the magazine spring to eject all the cartridges from the butt.

Roth died in 1909 and Krnka moved to another company, but one more pistol due to them was yet to appear; this was the Steyr M1912, and details will be found under that company's entry.

RUBIN / Switzerland

The use of lead bullets with rifled barrels led to problems with fouling—a deposit of lead left in the grooves of the rifling by the passage of successive bullets until the obstruction became so great as to prevent the rifle being fired. Various expedients were tried, such as enclosing the bullet in a paper sleeve or smearing it with lubricant, but none of these solutions were entirely successful.

In the late 1870s Major Rubin, director of the Swiss Military Laboratory at Thun, began to examine this problem, and from that he moved to a general review of the whole question of bullets and calibres. He eventually developed a small-calibre bullet composed of a lead core surrounded by a copper jacket. This

The 8mm Roth-Steyr automatic pistol, issued to the Austro-Hungarian Army in 1908.

A sectioned drawing of the Ruger Single Six.

gave a jacket soft enough to engrave in the rifling but which left far less deposit and thus gave the rifle barrel a greater useful life. In 1883 he submitted a 7·5mm calibre compound bullet to the Swiss Army, mated to a compressed black-powder charge in a brass cartridge case. In 1886, after Vielle had discovered smokeless powder, Rubin redesigned his cartridge to use the new propellant and then collaborated with Colonel Schmidt, a weapons technical officer of the Swiss Army, to produce the Schmidt-Rubin (*qv*) military rifle, which remained in Swiss service until the late 1950s. More important was the fact that Rubin's researches on small-calibre compound bullets was the key factor in the world-wide adoption of small-calibre rifles for military use in the 1890s, an advance which was only made against much conservative military opposition.

RUGER/*USA*

William B. Ruger took out his first patents for an automatic pistol in 1946. He then set up a company, Sturm, Ruger & Co., and in 1949 began manufacture of his pistol. It was an instant success, being inexpensive, reliable and accurate. With this project under way, Ruger saw that there was a great demand for single-action 'western-style' revolvers, which had been unsatisfied since Colt had ceased to manufacture their 'Frontier' model.

Ruger therefore designed and began production of a single-action revolver, not an imitation of the Colt but an original design, extremely well-engineered. The Ruger revolvers were such a success that Colt were forced to reconsider their decision, and many other companies went into the single-action revolver business, though few had Ruger's success.

In more recent years the company moved into the manufacture of double-action revolvers for defence and police use, to the manufacture of a single-shot falling-block sporting rifle, to a semi-automatic carbine in 5·56mm calibre (the Mini-14) and most recently, to a double-barrelled, over-and-under 20-bore shotgun of excellent quality.

The bedrock of all this was the original Standard ·22 automatic pistol. This uses a fixed, exposed barrel with a tubular receiver in which a bolt reciprocates in blowback action. Firing is by an internal hammer, arranged to give a short lock time. Variations in barrel length and weight are provided for target shooting purposes. The single-action revolver line began in 1953 with the Single Six, based on the lines of the Colt Frontier but with internal changes, such as the replacement of leaf springs by coil springs and the incorporation of a floating firing pin in the standing breech.

In 1968 the Gun Control Act was passed in the USA and in 1971 the US Treasury laid down stringent rules as to the safety of revolvers. No single-action revolver of the original Colt type could hope to pass these rules, and those on the market had either to be re-designed or withdrawn. The Ruger design, thanks to the floating firing pin, was half-way there. Modifying the hammer face so that it normally rested on the frame, clear of the firing pin, and adding a 'transfer bar' to the lockwork, was enough to bring the pistol into line with the new rules. Now the hammer could only touch the firing pin if the trigger was properly pulled back for deliberate firing, which forced the transfer bar up behind the firing pin and thus transmitted the hammer blow to the pin when the hammer fell. This is comparable to the Iver Johnson (*qv*) 'Hammer the Hammer' safety and the Colt 'Positive Safety Hammer' designs. In 1973 the Ruger revolver designs were modified to this new standard, and were thenceforth known by the additional designation of the word 'Super' in front of their names.

The Number One rifle was introduced in the middle 1960s, and uses an underlever to lower a vertical sliding breech block. This is by no means an innovative system, since similar mechanisms were in use almost a century ago, but it is well-engineered and immensely strong, capable of handling the heaviest sporting loads.

The Mini-14 carbine is a semi-automatic weapon resembling the US Army's M1 carbine, though having a slightly different system of gas operation. Chambered for the 5·56mm cartridge, it was originally restricted to police use but has since been placed on the open market.

S

SAUER/*Germany*

The firm of J. P. Sauer & Son in Suhl was founded in 1751, beginning Suhl's rise to eminence as a centre of gunmaking. For the most part the company has been concerned with the production of sporting arms, being particularly noted for 'drillings', or three-barrelled guns in which two barrels are smoothbored for shot and the third, below, is rifled in a suitable sporting calibre. From time to time the firm was given contracts for military weapons, producing Mauser rifles and being concerned in a consortium for the production of the Reichsrevolver (*qv*).

While the firm's long arms have been generally conventional enough, the same can hardly be said for the Sauer's various pistols. Their first commercial pistol was the Bär, a repeating pistol patented by a Russian, Burkhard Behr, in 1898. It was rather like a revolver in its layout but the barrel unit was a flat block with two superimposed barrels. Behind this, in the place where a revolver would have its cylinder, was a flat block with four chambers, and a longitudinal pivot through its centre. Behind this, inside the high frame, was a concealed hammer with a rotating firing pin. On pulling the trigger the hammer fell and fired the cartridge in the topmost chamber through the top barrel. The next pull on the trigger turned the firing pin unit during the hammer's rise and fall, so that when the hammer fell, it fired the lower chamber through the lower barrel. The chamber block was now rotated, bringing the two unused chambers to the top, so that two more shots could be fired. By half-turning the chamber block the pistol could be reloaded.

This remarkable weapon, in 7mm calibre, sold quite well in the early 1900s as a personal defence weapon, one virtue being that it was very slender and could be easily concealed. Eventually sales began to fall due to competition from pocket automatic pistols, and Sauer decided to go into this field, buying a design from George Roth. Like most of the Roth/Krnka designs it was too complicated and used the long-recoil system of operation,

quite superfluous since it was chambered for an exceptionally weak 7·65mm cartridge. This was marketed for some time as the Roth-Sauer but it does not appear to have achieved much popularity and specimens are not common.

Having survived these essays with other people's designs, Sauer then developed one of their own; it proved to be far more successful, but even then was slightly different from the usual. The pistol appeared in 1913 and was a 7·65mm blowback featuring a fixed barrel, annular recoil spring, lightweight tubular slide, and a separate breechblock retained in the slide by a knurled screw cap at the rear end. A seven-shot magazine fitted in the butt and the pistol was striker-fired. Shortly after the First World War the design was repeated in 6·35mm

calibre, but this model was only produced for a short time, being too complicated a manufacturing task in such a small calibre. It was replaced by a more conventional design, the WT (*westentaschen*, vest-pocket) model, which generally resembled the Baby Browning but still had the Sauer separate breechblock pinned into the slide.

In 1930 a new 7·65mm model was introduced, still to the same basic design as the 1913 version but with some small detail improvements. This was widely adopted by Police and similar bodies and became known as the *Behordenmodell* (Authorities' or Official Model). This remained in production until 1937 and was replaced in the following year by a completely new design, the Model 38H. (The 'H'

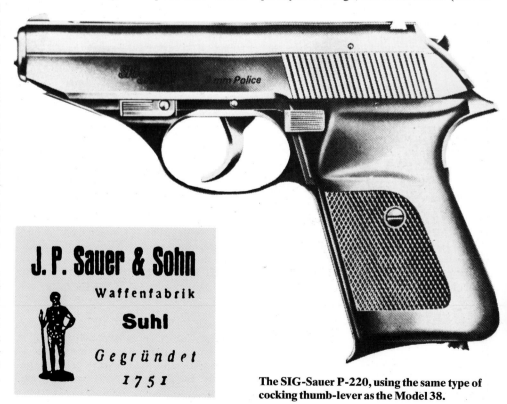

The SIG-Sauer P-220, using the same type of cocking thumb-lever as the Model 38.

J. P. Sauer & Sohn

Waffenfabrik

Suhl

Gegründet

1751

indicates 'hahn', i.e. using a hammer instead of a striker.) This was potentially one of the best pocket pistols ever made, and but for the war might have made a considerable impact on the commercial market. As it was, almost all the production was taken by the German forces. The 38H was a fixed-barrel blowback automatic with a double-action lock and with a novel control lever on the left side of the frame; this allowed a cocked hammer to be eased down on to a loaded chamber, or an uncocked hammer to be cocked. In conjunction with the double-action lock it gave the user full control over the options of firing double- or single-action at all times.

At the end of the Second World War Suhl became part of East Germany, and the Sauer factory became part of a state-owned consortium known as the VB Ernst Thalmann Werke. But sufficient numbers of staff and technicians had fled to West Germany to allow the Sauer company to be set up afresh in Eckernforde. Production there was resumed, firstly of sporting guns and latterly of pistols, in conjunction with the SIG (*qv*) concern of Switzerland. Two models have so far been introduced, and there is no doubt that the designs are not entirely from the SIG drawing office, since there are various Sauer features. The P220 pistol is a heavy-calibre locked breech model available chambered for ·45, ·38 Super, 9mm and 7·65mm Parabellum cartridges. Breech locking is by a heavy lug on top of the barrel allied to a shaped cam beneath the breech, basically the SIG-Petter system. The breechblock, in

Sauer fashion, is a separate component pinned into the slide. An external hammer is used and this is allied to a double action lock and the same cocking lever as used on the 38H.

The second new model is the P230, a fixed-barrel blowback with annular recoil spring; this too, has an external hammer, double action lock and side cocking lever. It is chambered for a new cartridge, the 9mm Police, slightly larger than the 9mm Short but not so powerful as the 9mm Parabellum. It would appear to be derived on similar lines to the Soviet 9mm Makarov round, a cartridge intended to extract the maximum power from a blowback pistol.

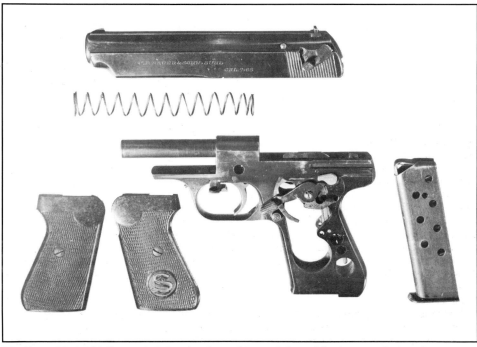

The Sauer Model 38 dismantled showing the cocking and de-cocking lever on the butt frame.

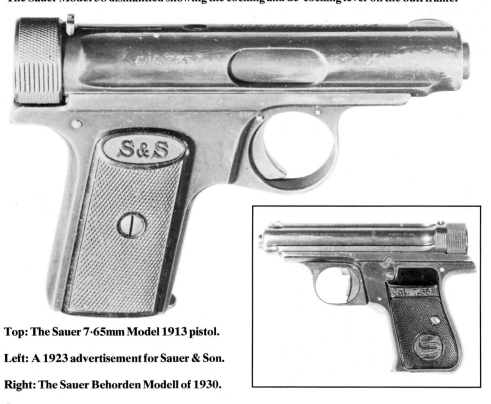

Top: The Sauer 7·65mm Model 1913 pistol.

Left: A 1923 advertisement for Sauer & Son.

Right: The Sauer Behorden Modell of 1930.

273

SAVAGE

SAVAGE, Arthur William *(1857–1941)*

The Savage Arms Company of Utica, New York, was begun in 1894 by Arthur Savage. (Note that he had no connection with Edward Savage or the Savage Revolving Fire-Arms Company mentioned below.) Savage had been born in Jamaica; he then went sheep-farming in Australia, coffee-growing in Jamaica, designed a naval torpedo which was adopted by Brazil, became Traffic Superintendent of a railway, and then designed a lever-action sporting rifle. He set up the company to make the rifle, and, with small modifications from time to time, this same rifle design has been the company's mainstay ever since. Once the company was well established, Savage sold his interest and returned to his wanderings; he went into the tyre business, grew citrus fruit, prospected for oil and gold, and died at 84.

The company he had founded continued until 1915, when it was bought out by the Driggs-Seabury Ordnance Company in order to cope with foreign war contracts, but in 1919 it was re-constituted as the Savage Arms Corporation. It subsequently bought out several small firearms companies and is today among the largest American manufacturers of sporting weapons.

In 1893 Savage patented a lever action rifle which went into production two years later as the Model 95. The action differed from other lever-actions—eg the Winchester and Marlin—in being truly hammerless, streamlined, and in using a rotary magazine. This latter feature allowed the use of pointed bullets in a lever action rifle for the first time; previous lever actions all used tube magazines beneath the barrel, and the close proximity of the bullet point to the cap of the cartridge in front was a

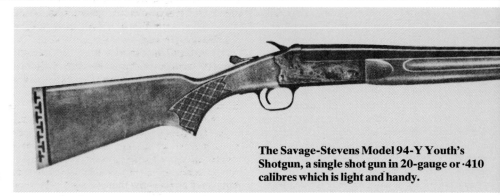

The Savage-Stevens Model 94-Y Youth's Shotgun, a single shot gun in 20-gauge or ·410 calibres which is light and handy.

dangerous feature and one which militated against the use of modern ammunition in these rifles. The Savage design changed this; it also made for a more slender and graceful weapon. The breech closure was done by a block which was thrust forward by the lever action and then lifted so as to lock into mortises in the receiver wall, being supported there by the lever during firing. The breech block contained a striker and spring.

Small improvements were made in the Model 99 (of 1899) and since then the design has remained relatively unchanged. It was followed by slide-action and bolt-action ·22 rifles in 1903, and in 1907 the company went into the production of an automatic pistol.

The Savage automatic pistol was largely the work of Major Elbert H. Searle, a former ordnance officer. The design used a rotating barrel which was linked to the slide by a lug riding in a shaped groove. When the pistol was fired, the lug held barrel and slide together, but reaction between a lug under the barrel and a cam track in the frame rotated the barrel

through 5° and unlocked the slide, after which it recoiled in the usual way. The opening of the breech was delayed, according to Searle, by the reaction of the bullet as it passed through the rifling, which resisted the turning movement of the barrel. This is a pretty thin story, and although the barrel and slide may be locked at the instant of firing, they certainly do not remain locked for very long afterwards, and to all intents the Savage is a delayed blowback pistol, in spite of Searle's claims to a locked breech.

Savage were working on this design in 1906 when the US Army canvassed for automatic pistols for the 1907 trials, and they made one in ·45 calibre and entered it. It survived the trial and a further 230 were delivered for troop trials between 1909 and 1910, but the decision was taken to adopt the Colt and the Savage ·45 was dropped. Meanwhile the commercial model in 7·65mm had been marketed in 1907. Minor changes in design occurred in 1915 and 1917, and it remained in production until 1926. Various reasons have been advanced for the end of production, but it was due, as much

The Savage Model 1917 pistol in 9mm Short calibre.

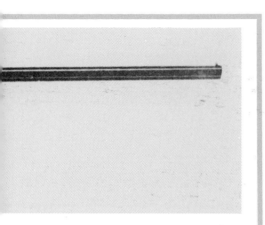

as anything else, to economic sense; the Savage was not a cheap pistol to produce, and the late 1920s were a hard time for quality guns in the face of cheap imports. The only official adoption of the Savage was by the Portuguese Government in the First World War when their supply of Parabellum pistols from Germany was cut off.

During the First World War the company received a contract from the British Government to manufacture Lewis (*qv*) machine guns, making over 70,000 during the course of the war. After the war Savage continued producing sporting guns, pistols and ammunition. In 1939 it received a contract from the Auto-Ordnance Corporation (*qv*) to make Thompson submachine guns, and in the ensuing five years made a million and a quarter of these. It also manufactured huge numbers of ·30 and ·50 Browning machine guns and over a million Lee-Enfield rifles for the British Army. At the end of the war it returned to the production of sporting arms, which it continues to the present day.

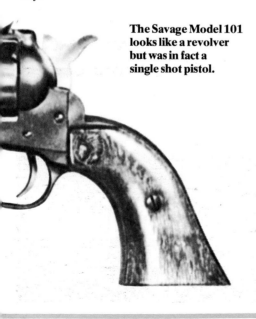

The Savage Model 101 looks like a revolver but was in fact a single shot pistol.

SAVAGE, Edward B. *(fl. 1850–1861)*
Edward Savage was the partner of James North whose son, Edward North, had patented a practical gas-seal percussion revolver. This was produced in the 1850s as the North & Savage revolver and is commonly called the Figure-8 model because of the peculiar double-ring trigger. North died in 1856 and Savage became sole owner of the factory and continued to produce the revolvers until 1859 when the Savage Revolving Fire-Arms Company was set up. Savage became president of the company but in 1861 he was displaced in a reorganisation; he sold the factory to the company and apparently then retired. The company then engaged in producing the revolver for sale to the Union Army during the Civil War, about 11,000 being supplied. However, there appears to have been some gerrymandering involved in the military contracts and the company did not survive for long after the war.

The pistol was a solid frame weapon in which pulling the lower ring trigger revolved the cylinder, thrust it forward to mate with the barrel and cocked the hammer. Pulling the top trigger then fired the pistol. Some were provided with shoulder stocks for use as carbines by cavalry troops.

SCHMEISSER / *Germany*
Louis Schmeisser (1848–1917) spent his early days as a journeyman gunsmith, in France, Germany and Austria, eventually settling in Jena and opening his own workshop. He designed a number of weapons, including a repeating rifle, and then entered into an agreement with Theodor Bergmann (*qv*) for the production of his designs. As a result of the agreement, Schmeisser's name vanished from

the weapons and they were sold under the Bergmann name. In about 1905 he severed his connection with Bergmann and went to work for Rheinmetall, developing the Dreyse (*qv*) pistols and machine guns.

His son Hugo Schmeisser began working for Bergmann during the First World War and was responsible for the design of the Bergmann MP18 submachine gun. After the war, when Bergmann was absorbed into the Lignose consortium, Schmeisser moved to the C. G. Haenel (*qv*) company, taking with him designs of a blowback pocket pistol which the company produced during the 1920s. During the 1930s the company became more and more involved in the production of military weapons, and during the war they were responsible for much production of the Erma-designed MP38 and MP40 submachine guns; Schmeisser managed one of the production plants, and, probably due to this, the Erma designs were widely known as the Schmeisser submachine gun on the Allied side. In 1945 the Soviet Army dismantled the Haenel factory and Hugo Schmeisser vanished behind the Russian lines.

SCHMIDT-RUBIN / *Switzerland*
This was the Swiss service rifle and carbine. It was developed in the late 1880s by Colonel Rudolf Schmidt, director of the Bern Arsenal, and Major Rubin, director of the military laboratory at Thun. Broadly speaking, the barrel, rifling and ammunition were due to Rubin, the bolt action and magazine to Schmidt. The rifle was introduced in 1889 and was in 7·5mm calibre, with a 12-round box magazine. The principal novelty was the straight-pull bolt action, one of the few such designs which ever prospered. The bolt handle was attached to an

Schmeisser's patent pistol, manufactured by Haenel.

operating rod which slid in its own groove in the body of the rifle; this rod carried a lug which engaged in a helical groove in the bolt sleeve. When the handle was pulled, the lug, by action in the helical groove, rotated the sleeve to unlock the bolt and then drew sleeve and bolt back together. The principal defect of this system was the length of the action, necessitated by the construction of the bolt and sleeve. The design was slightly modified in 1896 to give a shorter action. Another major change came in 1911 with the introduction of a new and more powerful cartridge, which necessitated adding forward locking lugs to the bolt. The final change came in 1931 when the whole action was redesigned, though still operating on the same general principle, to make the action shorter and the rifle more compact. The last Schmidt-Rubin design to be issued appeared as late as 1955, when a sniping rifle was produced. Generally, the Schmidt-Rubin rifles were extremely accurate, but it is open to question whether the system would have survived so long in service if it had ever been exposed to the ultimate test of war.

The Swiss service rifle, Schmidt-Rubin Model of 1889.

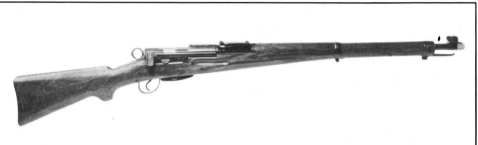

The Schmidt-Rubin Carbine of 1931 shortened the action and made a more compact weapon.

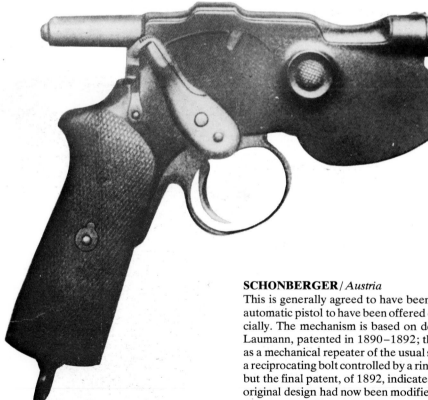

The Schonberger automatic pistol of 1893, the first automatic to be commercially marketed.

SCHONBERGER / Austria

This is generally agreed to have been the first automatic pistol to have been offered commercially. The mechanism is based on designs by Laumann, patented in 1890–1892; this began as a mechanical repeater of the usual sort, with a reciprocating bolt controlled by a ring trigger, but the final patent, of 1892, indicates that the original design had now been modified to produce automatic action. Where Schonberger comes into it is not at all clear; it has been suggested that he was, at that time, the works superintendent at the Steyr factory, where the pistol was made, and the naming of the pistol for him was a *quid pro quo* for getting it into production. Another theory is that he was Laumann's financial backer. In any event, it was produced at the Steyr factory in 1893–1894 in small numbers and sold; specimens are extremely rare, indeed it is doubtful if half-a-dozen exist, and the ammunition has not been seen for over seventy years.

The mechanism is absolutely unique in pistol design, since it relies upon the set-back of the cartridge cap due to the explosion pressure within the case. The bolt is locked by a cam surface on a forked arm; when the pistol is fired, the cap sets back about 0.18 of an inch, imparting movement to the heavy striker before the cap is stopped by the face of the bolt. This slight movement is sufficient to cause a lug on the striker to disengage the locking cam, so leaving the bolt free to recoil, swinging the forked arm back against a spring ready to close the bolt once more. The magazine was a clip-loaded box in front of the trigger, reminiscent of Bergmann designs.

SCHULHOF, Josef (1824–1890)

Schulhof was a farmer who, in 1870, threw up his farming career and moved to Vienna to become a gunmaker. In 1882 he produced a repeating rifle design intended for conversion of breech-loading bolt action single-shot weapons such as the Gras or Vetterli. The rifle butt was hollow and contained three compartments into which cartridges could be dropped. From here, they fed to a chute, up which they were fed to the bolt mechanism by a ratchet device actuated by the movement of the bolt. A total of 20 rounds could be carried in the butt. In the following year he produced an improved version which contained only ten rounds. Both these were tested by the Austrian Army but were turned down; he then attempted to sell the idea to Russia but without success.

In 1884 he developed a mechanical repeating pistol which used much the same sort of system, a magazine in the butt feeding up to a reciprocating bolt operated by a finger loop. This was also turned down by the military authorities but a small number appear to have been sold on the commercial market. He then abandoned the repeating arm and developed a single-shot target pistol with rotary breechblock and external hammer. A lever inlet into the rear of the butt operated the breech. This proved very popular on the continent and was made by others under license.

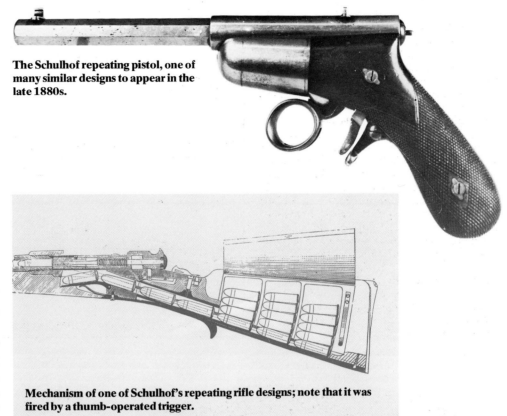

The Schulhof repeating pistol, one of many similar designs to appear in the late 1880s.

Mechanism of one of Schulhof's repeating rifle designs; note that it was fired by a thumb-operated trigger.

SCHWARZLOSE, Andreas William (1867–1936)

Schwarzlose was a farmer's son who served in the Austro-Hungarian Artillery, graduated from the Ordnance College with distinction and found a life-long interest in weapons. In 1892 he produced his first automatic pistol design, a remarkable weapon; it resembled the Remington rolling-block breech in some respects, though arranged for automatic operation. The barrel recoiled a short distance and the breech block was driven down and back. A tubular magazine beneath the barrel contained seven cartridges; a lifter seized one and the returning breech block rammed it into the chamber. A hammer was pivoted on the same axis as the breech block but was retained by a sear until the trigger was pressed. At least one specimen was made, but none were ever produced commercially.

His next design, in 1893, was for a long-recoil pistol but this was never made. By 1897 he had perfected a design which he considered fit for production and he set up a factory in Berlin. The pistol was a locked-breech weapon firing the 7·63mm Mauser cartridge; it used a rotating bolt, engaged and disengaged by a cam track in the frame. It was rather light for the cartridge it fired and was, by contemporary account, not particularly reliable. It suffered by comparison with the Mauser and did not gain commercial success. Production ended in about 1904, and apparently much of the remaining stock was sold to a Russian revolutionary group; the pistols were discovered while being smuggled into Russia, were seized by the

The 1898 Schwarzlose Standardt automatic pistol.

authorities and were later issued to various Russian police forces.

In about 1900 Schwarzlose developed a machine gun which was adopted by the Austro-Hungarian Army and which remained in service until the end of the Second World War. It was a heavy water-cooled weapon, comparable to the Maxim or Vickers of the day, but was a pure blowback weapon with no form of breech lock, the only such heavy machine gun design ever to succeed. It relied entirely on the mass of the breech block and on a semi-folded toggle arm which unfolded at a severe mechanical disadvantage so as to slow the opening of the block. The barrel was short to ensure that the bullet had left and the pressure had dropped before the block opened.

The machine gun design made Schwarzlose's name and fortune, and he turned again to the pistol business. This time he developed a unique blow-forward design in which the breech block was part of the pistol frame, and firing the cartridge caused the barrel unit to run forward. After loading, a spring sent the barrel back, collecting a cartridge nose-first from the magazine before coming to rest against the fixed breech. It is of interest to note that the only other blow-forward pistol ever to reach production, the Hino-Komura (qv), was being developed in Japan at about the same time, quite independently. The Schwarzlose model appeared in 1908, proved to be surprisingly popular, and remained in production until 1914, when the facilities of the factory were needed for more martial products.

The Schwarzlose factory was dismantled by the Allied Disarmament Commission in 1919, after which Schwarzlose became a free-lance firearms consultant until his death.

SCOTTI / Italy

Luigi Scotti (b. 1857) was a mechanical engineer who gravitated to firearms by way of military service. He then appears to have specialised in ammunition design and production, designing some of the service cartridges for the Italian Army in the 1890s. He became manager of a brass rolling mill in 1895 and in 1912 built an ammunition factory and ran it for the Italian Government during the First World War.

His son Alfredo qualified as an engineer and began designing prior to the war; he apparently

Schwarzlose's unusual blow-forward model of 1908.

was concerned with the Swiss engineer Birkigt in the design of the Hispano-Suiza aircraft cannon during the war, and in the 1920s he developed a number of machine gun and cannon designs for the Italian air force. Most of these depended on a delayed blowback system of his own design, in which a gas piston caused the breech bolt to rotate after which blowback completed the action cycle. He also dabbled with automatic rifles, coming up with the almost-inevitable conversion to permit a bolt-action rifle to become a gas-operated weapon. Like almost every other such conversion, it did not succeed. However his machine guns and cannon were used to some extent in Italian aircraft during the early part of the Second World War; much of the construction of his designs was undertaken by the Isotto-Fraschini automobile company.

SHARPS, Christian (1811–1874)

Sharps was a noted American designer who produced two weapons of considerable fame as well as several less well-known models. In 1848 he patented a falling-block rifle which was breech-loaded with a paper cartridge. As the underlever was raised, the breech-block

moved vertically up, the sharp front edge slicing off the base of the cartridge to expose the powder to a vent which passed through the block. A percussion cap fitted on a nipple and the cap was fired by an external hammer. Some were provided with ramrods so that when the inevitable powder fouling built up to the point where the breech could no longer be opened, the weapon could still be used as a muzzle loader. Rifles and carbines to this design were widely sold commercially, and then were extensively used in the American Civil War. After the war, when the metallic cartridge appeared, it was a relatively simple task to modify the design to accommodate them and the Sharps continued in use, notably in the American West, where its simplicity and strength were of vital importance. It has been suggested that the majority of buffalo were killed with the Sharps rifle.

In 1849 Sharps' other great invention appeared, a small four-barrelled pistol. This was made in ·22, ·30 and ·32 rimfire calibres from 1854 until Sharps' death and was also made under license in England by Tipping & Lawden of Birmingham. The four barrels were in a solid block which could be slid forward on the frame for loading, and the hammer incorporated a

The Scotti 7·7mm machine gun of 1938, made by the Isotto-Fraschini company.

rotating firing pin which turned through 90° at each shot so as to fire the four barrels in succession.

Other weapons produced by Sharps include a number of small-calibre percussion revolvers based on the tip-up design of the early Smith & Wesson rimfires; about 2000 of these were made in 1857–1858. He later took out a number of patents for cartridge-loading revolvers but seems to have made relatively few of them. A continental writer in 1894 stated that the army of Saxony was issued with a Sharps revolver M1873, but very little information on this weapon has ever appeared. It is unlikely to have been made by Sharps, however, and was probably using a Sharps-patented feature.

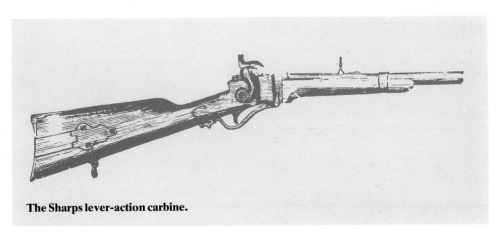

The Sharps lever-action carbine.

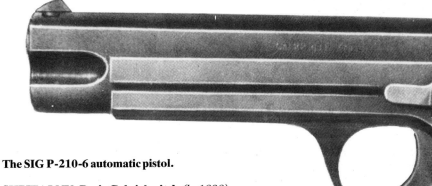

The SIG P-210-6 automatic pistol.

SHPITALNY, Boris Gabrielovitch *(b. 1898)*
Little is known of Shpitalny's early life, other than that he was actively connected with the Bolshevik movement before World War One. After the Revolution he went into the weapons design field. Here he was partly responsible for two well-known gun designs, was awarded a Stalin Prize for this in 1935, and in 1936 became head of the Bureau for Development of Automatic Weapons. He later wrote several technical papers on weapons design and was accorded various academic distinctions. The various honours seem, to the western observer, to be out of proportion to his design achievements and one is inclined to wonder whether or not they reflect his position as one of the 'Old Guard' Bolsheviks rather than his prowess as a designer.

Shpitalny's principal design was the ShKAS machine gun; the initials, in the usual Soviet manner, show that Shpitalny was assisted by another designer named Komaritsky; that the gun was an aviation (A) pattern; and that it had a high rate of fire (S = *skorostrel'nyi*, high speed). The development of this gun had gone on from the early 1920s and it entered service in 1932. Some were used in the Spanish Civil War and it was the standard Soviet Air Force gun until the middle of the Second World War, when it became apparent that rifle-calibre weapons were no longer sufficient to damage modern aircraft.

The ShKAS was a belt-fed, gas-operated 7·62mm gun which used an unusual rotating feed system, often called the 'squirrel-cage' system, in which the round was extracted from the belt and moved around a rotary feeder unit so as to be prepared for loading in easy stages, a system which gives a very smooth feed. It is this feed system which was Shpitalny's principal contribution to the design. The only other unusual feature is the provision of a mechanism to positively eject the empty case to the front of the gun, thus putting the empties over the side of the aircraft and not cluttering the cockpit or turret with empty cases. The rate of fire of the ShKAS was 1800 rounds a minute, stepped up in a later improvement to 2000 rounds a minute. Models were produced for flexible or fixed installation, and the fixed guns could be synchronised for firing through propellers.

Shpitalny's other design was the ShVAK 20mm cannon, designed in collaboration with Vladimirov in about 1942. This was, in general, a scale-up of the ShKAS machine gun, using similar gas actuation and rotary feeding; the result was a lightweight and sound cannon. Apparently attempts were also made to produce two other ShVAK designs, one a 12·7mm machine gun and the other a 37mm cannon, both being variations of the 20mm cannon design, but these were not successful and were never put into production.

SIG / *Switzerland*
The Schweizerische Industrie Gesellschaft of Neuhausen-am-Rheinfalls originated in 1953 as the 'Schweizerishce Wagenfabrik', manufacturing railway rolling stock. In 1860 there was an abortive attempt to produce a breech-loading rifle, the Burnard-Prelaz, but in 1864

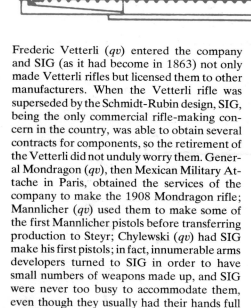

A sectioned drawing of the SIG P-210 pistol.

Frederic Vetterli (*qv*) entered the company and SIG (as it had become in 1863) not only made Vetterli rifles but licensed them to other manufacturers. When the Vetterli rifle was superseded by the Schmidt-Rubin design, SIG, being the only commercial rifle-making concern in the country, was able to obtain several contracts for components, so the retirement of the Vetterli did not unduly worry them. General Mondragon (*qv*), then Mexican Military Attache in Paris, obtained the services of the company to make the 1908 Mondragon rifle; Mannlicher (*qv*) used them to make some of the first Mannlicher pistols before transferring production to Steyr; Chylewski (*qv*) had SIG make his first pistols; in fact, innumerable arms developers turned to SIG in order to have small numbers of weapons made up, and SIG were never too busy to accommodate them, even though they usually had their hands full with military contracts.

It was not until after the First World War that SIG began to develop their own designs, following a careful analysis of the possible markets. In 1920, under license from Bergmann, they began making the Bergmann MP18 submachine gun, supplying 7·65mm calibre models to Finland and 7·63mm models to China and Japan. In 1930 they produced their own version, using a forward pistol grip and having the magazine enter the gun from the right side, possibly the only submachine gun to·use such a configuration. This model did not succeed—doubtless it looked too much like the 'old' Bergmann to offer promise of novelty—and SIG soon abandoned it.

One of the prime requirements in the 1920s appeared to be a reliable machine gun, and SIG produced the KE7 model, developed by Kiraly (*qv*) and Ende, two designers in their employ. This was a recoil-operated gun, quite light in weight, but the early 1930s were a poor time for machine guns on the open market and

apart from some sales to China the KE7 did not do well. The company then turned to gas operation and developed a gun having the most unusual feature of two magazines, one at each side of the body. Feed could be selected from either one, and one magazine could be changed while the other was being fired. It is believed that Ende had a hand in this design, but it was not taken beyond prototypes.

Meanwhile Kiraly had been helping to develop a submachine gun, the MKMO (Maschinen Karabiner Modell O), together with Ende and another designer named Gaetzi. The MKMO was a fully-stocked weapon resembling a short rifle; it had a forward-folding magazine and used the two-part bolt system derived from Kiraly's (*qv*) patents. This bolt consisted of a light head and heavy body; the head was forced back by the exploding cartridge but was held by a lug in the gun body. Its initial rearward impulse was transmitted to the heavy body which moved back and, by inclined faces, unlocked the head and allowed the whole bolt to recoil, thus giving a delay to the bolt opening.

The MKMO appeared in 1935 and was followed by the MKPO, a shorter model, and then the MKMS, a simplified model with one-piece bolt. They were all, as with every SIG product, beautifully made, and sold in small numbers until 1940. In that year SIG produced a much simpler and more compact design, the MP41, for approval by the Swiss Army, who were then looking for a submachine gun. But for various reasons the Army selected the Furrer (*qv*)

design, a far worse weapon, and the MP41 got no further.

SIG made a variety of prototype submachine guns in subsequent years. In 1958 they introduced the MP310, a simple design of modern form, using sheet metal and plastics, but even this has not received the attention it merited.

SIG began designing automatic rifles during 1942–1944 and in 1946 placed their first design on the market, the SK46. This was a conventional-looking wooden-stocked rifle, gas-operated but capable of having the gas port closed and being used as a bolt-action weapon. But in 1946 the market was flooded with war-surplus weapons and the SK46 had no chance. They then produced a remarkable weapon, the AK53, in which the barrel blew forward on

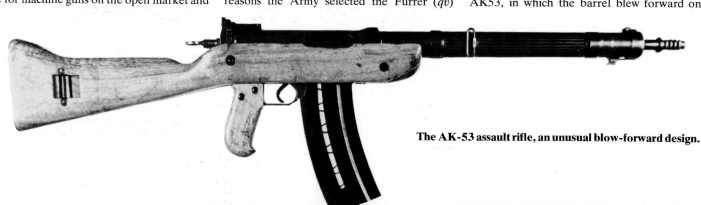

The AK-53 assault rifle, an unusual blow-forward design.

firing, leaving the cartridge case held by the fixed breech; the case was knocked clear and the barrel ran back to collect a new round. This is the same system as employed on the Hino-Komura (*qv*) and Schwarzlose (*qv*) pistols, and this was the only time it had ever been employed in a shoulder arm. There are some theoretical advantages to this system, but there are some practical disadvantages too, and the AK53 was never accepted.

Having got all these things out of their system the company then produced a very sound design, the SG57, which used a roller-delayed blowback system similar to that adopted by the CETME (*qv*) rifle and derived from the same source, the Mauser StuG45 assault rifle design. The SG57 selective fire rifle was capable of firing at 500 rounds per minute as a light machine gun, and it was adopted by the Swiss army in place of the Schmidt-Rubin bolt action. The basic mechanism has since been used in a slightly improved version, the SIG510, which is offered commercially in various models. A 5·56mm rifle, the SIG530, uses a modified roller-locking system in which the rollers are positively cammed in and out of lock by a gas piston, this system being better adapted to the pressure characteristics of the 5·56mm cartridge.

The source of inspiration for the rifle, a German wartime design, was also the source for the company's post-war machine gun designs. Their first was the MG51, which was little more than a cleaned-up version of the German MG42, a recoil-operated and magazine-fed weapon. The rollers of the MG42 were changed to locking flaps, but the general layout and feed mechanism were the same. This gun was bought by the Danish Army and by the Swiss, but it was soon replaced in Swiss service by the SIG710, a delayed-blowback gun using the same roller-locking system as the 510 rifle. This gun has, like the 510, gone into a number of variants to satisfy different potential markets; one of them, the 710–3, is specifically a low-cost version, using steel stampings as much as possible. This weapon has been sold in South America.

Shortly before the war the company ob-

The SIG MP-41 submachine gun, which was not adopted by the Swiss Army. The magazine folded into the wooden fore-end.

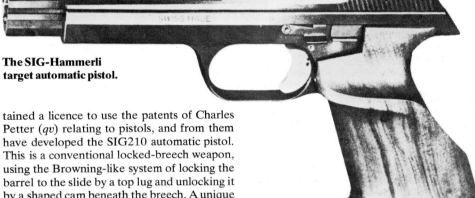
The SIG-Hammerli target automatic pistol.

tained a licence to use the patents of Charles Petter (*qv*) relating to pistols, and from them have developed the SIG210 automatic pistol. This is a conventional locked-breech weapon, using the Browning-like system of locking the barrel to the slide by a top lug and unlocking it by a shaped cam beneath the breech. A unique feature of the SIG design is that the frame supporting the slide is longer than usual and lies outside the slide, contrary to the usual practice. This gives excellent support and appears to have considerable bearing on the accuracy, which is formidable. This pistol first appeared in 1948 and was adopted by the Swiss and Danish Armies, but since then has established its position as probably the best automatic pistol in the world, being widely purchased by target shooters. In a way, this pistol is symbolic of almost all SIG's products; accurate, reliable, exquisitely made, beautifully finished—and expensive.

In recent years the political climate in Switzerland has become difficult for arms manufacture, and therefore SIG have found it necessary to operate in conjunction with German gunmakers, producing designs and perfecting

them and then turning them over to the Germans for manufacture and restriction-free export. The SIG-Sauer automatic pistols were the first fruit of this, and are described under SAUER.

SILVER & FLETCHER / *Britain*
One of the problems which many inventors tried to solve in the 1880s was the extraction and ejection of cartridge cases from solid-frame revolvers. The usual method was either to punch out the empty cases one at a time by means of an ejector rod or to remove the

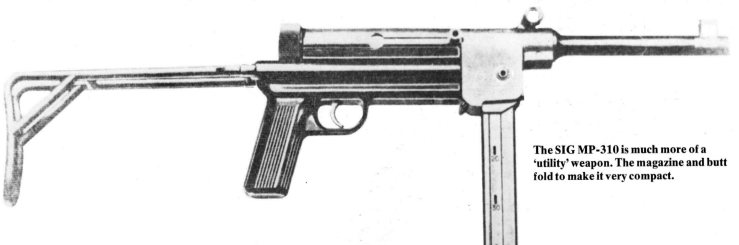
The SIG MP-310 is much more of a 'utility' weapon. The magazine and butt fold to make it very compact.

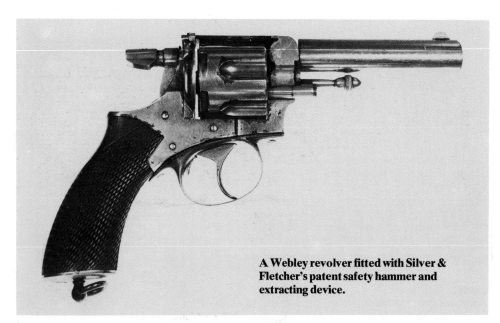

A Webley revolver fitted with Silver & Fletcher's patent safety hammer and extracting device.

cylinder and deal with the lot at one swoop, but several patents were issued for forms of automatic ejector, and that of Silver and Fletcher is a good example, since it was one of the few which was actually used.

In brief, a transverse lever lay across the top of the standing breech and terminated in a claw which aligned with the top right-hand cartridge in the cylinder. This, in the normal clockwise-revolving cylinder, was the last-fired empty case; the lever could be disengaged for the first shot to avoid ejecting a full cartridge. As the hammer fell, the tip struck the lever and caused the ejector claw to jerk the empty case out of the chamber and throw it clear, whereupon a fresh round could be inserted. This patent ejector was often found allied with a 'Safety Hammer' developed by the same two patentees which allowed the firing pin to be retracted and locked so as to prevent the revolver being fired. These fittings were most usually applied to Webley revolvers but could be fitted to other makes and have been seen on Colt revolvers.

SIMONOV, Sergei Gavrilovitch *(b. 1894)*
After leaving elementary school, Simonov was employed as a blacksmith in a foundry. Later he became a locksmith, and in 1915 attended technical school. In 1917 he assisted Federov *(qv)* in making the first Avtomat rifles. After the Revolution he studied at Moscow Polytechnic and in 1924 went to work in Tula Arsenal. By 1926 he was in charge of quality control, and in 1927 he went into the design department as Federov's assistant.

In the early 1930s he began work on a semi-automatic rifle which was approved for service in 1936 as the AVS-36. This was the first automatic rifle to be adopted by the Soviet Army, and it was a selective-fire weapon, capable of either single shots or automatic fire. It was gas-operated and used a vertically-moving block to lock the bolt and bolt carrier to the receiver. It suffered from excessive muzzle blast and recoil, and a two-port muzzle brake was fitted in order to alleviate this problem. However, it failed to stand up to the rigour of service life and it was not in service for more than about two years.

Simonov then turned his attention to the anti-tank field and developed the PTRS anti-tank rifle, issued in 1941. This, too, was a gas-operated weapon but it was far too complex for the job it was being asked to do and proved to be less robust, more heavy and more cumbersome than an alternative model designed by Degtyarev. As a result, relatively few of these weapons were manufactured.

Simonov's last design was a semi-automatic carbine to fire the 7·62mm short M43 cartridge, the first Soviet weapon developed for this round. The SKS appeared shortly after the Second World War and, like the 1936 rifle, was gas-operated with a tipping bolt. It was fully-stocked and carried a folding bayonet beneath the barrel. It was not a particularly inspired design, being somewhat too heavy, but considering it was developed under the stress of war, it was a serviceable enough weapon. Vast numbers were made, and although it is no longer in service with the Soviet Army it has been widely distributed to other Communist countries. It is used in Yugoslavia as their Model 59 and by the Chinese as their Model 56.

SKODA / *Czechoslovakia*
The Skoda company of Pilsen are more usually thought of as makers of artillery and similar heavy engineering tasks, but they were involved in small arms manufacture for a short period.

In 1888 the Field Marshal Archduke Karl Salvator and Colonel Ritter von Dormus, both of the Austrian Army, patented a machine gun. It was a delayed blowback weapon, the delay being imposed by a heavy spring and a system of pivoting blocks. This was adopted by the Austrian Army in 1893 and manufacture was entrusted to the Skoda works. It consequently became known as the Skoda machine gun, and it remained in service until shortly before the First World War. Early models used a peculiar overhead hopper to feed in the ammunition, though the model developed in 1909 used a cloth belt feed.

Salvator and von Dormus also patented an automatic pistol, though in fact Salvator died in 1892, before the patent was granted. This was a blowback weapon, clip-fed, and a small number were made, probably by Skoda. But in those days the military were insistent on locked breeches and the design was not pursued.

In the 1920s Skoda opened a subsidiary firm, the Zbrojovka Pilsen, with a view to making small arms; they produced a 6·35mm automatic copied from the usual Browning 1906 design for a few years, but then apparently thought better of it and closed the operation down.

The Simonov SKS-46 automatic carbine, the first Soviet weapon to use the short 7·62mm cartridge.

SKORPION / *Czechoslovakia*

A compact submachine gun, issued to elements of the Czech Army in 1962. It is, in fact, more of a machine pistol, since it is extremely small and fires a ·32 ACP bullet which is marginal as far as combat effectiveness is concerned. With the wire butt folded it can comfortably be fired in one hand, in pistol fashion, while with the butt opened out it can be fired at 700 rounds a minute. It is a blowback weapon and, with such light reciprocating parts, a high rate of fire might be expected, but the rate is slowed by a regulator set in the pistol grip which briefly retains the bolt after each shot, reducing the rate of fire to manageable proportions.

The Skorpion (properly known as the vz/62) was issued to armoured units so that it could be holster-carried by tank crews and yet allow them freedom of movement together with reasonable firepower for emergencies. Since its original introduction a heavier version in 9mm Parabellum calibre has been introduced and this, so far as is known, is for more general issue in the Czech Army.

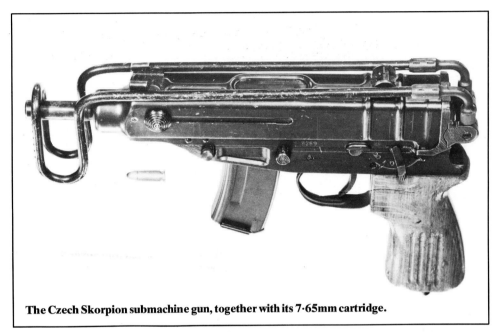

The Czech Skorpion submachine gun, together with its 7·65mm cartridge.

SMITH & WESSON / *USA*

Horace Smith (1808–1893) and Daniel B. Wesson (1825–1906) came to be associated in various early firearms ventures, notably that of the Volcanic (*qv*) rifle and pistol in 1854. Wesson, though, was shrewd enough to see that there was little future in that weapon and he left in 1856, took Smith with him, and the two sat down to design a revolver which they would be able to market as soon as Colt's master patent expired. In 1854 they had patented a small rimfire cartridge, which took them several years to bring to a workable state of manufacture. Wesson's brother Edwin had been involved in revolver manufacture and had been the loser in a long legal wrangle with Colt over patent rights; learning from this, Smith & Wesson carefully reviewed the patent field and discovered that Rollin White (*qv*) had a patent for cylinders with bored-through chambers which would be likely to hamper their new design. They therefore obtained this patent on advantageous terms and were able to market their own revolver in 1857 with cast-iron patent protection, which gave them a monopoly on cartridge revolvers for twelve years.

The Number One revolver was a ·22 rimfire, single-action, with the frame hinged at the standing breech so as to tip upwards when a latch at the front of the lower frame was released. The cylinder could then be slipped from its arbor, the empty cases punched out by means of a rod protruding beneath the barrel, re-loaded and replaced. Demand for this pistol was so great that by 1864 supply was lagging two years behind the orders, and several would-be pistol makers began producing copies. This led them into litigation, which Smith & Wesson invariably won, and the offending pistols were forfeited, being marked 'Made for Smith & Wesson by . . .', a useful accretion for the backlog of orders.

In 1869 the White patent expired and the field was open to all, therefore it behoved Smith & Wesson to produce something fairly spectacular to stay ahead of the field. This they did by producing a hinged-frame revolver with simultaneous ejection of the spent cases as the barrel was hinged down, a system based on patents of W. C. Dodge and C. A. King and held by the company. This was a heavy ·44 rimfire revolver known as the American, which appeared in 1870. In that year the Russian Army decided to adopt a modern revolver and chose the Smith & Wesson design, though with some small modifications. The most important change was in the cartridge, which the Russians redesigned to make it more accurate. Having settled the details, the Russians ordered 215,704 revolvers, an order which was to keep Smith & Wesson busy for the next five years and which effectively kept them too occupied to compete in the home market. In those years the American west was opening up, and Colt were the people who provided the majority of the handguns.

Once the 'Russian' was out of the way, Smith & Wesson turned back to the home market, but made relatively little impression on the Western trade; they therefore turned to making pocket revolvers of excellent quality. These were hinged-frame models in ·32 and ·38 calibre, with ribbed barrels and a simplified auto-ejecting mechanism, and they were widely copied. In 1887 they again scored a first with their New Departure model; this was the first 'hammerless' revolver to be successful, and it had the additional feature of a grip safety lever which protruded at the rear edge of the butt. The pistol did use a hammer but this was concealed from view by a rising frame, and thus there was no projecting hammer spur to catch in a pocket when the pistol was being drawn; indeed, as many people proved, it was quite possible to fire the pistol from inside the pocket when circumstances demanded. In a succession of models, this pistol stayed in production until 1940, and a similar pistol is still made.

The next advance in revolver design came from Colt, with their adoption of the swing-out cylinder, and Smith & Wesson adopted this form with a ·32 Hand Ejector model in 1896. The cylinder was locked in place by a pin which

TRADE
MARK
REG. U.S. PAT. OFF.

passed through the arbor and anchored into the standing breech, and the pistol was opened by pulling forward on the ejector rod which extended beneath the barrel. It was not a very strong design, and in 1899 a ·38 Hand Ejector was produced which had a thumb-operated catch on the frame which pushed the cylinder locking pin out of engagement. This still wasn't perfect and in 1902 the design was improved by placing a locking lug under the barrel into which the front end of the ejector rod engaged, thus locking the cylinder assembly at both ends.

In 1908 a final refinement was introduced, a third locking lug at the front of the cylinder aperture, into which the crane arm (which supported the cylinder) locked. The same thumb-catch, forcing the arbor pin forward, actuated all three locks, but as might be imagined, the manufacture and adjustment of the three locking surfaces was very precise and difficult. This system was introduced on the ·44 Hand Ejector of 1908, which inevitably became known as the Triple Lock model. More properly it was called the New Century model, and many authorities claim it to be one of the finest revolvers ever made. About 20,000 were made in all, and in 1914 the British Army purchased a small number which were chambered for the ·455 cartridge. The mud of Flanders soon demonstrated that some mechanisms can be too perfect for their own good; dirt in the shroud which surrounded the ejector rod in the Triple Lock models prevented them from closing. Nevertheless, they were a popular weapon and a surprising number of them survived the war. The company apparently noted this fault and dropped the Triple Lock feature in 1915.

In 1917 the US Army demanded a ·45 revolver which would fire the standard ·45 automatic pistol cartridge. Since it was normal practise of Smith & Wesson to machine a slight step in the chamber, against which the mouth of the cartridge case abutted, there was no

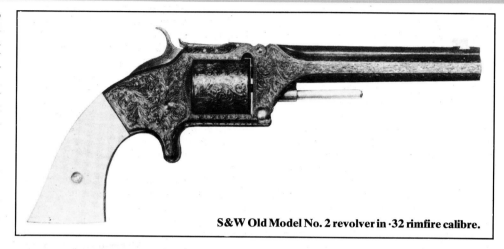

S&W Old Model No. 2 revolver in ·32 rimfire calibre.

A S&W ·38 Single Shot First Model of 1891, a notable target pistol of the time.

difficulty in loading and firing such rimless cartridges, but, of course, the ejector had nothing to grip and would not remove the empty cases. This was solved by developing a 'half-moon clip' which held three rimless cartridges; two such clips could be dropped in to load the chamber, the revolver fired and opened, and the ejector then bore on the clip so as to eject the cases. This model became the US Army's

M1917 revolver, and after satisfying the Army's demands the pistol was continued on the commercial market for several years, one ammunition maker producing a special ·45 cartridge with a thick rim, so that the special clips were no longer required.

In 1913, with the automatic pistol eroding their pocket revolver market, the company decided to compete in this field and purchased

S&W K-22 Masterpiece target revolver.

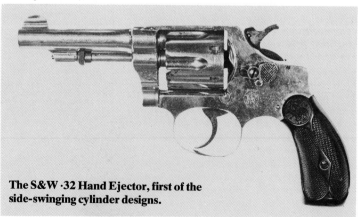

The S&W ·32 Hand Ejector, first of the side-swinging cylinder designs.

the French patents of Clement (*qv*). This used a blowback system, with a square bolt working in a slot in the body, but it was an awkward and expensive design to make and matters were complicated by the fact that Smith & Wesson chose to make it in the odd calibre of ·35, producing their own ammunition to suit. They persisted in manufacture until 1921, but the design was not very successful. In 1924 they produced a slightly simplified version which chambered the usual ·32 auto pistol cartridge, but it was still more expensive than its rivals and less than a thousand were sold before the company wisely killed it in 1926.

From then on their concern was entirely with revolvers, and the designs they produced were merely refinements of what had gone before, since there was little new that could be done. But in 1954 the company once again went into the automatic pistol business, with a modified Browning design, recoil-operated with the barrel locked to the slide by the usual rib. The lockwork was double-action, with safety catch on the slide in similar fashion to the system pioneered by Walther (*qv*) and the pistol was chambered for the 9mm Parabellum, the first time that an American manufacturer had recognised the existence of this calibre. An enlarged version, carrying a 14-round magazine, appeared in 1970, and this was followed by a special Master model chambered for the ·38 Special cartridge and intended solely for target shooting.

In 1934, with collaboration from ammunition experts, the company originated the Magnum idea in pistols. Their first model was the ·357 Magnum Hand Ejector, an extremely strong and heavy revolver chambered to accept a special cartridge of higher-than-usual power. Although the bore was the same as the normal ·38 revolver, the notation was ·357 in order to distinguish the super-power cartridge from the ordinary ·38 (which, in fact, is ·357 in calibre). Moreover the new cartridge had a longer case so that there was no danger of loading it into an ordinary ·38 revolver chamber due to the case fouling the chamber step. This weapon proved to be very popular, since not only was it powerful but it was also extremely accurate, and apart from an interval during the war years it has continued in production, though in slightly modified form. Other Magnum loadings pioneered by the company are in ·41 and ·44 calibre.

Although renowned for their pistols, it should also be noted that the Smith & Wesson company have a sound reputation in the shotgun field. They currently manufacture both slide-action and automatic guns in the standard bores, all of the highest quality.

The S&W Model 39 9mm automatic pistol.

The S&W Model 61 6·35mm automatic pistol.

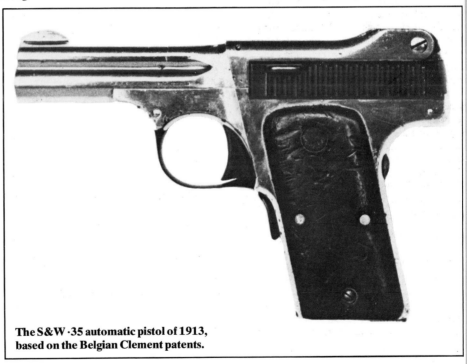

The S&W ·35 automatic pistol of 1913, based on the Belgian Clement patents.

A little-known venture of the Smith & Wesson company was this semi-automatic light rifle in 9mm calibre, used by the Royal Navy during the Second World War.

SNIDER / *Britain*

In 1864 the British government set up the Russel Committee, charged with investigating the possibility of adopting a breech-loading rifle for the British Army. The basic factor which was to influence their decision was the fact that the army possessed tens of thousands of Enfield rifled muskets, and it would be preferable to have a system which allowed these to be converted rather than adopt a system which demanded that they be scrapped and replaced by something entirely new. Some fifty or more systems of breech-loading were put forward, and in 1867 the proposals of Jacob Snider, an American, were accepted. The conversion consisted of cutting away the rear end of the Enfield barrel so as to fit a hinged breech-block which opened out to the right-hand side of the barrel. The block could then be slid back to actuate an extractor, and inside the block was a firing pin which was struck by the original Enfield outside hammer.

Snider produced a suitable self-contained cartridge for this rifle, with a metal base, cardboard body and central cap. It proved unsuccessful, largely because the bullet did not fly accurately, and it was completely redesigned by Colonel Boxer (*qv*) of the Royal Laboratory. Boxer's cartridge used an iron rim, brass and card rolled body and a fresh design of bullet, together with a new percussion cap of his own design. With this cartridge the Snider achieved considerable accuracy, and the Snider system was later adopted in various Balkan armies. It was replaced in British service by the Martini-Henry (*qv*) rifle.

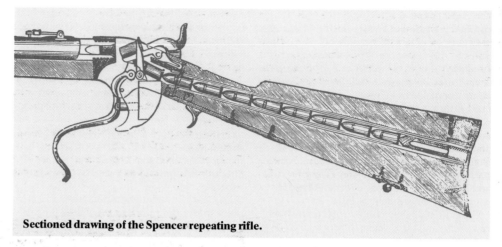

Sectioned drawing of the Spencer repeating rifle.

SOLA / *Luxembourg*

The Sola submachine gun represents Luxembourg's only contribution to the history of firearms. It was conceived in the early 1950s, reputedly by a man named Jansen, and was made in 1953–1956 by the Societe Luxembourgoise d'Armes SA of Ettelbruck. It was a conventional blowback weapon, using a number of steel pressings in its construction and notably only for having relatively few parts. The basic construction, with tubular receiver, firing mechanism and pistol grip unit, and barrel held in by a retaining nut, resembles the Erma MP38, though the shoulder stock was of heavy-gauge wire and appears to have been copied from the American M3 gun. Chambered for the usual 9mm Parabellum cartridge, the Sola sold in small numbers to various African and South American countries, but sales did not come up to the company's expectations and in the late 1950s they abandoned the firearms business and turned to the manufacture of plastics as being more profitable.

SPENCER, Christopher M. *(1833–1922)*

Spencer started his working life as a millwright and then went to work for Colt. He made his name with an automatic silk-spinning machine, but in 1860 patented a lever-action repeating rifle. The magazine was a tube inserted into the butt, and the breech was closed by a block which was rotated backwards by the action of

The Sola Super submachine gun from Luxembourg.

the under-lever. A spring-loaded section at the top of the block picked up a cartridge from the magazine and chambered it on the return stroke of the lever and an external hammer fired via a pin in the block. On operating the lever again, the empty case was ejected before a fresh round was collected. Re-loading could be done very quickly by carrying a number of ready-loaded tubes and slipping them into the butt when needed. A later improvement was the addition of a magazine cut-off which allowed the gun to be used as a single-loader while holding the magazine in reserve. To-

gether with C. E. Billings, he set up a company (Billings & Spencer) to manufacture these rifles. According to legend Spencer managed to gain access to President Lincoln and personally demonstrate his rifle in 1861, and as a result it was formally tested by the Navy and War Departments. The Spencer carbine in ·52 calibre was adopted by the Union forces and over 60,000 were manufactured during the Civil War. At the end of the war demand fell off, and in 1869 the company closed down, its remaining stock being bought out by Winchester.

SPIRLET, Alfonse (fl. 1865–1880)

Spirlet was a gunmaker of Liège who is chiefly remembered as one of the progenitors of the 'tip-up' revolver. His particular contribution to this class was an ejection system, patented in 1870, operated by striking a knob on the end of the cylinder axis pin so as to drive out the usual sort of star-shaped ejecting plate from the centre of the cylinder. The tip-up frame, with or without the Spirlet patent ejector, was widely adopted in Europe and hence tip-up revolvers are frequently called Spirlet models even when Spirlet had no hand in their making.

SPRINGFIELD / USA

In 1792 Congress instructed George Washington to organise two national armories; one of these was at Harpers Ferry, in what is now West Virginia, and the other was at Springfield, Massachusetts. Springfield Armory was founded in 1795 and in the first year produced

245 muskets, entirely hand-made. Thirty years later its output had risen to 15,000 muskets a year and it was also making pistols and carbines. In addition to its production facilities, Springfield has always been the home of American military small arms design, and from it have come the Garand and Pedersen rifles as well as the many designs carrying the Springfield name.

Among the most famous of the early Springfield designs was the 'Trap-door' rifle of 1868. This was a conversion from muzzle-loading on much the same lines as the contemporary Albini and Snider conversions. The rear of the barrel was cut away and a hinged block installed. This could be lifted, hinging forward, to allow a ·45 cartridge to be inserted into the breech. A firing pin inside the breech block was aligned with the cartridge when the block was closed, and an external hammer fired the weapon. Not only was it popular with the Army, but it also achieved a considerable following among hunters and trappers for its efficient simplicity.

In the 1890s the US Army adopted the Krag-Jorgensen (qv) rifle, but during the Spanish-American War discovered that the Mauser was a more efficient weapon, particularly when judged on the grounds of velocity and flatness of trajectory, factors which were the principal ones of their time and which still tend to weigh too heavily in American military thought. After extensive tests and studies of the Mauser, the Ordnance Department de-

cided that the Mauser system was the one to adopt, and reputedly paid Mauser $200,000 for the rights to manufacture. The first Springfield rifle was produced in 1900, using a new cartridge which proved not very efficient. This was redesigned and at the same time the rifle was shortened to become one of the first of the short rifles, doing away with the old-style division of long rifles for infantry and carbines for mounted troops. The final design was issued in 1903 as the Rifle US M1903, but Springfield it was called, and so it has remained. A further improvement appeared in 1906 with the adop-

The US Service Springfield rifle M1903.

tion of a pointed bullet, since which time the basic US Army cartridge has invariably been referred to as the ·30–06, relating its calibre and year of introduction.

The Mauser design was slightly modified in the Springfield rifle; the magazine cut-off was built in to the bolt release catch; a two-piece firing pin was adopted and other minor changes made. Americans insist that it is the finest bolt action rifle ever made; but they are unlikely to find agreement from any non-American soldier.

It might be noted here that, contrary to often-expressed opinion, no Springfield rifles were issued to the British Home Guard during the Second World War. They received numbers of M1917 Enfield rifles, and in many cases these were shipped from Springfield Arsenal; the markings on the packing cases led to the mis-naming of the rifles. The rifle was subsequently known as the P17.

Drawing of the action of the Springfield Trap-Door single shot musket conversion. The dotted outline shows the breech block in the open position.

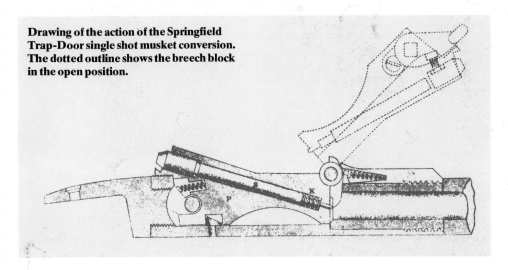

SQUIBMAN / *Philippine Islands*

Squibman is the trade name of the Squires, Bingham Manufacturing Company of Rizal in the Philippines who began operations in the late 1950s. Their products include ·22 bolt-action and semi-automatic rifles in both conventional and assault rifle configuration, shotguns and revolvers. The rifles are the Stirling bolt-action type or the Squibman M16, which is built to resemble the Armalite. The shotguns are sold under the name Bentley, and are slide-action 12-bores, one of which is a short-barrelled model sold as a riot gun. The revolvers are ·38 special solid-frame types with swing-out cylinders. The company's products are becoming more widely known.

STARR / *USA*

The Starr family were gun and swordsmiths in Middletown, Connecticut, in the first half of the 19th century. In the 1850s, Eben Townsend Starr, one of the sons, took out several patents relating to revolving pistols, both of the pepper-box type and the usual cylinder revolver type, and in about 1861 he set up the Starr Arms Company in Binghamton, New York, producing ·36 self-cocking percussion revolvers. His early models used an unusual double-trigger arrangement in which a front trigger was depressed to release the cylinder, allowing it to be revolved by hand, and then further depressed to cock the hammer, after which the rear trigger actually fired the pistol. The second trigger was a relatively small protrusion at the rear end of the trigger guard and can easily be overlooked at a casual glance. He later abandoned this system for a conventional single-action mechanism. Some 2500 or more of the first model were bought by the US Army in 1858–1861, and a further 47,000 were purchased by the Union Army during the Civil War, making Starr the third largest manufacturer of percussion revolvers. Some experimental revolving rifles and carbines were also made, though these were never put into production. At the end of the Civil War the firm got into financial difficulties and was wound up in 1867. Several thousand revolvers, surplus to military requirements after the war, were sold to France in 1870 when the French Government were desperate for arms in the Franco-Prussian War, this accounting for the presence of Starr revolvers in Europe in great numbers.

STAVENHAGEN / *Germany*

A type of pistol sight in which the rear sight notch is framed in white and the front sight blade has a white dot inlaid in its rear edge. This patented 'contrast' design was introduced in the 1960s and is claimed to facilitate rapid alignment of the sights in poor light. It is currently used on SIG-Sauer automatic pistols.

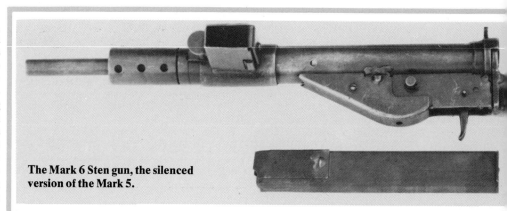

The Mark 6 Sten gun, the silenced version of the Mark 5.

STEN / *Britain*

The Sten submachine gun was the first 'cheap and nasty' weapon to see service in a western army. Prior to 1940 the desirable features of any military weapon included finish of a high standard and a quality of manufacture which would ensure that the weapon outlived several generations of soldiers. This was perfectly satisfactory when the rate of technological advance was relatively slow and warfare proceeded at walking pace. But when weapon developments began to appear faster than the old designs could wear out, and when the speed of warfare increased, it gradually became obvious that the old approach was no longer valid. Weapons had to be made cheaply and in vast quantities, so that they could be rapidly replaced when something better came along and could be turned out at sufficient speed to keep up with the wastage at the front. The ideal (which has not yet quite been reached) is the expendable weapon which is thrown away as soon as it malfunctions and replaced with a new one, on the grounds that this is cheaper than sending the broken one back to be repaired. And as far as the British Army was concerned, the Sten gun was the weapon which brought this question into focus.

In 1939 the British Army had no submachine guns; the Ordnance Board had tested every design which had appeared in the 1930s, but the principles outlined above—immaculate finish and permanent construction—were absent, and none were ever recommended for adoption. Moreover, there was only the haziest of ideas about where such an individualist weapon would fit into the tactical structure. The Army, however, wanted them, and the outbreak of war gave them the lever to demand some. They were issued with Thompson submachine guns bought from the USA at considerable expense and then set about trying to develop a home-made alternative. After much argument it was decided that the best way would be to copy the Bergmann MP28, and it was arranged to do this, calling the result the Lanchester submachine gun. While the prototype Lanchester was undergoing tests and production was being organised, in January 1941, the Design Department produced a greatly simplified model submachine gun for test. This had been designed by two men, Major R. V. Shepherd and Mr. H. J. Turpin; both were from the Small Arms Group at the Royal Small Arms Factory, Enfield, and from their initials and the place of origin, the name Sten was coined. Their prototype was tested and approved, and in a matter of weeks it was put into production.

The Mark 1 Sten was, compared to what followed, rather luxurious. It had a short wooden stock, a wooden fore grip and a flash hider on the muzzle. Mechanically it was simply a bolt with a fixed firing pin, travelling in a tubular receiver with a slot for the cocking handle, retained there by a bayonet cap at the rear end, and with a short barrel screwed into the front end. Subsequent models did away

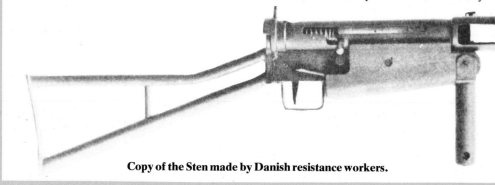

Copy of the Sten made by Danish resistance workers.

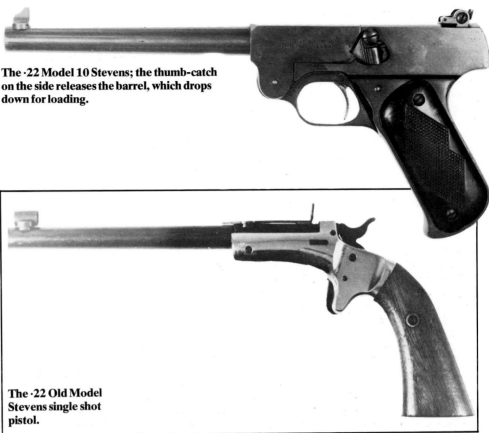

The ·22 Model 10 Stevens; the thumb-catch on the side releases the barrel, which drops down for loading.

The ·22 Old Model Stevens single shot pistol.

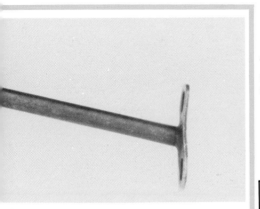

with the fore grip and the woodwork and eventually the Sten was being turned out by the tens of thousands for a price of about £2 each. Once the desperate urgency of 1940 was well behind, a somewhat more elegant version, the Mark 5, appeared; this had a wooden stock with (polishable) brass butt-plate and had the foresight guard and muzzle configuration of the Lee-Enfield Rifle so that the regulation bayonet could be fitted. In spite of all this, it was a Sten gun underneath.

The principal defect of the Sten lay in its magazine. This was a single-feed-position box containing 32 rounds; it was stamped from sheet steel and the lips, which were critical in their alignment for feeding, were easily deformed. Any dirt which got into the magazine could not get out again, and the vast majority of stoppages which occurred with the Sten were the fault of the magazine. Since the magazine design was never changed, the same problems followed every modification of the gun from the Mark 1 to the Mark 5. However, with good magazines it was extremely reliable; due to its loose tolerances it was far more tolerant of poor conditions than many ostensibly better weapons. This was proved more than once during the Korean War, when the Mark 5 Sten functioned reliably in sub-zero conditions which froze other weapons solid.

In addition to the standard models, there were two silenced versions of the Sten, developed for use by Commando and similar raiding parties. These used a short barrel, per-

forated to release gas and thus lower the bullet's velocity, and entirely surrounded by a casing containing baffles which oscillated the gases back and forth until they were released at low velocity without making any report. Due to the dangers of building up too much pressure inside the casing, it was normal to fire these weapons at single shot only, though automatic fire was possible in an emergency.

STERLING / UK

The Sterling Engineering Company made their start in firearms by manufacturing the Lanchester submachine gun for the British Navy during the Second World War. They then undertook the production of prototype models of the Patchett (qv) submachine gun and eventually adopted the design as their own, producing it as the Sterling. In recent years they have also negotiated license to permit them to manufacture other weapons, including the Ingram submachine gun and the Armalite AR-18 rifle, but little production of these weapons has yet taken place. The company is now known as the Sterling Armaments Company.

STEVENS, Joshua (1814–1907)

Stevens was trained as a toolmaker and then went into the gunmaking industry. He worked for Eli Whitney and made cylinders for the Walker Colt revolvers and then worked for Colt on the first Dragoon revolver. He was apparently found by Samuel Colt working on his own design of revolver in 1848 and was promptly fired. He joined forces with Edwin Wesson, and after Wesson's death worked for the Massachusetts Arms Company on percussion revolvers. In 1864 he founded his own company, which later became the J. Stevens Arms & Tool Company of Chicopee Falls, Massachusetts. He began by making a single-shot hinged-barrel pistol, which was the prototype for a long series of target pistols, and then expanded to make shotguns and rifles. The company eventually became the largest producer of sporting firearms in the USA for a short period prior to the First World War, but in 1920 it was taken over by the Savage Arms Corporation and has, since then, operated as an autonomous division within that firm, continuing to produce rifles and shotguns.

The British L34A1 silenced submachine gun.

STEYR/ Austria

The Osterreichische Waffenfabrik Gesell-schaft of Steyr was founded in 1853 by Werndl (*qv*) who, after visiting the USA to study production methods, established a 15-workshop complex to convert muzzle-loading rifles into Werndl breech-loaders for the Austro-Hungarian Army. After converting 80,000 rifles, he then obtained orders to manufacture 100,000 breech-loaders, and after that the orders came in profusion. By 1880 the Steyr factory's output exceeded that of any other rifle plant in the world, 13,000 rifles a week leaving its gates. After the First World War it became Steyr-werke AG and diversified into automobiles and other machinery. In 1934 it amalgamated with the Austro-Daimler-Puch combine to form Steyr-Daimler-Puch and was connected with the Rheinmetall company of Germany (*qv*). With the German annexation of Austria, the SDP became part of the Hermann-Goering-Werke 'paper corporation', but after 1945 much of the plant was removed and replaced by machinery for the production of motor-cycles, tractors and similar peacetime products. In 1950 the manufacture of sporting rifles began once again, and since that time various military weapons have appeared.

Steyr was the principal manufacturer of the Mannlicher (*qv*) rifles and pistols, and production of rifles to the basic Mannlicher pattern goes on to the present day. The current Austrian Army sniping rifle, the SSG, is an up-to-date Mannlicher-Schoenauer, using the same turnbolt and rotary magazine that was developed at the turn of the century. The modern aspect is reflected in the stock, which is entirely of plastic. The SSG is an extremely accurate weapon, and civil versions, for hunting, are available in various calibres.

The Steyr pistols were a mixed lot; the first products were to the designs of Pieper (*qv*), a

gas seal revolver very similar to the Nagant (*qv*), and produced in small numbers in the middle 1890s. This design did not prosper, and the factory then turned to automatic pistols. It had already worked on the Schonberger and Mannlicher designs (both *qv*), and now turned to the pistols developed by Roth (*qv*). For a pocket pistol it went back to Pieper, this time to Nicolas, and produced numbers of the tip-up barrel pistol in 7·65mm calibre prior to World War One. After the war it abandoned the pistol field, and it was not until the 1970s that a new design appeared, the Pistole Pi18. This is an unusual design of delayed blowback pistol, the delay being obtained by tapping a small portion of gas from the chamber and leading it to the interior of the slide. Here it enters an annular expansion chamber and brings sufficient pressure to bear on the slide to resist the opening movement due to blowback; the system is very similar to that first used on the Volksgewehr (*qv*). The lockwork is double action, and the pistol can be converted to full-automatic fire; in this case it is used with an over-length magazine and a short butt-stock, turning it into a compact submachine gun.

In spite of this, the company also produce a 'proper' submachine gun, the MPi69. This was developed in 1965 and was adopted by the Austrian Army in 1969. It is fairly conventional for its period, using an overhung bolt resembling that of the Uzi submachine gun. Much of the construction is of sheet metal, and the cocking system is unusual in that the gun is cocked by pulling the canvas sling out to one side and then pulling it sharply back; the forward sling anchorage is to the cocking piece of the bolt.

The Austrian Schwarzlose (*qv*) machine gun was also produced at Steyr, the factory having obtained a license from Schwarzlose's Berlin factory.

STONER/ USA

Eugene Stoner was the designer of the Armalite (*qv*) rifle, and in 1959 left Armalite to become a consultant with Colt. Shortly after this he conceived the Stoner System, and moved to the Cadillac Gage Company in California to complete its development. This is an ingenious idea, consisting of fifteen basic assemblies from which any one of a complete family of weapons can be assembled. The basic unit is a receiver with bolt, return spring, gas piston and trigger mechanism; on to this can be grafted different lengths of barrel, different butts, different feed systems, so as to build up six weapons—an assault rifle, a submachine gun, a magazine-fed light machine gun, a belt-fed light machine gun, a tripod-mounted heavy machine gun, and a fixed heavy machine gun

for use in tanks. All the weapons used the same gas-piston operating system; since machine guns form two-thirds of the system, the power available from a long-stroke piston is needed to actuate the belt feed mechanism, a load which simpler direct-gas systems (such as that in the Armalite) could not sustain.

The first weapon, known as the Stoner 62, was developed in 1962 and chambered for the 7·62mm NATO cartridge, but it was almost immediately apparent that the 5·56mm cartridge was going to assume greater importance in the future, and the Stoner 63 system, in 5·56mm, was devised.

The Cadillac Gage company manufactured the system and also licensed it to Mauser in Germany; they later gave it up and it was transferred to Nederlands Waapen et Muni-

tions de Kruithoorn in Holland. They publicised it and were very energetic in promoting the system throughout Europe, but in spite of testing by various armies, the idea was not adopted. The belt-fed light machine gun was adopted in small numbers by the US Marine Corps as the XM207 and was used by them in Vietnam, but no further adoption seems to have taken place. The Stoner system is a good idea and deserves close study; at present it seems that the need to compromise leads to some unacceptable features, such as the submachine gun being overweight and the assault rifle being rather more cumbersome than most of its competitors. These things may well be amenable to correction, but at the time of writing the Stoner system seems to be dormant, at least temporarily.

The Steyr factory's first venture into the automatic pistol business under their own name was this model of 1909, based on the Belgian Pieper patents.

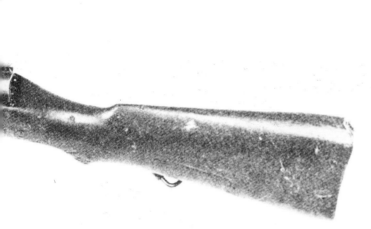

The German-designed, Austrian-produced, Steyr-Solothurn MP34 submachine gun, one of the finest quality weapons of this class ever made.

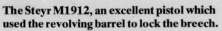

The Steyr M1912, an excellent pistol which used the revolving barrel to lock the breech.

The Steyr-Daimler-Puch company recently produced this Model SP pocket pistol.

The Stoner 63A1 in medium machine gun form; by suitable juggling with the basic components, other weapons can be constructed.

TATAREK, Edmund (*fl. 1905–1914*)

Tatarek was a First Lieutenant of the Austro-Hungarian Army, co-patentee with Captain Johann von Benko of a helical pistol magazine in 1911. This used a 'snail' type drum with a straight extension which could enter the pistol butt in place of the normal magazine, so giving extra ammunition capacity and (according to the patentees) served as an 'aiming rest'. This design appears to have been the basis of the well-known 'snail' magazine produced for the Long '08 (or Artillery) Luger pistol in later years. Tatarek was also linked with a number of other Hungarian officers in developing automatic rifles. One remarkable patent of 1913 covered the conversion of a Mannlicher automatic rifle back to hand operation, an unusual direction of effort.

In the years immediately after the First World War, the British Small Arms Committee tested a Tatarek-designed conversion of the ·276 Pattern 1914 Enfield rifle, turning it into a gas-operated automatic weapon, but the idea was not adopted or developed.

THOMAS, James (*fl. 1865–1880*)

Thomas was a Birmingham gunmaker who patented a revolver in 1869 having a system of simultaneous extraction. The revolver was of the usual solid-frame pattern, except that the aperture in the frame, into which the cylinder fitted, was about twice as long as the cylinder, and the barrel was a sliding fit in the frame. By means of a knob on the underside of the barrel, both barrel and cylinder could be pulled forward in the frame, the cylinder moving up to the front end of the frame aperture and a star-plate ejector remaining stationary so as to pull the empty cases out of the cylinder as it moved away.

Thomas then assigned his patent to Tipping & Lawden of Birmingham who produced revolvers in ·32, ·38 and ·45 calibre until 1877, when the company was absorbed by Webley (*qv*) and production of the Thomas revolver came to an end.

THOMPSON, John Tagliaferro (*1860–1940*)

Thompson (who, by the way, pronounced his middle name 'Tolliver') graduated from West Point in 1882 and entered the US Army Artillery, transferring to the Ordnance Department in 1890. He was concerned in the testing and adoption of the Springfield M1903 rifle, performed some famous tests on corpses and beef cattle which determined that ·45 was the only acceptable calibre for a handgun, and played a considerable part in the perfection and adoption of the Colt ·45 M1911 automatic. In November 1914 he retired from service, intending to devote his time to perfecting an automatic rifle, joining the Remington Arms Company as their Chief Engineer. There he was to be responsible for organising the construction, outfitting and operation of a rifle

factory at Eddystone, Pennsylvania, to produce the British Enfield rifle, and in 1916 he set up another factory to produce Mosin-Nagant rifles for the Russian Army. When war came to America he was recalled to service and was instrumental in adapting the British Enfield rifle to ·30 calibre and then producing it as the M1917. Promoted to Brigadier-General he was made responsible for the supply of small arms and ammunition to the AEF in France, and all accounts agree that he performed these manifold tasks with the utmost efficiency. He was awarded the Distinguished Service Medal 'for exceptionally meritorious and conspicuous service'. In December 1918 he retired for the second time.

During all this time, however, his aim was still an automatic rifle. He had rejected gas

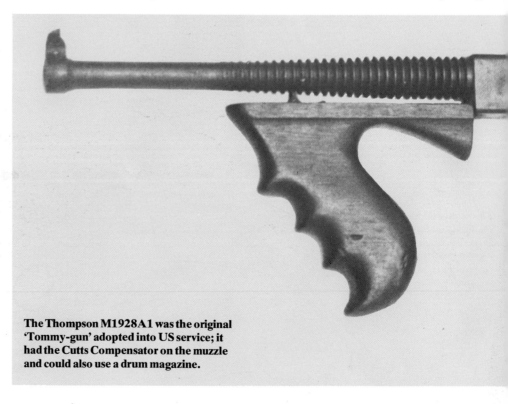

The Thompson M1928A1 was the original 'Tommy-gun' adopted into US service; it had the Cutts Compensator on the muzzle and could also use a drum magazine.

The Thompson M1 was a wartime version which did away with the controversial Blish locking system and the Cutts Compensator and could use only a box magazine.

operation as being too complicated for a shoulder arm, and recoil operation as being likely to produce too heavy a weapon. Blowback was no good for a powerful military cartridge, and that just about exhausted the available principles of operation. He was also anxious to come up with something untouched by the big companies, so as to avoid heavy patent license payments.

In 1915 Commander John Blish, serving in the US Navy, patented a delayed blowback breech system in which a sloping metal wedge interlocked the breech block with the gun body. Under high pressure, as when the cartridge fired, the angle of slope was such that the mating faces jammed solid; but when the pressure dropped, the faces were able to slip across each other, the wedge moved up due to the

slope, and the breech was unlocked. Thompson felt that this was the solution to his problem, and he offered Blish shares in a company in exchange for the patent. Blish agreed, and the Auto-Ordnance Company (*qv*) was founded. Two designer/engineers, Thomas Eickhoff and Oscar Payne, were hired to work on the design. After Thompson had been recalled to the Army, these two worked on, and eventually discovered that the system would not work with a rifle cartridge; they found, though, that it worked with a ·45 pistol cartridge quite well. On being told this, Thompson had the inspiration to change the design to a hand-held machine gun which he called the Trench Broom. After more design work, this finally appeared in 1919, after the need for it had passed; Thompson, not daunted, now called it

the Sub-Machine Gun and began to promote it as a police weapon.

The Thompson submachine gun was a delayed blowback weapon feeding from a characteristic drum magazine and with an outline which became well-known—a finned barrel, two pistol grips and a short butt. It was, after some unfavourable publicity in the hands of gangsters, adopted by the US Marines, but real success evaded Thompson. Ryan, the man who financed the operation, died in 1928, and his son wanted to be rid of the Auto-Ordnance Corporation. It was duly sold, and Thompson lost control of it. The Thompson gun, under the hands of its new owner, eventually went on to become a success during the Second World War, but Thompson died in 1940 without seeing its fulfilment.

THOMPSON-CENTER / USA

This company was formed in 1966 by Kenneth Thompson and Warren Center; Mr. Center had developed a design of single-shot pistol, while Mr. Thompson owned a tool company. The pistol produced by the company is known as the Contender, and is a single-shot, tip-up pistol of high quality. The unusual thing about it is that the barrel can be rapidly changed for one of another calibre without the need to change any other component; in order to cater for a change of cartridge, there is a dual firing pin which can be selected so as to fire centre-fire or rimfire cartridges at will. The pistol has been produced in over 20 different calibres, and so simple is the construction that a new calibre can be added to the range with very little difficulty.

After their success with the Contender the company went on to make muzzle-loading rifles and pistols in 'reproduction' style to cater for the growing army of black-powder shooters.

THORNEYCROFT / Britain

J. B. Thorneycroft, of Mauchline, Ayrshire, is a figure of whom little is known but, on the strength of a 1901 patent, deserves recognition as probably being the originator of the 'bull-pup' style of rifle. His patent described 'A rifle in which the barrel is carried rearwards into proximity with the butt end of the stock, the length of the weapon being thus shortened, whilst the length of the barrel . . . is retained.' He is believed to have built (or, more likely, had built for him) one or two rifles in this style for target shooting, and he developed a short-stroke bolt action to suit. This action later appeared in a cavalry carbine which he developed in 1904 in conjunction with Farquhar and Hill. In essence, it was an extremely short bolt which locked by means of multiple inter-rupted threads at the front end, the rear section of the bolt being shrouded in a wooden cover. This allowed the firer to take a firm grip, close behind the bolt, allowing the carbine to be somewhat shorter than usual, though without going to 'bull-pup' extremes. The carbine was submitted for military consideration, but since the Army had just decided to adopt the Short Lee-Enfield rifle, there was no demand for such a weapon.

The Hungarian-made Tokagypt, a 9mm conversion of the Soviet Tokarev design.

THUER / USA

Alexander Thuer was associated with the Colt company in the promotion of his patent, taken out in 1868, to permit the conversion of per-cussion revolvers to cartridge loading. Due to the restrictions of the Rollin White (qv) patent, Colt were unable to simply provide bored-through cylinders for their revolvers, as was done by many European makers who were not restrained by the White patent. The Thuer patent covered a cylinder which was blind at the rear end, except for a firing pin hole, and which was loaded from the front end. The cartridge could also be re-charged while in the cylinder, using various patented accessories, and the converted revolver was capable of being fitted with a special 'ejecting ring' behind the cylinder which carried a button; dropping the hammer on to this button caused the empty case to be forced from the front end of the cylinder.

The Thuer cartridge was a slightly tapered brass tube without any form of rim or groove and with a central cap in the base. Due to the taper it could be slipped into the cylinder chambers and was held there by friction of the bullet.

TOKAGYPT / Hungary

The Tokagypt pistol, as the name might imply, was a modified Tokarev (qv) TT33 manufac-tured expressly for the Egyptian Army. It was manufactured by the Femaru es Szerszamgep-gyar NV of Budapest in 1958, and was little more than the basic Tokarev design modified to fire the 9mm Parabellum cartridge. A safety catch was added (since the original Tokarev never used one) and a one-piece plastic butt grip gave the weapon a more dashing appear-ance. For reasons never disclosed, the Egyp-tian Army disliked the pistol, and passed them on to the Egyptian Police. After the first few batches had been delivered, the contract was terminated. Since the pistol was a sound and reliable weapon, one can only assume the reason for these manoeuvres was political. The Femaru concern, left with the pistols on their hands, disposed of them on the commercial market, most of them being sold in West Ger-many under the name Firebird.

TOKAREV, Feodor Vassilevitch (b. 1871)

Tokarev was apprenticed to a blacksmith at the age of eleven, then worked for a gunsmith, and

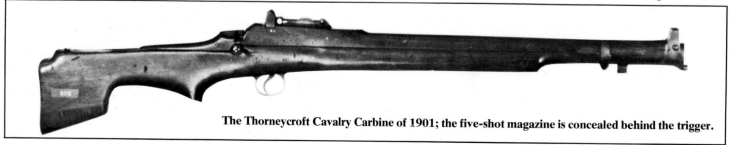

The Thorneycroft Cavalry Carbine of 1901; the five-shot magazine is concealed behind the trigger.

in 1888 entered a military trade school where he spent four years becoming an armourer. He went from there to be the unit armourer for the 12th Don Cossack Regiment. In 1907 he went to Officer School and after commissioning was posted to the Sestoretsk Arsenal. After the Revolution he became technical superintendent of the Tula Arsenal and thereafter devoted his time to weapons design.

He is said to have been working on a design of automatic rifle as early as 1909, though nothing ever came of this. His first major effort was a submachine gun which he put forward in 1926. This was a blowback weapon which fired the 7·62mm Nagant revolver cartridge at some 1000 rounds a minute. But the revolver cartridge was not well suited to an automatic weapon and the design was not followed up. In 1928 he developed the Maxim-Tokarev machine gun, an attempt to lighten and air-cool the standard Maxim gun. This weapon had an air-cooled barrel in a perforated jacket and a wooden shoulder stock and a bipod; a number were made for troop trials but they were not considered suitable and were not adopted. Most of them were, much later, off-loaded to the International Brigades in the Spanish Civil War.

In 1930 Tokarev produced the weapon which commemorates his name, the Tokarev TT-30 automatic pistol. This is basically the Colt-Browning swinging link design, though with some interesting modifications. The hammer and firing mechanism were contained in a removable module to simplify assembly and maintainance; the feed lips, normally on the magazine, were machined into the pistol frame so that slight damage to the magazine would not impair operation of the pistol. The lugs on the barrel were milled in the usual manner, but it was later decided to change this to ribs machined all the way round the barrel; this allowed the locking ribs to be turned on the lathe which finished the barrel, and thus removed a major machining process from the manufacturing sequence. With this adopted, the pistol became the TT-33 model. It was chambered for a 7·62mm rimless cartridge which is almost identical to the 7·63mm Mauser round, and it was to remain the standard Soviet pistol until the arrival of the Makarov in the late 1950s.

Tokarev then returned to the question of an automatic rifle, and developed a gas-operated weapon which was issued as the SVT38 model. This fired the standard 7·62mm Mosin-Nagant rifle cartridge, which was not a good design for such a weapon, and proved to be too fragile for normal service. A more robust version, the SVT40 was later developed but neither became general issue and were normally restricted to use by NCOs and snipers, who, presumably, were likely to give the weapons more care than the line soldier.

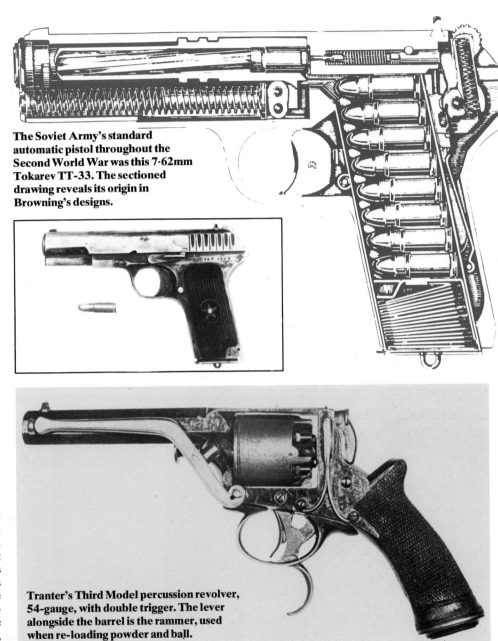

The Soviet Army's standard automatic pistol throughout the Second World War was this 7·62mm Tokarev TT-33. The sectioned drawing reveals its origin in Browning's designs.

Tranter's Third Model percussion revolver, 54-gauge, with double trigger. The lever alongside the barrel is the rammer, used when re-loading powder and ball.

TRANTER, William (d. 1890)

William Tranter was a Birmingham (England) gunmaker of considerable repute, an active patentee of many improvements, one of the first Directors of the Birmingham Small Arms Company and a prominent member of the Gun Trade Association. A large part of his business seems to have been the manufacture of weapons for sale by gunmakers and others under their own names, and the making of patented weapons for those firms without facilities for doing their own manufacturing. His scope covered all types of arms current between 1840, when he set up in business, and 1885 when he retired; shotguns, rifles, pistols and revolvers came alike from his factory. His

name, however, is principally associated with revolvers and he patented numerous improvements to mechanisms. He made revolvers in his own name, and several of the patents were licensed out to others, so that the words 'Tranter's Patent' on a revolver do not necessarily mean that Tranter made it.

His first revolvers were percussion models, introduced in about 1854, and the notable feature of them was a double trigger arrangement in which one trigger was pulled back to cock the hammer, and the other trigger was then pulled to fire the pistol. This idea obviously fascinated him, since he went on to develop a number of variants of this mechanism, re-arranging the triggers and lockwork; one of them was actually a triple-action, in which the hammer could be thumb-cocked and fired by the front trigger; or cocked and fired by simply pulling through on the front trigger; or cocked by the rear trigger and fired by the front, a plethora of options which surely had more novelty than utility.

With the arrival of metallic cartridges, Tranter devised conversion cylinders which allowed owners of percussion revolvers to adapt to the new system, and then went on to produce some excellent solid-frame cartridge revolvers. One of his first was adopted by the British Army as 'Pistol, Revolver, Breech-loading, Tranter' in 1878; this was a gate-loaded model in ·433 calibre which remained in service until 1887. Commercial models were offered in rimfire and centrefire calibres; some used variations of his original double-trigger, but the majority of his later designs adopted a fairly straight-forward double-action lock.

TURBIAUX / France

Jacques Turbiaux of Paris was the inventor of what is probably the best-known of all the 'palm-squeezer' repeating pistols, the Protector. The pistol took the form of a disc, some

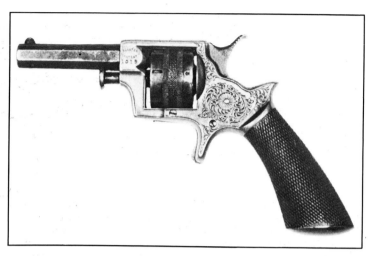

In the rimfire period, Tranter produced this elegant model in ·30 calibre.

two inches in diameter and half an inch thick, from one edge of which protruded a barrel and from the other edge a lever arrangement. The disc contained a revolving block with seven chambers for 8mm rimfire cartridges. The pistol was held in the palm of the hand, the barrel protruding between the first and second fingers and the firing lever resting against the heel of the palm. Squeezing the hand thus drove in the lever which rotated the revolving block to align a cartridge with the breech and then released a firing pin. On relaxing the hand the lever sprang out, ready for the next shot.

Turbiaux patented this in 1882 and it proved extremely popular in Europe, selling well into the 1890s. It was also licensed to be made in the USA, for details of which see under FINNEGAN, one of the American licensees.

UBERTI / Italy

The firm of Aldo Uberti of Gardone Valtrompia produces a wide selection of shotguns and in more recent years has produced a number of Frontier type revolvers aimed at the American market. These range from ·22 to ·45 in calibre, are available in a selection of barrel lengths, and are single-action models based generally on the Colt Model of 1873. Under such names as Buckhorn, Cattleman and Trailblazer they have attained wide distribution in the USA.

UNCETA / Spain

This famous Spanish company began in 1908 as Pedro Unceta y Juan Esperanza, manufacturing a blowback automatic pistol called the Victoria. In 1913 the firm moved to Guernica, became Esperanza y Unceta, and undertook the manufacture of the Campo Giro (*qv*) pistol for the Spanish Army. In 1914 the trade-name Astra was adopted, and during the First World War the company produced several thousand automatic pistols for the French and Italian armies. During this period they examined the Campo-Giro pistol most carefully and redesigned it to become their Astra Model 400 which they placed on the market in 1921. It was almost immediately adopted by the Spanish Army as their service pistol.

The Astra 400 has a characteristic 'water-pistol' shape, and is a pure blowback pistol, in spite of being chambered for the powerful 9mm Largo cartridge. This is achieved by a combination of heavy slide and strong recoil spring, and this pistol is also unique in that the chamber dimensions and firing pin length allow it to fire, without any adjustment or alteration, several different types of 9mm cartridge.

The basic design of the 400 was followed in several other models over the ensuing years, and fuller details will be found under ASTRA. In 1929 the company, which had now become Unceta y Cia, produced a copy of the Mauser Military pistol, chambered for the 9mm Largo cartridge, which was provided with a selective-fire option, allowing it to function as a sub-machine gun. These were supplied to the Guarda Civil, as well as being sold overseas, and continued in production until 1937. During the Civil War the factory made arms for whoever was occupying it, first the Republicans and then the Nationalists. After the War it was one of the three Spanish companies permitted to manufacture pistols and has continued to do so until the present day. The quality can be judged from the fact that when the Colt company of America found it inexpedient to manufacture their ·25 automatic any longer, they farmed it out to Unceta, who made the Colt Junior for sale in the USA.

UNIQUE/*France*
This was the trade name for a series of automatic pistols made by the Manufacture d'Armes de Pyrénées of Hendaye (see PYRENEES) from 1923 until the present day. From 1923 to 1939 the various models were numbered in a simple progression from Model 10 (the first, in spite of the advanced number) to Model 21, and all were simple blowback pistols more or less based on the Browning 1906 design. After 1945 the notation became more involved, and not all models are called Unique.

UNITED DEFENSE/*USA*
The United Defense Supply Corporation of America was set up in obscure circumstances by the US Government in 1940 and appears to have been a legal cloak to cover the supply of arms to friendly nations without jeopardising the country's neutral stance.

The company, in addition to its overseas sales, managed to develop two submachine guns which were submitted for military test during the war. The first was the UD M42, which had been designed in the late 1930s by Carl G. Swebilius, of the High Standard Manufacturing Co. Under contract from United Defense, this gun was made in some numbers by the Marlin Firearms Corporation, ostensibly for supply to the Dutch Government for service in the East Indies, though a large number apparently went to the Office of Strategic Services for supply to various clandestine organisations in Europe.

The UD M42 had originally been submitted to the US Army by High Standard in 1940, but due to other weapons being available there was no requirement and thus it passed to the United Defense organisation. The submachine gun was chambered for the 9mm Parabellum round in its production model, though the early ones were apparently for the ·45 cartridge. It was of the normal blowback type, fed from a box magazine, and provided with a wooden butt and either two pistol grips or one grip and a wooden fore-end. It is said to have been one of the best wartime designs, but since it was carefully made by machining, it could not compete with the cheaper stamped-out weapons, such as the M3 and the Sten gun.

The post-war Unique Model Bcf-66 in 9mm short calibre.

In 1943 a fresh model, intended to be a cheaply produced gun to compare with the Sten and M3, was offered for test to the US Army. This used a tubular receiver and a perforated barrel jacket, and was almost entirely stamped and pressed. A unique feature was that each gun was provided with two barrels, one in ·45 calibre and one in 9mm; by changing barrels, the weapon was immediately adapted to the fresh cartridge, no change of bolt being necessary. When one barrel was in place on the gun, the other was fitted into a socket at the rear, provided with a pad, and became the shoulder stock. It was an ingenious design, but it failed badly on test, being far too easily deranged by mud and dirt.

UZI/*Israel*
During the Arab-Israeli War of 1948 the Israeli Army felt the need for a reliable submachine gun, and in 1949 Major Uziel Gal began development of a native design. He had closely studied the several submachine guns available in the Middle East at that time, notably the Czech Model 23, and his eventual weapon shows evidence of this. The Uzi, which appeared in 1952, is a blowback weapon using an over-hung bolt, i.e. a bolt which is deeply recessed at the front end so that much of its bulk surrounds the barrel when the breech is closed. This reduced the length of the gun to no more than 17½ inches, and in this length the barrel length of 10¼ inches is accommodated quite easily due to the overhang.

The magazine of the Uzi enters the pistol grip, which allows the magazine housing to be exceptionally robust and also simplifies the problem of inserting a magazine in the dark, since one hand will always find the other. The butt is a folding metal unit, and the whole design utilises sheet metal stampings and plastic to the utmost. The standard magazine holds 32 rounds, but in order to increase the firepower, it has become the practice to weld two magazines together at right-angles; thus, when one magazine is entered into the grip, the other extends forward, beneath the barrel. It is immediately ready for changing with the inserted magazine, and it is also useful in adding weight to the front of the gun so as to keep the muzzle down during automatic fire.

The Uzi has also been adopted by the West German, Iranian and Venezuelan armies as well as the Israeli.

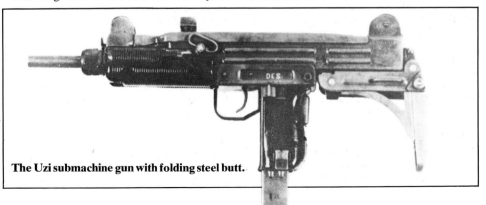

The Uzi submachine gun with folding steel butt.

V

VESELEY / *Britain*

Josef Veseley was a Czech engineer who had come to Britain to assist the BSA company in tooling-up for production of the BESA machine gun. On the outbreak of war in 1939 he stayed in this country, to work for BSA. In August 1940 he submitted sets of drawings of a submachine gun to the Chief Inspector of Small Arms. Although the design appeared to have some novel features, it was turned down because the decision to make the Lanchester submachine gun had been taken and the Sten Gun was also being examined. Nothing daunted, Veseley made a prototype gun and late in 1942 submitted it for test. It was a blowback weapon and had a novel magazine of two columns, one behind the other. Feed was from the first compartment until that was empty, after which the rear compartment automatically continued to feed until it, too, was empty; this gave a total magazine capacity of 60 rounds. The weapon was tested and was found generally good, though it failed the

stringent mud test, in which a weapon is thrown into liquid mud, is permitted to be wiped by hand only, and must then continue to function. This model became known as the V-42 and in 1944 a further six prototypes were made for more tests, certain small modifications having now been incorporated. Three of these were slightly different, having a removable stock and removable barrel so that they could be carried more compactly by parachutists, and these became known as the V-43. Trials were carried out in 1944–1945, but by that time there were better designs in the offing, and the Veseley was finally refused in October 1945.

VETTERLI, Friedrich *(1822–1882)*

Vetterli served his apprenticeship as a gunsmith and then became a journeyman, travelling throughout Europe and working with various gunmaking concerns to broaden his knowledge. In 1865 he was offered the post of manager of the weapons department of the

Schweizerische Industrie Gesellschaft (later to be known as SIG). Here he developed the Swiss Army's Vetterli M1868 rifle. This was a turnbolt rifle with a tubular magazine beneath the barrel, the bolt actuating the usual type of cartridge lifter. Chambered for a metallic cartridge, it was a considerable advance for its day and is generally conceded to be the first metallic-cartridge repeater to be adopted for military service. The bolt action was rather unusual in being entirely enclosed by the receiver, a tubular unit behind the barrel, pierced only by an ejection slot. Subsequent modifications kept this rifle in service until it was replaced by the Schmidt-Rubin in 1889.

The Italian government also adopted the Vetterli system, though they allied it to a box magazine developed by an inventive General named Vitali, and the rifles are therefore known as Vetterli-Vitali. A single shot Vetterli was adopted in 1871 and the magazine Vetterli-Vitali in 1881, serving until replaced by a Mannlicher design in 1891.

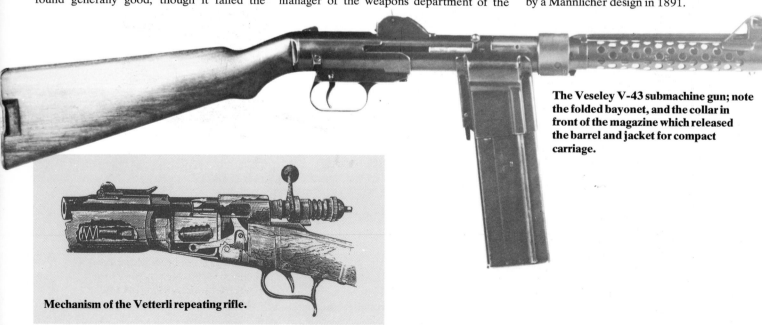

The Veseley V-43 submachine gun; note the folded bayonet, and the collar in front of the magazine which released the barrel and jacket for compact carriage.

Mechanism of the Vetterli repeating rifle.

VICKERS / *Britain*

This company began as steel-makers in Sheffield, then moved into ship-building. In 1883 Hiram Maxim (*qv*) entered into an agreement with Albert Vickers for the production of the Maxim machine gun, and the company later became Vickers, Son and Maxim. It gradually entered into every field of armaments, building battleships, tanks, aircraft and artillery and a full tabulation of its many products in these fields would take up several pages. In the small arms field, however, its output has been restricted and highly specialised. The company's name is, of course, best known for the Vickers machine gun, which formed the backbone of the British Army's automatic weapons from 1912 until 1968.

The Vickers machine gun was a re-design of the Maxim carried out at the Vickers factory at Erith in 1911–1912. The principal change was that the toggle was inverted so as to break upwards, and in addition the whole design was re-calculated so as to avoid excess weight. High-grade steel and aluminium alloys were used in place of the original Maxim's bronze and heavy steel, resulting in a considerable saving in weight without sacrificing strength or reliability. During the First World War the Vickers was in constant use and performed many legendary feats of sustained fire; 10,000 rounds non-stop was relatively commonplace. In addition to use as a ground gun, it was adopted as an aircraft weapon, the water-cooled jacket being replaced by a louvred jacket which cooled the barrel by the air-flow around the aircraft. In postwar years a ·50 calibre model, essentially an enlarged ·303 model, was adopted for use in tanks.

In the 1920s the company began producing the Vickers-Berthier (*qv*) machine gun, and also obtained a license for the patents of Pedersen, producing a slightly modified Pedersen (*qv*) rifle as the 'Vickers self-loading rifle'. Though frequently tested by various military authorities, it was never adopted and did not go into production.

The company was also instrumental in supplying several thousand Parabellum (Luger) pistols to the Dutch Government in the early 1920s. Vickers certainly could not have made these pistols, since they posessed none of the necessary machinery, and it seems most likely that the pistols were actually made by DWM in Germany, marked with Vickers' name, and supplied to the Netherlands. Reasons for such a manoeuvre vary between the desire to outwit the Allied Disarmament Commission, and the less nasty desire to obtain payment in sterling rather than in rapidly devaluing marks. The company history avoids the story altogether and it is quite probable that nobody now living knows the full story.

The Vickers gun in action during the First World War.

The Vickers Mark 1 medium machine gun, complete with water condenser. This gun remained in service, basically unchanged, for over half a century.

VICKERS-BERTHIER

VICKERS-BERTHIER / *Britain*

The Vickers-Berthier machine gun was designed by General A.V.P.M. Berthier (*qv*), his first efforts appearing in 1908. It was a gas-operated gun using a tipping bolt and fed from an overhead magazine, and had an unusual water-cooling system. After attempting to get this gun into production in the USA during the First World War Berthier came to Britain and sold the manufacturing rights to Vickers in 1925. Vickers then made one or two changes, notably doing away with the water-cooling system and turning it into an air-cooled gun with a finned barrel.

Manufacture of the Mark 1 gun began in 1928 and numbers were sold overseas. More improvements were then made; the barrel-change system was improved, the barrel lost its fins, the rear sight was simplified, and the result became the Mark 2, produced from 1930 onwards. The Indian Army then adopted the weapon and a subsequent model, the Mark 3, was made by them, under license, at Ishapore Ordnance Factory. The Vickers-Berthier was highly regarded, since it was a reliable, smooth-firing weapon, and in many quarters was tipped as the coming British Army light machine gun. However, in extensive trials during the early 1930s, it was beaten by the Bren gun and shortly afterwards Vickers gave up manufacture, leaving the Indian Army to continue making and using it until well after the Second World War.

VIGNERON / *Belgium*

The Vigneron submachine gun was designed by Colonel Vigneron, a retired Belgian Army officer, and produced by the SA Precision Liègeoise of Herstal. It was adopted throughout the Belgian forces in 1953 and is still in service.

The gun is a simple blowback weapon, well made from steel pressings, and with an unusually long barrel which carries a muzzle compensator. The butt is a folding wire affair, and the weapon is chambered for the 9mm Parabellum cartridge.

VILAR PEROSA / *Italy*

The Vilar-Perosa machine gun is often cited as the first submachine gun, on the grounds that it was a delayed blowback weapon of light weight, firing a pistol cartridge. These facts are correct enough, but the tactical function of the V-P machine gun and its actual physical appearance weigh against it being given status as a submachine gun.

The weapon was designed by A. B. Revelli (*qv*) and patented in 1915, the patents being assigned to the Officine de Vilar Perosa. It was adopted by the Italian Army as their M1915 and was also manufactured by FIAT, which led

The Vickers-Berthier Model 1928, used by the Indian Army.

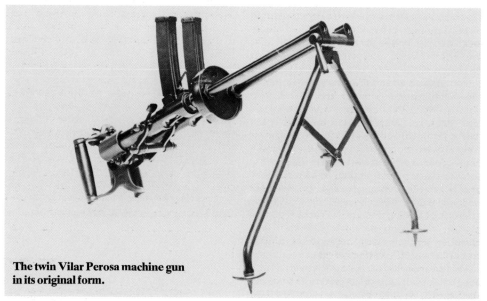

The twin Vilar Perosa machine gun in its original form.

to it being variously known as the V-P, the FIAT or the Revelli light machine gun. It was also made in Canada by the Canadian General Electric Company for the Italian government, in 1917–1918, but so far it has escaped being called the GEC.

The Italian Army were not well-equipped with machine guns in 1915, and in particular they desired a light gun for use by their Alpine mountain troops. As a result, the V-P was designed as an infantry support weapon; it was also used as an aircraft gun and for arming light coastal craft.

The gun actually consisted of two guns mounted side-by-side, each an independent unit. Each has a tubular receiver, barrel, and bolt unit, fed from an overhead magazine and chambered for the 9mm Glisenti pistol cartridge. Control was by a spade grip at the rear end with two triggers, one for each gun, and it could be placed on a light bipod or on a pivot mount. The bolt moved in the receiver, controlled by a lug engaging in a curved track in the receiver body. As the bolt closed up to the breech, so this track caused it to rotate through 45°, though the bolt did not actually lock to the breech. At almost the same time the striker was impelled forward, through the bolt; the striker also had a lug riding in the straight portion of

the groove, but was shaped at its head to relate to a slot within the bolt. Thus, only when the bolt had completed its 45° rotation could the striker pass forward sufficiently far for the tip to strike the cartridge. The rotation of the bolt was, therefore, primarily a safety device, but since, on recoil, it had to 'unwind' through 45° before it could move back, there was a slight element of delay in the opening.

The combination of light bolt and stiff return spring gave the gun an extremely high rate of fire; pressing both triggers at once brought both guns into action at a combined rate of almost 3000 rounds a minute. Since the two magazines held 50 rounds between them, this meant that both were empty within one second.

After much tactical thought, the Italians eventually hit on a method of using this gun in the assault, by mounting it on a platform suspended from a man's neck by straps, so that he walked into action firing the guns from the hip and looking rather like an ice-cream seller in a cinema. Some success was had with this tactic, but in 1918 the Army had had enough, and withdrew the guns, passing them to Beretta and to the Officine Vilar Perosa for conversion into single-barrel submachine guns. They thus became the Beretta M1918 and the OVP respectively, and original Vilar-Perosa guns are today comparatively rare, since most were dismantled to make these conversions.

VOLCANIC / USA

The Volcanic rifle, though a failure, deserves its place in any history of firearms since it formed a stepping-stone to better things. It had its origin in the Jennings (*qv*) rifle, a lever action weapon patented in 1849. Tyler Henry (*qv*) had worked on the original Jennings, and in the 1850s he was engaged by Smith & Wesson to build a new lever action combining some of the Jennings features with a double toggle lock system which Smith had patented in 1854. The result was a lever action rifle in which operation of the lever collapsed a toggle joint, retracted the bolt and lifted a cartridge from a tubular magazine beneath the barrel. The novelty lay in the cartridge, which was little more than an elongated lead bullet with the base hollowed out and filled with black powder and sealed with a pasteboard disc carrying a percussion cap. These were delivered to the cartridge lifter by a spring, rather than by gravity as in the Jennings design, but as might be imagined the whole idea fell down over the question of sealing the breech. This relied simply on the accurate mating of bolt and chamber, and once wear began to set in there was little hope of an effective seal.

This weapon was produced as a rifle and also as a pistol, both being marketed in 1854 under the Smith & Wesson (*qv*) name, but in 1855 the Volcanic Arms Company was set up, and the weapons henceforth were called Volcanic. Smith and Wesson left in the following year, and in spite of laudatory publicity the weapon failed to sell and the company went bankrupt in 1858. Oliver Winchester, one of the shareholders, bought up the remains, retained Henry, and from that beginning the Winchester lever-action rifle eventually appeared.

VOLKSGEWEHR / Germany

In 1944 the German government called upon various arms makers to develop Primitiv-Waffen, cheap, easily-made but effective weapons with which to arm the Volkssturm (home guard). The Gustloff company of Suhl were given the task of producing a light automatic rifle, and used a system developed by Barnetske, their chief designer, in 1943 but not hitherto used. It was a remarkable weapon.

The Volksgewehr consisted of a barrel surrounded by a tubular sleeve which carried the bolt at the rear end. The bolt recoiled into a casing which contained a hammer and trigger mechanism. The tubular sleeve maintained an annular space around the barrel, and inside this space was a recoil spring. About 2½ inches back from the muzzle were four gas ports in the

barrel, slanted forward into the annular space within the sleeve. A box magazine, that of the Sturmgewehr 44, fitted below the action, and on pulling back the bolt a round was fed into the chamber. Pulling the trigger dropped the hammer on to a firing pin and fired the round. The usual blowback force then tried to drive the bolt backwards, pulling the sleeve with it and compressing the recoil spring, but the propelling gas, following up the bore after the bullet, escaped through the four ports and impinged against the forward inner end of the sleeve, setting up a pressure which resisted the opening long enough to allow the bullet to get clear of the muzzle and the chamber pressure to drop, after which the blowback force overcame the resistance and the bolt was forced backwards, cocking the hammer and reloading the rifle on its return stroke.

Although the weapon appears to be cheap and shoddy, examination will show that it is well-built where it matters and that there is ample factor of safety. It works remarkably well and would doubtless have proved to be a useful weapon for the purpose envisaged. Its only defect was the probability of fouling between the barrel and the sleeve due to the gas and carbon products, and the possibility of barrel expansion causing the sleeve to jam.

As with many last-minute German designs, the war ended before it could be put into full production. Quite a number were made and several survive today.

VOLKSPISTOLE / Germany

As with the Volksgewehr (above) so with this weapon; it was hurriedly developed in 1944–1945 for arming of the Volkssturm. The designer is not known, nor the firm who made it, but the mechanism is almost identical with that of the Volksgewehr. The slide, around the barrel, encloses an annular space into which gas from the exploding charge is fed through ports just in front of the breech. This gas builds up pressure within the slide to resist the opening action long enough to allow bullet ejection and a drop in chamber pressure to safe levels. Chambered for the 9mm Parabellum cartridge, the magazine was the standard Walther P-38 model. An unusual, and unexplained, feature is the addition of a short smoothbored section to the barrel. It has been suggested that this might have been to sustain chamber pressure slightly longer and thus improve the locking (or delaying) action of the gas pressure system.

It was never put into production, and only one specimen of this pistol is known to exist.

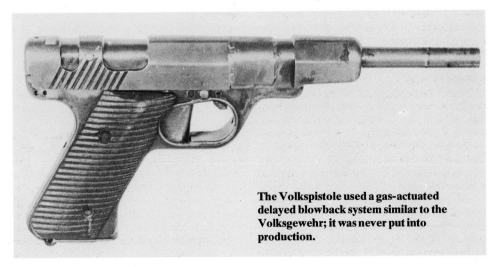

The delayed-blowback Volksgewehr, which used the Sturmgewehr 44 magazine and cartridge.

The Volkspistole used a gas-actuated delayed blowback system similar to the Volksgewehr; it was never put into production.

W

WALTHER / *Germany*

The Waffenfabrik Walther of Zella St. Blasii was founded in 1886 by Carl Walther, and for many years produced a variety of sporting rifles and shotguns. In 1908, assisted by his cousin Friedrich Pickert, a well-known revolver maker, Walther began production of a 6·35mm automatic pistol. This was followed by others and the First World War saw considerable expansion of the factory.

In 1915 Carl Walther died and the business was continued by his three eldest sons, and in post-war years production of small-bore target rifles, target pistols, automatic pistols, hunting rifles and shotguns continued. The company also developed a successful mechanical calculating machine. After the Second World War, the factory fell into Russian hands, and the company transferred its operations to Ulm-am-Donau, building itself up by its calculating machine production and licensing the production of its pistols to the French firm of Manurhin (*qv*). In the late 1950s pistol and sporting arm production was resumed once more, and a submachine gun was developed in the 1960s.

The early Walther pistols were all blowbacks of simple construction and first class quality, but it was not until the advent of their PP Model in 1929 that they really displayed anything outstanding. This introduced the double-action lock to common usage, and it was followed by the PPK model, a smaller version for plain-clothes police. (Fuller details will be found in the entries PP and PPK.) In the early 1930s the Army let it be known that they were looking for a new design to replace the service Parabellum and Walther first put forward a 9mm Parabellum version of the PP; as might be expected this was refused, since no army was willing to chance a blowback pistol in such a heavy calibre. The next attempt was the Model AP (for Armee Pistole), a locked breech weapon using a wedge beneath the barrel to lock slide and barrel together. This incorporated the double action lock of the PP and had the hammer concealed in the frame and under

the slide. While a successful pistol in its performance, the Army were reluctant to approve it since the unseen hammer meant that it was not possible to check whether or not the gun was cocked simply by looking at it. Walther went away and came back with the Model HP (for Heeres Pistole, which also means 'army pistol') in which the hammer had been moved to an external position. This was approved, and became the Pistole 38.

Other notable models include the pre-war Olympic Modell, a long-barrelled ·22 target pistol which gave an excellent performance in the Berlin Olympics, and the post-war OSP (or Olympic Schell-feuer pistole) also in ·22 calibre and also a target arm of the highest standard. One of the company's most recent products is the PP Super pistol. As the name implies, this is an updated Model PP, chambered for the new 9mm Police cartridge, and with the addition of a de-cocking lever on the left side of the frame.

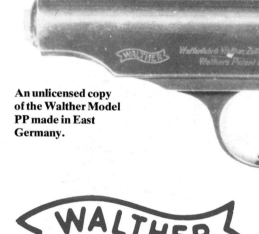

An unlicensed copy of the Walther Model PP made in East Germany.

The Walther Model 1 pistol of 1908.

The Weatherby ·460 Magnum De Luxe sporting rifle, typical of the company's products.

WARNANT / *Belgium*

The brothers L. & J. Warnant of Hognee, Belgium, established themselves in the latter half of the 19th century as jobbing gunsmiths, producing the usual sporting arms. Jean Warnant then began to experiment with revolvers and eventually perfected a double-action lock which was widely adopted by other makers. It appeared in the British Enfield revolver of 1882, but it seems that due to some dubious business deals, Warnant never received much profit from that particular application.

During the period 1870–1890 the Warnant concern produced a number of revolvers, largely based on contemporary Smith & Wesson designs. These had round barrels, folding triggers and automatic ejection and came in most of the usual commercial calibres. In the early 1900s they took to the automatic pistol with a confusion of patents and designs. They had, in 1890, attempted to market a mechanical repeating pistol, the Warnant-Creon, which used a hinged Martini-type breech block and tubular magazine, but this had no more success than any other of that pattern. Their first automatic pistol patent was taken out in 1905 and was then assigned to Pieper (*qv*) who produced it as their pistol for many years. However, the same patent covered the construction of the pistol as a fixed-barrel model instead of using the hinged barrel of the Pieper design, and this was produced by Warnants in 6·35mm for some years without much success.

In 1912 they produced another design, a 7·65mm model largely based on the well-tried Browning 1903 pattern but with the breech block section as a separate component, held in the slide by a heavy cross-bolt. This appears to have been quite a sound design and might well have succeeded, but before production could get under way the war broke out in 1914 and the Warnant pistol vanished during the German occupation of Belgium.

WEATHERBY / *USA*

In the late 1930s Roy Weatherby began questioning the accepted gospel that a heavy bullet was the only way to kill big game, and as early as 1940 he was making his views on small-calibre high velocity bullets known in the press. This caused a certain amount of argument, and Mr. Weatherby decided to prove his point by actually making such cartridges and, if necessary, the weapons to go with them. The cartridges were based on an existing case, that of the ·300 Holland & Holland Magnum; this was a very strong case, with a reinforcing belt around its base, and by reducing the neck diameter of the case Weatherby was able to fit smaller bullets and yet have a large chamber volume in order to contain a powerful charge.

Various calibres of cartridge were made and tried, and in September 1945 Weatherby began making rifles in these calibres for commercial sale. These were based on Mauser bolt actions for the most part, though Weatherby chambered whatever rifles his customers chose to send him, provided they were suitable for the heavy loadings. He eventually expanded his business and used FN-Mauser actions exclusively for several years, but the Mauser action was not entirely suited to some of the longer and more powerful cartridges, and in 1958 he introduced a rifle bolt action of his own design. This is a turnbolt mechanism in which locking is done by nine lugs on the bolt head, giving an immensely strong lock. The chamber is counter-bored, as is the face of the bolt, with the result that the cartridge case is entirely surrounded by steel once the bolt is closed. An unusual feature is that the action can be made in right-handed or left-handed form to suit the individual shooter. These actions are made for Weatherby by J. P. Sauer of Germany and are assembled to their barrels and the rifles completed in the Weatherby factory in South Gate, California.

The Weatherby rifle has, in the last thirty years, come to be accepted as one of the premier big-game rifles and his theories on high velocity and bullet weight have been thoroughly vindicated.

The 9mm Heeres Pistole, forerunner of the service Pistole '38.

The 6·35mm Warnant of 1905.

WEBLEY / *Britain*

James Webley set up in business as a 'percussioner and gun lock maker' in Birmingham, England in the 1830s and was later joined by his brother Philip. By 1853 they were making percussion revolvers. These were followed by rimfire solid-frame revolvers, and in 1867 their first official service contract was acquired for the Royal Irish Constabulary (RIC) model. This was also widely adopted by police and military forces throughout the Empire. It was a short-barrelled heavy-calibre weapon, extremely reliable and robust, and was eventually made available in several variant models and calibres, remaining in production until the end of the century. In 1877 the company, now trading as P. Webley & Son, began production of a hinged-frame self-extracting revolver incorporating the Pryse patents; these covered the rebounding hammer and cylinder lock, and the revolver also incorporated a double-bolted frame lock which kept the revolver securely locked against the power of the heaviest charges. In later years the company entered into working agreements with other firms and this resulted in the Webley-Wilkinson and Webley-Green revolvers.

In 1887 a Webley revolver was adopted as the British service pistol, beginning an association which was to last for many years. This first Mark 1 was a six-shot hinged-frame weapon in ·442 calibre with a 4 inch barrel. As more revolvers were needed, the Army came back to Webley and, since improvements were being constantly made by the company, the design of the military arm went through several changes over the years. The Mark 4 of 1899 introduced the ·455 cartridge and this continued through until the adoption of the Mark 6 in 1915. After the war the army elected to change to the ·38 calibre and adopted a pistol of their own, the Enfield ·38, but during the Second World War the supply of pistols fell short and large numbers of Webley ·38 were purchased, remaining in use until all revolvers were superseded by the Browning automatic in the 1950s.

In addition to service revolvers, of course, the company produced a wide variety of pocket revolvers in hammer and hammerless styles and in ·32 and ·38 calibres from the 1870s onwards.

In the 1890s the automatic pistol appeared on the scene and Webley were offered the Gabbet-Fairfax Mars (*qv*) pistol. After some trial with this they refused to adopt it as their own, and their designer Mr. W. J. Whiting began working on his design. His first experimental model appeared in 1903, chambered for a powerful ·455 rimless cartridge specially developed for it. The aim was to produce a heavy military weapon, and it was some years before the design was perfected. Meanwhile, a blowback automatic in 7·65mm calibre was introduced in 1906, a model which was adopted by the Metropolitan Police in 1911, and following this was to be widely adopted in Britain as a police pistol.

By 1909 the locked-breech design had been perfected and was offered to the Royal Navy. It was also marketed in ·38 ACP chambering and a version in 9mm Browning Long calibre was bought by the South African Police. The Royal Navy adopted the ·455 version in May 1913 and retained it until after the First World War; this model was also used by Royal Horse Artillery and Royal Flying Corps personnel to some extent during 1914–1916. These pistols are heavy and angular, and rely on inclined keys on the side of the breech mating with inclined grooves in the slide; as the slide and barrel recoil, the barrel is permitted to move downward so that the engaged faces come apart and allow the slide to move separately. One unusual feature is that the magazine can be slightly

The ·476 RIC Model of 1880.

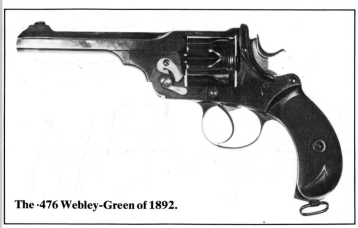

The ·476 Webley-Green of 1892.

A Webley single shot target pistol in ·22 calibre.

The Webley & Scott ·25 Hammerless model of 1909.

withdrawn from the butt and held locked in a special notch; the pistol can then be hand-loaded and fired as a single shot weapon, keeping the full magazine in reserve. When needed, a blow of the hand sends the magazine up into the top position and the pistol then functions as a self-loader once more.

Although the name of the company is primarily associated with revolvers, it must be added that their production of air pistols and rifles has started many youths into a lifetime of shooting, and that their shotguns enjoy a high reputation throughout the world.

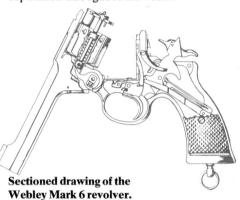

Sectioned drawing of the Webley Mark 6 revolver.

WEBLEY-FOSBERY / *Britain*
The Webley-Fosbery automatic revolver was derived from the invention of Colonel G. V. Fosbery VC (*qv*) as adapted by the Webley & Scott company. Fosbery's original idea was to make a revolver in which the barrel and cylinder were movable units, sliding across the top of the butt frame on recoil and thus cocking the hammer. Since the hammer controlled cylinder revolution, this would automatically rotate the cylinder and thus have the pistol ready for the next shot. The system worked but it was clumsy, and with the aid of Webley's designers, Fosbery next adapted it to the standard Webley revolver and changed the system of operation. He cut grooves in the exterior of the cylinder which engaged with a fixed peg in the pistol frame; as the barrel and cylinder recoiled over the frame, the peg forced the cylinder to revolve one-twelfth of a turn. On the return movement, another one-twelfth of a turn was made, bringing a fresh chamber into alignment with the barrel.

Fosbery took out his final patents in 1896 and in 1900 the Webley-Fosbery revolver was announced. Since most of these weapons were based on the current service Mark IV revolver, they were chambered and regulated for the service ·455 cartridge, but once the pistol was selling, models in ·38 Auto chambering were also made, these having eight-shot cylinders. After Fosbery's death in 1907 the Webley company continued to make small improvements in the design and continued to make and sell the revolver until some time during the First World War.

WELGUN / *Britain*
This submachine gun was developed by BSA Ltd. on instructions from the Special Operations Executive workshop in Welwyn Garden

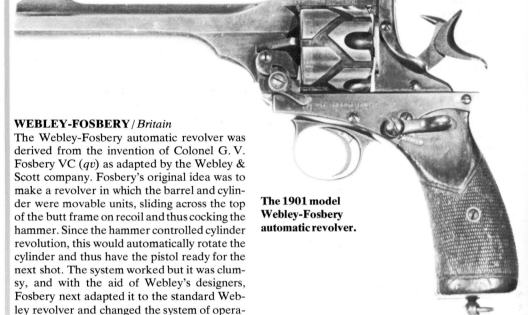

The 1901 model Webley-Fosbery automatic revolver.

City, Hertfordshire, from whence the name was derived. It was intended as a light and compact submachine gun capable of being carried by parachute-dropped secret agents, but it was later put forward as a possible weapon for normal parachute troops. It had some unusual features and in general was a sound and well-thought-out design. The bolt was attached to a recoil spring around the barrel, so that the spring pulled on the bolt rather than, as is usual, pushing it; this reduced the amount of body needed behind the bolt. The gun body was open on both sides and the bolt could be grasped through this gap and pulled back for cocking. A folding steel butt could be hinged to lie across the top of the gun, and the magazine fed from beneath. It was first tested in February 1943 and except for giving trouble under extreme cold conditions, performed well. But in spite of periodic re-tests it was never formally adopted, being considered inferior to other designs which were put forward in 1943–1944. It is not known whether any were made for clandestine operations, but it is extremely doubtful.

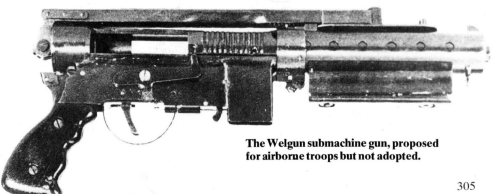

The Welgun submachine gun, proposed for airborne troops but not adopted.

The Welrod silenced pistol.

WELROD / *Britain*

The Welrod pistol is one of those shadowy weapons which were devised in great secrecy during the Second World War for use by clandestine organisations and of which little written record remains. It derives its name, like the Welgun, from being developed at the Special Operations Executive's workshop in Welwyn Garden City. It is simply a blowback automatic pistol but with a large and efficient silencer built on to the barrel. An unusual feature of its construction is that the magazine and butt are one piece, and the whole butt grip is removed in order to re-load the magazine. The silencer relies on the usual arrangement of baffles to reduce the noise of the emerging gases, and the pistol was chambered either for the 7·65mm or 9mm Short cartridges, both of which produced sub-sonic muzzle velocities. As a result, the pistol is almost entirely silent in operation.

WERDER, Johann Ludwig *(1808–1885)*

Werder was apprenticed as a locksmith, and then became a mechanical engineer, inventing and manufacturing every type of mechanism from machine tools to locomotives. In the late 1860s he was operating an arms factory in Nuremberg and came into contact with the Peabody (*qv*) rifle. While he admired the mechanism, he appreciated that an under-lever rifle was not a practical tool for a soldier who spent much of his shooting time lying on the ground. He therefore redesigned the mechanism so that the falling block was unlocked and dropped by a finger-operated lever inside the trigger guard, and then closed and locked by a thumb-operated lever which also cocked the internal hammer. This was adopted by the Bavarian Army in 1869, and a pistol, using the same mechanism was adopted shortly afterwards. From the speed of operation of these weapons, they received the nickname 'Bavarian Lightning guns'.

WERNDL, Josef *(1831–1889)*

Josef Werndl came from a family of gunsmiths and travelled widely after serving his apprenticeship, even as far as the USA where he worked for Colt and Remington. In 1853 he returned to Steyr to take over the family business there and, together with a gunsmith named Holub, began working on a design of

WINCHESTER / *USA*

Oliver F. Winchester (1810–1880) began his working life at the age of seven, on a farm. At the age of 14 he was apprenticed to a carpenter and at 20 became a master builder. In 1833 he went to work in a store selling drygoods and haberdashery, and in 1847 he patented an improved method of manufacturing men's dress shirts. In 1849, in partnership with one John M. Davies, he went into the shirt-making business and became a moderately rich man. Looking around for business investments, he chanced upon the Volcanic Arms Company and in 1855 purchased some stock in this company.

But the Volcanic (*qv*) rifle was not a commercial success, and in 1857 the company failed. Winchester, though, was convinced that the Volcanic design was capable of improvement, and for just over $39,000 he purchased the entire stock and assets. He then set up the New Haven Arms Company and hired Tyler Henry (*qv*) to re-design the Volcanic rifle. While this was being done, the Volcanic rifles and pistol were still made and sold, though only in sufficient numbers to keep the company functioning. Henry, meanwhile, developed a ·44 rimfire cartridge and then modified the rifle mechanism to suit, producing the result in 1860 as the Henry rifle.

The start of the American Civil War in 1861 appeared to present a golden opportunity for the Henry rifle, but to Winchester's dismay, the Union Army were not disposed to accept the idea of a repeating rifle of this degree of complexity. They already had the Spencer and saw no need to adopt another. As a result, military orders were extremely small, but this was compensated for by large purchases on the civil market by people living in areas liable to

suffer from the activities of raiders, and also by members of various State Militia regiments who preferred to arm themselves with the Henry rather than the government-issue muskets.

In the years after the Civil War, when many arms companies collapsed, Winchester actively promoted the rifle overseas and thus managed to build up his business; one notable purchase was by the Turkish government, who later used the rifles to good effect against the Russians at Plevna and, in so doing, provided Winchester with valuable publicity. In 1866 the company was re-organised as the Winchester Repeating Arms Company and a new rifle appeared, the Winchester Model 1866. This used much the same mechanism as the Henry but was improved by the adoption of King's magazine-loading feature, in which the cartridges were pushed into the rear of the magazine through a trap in the side of the action body, instead of being dropped into the front of the magazine tube. In 1873 came the Winchester 73, which introduced centre-fire ammunition in the lever-action Winchester rifle for the first time.

From that time onward the company has continued to promote the lever-action rifle, adding other weapons to its range from time to time. Lever-action and pump-action shotguns, bolt action rifles, automatic shotguns and automatic rifles have appeared. In the 1870s the company employed Hugo Borchardt (*qv*) for some years, and he developed some excellent revolver designs, but no orders were forthcoming from military sources and, according to legend, the idea of producing a revolver was dropped as a result of a 'gentleman's agreement' with Colt (*qv*), that Winchester would stay out of the revolver business if Colt left rifles alone.

military rifle. In 1863 he again visited the USA to study production methods, and upon returning he set up the Steyr (*qv*) arms factory to manufacture the Werndl rifle.

The Werndl rifle was a single-shot weapon which used an unusual form of breech closure. The breech block consisted of a solid cylinder of metal mounted with its axis parallel with the axis of the barrel and slightly below. A groove was cut along one side of this cylinder, and it was mounted so that it could be rotated through about 100°. A handle controlled the rotation. To load, the block was swung clockwise until the groove was lined up with the chamber, whereupon a cartridge could be loaded. The block was then swung in the opposite direction, bringing the mass of the block behind the cartridge and forming a very solid closure. In the block was a firing pin which, when the block was closed, aligned with an external hammer. A cartridge extractor was

fitted, which levered the case out by means of mechanical connection with the breech block. The Werndl system could be made new, or it could be applied to existing muzzle-loaders as a conversion. Either way, it was a strong and efficient system, and it is highly probable that it served as an inspiration to Nordenfelt, who later devised an artillery breechblock working on similar lines.

WHITE, Rollin *(1817–1892)*

Rollin White was an inventor who had worked for Colt. He was also given to taking out patents and including in a patent every conceivable aspect of employment or utility which could be claimed. In 1855 he took out a patent broadly entitled 'Repeating Firearms' which primarily encompassed a highly improbable design of repeating pistol, but in spreading his net as widely as possible, he claimed novelty in

The US Army's ·30 M1 Carbine, developed by Winchester.

WINCHESTER Western ®

Another famous name allied with Winchester was that of John M. Browning (*qv*) who, from 1883 to 1900, sold almost all his patents to Winchester. It is noteworthy that Winchester would never enter into a royalty deal with any inventor, but would purchase a patent outright for cash or, as was often the case with Browning, in goods which Browning and his brothers could then sell in their store. But in 1900 Browning developed an automatic shotgun and, doubtless considering that by that time he was sufficiently well-known in the firearms world to command his own terms, demanded a royalty. Winchester refused to alter their policy, and Browning parted company with them, taking his shotgun to Fabrique National of Liège. The company's history relates that the Winchester factory had assisted Browning to draw up his patent specification, and they had done such a good job that it took the Winchester engineers ten years before they could develop a shotgun which evaded the Browning patent.

During the First World War the company was involved in manufacturing Enfield rifles for the British and US governments. After the war it diversified into hardware, electric torches, refrigerators and innumerable other fields in order to keep the war-expanded plant occupied; among other things, it made radiators for Rolls-Royce. But this venture was not a success, and, with the depression years adding to their problems, the company went into receivership in 1931. It was bought out by the Western Cartridge Company and reorganized once again, this time with the intention of keeping to the manufacture of guns and ammunition. The company's fortunes gradually improved during the 1930s, continuing to the present day.

During the Second World War the company put forward a gas-operated military automatic rifle using a short-stroke piston arrangement invented by David Williams, one of their designers. Although favourably tested by the US Marines and by the British Army (whose report read 'with slight modifications this rifle would be suitable for adoption in the British service') it was not followed up, largely because the Americans were committed to the Garand and the British were reluctant to try a completely new rifle during wartime.

Nevertheless, the basic principle of the weapon was used when the US Army demanded a short carbine for arming supply troops, and this became the US Carbine ·30 M1, which is still in wide use throughout the world and which has been widely copied in other countries.

Mechanisms of the Winchester Model 1873 (top) and 1894 (bottom) lever-action rifles.

boring chambers in a revolver from end to end of the cylinder. Amazingly, there was no previous claim to this, and White obtained his patent. He offered it to Colt, but Colt, usually astute, missed the significant point, saw only the impractical pistol, and refused it. When Smith & Wesson began developing their rimfire revolver, they discovered the existence of White's patent, and very quickly secured sole rights to it. They did so on extremely advantageous terms; White was to receive a royalty on every revolver made, but he was to bear the expense of any litigation necessary to protect the patent. Since would-be pirates were thick on the ground, much of White's royalties were swallowed up in the lawsuits, and he came out of it a good deal worse than might have been expected. He patented various other firearms devices, none of any practical worth, and then got out of firearms entirely to patent a sewing machine which made him a sizeable fortune.

ZEHNA / *Germany*

This 6·35mm blowback automatic pistol was produced by Emil Zehner of Suhl in 1921–1927. The only interesting feature about it was the method of assembly, in which the backstrap of the butt is a removable unit and can be removed complete with the mainspring and sear. It is frequently alleged to be the same pistol as the Haenel/Schmeisser, but though the two have a similar external appearance, their construction is quite different.

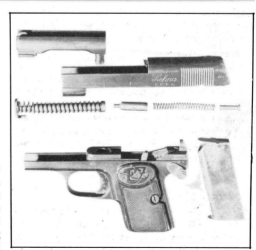

The Zehna automatic pistol, demonstrating the method of attaching the barrel by a longitudinal pin.

MAJOR WEAPONS FROM 1830 TO THE PRESENT DAY

REVOLVERS

Name	Calibre	Shots	Barrel length mm	Weight gms	Date of Introduction	Country
ABADIE	9·1mm	6	113	750	1878	Portugal
ADAMS	·45	6	152	985	1872	UK
ARMINIUS (Pickert) No. 1	·22	7	50	225	1920	Germany
ARMINIUS (Pickert) No. 7	·32	5	60	480	1920	Germany
ARMINIUS (Weirauch) HW3	·22	8	70	680	1960	Germany
ARMINIUS (Weirauch) HW5	·32	6	100	900	1960	Germany
ASTRA 357	·357	6	102	1100	1970	Spain
ASTRA CADIX Model 384	·38	5	102	680	1958	Spain
BODEO	10·4mm	6	160	755	1889	Italy
CHARTER ARMS Bulldog	·44	5	76	540	1970	USA
CHARTER ARMS Pathfinder	·22	5	76	524	1967	USA
CHICAGO PROTECTOR	8mm	7	30	255	1892	USA
COLT: Paterson	·34	5	140	1250	1836	USA
COLT Walker	·44	6	228	2040	1847	USA
COLT Navy	·36	6	190	1135	1861	USA
COLT Single Action Army	·45	6	190	1140	1873	USA
COLT Bisley	·45	6	140	1135	1894	USA
COLT Cloverleaf	·41	4	100	410	1871	USA
COLT New Line Pocket	·22	7	57	200	1873	USA
COLT Lightning	·38	6	115	650	1877	USA
COLT Navy	·38	6	152	685	1889	USA
COLT New Army	·38	6	115	995	1892	USA
COLT New Service	·45	6	140	1190	1898	USA
COLT Police Positive	·32	6	89	525	1907	USA
COLT Banker's Special	·38	6	51	400	1928	USA
COLT Cobra	·38	6	101	1035	1950	USA
COLT Trooper Mark III	·38	6	101	1020	1969	USA
DARDICK	·38	11	76	700	1955	USA
DECKER	6·35mm	5	50	255	1912	Germany
DIMANCEA	·45	5	140	920	1886	UK
ENFIELD	·476	6	150	1150	1880	UK
ENFIELD	·38	6	127	800	1932	UK
FAGNUS	·45	6	143	1025	1875	Belgium
FOREHAND & WADSWORTH Perfection	·32	5	76	470	1880	USA
FOREHAND & WADSWORTH Russian	·44	6	190	997	1880	USA
GALAND	9mm	6	95	1100	1874	Belgium
GARATE, ANITUA	·45	6	130	680	1914	Spain
GASSER Montenegrin	11·3mm	6	225	1450	1870	Austria
GASSER-KROPATSCHEK	9mm	6	115	770	1876	Austria
GRAND	·357	6	102	980	1957	Czechoslovakia
HÄMMERLI Virginian	·357	6	140	1135	1970	Swiss
HARRINGTON & RICHARDSON Defender	·38	5	101	878	1950	USA
HARRINGTON & RICHARDSON Young America	·22	5	114	300	1892	USA
HARRINGTON & RICHARDSON Sidekick	·22	9	101	793	1955	USA
HARRINGTON & RICHARDSON Premier	·32	6	101	340	1900	USA
HIGH STANDARD Sentinel	·357	6	102	1075	1960	USA
HIGH STANDARD Double Nine	·22	9	140	905	1968	USA
HIGH STANDARD Sharpshooter	·22	10	140	1190	1970	USA
HOPKINS & ALLEN XL No. 2	·22	5	60	315	1872	USA
HOPKINS & ALLEN D.A. No. 6	·32	5	100	430	1880	USA
HOPKINS & ALLEN Safety Police	·32	6	76	400	1907	USA
IVER JOHNSON Sealed Eight	·22	8	152	680	1922	USA
IVER JOHNSON Trailsman	·22	8	152	950	1955	USA
IVER JOHNSON Sidewinder	·22	8	152	880	1955	USA
JAPANESE Model 26	9mm	6	120	880	1893	Japan
KYNOCH	·45	6	152	1375	1886	UK
LANDSTADT	7·5mm	7	115	1020	1900	Norway
LEFAUCHEAUX	11mm	6	152	1400	1871	Sweden
LE NOVO	6·35mm	5	30	345	1907	France
LIBERTY CHIEF	·38	6	64	500	1976	Japan
LLAMA Model 26	·38	6	102	935	1959	Spain
MARLIN XXX	·30	5	76	335	1875	USA
MAUSER Zig Zag	9mm	6	136	750	1878	Germany
MERWIN, HULBERT	·44	6	100	1060	1877	USA
MINI-REVOLVER	·22	5	25	285	1974	USA
MODELE D'ORDONNANCE	8mm	6	114	840	1892	France
NEW NAMBU	·38	5	76	680	1975	Japan
RAST & GASSER	8mm	8	116	980	1898	Austria
REICHSREVOLVER, Officer's	10·6mm	6	126	920	1883	Germany
REICHSREVOLVER, Trooper's	10·6mm	6	183	1030	1879	Germany
REMINGTON New Line	·38	5	62	445	1873	USA
REMINGTON Army	·44	6	140	1160	1874	USA
ROHM RG-10	·22	6	60	325	1955	Germany
ROHM RG-38	·38	6	100	965	1960	Germany
ROSSI	·38	6	76	625	1974	Brazil
RUBY EXTRA	·38	6	125	820	1970	Spain
RUGER Single Six	·22	6	165	978	1953	USA
RUGER Blackhawk	·44	6	190	1360	1955	USA
RUGER Security Six	·357	6	102	950	1968	USA
SMITH & WESSON American	·44	6	203	1160	1870	USA
SMITH & WESSON SA Frontier	·44	6	165	1130	1885	USA
SMITH & WESSON Hand Ejector	·32	5	82	510	1903	USA
SMITH & WESSON Military & Police	·38	6	101	865	1899	USA
SMITH & WESSON Russian	·44	6	165	1135	1870	USA
SMITH & WESSON Service M1917	·45	6	140	1020	1917	USA
SMITH & WESSON New Century	·455	6	165	1075	1915	USA*
SMITH & WESSON 357 Magnum	·357	6	152	1245	1935	USA
SMITH & WESSON New Departure	·38	5	82	510	1887	USA
THOMAS	·38	5	126	700	1870	UK
TRANTER	·45	6	146	1077	1878	UK
VELO DOG	5·5mm	5	47	295	1895	France
WARNANT	·38	6	150	645	1880	Belgium
WEBLEY Army Express	·45	6	152	965	1878	UK
WEBLEY Bulldog	·442	5	64	454	1878	UK
WEBLEY RIC	·45	6	82	645	1872	UK
WEBLEY Mark IV Pocket	·32	6	76	625	1929	UK
WEBLEY Police & Civilian	·38	6	101	545	1896	UK
WEBLEY Service Mk I	·442	6	101	985	1887	UK
WEBLEY Service Mk VI	·445	6	152	1075	1915	UK
WEBLEY Tower Bulldog	·45	5	61	500	1885	UK
WEBLEY-FOSBERY	·455	6	152	1155	1901	UK
WEBLEY-GREEN	·455	6	190	1185	1892	UK
WEBLEY-WILKINSON	·45	6	165	1090	1880	UK

AUTOMATIC PISTOLS

Name	Calibre	Shots	Barrel length mm	Weight gm	Year	Country
ADLER	8mm	8	86	680	1905	Germany
ASTRA 400	9mm	8	150	1150	1921	Spain
ASTRA 600	9mm	8	134	910	1944	Spain
ASTRA 900	7·63mm	10	145	1400	1933	Spain
ASTRA 3000	7·65mm	7	100	620	1954	Spain
AUTO MAG	·44	8	165	1665	1970	USA
BALLESTER MOLINA	·45	7	150	1140	1940	Argentina
BAYARD	7·65mm	6	57	470	1910	Belgium
BAYARD	9mm	6	85	520	1923	Belgium
BEHOLLA	7·65mm	7	74	640	1915	Germany
BERETTA 1915	7·65mm	7	85	570	1915	Italy
BERETTA 1934	9mm	7	95	690	1934	Italy
BERETTA 948	·22	8	47	480	1948	Italy
BERETTA 951 Brigadier	9mm	8	115	890	1955	Italy
BERETTA M81	7·65mm	13	97	680	1977	Italy
BERETTA M92	9mm	15	125	965	1977	Italy
BERGMANN No. 3	6·5mm	5	112	750	1894	Germany
BERGMANN-BAYARD	9mm	10	100	1020	1910	Belgium
BERNADELLI Model 60	7·65mm	8	90	670	1959	Italy
BORCHARDT	7·65mm	8	165	1160	1893	Germany
BRIGADIER	·45	8	140	1925	1950	Canada
BROWNING 1900	7·65mm	7	100	650	1901	Belgium
BROWNING 1903	9mm	7	127	910	1903	Belgium
BROWNING 1906	6·35mm	6	54	375	1906	Belgium
BROWNING BABY	6·35mm	6	54	285	1922	Belgium
BROWNING 1910	7·65mm	7	90	610	1910	Belgium
BROWNING 1922	7·65mm	9	115	730	1922	Belgium
BROWNING GP35	9mm	13	118	990	1935	Belgium
BROWNING NOMAD	·22	10	171	1050	1958	Belgium
CAMPO GIRO	9mm	7	165	950	1913	Spain
CHAROLA y ANITUA	5mm	6	104	570	1897	Spain
CLEMENT	6·35mm	6	50	350	1907	Belgium
COLT Pocket Hammerless	·32	8	100	650	1903	USA
COLT Military	·38	6	152	1050	1902	USA
COLT Hammerless	·380	7	96	650	1908	USA
COLT Junior	·25	6	50	370	1960	USA
COLT Service	·45	7	127	1105	1911	USA
COLT Super 38	·38	9	127	1110	1929	USA
COLT Commander	·45	7	108	935	1950	USA
COLT Woodsman	·22	10	115	737	1915	USA
CZ24	9mm	8	90	680	1924	Czechoslovakia
CZ27	7·65mm	8	97	710	1927	Czechoslovakia
CZ38	9mm	8	118	940	1938	Czechoslovakia
CZ45	6·35mm	7	64	425	1945	Czechoslovakia
CZ52	7·62mm	8	120	850	1952	Czechoslovakia
DOMINO OP601	·22	5	142	1150	1975	Italy
DREYSE	7·65mm	7	93	710	1907	Germany
DREYSE	9mm	8	126	1050	1913	Germany
DUO	6·35mm	6	54	425	1926	Czechoslovakia
DWM	7·65mm	7	88	570	1920	Germany
ECHASA	7·65mm	7	81	680	1952	Spain
ERIKA	4·25mm	6	42	255	1913	Austria
ERMA Olympia	·22	10	200	1100	1937	Germany
ERMA KGP-68	7·65mm	9	89	638	1968	Germany
FAST Model 761	7·65mm	8	80	710	1955	Spain
FIEL	6·35mm	5	40	375	1919	Spain
FRANCOTTE	6·35mm	6	55	410	1912	Belgium
FROMMER Baby	7·65mm	5	55	498	1912	Hungary
FROMMER Stop	7·65mm	7	100	610	1919	Hungary
FROMMER Lilliput	6·35mm	6	55	300	1921	Hungary
FROMMER M29	9mm	7	100	750	1929	Hungary
FROMMER M37	7·65mm	7	110	770	1937	Hungary
GALESI Model 9	7·65mm	7	85	700	1950	Italy
GARATE	7·65mm	9	80	620	1914	Spain
GAVAGE	7·65mm	7	75	600	1936	Belgium
GLISENTI	9mm	7	103	850	1910	Italy
HAENEL (Schmeisser)	6.35mm	6	63	380	1921	Germany
HÄMMERLI Model 208	·22	8	125	750	1965	Switzerland
HARRINGTON & RICHARDSON	7·65mm	8	85	565	1912	USA
HECKLER & KOCH HK4	9mm	7	85	485	1958	Germany
HECKLER & KOCH P9	9mm	9	102	880	1970	Germany
HECKLER & KOCH VP70	9mm	18	116	823	1972	Germany
HIGH STANDARD Supermatic	·22	10	171	1088	1951	USA
HIGH STANDARD Sports King	·22	9	115	1105	1950	USA
HIGH STANDARD Victor	·22	10	115	1360	1970	USA
JÄGER	7·65mm	7	79	440	1915	Germany
JAPANESE Model 94	8mm	6	96	820	1934	Japan
JIEFFECO	7·65mm	8	90	650	1911	Belgium
KIMBALL	·30	7	127	1133	1957	USA
KIRRIKALE	7·65mm	7	95	700	1951	Turkey
KOLIBRI	3mm	6	30	220	1914	Austria
KOMMER Model 4	7·65mm	7	76	570	1940	Germany
LAHTI Model 35	9mm	8	107	1220	1935	Finland
LANGENHAN Army	7·65mm	8	105	670	1917	Germany
LE FRANCAIS Pocket	6·35mm	7	60	300	1913	France
LE FRANCAIS Military	9mm	8	127	1080	1928	France
LIGNOSE Einhand Nr. 2A	6·35mm	6	55	410	1922	Germany
LITTLE TOM	7·65mm	8	90	585	1914	Austria
LLAMA Model 3	9mm	7	92	550	1936	Spain
LLAMA Model 11	9mm	8	127	1075	1936	Spain
LLAMA Model 18	6·35mm	6	58	395	1958	Spain
MAB Modele A	6·35mm	6	53	368	1921	France
MAB Modele D	7·65mm	9	100	710	1933	France
MAB Modele PA-15	9mm	15	152	1100	1968	France
MAKAROV	9mm	8	91	675	1960	USSR
MANNLICHER Model 1901	7·65mm	8	160	910	1901	Austria
MANNLICHER Model 1903	7·65mm	6	115	1020	1903	Austria
MARS	9mm	10	222	1475	1901	UK
MARS	·45	8	241	1415	1901	UK
MAS 35	7·65mm	8	105	790	1935	France
MAS 50	9mm	9	112	860	1950	France
MAUSER Military	7·63mm	10	140	1250	1912	Germany
MAUSER 1910	7·65mm	9	87	595	1910	Germany

TECHNICAL SPECIFICATIONS

Name	Calibre	Shots	Barrel length mm	Weight gm	Year	Country
MAUSER 1934	7·65mm	8	87	600	1934	Germany
MAUSER WTP-2	6·35mm	6	55	300	1938	Germany
MAUSER HSc	7·65mm	8	86	600	1940	Germany
NAMBU Baby	7mm	7	84	650	1930	Japan
NAMBU 4th Year	8mm	8	120	900	1915	Japan
NEW NAMBU	7·65mm	8	90	595	1957	Japan
OBREGON	·45	7	127	1140	1940	Mexico
ORTGIES	7·65mm	8	87	650	1920	Germany
ORTGIES	9mm	7	100	850	1922	Germany
PARABELLUM Swiss	7·65mm	8	100	840	1900	Germany
PARABELLUM Marine	9mm	8	150	1000	1904	Germany
PARABELLUM Pistole 08	9mm	8	102	850	1908	Germany
PARABELLUM Long 08	9mm	32	200	1060	1913	Germany
PARABELLUM Mauser	7·65mm	8	150	910	1972	Germany
PIEPER	6·35mm	6	51	312	1909	Belgium
PIEPER	7·65mm	6	73	570	1909	Belgium
RADOM	9mm	8	115	1050	1935	Poland
REMINGTON Model 51	7·65mm	8	89	600	1919	USA
ROTH-SAUER	7·65mm	7	100	655	1905	Germany
ROTH-STEYR	8mm	10	131	1030	1907	Austria
RUBY	7·65mm	9	85	670	1914	Spain
RUGER Standard	·22	9	120	1020	1949	USA
SAUER WTM	6·35mm	6	50	300	1928	Germany
SAUER Old Model	7·65mm	7	75	570	1913	Germany
SAUER Behorden Model	7·65mm	7	77	620	1930	Germany
SAUER Model 38H	7·65mm	8	83	720	1938	Germany
SAVAGE	9mm	10	96	570	1915	USA
SCHONBERGER	8mm	6	127	895	1892	Austria
SCHOUBOE	11·35mm	6	130	890	1905	Denmark
SCHWARZLOSE	7·63mm	7	163	940	1896	Austria
SIG P-210	9mm	8	120	960	1948	Switzerland
SIG-SAUER P-220	9mm	9	112	750	1976	Germany
SIG-SAUER P-230	9mm	7	92	535	1976	Germany
SIG-HÄMMERLI P-240	·38	5	150	1170	1976	Switzerland
SMITH & WESSON	·35	7	89	625	1913	USA
SMITH & WESSON Model 39	9mm	8	101	750	1954	USA
SMITH & WESSON Model 41	·22	10	187	1235	1951	USA
SMITH & WESSON Model 52	·38	5	127	1165	1954	USA
STAR Model 1914	7·65mm	8	112	850	1914	Spain
STAR Model B	9mm	9	122	1085	1928	Spain
STAR Model PD	·45	6	95	680	1975	Spain
STECHKIN	9mm	20	127	1030	1960	USSR
STEYR	7·65mm	7	92	630	1909	Austria
STEYR	9mm	8	129	1020	1911	Austria
STEYR-DAIMLER-PUCH Pi18	9mm	18	140	950	1974	Austria
TOKAGYPT	9mm	7	115	910	1958	Hungary
TOKAREV	7·62mm	8	116	840	1930	USSR
UNIQUE Model 10	6·35mm	6	53	370	1923	France
UNIQUE Model 17	7·65mm	9	85	785	1925	France
UNIQUE Model Bcf-66	7·65mm	8	100	680	1966	France
UNIQUE Model Rr-51	7·65mm	9	80	735	1951	France
VOLKSPISTOLE	9mm	8	130	960	1945	Germany
WALTHER Model 1	6·35mm	6	52	370	1908	Germany
WALTHER Model 8	6·35mm	8	72	370	1921	Germany
WALTHER Model PP	7·65mm	8	85	710	1929	Germany
WALTHER Model PPK	7·65mm	7	80	580	1930	Germany
WALTHER Model Pistole 38	9mm	8	127	840	1937	Germany
WALTHER Model TPH	6·35mm	6	71	325	1971	Germany
WALTHER Model GSP	·22	5	115	1270	1968	Germany
WEBLEY & SCOTT	·455	7	127	1105	1913	UK
WEBLEY & SCOTT	6·35mm	6	54	290	1906	UK
WEBLEY & SCOTT	7·65mm	8	90	575	1906	UK
WELROD	7·65mm	6	110		1943	UK
ZEHNA	6·35mm	6	60	375	1910	Germany

MILITARY MAGAZINE RIFLES

Name	Calibre	Magazine capacity	Length overall mm	Weight Kg	Country
ARISAKA 30th Year	6·5mm	5	1275	3·85	Japan
ARISAKA 38th Year	6·5mm	5	1275	4·31	Japan
ARISAKA 38th Year Carbine	6·5mm	5	978	4·01	Japan
ARISAKA Type 99	7·7mm	5	1143	4·19	Japan
BERTHIER 1890 Carbine	8mm	3	945	3·02	France
BERTHIER 1892 Mousqueton	8mm	3	937	3·06	France
BERTHIER 1907/15 Rifle	8mm	3	1303	3·79	France
ENFIELD Pattern 1917	·30	5	1175	4·36	USA
KRAG-JORGENSEN 1889	8mm	5	1330	4·42	Denmark
KRAG-JORGENSEN 1894	6·5mm	5	1270	4·05	Norway
KRAG-JORGENSEN 1892	·30	5	1248	4·24	USA
LEBEL 1886	8mm	8	1295	4·28	France
LEBEL 1935	8mm	3	944	3·10	France
LEE Navy	6mm	5	1194	3·63	USA
LEE-METFORD Rifle Mk I	·303	8	1257	4·37	UK
LEE-METFORD Carbine Mk I	·303	10	1014	3·42	UK
LEE-ENFIELD Rifle Mk 1	·303	10	1257	4·19	UK
LEE-ENFIELD Short Rifle Mk 3	·303	10	1132	3·71	UK
LEE-ENFIELD Rifle No. 4	·303	10	1128	4·17	UK
LEE-ENFIELD Rifle No. 5	·303	10	1000	3·24	UK
MAS 1936	7·5mm	5	1020	3·78	France
MANNLICHER 1886	11mm	5	1320	4·53	Austria
MANNLICHER 1895	8mm	5	1270	3·78	Austria
MANNLICHER 1893	6·5mm	5	1232	4·00	Romania
MANNLICHER 1895	6·5mm	5	1295	4·39	Netherlands
MANNLICHER 1935	8mm	5	1110	4·04	Hungary
MANNLICHER-CARCANO 1891	6·5mm	6	1290	3·80	Italy
MANNLICHER-SCHOENAUER 1903	6·5mm	5	1225	3·78	Greece
MAUSER 1884	11mm	8	1295	4·60	Germany
MAUSER 1887	9·5mm	8	1250	4·22	Turkey
MAUSER 1889	7·65mm	5	1295	4·01	Belgium
MAUSER 1890	7·65mm	5	1235	4·11	Turkey
MAUSER 1893	7mm	5	1235	4·28	Spain
MAUSER 1895 Carbine	7mm	5	940	3·27	Spain

Name	Calibre	Magazine capacity	Length overall mm	Weight Kg	Country
MAUSER 1896	6·5mm	5	1255	3·97	Sweden
MAUSER Gewehr 98	7·92mm	5	1255	4·14	Germany
MAUSER Karabiner 98k	7·92mm	5	1110	3·90	Germany
MOSIN-NAGANT 1891	7·62mm	5	1304	4·43	Russia
MOSIN-NAGANT 1910 Carbine	7·62mm	5	1016	3·40	Russia
MOSIN-NAGANT 1938 Carbine	7·62mm	5	1016	3·54	Russia
REICHS COMMISSION 1888	7·92mm	5	1240	3·82	Germany
ROSS Mark 3B (1915)	·303	5	1285	4·48	Canada
SCHMIDT-RUBIN 1889	7·5mm	12	1302	4·44	Switzerland
SCHMIDT-RUBIN 1911	7·5mm	6	1312	4·59	Switzerland
SCHMIDT-RUBIN 1931	7·5mm	6	1105	4·01	Switzerland
SPRINGFIELD 1903	·30	5	1097	3·94	USA

AUTOMATIC RIFLES

Name	Calibre	Magazine capacity	Length overall mm	Weight Kg	Rate of fire	Country
ARMALITE AR15	5·56mm	30	990	2·86	800	USA
ARMALITE AR18	5·56mm	20	965	3·04	750	USA
BERETTA BM59	7·62mm	20	1095	4·40	800	Italy
BROWNING 'BAR' M1918	·30	20	1219	7·28	500	USA
CAL	5·56mm	20	978	2·94	850	Belgium
CETME	7·62mm	20	1015	4·50	600	Spain
CZECH VZ/58	7·62mm	30	820	3·82	800	Czechoslovakia
DRAGUNOV	7·62mm	10	1225	4·31	SS	USSR
ENFIELD EM2	7mm	20	889	3·41	SS	UK
ENFIELD 4·85	4·85mm	20	770	3·89	SS	UK
FAL	7·62mm	20	1053	4·31	SS	Belgium
FG42	7·92mm	20	940	4·50	750	Germany
FABRIQUE NATIONAL M1949	7·65mm	10	1116	4·31	SS	Belgium
GALIL	5·56mm	35	970	3·90	650	Israel
GARAND	·30	8	1103	4·37	SS	USA
HECKLER & KOCH G-3	7·62mm	20	1016	4·25	550	Germany
HECKLER & KOCH HK33	5·56mm	30	920	3·50	600	Germany
HARRINGTON & RICHARDSON Model 60	·45	12	1022	3·35	SS	USA
HIGH STANDARD Sport King	·22	12	978	2·49	SS	USA
KALASHNIKOV AK-47	7·62mm	30	880	4·30	600	USSR
LJUNGMAN AK-42	6·5mm	10	1215	4·74	SS	Sweden
MAS M1949	7·5mm	10	1105	4·54	SS	France
MAS M1977	5·56mm	25	757	3·70	950	France
MOSSBERG 351C	·22	15	978	2·49	SS	USA
MONDRAGON	7mm	8	1105	4·18	SS	Mexico
MARLIN 49	·22	14	1028	2·95	SS	USA
REMINGTON 81	·35	5	1040	3·74	SS	USA
RUGER MINI-14	5·56mm	5	946	2·89	SS	USA
SIMONOV SKS-46	7·62mm	10	1022	3·86	SS	USSR
STURMGEWEHR 44	7·92mm	30	940	5·10	500	Germany
SIG AK-53	7·5mm	30	1000	4·90	300	Switzerland
SIG 530	5·56mm	30	940	3·45	600	Switzerland
TOKAREV SVT-38	7·62mm	10	1222	3·95	SS	USSR
US Carbine M1	·30	15	905	2·48	SS	USA
WINCHESTER Model 1907	·351	10	1065	3·72	SS	USA

NOTE: 'SS' in Rate of Fire column indicates single shot capability only, no automatic fire.

SUBMACHINE GUNS

Name	Calibre	Magazine capacity	Length with butt unfolded	Weight	Rate of Fire	Country
ATMED	·45	30	876	4·31	550	USA
AUSTEN Mark 1	9mm	28	845	3·96	500	Australia
BERETTA M1918	9mm	25	850	3.27	900	Italy
BERETTA 38/42	9mm	40	800	3.26	550	Italy
BERETTA Model 12	9mm	40	645	2·99	550	Italy
BERGMANN MP18	9mm	32	815	4·17	500	Germany
BSA M1949	9mm	32	698	2·54	700	UK
CARL GUSTAV M45	9mm	36	808	4·20	600	Sweden
COLT COMMANDO	5·56mm	20	796	2·72	750	USA
CZ23	9mm	40	686	3·08	600	Czechoslovakia
ERMA EMP	9mm	32	950	4·17	500	Germany
ERMA MP38	9mm	32	835	4·08	500	Germany
FURRER MP41	9mm	40	775	5·22	900	Switzerland
HECKLER & KOCH MP5	9mm	30	660	2·54	650	Germany
HUNGARIAN M39	9mm	40	1047	3·72	750	Hungary
HYDE Model 35	·45	20	890	4·31	725	USA
INGRAM Model 10	9mm	32	548	2·61	900	USA
JAPANESE Type 100	8mm	30	865	3·41	450	Japan
MAUSER M57	9mm	32	610	3·18	800	Germany
OVP	9mm	25	900	3·63	900	Italy
OWEN Mk 1	9mm	33	813	4·24	700	Australia
REISING Model 50	·45	12	908	3·06	550	USA
REXIM Favor	9mm	32	870	3·81	600	Switzerland
RUSSIAN PPD-40	7·62mm	71	788	3·63	800	USSR
RUSSIAN PPSh-41	7·62mm	71	840	3·63	900	USSR
RUSSIAN PPS-42	7·62mm	35	907	2·95	700	USSR
SIG MP41	9mm	40	798	4·35	850	Switzerland
SIG MKMO	9mm	40	1022	4·45	900	Switzerland
SIG MP310	9mm	40	735	3·18	900	Switzerland
SKORPION VZ/61	7·65mm	20	510	1·54	850	Czechoslovakia
STEN Mark 2	9mm	32	762	3·01	450	UK
STEN Mark 5	9mm	32	762	3·54	475	UK
STERLING L2A4	9mm	34	711	2·72	600	UK
STEYR-SOLOTHURN	9mm	32	850	3·90	500	Austria
SUOMI M1931	9mm	50	870	4·67	900	Finland
THOMPSON M1928	·45	50	857	4·88	675	USA
UNITED DEFENSE M42	9mm	20	818	4·14	700	USA
US Service M3	·45	30	757	3·70	400	USA
UZI	9mm	32	635	3·46	600	Israel
VIGNERON	9mm	32	885	3·29	600	Belgium
VILAR PEROSA	9mm	2×25	535	6·48	2400	Italy
WALTHER MPK	9mm	32	660	2·86	550	Germany

MACHINE GUNS

NOTE THE FOLLOWING ABBREVIATIONS
Feed: B = Belt; the number indicates the number of rounds in the belt; where no number is given, the belt may be of any convenient length.
BX = Box magazine. D = Drum magazine. S = Strip feed. H = Hopper feed.
Cooling: A = Air cooled. W = Water cooled.
Operation: R = Recoil operated. G = Gas operated. B = Blowback or delayed blowback operation.
Weight: weight given is weight of gun, without tripod or other mountings, cooling water, etc.

Name	Calibre	Feed	Cooling	Weight Kg.	Rate of fire	Operation	Country
AAT-52	7·5mm	B.200	A	10·88	600	B	France
ALFA M1955	7·62mm	B.100	A	12·92	800	G	Spain
BEARDMORE FARQUHAR	·303	D.77	A	7·37	500	G	UK
BERGMANN MG15nA	7·92mm	B.200	A	15·42	800	R	Germany
BESA Mk 1	7·92mm	B.225	A	21·31	450	G	UK
BREDA M37	8mm	S.20	A	19·27	500	G	Italy
BREN Mk 1	·303	BX.30	A	10·10	500	G	UK
BROWNING M1917	·30	B.250	W	18·50	500	R	USA
BROWNING M1919A6	·30	B.250	A	14·75	500	R	USA
BROWNING M2HB	·50	B.110	A	38·10	575	R	USA
CHATELLERAULT 1924/29	7·5mm	BX.30	A	9·98	475	G	France
COLT-BROWNING M1895	·30	B.250	A	18·14	400	G	USA
CHAUCHAT	8mm	BX.20	A	8·16	240	R	France
DARNE M29	7·5mm	B.250	A	8·39	1200	G	France
DEGTYAREV DP	7·62mm	D.47	A	9·07	550	G	USSR
DEGTYAREV DT	7·62mm	D.60	A	9·07	550	G	USSR
DEGTYAREV DShK	12·7mm	B.50	A	33·34	600	G	USSR
DREYSE 1912	7·92mm	B.200	W	17·01	600	R	Germany
FIAT-REVELLI M1914	6·5mm	BX.50	W	17·23	500	B	Italy
FIAT-REVELLI M1935	8mm	BX.50	A	10·88	500	B	Italy
FABRIQUE NATIONAL MAG	7·62mm	B	A	10·15	850	G	Belgium
FURRER M1925	7·5mm	BX.30	A	10·59	450	R	Switzerland
GAST	7·92mm	2 × D, 180	A	27·22	1800	R	Germany
GORYUNOV SG43	7·62mm	B.250	A	14·51	700	G	USSR
HECKLER & KOCH HK13	5·56mm	BX.30	A	5·40	650	B	Germany
HECKLER & KOCH HK11	7·62mm	D.80	A	6·20	850	B	Germany
HOTCHKISS 1914	8mm	S.30	A	24·94	450	G	France
JAPANESE Type 3	6·5mm	S.30	A	27·21	500	G	Japan
JAPANESE Type 11	6·5mm	H.30	A	10·21	500	G	Japan
JAPANESE Type 97	7·7mm	BX.30	A	11·79	500	G	Japan
JAPANESE Type 99	7·7mm	BX.30	A	10·43	850	G	Japan
JOHNSON M1941	·30	BX.20	A	5·89	400	R	USA
KPV	14·5mm	B	A	48·98	600	R	USSR
LEWIS	·30	D.47	A	11·80	500	G	USA
MADSEN	8mm	BX.30	A	9·08	450	R	Denmark
MAXIM M1892	·45	B.334	W	27·22	600	R	UK
MAXIM M1908	7·92mm	B.200	W	18·37	600	R	Germany
MAXIM M1910	7·62mm	B.250	W	19·95	500	R	USSR
MG34	7·92mm	B.250	A	11·11	750	R	Germany
MG42	7·92mm	B.250	A	10·88	1200	R	Germany
PARABELLUM	7·92mm	B.250	A	9·80	700	R	Germany
PK	7·62mm	B.200	A	9·52	800	G	USSR
RPD	7·62mm	B.100	A	7·03	700	G	USSR
RPK	7·62mm	D.75	A	6·35	600	G	USSR
ST ETIENNE	8mm	S.25	A	20·86	500	G	France
SCHWARZLOSE M1912	8mm	B.250	W	19·91	400	B	Austria
SIG KE-7	7·92mm	BX.20	A	7·80	550	R	Switzerland
SIG M710-3	7·62mm	B.200	A	9·65	900	B	Switzerland
US SERVICE M60	7·62mm	B.200	A	10·50	600	G	USA
US SERVICE M73 (Tank)	7·62mm	B.250	A	13·29	500	R	USA
US SERVICE M85 (Tank)	·50	B	A	27·90	400	R	USA
VICKERS Mk 1	·303	B.250	W	18·14	500	R	UK
VICKERS-BERTHIER	·303	BX.30	A	9·98	600	G	UK
ZB26	7·92mm	BX.30	A	9·60	500	G	Czechoslovakia
ZB59	7·62mm	B.50	A	9·60	750	G	Czechoslovakia

PISTOL & SUBMACHINE GUN CARTRIDGES: METRIC SIZES

Ammunition tables are divided according to whether the cartridge is familiarly known by a metric or by an 'inch' designation. All dimensions are in metric units; the 'Actual Calibre' given is the actual measured diameter of the bullet, which rarely coincides with the 'nominal calibre'. Bullet weight is in grammes, muzzle velocity in metres per second. The date is that of the first introduction of the cartridge. Type of cartridge case is shown as 'R' for rimmed', 'RL' for 'rimless' and 'SR' for 'semi-rimmed'.

Nominal Calibre & Name	Actual calibre	Bullet weight	Muzzle velocity	Year	Type
3mm KOLIBRI	3·048	0·200	183	1914	RL
4·25mm LILLIPUT	4·267	0·776	236	1913	RL
5mm BERGMANN No. 2	5·156	2·329	176	1894	RL
5mm CHAROLA y ANITUA	5·156	1·941	305	1897	RL
5·5mm VELO DOG	5·588	2·912	198	1894	R
6·35mm AUTO PISTOL	6·350	3·235	250	1906	SR
6·5mm BERGMANN No. 3	6·604	5·176	215	1894	RL
7·62mm NAGANT	7·823	7·117	290	1895	R
7·62mm SOVIET AUTO PISTOL	7·823	5·500	457	1930	RL
7·63mm MAUSER	7·823	5·500	457	1896	RL
7·63mm MANNLICHER M1900	7·823	5·500	312	1900	RL
7·65mm AUTO PISTOL	7·874	4·852	300	1900	SR
7·65mm BORCHARDT	7·823	5·500	380	1893	RL
7·65mm FRENCH LONG	7·823	5·500	360	1925	RL
7·65mm PARABELLUM	7·849	5·823	365	1900	RL
8mm LEBEL REVOLVER	8·255	7·765	220	1892	R
8mm RAST & GASSER	8·128	7·765	240	1898	R
8mm NAMBU	8·128	6·470	320	1909	RL
9mm BERGMANN-BAYARD	9·017	8·088	340	1903	RL
9mm BROWNING LONG	9·068	7·117	312	1907	SR
9mm JAPANESE REVOLVER	9·017	9·640	200	1893	R
9mm MAUSER EXPORT	9·068	8·282	420	1908	RL
9mm MAUSER REVOLVER	9·398	10·352	245	1878	R
9mm PARABELLUM	9·017	8·088	380	1903	RL
9mm POLICE	9·145	6·470	320	1976	RL
9mm SHORT	9·068	6·145	295	1908	RL
9mm SOVIET AUTO PISTOL	9·220	6·147	335	1960	RL
9mm STEYR	9·017	7·440	365	1912	RL
10·4mm ITALIAN ORDNANCE	10·795	11·322	250	1874	R
10·4mm SWISS ORDNANCE	10·922	12·487	182	1878	R
10·6mm GERMAN ORDNANCE	10·920	16·175	205	1879	R
11·3mm MONTENEGRIN	11·430	19·410	215	1870	R

PISTOL & SUBMACHINE GUN AMMUNITION: INCH SIZES

Nominal Calibre and Name	Actual calibre	Bullet weight	Muzzle velocity	Year	Type
·22 LONG RIFLE	5·664	2·588	334	1887	R
·221 REMINGTON FIREBALL	5·690	3·235	807	1963	RL
·25 AUTO PISTOL	6·350	3·235	250	1906	SR
·256 WINCHESTER MAGNUM	6·528	3·882	720	1962	R
·32 AUTO PISTOL	7·874	4·852	300	1900	SR
·32 COLT NEW POLICE	7·975	6·470	242	1896	R
·32 SMITH & WESSON LONG	7·950	6·340	242	1896	R
·32-20 WINCHESTER	7·925	6·470	312	1873	R
·35 SMITH & WESSON AUTO	8·128	4·917	260	1913	RL
·357 MAGNUM	9·068	10·223	442	1935	R
·38 AUTO PISTOL	9·119	8·411	365	1900	SR
·38 COLT NEW POLICE	9·119	9·705	210	1905	R
·38 LONG COLT	9·068	9·730	243	1887	R
·38 SPECIAL	9·068	10·223	265	1902	R
·380 AUTO PISTOL	9·068	6·145	295	1908	RL
·38-40 WINCHESTER	10·160	11·646	290	1873	R
·380 BRITISH REVOLVER	9·068	12·940	183	1929	R
·41 LONG COLT	9·830	12·940	227	1896	R
·41 MAGNUM	10·414	13·587	350	1964	R
·44 COLT	11·277	13·587	200	1871	R
·44 MAGNUM	10·922	15·528	442	1955	R
·44 SMITH & WESSON RUSSIAN	10·947	15·916	229	1870	R
·44 SMITH & WESSON SPECIAL	10·947	15·916	240	1907	R
·44 AUTO MAG	10·920	15·528	512	1970	RL
·44-40 WINCHESTER	10·820	12·940	285	1873	R
·45 AUTO COLT PISTOL	11·455	14·881	262	1911	RL
·45 COLT REVOLVER	11·531	16·175	265	1873	R
·45 MARS	11·430	14·234	365	1901	RL
·45 WEBLEY	11·430	14·881	168	1875	R
·455 ENFIELD	11·557	17·145	177	1881	R
·455 WEBLEY & SCOTT AUTO	11·557	15·786	215	1912	RL
·476 ENFIELD	12·115	17·145	185	1882	R
·50 REMINGTON ARMY	13·081	19·410	180	1871	R

RIFLE & MACHINE GUN AMMUNITION: METRIC SIZES

Nominal Calibre and Name	Actual calibre	Bullet weight	Muzzle velocity	Year	Type
5·6mm×61	5·766	4·982	1080	19?7	RL
5·56mm×45	5·689	3·559	1005	1957	RL
6mm LEE	6·197	7·246	780	1895	RL
6·5mm GREEK SERVICE	6·680	10·350	745	1903	RL
6·5mm DUTCH & ROMANIAN SVC	6·680	10·095	745	1892	R
6·5mm JAPANESE SVC	6·680	10·095	630	1905	RL
6·5mm SWEDISH SVC	6·705	8·995	790	1894	RL
6·5mm ITALIAN SERVICE	6·731	10·355	700	1891	RL
6·5mm×57 MAUSER	6·705	7·700	860	1893	RL
7mm×57 MAUSER	7·214	11·190	700	1892	RL
7·35mm ITALIAN SERVICE	7·569	8·280	760	1938	RL
7·5mm SWISS SERVICE	7·722	12·290	775	1889	RL
7·5mm FRENCH SERVICE	7·823	9·705	815	1929	RL
7·62mm NAGANT, RUSSIAN SVC	7·874	9·705	850	1891	R
7·62mm SOVIET M43 SHORT	7·874	7·894	730	1943	RL
7·62mm NATO	7·823	9·317	823	1954	RL
7·7mm JAPANESE SVC	7·899	8·410	855	1939	SR
7·92mm GERMAN SVC	8·204	9·964	875	1888	RL
7·92mm GERMAN M43 SHORT	8·204	8·088	650	1942	RL
8mm FRENCH LEBEL	8·204	12·810	725	1886	R
8mm AUSTRIAN SERVICE	8·204	15·786	610	1888	R
8mm HUNGARIAN SERVICE	8·357	13·328	700	1931	R
8mm DANISH SERVICE	8·179	12·681	750	1889	R
9·5mm TURKISH SERVICE	9·880	18·440	535	1887	R

RIFLE AND MACHINE GUN CARTRIDGES: INCH SIZES

Nominal Calibre and Name	Actual calibre	Bullet weight	Muzzle velocity	Year	Type
·22 LONG RIFLE	5·664	2·588	334	1887	R
·220 SWIFT	5·689	2·912	1250	1935	RL
·223 REMINGTON	5·689	3·559	970	1957	RL
·25-35 WINCHESTER	6·528	7·570	705	1895	R
·257 WEATHERBY MAGNUM	6·528	7·570	1005	1944	B
·270 WEATHERBY MAGNUM	7·036	8·411	1030	1943	B
·280 ROSS	7·290	9·058	885	1910	RL
·300 WINCHESTER MAGNUM	7·823	9·705	975	1963	B
·30-06 U.S. SERVICE	7·823	11·258	815	1906	RL
·30 CARBINE M1	7·823	5·988	580	1941	RL
·30-30 WINCHESTER	7·823	11·028	675	1895	R
·303 BRITISH SERVICE	7·925	11·257	745	1887	R
·308 WINCHESTER	7·823	9·317	823	1954	RL
·32-20 WINCHESTER	7·925	6·470	820	1882	R
·340 WEATHERBY MAGNUM	8·585	12·940	975	1962	B
·351 WINCHESTER SELF-LOADER	8·915	11·646	565	1907	RL
·360 NITRO EXPRESS	9·322	20·704	670	1910	R
·375 WEATHERBY MAGNUM	9·525	17·469	860	1945	B
·38-40 WINCHESTER	10·185	11·646	520	1874	R
·400 NITRO EXPRESS	10·363	25·880	640	1900	R
·44-40 WINCHESTER	10·846	12·940	550	1873	R
·45-70 U.S. GOVERNMENT	11·068	26·275	400	1873	R
·45 MARTINI-HENRY	11·303	31·056	412	1871	R
·450 NITRO EXPRESS	11·557	31·056	665	1900	R
·500 NITRO EXPRESS	12·878	36·879	655	1892	R
·577 SNIDER	14·478	31·056	380	1867	R

NOTE: In this table, the letter 'B' indicates a 'Belted' cartridge case, i.e., one which is rimless and in addition carries a raised belt just in front of the extraction groove in order to give additional strength.

GLOSSARY

ACCELERATOR
Component of recoil-operated weapons intended to give extra velocity to the bolt or breechblock during the recoil movement. Best-known application is in the Browning machine gun, where it takes the form of a curved arm hinged at its lower end. When struck on the curved face by the returning barrel, the curvature gives an increase in leverage and thus the tip of the arm moves faster than the barrel. The tip strikes the bolt just as the latter has been unlocked and thus imparts to it a higher velocity than it would receive from the barrel alone. This speeds up the rate of fire and also gives the bolt a reserve of energy to overcome stiff extraction problems.

ADVANCED PRIMER IGNITION
Also called 'differential locking'. A system of operation applied commonly to submachine guns in which the primer is struck and the cartridge fired while the bolt is still moving forward and the cartridge still being inserted into the chamber. The advantage in this system is that the rearward pressure of the cartridge case due to the explosion of the charge must first arrest the forward movement of the bolt and then begin the 'blowback' movement. This introduces a fractional delay between firing and the start of the ejection stroke of the bolt, which is sufficient to allow the bullet to leave the barrel and the breech pressure to drop to a safe level. It also absorbs a certain amount of the recoil force and makes the gun easier to handle.

In slightly different form it has been used in locked breech machine guns (e.g. the BESA), where the cartridge is fired while the barrel and breech, locked together, are moving forward into battery. ('Battery' is an American military term which means 'firing position'.) Causing the cartridge to be fired while the locked breech-and-barrel are still moving forward reduces the recoil stress on the gun and its mountings.

AIR COOLING
A firearm is a form of internal combustion engine, and as such it generates a great deal of heat. Single shot weapons generally have sufficient time between shots for this heat to dissipate, but an automatic weapon builds up heat in the barrel very rapidly, over half the energy developed by the explosion of the cartridge being transformed into heat. Since the steel of which the barrel is made will melt at temperatures in excess of about 550°C, it is necessary to cool the barrel so that excessive wear does not take place and also to keep the chamber below the temperature at which induced heat will fire the inserted cartridge ('cook-off').

Air-cooling is at its best in aircraft weapons where the motion of the aircraft generates a stream of cold air across the gun. In ground weapons the system is less reliable, though designers have attempted to improve matters by various arrangements of fins and shrouds to direct air or to produce a larger heat-dissipating surface. In general terms, the greater the amount of metal in the barrel, the better radiator it becomes, but practical considerations place a limit on this.

In general, air-cooled automatic weapons have to be provided with a method of changing the barrels rapidly so that a cold spare barrel can be placed on the gun while the hot barrel is given time to cool down. Where this is not possible, restrictions must be placed on the rate of fire.

ASSAULT RIFLES
Class of military rifle generally characterised by the use of a short cartridge and the ability to fire either single shots or automatic fire. The assault rifle came about from the development, in Germany, of a short cartridge; this was predicated on the analysis of First World War experience which indicated that the average infantry soldier rarely used his rifle at ranges greater than 400 yards and, indeed, could rarely distinguish a target at all at ranges greater than this. From this arose the question of the utility of the standard military cartridge which was capable of delivering accurate fire to ranges of up to 2000 yards. Since this sort of range was not used, it followed that by shortening the cartridge case and reducing the propellant charge, though retaining the standard calibre of the bullet, the performance would be adequate for the short ranges envisaged, while the recoil force on the rifle would be reduced. Moreover, the cartridges would weigh less and therefore the individual soldier could carry more, and since the cartridge was shorter the rifle action could also be made shorter.

This reasoning eventually produced the Sturmgewehr 44, the first use of the phrase 'assault rifle', which was issued to the German Army in 1943–1944. It proved to be a highly effective weapon, bearing out all the forecasts of the designers. The short cartridge was then copied by the Soviet Army in 7·62mm calibre and used as the round for the Kalashnikov AK-47 rifle. Since then, various short cartridges have been designed, together with appropriate rifles; the British EM2 rifle and 7mm cartridge of the late 1940s was one of the first, followed by various Swiss and other designs, but there was considerable resistance to the whole idea in postwar years, which led to NATO standardisation of the 7·62mm cartridge, a round which was only slightly less powerful than the ·30 and ·303 rounds which it replaced. In the late 1950s, though, the Armalite company developed the 5·56mm round, together with their AR-15 rifle, and this brought about a resurgence of interest in assault rifle and short cartridge design. At the time of writing, a full-scale trial is being conducted by the NATO countries to decide upon a short cartridge for future standardisation.

The small size of the assault rifle, together with its ability to fire automatic at rates up to 800 rounds a minute, has led to it being adopted by various forces as a replacement for the submachine gun, and there is every likelihood that this trend will continue in the near future.

AUTOMATIC PISTOL
As commonly used, a pistol which, on pressure of the trigger, will fire and re-load ready to fire the next shot. This is, strictly speaking, a self-loading pistol, and the term 'automatic' should only be applied to those pistols (and other weapons) which will fire and continue to reload and fire so long as the trigger is pressed and there is ammunition available—e.g. machine guns. Such pistols have been made, but they are impractical weapons. So far as this volume is concerned, the common usage is accepted, and where a pistol is of the full-automatic type, this is specifically pointed out.

Automatic pistols can be divided into two broad classes: those with locked breeches and those without, the latter being generally called 'blowback' types. The distinction is somewhat blurred by a twilight class of 'delayed blowback' pistols in which there is a form of breech locking which is of limited effect.

The necessity for a locked breech arises with the more powerful calibres, in which lack of restraint of the breech mechanism would lead to the cartridge case being blown violently from the breech immediately upon firing. It is therefore desirable to lock the bolt or other type of breech closure securely to the barrel and keep it locked until the bullet has left the barrel and the gas pressure in the breech has dropped to a level at which it is safe to open the breech and begin extracting the cartridge.

In smaller calibres—9mm is roughly the dividing line—the relative sizes of the bullet and the breech mass are such that inertia will hold the breech closed for the fraction of a second needed to allow the bullet to escape, after which the residual pressure in the chamber, acting against the base of the cartridge case, will force the breech back against some form of spring, extracting the empty case.

Locked breech pistols are operated by the force of recoil; gas operation has been attempted, but has never been successfully applied. Locking may be done in various ways, but at the present time the most common method is the 'swinging link' system pioneered by John M. Browning and best exemplified by the US Army's Colt M1911A1 pistol. In this system the pistol barrel is loosely attached to the pistol frame by a hinged link, in such a manner that as the barrel moves rearward under recoil, it is constrained by the link to move also in a downward arc. The top of the barrel has formed upon it a number of cross ribs which, when the barrel is raised to the full extent of the link's movement, engage in rib recesses cut in the interior of an enveloping 'slide' which also incorporates the breech block and firing pin in its rear section. A powerful spring forces the slide forward, thrusting a cartridge from the pistol magazine into the breech of the barrel and also forcing the barrel forward to the limit of its travel, when the ribs engage in the recesses. By virtue of this engagement, the barrel and slide—and hence the breech block section—are locked together, and any movement of one must be accompanied by movement of the other.

When the pistol is fired, the rearward force on the base of the cartridge—the recoil—pushes the slide back, but the ribs and grooves cause the barrel to move back as well, the two being locked together. As the barrel moves back, so the link causes it to drop until the ribs disengage from the grooves, whereupon the barrel stops moving but the slide and breech block are free to continue the recoil stroke. Although the period of locking is extremely brief, it is sufficient to permit bullet exit and the necessary reduction in chamber pressure.

A typical blowback pistol, on the other hand, while using the same configuration of slide and breech block unit in one piece, has the barrel firmly fixed to the pistol frame and there is no locking connection between barrel and slide. The only thing which holds the breech closed is the mass of the slide, assisted by the power of the return spring forcing it against the breech.

Within these basic parameters, of course, individual designers have permutated design features so as to produce individual pistols, and the peculiarities of the various designs and systems will be found in greater detail in the entries relative to specific pistol types.

AUTOMATIC REVOLVER
Class of revolver in which the rotation of the cylinder and the recocking of the hammer or firing pin are achieved automatically rather than by manipulation of the trigger. Automatic operation was attempted at an early date; the Museu de Armas at Eibar in Spain had a gas-operated revolver by Orbea tentatively dated in the 1860s, while the British designer Paulson patented a gas-operated weapon in 1886. On both these, a gas piston was used to force the pistol hammer back to the cocked position, a pawl on the hammer acting to rotate the cylinder.

The only successful automatic revolver was the Webley-Fosbery, based on the patents of Col. G. V. Fosbery VC. This relied upon the recoil of the barrel and cylinder across the pistol frame; a fixed pin on the frame engaged with grooves in the surface of the cylinder so as to rotate the cylinder after every shot, while the rearward thrust of the barrel unit served to cock the hammer. A similar design, based on the patents of Lefever, was produced by the Union Arms

Company of Toledo, Ohio in about 1910.

An unusual approach was that of the Landstadt revolver, patented in 1899. In this weapon the 'cylinder' was a flat-sided unit with two chambers, while the pistol magazine was a box fitted inside the butt. The weapon was manually cocked for the first shot by pulling out and releasing a bolt unit which thrust a cartridge from the magazine into the lower chamber of the 'cylinder' unit. On pressing the trigger the 'cylinder' revolved through 180°, aligning the loaded cartridge with the barrel, after which a striker fired it. Subsequent action was by blowback of the bolt unit, which automatically re-loaded the lower chamber. Landstadt's principal object appears to have been to produce a revolver which was unusually safe, insofar as the cartridge was never aligned with the barrel or the firing pin except by pressure on the trigger.

BARREL EXTENSION
In a recoil-operated weapon, a frame attached to the barrel and carrying the breech block or bolt and usually also carrying a means of locking the bolt to the barrel extension and therefore to the barrel. As this complete unit recoils in the weapon frame or body, the breech lock is released; thereafter the barrel and extension are halted and the bolt or block is free to move.

BELT FEED
System of supplying ammunition to a machine gun in the form of a continuous belt. In early designs these belts were simply two strips of canvas stitched together at intervals to form pockets, into which the cartridges could be pushed. This meant that the cartridge had to be withdrawn backwards from the belt, lifted or lowered to align with the bolt, and then loaded into the chamber. The belt was automatically advanced so as to bring the next cartridge into position. The next step was to develop the 'open loop' belt in which metal clips, riveted to the canvas belt, held the cartridges in position. These clips, being open at the top, allowed the bolt to push the cartridge (if it was rimless) straight forward out of the belt and into the chamber, thus simplifying the design of the gun mechanism.

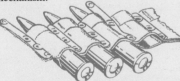

Once emptied, the belt tends to flex easily and can jam itself in the exit from the gun unless guided out; when aircraft machine guns became common, the 'disintegrating link' belt was developed to avoid this kind of jam. This belt is formed of independent metal clips which are connected together by the cartridges themselves. Thus, as the cartridge is removed from the belt, the clip falls away and can be discarded from the aircraft through a chute; there is no need to provide a receptacle for the empty belt.

One point about belt feed which is frequently overlooked is the need for the gun mechanism to generate sufficient power to lift and move the belt; in aircraft installations where the belt may have to run some distance before reaching the gun, and do this irrespective of attitude of the aircraft, this is of considerable importance.

BLACK POWDER
Formerly used as a propellent for guns, black powder (also called gunpowder) is now almost entirely restricted to use in pyrotechnic compositions. However, in recent years there has been a resurgence of the shooting of black-powder arms for amusement.

Black powder is a mechanical mixture of charcoal, sulphur and potassium nitrate in the proportions 15:10:75. While frequently regarded as a plaything, it must be borne in mind that black powder is a powerful explosive and one which is among the most sensitive; any spark or impact will initiate it. As a gun propellent its principal faults are (1) liability to damp; (2) the dense cloud of white smoke given off and (3) the quantity of fouling generated by the explosion, which can soon jam any weapon.

BLOWBACK
System of operation of an automatic firearm in which the breech block or bolt is not physically locked to the barrel. On firing, the explosion pressure in the chamber causes the cartridge case to be expelled rearwards, where it impinges on the face of the bolt or block and drives it to the rear. Safety is achieved by arranging that the mass of the bolt, and the usual recoil spring backing it up, form an inertia load sufficient to resist movement for the short period in which the bullet is in the barrel. Once the bullet leaves the muzzle the propelling gases follow it and the chamber pressure drops instantly, but by that time sufficient momentum has been imparted to the bolt to allow the action to continue in the absence of sustained pressure.

BLOW-FORWARD
System of operation of an automatic arm analogous to blowback (*qv*) but in which the breech block is firmly anchored to the weapon frame and cannot move. Therefore the chamber pressure causes the barrel to move forward, away from the breech block, due to the cartridge case being forced back and the bullet and barrel forward. It is theoretically quite workable, but there are numerous practical problems. The action of cocking such a weapon, by forcing the barrel forward, is awkward; the actual movement of the barrel tends to upset weapon balance more than the equivalent rearward movement of a bolt; and since the sliding surfaces are generally more exposed than in a blowback weapon, wear sets more easily. It has been used only occasionally; see under SCHWARZLOSE, HINO-KOMURA, and SIG for details of weapons using this system.

BOAT-TAILED
Term used to describe a bullet in which the base diameter is less than the maximum diameter and the base is tapered. The object of this is to cause the airflow over the bullet to meet quickly and smoothly behind it, reducing the low-pressure area behind the base and thus reducing drag. In British terminology, such bullets are described as 'streamlined'.

BOLT ACTION
Form of breech closure performed by a bolt moving in prolongation of the weapon's barrel axis. May be a *turnbolt* in which the bolt is manually pushed forward and then rotated in order to lock by means of angular lugs; or *straight-pull* in which the manual action is a simple reciprocating movement and usually the turning of the bolt is accomplished by cams. In some cases a straight-pull bolt does not rely on rotation for locking but is locked by a cam block arrangement beneath the bolt which braces it against the body of the weapon.

BOX MAGAZINE
Form of ammunition supply which takes the form of a metallic box, either detachable from the weapon and held in a *magazine housing* or actually forming part of the weapon body. Inside this box is a *follower* or *platform*, a plate shaped to place pressure on the ammunition contained in the box, this pressure being

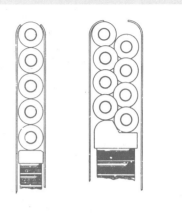

sustained by a spring. The magazine may be single or double column: either the cartridges form a single column or lie staggered on alternate sides to form a double column. The design of the open end of the magazine—the *feed lips*—will position the topmost round to align it with the bolt or breech block.

Box magazines may be loaded by *clips* or *chargers*; both are metal grips which hold a number of cartridges by their rims or bases. The clip is inserted into the magazine with the cartridges and remains there, forming part of the magazine mechanism, so long as there is one cartridge left in it. When the last cartridge is removed, the clip is expelled from the magazine. The charger is presented to the magazine mouth, held in *charger guides*, and while so held, the cartridges are manually pressed out of the charger and into the magazine. The charger is discarded manually when empty. Box magazines of large capacity—e.g. for machine and submachine guns—may be loaded by hand with individual cartridges, or may be provided with a loading device.

BUFFER
A resilient unit at the rear end of a machine gun body, against which the recoiling bolt strikes; the resilience may be achieved by springs, soft material or an air chamber, and serves to arrest the movement of the bolt in a comparatively gentle manner. In some cases, e.g. in spring buffers, the reaction of the buffer gives additional impetus to the return of the bolt, and this may be deliberately engineered in order to speed up the operation of the weapon. In other cases additional resilience may be allowed in order to slow down an otherwise inherently fast mechanism.

CALIBRE
Diameter of a weapon's barrel, measured internally from *land to land*. The land is the area of barrel left between the grooves; thus the calibre is the diameter of the bore excluding the depth of the rifling grooves. In British and American usage calibre is expressed in thousandths of an inch; e.g. ·303, ·357, ·45 etc. In continental usage the calibre is expressed in millimetres; e.g. 7·65mm, 9mm etc.

CANNELURE
A groove cut into the body of a bullet and into which either (a) lubricant can be pressed in order to lubricate the passage of the bullet up the bore, or (b) the mouth of the cartridge case can be pressed so as to grip the bullet more firmly.

CARBINE
A short rifle, usually for use by cavalry, artillery, engineers, or others whose primary task is not that of

using a shoulder arm but who require a weapon for self-defence and for use in emergencies. The carbine was shorter than the rifle so as to be more conveniently carried in a saddle-bucket or slung while performing other duties. Since it was invariably chambered for the same cartridge as the longer rifle, its accuracy and regularity of ballistics were never as good as those of the rifle.

CARTRIDGE HEADSPACE

Critical dimension in the assembly of a weapon. It is, basically, the distance between the face of the bolt or breech block and the base of the cartridge case, and it is measured in tens of thousandths of an inch. If the headspace is excessive, the cartridge case will be able to move out of the chamber when fired and may burst or expand; if headspace is insufficient the bolt or breech block may be prevented from locking.

CASELESS AMMUNITION

Term reserved for use to describe small arms ammunition which does not use the conventional metal cartridge case. Instead, the propellant powder is pressure-formed into a solid mass and attached to the bullet. At the base of the powder pellet is a cap, either percussion or electrically fired. Obviously, the powder pellet has to be highly resistant to fire and abrasion, and must be capable of being accurately formed and keeping dimensionally stable. This design has been pursued for the last forty years with varying degrees of success; the principal drawbacks are that it complicates the design of the weapon insofar as some positive breech sealing has to be used in place of the sealing normally obtained from the metal case, and that it poses problems of storage and transport, when considered in bulk. On the plus side, the weapon designer has no need to worry about extracting and ejecting the case, and the weight of a quantity of ammunition is considerably lessened by the absence of metal cases. At the time of writing, a caseless cartridge designed in Germany is being tested by NATO authorities.

CENTRE FIRE

Cartridge in which the percussion cap is mounted centrally in the base of the cartridge case. The cap may be visible or, on some early designs, may be completely concealed within the case, in which event it is described as being 'inside primed'.

CHAMBER

Enlarged and specially shaped portion of the barrel at its rear end, into which the cartridge is placed prior to firing. The chamber holds the cartridge and, by its 'leed' or blending-in to the rifled bore, directs the bullet into the rifling in proper alignment.

CHOKE

A constriction in a shotgun barrel designed to cause the shot to leave the bore in a more dense pattern and retain this pattern for a longer range. Almost every gunsmith has his own ideas on how much the constriction should be and how far back in the barrel it should be placed, but in general the muzzle of the gun is some ·04 of an inch less in diameter than the rest of the barrel. In recent years muzzle attachments which can be adjusted to give various degrees of choke have been made to be fitted to cylinder-bored (i.e. chokeless) guns.

COMPENSATOR

Device screwed to the muzzle of an automatic weapon, or formed integrally with the barrel or jacket, which deflects some of the emergent gas

upwards. This tends to drive the muzzle down, and counters the tendency for the muzzle to rise during automatic fire due to the axis of thrust being above the point of resistance — e.g. the firer's shoulder.

COOK-OFF

Colloquial expression for premature ignition of a cartridge due to heat induced through the case from a hot barrel. This can occur quite readily in light automatic weapons which, after a prolonged burst of fire, heat up barrel and chamber to a considerable temperature. If a cartridge is loaded into the chamber and not fired, the induction of heat is likely to cause spontaneous ignition of the powder in a very short time. For this reason, most light automatic weapons are designed so that when the trigger is released, the bolt is held back from the chamber to allow air to pass down the barrel and assist in cooling, as well as to prevent the loading of a cartridge.

CYLINDER

Component of a revolver in which the chambers are bored. This is held behind the barrel on an *arbor* or central axis, so that it can be revolved by some mechanism, usually connected with the trigger, so as to present the chambers to the barrel in succession.

DELAYED BLOWBACK

Automatic arm in which the breech block or bolt is not positively locked to the barrel for the entire period of the bullet's travel up the bore and until the chamber pressure has dropped. It is basically a blowback (*qv*) weapon in which some means of slowing down the opening movement of the bolt is employed. This may range from having a spring press on the bolt so as to slow it, to various types of lock mechanism which actually begin to unlock as soon as the recoil force is felt but which take a short time to complete the unlocking and thus delay the bolt's opening.

DISCONNECTOR

Part of the firing mechanism of a self-loading weapon which disconnects the trigger from the remainder of the mechanism as soon as the shot is fired and does not re-connect it until the firer positively releases the trigger and takes a fresh pressure for the next shot. This prevents the gun firing more than one shot for one pressure of the trigger. In automatic weapons, the disconnector is thrown out of engagement by a 'selector' which allows the firer to select single shots or automatic fire.

DOUBLE ACTION

A firing mechanism for a pistol which offers the firer two methods of discharging the shot; either he may pull back the hammer to the full-cock position and then release it by pressure on the trigger; or he may, by pulling the trigger alone, raise the hammer to full cock and then release it. In general, the latter option is used for hasty fire, the former for deliberate fire.

DOUBLE RIFLE

Form of sporting rifle in which there are two barrels, mounted side-by-side, as in a shotgun. Popular as a big game rifle in heavy calibres in years gone by.

DOUBLE TRIGGER

This expression has two meanings: 1. A firing mechanism for revolvers in which two triggers are

provided, one to cock the hammer and the other to release it; examples are the revolvers of Tranter and Kynoch. 2. A firing mechanism used with machine and submachine guns in which one trigger is provided for firing single shots and another trigger for automatic fire.

DROPPING BLOCK

General term for those single-shot rifles in which the breech block moves vertically in guides, impelled by an operating lever, to expose the rear of the chamber for loading and unloading. The guides are milled into the barrel extension and therefore this type of action is usually very strong and capable of handling the most powerful cartridges. It was extremely popular in the 19th century, when the bolt action was in its early days and not considered trustworthy with powerful cartridges used for hunting, but it is uncommon today.

DRUM MAGAZINE

Magazine for an automatic weapon in the form of a shallow cylinder or drum. It may be fitted to the gun in almost any way: the Lewis and Degtyarev guns have the drum flat on top; the Thompson and Suomi submachine guns have the drum vertically beneath;

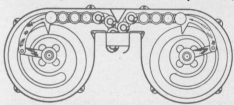

the Gast and Chatellerault machine guns have the drums mounted alongside. The casing of the drum may or may not revolve; in most cases it does not, and the cartridges inside are impelled by a powerful spring towards the magazine mouth. In other cases the drum revolves and carries the cartridges to a stripping device on the gun which removes them as they pass — e.g. the Lewis gun. In general, the drum is no longer in common use; in submachine guns it was found to be heavy and also noisy, due to the cartridges rattling inside; in light machine guns it is generally too prone to accidental damage which will inevitably jam the gun. It is also much more expensive to make than a box magazine (*qv*).

DUPLEX CARTRIDGE

Round of small arms ammunition which contains two or more bullets in one cartridge case, though only one is visible. This bullet is generally the standard bullet for the weapon; behind it, concealed in the case, will be a lighter and shorter bullet, usually with the base cut away at a slight angle. On firing, both bullets are blown up the bore; the first leaves on the normal trajectory; the second, due to the cut base, tends to deviate slightly from the line of the bore. By careful design this deviation can be held within certain limits. The object is to improve the chance of hitting a random target.

Duplex bullets have appeared many times in the last hundred years; George Luger patented one in the 1900s. At present, the US Army has developed a duplex round which has been on limited issue for some time; in this, the second bullet will always strike within a one-foot circle of the first at 100 yards range.

EJECTOR

Weapon component, the function of which is the physical expulsion of the cartridge case from the weapon after the shot has been fired. In most cases it is simply a protruberance of metal so placed that the bolt or breechblock will carry the fired case up against it, thus causing the case to be knocked from the bolt and out of an ejection port. In some weapons, particularly long-recoil weapons, it is often necessary to arrange for the ejector to move in order to do its work and then retract so as not to interfere with the movement of the recoiling parts.

EXPRESS
British term used to describe high velocity hunting rifles. The term is said to have originated in 1856 when Purdey, the gunmaker, produced a rifle which he advertised as the 'Express Train' model. The term was soon shortened to 'Express' and was used to indicate that a rifle so called would develop a higher power than was usual with that calibre. This, of course, was provided by specially powerful cartridges, also known as 'Express'. In more recent years the term has fallen into disuse, being replaced by the word 'Magnum'.

EXTRACTOR
A component of a weapon which is generally attached to the bolt or breech block and which pulls the empty cartridge case out of the chamber and presents it to the ejector. In some older weapons, e.g. the Martini rifle, the ejector is a separate unit mounted under the breech but is actuated by movement of the breech block to force the cartridge case from the chamber.

FERMETURE NUT
System of breech locking developed by Benet & Mercie of Hotchkiss (qv) for a light machine gun. Briefly, it consists of a sleeve around the gun chamber, secured from moving rearward. The inner surface of the sleeve is cut into interrupted threads and the sleeve can revolve through a definite arc, impelled by the gas piston of the gun. The breech bolt is formed with mating interrupted threads and thus, with the fermeture nut in its 'unlocked' position, the breech bolt can close; the gas piston then turns the nut so that the threads engage and the bolt is thus locked to the barrel during the firing period. As the piston moves, the nut is revolved to unlock the bolt which is then driven back by further movement of the gas piston. It is an effective system but one which requires very precise machining and fitting, and it is not suited to today's cost-conscious gunmaking.

FLECHETTE
Type of military ammunition in which the conventional bullet is replaced by a thin dart-like projectile, pointed and with fins. In order to make this function in a conventional barrel it is necessary to fit it into a plastic carrier which fits the bore of the rifle. On leaving the muzzle, the plastic carrier is discarded, due to air drag, and the flechette is left to fly to the target. Weights of flechette are around the region of 5 to 10 grains, and they therefore take on extremely high velocities, in the 4000+ feet a second region. Although light, due to their speed they have a considerable wounding effect when they strike. Much experimental work has been done in this area, including multi-flechette rounds which discharge several such missiles for an area effect, but none, so far, have been standardised for issue.

FLUTED CHAMBER
A chamber of a firearm which has thin grooves cut longitudinally throughout most or all of the length and which extend past the neck of the cartridge case when loaded. In such a chamber, when the cartridge is fired, a proportion of the propelling gas passes back along the flutes and thus equalises the pressure inside and outside the cartridge case, literally floating the case on a layer of gas. This system, attributed to the Italian designer Agnelli, is used in blowback weapons in order to prevent the cartridge sticking in the chamber. A blowback weapon which uses a plain cylindrical cartridge case rarely gives trouble, but one which uses a bottle-necked case frequently gives problems in extraction; this is because the pressure in the case expands it against the chamber and keeps it there as the bolt begins to open. In such a case the extractor pulls and the base of the case moves back under chamber pressure, but the neck of the case is still tightly expanded against the chamber wall, and the result is either that the case rim is torn off or the case splits in the middle; either way the gun jams when the next cartridge is lined up for loading. Floating the case on gas equalises the pressure and prevents this happening.

GAS OPERATION
One of the basic methods of operating an automatic or self-loading arm. A portion of the propelling gas is tapped from the barrel via a port and directed to a cylinder in which a piston moves. The pressure of the gas drives the piston back, and this movement is then applied to the breech block so as to open the breech and re-load the weapon.

There are innumerable variations on the idea. The piston, for example, may make a full stroke, or it may be a 'tappet' piston which has a stroke of no more than half an inch, striking an operating rod and giving that sufficient impetus to carry out the reloading cycle; this is done in the US Army's M1 Carbine, for example. The gas may be piped into the cylinder and there left to its own devices, sustaining pressure until the bullet leaves the barrel and the gas is able to run back into the rifled bore; or the first movement of the piston might cut off further supplies of gas and leave that portion trapped in the cylinder to expand and provide the thrust in that manner. The piston may be provided with vents which allow the gas to escape to the atmosphere after a short stroke. Alternatively, there may be no piston at all and the gas simply piped back to strike directly on the bolt or some other part of the mechanism.

GAS SEAL
A type of revolver in which the cylinder is moved forward along its arbor so that the rear end of the barrel enters into the mouth of the aligned chamber to form a positive seal. In addition, the cartridge case is abnormally long, extending past the bullet, so that the mouth of the chambered case enters the rear end of the barrel and overlaps the connection between barrel and chamber. Thus when the cartridge is fired, the case mouth expands to permit the egress of the bullet and forms a complete seal at the chamber-barrel joint, preventing any leak of gas. For examples of this type of revolver see PIEPER and NAGANT. Generally speaking, the results are not worth the complication.

GENERAL PURPOSE MACHINE GUN (GPMG)
A machine gun is designed so as to be able to function either as a squad light automatic weapon, mounted on a bipod and fired from the shoulder, or as a sustained fire long-range weapon, mounted on a tripod and provided with some form of optical sight. The concept was first explored by the German Army with their MG34 and MG42 designs, and was adopted by several armies in post-1945 years. The Fabrique-National MAG machine gun is known in British service as the GPMG since it is used in both roles, and several other armies use it in similar fashion.

GRIP SAFETY
A lever or plunger let into the grip of a pistol or submachine gun in such a manner as to positively lock the bolt or hammer or trigger unless the weapon be properly held so that the grip is consciously depressed. Acts as an automatic safety device and prevents the weapon being accidentally discharged if dropped or mishandled.

GUNPOWDER
See BLACK POWDER.

HAMMERLESS
A somewhat ambiguous term which only really means that the hammer cannot be seen. Strictly speaking, it should mean what it says and imply that the firing of the cartridge is done by an axial striker or firing pin, but in practice the word is often applied to shotguns and revolvers which in fact do have hammers concealed within the frame.

HANGFIRE
A malfunction of ammunition in which the ignition of the cartridge takes place some interval after the strike of the hammer or pin against the cartridge cap. The amount of interval may be anything from a fraction of a second to several seconds or even minutes; in British military specifications, any delay of greater than 0·1 second is a hangfire. Hangfires are extremely dangerous, since the instinctive reaction when the weapon fails to fire is to put it down, or at least move it off aim, in order to examine it, and then accidents follow.

HINGED FRAME
Type of revolver in which the barrel and cylinder form a movable unit which is hinged to the butt frame by a pivot pin at the front edge of it. When closed, the two sections are locked together by some form of catch which holds the top strap (that part of the barrel section passing over the cylinder) to the standing breech (that part of the butt frame unit which lies immediately in front of the hammer). By releasing the catch and pressing down the barrel, the two units are hinged about each other and the rear of the cylinder is exposed for loading.

Hinged frames can also be hinged at the top of the standing breech and latched at the bottom front of the butt frame unit, but in this case they are known as 'tip-up' revolvers.

KNOXFORM
British expression which refers to a flat surface ground on the breech end of a barrel which is to be screwed into an action body, e.g. the barrel of the Lee Enfield rifle. This flat is formed as a reference point in order to ensure tht the barrel is correctly fitted and the sight is upright. The name is a corruption of 'Nock's Form', and came from an 18th-century gunmaker named Nock, who devised this system.

LEVER ACTION
A rifle breech action operated by a hand lever which lies beneath the weapon and generally forms an extension of the trigger guard. Best exemplified by the Winchester and Marlin rifles.

LONG RECOIL
System of operation of an automatic or self-loading weapon in which the barrel and breech block are securely locked together at the instant of firing and then recoil, still locked, for a distance greater than

the length of a complete unfired cartridge. Having so recoiled, the breech is unlocked and the breech block is held fast while the barrel returns to the forward position. Once it has done so, the breech block is released and runs forward, chambering a round from the magazine, and then locks into the breech once more, ready for the next shot. Notable weapons using this system are the Chauchat machine gun and the Frommer 'Stop' pistol.

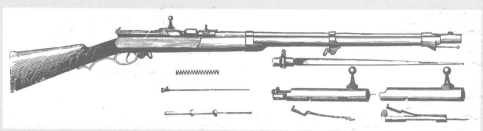

MAGAZINE SAFETY
A form of safety device used with automatic pistols in which the pistol cannot be fired if the magazine is removed. One of the most frequent causes of accident with automatic pistols is the cartridge left in the chamber when the magazine is removed; this is frequently forgotten or overlooked, and the pistol trigger is pulled, with unfortunate results. A magazine safety device ensures that this cannot happen.

MAINSPRING
The spring in a pistol which propels the hammer.

MECHANICAL REPEATING PISTOL
A pistol which is adapted to fire a succession of shots but by physical effort on the part of the firer and not by any self-powered agency such as recoil or gas. The simplest sort is the multi-barrel pistol such as the Sharps or Lancaster which has a firing pin which moves round to fire the various barrels in succession. More involved are the bolt-action pistols of Reiger, Passler & Seidl and similar inventors which were operated by pushing and pulling on a ring trigger. By strict definition, of course, the common revolver is a mechanical repeater, but by general agreement they are considered as revolvers and the mechanical repeater class is confined to the oddities.

MUZZLE BRAKE
An attachment on the muzzle of a gun which deflects some of the emergent gas to the sides and slightly backwards so as to exert a pull on the muzzle to counter some of the recoil force. Muzzle brakes can be made to very high degrees of efficiency; 85% is not unheard of in special artillery applications. But

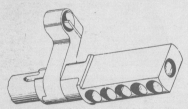

for small arms, their efficiency cannot be very high, otherwise they direct too much blast back at the firer or towards men at his sides. Nevertheless, a well-designed brake can make an appreciable difference to the recoil felt from a shoulder arm.

NEEDLE GUN
The von Dreyse Needle Gun, to which reference has been briefly made in the body of the book, was the first practical military breech-loading bolt-action weapon. The bolt was based on the domestic door-bolt, being secured in place behind the barrel by being turned down in front of a lug in the weapon frame. Inside the bolt ran a pointed needle or striker of considerable length. To operate the Needle Gun the striker was first drawn back and then the bolt opened. A cartridge was inserted in the breech and the bolt then pushed closed and turned down to lock.

The striker sleeve was then pushed forward so as to compress a spring around the striker. Finally the trigger was pressed, which released the striker. This ran forward, impelled by its spring, to enter the chamber, pass through the paper cartridge, and strike a percussion cap on the base of the bullet. This fired and ignited the powder in the cartridge, expelling the bullet. The breech was then opened by pulling back the striker and sleeve and opening the bolt. Sealing of the breech was by the face of the bolt being slightly tapered and entering tightly into the chamber mouth.

The defects of this system were that the powder fouling on the long exposed needle eventually corroded it to the point of breaking, and the joint between bolt and chamber leaked gas. Nevertheless, it was a notable advance and was instrumental in forcing breech-loading onto a reluctant military world.

OPEN FRAME
Type of revolver in which the barrel section is attached to the bottom of the butt frame, and there is no top strap passing from the barrel to the standing breech. Best known examples of this are the early Colt percussion revolvers. With low-powered cartridges the system was satisfactory, but it did not long survive the arrival of the metallic cartridge.

OVER AND UNDER
Type of shotgun in which the barrels are arranged one above the other. While preferred by some shooters for game shooting, the over-and-under is most often seen as a trap-shooting gun, since it is claimed that the single width of barrel allows better alignment with the target.

PATRIDGE SIGHT
Type of pistol sight named for a Mr E. E. Patridge, who invented it in 1898. The foresight is a rectangular blade with a vertical rear face, and the rear sight is a plate having a rectangular notch. When aiming, the flat top of the front sight is aligned centrally in the notch of the rear sight and level with the top of the rear sight notch. It is frequently mis-named the 'Partridge' sight, but has nothing to do with game-shooting.

PERCUSSION
While almost all firearms, with the exception of some specialised military weapons, are fired by the application of a percussive blow to a sensitive cap, this term is applied solely to weapons fired by the use of a separate cap placed on a nipple communicating with the chamber, and thus implying a black-powder muzzle-loading gun.

PINFIRE
A type of cartridge in which ignition was done by a percussion cap concealed within the cartridge body and struck by a pin which formed part of the cartridge construction. When loaded into a firearm, the pin was exposed and was then struck by a hammer so

as to fire the cartridge. By extension, any arm adapted to firing pinfire cartridges.

PRIMER
American term for the percussion cap in the base of a cartridge.

PUMP ACTION
Term given to a mechanism used in rifles and shotguns in which a reciprocating action is given to a grip beneath the barrel. Pulling this back and pushing it forward again opens the breech and reloads the weapon from a tubular magazine under the barrel. The tubular magazine usually forms the frame along which the 'pump' grip moves. Most commonly seen on shotguns and small-calibre rifles. Also called 'slide action' and 'trombone action'.

RECEIVER
The 'body' of a firearm, to which the barrel, stock, pistol grip, sights etc. are fixed and within which lies the firing and breech closing mechanism.

RECOIL INTENSIFIER
A device attached to the muzzle of an automatic weapon which impedes the muzzle blast and turns some of the gas back against the barrel face. This gives the barrel additional rearward velocity and thus intensifies the recoil action, making the automatic operation more positive.

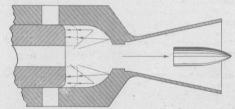

RECOIL OPERATION
System of operation of a self-loading or automatic weapon which relies on the recoiling of the barrel, due to firing, to generate the necessary power to operate the reloading cycle. May be subdivided into long recoil (qv) or short recoil, the latter being far more usual. In short recoil systems the barrel and locked breech recoil for a short distance, whereupon the breech block is unlocked while the barrel is halted. The impetus given the breech block by the short recoil movement is sufficient to drive it fully back to extract the fired case, and a recoil spring then drives it forward again to reload.

RECOIL SPRING
That spring in an automatic or self-loading weapon which returns the bolt or breech block after recoil; sometimes known as the 'return spring'.

RETARDED BLOWBACK
Same as 'delayed blowback' (qv).

REVOLVER

A repeating arm in which the barrel is fixed and the ammunition is contained in a rotary cylinder behind it, with a mechanism which will index the cylinder round so as to present a fresh cartridge to the barrel for each pressure of the trigger.

RICOCHET

A bullet which strikes against any object and bounces off at an angle is said to 'ricochet'. The angle at which it bounces and distance to which it flies is completely unpredictable. It is a factor which has to be taken into account when planning a firing range, so that any ricochetting bullet falls clear of nearby habitations. The danger is more pronounced with jacketed bullets.

RIFLING

Spiral grooves cut into the bore of a firearm so as to impart rotary motion to the bullet during its passage. The object is to gyroscopically stabilise the bullet's flight so that it travels point-foremost. Rifling permits the use of long bullets; were these fired in a smoothbore weapon they would not be stable in flight. The degree of twist of rifling is determined by the weight and length of the bullet and the velocity at which it is to be fired; too much twist can 'over-stabilise' a bullet so that on striking an animal it passes cleanly through without doing much damage; too little twist leaves the bullet with insufficient stability and it can be easily deflected from its course by wind or by grazing a leaf. The bullet tends to 'drift' off to one side because of aerodynamic effects caused by its spin, and the rifle sights must compensate for this.

RIMFIRE

A type of cartridge in which the case is formed into a rim at the base by pressing, so as to leave the rim area hollow. This is then filled with a sensitive percussion composition, and the body of the case filled with propellant powder, the bullet then being seated on top. When loaded the rim rests against the face of the chamber; the firing pin is arranged to strike on the rim and thus nip the composition between the pin and the chamber, producing sufficient friction to initiate the propellant. Some rimfire weapons, notably the early Henry (*qv*) rifle, had a double firing pin which struck the rim in two places at once in order to ensure efficient ignition. The principal defect of the rimfire is that the case metal must be malleable to permit the firing pin to compress it and so nip the composition, and this, in turn, implies a weak metal which will not withstand powerful loadings. In consequence rimfire cartridges are only used with low-pressure cartridges, and at the present day are confined to ·22 calibre rifled arms and the 9mm 'garden' shotgun.

SEAR

That part of a firing mechanism, linked to the trigger, which engages with the hammer or striker against spring pressure and, when pulled clear by trigger action, allows firing.

SELECTOR

Device which operates the disconnector (*qv*).

SELF-COCKING

Form of revolver firing mechanism in which pressure on the trigger cocks the hammer and then releases it to fire. This type of firing mechanism, though normally associated with revolvers, is also used on automatic pistols with an axial striker.

SELF-LOADING

Any firearm which, for a single pressure of the trigger, fires and then by its own agency re-loads. The trigger must then be released to fire the next shot. In this they differ from an automatic weapon, since an automatic weapon would continue to fire. The commonly defined 'automatic' pistol is, in fact, a self-loader.

SET TRIGGER

Form of trigger mechanism found on target weapons. As well as the firing trigger there is usually a second trigger or stud or lever of some sort which is operated first so as to cock the arm and 'set' the firing trigger so that a very light pressure on it will discharge the weapon. This method is adopted so that the actual firing trigger is not called upon to raise hammers or do any other heavy work for which stiff springs or difficult linkages might be needed; all this is done by the setting trigger or lever, and the firing trigger merely has to release the firing pin. By so arranging the mechanism, the release pressure can be extremely light, as is often desired by target shooters.

SHEATHED TRIGGER

Form of trigger commonly found on American revolvers of the 1860–1880 period, and occasionally on European revolvers. The frame of the pistol has an extended spur, which is slotted at the front and which contains the trigger. When the hammer is down, the trigger is concealed within the spur or sheath; when the hammer is cocked ready to fire, the trigger is forced out so that it can be pressed. Obviously restricted to single-action weapons. Also known as a 'stud trigger'.

SILENCER

Device attached to the muzzle of a firearm in order to reduce the noise of discharge. The first practical silencer was invented by Maxim. Its usual form is a large cylinder containing a number of metal plates, pierced to permit the passage of the bullet. The emerging gases are caught by these plates and swirled round inside the casing, so that by the time they emerge their velocity is reduced to the point where they do not generate sufficient disturbance of the air to cause a noise. The internal arrangements of the baffles vary according to the ideas of the designer, but the principle remains the same. If gas is permitted to escape from any other part of the gun, with sufficient velocity to cause noise, the effect of the silencer is reduced; thus, it is not practical to attempt to silence a revolver, since sufficient gas escapes from the cylinder-barrel joint to make a noise.

It should be pointed out that the noise of the emergent gas is only a part of the noise heard at the target; if the bullet is travelling at above the speed of

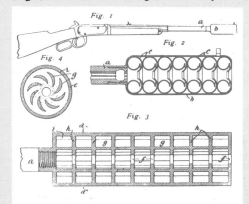

sound, as it usually is except for low-velocity pistols, then it will generate a shock-wave which is heard as a sharp crack. To make a silent weapon it is necessary to reduce the muzzle velocity of the bullet so as to avoid this. Such reduction can be done by boring holes in the barrel to bleed off gas (into the silencer, of course) or by producing special low-powered ammunition for use in silenced weapons.

SINGLE ACTION

Term used to describe a revolver firing mechanism in which the hammer must be pulled back and cocked by hand, after which the trigger can be pressed to release the hammer and fire the pistol.

SLIDE ACTION

A more formal term for what is popularly called 'pump action' (*qv*), a reciprocating fore-end on a shotgun or rifle which, when pulled back, opens and closes the breech.

SMOKELESS POWDER

Propellant powder for cartridges based upon nitrocellulose and with various additives. It is not entirely smokeless, but in comparison to gunpowder the appellation is appropriate. It is considerably more resistant to damp, more powerful for a given bulk, more consistent, gives less fouling in the bore, but tends to be more erosive. It can be found in various shapes, selected to permit some degree of control over the rate of burning; it may be in flakes, discs, balls, thin tubes or cords. In general it is more difficult to ignite than gunpowder and demands a more powerful flash from the initiating cap.

SOLID FRAME

Form of revolver construction in which the frame is in one piece, with a rectangular aperture for the cylinder. It follows that to empty and load the cylin-

der either there must be a prepared 'gate' at one side through which the chambers can be reached one at a time, or the cylinder must be removable in some way. Current manufacture by almost all makers is to use a solid frame and mount the cylinder on a crane so that it can be swung out of the frame for loading.

SPENT CASE PROJECTION

Another way of describing 'blowback' action, since the breech block is 'projected' by the chamber pressure acting via the spent cartridge case. A somewhat formal term which is usually only met with in military phraseology.

SQUEEZEBORE

Type of rifle barrel in which the calibre is suddenly reduced and then continues at this reduced figure to the muzzle. When used with deformable bullets, this system boosts the muzzle velocity since it reduces the area of the bullet base presented to the pressure of the propellent gas. If, for a given pressure of gas, the base is reduced in area, then the pressure per unit of area must increase, and this increases velocity. It has been used experimentally but never in a production weapon.

STANDING BREECH

That part of a revolver frame which is immediately behind the cylinder and acts as resistance to the recoil of the cartridge as it is fired. It is generally either pierced to admit the passage of the firing pin attached to the hammer, or carries a separate firing pin which is struck by the hammer. The sides of the standing breech are extended to cover the rear surface of the cylinder so as to prevent the cartridges from either falling out or being jarred out by the recoil of the pistol, and these extended sides are known as 'recoil shields'.

STIRRUP LATCH

Form of latch which holds the two sections of a hinged-frame revolver together. It is in the form of an inverted 'U', running up, across and down the side of the standing breech and controlled by a thumb lever. The top section passes across the top of the top

strap and thus anchors it securely to the standing breech. Devised by Edwinson Green, an English gunmaker, it was later widely used in Webley revolvers. One advantage of this system is that if the hinged section is not properly positioned, the stirrup does not close and impedes the fall of the hammer; in which case, either the pistol does not fire or the hammer knocks the stirrup forward and latches the gun before firing takes place.

STRAIGHT-PULL

Type of bolt action (qv) in which instead of lifting the bolt handle so as to rotate the bolt from engagement, the handle is pulled straight back, bolt rotation being achieved by a cam arrangement. Some straight pull systems (e.g. the Lee) did not rely on rotation of the bolt but used a locking lever attached to the handle which braced the bolt against the receiver.

STRIKER

Alternative term used for the firing pin of a weapon, when that firing pin is axially mounted and spring-propelled, as, for example, inside a rifle bolt.

STRIP FEED

System of providing ammunition for machine guns in the form of metal trays or strips into which the cartridges are clipped. The tray is fed into the gun at one side, the cartridges are stripped out and fired, the cases ejected, and the empty tray ejected from the other side of the gun. Commonly used on the Hotchkiss machine gun. A variation was to make the strips very short, holding three to five cartridges, and then link them together to give a form of flexible belt. On one Breda machine gun design the empty cartridge cases were replaced in the strip before it was fed out of the gun.

SUBMACHINE GUN

A submachine gun is a lightweight one-man weapon, capable of automatic fire, firing a low-powered pistol cartridge, and hence having limited range and accuracy. The definition tends to merge into other weapons at either end of the scale; thus, an automatic pistol provided with the means to fire in the true automatic mode and given a shoulder stock, can qualify as a submachine gun, while an assault rifle, firing a more powerful cartridge, is very close to being a submachine gun in the tactical sense.

SUICIDE SPECIAL

Name coined by American authority Donald B. Webster Jr., and used to collectively describe the common single-action, sheathed trigger, rimfire revolvers, invariably of cheap quality, which flooded the US market after the expiry of the Rollin White patent. Such weapons were made to sell at prices as low as sixty cents apiece, but they have survived in remarkable numbers.

SYNCHRONISER

A device used with aircraft machine guns in the days when fighter aircraft had propellers on the front and machine guns mounted so as to fire through the propeller arc. The most usual system was an hydraulic pump attached to the propeller spindle and connected by a pipe-line to a piston arrangement linked to the gun trigger. As the propeller spindle revolved, the pump sent impulses down the hydraulic line so as to depress the gun trigger at times when the propeller blade was not in the line of fire. An electrical system was later devised, with contacts on the spindle controlling a solenoid on the trigger. Synchronisers were no longer needed during the Second World War when it became normal practice to mount the guns in the aircraft wings, well outside the propeller arc.

TAPE PRIMING

System of delivering percussion priming caps to the nipple of a firearm by affixing them to a flexible tape and linking the feeding of the tape to the actuation of the hammer. See under MAYNARD for the successful application of this system.

TAPER BORE

Rifle in which the calibre gradually decreases from the breech to the muzzle. This allows a higher velocity to be attained, and the principle is the same as that of a squeeze-bore (qv). The difference is that here the taper is gradual, whereas with a squeeze bore the change in calibre takes place over a short section of the bore. Rifles of this type were developed in the 1920s as high-velocity hunting rifles, but they were not entirely successful, largely due to problems with ammunition, They were also tried as sniping rifles by various countries, but the idea was discarded. It was finally used in artillery calibres for anti-tank guns during the Second World War.

TIP-UP REVOLVER

See HINGED FRAME.

TOGGLE LOCK

System of breech locking for recoil-operated arms, notably the Maxim machine gun and the Parabellum (Luger) pistol. The system requires a barrel with barrel extension; inside the barrel extension is the breech block, and behind this are two arms. One is hinged to the breech block, the other is hinged to the barrel extension, and the two are linked by a hinge bolt in the middle—thus, breech block-hinge-arm-

hinge-arm-hinge-barrel extension. When the bolt is closed, the central hinge lies below the axis of the barrel by a slight amount, so that any pressure on the block tends to force this hinge down, where it is stopped by the surface of the barrel extension. When the gun fires, therefore, the whole unit recoils, the opening action of the block being resisted by the toggle arms lying slightly depressed. If, however, a ramp on the weapon frame is now arranged so as to kick up the central hinge, all resistance ceases and the breech block is free to recoil in the barrel extension, folding up the toggle joint as it does so.

There have been other applications of the toggle joint, usually having the toggle folded and then causing the moving breech block to unfold it at a mechanical disadvantage, so as to impart some delay to a blowback mechanism. This was successful in the Schwarlose machine gun, but no other application of it has been successful.

TUBULAR MAGAZINE

Magazine in a repeating arm, usually a rifle or shotgun, in which the cartridges are carried end-to-end in a tube mounted beneath the barrel. Only suited for use with blunt bullets, since pointed bullets, in contact with the percussion cap of the next cartridge, can fire the cap due to the shock of recoil when the gun is fired.

VELOCITY

Measure of the speed of the bullet. May be defined as muzzle velocity when referring to the speed at which the bullet actually leaves the muzzle; observed velocity, when the speed is determined at some specific point in flight; or remaining velocity, which refers to the speed of the bullet at the end of its flight. Abbreviations for these are 'MV', 'OV' and 'RV' respectively, though continental usage prefers 'Vo' for muzzle velocity.

WADCUTTER

A type of bullet used in target shooting with certain types of pistol. It is of lead, cylindrical, and designed so as to punch a clean hole in the target card at the specified practice range, so avoiding arguments due to ragged holes.

WINDAGE

Term used in two senses: 1. The clearance between a muzzle-loaded bullet and the calibre of the barrel, which allows the bullet to be loaded easily. 2. An allowance given in taking aim in order to compensate for the effect of wind upon the bullet's flight. This can generally be compensated for by adjusting the rear sight to one side or the other, and such adjustment is called 'windage'.

ZERO

A firearm is said to be 'zeroed' when the sights are adjusted so that the bullet will strike the point of aim at some specified distance, usually 200 yards or so. From this 'zero point' the sight adjustment mechanism will be able to alter the sight line for different ranges so that the bullet strike still coincides with the aiming point, but unless the sight is adjusted to suit the individual firer, his method of aiming, and the ammunition in use, before anything else is done, further adjustment of the sight will merely be adding unknowns to unknowns. 'Zeroing' a rifle for an individual may involve fitting different heights of sight blade, changing the rear sight aperture and setting in false values before the bullet strike coincides with the point of aim, but once this has been done it gives a firm base for further shooting, and adjustments for different ranges can be made.

Acknowledgements

The majority of the illustrations in this encyclopedia are from the author's personal archive. The publisher and author would also like to thank the following institutions and organisations for providing illustrations: Ambrosiana, Milan; Austrian National Library, Vienna; Bayerisches Nationalmuseum, Munich; Bradford City Museum; British Museum, London; Christie, Manson & Woods Ltd., London; National Army Museum, London; National Historical Museum, Stockholm; Palazzo Ducale, Venice; Radio Times Hulton Picture Library; Service d'Information et de Relations Publiques des Armées; Sotheby's, London; Tøjhusmeet, Copenhagen; Tower of London (Crown Copyright, Department of the Environment, London); University of Gottingen; Victoria and Albert Museum, London. Special diagrams and drawings are by Helen Downton.